OLIVER TAMBO

Beyond the Engeli Mountains

OLIVER TAMBO

Beyond the Engeli Mountains

Foreword by
PRESIDENT THABO MBEKI

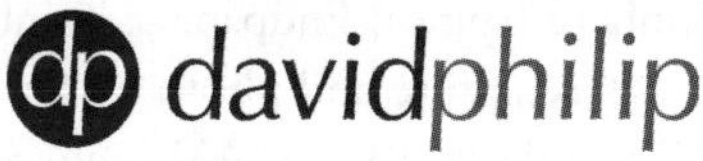

LULI CALLINICOS

DEDICATION

For Nicholas, Zoë, Luc, Eleni and Zac,
and for the youth of Africa, so that they will know their heritage.
For all the world to understand and celebrate Oliver Tambo's
multifaceted struggle against apartheid and the role he played
in its wise and humanist resolution.

First published in 2004 in southern Africa
by David Philip Publishers,
an imprint of New Africa Books (Pty) Ltd,
99 Garfield Road, Claremont 7700,
South Africa

Second Edition 2004

ISBN 0-86486-642-9 (hardback)
ISBN 0-86486-666-6 (paperback)

MANAGING EDITOR: Sean Fraser
DESIGN: Peter Bosman
INDEXER: Mary Lennox
REPRODUCTION BY House of Colours
PRINTED AND BOUND BY ABC Press, Cape Town

PHOTOGRAPHY
COVER: ANC DIP (inset), Roger de la Harpe/AfricaImagery.com
(background), Eli Weinberg (spine); Endpapers: Tambo Family Album;
HALF-TITLE PAGE: sculpture and photo by Ian Wallens;
TITLE PAGE: Eli Weinberg; PART 1: AM Duggan-Cronin;
PART 2: Dr Lancelot Gama; PART 3: Bailey's African History Archives;
PART 4: Peter Magubane

AUTHOR ROYALTIES FROM THIS VOLUME ARE TO BE DONATED TO
THE OLIVER TAMBO FOUNDATION

CONTENTS

FOREWORD

As we celebrate Ten Years of Democracy, it is right and fitting that we honour the memory of one of Africa's most illustrious sons, our own Oliver Reginald Kaizana Tambo – OR. More than any other, it was Oliver Tambo who kept our movement together through his skilled and sensitive leadership of the African National Congress during its 30 years of illegality and exile. It was during these trying times of struggle and sacrifice that Comrade OR became our exemplar, both to those in exile and to the millions of members and grass-roots supporters at home, including political prisoners.

But, sadly, this key architect of our revolution who carried the South African nation to the eve of freedom and democracy, succumbed under the heavy burden of decades of selfless commitment, and passed away on 23 April 1993.

Oliver Tambo's life and character are a metaphor of our struggle for freedom and democracy. His life began in a small rural community in Pondoland, but moved inexorably in the next 75 years towards an ever-growing national and international reputation.

He played a historic role, helping to develop and mature the ANC into an inclusive, democratic African organisation. He was present and active at many key moments in its history, from the conceptualisation and formation of the Youth League, the adoption of the 1949 Programme of Action, the widening of the mass base of the ANC in the 1950s, the adoption of the Freedom Charter, to the historic defeat of the brutal repressive campaign of the apartheid regime to destroy our movement, at home and abroad.

He played a central role in shaping the ANC constitutions from the 1940s through to the 1980s, which, among other things, placed respect for human rights at the centre of ANC policy. Similarly, Oliver Tambo masterminded the road map of our negotiations, the Harare Declaration in 1989, and the strategic outline and structure of our new democracy.

More than anyone else, OR personified the leadership of the ANC when many of its leaders were in prison or exile, and when some had been hanged or murdered in police cells. And he served in this capacity with humility, without thought of personal gain, always insisting that it was incorrect to present him as the President of our movement. Without ever wavering, he always argued that he was merely the Acting President of the ANC.

A key to Comrade OR's character was that he was an intellectual in the best meaning of that word. He was a person of reason, a person of rational thought and creative but rational action. This great ability, this gift of reason, was central to Comrade OR's make-up and central to his behaviour. It meant that here was a leader who could deal with both the concrete and the abstract. With the scientist's level of precision, he would always master the specific, the particular, while equally comprehending the general, the whole. As a political activist and leader, he could grapple with both strategy and tactics, with a full grasp of the interconnection between the two. This is a dialectical interaction, a synergy, which governed Oliver Tambo's political conduct and informed his diplomacy. This was made possible by the fact that he was a person of rational thought. His keen mind, his dedication to the liberation of our people, together with his deep humanism, enabled him to mobilise both the East and the West into the international struggle against apartheid, despite the fact that they were strategic opponents.

In the exercise of his leadership, Comrade OR was always ready and willing to listen to everybody, whatever their rank within the organisation. He would come to meetings having researched the topics that were to be discussed, having formulated a view, having thought through what it was that we had to do and what it was that we ought not to do.

He would not, however, air his views at the beginning of the discussion, but would rather wait, listen to people, take copious notes, and let everybody speak as they saw fit. Once he had heard what others had to say and reflected on it, only then would he speak. Nobody who worked with OR could ever claim that he did not consider their views when arriving at a decision.

The ANC is proud of its tradition of collective decision-making and leadership. But if there were one person who symbolises 'the crystallisation and personification of what the ANC is and became', as his legal partner, friend and comrade, Nelson Mandela put it, 'that person would be Oliver Tambo'.

Madiba explained, 'When we assess the processes that brought about the watershed events of February 1990, we should never underrate the great importance of the individual personality in determining the pace at which matters moved to that turning point'.

Yet, Oliver Tambo has not taken his rightful place in our national memory. In the tumultuous events that followed his death and the 10 years of our democracy, the contribution of this humble but brilliant patriot and mentor of our movement has been overlooked. Together with many other comrades, I was deeply moved when our government decided to name our most prestigious international friendship award the Order of the Companions of OR Tambo.

Luli Callinicos' timely and well-researched social biography begins the process of reducing the yawning deficit caused by the unintended consignment of the memory of Oliver Tambo to the dark shadows of a forgotten history. In her previous work, she has meticulously documented and made accessible to generations of readers, the neglected struggles of our working people. In this biography, she has captured the outstanding qualities of Comrade OR extremely well. Her biography is a welcome and fine beginning to a new historiography of OR Tambo.

One of the strengths of social biography is its emphasis on the whole person. In this context, I am especially pleased that the contribution of his wife, Adelaide Tambo, is included and acknowledged.

I trust this work will be widely read, not only by the members of our movement, but also by all South Africans, so that all of us can learn about the heroes and heroines who gave us the freedom we enjoy.

Undoubtedly and deservedly, this book will stimulate debate and lead to further analyses, as befits the memory of a man whose historic contributions touched the lives of so many people.

Comrade OR's dear friend, Archbishop Trevor Huddleston commented: 'History is never simply a chronicle of the past. It is always a challenge to contemporary thought for the future.' The life, character and contributions of Oliver Tambo to our national wellbeing, a better Africa and a better world, will continue to be relevant to future generations, because the values he personified are universal values that underlie all great struggles for freedom, and the universal effort to build a people-centred human society.

For the sake of our heritage, identity and pride as a nation, all of us, South Africans, dare not allow ourselves to forget what Oliver Tambo did so that we could reclaim our human dignity. Without the memory and spirit of OR Tambo in our midst, serving as our guide, our present and future will carry the taint of barrenness, because they will be deformed by a poverty of meaning.

On 28 May 1987, Oliver Tambo delivered the 'Canon Collins Memorial Lecture'. Among other things, he said: 'Such was the durability of his good works that it was inevitable that they would outlast the short life that is given to us all, and thus serve to turn the memory of the man into a material force that will continue to transform the destinies of the living.'

Such is the durability of Oliver Tambo's own good works that they have served to turn his memory into a material force that continues to transform the destinies of the living.

PRESIDENT THABO MBEKI

ACKNOWLEDGEMENTS

A BIOGRAPHY IS A GENRE THAT is not quite a history nor quite a novel. Like history, it requires empathy and imagination to try to understand the social and political landscape of that 'other country', the past, and a particular life within it. Like a novel, the reader requires the character (in this case, Oliver Tambo) to come alive, to develop; the reader wants to get to know what moved him, how he coped with the struggles of his own life as well as the movement's, what sort of a person he was.

In the absence of adequate written records, I interviewed and spoke to hundreds of people. More than 195 men and women were interviewed formally, each session lasting well over an hour, with many giving two to five hours of their time. Some were – or were about to become – well known in politics or government, others had been foot soldiers in the struggle. Sadly, more than 20 have passed away since I spoke to them, some in dire circumstances. Chris Hani and Carlos Cardoso were assassinated mere weeks after my interviews with them. To all these individuals, who spoke so earnestly, from the heart, about their memories of Oliver Tambo, I am deeply grateful. This book could not have been written without their memories, and their generous sharing of them.

In order to reach all these people, I was guided by suggestions given to me by the late Comrade OR himself, as well as Dr Adelaide Tambo. Eleanor Kasrils, who had herself worked with Tambo in Tanzania in the early sixties, arranged many interviews for me in the first two years of the undertaking. Warm, perceptive and with an infectious sense of fun, she was unfailingly encouraging, knowledgeable and proactive, and of immense assistance to me. I am also moved to recall, with appreciation, the late Rusty Bernstein, who on one occasion made a special trip to see me and to argue that Oliver Tambo deserved 'a substantial biography'. During the long gestation period of this biography, the patience of the Tambo family was sorely tried, and I must thank particularly Mrs Tambo, Thembi, Dali and Tselane for their endurance.

I relied too on the collegial encouragement of many people. I benefited greatly from being a member of the History Workshop, whose pioneering approaches to history in South Africa since their foundation in 1977 have been an intellectual inspiration to me. A number of colleagues remembered me when they came across relevant material in their own research and shared it with me. In this respect I am indebted to Rachidi Molapo of the University of Venda for his comprehensive bibliography; Dr Robert Edgar of Howard University in Washington, USA, for many documents and insights; Dr Tom Karis and Dr Gail Gerhart for their interest in the project and for copies of interviews with Oliver Tambo and others over a period of 40 years; Judge Albie Sachs for making me a copy at his own expense of ES Reddy's weighty collection of Oliver Tambo's speeches and private letters and for his thoughtful feedback on the manuscript; to Dr Reddy himself for a valuable e-mail correspondence on his relationship with Tambo; to Elinor Sisulu for sharing with me the fruits of her own research work and the prison memoirs of Walter Sisulu; to Dr Sifiso Ndlovu, Professor Bernard Magubane, and Dr Greg Houston of SADET; to Professor Peter Delius for his insights into Sekhukhuneland struggles, and to Raymond Suttner and Professor Phil Bonner for reading some of my draft chapters and providing feedback. To Professor Eddie Webster I owe special thanks for his academic advice and for reading the entire manuscript and making constructive suggestions as to where I might cut down and create a new chapter.

I benefited from discussions with fellow biographers Mark Gevisser, Ronald Suresh Roberts, Elinor Sisulu, Joyce Sikhakhane-Rankin, Tim Couzens, John Matshikiza and Dr Jonathan Hyslop, and also from discussions on the legacy of Oliver Tambo with Max Sisulu, Zeph Mokgetle, Dr Sakhela Buhlungu, clinical psychologists Tony Hamburger and Hillary Hamburger and, yet again, Raymond Suttner and Eddie Webster. I owe thanks, too, to Lionel Abrahams and Phillip Daniel for their responses to some early chapters and, in particular, Nelson Mandela for his input on the chapters on OR's childhood.

In addition, I want to express my appreciation to Albie Sachs, whose literary eye and insights, both in interviews and in his comments on the manuscript, raised the quality of my own perceptions. Then, too, I am indebted to Dr Pallo Jordan, who has both an experiential and academic grasp of the history of the ANC, and who read through some of the draft chapters before I had finished the entire manuscript. He helpfully pointed out some inaccuracies of fact and sequence of events in some of the chapters.

His comments made me realise how the rich and complex source of oral history confirms another long-held ANC tradition – that both its strength and its challenge consist of many perspectives and interpretations, bound together by a broad common vision. It was precisely this aspect of the movement that Oliver Tambo was obliged to confront and negotiate, from the 1940s until the end. It also confirmed for me the multiple experiences of life in exile during the struggle, and the impossibility of conveying the voices of even a couple of hundred people in one study. This is yet another confirmation for me of the skill and sensitivity of Oliver Tambo in being able to touch so many diverse people with a common goal, in a personal way.

In particular, I owe an enormous debt to Ronald Segal, who generously gave his time and shared his wealth of creative experience as a writer and editor with me, especially in response to five particular chapters. I learnt a great deal from our interesting and stimulating discussions in London, Walton-on-Thames and Johannesburg, and his encouragement was a constructive incentive.

In addition to benefiting from the knowledge of others, in my own research work I have been assisted by Kimon Webster, Thalia Hambides and Alexia Webster. I am most grateful to them for their hands-on help when I was under pressure. I also received assistance from the archives of the Mayibuye Centre at the University of the Western Cape, from Wits University's Historical Papers (with particular thanks to Michele Pickover, Carol Archibald and the late Miriam Hepner), from the Oliver Tambo Archives at the University of Fort Hare (Yoliswa Saul, Sadie Forman, Mosoa Buli Maamoe), archivists Narissa Ramdani, Razia Saleh in the ANC's Luthuli House, as well as Zeph Mokgetle for video sources. I must also thank Mrs Adelaide Tambo not only for being a gifted story-teller but for allowing me to encroach into her life and the lives of the Tambo family, read correspondence and page through personal photo albums.

I am also grateful to Thomas Mathole, in particular, as well as Mukoni Ratshitanga, Coleen Barker, Madhu Kanji, Sheila Weinberg, Edward Rapao and Alexia Webster for their labour-intensive transcriptions of interviews. In addition, there were friends and colleagues who helped to accommodate me when I was conducting research far from home. Margaret Castle was a warm and munificent hostess in London, Ann Perry and Antony Swift in Oxford, Marilyn and Richard Honekman in Cape Town, Janette and Hillary Deacon in Stellenbosch, Helene Zampetakis in Sydney, Nozipho Diseko and Dr Beth von Schreeb in Stockholm, Michael Burawoy in San Francisco. Josh and Daniel Brown and Julie Joslyn in Manhattan, Tom Karis in White Plains, New York, and Thesa Kallinicos in Longmont, Colorado, also provided generous hospitality. To them all, I owe a sense of a caring, First World community.

Financial support came initially from Friedrich Ebert Stiftung, from whom I have had many years of warm support for my other research work and writing. The University of the Witwatersrand, through a grant by Deputy Vice Chancellor (Academic), Professor Malegapuru Makgoba, also made available to me eight months' salary in 1996, after my first grant had been used up. From 1999 to 2002, the Ford Foundation assisted me with a generous grant that allowed me to make headway with the writing of the second half of the book, followed by grants by the Netherlands Institute of South Africa (NIZA) and one by the Oliver Tambo Foundation in 2003. In between and indeed throughout the writing of this book, my partner Eddie Webster supported me financially – during times of illness and short breaks, and also assisted me with research and running costs.

Finally, in the last part of this extended labour process, I would like to express my appreciation for the goodwill and patience of, firstly, the project manager of this undertaking, which has formed part of the run-up to the launch of the Oliver Tambo Foundation, Dr Morley Nkosi, as well as Dr Joanna Nkosi. I am also grateful for the fortitude of my editor Sean Fraser and Brian Wafawarowa, publisher of David Philip and New Africa Books.

There are also organisations that unwittingly assisted me in my research – as a member of various boards and committees such as the National Monuments Council, the South African Heritage Resources Agency and the Noma Award Adjudication Panel, as well as the recipient of a USIS trip to the USA in September/October 1993, I was over the years able to conduct out-of-town research in Cape Town, Durban, London, Stockholm, Boston, Washington and New York, as well as Boulder, Colorado, and Los Angeles, California. To all of these people, resource centres and organisations I owe my thanks. They prove yet again that knowledge is a most satisfying, collective undertaking.

Nevertheless, notwithstanding the goodwill and help that I have enjoyed, I need to take responsibility for the finished product. Any flaws or interpretations that might be faulty must fall on my shoulders alone, for ultimately the telling of any story, no matter how well researched, relies on both interpretation and selection. This inescapable fact confirms yet again that no scholar or historian can be value-free – for good or ill, the final product is the responsibility of the writer, even though she is drawing from the work and memories of those who have climbed the path before her.

LULI CALLINICOS
JOHANNESBURG, SEPTEMBER 2004

PREFACE

IT WAS A FINE APRIL EVENING in Perth, 1987. Outside the hall an anti-ANC protest was in full swing.[1] Demonstrators were sporting tyres around their necks and held banners asking 'Is this the ANC's freedom struggle?'[2] Inside, Oliver Tambo, dressed in his neat, finely cut suit, tribal markings clearly evident on his face, gave a calm, logical speech. He had barely finished when a furious, red-faced heckler, leading right-wing activist Brian Huckston, burst out with:

'I resent, as a taxpayer, your being in Australia at my expense. I believe you are masquerading – you are a terrorist, masquerading as a suave black gentleman!'

Tambo's response was a smile, then a chuckle. He seemed genuinely to appreciate the paradox of the metaphor.

The detractor continued: 'It should be known that you are responsible for killing thousands – the majority are blacks; your organisation is responsible for annihilating all these people.'

Tambo, he informed the audience, was 'closely linked to the Soviet Union and the South African Communist Party'.

Tambo replied to these charges point by point. In 10 years, he remarked, quoting from the Institute of Strategic Studies at the University of Pretoria, 80 people had died at the hands of the ANC. Government action had killed 2 340 in the years between 1982 to1986 alone.

'It's the other side who have killed, not the ANC...'

He went on to explain, step by step, the reasons for the armed struggle and the stratagem of a 'People's War'. He spoke about the 1955 Freedom Charter and the ANC's non-racial principles, 'to counter any notion that we want to drive whites out of the country'. He referred to the 'necklace' protestors outside, and spoke of executions by necklacing by the South African Special Police, who then went on to 'discover' the body'.[3]

'We don't condone [necklacing] – we disapprove of it.'

This exchange in Perth captures the character of Oliver Tambo: his unfailing courtesy, his lack of vanity, and his ability to fix his gaze on the goal of liberation. Tambo had the capacity to transcend the incidental: to submerge his ego into the larger goal of serving the liberation struggle. Typically, he made his case with facts, drawn from an authoritative source. His personal, open and unassuming style was to draw his opponents, as it did the audience in Perth, into a consideration of the challenge, so that they left the meeting with a deeper understanding of the South African struggle.

The Perth bigot, however, had not been entirely wrong. Tambo was indeed both a gentleman and a 'terrorist' – a deeply religious Christian and, simultaneously, a revolutionary, a distinguished professional and the architect of the African National Congress's strategy to overthrow the apartheid regime.

The conventional wisdom is that Oliver Tambo was the glue that held the ANC together in its 30 years of exile. While this is a proper tribute, it underestimates his vital contribution to the ANC and to the new South Africa. He played the pivotal role in the transformation of the ANC from a small group of well-educated petitioners to a broad-based militant liberation movement equipped with a Programme of Action to remove apartheid. He bridged the gap between the political generation that founded the ANC and the current generation that governs a new and inclusive South Africa.

This book seeks to demonstrate this argument by examining the central role of Oliver Tambo in the major organisational innovations that enabled the ANC to achieve its historic role. Let me summarise these innovations.

- He consolidated the organisational practices of consensus-making and collective leadership inside the organisation for the ANC.
- He was a key figure in the formation of the Youth League, whose call for a Programme of Action was to transform the ANC from its dependency on the goodwill of the oppressors to direct action by ordinary members.
- He, and the political generation of which he was a part, broadened the constituency of the ANC by establishing a close working relationship with the Communist Party (and continuing this relationship in exile) and its working-class base.
- He embraced an inclusive, non-racial project and consolidated it both inside South Africa and in exile, over many years.
- He developed a diplomatic strategy that isolated the apartheid regime.
- He consciously instilled in a generation of young people a love of intellectual enquiry and professional excellence, to be placed in the service of a future, free and democratic South Africa.
- And, most significantly, through his commitment to human rights and reconciliation, he laid the basis for the South African constitution and, by means of the Harare Declaration, an ANC-led negotiated resolution of the struggle.

This book is, however, not a political history of the ANC. It is a biography of the life and times of one man. It is here where the biographer can inform, I believe, the reader of a social context. The life of Oliver Tambo then becomes a prism through which to view a historic era. Biography combines history with story-telling and empathy. It contributes to the memory of a shared national history. It offers an additional interpretation of the human condition. It is a life in a particular time, a particular context. And it teaches us something more about ourselves, as members of the human race. For, as Oliver Tambo firmly believed and practised every day of his life, '*Umuntu ngumuntu ngabanye abantu*' – 'a person is a person through other people'.[4]

But biography also bestows agency. When we focus on one individual, we are given the opportunity to examine the particular circumstances, the life choices and values chosen in a particular life. It is here where personality, character and an inner life are revealed. Insights into the particular strengths, weaknesses and the nature and ambiguities of relationships enrich our understanding of a person and their times. We begin to understand, for example, that what is a strength in most situations can be a weakness in an exceptional moment. Details of Oliver Tambo's personal life are therefore far from irrelevant or an obfuscation of his central goal. The connection between the personal and the political reveals more of the perpetually elusive, whole person.

I first met Oliver Tambo in the home of Ruth First and Joe Slovo in 1959. I was a young activist and he was an attorney. We both lived in Benoni – I in a 'white' suburb overlooking a lake teeming with bird life, and he in the dusty, treeless township of Wattville. Tambo had a captivating smile, yet I remember being somewhat awed by his self-contained air. He had a calm, inner stillness. He did not speak much; it was mostly the genial Joe Slovo who spoke about the role that white South Africans could play to contribute to social change. He told us young whites about the Freedom Charter and the Congress of Democrats, the tiny white organisation allied to the Congress movement.

The next time I saw Tambo was in March 1960, in a small school hall in Actonville, where trade unionist Mary Moodley was giving a 'party' – in reality a preparation for the impending ANC campaign against the pass system. As we sat on straight-backed chairs drinking coloured cool drinks, I saw Tambo standing a pace away from the doorway, his face half in the dark, looking serious yet not disagreeable. I knew that as he was banned, he was risking arrest. When I next looked, he was gone. I was disappointed. I had hoped to speak to him. Three weeks later he left the country, the beginning of his 30-year exile.

It was more than 30 years before I met him again. In the intervening years, he had become an international figure. In about 1985, I had caught a glimpse of him on BopTV. I recognised him instantly. He had grown a short beard and a moustache, and the outline of his face was a little softer; but he was still the neatly formed, elegant man I remembered. As part of a newscast, Tambo was explaining, in a 30-second sound bite, why the ANC supported sanctions against South Africa. The following day the South African government expressed violent objections to the Bophuthatswana homeland's gratuitous exposure of a banned 'terrorist'. The SABC threatened to cut off BopTV's special access to its Soweto audience.

But Tambo's image and stature were growing without Bophuthatswana's help. He was inspiring young people with his broadcasts on Radio Freedom. His call to 'make the townships ungovernable' became the tantalising popular slogan that helped to mobilise activists during the intense, final years before the unbanning of the ANC. Once a militant 'young lion' himself, he had became the symbol inside South Africa – perhaps more than the imprisoned Nelson Mandela – of People's Power and the People's War, the course of action to be taken towards liberation.

In November 1992, I was deeply honoured to be asked by Oliver Tambo and Mrs Adelaide Tambo to write his biography. As there was also a political biography in the offing, I drew up for the family my concept of a gendered, social biography in which 20th-century South African history would be explored through the prism of the life and experiences of Oliver Tambo.

'The biography,' I wrote, 'will examine the ways in which Tambo's own life experiences instilled in him diverse repertoires – homestead culture; Christian morality and the education of the missionaries; and the radical, revolutionary discourse... In an organisation with a strong consensus of tradition and a culture of collective leadership, Tambo was able to manage the diverse repertoires and came to personify the coherence and "moral high ground" of the ANC. A conventional wisdom may be said to prevail. I am concerned to interrogate the reasons for this almost universal approval.'[5]

There were all too few secondary sources, for many of the events were too recent for much historical scholarship. But I was delighted to receive from Thembi Tambo the rich archive of taped and partly transcribed memoirs of Oliver Tambo of his childhood and youth. There were also many boxes of official documents and correspondence, although many records were missing or were scattered around the world. One treasure trove of 12 briefcases stuffed with papers was recently discovered in a 'safe house' in Lusaka, but has not yet been catalogued. Of special value are the handful of surviving notebooks in which Tambo scribbled reminders and comments, both his own and others' during meetings over the years.

My chief historical and fascinating source, though, lay in memory; and in the oral research work that ensued, a remarkable portrait emerged. Overwhelmingly, the respondents expressed pride in their association with Oliver Tambo. For them, Tambo represented their own 'age of innocence'. He seemed to have succeeded in interpreting for them the brave and dedicated new men and women that the liberation movement required. He affirmed the value of their lives. He symbolised the transformation of dreary, unfulfilling township living into the noble pursuit of freedom for all. Together with the other leaders, he had invented – and continually adapted – the movement, drawing on traditional rural discourses, Christianity, Western know-how and revolutionary strategy. He personified, by his unwavering focus on national liberation, the lure of altruistic ideals, spiritual affirmation and allegiance without material reward to which they had committed themselves when they first joined the movement.

The respondents' own life stories were fascinating and stirring. It became clear that these ANC 'stalwarts' were a self-selected band. Clearly, these exiles were not ordinary men and women. Through the long years of exile, many had experienced hardship, uncertainty and tragedy. Many had received valuable training. Through travel, they had been exposed to other cultures and societies. And perhaps some, as members of a beleaguered, exiled resistance movement, had become involved in shabby compromises. But when they recounted their memories of Tambo, and recollected their own experiences, their entire body language reflected their feelings. Their faces glowed, their bodies leaned forward, they gestured eloquently with their hands, they engaged in lively eye contact. Oliver Tambo represented for all these ANC members the best component of themselves.

Tambo's wide and inclusive national embrace enabled the vast majority of the ANC in exile to identify experiences significant to themselves. As with all experiential or oral testimony, the respondents recalled the qualities and characteristics most relevant to their own life stories. Mosie Moola, son of a devout Muslim and supporter of Gandhi, was profoundly touched by Tambo's 'most endearing feature', his 'simplicity'. Constitutional Judge Albie Sachs's absorbing narrative depicted Tambo as 'a natural democrat' who facilitated civil rights for all. Bridgitte Mabandla dramatically described Tambo's intelligent, subtle and successful intervention on her behalf with a hostile, all-male legal committee. Jacob Zuma saw in Tambo a rural wisdom. Ngoako Ramatlodi and Jonas Gwangwa were stirred by Tambo's love of music and his creative use of culture to further the cause of the movement. Thabo Mbeki was deeply influenced by Tambo's intellect and his strategic diplomacy; and so on. There was a part of Tambo in them all.

The universal esteem and affection, expressed almost without exception (and not excluding opponents and observers from around the world), raised challenges.

First, there was the danger of a lapse into hagiography – not necessarily only on political grounds, but because the reader will not be satisfied with a portrait of a two-dimensional 'saint'. Oliver Tambo himself wished to avoid such a construction. In any case, 'There is more to me than just politics', he once wrote.

But it is all too easy, in Tambo's case, to underemphasise his qualities. A reluctant leader, content to commit 'quiet acts of unrecorded heroism', Oliver Tambo was obliged to contradict his natural inclination of reticence. Perhaps it is for the reader – given an opportunity to examine his formative years: his family foundations, his cultural roots and the development of his aspirations and values before he committed his life to politics and the ANC – to form an opinion of Oliver Tambo the man. Tambo's biography reveals the influences and values of his roots, and his ability to utilise these, in tandem with the skills required in a modern world, moulded him into a unique blend that benefited the ANC both at home and in exile.

The second challenge was to disaggregate the role of the individual from the political tradition of the collective in the ANC, an organisation deeply embedded in the collective African traditions, reinforced by the 20th-century ideology of Marxism-Leninism that so emphatically rejected Western individualism.

Per Wastberg, the Swedish writer and long-time friend of Oliver Tambo, commented: 'OR fades in and out of focus; it is hard to hold on to the "real him". Like Nelson Mandela, who also submerged his identity into the ANC (though singled out and built up by OR and the ANC in exile), he is difficult to identify. The reality is that there is seldom a single identity.'[6]

The story of Tambo, whose political life coincided with a greater part of the 20th-century history of the ANC, raises questions beyond the personal and the political: the interplay between 'family and nation' introduces itself. As 'father of the nation', how did Tambo distinguish between his family and the movement? To what extent did he conflate his deeply embedded insights into the extended family with the nation itself – even as his concept of the nation grew exponentially over the years? In what ways did he combine African and modern customs and values to the benefit of himself, his family and his organisation?

Oliver Tambo, as we have observed, has been called the 'glue' that held the ANC together in exile under very difficult circumstances for 30 years. How was he able to achieve this? During these long years, restructuring and strategic shifts to armed struggle and its relation to the political and, later, the nature of negotiations, were needed. How did the leader handle the custom of patronage? How democratic could the movement under Tambo have been in a situation of security risks, with widely dispersed, diverse members?

How did Tambo oversee the uneven growth of the movement into a mass movement inside South Africa, benefiting from a worldwide support base?

To what extent did his traditional, rural roots combine with his own modern education to form the inspiring intellectual he became? And how did Tambo's inner spiritual life and his personal character imprint his own distinctive style on the liberation movement?

The ANC was blessed with a panoply of impressive and dedicated men and women in the struggle for liberation. Yet a remarkable number of people regard Oliver Tambo as the only person who could have held together the ANC and simultaneously retain the respect and affection of its members.

Far from considering Tambo's personal life as irrelevant or an obfuscation of his central goal, my approach has been to explore the relationship between the personal and the political in order to enrich our understanding of both the man and the movement.

In 1988, Oliver Tambo began to record the story of his life. For some time before, he had resisted entreaties by family and friends to commission his biography. For security reasons, as well as a wish to avoid a two-dimensional eulogy as President of the ANC, particularly at a time when the collective culture of the ANC needed to be highlighted, he felt that the time was not right. Certainly, he had been at the centre of the ANC's leadership throughout his political life, and his biography could not be separated from the history of the ANC, particularly during the exile years.

'My biography becomes inseparable from the day-to-day activity of the ANC during the course of these years,' he admitted. But, he argued, there was also another side to his life. 'I believe I have a fascinating story to tell,' he wrote. 'It is not a self-glorifying story, but certainly one that is worth telling. Nor is it all about political meetings.'[7]

Tambo made a counter-suggestion: that he work with his elder daughter, Thembi, in preparing his story – although, he said, 'I would not want it published during my lifetime.'[8] He began, consciously and systematically, to recollect memories of his far-off and far-away birthplace, nestling under the Engeli Mountains in Pondoland.[9] He began speaking into a tape recorder, describing nostalgically his family background, his homestead life and the community values, culture and influences that were to have a profound bearing on him.

Tambo undertook to do this at a time when his work was greatly increasing in intensity. Both internally and worldwide, resistance to apartheid was surging, unstoppable, towards a climax. As President of the African National Congress, Supreme Commander of the armed wing of the ANC and Chairman of the Revolutionary Council, Oliver Tambo conducted regular visits to the camps, carried out administrative work, held sessions with the National Executive and all the subcommittees in Lusaka and elsewhere in Africa. He addressed gatherings of anti-apartheid support groups in many countries. In addition, as the ANC came increasingly under the international spotlight, he was meeting with heads of state and major officials in both the West and the East – late at night, in hotel rooms in Stockholm, Washington or Moscow; in 'safe houses' in Lusaka; in airports or aeroplanes, Tambo made time to reflect on his hitherto little-known childhood and youth, paying tribute to his family, and the homestead and community culture of his early childhood:

'This was my world,' he explained.[10] He traced his steady projection, after the age of six or seven, further and further away from the Engeli Mountains, at the foot of which the Thambo[11] homestead nestled.

Tambo began to describe how the world of his homestead and community in Kantolo[12] laid his foundations. Inexorably, however, he was propelled by historical circumstances, and in ever-expanding circles, towards that other world beyond the rural village of Kantolo, beyond the town of Bizana, beyond the embrace – and the confines – of the Engeli Mountains.

Oliver Tambo's early life was not directly political, but his reminiscences are important for at least two reasons. Firstly, they provide a record of a personal and family history formerly unknown; and they point towards key influences on his making. But perhaps even more significantly, Tambo's reconstruction of his childhood gives us an insight into the events that he selected, consciously and unconsciously, to reconstruct and explain the man that he became. These experiences of his formative years stood out in his memory at a time when he was at the pinnacle of his productive life.

Oliver Tambo's family history, like that of other contemporary Africans, reflects the rapid economic and social change of 20th-century South Africa. Some of the key experiences of his time – land dispossession, political exclusion, religious conversion, Western education, migrant labour and abrupt urbanisation – were all directly experienced or acutely observed by OR himself. And, before he had finished his formal education, organised resistance was renewed. His participation in black opposition accompanied the making of a generation of leaders whose approach to their society and its challenges was to resonate with hundreds of thousands, indeed millions of people over the following 50 years.

Part One of this book recounts Oliver Tambo's early life, drawing on his own memoirs, which he wished to be called *Beyond the Engeli Mountains.* Not insignificantly, his memoirs stopped with his expulsion from the University of Fort Hare in 1942 – at the very point when he was becoming politically active. It was then (1988) that contemporary events overtook Tambo the story-teller, and he had to put the tape recorder away.

This biography continues in the spirit of Oliver Tambo's approach of an unfolding, incremental narrative. It links the personal with the political for a more layered insight into a man who made a great and historic contribution to South Africa. Part Two deals with the momentous years of the Youth League, Tambo's religious development, his courtship and marriage as well as the mass campaigns of the fifties and the making of the path-breaking Freedom Charter. Part Three deals with Tambo's management of the ordeal of exile in the early years, and the organisational challenges confronting the movement outside South Africa in their battle to return home. Part Four includes two thematic chapters, which explore the condition of exile and Tambo's particular approach to diplomacy; in addition, it covers the tumultuous eighties, culminating in the management and the strategy of negotiation with the apartheid state. It was a mammoth effort. It cost Tambo his health, and ultimately his life.

As one reflects on the life of Oliver Tambo, it becomes clear that here was a man of consistent and substantial character – a more encompassing word than its modern offspring, 'personality'. Character embraces integrity and sensitivity to others, intrinsic worth that endures through difficult times and 'focuses upon the long-term aspect of our emotional experience'.

'Character,' Richard Sennet writes, 'is expressed by loyalty, and mutual commitment, or through the pursuit of long-term goals, or by the practice of delayed gratification for the sake of a future end.'[13]

It is this essential quality that gleams through as the eventful story of Oliver Reginald Tambo unfolds. His eyes fixed on the horizon of a distant mountain range, 'beyond the Engeli Mountains', he sustained a steady gaze during the long and arduous pilgrimage towards the pinnacle of freedom and democracy. It is a life from which we can learn many lessons.

Part One

At the Foot of the Engeli Mountains

1918–1939

CHAPTER ONE

'This Was My World'

OLIVER TAMBO BEGAN HIS MEMOIRS with these words: 'Looking out from my home, the site of it commanded a wide view of the terrain as it swept from the vicinity of my home and stretched away as far as the eye could see – the panorama bordered on a high range of mountains that faced [me]. The Engeli Mountains were a huge wall that rolls in the distance to mark the end of very broken landscape, a landscape of great variety and, looking back now, I would say of great beauty... You had this sweep of terrain stretching to the foot of the mountain range that then rose gracefully in the distance, cutting your view from everything else beyond the range...

'But the nagging question was, what lay beyond the Engeli Mountains? Just exactly what was there? Were there people? What type of people? Were there towns? Were they like Bizana?... How far would one be able to walk over the mountains to Egoli, Johannesburg? What sort of world would it be? This was an unavoidable question whenever you looked in the direction of this range. What did it conceal from my view?

'I saw two worlds. The one in the vicinity of my home, which bordered this range of mountains, and its continuation eastward and westward. This was my world. I understood it from my mother's rondavel outside its precincts to the neighbours [in] Kantolo... I was part of this world. There was obviously another one, beyond the Engeli Mountains.'[1]

In African epochs, long before the coming of the colonial masters from their northern climes three or four centuries ago, men and women moved skilfully and purposefully across the terrain, plucking from the earth its bounty. Trained to utilise a variety of means for their survival, they employed the art of the hunt, the judicious selection of the fruits of the wild, the identification of the lushest pastures for their livestock, the cultivation of the most reliable staple foods; the growth of trade, the establishment of collective social structures and a world view, despite the occasional clash of interests between one clan and another, of the practical value of warm relationships and a deep respect for a shared humanity.

In this changing landscape across history, let us fix on the image of one man in the late nineteenth century. He is in the prime of his life, proceeding with his wife Mabewane and his children across mountainous terrain somewhere near the southeast coast of southern Africa. The travellers carry bundles of food and gourds containing sweet water, meted out carefully in sips. The youngest children are carried in turns, but are also learning to tread carefully on uneven surfaces, avoiding sharp stones, dangerous insects, reptiles, thorns and stinging plants. In his lifetime, the head of this little family, Nqwatshu – or Thambo (for, like others, he has many names) – and Mabewane of the Amachi people from south of Harding in the Natal Colony, have witnessed the attacks on the Zulu kingdom to the north by colonisers, and observed the consequences of war with the British colonials – the imprisonment and the summary replacement of the Zulu king Cetswayo, the drastic diminution of royal territory, and the proletarianisation of the monarch's warriors on the railways and the coal mines of Natal.

We do not know the reasons for Oliver Tambo's grandparents' decision to move. It may have been the immediate crisis of the rinderpest, that fatal cattle disease that swept the colony in the 1890s, or perhaps the even more severe and long-term problem of overcrowding in the rural locations, visited by the conquest and increasing regulation of land and chiefs by the Colony of Natal. Or, as a younger son, Thambo may have been striking out for an independent life of his own. Be that as it may, beyond the mountains lay sparsely populated Mpondoland, known for its fertile lands. King Sigcau, who resided in his Great Place of Lusikisiki, led this last outpost of independence. To the north, south and west stretched the land of subject peoples. There, traditional leaders deferred to the colonial magistrates established in their districts. Their traditional duties had been usurped, and they themselves had been bought over by an annual stipend.

Across the Engeli Mountains Thambo carried with him an ancient heritage, the customs and traditions he sought to preserve and sustain. Ahead lay the Engeli Mountains, and new opportunities.

Early one spring morning on 27 October 1917, a son, Kaizana, was born in a Kantolo homestead to Mzimeni, the eldest son of Thambo, and his third wife, Julia. To the world at large, Kantolo was little more than a tiny, remote village watered by the Umtamvuna River in a valley southwest of the Engeli range, which separated Natal from Eastern Pondoland. Much had already changed since the arrival of the child's grandfather more than a quarter of a century earlier. In 1895, Pondoland had been annexed by the British colony at the Cape. Its then prime minister, Cecil John Rhodes, could not abide this pocket of independence and loudly denounced the instability this caused in the colonial realm. A further irritation was the temerity of the king of Pondoland who was in the process of exploring the possibilities of trade relations with that new and growing industrial country, Germany. Rhodes – imperialist, mining magnate and prime minister of the Cape Colony – was determined to keep out Britain's commercial and political rival.

In addition to this external threat, the Cape authorities were determined to gain control of Pondoland as a reserve of labour before Natal could annex the territory. Rhodes used an ongoing dispute between the late King Mqikela's senior councillor, Mhlangaso, and the new successor, Sigcau, as an excuse to intervene. By threats, acts of aggression and intimidation, Rhodes persuaded the new king that it was in his interests to submit to colonial authority or face imprisonment on Robben Island and almost certain death. Sigcau thus became 'Paramount Chief' and the territory under his care was thenceforth a protectorate of the Cape Colony. The annexation of Eastern Pondoland was followed by the imposition of the 'hut tax' – to be paid in cash (to encourage at least one member of each homestead into wage labour), and Rhodes congratulated himself on this 'peaceful transfer from a barbarous to a civilised government'.[2] On the eve of the annexation, he declared that 'the Natives [will] no longer be destroyed by tribal wars and their increase [will] become a very serious matter. We can only hope that we shall be able to deal with them and show them that there is dignity in labour and that we pay the highest price for labour of any country in which the manual work is performed by Natives'.[3]

The annexation of Pondoland had taken place within the lifetime of Oliver's Tambo's parents. It was an act that symbolised the ills of dispossession afflicting South Africa as a whole. It also, in a contradictory way, offered new opportunities. For a number of years, the new labour system served to enrich the homestead economies, for returning wage labourers were able to buy cattle and so increase their stock. At the same time, the new economy foreshadowed the devastation of their culture and cohesion. Ultimately, Oliver was to devote his life to overturning the system of racial capitalism that colonialism had spawned.

Since the annexation, the little settlement had grown. A post office had been erected very close to the Thambo homestead, which itself was set in idyllic surroundings in a protected, green pocket of land with a view of the mountain range that soothed the soul. For the villagers, the mountain tops were sites of singular spiritual significance, burial places where the most illustrious ancestors resided. Timeless and ancient, the boulders were the very bones of the earth, preceding human beings by many aeons. They held secret networks, messages and sustenance from the past.[4] The village itself became known as 'the place of the post office' – 'Kantolo', from the Dutch word *kantoor*, meaning 'office'. A white man, who was also the resident trader, ran the post office, increasingly significant for administrative purposes, but also for facilitating fitful communication between the homesteads and their migrating sons. The postmaster/trader was to become the living personification of modern, colonial life and the fateful transformation that this heralded.

Despite the remote location of their homestead, international events had already made an impact on the Thambo family: the baby's first name, Kaizana, was a tribute to Kaizer, the German king, who at this time was challenging, through the First World War, the power and sway of Pondoland's colonisers, the British Empire. Later, in his birth registration, the names 'Oliver Reginald' were added and indeed, in time, were to replace his first, home name.

Nqwatshu and Mabewane's eldest son, Mzimeni (known locally by his clan name, Manchi), had been a mere youth at the time of their trek, and yet, enterprising and aspiring, it was he who located what everyone agreed was 'a brilliant choice for a homestead'.[5] And it was he, together with his father, who obtained permission from the chief of the Bizana district to build their homestead in Kantolo.

The site that Manchi had chosen was near the trading store. It was known as the Ntlazukazi Trading Store, because it was situated next to the river of the same name, a tributary of the Umtamvuna. Less than a kilometre away, facing the store, the land dipped into a 'saddle'. This green and idyllic setting, Oliver Tambo recorded, was 'where I was born, and where I first became conscious of my environment, and my surroundings and the people around me'.

The *umzi*, or homestead, was unusually large: 'a big kraal, as distinct from a two-hut home, of which there were many'. Because the Thambos were relatively recent arrivals, the family could not immediately obtain permission for the use of further land. The brothers stayed together until the following generation. The homestead thus consisted of the paternal grandparents, and their three sons, with their wives and children. (The eldest sibling, a daughter, had married and moved away.) Oliver's father, Manchi, was not a Christian and had four wives – however, he married his youngest wife, Lena, only after the untimely death of his second wife.

Manchi's family relationships were harmonious. Oliver Tambo recalled:

'We were very lucky. My mother and stepmothers were on very, very good terms – and so we, the children, grew up as brothers and sisters. You did not always have your meals in your mother's house; you ate together with the others, anywhere in the home, and my stepmothers would bring us together and just feed us; and we would play together, except for going to bed, and then you would go to your mother's hut to sleep... Very good atmosphere. We learnt to forget our mothers were different... I think we owe this kind of family to my father.'

Manchi's first wife bore him four children – a girl, who died, and three boys, whose English names were Willy, Wilson and Alan, the latter being youngest son, younger than Oliver. Willy, the eldest, though uneducated, left home to work as a labourer for wages, and for some years paid towards Oliver's education. Manchi's second wife gave birth to a son, James (Zakhele), before she died. Then came Lydia and Oliver, born to Julia, the third wife, and to Manchi's last wife, Lena, 'the youngest of our mothers... an absolutely wonderful person', were born Gerty, Florence and Connie.

Manchi, it seems, was comfortably off, and Oliver recalls that his father owned at least 50 cattle at one time, several fine horses and an ox-wagon.[6] These resources led to other opportunities:

'My father had trading connections that stretched to different parts of that world and he often took me along, so I knew a number of places. Sometimes we travelled by ox-wagon, which again was only possible because he had an adequate number of cattle, and he did transportation, carrying goods from one store to another. So he travelled long distances and often he took me along. Sometimes he would be going on horseback and we would ride side by side.'

Manchi was also well respected. On many occasions, he shared his resources with poorer neighbours or newcomers, lending them a cow or two for a few years, for ploughing and milking. When they returned the stock, he allowed them to keep the offspring. In 1993, a neighbour recalled how once, when Gazula, the headman of Kantolo, was convicted of an offence, a replacement was required for the duration of Gazula's prison sentence and Manchi was one of the three individuals nominated by the community. The magistrate, however, chose one of the other nominees, a Christian who could read and write.[7]

Manchi was not literate – 'My father had not seen the inside of a classroom,' said Oliver – and his prosperity was largely due to his own enterprise. Shrewd, creative and quick to seize an opening, Manchi sought and gained employment as an assistant salesman at the trading store. This exposure to a commercial economy taught him a number of skills and widened his world.

Oliver's mother was a Christian. A sociable and energetic person who could read and write, her home became the local headquarters of the Full Gospel Church. Tambo, in fact, recalled occasions when large, bustling groups of worshippers gathered in his mother's hut. He also remembered times when she and her friends would take a whole day to walk to Harding to buy fabric to make dresses for church. Eventually, perhaps because of his wife's influence, Manchi himself converted to Christianity, and had all his dependants baptised.

In that somewhat large and busy homestead, Kaizana had an active, happy and traditional childhood. As was customary in some clans, he had, in infancy, undergone *ukuchaza*: the scarification of his face, either to ward off or cure childhood illnesses.[8] Surprisingly, however, Tambo never mentioned his facial scars in his memoirs, despite the fact that it was a distinctive attribute that was often noted in his international travels, and regarded by some as a rather romantic and exotic symbol of the modern African revolutionary.

From as early as three or four years of age, the little boy learnt the essential skills of the rural economy, and the practical discipline that went along with it. Each morning, the bigger boys took out the cattle and drove them away for grazing. They would be away until early afternoon. The younger boys led the calves out of the pen to graze around the home. There was considerable skill for a youngster to learn in this task.

'Our task during the milking was to let out each calf, and during the milking we would stand around keeping the calf away from sucking while the milking would be going on. There was consideration for the calf; it was allowed, first of all, to suckle, and then removed. The milking would then go on, but before the cow had been completely drained of milk, the milking would stop to enable the calf to feed further from its mother's teat. This was a school too, because it was seen as an act of irresponsibility to allow the calf to reach the mother's teat to compete with the milkman. It invited very severe rebuke, so one had to concentrate and make sure you performed your duty properly, while the milkman did his.'

As the boys grew older and were able to accept more responsibility, they were given the task of herding the cattle. Kaizana was thrilled when he was given this additional duty. He made a point of scouting around for the best grazing sites, and discovered that the best spots were in between the cultivated fields. He particularly enjoyed taking the homestead cattle to these lush grazing areas, and watching them grab at the grass with gusto. Kaizana's inventiveness and strategic patience were thus discernible at an early age:

'Most herd boys would not want to approach these areas, because there was a risk of the cattle trespassing, and I started training my herd for moving through narrow lanes separating cultivated lands, but leading into open areas which were, for the purposes of grazing, untouched. This took some time to teach the cattle how to behave, but indeed they did learn, although there were the clever ones who tried to cheat. But we developed a system where they would move properly through a narrow strip of grass onto an open field and confine themselves to the grass.'

Tshongwana Mchitwa, who spent the day herding with the young Kaizana, recalled many years later two things about him: that he was very sociable – 'He loved being with friends' – and that he was a perfectionist.[9] Oliver Tambo, the innovative, patient and perceptive teacher of later years, thus received his apprenticeship in the pastures of Kantolo:

'Now and again some tried to steal, and the way they did it showed they were aware of the rules. A cow would approach the lanes, and I would be standing some 15 feet inside the field and watching; and the cow would approach a stalk, a mini stalk, and carefully eat all the grass around it very quickly, and move onto the next one, eating very rapidly, then snatch at the third and dash away as soon as it had done so, because if it hadn't, it knew by then that my stick would land on its nose! I did this often. It was my way of teaching them to leave the mealie stalks alone. It was interesting, the way they got to understand this and it made me enjoy grazing cattle. And of course the particular satisfaction I had was when I then returned home after watering them. Their tummies would be bulging and their milk would be in very good condition.'[10]

But the young Tambo also took pride in many other achievements. For him, the attraction lay in the fact that his accomplishments were not in the realm of play and fantasy, but were real and practical. He delighted in taking responsibility for tasks that helped him emulate grown men. He learnt to plough, and mastered the craft of spanning a team of oxen, controlling their speed, particularly on a slope in wet weather. He also taught the oxen to obey commands 'in such a way as the whole team pulls together'.

These accomplishments were facilitated by both the extended family and the community, which functioned as a coherent whole. In the homestead economy, work was both relevant and rewarding. Unlike labour in industrial society, it was not separated from home or community. Herding, like other productive activities, would be done in groups, and would include social interaction and the joy of satisfaction. Nor were opportunities for creative imagination bypassed. In his memoirs, Tambo lovingly recalled in some detail the inventive and creative pastimes and many games played by the herd boys during the long summer days. These included games of marksmanship; hunting birds by the surprisingly effective method of stick throwing; stick-fighting championships; and fashioning cattle and wagons from clay, 'binding them together so they moved like a span of real oxen'. But sometimes the games 'were a little too exciting for one's liking'. Mouse hunting, at the age of six, was a case in point:

'One group of boys would form a skirmish line and move slowly forward, singing some tune, and beat the grass so that the mice would run away in the direction that the boys were moving. In the meantime, a little further on, another group had placed themselves each at the mouse route – the track which the mice would take, because as they moved around they had their own system of roads – and you would position yourself with your bow and arrow and wait for the mice to emerge, and then pull and let go. Sometimes the mouse was so big that you had to scream and run away! But worse still, what appeared was not a mouse but a snake, which changed the whole scene completely then, and made the game less attractive than it might have been.'

But adults also worked in groups or parties:

'All the houses combined, not only in the ploughing but also in the weeding process. With fairly big fields, the neighbours were invited to come on a particular day for a whole day's weeding. We would have beer, and other drinks would be provided. We would perhaps slaughter a goat or a sheep. These were thrilling because there were so many people involved. We moved from work on a particular home's field to the next one, and with this kind of giant action, this facilitated the task and made it less strenuous.'

Those in the community who were better off were expected to assist poorer families. What helped the Thambo family was that it was a big family – even children were an asset in the homesteads. Tambo remembered that from time to time his father would slaughter a cow in order to provide a feast for the community: meat was a scarce commodity and therefore a luxury.

'You slaughtered a cow, usually in the afternoon and the neighbourhood was warned that a cow was going to be slaughtered... So that evening visitors came and had a portion of the meat; but the big day was the following day when the meat would be put into big pots, and around midday, early afternoon, everybody would start arriving from all directions, and then the meat would be served out to them; either according to clans or according to the areas from which they came. But the event was a social occasion, a feast.'

He recalled the generous portions of meat distributed. A group of men or women seated around a chunk of meat placed on a mat would help not only themselves but others beyond the circle too. 'Not infrequently,' said Tambo, 'a man would see someone, possibly a young boy, standing or sitting somewhere and call him, cut a large chunk of meat from the portion that lay there for them, and give it away. You could do that more than once without anyone complaining that he was in effect taking more than was due to him.' There was also always a little left for the following day, when a few of the men or women returned to pick up whatever else remained.

Like the festive gatherings to share beer, which Tambo also remembered with pleasure and nostalgia (despite his strict abstinence from alcohol as an adult), these feasts were a way of distributing some of the luxuries throughout the community, especially among those who were considered hard up. The community respected those who, in prosperous times, shared their good fortune, and status was accorded to those who shared with the community or who could benefit the community.

'To that extent, the profit motive could not be found. The practice of exploitation of others therefore was very remote from social practice. Everyone helped everyone else, and everyone shared what they had with others. Indeed the land on which the cattle grazed was communal property. It was owned by no one. It was nobody's private farm. It was the common property of the people, shared by the people. So the practice of sharing was central to the concept of ownership of property.'

This culture of sharing prevented an uneven distribution of wealth, and ensured a loyal commitment by all to the wellbeing of the community. One could not easily accumulate large herds by cheating anybody – and certainly not by stealing – simply because the neighbours would immediately notice. Tambo specifically recalled a neighbour known as Natinga, meaning 'Nothing'.

'He was a new immigrant into our area and at first he stayed at my home, with his wife and children and he had arrived with nothing. We gave him a goat or two – I can't remember how many – and helped him to set up a home about three quarters of a mile from our home... [Natinga had] no cattle to begin with. And he was loaned some cattle in keeping with the practice of the time of lending cattle out, on condition that the beneficiary would look after the cattle and see to their natural increase, and then after so many years, there would be repossession of the original number – the individual cattle – leaving the rest of the increase with the person who had been looking after the cattle... Within a few years, Natinga was a fairly well-off man; he had married two more wives, had a lot of children and his herd of cattle had increased. He had many goats and was a well-established, respected man... To achieve that position, he had cheated no one. He had robbed nobody, and he was in turn willing to help others who were less able to solve their problems than he was.'

In a society in which everyone knew almost everyone else, group pressure was a potent form of discipline. The most common disputes were those involving succession to property:

'All of these were based on people's interpretation of the law; and these cases were genuine – certainly most of them – and were brought before the customary court and discussed by the elders of the community and resolved.

In some cases they went as far as the magistrate's court, but virtually all litigation arose from mistaken ideas about rights or obligations. Seldom did they arise out of an attempt to cheat.'

Oliver Tambo did not, however, wish to romanticise his rural culture; the society was not perfect, he was careful to point out. 'There were,' he insisted, 'as there always must be, offenders but the social system as a whole was one which was inspired by fairness and fair play, mutual assistance and support – the sharing of property rather than unjustified acquisition at the expense of others.' And indeed, in a culture where personal relations were very meaningful for the wellbeing of a small community, understanding and mercy were far more important and constructive than retribution and punishment[11] – a custom that was to be pertinent to the culture of the African National Congress in exile too.

Theft and other criminal activity would be swiftly followed by arrests made by the government police. In many instances, though, the traditional form of collective action was used as an alternative to the official system of white retribution. For example, in the 1950s, stock theft in the districts of Qumbu and Tsolo reached such proportions that the community responded with its own combined form of justice. Suspected thieves would be summoned to secret places in the mountains and there they would appear before a tribunal. If the accused were found guilty, they would be fined, either in money or livestock. And if they failed to pay, their roof thatches would be set alight.[12] Interestingly, this same form of punishment against antisocial behaviour was used in Pondoland in the early 1960s against those chiefs and 'collaborators' who went along with the apartheid system of the Bantu Authorities Act – they too were seen to be committing acts against the interests of the community as a whole.

The Amapondo, like many polities in southern Africa, had a consensus approach to decision-making, a feature that was to become characteristic of resolutions passed in the African National Congress, particularly under the presidencies of Chief Albert Luthuli and Oliver Tambo. Between headmen and the community, as well as between the chiefs and the people, there was a balance of power. Consensus was the aim and method of reaching a decision. After a long discussion in which all the parties participated, the chief and his advisers would 'get the feel of the meeting'. Opponents of the plan were encouraged to speak out because, as the saying went, 'people should not be like a stream that flows in only one direction'.

'It is clear that chiefs relied on their councillors to prevent them from acting contrary to popular will... It was in the meetings of the *ibandla* [advisers] that the chief was able to test the loyalty of the people to him. If he found that the opinion of the councillors was rejected on many occasions, then he had to do something about the composition of his council. It meant they were no longer a yardstick by which he could test the loyalty of his people.'[13]

This supremely prudent practice of never straying too far away from their constituencies was to play a profoundly important role in the African National Congress under Tambo's guidance during the exile years. The culture of community involvement and answerability was thus inculcated from childhood. Tambo described how he was imbued with a sense of responsibility from an early age: 'Responsibility for the proper conduct of children was not confined to their parents only. When they misbehaved, they misbehaved against the community. And a senior member of the community was expected to do something about it. Any grown man had not only a right, but a duty to make sure that boys herding cattle did their job properly. Once or twice I had to flee a stranger, because the cattle that I was herding had strayed into a field at one end, and he chased me for quite a distance! At some point he gave up and I was saved from quite a severe beating.'

Among Oliver Tambo's most significant memories were those that revolved around cultural events. The interaction between traditional and Western lifestyle was just beginning to impinge on the community of Kantolo at this time. These recollections are significant because they reflect Tambo's deep interest in culture and his awareness of its power. During the ANC's 30-year exile, he was to utilise culture imaginatively to help mobilise resistance against apartheid on an international scale.[14]

One of Tambo's most vivid memories of social life in the Bizana district was the impact made by groups of young men and, in some cases, women, who sought ways in which to direct their energy and high spirits. There were two distinct styles of youth culture: the traditionalists, who had not been to school, and who formed themselves into loose organisations (Oliver's brother Zakhele belonged to one of these) and were, recalled Tambo, 'much less troublesome' than the other, schooled, group.

'What kept [the traditionalist group] together was singing clubs. On special occasions, each group would be singing its songs and moving with rhythm as they sang, carrying their sticks... You identified them, not only from the area from which they came, but because they were organised into these singing groups and groups of friends... moving from place to place and identifying themselves actually by the songs that they sang.'

Women, with their long, tightly plaited hair and stylish clothes, also participated in the groups. Choral music was always prominent at weddings, which inevitably included as part of the festivities a competition between the bride's choir and that of the bridegroom.

'It wasn't singing you'd find in a school choir or anything like that, but they were dancing to the music they were singing... graceful motions performed uniformly; and the test was largely the quality of the singing, the beauty of the composition and the grace, especially of the girls as they acted out the song.'

Many years later, what struck Tambo – himself a keen choral singer and teacher – was that 'that type of singing which was, well, unique, certainly to my area, has not been developed, has not been picked up by musical recorders. Where so much has been contributed to music by our traditional singing, this particular type seems not to have made any headway... Perhaps someone, someday, will, as the saying goes, "discover" this form of music'.

Western culture was, however, already making inroads into Mpondo society, and Tambo recalled a popular English song, which he sang at his sister's wedding. It went something like 'I say longy to Jelico, ha bla am I odiss'. But, said Tambo, 'it was many, many years later that I solved the problem of what the song was about, and the true words occurred to me one day. What the singers were saying was: "I sail on a ship to Jericho, how proud am I of this." Of course, they were singing the song in English... It didn't matter what it meant. It was the sound of it, the action that went with it and the fact that it was in English that mattered. English was largely like Greek – they didn't understand it – and it did not matter: the song was good.'

Christmas Day was another prominent event, one that was introduced to the village by the local trader-cum-postmaster.

'Early in the morning we kids would go round from house to house and our own homes and to other homes, calling out "*Kisime si bolise*", meaning "Christmas Box". This was asking for a Christmas present, which invariably came in different forms; but seldom was the quest ignored. Later in the day, the people would assemble at the trading store to exchange Christmas gifts.'

The trader would bake large quantities of small loaves and stock other little items, which were all reasonably priced, to be bought as Christmas gifts – 'to a sister, a brother, a cousin, a lover, to a lover's relative' – and the recipient was then expected to reciprocate. In fact, it was in ways such as this that a cash economy began to infiltrate the area. Young men, especially those who had had some schooling and were not yet earning wages, thus became restless and formed the second group described by Tambo:

'They were called "a column" and you could see them, winding their way around in a single file, singing and moving to the rhythm of the song, and then settling down for a chat... before they moved on to the next place.

'They would turn up at wedding parties, and make their presence felt, by engaging in disruption to a greater or lesser extent. The community would, of course, not be over-upset by this, because they know that it is part of this group that engage in a certain amount of misconduct.'

Oliver's older brother, Wilson, was very popular and, as a group leader, was known to provoke fights:

'In evening parties, it was often said of him – where they had gathered for some social event, late in the night with a candle being the only source of light – he would quietly sort out his group, and get them to sit in one part of the room, which would usually be crowded. The candlelight would be attached to the central pillar. There was one door out of the place, and on many occasions he was reported to have stood up and blown out the light, of course plunging everybody into darkness and started striking away at opponents or those who were not friends. A ferocious battle would take place, with people not sure who they were really hitting! Some of them would position themselves at the door and lash away at anybody who tried to get out. But it was all in good spirits, and the following day people would be walking about carrying wounds, but there was no question of revenge. It was the kind of thing that was expected to happen. All this was a way fairly young people, who are of working age but have no particular work to do, occupied themselves.'

Regularly, young men from Kantolo who could find no work would make the 25-kilometre trip to Bizana, where there was a recruiting station for the coal and gold mines. The recruiting agent, colloquially known as the *galajane*, or 'deceiver',[15] used various enticements to persuade young people to accompany him back to the mines. 'This man,' said Tambo, 'went round collecting workers and [would] sometimes pay them, even before they left... And this, of course, committed them to going.'[16]

In fact, even the custom of *lobola* was used to entice young men into labour: 'Young people went to work at sugar plantations, the gold mines – wherever – to raise money so they could purchase cattle with which they would be able to get their young brides. And it was almost a reason for seeking work – some day you've got to get married and then you would have to make this payment.'

All of Oliver's older brothers became wage labourers, both the traditionalists, such as Willy and Zakhele, and the younger Christians, such as Wilson and Alan. The migrant labour system was indeed an integral part of the homestead economy, and became even more important when Manchi's fortunes began to decline in the late 1920s. It also influenced the homestead's marriage patterns, even the timing of pregnancy and childbirth. But migrant labour brought both risk and adversity. Wilson, Oliver's older brother, for example, contracted tuberculosis in the compounds of the sugar plantations and had to return home, permanently unfit for strenuous work. In 1929, migrant labour resulted in a severe tragedy for the Thambo family:

'My father's youngest brother, Mbizweni, together with the son to my father's second wife, James [Zakhele], and our eldest brother, Willy, these three left home to find work somewhere away from home and would be away for some time. We did not know where they had gone to, until my father quite some time later, perhaps several months later, broke the tragic news that Mbizweni and James had died in a mine – a coal mine that caught fire – and the miners who were on shift at the time were killed. Willy had escaped because he was on a different shift. As my father reported this, he was a broken man. We all felt broken. James [Zakhele] was popular in the family, a delightful young man – self-confident and very active. Mbizweni had just got married and had had a son. He was also a very prominent figure among the young men in the area. He was the song leader for the local group.

'My father complained bitterly, but side by side with the information received, he had been told that compensation would be paid for his brother and son to the amount of £30 each. He said something to the effect that this was adding insult to injury. For us it brought a new understanding to the true value the white man attached to the black man. With such a painful death of young people with a future, all the company had paid was a miserable £30 each.'

Aside from the heartbreak and personal anguish, the death of two healthy and productive members of the homestead was a severe economic blow, and further hastened the decline of Manchi's prosperity. The tragic loss remained deeply imprinted in Oliver Tambo's mind, even to the last years of his life. It was not difficult to make the connection between his personal pain and the system of cheap and migrant labour in South African mines in general:

'Whenever, since then, I heard of mine accidents, a fire in the mine, such as those we had recently [1987] or a rock fall killing miners, my mind goes back to a name I did not know before the death of James and Mbizweni but which I remembered later – this was Dan Hauser. It was the Dan Hauser coal mine that caught fire and consumed hundreds of lives – people who were virtually working for nothing anyway. The striking feature about the way mining companies treat their black workers is that death due to accidents has not abated since... The toll of life in the mines is easily the highest for an employer group in the township, and in relative terms it is surely the highest in the world.'

Oliver Tambo's memories of his early life illustrate the shaping of his own identity, through his community values and experiences in the homestead, the culture of the *umzi*. The high motivation for work the Thambo family cultivated was, in time, to lead to a lifelong habit of tackling challenges with unshakable determination, and heralded the characteristics that were to mark Oliver Tambo's particular style of leadership in later years.

The changes associated with colonialism and industrialisation could be discerned in Kaizana's early childhood. Already, the community was beginning to assimilate different experiences and new cultural groupings, and it seemed that the young boy readily absorbed these new phenomena as well as the old. The influence of the missionaries, too, was extremely powerful. They brought with them not only a new theology – with all its social implications – but also offered the allure of knowledge and access to a new technology. The Thambo family, through Manchi, as the homestead head, was one of the first to discern their potential for self-empowerment. But very soon the entire community was to become inextricably involved in the rapid and far-reaching changes taking place in South Africa.

During Kaizana's early childhood, Manchi's family was fairly comfortably off, and they were able to resist surrendering their economic independence to wage labour in the 'white' cities. But the homestead could not remain untouched by the extensive grip of the system of cheap black labour that was emerging. The cash economy, with its industrial expansion and ever-growing demand for wage labour, was impinging more and more on the structure and productive power of the homestead itself. These changes made a deep impression on the child.

Even more profoundly, however, the character of the young Kaizana was a product not only of his parents' care, but also of his homestead culture. As a member of a large extended family, the little boy – even as an infant – had had to share his mother with many others.[17]

Unlike most Western middle-class children in a nuclear family culture, little Kaizana did not have the exclusive attention of his mother. Consequently, he had to sacrifice some of his own ego, his own sense of individual identity. But at the same time, the little boy was compensated by having access to other mothers, aunts, uncles and older brothers and sisters. The child's growing sense of himself was thus intimately tied to his extended family, to his neighbours and to his community. The day-to-day lifestyle, and hence the value system, was one of sharing.

'The wider family,' observes Gandhi's biographer Erik Erikson, 'permits a closeness, often expressed physically and affectively in a true "togetherness", deeply touching and yet somewhat disturbing to the Western observer. To hurt or abandon the uncle or the aunt or the older brother or older sister, therefore, can provoke a peculiar or lifelong guilt; and to be hurt by them, forever gnawing resentment.'[18]

In the case of Oliver Tambo, this sense of obligation was magnified. Over the years, his concept of the 'community' was to grow, little by little but steadily, along with his increasing exposure to that wider world beyond the Engeli Mountains. His sense of personal responsibility for the welfare of the community continued to grow – until it reached a point where the identification of his kinfolk, and his obligation to them, expanded to include all African people, indeed all the oppressed and exploited of South Africa.

CHAPTER TWO

The Reluctant Schoolboy

MANCHI, OLIVER TAMBO'S FATHER, was an astute man who well appreciated the value of Western education. Working in the trading store for so many years, he had been impressed by two aspects of Mr Mountjoy, the white trader: that his learning enabled him to run an independent business and keep its books; and that his relative wealth gave him both power and status. People would come from all around to buy, explained Oliver Tambo. 'He had a car, horses – he was a reference point to the community – and he had servants. In general, he was a chief in his own right. He certainly was something above the level of ordinary people. It was exactly this difference of levels that my father was targeting in insisting that his children should go to school.'

This, however, was not to say the community was overawed by the trader's rank. Oliver recalled with amusement a memorable occasion when a trader was disciplined – an incident that quickly became imprinted in the local memory:

'At one time, the trading store was owned... by a man called Mkobeni by the people. The store was known as Qua'Mkobeni – Mkobeni's place. He was the stout, bulky, bullying type. He was very short-tempered and had crossed words with many of the people who frequented his shop. One day he was offended by a man from the locality. He got very angry and a fight broke out in which this man hurt Mkobeni and immediately broke contact and ran towards the river in the direction of his home. Mkobeni wanted to deal with him and so ran for his horse – a big stout animal – saddled it up, jumped up on it and raced after this man. By that time the man had crossed the river and was running on a slight incline. Mkobeni chased and caught up with him one to two miles from the shop. He jumped off the horse and tackled him, bringing him to the ground. He started to pound him, with Mkobeni on top and the man underneath. The man grabbed and held on to Mkobeni's testicles and squeezed, at which time Mkobeni yelled with his booming voice, attracting the attention of people who wondered what was going on. He yelled, begging this man to let him go. After some time, the man seemed convinced that Mkobeni was indeed surrendering, and let go... By this time a number of villagers had gathered to watch, and Mkobeni quietly went to his horse, got on it and rode back to his trading store... The news of this fight spread like wildfire through the locality.

'After this incident, Mkobeni became quite a different person. More respectful to the Africans, in better control of his temper and was never near trying to beat up anyone. I say he was the first to be there and had been there a long time. Those who came after him may have picked up something of this story, but as I have said, their attitude to the people was correct and there were no incidents of that kind. It was very interesting to us youngsters; it took away some of the apparent superiority of the white person who had everything.'

But Manchi was wise enough not to allow the insolent behaviour of some white traders to deflect him from an understanding of one of the major keys to their power – education. Manchi himself had bold ideas. He developed his own capacities in the form of a transport business and built up the resources in his homestead. While he had indeed managed the trading store under a previous owner, he was considered little more than an assistant salesman. Nevertheless, he was well aware of his own capabilities and knew that he could do anything the trader did. The store, for example, boasted a large garden, fenced in and cultivated with fruit of various kinds.

'My father,' said Tambo, 'had exactly the same thing. He had fruits, he had fenced his garden and worked very hard.'

Manchi had clearly grasped the advantages of agricultural and other modern practices, and adapted these as far as his vision and abilities would allow. 'He entered into a variety of contracts and did very well to begin with,' recalled Tambo. His disadvantage, however, was that his lack of literacy limited his opportunities, and he was very conscious of the necessity to master the skills of the colonials. 'He understood that the best thing was to be independent, and he did not want us to be employed as he had been. He did not want us to suffer the handicap that he did, and so pushed and pressed that we go to school, so that ultimately we could be independent and not be employed.'

In fact, so keen was he that his children gain some measure of independence that he did not particularly want them to become employees even if they acquired a trade or profession. This was a singular approach in the community. This challenging attitude expressed itself remarkably differently as far as the rest of the village was concerned. '[The community] distinguished between themselves and the white man. They didn't really need him – they could get along without him. There was no need for education if you could span oxen, plough, weed the fields; and if you were well enough to find employment if necessary, that was sufficient.'

Young Tambo and his brother Alan sometimes played with the two Du Toit boys, whose father now ran the Kantolo store. They were friendly and spoke the local language.

'I envied their attire – a pair of trousers, a shirt, a pair of shoes especially. I, on the other hand, was of course going barefoot and my attire consisted of a piece of clothing material which I tied around my waist so that it formed a kind of baggy underpants. The rest of the attire consisted, if anything at all, of a light blanket, which hung over the left shoulder and body, and was secured around the neck with a knot so that the right shoulder and the right hand, the hand that would always carry a stick, would be free and could move without being hampered by this blanket.'

One day, when Kaizana was about six years old, Manchi told his young son that he would start school the following morning. Kaizana at once discovered its powerful potential for change. To his great excitement, 'my mother dressed me up in the new clothing, which had been bought for me, a pair of shorts and a shirt'. The school on the hillside was less than a kilometre from the family home, and had only recently been opened. It boasted a Sub A and a Sub B class. On his first day of school, Kaizana discovered something that was as important as the reading, writing and arithmetic his father hoped the teacher would instil in the young boy. He learnt that schooling also required him to manage another identity.

'The teacher approached me and asked me for my name. I gave him my name and he said, "No, you are giving me your home name. I want your school name." I told him I did not know my school name. "Well then," he said, "you must go back and ask your parents to give you your school name. You must also have a second name, which should be the name of one of your ancestors who has died. So tomorrow you bring your name and surname."

'Returning home, I told my parents that the teacher did not want my name... The following morning, my father told me that my school name would be Oliver and the second name, Tambo. I, of course, did not know how Oliver was arrived at, but I knew that Tambo was my father's paternal grandfather. Armed with the two names, I returned to school and duly submitted them to my teacher. As I learnt to read and write, I came to know that Oliver was spelt "Oliga"! I do not recall at what stage the spelling was changed.'[1]

Several months after Oliver started his schooling, an epidemic – possibly diphtheria – broke out, and many children died. Fearing for the lives of Oliver and Lydia, Manchi sent them to stay with their mother's cousin, Stanford, so that they could attend the local Kanero School. It was here that the two received their first taste of institutional life at its worst. No doubt, it was to be a painful lesson for the future educator on how not to instil knowledge to young minds. Certainly, many decades later the experience was still carved in Tambo's mind in vivid detail.

'I cannot say if the only teacher at this junior school was a good or bad teacher. But I've never had anything to do with a more cruel teacher. He was a sadist if he was nothing else. Mr Godlwana moved up and down his single classroomed school, with his trouser belt in his hand, and throughout the day he would beat one child or another.

'His favourite way of punishing the children was to double-fold the belt – leather, heavy leather – so that it formed a loop; and he would throw this, standing in front of you so that it would land on the neck behind. I went to school every day with a stiff and painful neck and every day I knew that I, like the others, would get the taste of Mr Godlwana's belt. During the 11 o'clock interval, when the time approached for him to ring the bell which called the children into the classroom, the children would be playing around and he would quietly creep up to the bell, which was not far away from the entrance to the classroom, then he would pull the bell and ring it and immediately rush to stopper the door and if he got there before you did, you were late.

'This time he used a small stick, and made you hold your hands, fingers together, facing up and he would strike the tips of the fingers one or two or three times as he pleased. He enjoyed this – that he was inflicting indescribable pain on his victims – and daily we were treated to this treatment. It was easily the worst year I have spent anywhere, in any school since then.'

At the end of the year, Oliver passed Sub A, a milestone the youngster was to appreciate at the end of the following year, when he returned home to yet another school, further away than Kantolo, at Embhobeni. The move was a happy one for the boy. It was there that Oliver was introduced to formal music lessons: 'One of my fascinations at the time was tonic sol-fa, which we were taught there – how to read and sing in tonic sol-fa. I even made a practice of composing and writing up songs for myself – nothing to be presented to anybody, but I enjoyed doing it and this was the beginning of my interest in choral music and other types of music.' In fact, the influence of Western music on traditional singing was to expose the boy to a syncretic enjoyment, in time to come, of all kinds of music.

Nevertheless, despite Oliver's relish for his musical education, a white school inspector decreed at the end of his second year that Oliver had failed Sub B. Manchi's anger at the school for failing to teach his children to the required standard made a deep impression on Oliver. It is perhaps at this stage that the child began to associate achievement with hard work – a striking characteristic that was to be developed more consciously and systematically when he was a little older. Manchi, in the meanwhile, decided to move his children to a more established school, the Ludeke Methodist School, some 16 kilometres from the homestead. '[But] to cover that distance twice a day took away from the excitement of going to school,' remembered Tambo. In the rainy season, the children arrived at school drenched to the skin after the two-hour walk and, as a result, Oliver became increasingly reluctant to walk this distance daily. In any case, he was still very attached to cattle and oxen, and this tended to compete with his interest in going to school.

'I did not like going to school, firstly because it was far, and I didn't enjoy it. My father was aware of this and he sometimes lent me his horse to go to school just to encourage me. But of course, if I was going on horseback it was great fun; but when I didn't have the horse, I would find excuses not to go. I would play sick, and I found the weather a great ally of mine. If it was raining then my parents would say, "No, don't go to school."

'So my best day was rain. And I came to study the weather, the movement of the clouds every afternoon to try and make out what kind of weather it was going to be the following day. I became quite an expert. I had a deep interest, and I was absolutely accurate about whether it was going to rain or not. Always accurate. That stayed with me even when I was no longer home. I looked at the clouds and I could say to people, "It's going to rain", and it rained. It's still the same today. I usually can tell long before people are aware of it. That's how I learnt it – because I didn't want to go to school.'

To overcome this problem, Manchi boarded Oliver with three families in turn, all of whom lived near to the school. But he found that the cost of supplying entire homesteads with bags of maize proved too much for his resources, and Oliver was finally called back home, to travel to school on foot, or, whenever Manchi could spare an animal, on horseback.

The trouble he took to ensure that his children were able to attend school says much for Manchi's commitment to their education, particularly in the face of growing criticism from some members of the community. As Oliver and his brother Alan moved to the higher classes, disapproval became increasingly overt. There was indeed, commented Tambo, 'a general hostility to education at that time.'

'[My] younger brother and I, and certainly I on several occasions, would meet people who would ask why we were still at school – we were only in the early primary and they would say, "Well, but can't you read and write yet?" – and the test of whether you could read or write was contained in a question: "Are you not as yet able to write a letter that would go to Johannesburg and come back?" That was another way of saying, Can you write a letter to which there would be a reply? And, of course, if you could do this, this was just about what was required. It was necessary to have somebody who could do this, because then the people would be able to dictate letters, as we did so many times. They dictate a letter which you write out addressed to the husband or son or brother who is working in some mine in Johannesburg. If you wrote that letter, it was posted and there was a reply. Then the expression would be: "The letter reached Johannesburg and came back."

'This was a very, very big test whether one had really done enough or not at school; beyond that they didn't understand, it didn't make any sense. What more would one want?'

The attitude of the community, coupled with the prospect of the long walk to and from school, had an adverse impact on Oliver. He was also becoming increasingly concerned that he was not contributing his fair share to the productivity of the homestead. 'My father now had to look after cattle as if he were a herd boy,' recalled Tambo. '[His friends] thought he was silly and stupid. "He's got so many boys and here he is looking after cattle himself," they said – and he was just about the only one who did that. Our age group were at their homes looking after cattle; their parents had no problems looking after cattle themselves. But we weren't there. My father was determined that we should go to school.'

Young Oliver was a sensitive child: he was eager to please, keenly responsive to social relationships and conscious of his family duties and obligations. In 1925, when Oliver was just seven years old, Manchi's fortunes began to decline markedly. In his recollections, Tambo did not explain precisely how this reversal came about, except to refer indirectly to his father's lack of literacy as a disadvantage in business. But Manchi was not alone in his financial difficulties. Pondoland homesteads were, in general, hit by the effects of the Native Taxation and Development Act, which imposed a £1 poll tax on every African male aged 18 and over. In addition, there was a host of other burdensome levies designed to propel peasants into a cash economy and finance the administration of Pondoland. These included the 10-shilling hut tax for every wife in the homestead, the two-shilling education tax, and the six shillings and sixpence dipping levy for stock (which, in turn, was further increased a few years later).[2] Even for full-time wage earners, these were hefty amounts in the 1920s, and for homestead economies without an external source of cash they were extremely prohibitive.

The years that followed, 1926 and 1927, were equally bad years in market production in Pondoland.[3] The Bizana district would almost certainly have been affected, and Manchi's transport business would have suffered too.

Manchi began to sell off some of his stock, and eventually also his ox-wagon, the means of his transport business. And the rest of the Tambo household would also suffer under these harsh conditions. Manchi's brother and older sons were obliged to find work in Natal – three of them in the coal mines and one in the sugar plantations. Oliver could not fail to be affected by this shift to wage labour and was keen to make his own contribution to the family fortunes. But the decisive moment in his future plans seem to come with an incident when he was unjustly punished by his father.

'[My father] had grease, which he had put on the fire, melting. It was in the fireplace and my father left it to go to Bizana. This was in an open pot, and my younger brother [Alan] started playing around, swinging his leg backwards and forwards above this pot.' The more alert and conscientious older brother reprimanded him: 'You know you're going to kick this thing over and it will spill.' 'But he ignored me, and he did kick it, and the grease got spilt and I said, "But I told you!"' When the boys' father returned and discovered the mess, he was livid and asked, 'Who did this?' Oliver looked at Alan to admit to it: 'Talk.' But the youngster denied any involvement in the mischief. 'I was surprised,' recalled Oliver, 'and my father concluded that I did it, and he beat me up. I felt it was so unjust. It annoyed me. I was waiting for that kind of thing to happen again and the next time it happened, that same night I would disappear from home.'

Clearly, Oliver was already, at that tender age, showing a determined and unshakeable sense of fairness. He was intensely protective of his own rights to the extent that he was not willing to allow even his esteemed father to impose an injustice, however well intentioned, on himself. He thus began to at least consider moving away from his father's ambit. Oliver was now going on for 12, and a number of options were opening up for him. 'Some of my age group,' he explained, 'had already left their homes, crossed the Umtamvuna and went to Natal to work – some in the plantations. And some were coming back, big stout chaps already. They were young men, and I was still going to this school. So I began to think in terms of leaving, escaping to go and work there as a garden boy or even in the sugar plantations. I would work there and bring back money to my parents – that's what everyone else was doing.'

In fact, one of Oliver's older herd mates, Tshongwana Mchitwa, was already preparing to go to work in the Natal sugar fields.[4] But not long after Oliver had received his unmerited beating, another experience made him delay his decision to leave school:

'There was a practice in the school of the senior classes having debates in English and continuing these debates outside the classroom; and there was this particular chap who was so extremely fluent that it was like an English person speaking, and we all said, "But where did he learn English? Where did he go?" And somebody said he went to school in Kokstad. Now Kokstad is outside the Bizana district. I said to myself, "My goodness, I would like to go to that school!" So again, I had no interest in the school I was going to and I thought, if I don't go to work I will go to that school in Kokstad to learn English.'

This was a significant turning point in Oliver's thinking – in his recollections, it symbolised the process of change in his attitude towards schooling, and by implication, his culture. At that age, he was beginning to assert himself and pit himself against his father's will, where it had been unjust. Yet the boy was also absorbing from his father (contrary to the more conservative opinion of the community) that the ruling class had powers that could be assimilated usefully into his own culture. Oliver had discovered in himself a love of disputation, reason and debate, and English seemed to be the key to these ruling-class skills. The English language provided new words, and therefore labels for new concepts. The boy at the school debate demonstrated, unexpectedly, to Oliver that the initiation of approaching manhood (for the Amapondo did not emulate the traditional initiation rites of other Nguni-speaking chiefdoms) did not need to be confined to wage labour in the 'white' city. It could take the form of trial by knowledge. In leaving home, new choices would present themselves to him; a new, alluring identity would open doors to power through knowledge, to adventures of the mind.

Said Tambo, 'I didn't know how to get to Kokstad, who to say I was when I got there, and so I was working on two choices: either to go to Kokstad and learn and bring myself up in English, or to go and find work. I was waiting for something to happen that would decide.'

Then 'something' did happen. In exile decades later, Oliver Tambo – relating the story in the present tense – bestowed on the incident a vivid sense of immediacy: 'One day my father has a visitor and I see him, sitting outside the house talking to some man. This happened so often I hardly took notice. But after a time my father calls me so I go there, sit down. And he says, "This man comes from a place known as Holy Cross. He says there are white Fathers at this big school who are willing to take on and educate children whose parents cannot afford to pay for the schooling of their children." (By that time, my family's relative prosperity has diminished considerably.) And he says, "Would you like to go there?"

'It was the biggest piece of news I had heard for a very long time. The excitement of being away from those conditions of going to school; the excitement of being in another part of the country – not so much the fact that I would be at school, but that I would be away – somewhere... I jumped at the idea and from then on I was pestering him about when we were going... That was the first time that I took an interest in the prospect of going to school.'

Who was the visitor and why had he taken the initiative to intervene in Oliver's education? Uncle Thomas had been a nonbeliever who had never been to school, until one day the wheel of an ox-wagon fell on his head. He was then rushed to the Holy Cross Mission hospital, where he was treated, and in due course Thomas converted to Christianity. He remained at the mission, working and attending school. During one of the holidays, he decided to visit his neighbour Manchi to recruit his school-going children for Holy Cross.

So it was that, after a few impatient weeks, one April morning in 1928, Oliver and his brother Alan left with their father and Uncle Thomas. It took them the entire day on horseback to reach the mission. In describing the journey nearly 60 years later, Oliver Tambo saw it as 'the beginning of a new era' and again relived that momentous experience: 'I have now left the district of Bizana where I have lived for about 11 to 12 years, and will never go back there again except on school or other holidays.' It was as if Oliver realised that his symbolic universe was about to be irrevocably altered, and his senses avidly absorbed the new sights. His first impressions were of the size and design of the land and the buildings, which, for him, took on a deeply symbolic and spiritual dimension.

'Holy Cross is built on land in the shape of a "T" – significantly, in the shape of a cross without the top section. The main section of land lies east and west and then winds north-south. At a point roughly where the sections meet, and certainly on a line running east-west through the centre of the longer section is a church that towers over the entire mission ground... As you curve to the right into the inner road, if you are coming from the north, immediately to the right, next to the church, there is a huge wooden cross that rises tall like a great big sign telling where you now are – Holy Cross.'

Tambo then went on to describe in graphic detail the layout of the buildings – the hospital, the classrooms, the pupils' hostels and the residences of priests, doctors, nurses and teachers, the sports grounds and the inner roads and paths that connected them all.

'This then is the new world which opened to us, as a group of horsemen led by my father and including Thomas, Alan and myself, rounded the great course at the entry point. We rode on without following the curve of the inner road. This took us past the school buildings on our right, and further on our left a cluster of two or three rondavels, and we ultimately reached a point with St John's Kraal on our right which was a built-up area comprising some more rondavels. Here we unsaddled, here was our journey's end.'

Oliver Tambo's next indelible impression was the Anglican Church Easter ritual, a pageant in all its glory of colour, rhythm, finery, and the exotic aroma of incense.

'It turned out to be Saturday of the Easter Weekend, the eve of Easter Sunday. Indeed, I had observed standing outside the entrance to the church, which would be about 200 yards away, a group of people who were wearing what I came to know were red cassocks and white surplices. I did not know what the uniform represented at the time, but found out it was the evensong which preceded Easter Sunday. And so it was very early the following morning that I was woken up and told to go to church; and there we found a church that was overflowing with people, notwithstanding its big size, and I have [sic] never been inside such a long, high building.

'A procession soon started which moved within the church to begin with, accompanied by a drum, and moved out into the open, wound its way round the cross onto the main road leading north with singing and the beating of this drum. It finished up at a cemetery. All this was quite mystifying to me... It was headed by a boy clad in this uniform who was swinging a smoking object followed by someone else who was carrying a cross.'

This was Oliver's first experience of the church to which he was to make a lifelong commitment. But, after the enticement of the Sunday service and the warm interest shown by the boys at the hostel of St John's Kraal, the next morning was to bring acute disappointment for Oliver. Uncle Thomas had been mistaken, Manchi was informed. The school could not afford to take on more pupils without means, although their go-between, Brother S'Kumbu, indicated that the staff would try to raise bursaries for the boys.

'As day followed day, the gloomy prospect of returning [loomed] larger and larger and my father and the rest of us were increasingly giving in to despair and sadness; but the school, Boetie (meaning brother) S'Kumbu, did not seem prepared to give up, and indeed after several painfully anxious days, he brought the great news that we were to be admitted to the school and would stay at St John's Kraal as boarders... We came to know that the relief which thus came to us was provided by two women, Joyce and Ruth Goddard, who lived in England.'

While some black pupils, who had been similarly assisted, grew up to express suspicion and mistrust of the motives of their white benefactors, in all of Oliver Tambo's life, even during his most sharply nationalist period, he always expressed unambiguous appreciation for those two faraway English ladies. They were the first of a number of benefactors in the tradition of intrepid British Victorian female missionaries and explorers. In his recollections many years later, Tambo linked their action to the international support 'for those engaged in the struggle for liberation from oppression and the apartheid system in particular' in the years to come.

'[The sisters] were total strangers to us as we were to them. They intervened tirelessly to save the careers of two unknown youngsters who but for their intervention, might have had to say goodbye to Holy Cross and goodbye to education as well as goodbye to a future of possible usefulness to humanity... They had stretched a couple of hands across the lands and oceans to the south of the continent of Africa to give aid and support to two unknown children. Two unknown African children.'

Oliver's letters to the sisters over the years are revealing. The following is his first letter to them, dated 27 October 1928, on the day he turned 11 years old.

> Dear Friend,
> I thank you all about what you are doing for me, to pay money for me, and above all, I stay here at Holy Cross by your money. I am glad because I learn by your money. There is a good thing I want to tell you, that there was a Bishop here and he baptised me, and I am glad for that. It is nice here at Holy Cross, we play some certain games, and our kraal is well made. I hope that sometimes you will come here and I shall see you. On November we shall be examined by Mr Pope and I am in Standard 4 but I do not know whether the inspector will be very strict, and I hope that you will pray for me.
> I remain there
> Yours
> lovely child
> Oliver Tambo

In spite of the difficulty that Oliver must have had in writing a letter of thanks in English to remote strangers, his additional items of news signified a desire to communicate something of himself to which the sisters themselves could relate – the importance of his baptism, his nervousness about the coming examination by the white school inspector, his observation of the school buildings – more substantial than any he had ever seen – and his enjoyment of sports. Doubtless, his teacher helped him with the spelling and construction, but the content itself and the great effort it must have demanded, was an indication of a little boy's efforts to reach out to his benefactors, to reciprocate in some way, and engage them further by asking for their prayers.

The Goddard sisters could not, in fact, afford the full amount needed for the boys' education, so Oliver and Alan's oldest brother, Willy, who was working in the coal mines in Natal, undertook to provide £6 a year, to match the £6 donated by the English sisters. Their financial help was to continue, to a greater or lesser extent as far as their means allowed, until 1940, by which time Oliver was a student at Fort Hare.

Thanks to the Misses Goddard, Oliver was now able to stay on at Holy Cross, and was delighted at the prospect of the new world that was opening up before him, but there was nevertheless a little sadness in his heart:

'As my father took the left-hand curve around the cross and disappeared behind the church as he joined the main road leading to Flagstaff and the north, I suffered an attack of homesickness. He was flanked on his left by the two horses that had brought Alan and myself, each complete with saddle and bridle. I suddenly thought of my mother, sister and all the world that had meant home for me, and wished I could be riding back with my father.'

Never again would he spend more than a few weeks in Kantolo with his immediate family, in the shared bed and the warmth and intimacy of his mother's hut. This was his moment of initiation into adolescence, the first step towards a journey to self-reliance.

But the boys very quickly adjusted to the social life of the hostel. Alan, too, 'settled down to make many friends at St John's Kraal. He developed to become a good cricketer and a strong and lively full-back in soccer. He did not do badly at school, although that was not exactly his favourite pastime'.

In fact, the young Oliver grew to love Holy Cross, which he significantly called his 'second home'. St John's Kraal became a projection of his *umzi*, his homestead in the outer world, and the staff members and the boys and girls, his surrogate family. His detailed recollections of his peers are lively and affectionate, and of the many individuals he remembered so vividly was one Van der Berg Ngeyane.

'He was a great entertainer, one of those people whose absence you would feel but as soon as he comes you know he is around, laughing and joking, talkative. I had frequent bouts of stick fighting with him, and even this he turned into quite an entertainment. Frequently breaking contact, running around the grounds, shouting and boasting to draw the attention of everyone to what was happening. So it came to involve everybody.'

Oliver, in fact, retained his fondness for Ngeyane's exuberance. According to one of his ex-pupils, Mr Rumford Qwalela, when KD Matanzima – head of the first 'independent homeland', the Transkei – visited Tambo in England in the 1970s, Oliver asked Matanzima's bodyguard, Ngcayi, to 'please give my love to Mr Ngeyane. This is the present I am giving him.' The gift was a hat, a Battersby hat, from London.[5]

It was stick fighting that inducted Oliver as a new boy to boarding school. At home, Oliver and his peers never ventured out without a stout stick. It was part of their traditional accoutrement, their presentation of themselves as purposeful young men on the move. On his first morning at the hostel, Oliver was assigned to wash the dishes with his friend, Madhlamba.

'As we washed dishes he said something which amounted to an invitation to a stick fight which I readily accepted. So he gave me my two sticks and got hold of his and we abandoned the dish-washing for a test of each other's prowess. In Bizana, I had had quite a few of these with various other boys and except for the experience with Ganavi [who had defeated him] I had good reason to be self-confident. Some of those who had faced me had had to flee after an encounter in which I of course took some beating, but I had clearly given more than I took and I was respected among my age group and so I accepted the challenge gladly and started.

'Five minutes can be a long time. But it can also be a short time, depending on how the going is. I think we were about five minutes in a furious exchange of blows, many of which were landing on the flesh on both sides. It was a fast, hard, give-and-take affair. We reached a point where we both broke with the encounter, we smiled at each other. I knew he was a man and he knew I was a man. I came to find Madhlamba was very fond of provoking stick fights with all kinds of people, and of course he was very good, but he never ever, not once invited me to a fight, nor I him. We had tested one another and we knew what each one was. He became from that moment when we called off the exchange, fast friends, intimate in a remarkable manner. Never so much as a difference and we understood each other so very well. The friendship with all its intensity lasted until long after I left South Africa to go abroad.'[6]

Sindiso Mfenyana, Tambo's long-time comrade from the early 1960s, was in later years to insist that Oliver's qualities of personal courage and endurance were first engendered by his training in stick fighting.[7]

Oliver also fondly remembered the teaching staff at Holy Cross. He had lively recollections of the principal, Mr Ntongana, as well as teachers Mr Mti, Mr Fitzgerald Ndelu, and the St John's Kraal housemistress, Miss Hill, who had contacted the Goddard sisters to obtain financial support for Oliver and Alan. He recalled, too, 'a lady teacher in charge of sub-standards A and B in a third classroom, which, unlike the other two, was a rondavel. This post was held by a Mrs Bam, whose son – a very bright and neatly dressed little boy – was known as Fikile...'[8]

Once committed to schooling, Oliver was determined to excel. In his earlier reluctance to attend school, he had not avoided the classroom out of indolence. From early on, since his herding days, he had enjoyed the satisfaction of work well done, and reaped its rewards. Homestead life had prepared the child well for responsibility and industriousness. Furthermore, his father's steadfast faith in education had sustained Oliver's own belief that what he was learning at school would count with the new authority figure, the teacher, and would be relevant for his future life. And so, despite the cleavage in his world, Oliver was able to integrate, both symbolically and practically, the world of his home, the *umzi*, with the world of school and Western knowledge. He thus tackled the challenge to excel with conscious resolution:

'Of course, it took many months of hard work before I could build myself into a position where I was counted among the top four in the higher classes. The conditions were relatively most favourable. In Holy Cross, I came to like school, to like studying in a way I had never done before. The nagging problem of walking 10 miles every morning, starting early and repeating the 10-mile journey back, arriving back home late afternoon – all of this was now a thing of the past. It took just about two minutes to walk from St John's Kraal to our classroom. That made a substantial difference. And then I was outside school among other schoolboys all the time, which facilitated concentration on school work.'

Johnson Makaula, the head prefect, recalled how he too benefited from the switch from part-time herd boy to full-time scholar. 'I came to Holy Cross, where I started learning. There were no sheep here. I just concentrated, carried on with my education till I passed my Standard 6.'[9] In January 1993, at the age of 80, Makaula travelled to Holy Cross to see his old friend again, and remembered Oliver as 'a very clever boy... he used to pass with first grade, distinction'. He recalled, too, that from that early age, Oliver had a litigious tendency, and a love of debate that indicated the makings of a vocation different from his own:

'Oliver used to argue a lot. With his friend, Robert Sonqishe, who later became a priest... He used to argue, saying gold will be finished some day, and they used to argue about that. And I used to say, gold will never be finished... He had to dig up a lot of arguments about a lot of things... and one day he became a lawyer, and a politician... I didn't like arguments. If I want to say a thing, I just say, this is wrong, this is right... We were told that teachers had no part in politics, so we had to stick to that, otherwise we would be sacked.'

But Oliver's conscientiousness in his studies was extended to his extramural activities too. One story – almost a parable, which he related with humour –

revealed the boy's obsessive meticulousness, a trait remarked on with some affectionate exasperation by some of his speech-writers in the ANC during the exile years. Along with the other boys, Oliver was assigned a small plot of ground to grow vegetables:

'I took *extreme* care of it, and ensured that it was among the neatest of the plots. The top was always kept flat as a table, virtually spotlessly clean. Father Hartley, the priest in charge, would visit St John's Kraal periodically and take a look at the plots. He would find tomatoes, cabbages, carrots, potatoes sometimes, beetroot and so on. The second time he came round to my plot, having visited it on an earlier occasion, he said to me, "My dear Oliver, your plot is very neat indeed. But nothing ever seems to grow on it. Why don't you plant something?"

'I gave no reply, but I knew that to begin to plant anything would spoil the look of my plot. I would have to dig holes on its flat surface, and possibly have to step on the ground and spoil the surface. But he passed on. The most I'd do with my plot was to dig it up from time to time but then level it up, and use the rake to restore it to its unspoilt beauty and plainness. I treated the plot as a toy. I was used to growing big fields, not an eight by six piece of land.

'My father did plant potatoes and cabbages, but there again it was not such a tiny piece of land. The whole thing generally was not very serious to me. I did, however, in due course persuade myself to grow something on that plot, and then it lost, of course, what I regarded as its neatness; it assumed the beauty of productivity.

'Reflecting upon it in after-years, I remember the biblical story of the master who gave equal amounts of money to each of his subjects and, returning some months or even years later, he said to the one, "What did you do with the money I gave you?" So he proudly produced it, saying "Here it is. I've kept it very safe." And to the other man he said, "And what did you do with the money that I gave you?" He said, "I invested it and it has multiplied itself manyfold. Look how much I have now." I'd been keeping my plot nice, beautiful, safe – [chuckles] unproductive.'

At the end of the term, Manchi came to fetch the boys to take them home for the holidays. There, they found 'big changes in the religious life' of the family. Manchi and his family had been converted to Christianity. The 1920s had witnessed a burgeoning of competing missionary zeal, and each religious movement vied for members. Oliver himself had been exposed to a number of different interpretations of Christianity.

'Preachers would come round from time to time and they would say, "The Gospel says so and so, everything else is wrong. We are members of this church because we are following what the Gospel says here." And they would read it and it was convincing, so my parents would join. Then, later, a different preacher would come along with a different verse, equally convincing, and my parents would change over to this new faith...

'[During my first holiday from Holy Cross] there arrived at home a religious group... calling themselves by a new name. There was something new about them. They prayed for the sick and they healed the sick... The great thing is people actually got healed – some blind person who started seeing; others came with ailments, who were known to have these ailments, were prayed for and they got healed.'

The evangelical movement had arrived in Kantolo. Its fervent and even impassioned approach to spiritual life and to prayer were much closer to the traditional consciousness of a world penetrated by sacred forces beyond human reason than the more formal, rational outlook of most of the missionaries of the mainstream churches.[10] Both Oliver and Lydia were impressed by the passion and commitment of its followers. Influenced also by their mother's active devotion, both children were to continue to be personally involved in their respective churches for the remainder of their lives. 'My sister had some ailment and convulsions that she suffered from and she had been sent to some place to go and get healed there. She was brought back and prayed for by those people. She recovered – in fact she grew to be an Evangelist in her own right, healing people and travelling around.' Oliver himself was highly impressed with these Christian visitors:

'There was something which, somehow, keeps working up the leader, and then of course they had a way of speaking in new tongues also, almost automatically, just uttering, not an intelligible language, but you could see that they're not controlling it and you'd feel the spirit keep on rising... Now how this affected me was that, until then, you went to church and sang hymns. You said "Our Father", but were not a part of it. I was affected by an experience I had had with this leader called Matthew. They don't wait until 5 o'clock for prayers. If you feel like praying, you go out and just kneel there and pray, aloud. You can't imagine it happening here. People would think you were crazy; it didn't happen here. Like the Moslem travels around with something he spreads and kneels there. They did that. So one day Evangelist Matthew was kneeling, facing east, talking. So I knew he was praying; but what struck me about his prayer was that he was talking to somebody, and now and again he would be laughing. I was thunderstruck. It seemed he was talking to a friend! This was more than the prayer as I understood it. He was talking to somebody. I said to myself, "Yes. Why are we always crying when we are praying? What sort of God is it who asks us to cry all the time? Why can't we talk to him as a friend, and converse, talking to a person?"

'That struck me, and it introduced a new dimension to my own prayer. Even as I now went back to school, some of the results were remarkable. And I knew that my prayer was very powerful.'

Oliver thus developed a rich spiritual life that was to be a vital source of sustenance in times to come. It was also to be nurtured by his environment at Holy Cross, for – despite his attraction to spontaneous and individual prayer – here he was potentially open to all forms of spiritual expression. Besides, the will to be a fully accepted member of the school community was powerful. Oliver consequently responded to more formal worship too. Churchgoing was a regular feature – during the week, certainly on Saturday evenings and on Sunday mornings.

The mission prepared to baptise the two Tambo brothers and other new boys. Oliver was very eager to be accepted into the Anglican fold, even though he had already been dramatically baptised by one of the sects that had visited Kantolo.

'One of these [church leaders] took us to the Umhlalikazi River, together with several people. The priest stood in the water, which was at a level above his knee, and would take each person being baptised, hold him by the neck and plunge him into the water head foremost facing down and immerse the head, and of course unavoidably part of the body. This done, I had become a Christian, an acknowledged Christian who was at the same time a new member of this particular denomination.'

Back at the Ludeke Methodist School, Oliver had been prepared for his christening by attending catechism classes, but before he could complete the process, he had left to become a pupil at the Anglican Mission School of Holy Cross. Here the priest, who refused to acknowledge the validity of the boy's earlier baptism, reconfirmed the young Oliver Tambo to Christ.

'The procedure,' said Tambo, 'was quite simply pouring water over my head and uttering the relevant accompanying words. That done, with a few additional elements of ceremony, I was now a Christian and a member of the Anglican Church.'

The ceremony was followed by Oliver's confirmation into the Church, and his response to this event throws some light on the importance to Tambo of inclusiveness, a practice that was to be a mark of ANC policy during his – and his predecessor's – presidency.

'On a particular Sunday, the Bishop of St John's, Bishop Etheridge, was there to lay his hands in confirmation of a pretty large number of boys and girls. It was an exciting occasion. It meant, among other things, that we would no longer suffer the humiliation of being asked to leave the church when communion was being taken by those confirmed. It meant we would be full participants in the act of worship. And so indeed, I became a fully fledged member of the Anglican Church.'

Yet, despite Oliver's ardent embrace of the spiritual world, there remained an element of shrewd pragmatism that was to be yet another characteristic of his political adulthood.

'As far as I was concerned, it made no difference if I was a Methodist or an Anglican. Indeed, in later years I narrowly missed going to Marianhill in Natal, which is a Roman Catholic secondary school. If I had gone there, would I have identified sufficient of a difference between the Anglican and the Roman Catholic Church to prevent me identifying with the religious practice of those among whom I stayed? I do not see what it would have been.

'So, as things worked out, I was Anglican. And I have no regrets. On the contrary, unable to say what would have happened if I had not gone to Holy Cross Mission, I am able to say it was a jolly good thing I did! And a jolly good thing that I was put through the institutions run by the Anglican Church, which became part of my experience, including an Anglican hostel at Fort Hare. All these have served to define my life in a way, I have reason to believe, to be different from how I would have developed otherwise. Except that I have no reason to suppose that whichever I had developed I would have cause to regret whither had I come up through a different religious practice.'

These various inductions thus exposed Oliver to the arbitrary nature of his endorsement as a Christian.

'I certainly continued to be unable to say what the justification is for having Methodist Christians, Roman Catholic Christians, Anglican Christians, Baptist Christians, Congregational Christians, Church of Nazareth Christians and all these. I still am unable to appreciate... the need. I certainly find myself as much at home in a Methodist service as in an Anglican one, to the extent that apart from detail, these services are about the same thing and serve the same purpose, and participants do the same things. They talk about the same things to the Maker. They sing hymns that say the same thing. They say prayers that convey the same thought. And so it is that having through circumstance identified more with the Anglican Church than the others, I found no need to move from the one to the other; that if as a young boy I found myself as a member of the Anglican Church, in circumstances which made it virtually impossible for me not to be... Now as a grown-up, [if I had] come to find anything about the Anglican Church which, if I had known it as soon as I was able to exercise my choice, would have led me to walk out of the Church.'

Oliver, then, was well aware of the role chance had played in the eventual outcome of his church affiliation, and the extent to which he himself had been excluded from the decision to be initiated into each particular church. The social context of the missionary influence pervading Pondoland, and indeed the Eastern Cape as a whole, surely made a powerful impact on Oliver's entire generation of Xhosa-speaking ANC leaders. As colonised Africans, they were more likely to be sensitive to the fact that culture and religion were socially constructed and controlled. Yet, this missionary background also contributed to the distinctive social and political culture that the ANC was to develop.

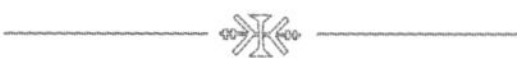

The following five years were to be years of rapid and eager development. Oliver continued to flourish, both in the classroom and on the playing fields. In 1930, he was promoted to Standard 5, finishing among the top four in his class, and then on to Standard 6, the final year in primary school. But at the end of the Standard 6 year, he was to endure a severe setback:

'We acquitted ourselves most creditably, passing with very good marks. And now we were looking with great expectations and hopes and much engagement of our imagination about what would be coming... One of my close friends, Captain Flatela, was already a secondary-school student at St John's College at Umtata. I looked forward to joining him there the following year...

'Naturally, after the exams, the big question was, "What next?" Following up enquiries about what the exact arrangements were for my going to St John's College, I uncovered a shock. No arrangements had been made for me to go, because there were no funds. I was staggered. I was informed that I would, however, be able to enter St John's College in 1933, when the necessary funds would have been found. Did this mean that I was to spend a whole year at home before going to college? No. There were others in my position, I was told. We would all come back to Holy Cross the following year.

'But, to do Standard 6 again when we had passed so well, when we had learnt everything there was to know – to repeat Standard 6! Not quite. A special class was to be set up in which we would do studies just above the Standard 6 level. A retired teacher, a Miss Tidmarsh, was coming out specially from England to take charge of the class. I pondered the meaning of it all. I would now enter college in the same class as those who were in Standard 5 when I had passed my Standard 6. They would have caught up with me as though I had failed Standard 6! I would be a year behind the colleagues who were with me when we wrote Standard 6, and with whom we wrote and passed the Standard 6 examinations. I was getting left behind. I would be junior to them. Whereas at Holy Cross I was, in terms of my performance, their senior... But the reality was that there was no college for me the following year.'

Despite the blow to Oliver's well-developed sense of decorum and the well-deserved regard in which he was held, he soon adjusted to this reality and appreciated the merits. They were operating at a level somewhat above that of Standard 6. There was greater concentration, a greater demand and the studies went deeper and further than was the case during what was essentially their last year at primary school. Of course, it certainly helped that the new teacher, Miss Tidmarsh, was extremely strict, but because there were only seven students in her class, she could in turn offer each one personal attention. 'The top marks,' said Oliver Tambo, 'regularly went to Meshack and myself, with the rest by no means far behind. The general standard, I would say, was high. Suddenly, no one felt he was wasting his time doing "Ex-Six". We were, in fact, being prepared for secondary school, the year following.'

Oliver was also appointed prefect at St John's Kraal, but despite the immense pride and sense of achievement that must have come with it, it also led to an event that would serve as a further blow to his self-esteem.

'On one occasion the cricket team went to Flagstaff for a match. We walked back and arrived at St John's uneventfully. At least, not until [head prefect] Johnson Makaula suddenly confronted me with a ridiculous accusation... He said he had seen me smoking. I told him that was absurd! He couldn't have seen me smoking because I did not smoke as we were walking back, or indeed at any time during my entire stay at Holy Cross. I was no smoker. Johnson insisted and proceeded to cause me to be demoted from the position of prefect.'

Oliver's sensitivity, his pride in receiving recognition for worthy endeavour and behaviour, and his keen sense of honour and justice were profoundly shaken. The experience imprinted itself in his memory:

'I still cannot explain what it was he saw. He was wrong, and for a second time, I was getting punishment for an offence I had not committed – the first being when my father gave me a beating over grease Alan had kicked over and spilt. Although I have since known many instances of innocent people being executed, hanged, let alone jailed, I have never forgotten those instances when I first experienced this injustice. I feel no bitterness about it because those who punished me believed I was guilty. [But] they acted without investigation. The true facts are not always obvious. They often have to be looked for.'

But in the meantime, the year was drawing to a close, and Oliver had no indication that he was to be enrolled at St John's in Umtata. He decided to take the initiative and apply to Marianhill, a Roman Catholic secondary school in Natal. To his delight, Marianhill accepted him, informing him that the fees were £7 a term. When Oliver returned home for the Christmas holidays, he showed his father the letter.

Although Manchi had no money, not even for the railway fare to Natal, he was nevertheless anxious to accommodate his young son's desire, and thus arranged for Oliver to fetch the horse Manchi had lent to neighbours. In the meanwhile, he borrowed a horse to collect Oliver's clothes and books from Holy Cross.

Oliver's mission to recover his father's horse was unsuccessful as the man was away for three weeks, and had taken the horse with him, but Oliver was confident that his father would find a way of procuring the money – perhaps he would sell a cow in order to further Oliver's education. When Manchi returned, however, he brought disconcerting news: 'The white people are fighting at Holy Cross.' Oliver was stunned. What could they be fighting over? He could not imagine such a thing taking place at Holy Cross and wondered exactly who was fighting who. But he had misunderstood his father. Manchi explained, 'They just will not hear of your going to Marianhill. They want you to go back to Holy Cross for another year.'

'"Go back?" I exclaimed. "Go back for another year?" I repeated. I could not stand the very thought of it. It was something out of this world. I could *not* imagine myself going back to Holy Cross again! The very thought of it was maddening. How could I? Who had ever been asked to mark time for two years, awaiting funds? In any case, I had been admitted at a college and it was only a matter of my father raising the necessary funds for me to proceed. Why should I go back to Holy Cross? All these questions poured into my head. My father, keeping quite calm, went on to say he thought I should leave for Holy Cross the following morning, because, as he said, the school had already opened and I was expected. He said he himself thought I should go back. I walked away from him, and kept away until the following morning.

'In the meantime, sleep did not come that night. I was faced with having to obey, or disobey. I had never disobeyed my father before. But then he had never ordered me to do anything quite so impossible as going back to Holy Cross. I had a college to go to. Why should I go back to Holy Cross, I asked myself. The authorities were promising to send me to college in 1933. How did that promise differ from their promise to send me to college in 1932? Would I ever go to college at this rate? And what would I spend the year 1932 doing at Holy Cross? Not Ex-Six again! I found the whole thing most difficult to swallow. My only problem was how not to disobey my father. And, in the end, I decided I would have to obey; I would have to go back to Holy Cross, quite unwillingly.'

Oliver's ingrained respect for his father and his intrinsic sense of duty did not, however, prevent him from showing his silent anger.

'And so the following morning I dressed up and went to my parents' hut. I found my mother had packed up a suitcase for me, that she had breakfast ready for me. My father proceeded to tell me what route I should take and described the kraal along the way where I should spend the night. I would be walking to Holy Cross this time, not going on horseback. Having heard him, and without taking breakfast, I picked up my suitcase and walked out, without saying good-bye to my parents.'

But yet again, Oliver found that, in spite of himself, he enjoyed this third, undeserved year in Standard 6. The class realised that they were gaining more and more knowledge, becoming more and more proficient in the subjects they were learning, limited in number as they were, for they included neither Science nor Mathematics. But not everything was repetition. Miss Hill had left St John's Kraal, and had been replaced by Miss Motutu. Sadly, Boet S'Kumbu had passed away of tuberculosis, but Oliver's eldest brother Willy, who had been stricken with TB in the Natal sugar plantations, had now been offered a job as a driver at Holy Cross. Although Willy was not earning enough to contribute to Oliver's schooling, the Goddard sisters had agreed to continue their support. It was at this time, too, that a lifelong friend – Robert Sonqishe – was admitted to the school. Of their great friendship, Oliver Tambo said, 'a friendship of the same strength as I had with Eliot [Madhlamba]'.

In the second half of the year, Oliver developed a growth in his chest, which the doctors decided to remove. He was duly hospitalised for some weeks, and Miss Hill reported this turn of events to the Misses Goddard:

'I am very sorry to report that Oliver... quite suddenly developed a TB chest... However as it's so much the beginning and he's so young and fit generally, I quite hope he'll soon be quite cleared. We've got sudden expectations from him as he's quite the cleverest boy in the Kraal and school! He lives on a bed on the verandah at the Hospital: so has plenty of air!'

Convalescence was, in fact, quite an adventure for the boy. It became even more memorable by some unexpected news from a member of staff, another British missionary:

'One day I was visited by Miss Tidmarsh. She told me she had just returned from a holiday in the Transvaal. She had been to the Kruger National Park as well as to a secondary school in one of the suburbs of Johannesburg known as Rosettenville. She had been shown around this school and had liked it very much. She thought if I had any chest complaint, the higher altitude of Johannesburg would be very good for me and she would recommend to Miss Whittington that she applies to this school, known as St Peter's Secondary School, for my admission for the next year.'

To the young Oliver Tambo, this was a thrilling idea indeed. To go off to Johannesburg, the famed Egoli, though not as a miner but as a scholar, was surely a pioneering move.

'Having missed St John's College and Marianhill, would I be the first student from Holy Cross and possibly even Bizana and Flagstaff to be admitted at a secondary school in Johannesburg? It was an exciting prospect. But then, who would pay for my travelling all the way to Johannesburg? Who would pay the fees? Why would Johannesburg succeed where Umtata and Durban had failed? Lest another shock should be in the wait for me, I decided not to be overly optimistic, and to wait and see what happened.'

But towards the end of the year, Oliver learnt that he had indeed been admitted to St Peter's, along with his best friend Robert Sonqishe. 'This was by far the most exciting news I had heard since coming to Holy Cross in 1929,' he said. 'I doubt if sleep came that night. My gratitude to my father for his insistence that I return to Holy Cross yet again was boundless!'

As had happened before, Oliver found himself in a situation in which he relied on the power and goodwill of strangers. He had been forced to take on a passive role, and to try to deal with the circumstances as constructively and creatively as possible. Oliver interpreted this significant event in his life – as he was to do with other important moments in the future that were beyond his control – by discerning a divine intervention.

'My mind raced back to the year 1931 when I had completed my Standard 6 and was expecting the following year to proceed to St John's at Umtata. Would I have been in this happy position if I had not been prevented from going to St John's College; if a year later my father had not forced me to go back to Holy Cross for one more year of waiting; if I had not been taken ill with Miss Tidmarsh returning from a visit to the Transvaal, and finding me in bed at Holy Cross...? It was as if every gigantic step forward started with a setback; or to look at it differently, every setback was countered with a big leap forward.'

This was an observation that was to sustain him during countless setbacks in the turmoil of the future, and developed in him a rare skill that was to prove invaluable in the years to come.

And so it was that, armed with some symbols of the big city – a suitcase, and his first pair of shoes, which was bought for him by his brother Willy – Oliver Tambo crossed the Engeli Mountains on his journey to Egoli and that 'other world', geographically and culturally so far away from home.

'Accompanied by a member of the family to help me with my suitcase, I left home. We walked about five hours to catch the Flagstaff/Kokstad bus... We were in time for the bus, and I was soon on it, leaving my companion behind. After running some distance, the bus started winding its way down to Brooksnek, another trading store-cum-bus stop. From here the road zigzagged and twisted as the bus followed it in a long climb to the top of a mountain slope. As the bus began the descent, a big town came into view in the distance below. It was Kokstad. I had crossed the Engeli mountain range. As a child, at possibly four years of age, my father, on the very first of my trips with him, had brought me to Brooksnek in a jolly ride on his ox-wagon. Now, Brooksnek was the last stop on my way out of the world I had come to know since then – that world was now behind me.

'According to a Chinese saying, "The journey of a thousand miles begins with one step." For me, that step was accomplished when I arrived in Kokstad.'

CHAPTER THREE

The Mountain of Knowledge

THE TRAIN FROM KOKSTAD, carrying two anxious and excited country boys from the Bizana district, steamed its way into greater Johannesburg late one afternoon in January 1934. Looking out of the train window, the youngsters were confronted by one bustling railway station after another, the platforms crowded with newcomers to Egoli, the 'place of gold'.

By the mid-1930s, thousands of men and women were arriving from the increasingly strained rural areas. Some passengers, many of them young men and women, avidly sought out the 'home-boys and -girls' waiting to meet them, to instruct them in negotiating the city streets and to help them to find jobs as domestic servants, gardeners, night watchmen or labourers. Whatever low wage they might earn in the city could only be an improvement on the conditions at home. Many of these young people were fleeing white-owned farms where dispossessed sharecroppers and labour tenants were unwilling or unable to pay cash wages for labour.

Men, married or single and wearing the guarded expressions typical of migrant workers, climbed out of the third-class compartments with their bundles of clothing and sleeping mats. They intended to stay only temporarily, long enough to earn the money needed to fortify their rural communities and homesteads. Also disembarking were a few proper but poorly paid ladies and gentlemen, church ministers or teachers, respectably dressed for their occupations in spotlessly maintained but often threadbare suits. And on the platforms waited assorted working people – friends, hawkers, touts and ragged adults and children hoping to cadge a few pence for services rendered.

At the end of the line, Oliver and Robert Sonqishe disembarked. A guard paraded up and down the train passages, shouting 'All change! All change!' They had arrived at last! The boys eagerly scanned the throng on the platform for signs of other schoolboys and -girls and the St Peter's escort they were promised would meet them at the station. But after waiting for more than half an hour, they were dismayed that no one had come forward to greet them.

Robert thus volunteered to go outside to look for help, while Oliver stayed behind to guard the luggage. When Robert returned, he announced enthusiastically, 'He has come!'

Their attendant had arrived with a horse-drawn cart – 'one of those where the passenger sits behind and below, under a hood, while the driver sits on top, holding the horses' reins'.

But their relief was to be short-lived. They were quickly to learn their first lesson about Egoli: that what in the countryside counts for simple neighbourliness becomes a commodity in the city.

'We had been on the road for some 10 to 15 minutes when the cart came to a stop. Had we arrived at last? we wondered, looking out to see if we were near anything that looked like a school. Meanwhile, our friend climbed down from the top, and standing next to me with Robert sitting on my left, he bent over and said: "By the way, do you know where this place, St Peter's Secondary School is?" I was astounded.

'"But you know where this place is. You come from there," I snapped.

'"No," he replied. "I don't come from there."

'"Surely you've been sent by the school to come and meet us?"

'"No, I'm a cab."

'We wondered what he meant by "he was a cab".

'So there we were, at night, in the middle of nowhere, stuck with a strange man who came from nowhere. What was to happen? He then came up with the answer.

'"All right, I'll try to find it. I think I know where it is. I'll charge you 12/6."

'This was a frightful surprise for us: "How can you charge us anything when you offered to take us in your cart?"

'"Of course I offered to take you," he said, "I am a cab."

'What on earth did he mean "he was a cab"? What was a "cab"? In any case, we told him, we did not have 12/6 to pay him. (We actually had only 5/– between us.)

'"In that case," he said, "I'll drop you here. But you must pay me 2/6."

'We insisted we would not pay him anything.

'"In that case, I'll take you to Marshall Square. There you'll pay 7/– or get locked up."

'We were puzzled. Who, or what was the "Marshall Square" he was talking about? Seeing we were likely to end up in a worse situation than we were already in, I offered two shillings. Robert insisted we don't pay. But I ultimately persuaded him that it might save us endless trouble to pay him two shillings if he is willing to accept it. He did. And so we got out of the cart.'

The boys were lost somewhere in the vast expanse of Johannesburg. The city could be a perilous place of predators, and one trembled to think of what might have happened to these young newcomers, wandering alone at night in the streets. But the boys were not stranded – 'the cab' might have been a resolute businessman, but he was neither an exploiter nor a robber.

'Communication was now friendly, and he lost no time in directing us in how to get to Rosettenville, where we could ask people to direct us further to St Peter's... After an hour's walk through a largely unbuilt area, we reached the end of the line. We were in Rosettenville. Here we soon met very friendly African boys who asked eagerly if we were going to St Peter's. It turned out they were themselves St Peter's students, arriving back from home that evening, and waiting around Rosettenville to be joined by their friends, also returning from the holidays. They directed us to St Peter's and within about 10 minutes we were indeed, at last, at St Peter's Secondary School, the Priory, Rosettenville, Johannesburg.'

In their first excursion in Johannesburg, they had already absorbed a few lessons: that they had missed their school transport at Park Station, where they should have disembarked; that they had climbed off at Braamfontein; and that Marshall Square was not a person, but Johannesburg's central police station.

The late arrival of Oliver and Robert at St Peter's aroused good-natured interest among the more cosmopolitan boys. As they walked up the front steps of the main building, one of them, Victor Sifora, was struck by the fact that both boys, who had clearly been walking some distance, were carrying their shoes, laces tied together and slung around their necks. Victor was the one chosen to show the boys to the hostel.[1] The buildings were as Miss Tidmarsh had described them, of stone and brick, cloistered by a long courtyard.

The school had first been established as St Agnes, a residential training school for female domestic workers for white households in 1909. This had been the pet project of Lady Selborne, the wife of the High Commissioner. At the time, the land to the south of Johannesburg was sparsely populated and regulations restricting black urban residence did not apply. From the rocky outcrop of the *koppie*, the view spanned nearly a hundred kilometres of the highveld's yellow-brown, rolling plains. The scheme, however, was apparently unpopular with middle-class Johannesburg, most of whom were hostile to educating Africans, and whose households at the time were being maintained mainly by white domestic workers. A Miss Boyle expressed concern that low-paid black servants would force white women out of jobs, driving them into 'destitution or even prostitution'.[2] But St Agnes's powerful patroness was able to quash opposition: 'On the correct treatment of the native does our existence as a white nation in South Africa depend,' declared the committee secretary; and the project was handed over to the care of the Community of the Resurrection (CR), an order of the High Anglican Church. Two years later, Father Osmund Victor, principal of the CR's seminary, moved the entire operation from the city centre to Rosettenville. In those days, the little suburb fringed with rows of Johannesburg's ubiquitous Australian gum trees was more conducive for quiet study. Besides, it would provide ample space for additional buildings.

By the end of 1925 the new campus, built largely by the theology students, was ready to be opened. A stone taken from the house of the famous Protestant missionary, David Livingstone, in Mabotsa in the western Transvaal was set in the aisle wall of the church – a gracious interdenominational gesture. In the same year, a start was also made with a secondary school, which included a hostel for 40 boarders. In 1931, St Agnes, which 'had outlived its usefulness as an industrial school', was converted to a hostel for girls – 'girls now also wanted secondary education'.[3]

The 1930s was a decade of rapid urbanisation for both blacks and whites – the devastating drought of 1933 had driven many small-scale white farmers to the cities and, lacking industrial training and artisan vocations, their sons and daughters became semi-skilled workers in the factories, mines and railways. But as South Africa's economy began to take off, the white working class improved their prospects – aided, no doubt, by a combination of trade-union organisation and a racially discriminatory social welfare system augmented by the new United Party of JBM Hertzog and Jan Christiaan Smuts. In the course of a decade, Rosettenville was speedily transformed into a white suburb with solid brick houses, and it was through these residential streets that Oliver and Robert traversed on their first, nocturnal journey to the school.

St Peter's, a missionary school like Holy Cross, differed from other such schools in South Africa. Though located outside the city's boundaries in its early years, the school was now situated in the heart of South Africa's metropolis. The culture of St Peter's (these rookies were to discover) was to prove far more multifaceted and sophisticated than the customs of schools in Pondoland. Its discourse and language reflected more closely black, multilingual South Africa as a whole. The school's impact was immediately made apparent to Oliver within the first hours of his arrival:

'What had struck me already, and especially as we listened to people talking in the dormitory, was that where at Holy Cross we spoke in the vernacular, Xhosa, as the language of ordinary conversation, here at St Peter's, everybody seemed to speak in English, and to speak the language fast and fluently, as if it was their mother tongue. I remembered Sokane. I was to learn later that, before going to Flagstaff, he had been a student at St Peter's.'

Oliver's active mind was already making conscious observations about this new milieu and its unfamiliar methods of communication:

'There were several boys in the dormitory. One of them, quite a big boy, who kept up a lively conversation with the others as everyone was preparing to get into bed, saw me undress and sleep under my blankets. He shouted: "Don't get into that bed before you put on your pyjamas!" As it happened, I had no pyjamas to put on. I had brought none. But what struck me was not so much the outburst, but rather, and firstly, the effortless rapidity with which he uttered the words. Secondly, the thought process was strange to me. I would have expected him to say something to the effect of "Put on your pyjamas first before going to bed". This is how the idea would normally have been conveyed in Xhosa, because that indicates the order of action. Olifant had mentioned bed first, and the pyjamas last. I was left with the feeling that I had a great deal of English to learn yet.'

The sharp rebuke was also an intimation of the institutionalised behaviour required of the scholars. The next morning, Oliver and Robert were summoned to see Boet Dudu. The boys were escorted by a fellow classmate, Peter Nchaupe, across a courtyard and into what turned out to be the boys' dining hall. Suddenly, Oliver felt a harsh *klap* (blow) across his cheek.

'Go and peel those bloody potatoes!' shouted a man's voice as he pushed Oliver towards a group of three boys peeling potatoes.

'The assailant was Dudu, the cook, alias Dan Pooe, possibly in his thirties. Outside of my dormitory that morning, he was the very first person to receive me at St Peter's School. And what a reception! Until he struck, he did not have the foggiest of who I was or what I looked like. I had angered simply by being a newcomer. But if Dudu gave me more than I deserved, other newcomers had their full share of entertainment. As for Dudu, it seemed he expended all his energies on me, and did not touch Robert.

'But soon enough I was to see Robert being marched on one leg across the football ground by Christopher Nkumbane, one of the senior boys at the hostel – and incidentally, the finest among many fine singers at St Peter's. None of us as newcomers fought back or did anything about our humiliation because we knew our turn would come when we would take it all out on the next batch of newcomers at the beginning of the following year.'

As it happened, somewhat to Oliver's rueful amusement, in the following year Brother Roger, the warden, abolished the system of exploiting new boys through the system of 'fagging', and so Oliver and Robert never did get a turn to 'do unto others what had been done unto them'. Nonetheless, if the price of discomfort and loss of dignity meant self-improvement, they were prepared to endure the cost. Said Tambo, 'It was becoming clear that, from being at the top at Holy Cross, we were at the bottom at St Peter's. Objectively, this was very good, for it offered us a challenge and an opportunity to grow if we were ready to take it; and we surely were.'

Apart from the unfriendly cook – who, according to a schoolmate, bullied Tambo 'because he is a Pondo'[4] – Oliver perceived both the fellow students and the staff to be friendly and welcoming. Their attitude was perhaps partly influenced by Oliver's eagerness to connect with them. They presented him, he felt, with boundless opportunities for learning.

'The teaching staff consisted of blacks and whites, and the students came mainly from the Transvaal, but there were some from Natal and one or two from the Cape Province – that is apart from Robert and myself, who came from Eastern Pondoland. There could also be some from the Orange Free State. Between them, the students spoke most of the country's African languages or dialects. Many of them, perhaps even most of them, also spoke Afrikaans. I had moved from a local school at Ludeke, to Holy Cross, which was attended by students from different parts of Eastern Pondoland, with members of the teaching staff drawn from within that area, and I was now at an institution that was representative of the whole country, the whole of South Africa – a school that had most of the attributes of a national, as distinct from a local institution. I had entered a wider world.'

St Peter's was indeed a wider, and a very different, world. The monastic order of the Community of the Resurrection drew mainly from the upper middle-class British graduates of Oxford and Cambridge. The Community had been founded, in fact, by the Oxford academic and Anglican Bishop, George Gore, in 1892, partly as a response to the fragmentation of community life brought about by Britain's industrial revolution, and the dislocation and urbanisation that accompanied it. The aims of the Community were 'to reproduce the life of the early Christians as recorded in the Acts of the Apostles'.[5] In addition to the vows of obedience, poverty and celibacy, its members also committed themselves to 'a brotherhood life, a fellowship of those who were devoted to the Truth', and to 'the language of self-sacrifice'.[6] But, in the words of Trevor Huddleston, it 'was not a reclusive community, it was an active missionary order'.[7] To translate this into practical terms, the members ministered not only to communities in the far-flung colonies of the Empire, but also to Britain's own labouring poor. This consideration of the working-class people, together with a broader, more intellectual and flexible view of the message of the Bible than was generally accepted at the time, marked members of the CR as socially radical.[8]

In South Africa, however, the CR frequently came upon the contradictions of British missionaries ministering to a dispossessed, impoverished and colonised people. While, for example, the CR in the Transvaal ran a diocese in rural Sekhukhuneland, another in Sophiatown, and a seminary and school at St Peter's Priory in Rosettenville, some of the brothers and sisters expressed an uneasiness with the Community's deep involvement in 'one of the most famous white public schools in Africa', St John's, 'housed in probably the finest school buildings in the southern hemisphere'.[9] The justification that the CR was setting a worthy example to the children of the rich by their selfless and simple lifestyle was countered by the rejoinder that, by working for St John's, the Community was simultaneously endorsing class and racial segregation in a grossly exploitative society. And the contradictions were not lost on Afrikaner nationalists. 'When bishops attacked the country's racial policies, government ministers would retort by pointing to the exclusive white church schools. It was not until 1980 that the first black pupils were admitted to St John's.'[10] The CR finally withdrew from St John's at the end of 1934.

On the whole, though, the Community of the Resurrection were not typical of other missionaries in South Africa. They were more intellectual, more sophisticated and possibly less socially skilled, as most of them had been reared in public schools and the semimonastic culture of Oxbridge. There was something almost adolescent in their humour and their style of rebelliousness. Ezekiel Mphahlele recalls, for example, Brother Roger Castle, the boarding master at St Peter's, entertaining the boys with his irreverent Freudian cracks at age, women and authority.[11] Castle, whom Oliver described as 'a very interesting personality as well as being a very good boarding master indeed', was said to have 'achieved an extraordinary hold over the boys'. It was Brother Roger, Oliver recalled, who had provided him with his first pair of pyjamas, 'no doubt to the satisfaction of Olifant'. Castle was remembered by his peers as having an 'artistic personality, un-English spontaneity, authentic spirituality and total unconventionality'.[12]

From its earliest years in South Africa, the Community had committed itself to cultivating a black ministry. In 1900, the black Order of Ethiopia was recognised by the Anglican Archbishop, and in 1907 the CR was asked to look after the Order in the diocese. But it was only in 1983 that the Order received its first bishop, Sigqibo Dwane, grandson of the founder of the church and principal of St Peter's Theological College since 1976.[13] Alban Winter, Oliver's first headmaster at St Peter's, was adamant that 'separate development' was the right policy for the Church. Africans, he maintained, needed priests who had the right approach, to convert them and to substantiate their faith: 'Africans wanted more colourful worship in their own languages. They needed their own organisation within the church so that they could develop their own leaders.'[14]

At the same time, though, he objected to segregation, because '"the easy-going" African needed to be roused by the "dynamic of the West"';[15] he was horrified when, after 1948, the philosophy of separate development was used to provide a cover for the crude policies of apartheid.[16] In the process of struggling for resources from the white community and the authorities, he became particularly known for his irascible temper. 'His tactic was usually to make himself so objectionable to the bullied officials concerned that, in sheer desperation, they would finally agree to his requests.'[17] Oliver Tambo, too, recalled Father Winter's unpredictability – but his response was somewhat different: 'Father Winter [was] a most fascinating person – most popular. The ease with which he lost his temper seemed to contribute to his popularity. We loved him for it!'

Despite the boy's admiration, however, it was Father Winter who was the cause of Oliver's third unjust punishment. The arbitrary retribution was dispensed to Oliver and Joe Mokoena, the two great mathematicians in the class:

'It was during a free period, and students were working at various things in the classroom. I was working on Algebra. Father Winter, who was our teacher in Mathematics, came in in a furious temper and asked who had been making a noise in the classroom. There was dead silence. He then asked me who had been making the noise. I said I did not know; I heard no noise. He asked Joe Mokoena. He did not say who had been making the noise. And he said we were telling lies. We must have known. He called us to follow him to his office, and there he called me to bend over a table and gave me 10 strong lashes with a cane. He gave Joe Mokoena the same punishment.

'As a rule, if I was studying or otherwise doing schoolwork on my own, I would be so absorbed with what I was doing that I seldom heard any noises around me and on this occasion I had heard none. There must have been noise, because the principal wouldn't have come in to enquire but I had not heard it. He disbelieved me and punished me for not being truthful. Of course, neither Joe nor myself were monitors. There was a monitor, a certain Nofala, who was in the classroom at the time, whose duty it was to keep order in the classroom and report any misconduct. The principal did not confront him, and as we came to learn afterwards, he was causing the noise. [As at] Kantolo and Holy Cross, this was the third time I was found guilty in my innocence. Having given us 10 lashes each, Father Winter gave us some grapes and sent us off with a smile as if nothing had happened. But he was like that. His flashes of anger evaporated very quickly, giving in to a smile.'

Undoubtedly the Community of the Resurrection attracted a fair share of eccentrics and inspirational figures and, in general, the fathers, though easy-going, friendly and relatively tolerant of individual expression, were an alien if benevolent species. The poet William Plomer, who had attended St John's College during the reign of the CR brothers, described delightfully the impression they made on their pupils there:

'The fathers were mostly excellent creatures... Neither cranks nor fanatics... they were mostly like large good boys than schoolmasters. Their cassocks and birettas lent them an air of distinction. As soon as we were dressed every morning we assembled in the chapel and sang, as plainsong, the simple hymn: "Now that the daylight fills the sky, We lift our hearts to God on high..." After the brief early service we ran like stags, headed by an athletic long-legged Resurrection father in a flapping cassock, across the main playing field and back to our breakfast, which always began with maize-meal porridge.'[18]

At St Peter's, the routine was much the same, with the difference that at the black school the pupils had to undertake school maintenance. Oliver recalled that 'every morning before breakfast, we did our cleaning – the grounds, dormitories, bathrooms etc. and part of the afternoon was devoted to sport'.

The teaching staff at this 'Black Eton' was almost equally divided between white and black, although none of the black teachers was ordained. Brother Roger was both gratified and discomfited to observe that St Peter's was 'the only institution in the land where a European eats with his pupils'.[19] The CR educational policy was firmly an integrationist one, although it became clear from the beginning of the brothers' arrival in South Africa that much as they may have preferred it, racially integrated schooling 'would have created such an outcry that the whole venture would have been imperilled'.[20]

'St Peter's,' declared Brother Roger, 'is trying to produce an educated, self-disciplined, Christian youth, capable of becoming the leaders of the New Africa.'[21] And certainly, to the more intellectually inclined boys and girls, the vision of attaining academic skills and understanding was enticing. On a wall of St Peter's hung a drawing of a concept of 'The Upward Path of Native Education', based perhaps on John Bunyan's *The Pilgrim's Progress.* At the foot of the range of mountains, the peaks of which are surrounded by glorious sunshine, are images of 'the homes of the people' and a path leads through a series of peaks – labelled Primary School ('sub-standards'), Intermediate School and Secondary School (Junior Certificate) – to a shining arch, which graces the summit of one of the mountains, embracing 'Fort Hare' and emblazoned with the words 'The South African Native College'. The remaining mountain range rises above this educational peak, promising glorious possibilities. The entire representation is a clear, graphic illustration of the steps needed to reach the apex of the shining, upward path. Many boys and girls must have studied the familiar icons, its inspiring message laid out so clearly and unambiguously.

To what extent the brothers were able to separate their Christian beliefs from Victorian middle-class culture in influencing this 'New Africa', however, is hard to say. Early in 1938, in Oliver's matriculation year, the St Peter's Priory magazine, *The Bulletin*, published an article by an African ordinand, Edmund Maponya.[22] In it, Maponya offered a parable of Christian transformation to which young people could relate and aspire – certainly it was a success story that resembled Oliver's own. But Maponya also conveyed an additional message. Despite the hero's forsaking of the 'heathen kraal', the world of the homestead should not be totally discarded, for it cultivated many social virtues and special skills forgotten by 'civilisation'. Ultimately, Thoko – the subject of this parable – was able to combine what was finest in his own heritage with the Christian message, in order to go out into the world searching for a path on which to shed his own, special light. This was the syncretic challenge that Maponya was delicately raising, and with which many African Christians were increasingly wrestling. Its import was also making an impact on the highly receptive but critical mind of the newcomer Oliver Tambo, who was just then entering a stage of his mental development that was grasping concepts and grappling with them.

The CR was more sensitive to cultural identity than the vast majority of missionaries. 'Christianity for most of the churches and communities meant abandoning and foregoing what we were,' remarked Victor Sifora, 'your culture, your custom; your song, your dance, your dress.' He said: 'All those things went overboard. Now the Anglican Church and the Community of the Resurrection also were contaminated to a certain point with that idea. But more than anybody else, they could not bring up a truly educated, liberated people if in the process they made certain that those people lost their culture.'[23]

Despite the best of intentions, though, the brothers of the CR itself, as proselytisers, were inevitably paternalistic. Ezekiel Mphahlele expressed his disappointment with the fathers: 'The idea that they came to receive did not exist... They came to uplift, they were doing you a favour and that's why you were not allowed to talk back and say how certain things hurt... I often felt cheated myself in later years.'[24]

Certainly, sensitive and supportive as they were to their black congregations, in their reports to the CR headquarters the brothers constantly detailed the progress they were making in providing spiritual direction for their charges. An awareness and appreciation of the qualities prevalent in African culture tended to come much later, with the community and cultural involvement of CR brothers Trevor Huddleston and Martin Jarrett-Kerr in the 1950s and 1960s.[25]

But the white brothers were not the pupils' only educators. Besides the black teachers in the school, every Wednesday afternoon, recalled Victor Sifora, Selope Thema – journalist and subeditor of *The Bantu World* – would come to St Peter's and give them an African history lesson that included a precolonial past as well as the recent history of the struggle against colonialism and oppression. 'Today we talk of them as workshops,' added Sifora. Thema also 'inculcated' into the boys that they had a role to play: 'That we can make our own decision as to which way, or from which side we give our support but that we have a role to play. And that the decision of South Africa that the ANC from 1912 had been fighting, that decision is going to be made by us.'[26]

Sifora appreciated the progressive educational role played by St Peter's, particularly as more and more black educators joined the teaching staff. Thema, he was certain, 'was already conscious that no other institution anywhere, was giving out the education and the guidance and the freedom of thought and the freedom of expression and association as St Peter's'. These were thrilling and exciting ideas. Even so, Oliver kept a cool head, often playing the devil's advocate to test the imperfections of these and any other ideas – he was an intellectual even then. Sifora remembered Oliver's response, not only in Thema's discussions, but also in debates generally:

'When it came to organised discussions, whether it was an argument on some topic, Tambo took a side that would be opposed to the side taken by most of you. He'll rally his arguments, [and] when he did reply after all the noise you have been making for hours, you'd realise [he was] a thinker. You had not been thinking, you realise for the first time that a thinker is now addressing the subject, analytical. Tambo was a great listener; that's where he beat us.'[27]

Holy Cross had partially prepared Oliver for a Western style of cooperative, institutionalised living. Accustomed to the routine at Holy Cross, the boys easily fell into the school's routine of daily chores. In sport, Oliver and Robert were among the best cricket players. They played against other schools and institutions, including Alan Paton's Diepkloof. An entry in the school's logbook for 1937 reads: 'Feb. 13: School played Diepkloof Reformatory. Won by 36 runs.' Two weeks later, the return match resulted in a draw.[28]

Both boys also played an adequate game of tennis and soccer, though at St Peter's 'the standard of soccer was relatively very high' and Oliver did not make the college team. Both sang in the school choir, which had an impressive reputation. In 1926, a visitor to the College had enthused over the church choir's singing as 'what that of black velvet would be, could it sing. The rich, blurry effect is increased by the fact that... they sing to English, Dutch, Sechuana and Sekosa [sic] words all at once... The fire and emphasis imparted to one's halting words by the interpreter is something wonderful'.[29]

Academically, Oliver rapidly climbed the class ladder, and in the June 1934 examination, he passed with an aggregate of 88 per cent.[30] Looking back, he found the ever-growing 'wider world' never failed to bring him intellectual and experiential expansion. Once motivated, Oliver was clearly equipped to work hard to reach his goal, and he revelled in the outcome. His favourite subjects at Holy Cross had been English Grammar and Arithmetic.

'At St Peter's, largely because of this, Latin became my best subject, followed by Mathematics and Science. In these subjects particularly, I quickly rose to the top, competing for that position with Joe Mokoena, who was ahead of me most of the time. One hundred per cent marks in Latin was the normal thing and we both felt disappointed if we made only 98 per cent. In Mathematics too, particularly Algebra, you're either right or you're wrong, and if you're right you obtain 100 per cent marks. Science was a fascinating subject where we also scored very high marks. Joe Mokoena had a wonderful brain. He did rarely work outside the classroom; whereas I had to work hard. He certainly had a fabulous memory. I also have no doubt that the years I had spent doing Ex-Six One, Ex-Six Two, provided me with a most useful foundation. I had problems with no subject whatsoever.'

But the boys' experiences were not confined to the insular world of St Peter's. It was the school's practice to allow the senior pupils to take turns on the weekends to 'go out'. During these excursions, Oliver and Robert began to be exposed to new values and social attitudes. The culture of consumerism, though in its infancy in the 1930s, soon made a sharp impact on the two.

'When it was the turn of Robert and [myself] to be out, we would wear our khaki shirts and shorts and, of course, shoes. I mention shoes because it took us time to get used to them. At school we did not have to, but it was the practice when you went out you did wear shoes. In our case, we would soon enough take them off. For me, not only was I not used to walking in shoes, but my shoes were slightly too small for my feet and it was a constant pain wearing them. And so we would meet many fellow students in town dressed in their best, while we walked barefoot carrying our shoes in our hands.'

The majority of the pupils at St Peter's were from homes that were more urban than rural. Their parents tended to be wage earners (however modest), with better access to cash resources than were peasants from agrarian homesteads. Characteristically adolescent – and all the more because they were 'new boys' – Oliver and Robert were anxious to be accepted by their peers. Yet they did not have the means to conform to the schoolboys' current fashions. Oliver and Robert thus learnt to play a strategic game of concealment:

'Actually, the other boys thought we were making a joke about ourselves. But there was, in fact, another reason. We could not afford the sports jackets and the flannel trousers, certainly not at the beginning. For our approach to the expenditure of money seemed to be the opposite of the general conception amongst students at St Peter's at least. Every so often, we would hear someone boasting that his shirt was worth 27/6 and not a mere 3/6 that some of us were wearing. It seemed odd that some of us were proud of spending a fortune on a shirt when there was one available very cheaply. My mother and her friends would go to Harding, a whole day's journey there and back, to buy clothing material at 9d a yard rather than pay 12d a yard at the local trading store. The distance, the time, the energy expended on going to Harding was not important – what was important was that they [would otherwise be] paying 12d instead of 9d, and it was not as if they were buying huge quantities. Perhaps they were buying four or six yards each.

'In Johannesburg the suits [that] students were wearing cost them upward of three pounds each. I knew that for three pounds you could buy a whole cow at home. I couldn't imagine myself giving away a cow in exchange for a pair of trousers or a jacket – the people of Kantolo would think I was mad! And so the purchase of a suit in Johannesburg was something quite remote as we started our life there.'

But the boys realised that sooner or later they would have to conform to the urban image if they were to be accepted as part of the group, and they thus began to devise ways of making money. They started a school hair-cutting service, working hard at mastering the current style in fashion at the time, and eventually earned enough cash to be able to keep up with the other scholars.

The city itself had all the allure of the 'bright lights'. On the first leg of their train journey to Johannesburg, Oliver and Robert had already been enchanted by the novelties of Kokstad, 'all lit up with countless street lights'. At Pietermaritzburg there had been an overnight stop, where the boys were exposed to some fast-talking repartee and the good-humoured exchange of insults in a street lingo, which, to their amazement, had not resulted in a knockdown fight. They had also met on the pavement a 'magic man', his wares on display, who offered to arrange for them the instant death of their enemies through his bewitched mirror. In the city, it seemed, fascinating games with evil and power were seemingly as possible to come by as the 'good things', such as access to learning, esteem and material comforts – if one had the means. 'For us,' commented Oliver, 'this was not only new, but complicated stuff.' The result was that both Oliver and Robert thoroughly enjoyed their weekend outings in Johannesburg: 'We had come to realise what a tiny little spot Kokstad was in comparison with the vast expanse of Johannesburg, whose street lights at night seemed to stretch out to the end of the world. They were everywhere, and I liked to stand outside in the evening and take it all in, for it never ceased to be a great attraction for me.'

But Johannesburg also exposed them to the bleak world of urban segregation. Oliver was struck by the stark difference in race relations between the sheltered mission-school environment, and Johannesburg's 'concrete jungle'. He retained vivid memories of the hostility that he encountered, even in those pre-apartheid years. These specific experiences were brought home particularly sharply because of the school's location in a white working-class suburb that reflected the wider racist context that prevailed throughout South Africa.

'[You] got to know you did not belong. You were not wanted. You were, at best, tolerated. You had to be constantly on your guard, like an animal in a jungle full of beasts of prey. You experienced it all within the short distance of five miles from the gates of St Peter's to Park Station in the City.

'As you leave the school, you already notice the gate of the house, "Dogs and Natives Not Allowed". You walk on and see a baby, barely two years old, sitting at a pavement with an African woman; [the baby] looks up at you as you walk past, and with the full tenderness of her little voice, shouts: "You kaffir!" – a phrase which must comprise the first few words she has learnt from her mother. You reach Rosettenville corner to catch a tram or the bus, you occupy a seat reserved for Natives at the back – out of sight. You reach the terminus, you start walking down Eloff Street which leads to Park Station, but you often find it wiser to get off the pavement and pick your way among the heavy traffic to avoid rubbing shoulders with a so-called "Missus", or a so-called "Boss", which could bring you a lot of trouble.'

Historically, 1934 is remembered as the year of 'Fusion'. The two leading parties, the ruling Afrikaner National Party and the opposition South African Party, had merged to form the United Party in the wake of the Depression and the subsequent economic crisis produced by going off the international gold standard. Both parties were, of course, white, although a few thousand black male property owners and professionals were entitled to vote in the Cape (but in no other province). In order to become part of the new United Party government, the leader of the opposition, Jan Smuts, agreed that the African voters in the Cape Province could be deprived of the franchise. More than two thirds of a joint sitting of both houses of Parliament voted to change the constitution and, in return for losing this remaining political access, all Africans were to be represented by four whites in the Senate. In addition, a few thousand hectares of land were to be added to the 'Reserves', as defined under the 1913 Land Act. This new arrangement was to be made law by the Native Land Act in 1936.

Black opposition was, however, not slow to react. A number of respectful but fervent protests and deputations to government officials were organised by various organisations, including the African National Congress – but they failed to prevent the passing of the Act. South Africa, long before 1948, was thus unashamedly segregationist. The 1923 [Natives] Urban Areas Act, in response to the growing number of black townspeople, had already defined the cities as 'white' and had devised a law to confine the right of black people (Africans in particular) to remain in the urban areas only as long as they were 'ministering to the white man's needs'. The vast majority of whites, of all classes and ethnic origins, did not for a moment doubt their own superiority over Africans. All the institutions and public spaces outside of the 'Native Reserves' proclaimed this in thousands of ways in everyday life. For example, as Oliver remembered:

'There are two approaches to the railway platforms at Park Station – one for "Europeans" and another for "Non-Europeans". Each platform has a European and a Non-European section. Similarly, the train is divided into European and Non-European coaches, the latter looking vastly inferior to the former. This separation pursues you relentlessly as long as you are outside the school premises or within the borders of an African township. Indeed you are presumed to be committing a crime anywhere. Your very existence is an illegality. Unless you can establish the contrary by producing a piece of paper, a pass, or other identity deemed to be valid and to do so on demand by a policeman, thereby showing that you have permission to be where you happen to be, when he meets you or finds you.'

These encounters, so at variance with the foreign yet relatively accepting environment of Holy Cross, could not fail to arouse some indignation in the youngster. But Africans were not merely victims; and even Oliver, not as yet systematically exposed to a political culture, was becoming dimly conscious of the contest that inevitably lay ahead. 'There was something challenging about this,' he said. 'Something wholly unacceptable, but I did not know at the time what, if anything, could be done to meet that challenge. My primary focus and challenge was my studies, which would lead to the Junior Certificate examination in two years' time. It was clear, however, that the African people were not prepared to be and remain the underdog of society.'

The deep and lasting perception of injustice – a 'sense of moral legitimacy',[31] which was spreading throughout colonial Africa – was trickling down into even the most respectable black Christian schools. In the more suggestive lessons, sermons and songs, invocations of resistance could already be discerned.

'I came to know a plethora of choral music in the vernacular whose theme focused on and deplored the social, economic and political status of the African – of the black person. Virtually all these songs, many of them prepared by some of the most famous composers in the country, urged the African to rise up and take his proper place among the nations of the world. The first of these that I came across was a song by the St Peter's Secondary School choir, conducted by Mr Nonqausa who was the choirmaster in 1934: "Awake, awake ye nations of Africa, Why are you content to remain in darkness?" These were the opening words. [But] there were scores of other songs pursuing the same theme: "Masizas Vukane Ma Wethu, Vukane Ma Wethu."

'"Awake, O My People", which begins by lamenting the sad plight of the black person in Africa and ends with a rousing call to the people to awake and unite in action, is one of the classics in South African choral music. It is a striking and even central characteristic of the culture of the black people of South Africa that at moments of joy, grief or danger they resort to singing. The end result is that the country resounds with song, much of it dedicated to our hopes for the future.'

Oliver thus found himself having to reconcile his two sets of experiences. This was particularly noticeable when he returned home in June 1934. In the harsh metropolis, he was a scholar; at home, he was a member of a rural community. In his struggle to become a whole person in his own right, he consciously tested himself with goals and boundaries. At Kantolo, Oliver participated in the harvesting season with his customary zeal. But it was soon over, and he was then free to visit age-mates – in particular other school-going or educated friends – to compare new identities with them, and to compare his experiences of Western education with theirs. 'In the course of these visits,' he observed, 'I found that other students had not had the exposure I had had; they continued to do things the old way. Their habits, tastes and standards had not changed and I felt the difference. Perhaps this was natural. I had for the first time been thrust into an environment which was urban rather than rural.'

Like any other 16-year-old, Oliver was in the process of shaping his own identity. But his was one that would develop a unique social responsibility in an attempt to accommodate his own two very different worlds of school and homestead. He tried hard to harmonise these by creating a new reference group with his peers, just as the 'column' or traditionalist singing groups had interpreted their identities and, in the process, empowered themselves. But, he learnt, leaders were required to take responsibility for maintaining impetus:

'After consultations among students during these holidays, it was decided that we form a students' organisation known as the Bizana Students Association, the BSA. Caledon Mda was elected Chairman and I became its Secretary. The principal aim of the association was to mobilise the Bizana students into a conscious collective, with activities to be organised during holidays. Although the Association succeeded in organising meetings and social gatherings, it suffered from the fact that the Secretary was hundreds of miles away and unable to return home every six months, as other students were able to. The result was that the Association weakened and ultimately folded after a few years.'

It was not enough simply to take the initiative – that initiative needed to be backed up with long-term application, a lesson that Oliver would implement at Fort Hare and beyond.

At this time, Oliver was also exploring his own moral boundaries. Many years later, when he was in exile, Tambo would regale his comrades with the story of how, as a youngster of 15 or 16, he had come to renounce alcohol.[32] By then Oliver was already becoming known in Pondoland for his academic achievements and had been invited to accompany the chief's son to a drinking party. At the party, he was offered a turn at the drinking bowl. At first he hesitated, but his father reprimanded him – it would be the height of bad manners to refuse this hospitality, particularly as he had arrived with an honoured guest. Not wanting to offend, Oliver dutifully drank, and then had another taste, and another – each time the beer came round to his side of the circle. Finally, late at night, Oliver (who had never before had more than a taste of alcohol) unsteadily mounted his horse and rode home with his group. But the ground was uneven, and in his intoxicated state Oliver was unable to keep control of his mount. He fell off, much to the amusement of the others, and was carried home. Oliver felt a burning sense of shame. He had prided himself on his horsemanship; he hated to be mocked, or to lose control of himself. Furious, he vowed never to touch alcohol again. Despite the many social and international occasions in times to come, Tambo – with just one exception – kept his word until the end of his days.

The task of blending two worlds was not an easy one for the growing boy. On a practical level, too, he experienced great difficulty in physically moving from the one to the other. Oliver recalled his return trip to school at the end of the June holiday.

'[As] we were about to leave, we were asked to take some tea. I suggested it would delay us, but my father insisted that we take tea before we leave, so I sat down and proceeded to drink the tea, but found it very hot and so once again I said, "No, I think this is too hot and is going to delay us". I was still pressured to drink up the tea, which I did, ultimately, and we left. We arrived... There is a trading store at Fort Donald and the bus stop is on the main road in front of the store which faces west. We were approaching the bus stop from the east, along a path which ran parallel to a wall on our left which obstructed our view of the bus stop. As we turned the corner of this wall, the bus, some 10 paces away, was moving off. We waved, we shouted and ran frantically but all in vain. The next bus would be the same time, the same place, the next day. We had missed the bus by a small fraction of the time it had taken me to drink the cup of tea before we left home. As the bus disappeared behind a cloud of dust, I made a silent pledge. There was nothing we could do but return home, which meant we were to travel the distance between Kantolo and Fort Donald two more times before leaving for Kokstad. My parents were stunned when we arrived back in the late afternoon. All I could tell them was that I would never drink tea again, and I did not – at least for the next six months!'

This occasion, however, was to be the last time Oliver was to see his mother. Back at St Peter's, he nevertheless continued to meet the challenges of school life, preparing for the Junior Certificate examination, due at the end of the following year. But during the course of the term, Oliver and Robert received an unexpected visitor, a Mrs Elaine Melville, who had called on the Holy Cross Mission and had been asked to get in touch with the two boys. Oliver, rather significantly, described her as 'most charming and motherly'.

'She lived in Bellevue, a suburb of Johannesburg eight miles from St Peter's, and invited us to visit her at her home whenever we wished. She also invited us to spend the December holidays with her, which we gladly accepted as it would save us the expense of travelling to Bizana. By the end of the year, Mrs Melville's home had become a [second] home and she treated us as her two sons. She herself was a widow. Her husband, a medical practitioner, had died in service during World War One, survived, I think, by a boy and girl, both of whom were now married.'

This happy discovery of a proxy mother was, however, shortly to be followed by tragic loss:

'We were beginning to look forward to our Christmas holidays with Mrs Melville when one heart-rending afternoon in late November I received a short telegram informing me that my mother had died in September. No further details were given. Naturally, this was a most staggering blow. She was perfectly well when I left her in June and I could not imagine what had suddenly gone wrong. She was generally a healthy person.'

Almost inaccessible to his family, Oliver was left to cope with his stunned incomprehension, his sense of abandonment, guilt and grief, on his own. It was only in the June holidays of the following year that Oliver learnt about the immediate cause of his mother's death. She had had a problem with her leg, possibly a thrombosis, a condition that might have been cured had there been medical services. 'There was no doctor anywhere nearby,' explained Tambo. '[And] even if there was, she would probably have refused to receive medical treatment because she was a member of a church denomination, the Full Gospel Church, whose members did not believe in and did not use medicine. Rightly or wrongly, they relied exclusively on faith healing.'

Oliver had thus lost his mother in her own process of migrating from one universe to another. As a fervent evangelical Christian, she had abandoned traditional healing but had also rejected Western medical science. Oliver lost her at a turning point in his life. Not yet 17 years old and still learning to manage his emotions as well as his identity, he was on the threshold of realising his parents' dream for him – scholastic honours in order to acquire an independent profession for himself. When he finally returned home the following year, her funeral had long since passed, depriving him further of the necessary ritual of mourning; but, in any case, the boy would not have had the means to travel home had he been informed in time. He remained nevertheless heartbroken: 'I had lost her before I was able to repay her love and care for me – before I could do any of the things which I promised myself I would do for her when I started working. For weeks, the thought of her death haunted me.'

Oliver spent many hours in St Peter's church, 'the church with two chapels in it... a stone's throw from my room'. Christian instruction taught him that he had to accept his loss as an act of divine will. It is not clear to what extent Oliver was given the opportunity to share his grieving with others – friends or ministers – or to talk about his mother and express the meaning of her loss to him.

Oliver did, however, write to another of his secondary mother figures, Miss Hill, who was away in England. 'It was very sad that you are not able to come back yet...' he wrote. 'Well, we cannot help feeling sorry when things go against our will. The same has happened to me, because I received a telegram from my father saying that my mother was dead... Please pass my best wishes to Miss Gee and Misses Goddard to whom I owe a big lump of gratitude for the kindness they show to me by helping to pay my fees.'[33]

In June 1935, Oliver was able to return to Kantolo for a month. There he learnt that the mother of Wilson, Willy and Alan had also passed away. The homestead was changing, and he was distressed to be losing his childhood bonds. Then, back at school, in September of that year, another devastating telegram arrived – Manchi had died. 'I was less unprepared for this news than in the case of my mother,' said Tambo. 'I had noticed during the June holidays that my father was very ill. He was receiving no medical treatment and yet was overworking himself. And so he passed on.'

At this stage of Oliver's developmental life, Manchi's influence as a father and role model had to a large extent been replaced by the boy's new mentors at school and in church. But Oliver needed to affirm for himself his father's blessing. Many years later, Tambo remarked that his father had particularly wanted him, of all the boys in the family, to continue with his education.[34] Whether this observation was a fervently desired impression or the outcome of more direct evidence of the boy's clear ability, Oliver was clearly motivated by his father's approval. In an extended family such as Oliver's – three mothers, eight siblings, two younger uncles, a number of aunts and cousins, and his father, the head of the homestead – it was likely that a sensitive and perceptive boy would make a singular effort to win that father's approval. Oliver reassured himself that his father had a special regard or plan for him. In his recollections of his childhood, Tambo recalled more specific incidents of his father than of his mother. He relived the scenes of the ox-wagon rides, the horse-riding lessons, the visits to other towns and homesteads; these seldom pictured any of the other siblings in the scenes – he had his father to himself and clearly the old man was proud of his highly intelligent, dependable son. During that last holiday at home, Tambo recalled:

'We were very good friends. He had always wanted me by his side as he went about doing odd jobs around the home, planting fruit trees, mending fences, digging trenches, or when he took a sport with his guns at crows that had made the trees around our home their habitat. I travelled around with him on horseback... among the many people who knew him, I found none who didn't have a good word to say about him.'

Far from home, in surroundings alien to his father's world, Oliver was left to treasure his memories and reflect on his bond with his parents.

'And so it was that my first two years at St Peter's were witness to my losing that which had been my greatest ambition and my primary motivation –

to give my parents a new and better life; to reward their great vision in encouraging me to go to school when few children of my age and in my area did so, that I might understand the world better, so that I might be somebody in society – a position I was determined to use to their fullest benefit. Both were now gone. The only thing they had ever received from me was the four weeks' wages totalling the sum of 10 shillings, which I had earned from Sister Margaret Tracy at Holy Cross Mission during the June holidays some six years earlier.'

Following these two critical blows in such rapid succession, Oliver's studies began to suffer a moderate relapse. The young man wrote to Miss Hill: 'I am now in Form 2, the second year of the Junior Certificate; and if I am promoted this year, I shall take my final exams next Christmas. I am getting on quite well at school, though I am not doing as well as I did when I first came... In June 1935 I passed with 77%. In these tests I have always come out second in our class of about 30 students. Now I am struggling for a higher percentage mark.' About his future plans, he confided that he was 'not sure about what to do when I leave school, but there is still plenty of time to think it out. I wish to go in for matric. when I pass JC [Junior Certificate] and if possible, to take BA privately.'[35]

But shortly after this letter, Oliver received the news that the means to further his education was coming to an end. Willy Tambo was finding it quite impossible to continue his contribution to the fees at St Peter's. The other donations had been used up, the exception being the regular amount sent by the Misses Goddard, but their subsidy was not enough to keep Oliver at the school. He thus began to cast around for alternative financing and, early in 1936, he stumbled across information that gave him renewed hope:

'I got to know that Lovedale, a famous high school in Alice, Cape Province, offered a three-year scholarship, tenable at Lovedale, enabling successful candidates to study for the final year of the Junior Certificate and the two-year matriculation course... Interested second year JC students, that is Form 2 students across the country, are required to write a qualifying examination and the scholarship goes to the six best students. I wondered how I could make contact with Lovedale; but fortunately, on one hopeful afternoon, our Form 2 class was informed that the principal, Mr Shearsmith, would be issuing application forms to those students who wished to enter the contest... I was among those who joined the queue.'

But luck was not with Oliver that day. Mr Shearsmith (a lay headmaster who had succeeded Alban Winter in 1935) handed the last application form to a student two places in front of Oliver.

'With a broad smile Mr Shearsmith immediately turned and faced us saying, "Finished," as he threw his arms apart. Quite shocked, I said, "But Sir, there must be more forms!"

'"Finished", he repeated, again throwing his arms apart.

'He was obviously very happy at my ill-luck; for that was all it was. An ill-luck. Disappointed and in despair, I walked away, pondering my future. It occurred to me that Joe Mokoena was not in the queue and wondered why. It turned out that he was already on a scholarship to St Peter's and did not need another. This made it all the more difficult for me to understand why the Principal was so gleeful in the shortfall in the number of application forms for the Lovedale Scholarship.'

Wounded by this insensitivity, Oliver concluded that the principal obviously did not wish to lose a good student who had the potential to enhance the prestige of St Peter's. 'Of course, he could not have known of the problem,' Oliver pondered, demonstrating his natural reticence. 'Should I tell him, I wondered. I decided not to.'

Later in the year, the applicants duly wrote the exam and Cecil Nolotshungu was among the top six, and was accordingly accepted for the bursary at Lovedale. 'This was very painful,' recalled Tambo. 'Not that he should not have been among the best six, but that I would not have failed where he succeeded. Why did I have to miss such a scholarship by only two application forms? Very bad luck. Anyway, we felt proud of Cecil Nolotshungu, congratulated him on his success and wished him more success at Lovedale.'

The year 1936 was one of nagging anxiety. Towards the end of the year, Oliver learnt of the offer of the Bhunga (the United Transkei Territories General Council) of a five-year scholarship to Transkei children. He immediately posted off a letter of application, indicating that he wanted to train for a medical degree. Afterwards he learnt that, in practice, bursaries tended to go to the children of the establishment – 'of wealthy, well-known or otherwise prestigious parents in the Transkei'. It was clear, too, that Oliver's parents did not fall within any of these categories. 'The people who would receive my letter of application would not have the foggiest idea who I was, so I did not have a chance in a thousand to win this scholarship,' said Tambo. 'I was therefore left to hope against hope that Miss Tanqueray would somehow strike some luck. If the worst came to the worst, armed with a JC certificate, I could surely obtain employment as a clerk somewhere on the mines.'

But shortly before the end of term, Oliver was presented with yet another dilemma – and his response was an indication of the type of role he was to map out for himself in the political hierarchy in years to come. Brother Roger informed Oliver that he had been selected to become the new head prefect for the following year. This immediately threw Oliver into a quandary, as he examined his own disposition and reflected on his aspirations for himself. He knew at once that he did not want the spotlight – though ambitious, and even competitive, public aggrandisement was not for him. Perhaps his deep sense of commitment to the group, to the collective, fostered by his rural background and further encouraged by the boarding-school culture that mocked 'show-offs' made him shy away from prominence.

'I battled to overcome an aversion I had always felt for the limelight... There was certainly no doubt that the position of Head Prefect of St Peter's carried much prestige, power and authority. It was the highest position to which any student could rise. But none of these held any attraction whatever for me. I had no use for being an important person. Except in the case of my school work, I had never been, nor consciously sought after being, *primus inter pares.*'

Nevertheless, Oliver was not entirely exalted: his imagination did dwell on thoughts of vindication that fell just short of vengeance:

'There were more reflections, some of them quite petty. I recall, for example, my blistering reception by Dudu, the cook on my first morning at St Peter's. I was at the bottom of the social heap then. To be Head Prefect would mean that I had risen through the ranks to the very top. Indeed I could invite Brother Dan, alias Dudu, to be my guest during a luncheon, so that I could prove to him that I had forgiven, but not forgotten what Peter Mchaope had meant when he said to me and Robert, "Boet Dudu wants you in the kitchen". I thought of Johnson Makaula, Head Prefect at St John's Kraal, Holy Cross Mission, who had caused me to be relieved of my duties as Prefect. It would be sobering for him to know that I was the Head Prefect of a big and famous secondary school in South Africa's biggest city, Johannesburg, next to which Flagstaff was barely visible.'

His fertile mind was also engaged, however, in finding a constructive way to turn down the honour with grace.

'The question which Brother Roger's intention posed for me was how to divert his focus away from me to someone else without my appearing to decline to serve when I was required to do so. But I felt at all costs I must not be Head Prefect, and so the following day I returned to Brother Roger with what I thought might be acceptable to him. I proposed that I serve as deputy Head Prefect and told him that most of the senior students were my personal friends and I could get along with any of them... I sought to impress upon him my reluctance.'

Ultimately, Brother Roger appointed David Mankazana, 'a local boy' – tall, handsome and socially confident – who had been born and bred in the city, according to Mankazana's own description of himself.[36] Mankazana would thus be head prefect and Oliver his deputy – 'the Cabinet', as school friends called the team.[37] It was, Tambo commented, 'a good partnership'.

One of their achievements, he particularly remembered, was to unite the students through an uplifting project. One afternoon, Oliver came across two elderly African women sitting despondently on the pavement outside the school. After initiating a conversation with them, he discovered that they were penniless rural women who had lost their way from their friend's room and had spent the previous two days and nights wandering about without food and drink.

'They looked dilapidated. A truly sad sight. I could well understand their position, having myself grown up in the rural areas. You don't need any money when you leave your home to go visiting; or even travelling long distances... Unknown to these two old ladies, this was not the practice in the urban areas. Certainly not in the white suburbs in the city of Johannesburg as distinct from perhaps the townships or – as they were called at the time – "locations", where Africans stayed segregated from white residents in the city. And so I could imagine how these two would have gone shuffling past a succession of shop windows displaying stacks of bread, drinks and fruit. All of it so near to them; but so inaccessible. I reflected on a situation where a person could die of hunger in the midst of so much food.'

Typically, Oliver's response was a collective one. He called the head prefect and together they gave the women food and drink. Then they decided to raise money for them from the students, who gave generously and without hesitation. Some, Tambo reported, said 'It could have been my mother or my aunt'. As a result, within the hour, the two women not only had a big meal, but were also presented with a substantial sum of money collected from virtually every student in the school. 'It was so satisfying,' said Tambo, 'to see the surprised disbelief and joy in their brightened eyes... The students felt good about playing the Good Samaritan.' For Tambo, here was yet another example of the overlap of Christian charity with the traditional values of *ubuntu* (concern, generosity and humanity), and he immediately made the connection between these beliefs and the need for social change: 'The incident was for me a sharp reminder of the suffering that the African people were experiencing outside the comfortable grounds of St Peter's School and its cosy hostels. But I was pleased by the students' collective demonstration of sensitivity to human suffering and misery. I wished that sensitivity would manifest itself as each of us left St Peter's for the outer world.'

But Oliver's talents also included an investigator's bent. At Holy Cross, Johnson Makaula, with an eye on Tambo's ultimate profession, had observed the youngster's love of logical argument. At St Peter's, Nimrod Tubane extended the metaphor.

'Oliver was appointed head prefect [sic], [and] his succession gave me a chance to learn more about Oliver Tambo, who displayed his thinking powers. Boys being boys in their behaviour, you needed Tambo to solve the various cases like theft, dishonesty among the boarding inmates. With the arrival of the prefects Tambo decided that it should be called the "Cabinet". He was in effect a prosecutor in his questioning of a culprit, ending up by the boy owning up, ie. accepting the verdict of guilty. At the time of questioning a boy, Tambo could put his mind on the problem; his eyes would move from left to right rapidly and firing questions like you were in court. All this performance would end with the boy failing to answer and finally admitting his guilt, eg. stealing keys from another boy, with intent to steal from his trunk. We found Tambo an effective FBI and a successful detective to solve mysterious cases.'[38]

Head prefect David Mankazana also remembered Tambo's oscillating eyes when he was intellectually aroused. Tambo, he said, was interested in Science and Mathematics: 'That's why his eyes went like that, you know sort of like a computer... But he was a deep, a very deep thinker.'[39]

In November 1936, Oliver wrote his JC examinations, along with other black and white students throughout the Transvaal, who all sat for the same examination. He clearly relished the honour and publicity bestowed on him after the highly successful results were announced. This was public notice in which he indeed exulted – he had worked hard at his studies, and felt he deserved the accolades that followed.

'The results showed that Joe Mokoena and I had made history. For the first time in the history of education in South Africa, two African students had passed the JC with a First Class degree, regarded as a rare achievement for any student. For a society steeped in racist beliefs about European superiority, this incredible news – this "incredible news" – rocked the whole country, including the Transkei and, in particular, the Bhunga. Proud to claim the unknown but "known" famous boy as one of its children, the Transkeian Bhunga promptly awarded me a five-year scholarship amounting to £30 per annum, tenable with immediate effect. Some other body in the Transvaal [the University of South Africa] also immediately granted me a two-year scholarship totalling £20.'

The effect was indeed dramatic because it contradicted the racial stereotypes held by most white South Africans – so much so that it warranted comment in the newspapers. For the African community, in particular, this was exhilarating news. For the St Peter's students, these results served as a model to strive after.

'This group was the best in the history of St Peter's among whom we beheld the glory of St Peter's by way of distinctions in Maths, Science, Latin and History,' wrote an inspired Nimrod Tubane, who two years after Oliver and Mokoena's success, himself achieved a First-Class Pass in his JC examinations.[40] Oliver's classmate, Lancelot Gama, described the impact of the results:

'We were writing then the same examinations as any white school in those days... They excited the whole of South Africa that for the first time two black students can get First Class, First Division and come out with distinctions; the examiners in Pretoria were very surprised. They had to come and inspect the school, because they couldn't understand how black people could acquire such high standards. Then fortunately, when they got there to find out where they were sitting, because they suspected that they may have been copying. [But] they had been sitting far from each other when they wrote the exams.'[41]

Intellectual distinction was highly valued, and decades later scores of ANC members interviewed about Tambo alluded to their admiration for his fine mind and his academic excellence. It had become conventional wisdom in African circles that the educated should be in the forefront of uplifting their people. KT Motsete, the first African to obtain a Bachelor of Divinity at the University of London, wrote for St Peter's magazine (which Tambo would have read): 'With a Booker T Washington, or Dr Carver, a John Knox Bokwe, a Jabavu, leisure time is another opportunity for self-improvement, for inventing or creating a new source of benefit to others... Remember it is to such brilliant students that the African communities must look for future leaders.'[42]

The Anglican community was also impressed with Oliver's success. Miss Whittington from Holy Cross wrote to Joyce and Ruth Goddard of Oliver's 'splendid' success: 'He is truly humble with it all. I got him to speak to the boys in the Chapel one evening when he was here, and he puts down his success all through his course to the training and influence received at the Mission...'[43] And a jubilant Brother Roger reported in the *CR Chronicle*:

'Some people think it isn't worth while educating the black man; judge that for yourselves... In the [JC] examination, 2 years before matriculation, 2 boys passed in the First Class, First Division, which means that they got over 80%. Only one other boy in the Transvaal managed to equal that – and he was white. These marks have never before been got by an African.'[44]

Naturally, the school as a whole was equally delighted. 'The announcing of the results was truly African,' Brother Roger observed. 'When the morning papers came with the results in them, Shearsmith... could not contain himself any longer and read them from the steps of his office – unofficially, amidst wild enthusiasm. Then they were read again, officially in church, amidst fairly reverent stirrings and murmurings. Surely the matter could have ended there. But no, at dinner time in the dining hall, there were fresh scenes of delirious excitement when the Head Prefect read them out once more.'[45]

But, though excited and proud, Tambo recalled: 'I felt I missed my parents. I would have loved to have been able to share this moment of triumph with them.'

At home for the holidays, Oliver found ways of keeping his parents' presence alive. The loss of his mother was an irreversible blow, but the extended family compensated with a surrogate. Lena Tambo, Manchi's fourth wife, was to play a major role in helping Oliver achieve a relatively healthy recovery. 'We were now left with the youngest of our mothers – the latest one,' explained Tambo. 'Because there had been Mother Number 1, Mother Number 2, Mother Number 3, she fitted. Because I was still attending school, she fitted exactly into my mother's position... Absolutely wonderful person. There is no way in which my mother could have related to me, other than the way [Lena] did – no way.'

Over the years, with an ailing husband much older than her, Lena developed resourceful ways of swelling the family income. Her daughter, Gerty Tambo, remembered how her mother 'took over' the management of the family. She worked in the trading store as a cleaner. In addition, she baked bread to sell to the store, and also supplied it with meat and home-grown vegetables. Like most other peasant women, Lena conserved her assets by making instead of buying. She wove grass mats, moulded clay pots and carefully preserved and recycled her possessions, teaching her daughters and the other children these skills.[46] Lena's energy, initiative and warmth evoked Oliver's admiration and gratitude – and he remained attracted to strong, competent yet nurturing women.

Oliver's father was not so obviously replaceable, however – the homestead was showing signs of decay. The older brothers were working as migrants; like Oliver, they were away from home for most of the time, and struggling to make sense of their lives. Nevertheless, it was a matter of course that all the brothers should – and did – take over their father's responsibilities in whatever ways they could. Their attention was necessarily uneven, however. Wilson, the eldest, was 'working somewhere in the sugar canes', Gerty recalled. Brother Willy, 'that one was the rolling stone, he never stayed in one place. From town to town – he used to work in Kokstad, went to Maritzburg, went to Flagstaff, went to Umtata, and then he came back home, where he passed away'.

Japan, the son of their brother Zakhele, who had died in the fire in the coal mines, was one of the children Oliver sent to boarding school. Alan Tambo had finished his Standard Six and was training as a driver. In 1939 he joined the army and went 'up North' until the end of the Second World War, in 1945.

In paying tribute to her brothers, Gerty described, with respect and humour, Oliver's conscientious tutelage during his visits home. Primarily, he taught by example, she explained. 'Whenever he had school holidays, he used to work just like everybody here and around me, ploughing, and all sorts of things, doing all the hard work.' He took his duties as *loco parentis* very seriously:

'He was a quiet person, and honest and strict. Because, you see, we were a bit naughty. I remember we usually go to school, [but] when he's on holidays, we usually dodge – don't go there. We pretend as if we have gone to school. And one day he caught us, because the teacher wrote a letter... And he found we don't go perfectly well to school. He gave us a hiding. Yes, he gave us a hiding!'

Oliver's cousin, Elias Bantshi, referring to Tambo as 'my father', confirms: 'He was very strict. He wanted to bring us up nicely... He would take the oxen and push the reaping from the fields. He would send me to go and fetch the oxen... But if I delayed – didn't come straight away – I would get a hiding...'

But Oliver's corporal punishment was not always unquestioningly received. Bantshi recalled that once he ran away from the homestead, reporting Oliver's treatment to his own mother in Harding, who laughed and packed him off back to Kantolo. But, in later years, Bantshi saw in Oliver's combination of encouragement and discipline a method of character building. His participating in the tasks himself, claimed Bantshi, heralded his success as a teacher:

In February 1937, Oliver had received the news that the Bhunga had awarded him a bursary of £30 per annum for five years 'for Matric and Degree'.[47] His future was thus assured. Matriculation was a two-year course and, together with eight other students, he wrote his examinations in December 1938. Six students passed. 'In general our class was in good hands,' said Tambo, 'and predictably we obtained good pass marks at the final matriculation exams – although we did not reach the levels of two years earlier when we wrote the Junior Certificate examinations.' Oliver was awarded a First-Class Pass with a distinction in Mathematics, while Joe Mokoena received three distinctions.

Oliver was now ascending new heights. In his mind, he had already crossed the Engeli Mountains to face fresh challenges. The symbol of the mountains had, by this time, probably taken on an added meaning from Osmund Victor's 'The Upward Path of Native Education', which sketched out its progress:

'Here then is the Mount of Knowledge, with the path of Native Education winding up its slopes, while round about it at the foot are the homes of the native people; country homes on one side, and town houses on the other. From these homes the children sally forth morning-by-morning to climb the mountain as far as they may. Several things you notice at once as you watch them going. In the first place, that three-quarters of the children are left behind to play about or get into mischief, for though all their parents are bound to pay poll tax and therefore have a right to some return for their money, there are not schools to go round... Secondly, though this cannot of course be made plain in the picture, that the crowd of children emerging from town homes is a very large one, while the country homes are sending out the merest trickle...

'So we pass on up the mountain to intermediate schools at whose moderate level all but 1 per cent drop-off; there may have been some congestion on the lower slopes, but on these more rarefied heights numbers thin rapidly...

'In some instances [some secondary schools] may find their pupils passing the Junior Certificate or may in even still rarer instances carry them right up to matriculation itself, though only a very few in the whole of South Africa are found capable of passing it in each year. So to the top of the mountain and the giddy heights of the Native University College at Fort Hare with its 150 students... Fort Hare then shines like a guiding star in the educational firmament of South Africa... Fort Hare offers them the chance; the way is at last open to the highest of which the individual is capable.'[48]

The message was simple and developmental but, once more, it was a missive that Oliver's personal history seemed to confirm. He began to reflect on his future career, and was particularly interested in combining the two legacies of homestead culture and Western schooling. At St Peter's, there had been some lively discussion on the importance of 'Bantu customs'. In the school magazine during Oliver's matric year, for example, the Reverend Jolingana wrote of an experiment he had conducted in a rural area with the approval of Father Yates. Jolingana offered a ritual service for 'Christian circumcision' in which he would be both 'Nurse and Christian Instructor for the initiates'. Circumcision, he perhaps felt obliged to explain, was an example of the 'primitive customs of the Africans which could be made to fit in with the Christian religion'. 'I am persuaded,' he wrote, 'that an African will never give up a custom unless he is convinced that it is wrong.' The result was an intriguing synthesis of two rites of passage, with access to special Western amenities as a bonus.

'Two weeks before Lent, the boys were taken to the doctor's surgery and from there were conveyed in a car to their school, which is situated between Holmdene and Cedarmont on Mr Reed's farm... [The boys] were given instruction for confirmation while at the circumcision lodge. Every day we had religious class and Bible teaching... At the end of the school course, we took the boys to our Church where we all received the Holy Communion with the other members of the congregation. With the permission of the Bishop, I dismissed the initiates with a blessing, after having presented each one of them with a copy of the Zulu New Testament.'[49]

It is clear that syncretic investigation held a special appeal for Oliver. For years, since his days at Holy Cross, he had wanted to heal people, to become a medical doctor. Since the death of his parents, particularly as a response to his mother's rejection of all medications, this aspiration was perhaps intensified. But his ambition went beyond Western orthodoxy. 'I had wanted to study medicine,' he explained, 'and on completion as a medical scientist to get myself apprenticed to a "Witch Doctor" and "Herbalist", with a view to doing research into a field of knowledge which I was certain had great potential for medicine and possibly even the natural sciences.'

Despite the constant exposure to Western culture for close on a decade, Oliver believed that even in the field of science – that form of knowledge that the West claimed for itself – there was much to be learnt from Africa.

'I had had experience of this level of [African] medical practice. And I had accepted it, and although later, as I climbed the ladder of education and was exposed to wider experiences... I had myself begun to dismiss these practices, I nonetheless felt some of them had a great deal that needed studying, instead of dismissing them as the results of superstition. I was certain there was a need to prove that everything these "Witch Doctors" and doctors and herbalists said and did was indeed based on pure suspicion, or whether science had anything to learn from it.'

But then he learnt that Fort Hare did not offer a medical degree. Instead, it advanced a four-year medical auxiliary diploma, designed for Africans only.[50] His future was thus to be directly affected by the institutionalised race discrimination in the universities themselves: 'White students in the country proceeded from matric to medicine if they wanted to do that, but certainly at Fort Hare the most that Africans were allowed to do was this "Medical Aid", after which they could either practise as semi-doctors, or begin afresh a full medical course at those white universities that would accept African students.'

In principle, the medical schools at the relatively liberal universities of the Witwatersrand and Cape Town had indeed agreed to accept black students, but in practice there was no opportunity for Africans to study for a medical degree in South Africa in the 1930s. The Loram Committee commissioned by the University of the Witswatersrand in 1928 admitted that 'the Natives themselves demand the same standard of training and are unwilling to accept anything inferior'.[51] But it added:

> '(b) (i) In view of the strong prejudices of the Community, Non-European students cannot be admitted to the existing medical classes for European students; but they must be taught in separate classes...
>
> '(b) (ii) As the finances of this University cannot support the additional burden entailed by the establishment of Non-European Medical Students, full provision should be made for such additional cost, including all the necessary buildings and equipment as well as the recurring expenses.'

Not surprisingly, nothing was done to establish these classes. It was only in 1942 that the first intake of black students was admitted to the Wits and University of Cape Town medical schools.[52] In the meantime, blacks who wanted to qualify as fully recognised doctors were obliged to find a way of proceeding abroad to be trained. In a very few cases, some exceptionally bright and hardworking students had the good fortune to attract the attention of private benefactors and, after a preparatory year of science courses at Fort Hare, proceeded to Edinburgh.[53]

A patron who was in a position to provide the major outlay required for an overseas training was clearly not available and, unwilling to study for a second-class qualification, Tambo abandoned the idea of studying medicine. He began to look for alternatives. Invariably socially minded, he observed that very few university-educated Africans had qualified in the sciences, compared with the Bachelor of Arts degree.

'There were only about six Africans who had the Bachelor of Science degree,' he said, 'and I decided to reinforce this small group and wished others would do the same so as to correct the imbalance. Virtually all African graduates were school teachers, which was the only meaningful avenue of employment open to them... Since I was not going to study medicine as a profession, then I had to prepare myself for the teaching profession.'

Oliver then conducted a personal survey. Talking to other students, he discovered that science students tended to major in Botany, Zoology and Chemistry. 'There was no mention of Maths and Physics,' he discovered. 'Here I saw another imbalance and decided to major in Maths and Physics.'

When students warned him against taking such a difficult combination, Tambo 'was particularly reassured'. He wanted a challenge, he said; he wanted to fill a gap, and was delighted when two other St Peter's boys, Joe Mokoena and Lancelot Gama, opted for the same majors in the Bachelor of Science degree at Fort Hare.

Part Two

The Ascent

1939–1959

CHAPTER FOUR

'The Starting Point'

FORT HARE COLLEGE RAG was a significant fundraising event on the campus calendar, and many students looked forward to the opportunity to wear traditional dress. On each occasion, Oliver wore a Mpondo costume, finished with an intricate beaded collar. For the students, regional identity was an important part of their make-up. But despite first impressions – Tambo's tell-tale facial scars and his reticent manner – he was far more sophisticated in his outlook than the vast majority of his peers. Unlike most of his generation, including the missionary-educated sons and daughters of chiefs and headmen at Fort Hare, Tambo had grown up in an urban school in the heart of the metropolis. For him, the College – which was to receive official 'university' status only in the 1960s – was undoubtedly another step in the ongoing widening of his world rather than uncharted, threatening terrain. Indeed, as soon as he arrived, Tambo was delighted to see that 'apart from African students, there were also "coloured" and Indian students'. The students came not only from the Union of South Africa, but also from the British protectorates of Bechuanaland [Botswana], Basotholand [Lesotho] and Swaziland. There were even students from as far north as Uganda.

Notwithstanding this diversity, there were fewer than 200 students at Fort Hare in 1939.[1] 'It did not take me long, therefore, before everybody knew everyone else, and I did not have the problems of social adjustment and adaptation that faced me when I first arrived in Johannesburg five years earlier,' reflected Tambo. He felt a close association with his black fellow students, regardless of their origins. St Peter's had prepared him for a broader African national culture. Half a century later, looking back on his student days, he recalled with unmistakable satisfaction:

'I belonged with every group. Those students, for example, who came from what were known as the northern provinces, namely the Transvaal, Orange Free State, the then British Protectorates, were amicably referred to as "Northerners", and would proudly refer to themselves as such. I belonged with them, having taken my secondary school education in those areas. But my home was in the Cape Province and in particular in the Transkei, situated a few miles from the border between the Cape and Natal provinces. I soon found and made friends in all the residences; but this could not have been peculiar to me only – Fort Hare had a very friendly atmosphere.'

In Beda Hall, the residence for Anglican students, Tambo remembered a similar combination of unity and diversity. The hostel accommodated 'ten coloured men and six Indians', reported the warden to the Archbishop of Cape Town: 'The rest were Bantu.'[2] Notwithstanding Tambo's deep religious convictions, he had no problem belonging to an extensive community beyond the confines of his own heritage, an approach that was to become analogous to the 'broad church' of the ANC that he was to head in years to come.

'At Beda Hall it did not matter to me if the student occupying the room next to me was a Roman Catholic, a Muslim or a Hindu,' said Tambo. 'I did not even bother to ask; nor was there anything to suggest that any of us at Beda Hall would have had any objection to having his room in Wesley Hall or Iona. Because we found ourselves at Beda Hall, we liked and were proud of our residence, and had no call to wish that we could be accommodated elsewhere.'

Ironically, Fort Hare had been founded specifically to educate the young Christian men and women of Africa, and all the members of staff had to be 'professing Christians and of missionary sympathies'.[3] It was the product of many layers of history. The College adjoined the small town of Alice, accessible by a bridge across the Tyumie River, which also hosted Lovedale Press and Lovedale College as well as the famous Methodist school, Healdtown. Fort Hare was situated next to the crumbling ruins of the old colonial fort built in 1846 as a white bulwark against attempts by Maqoma's people to reclaim the land seized during the wars of dispossession. The significance of the site was not lost on the prime minister, General Louis Botha, when he declared the College open in 1916. A more lasting monument, he announced, was being erected on the relics of Fort Hare, 'the place where the struggle between white and black was settled with blood and tears'.[4]

For many, this exposure to a multilingual and multinational institution posed something of a challenge to their identities. The majority had accepted, perhaps uneasily, the ambiguity of an assimilationist model, which in time to come might embrace them as an elite class of 'civilised natives'. As educated Christians, they consciously distinguished themselves from the unconverted, whose place in the social structure was destined to be confined to the role of migrant worker and common labourer. The more politically minded were aware of the African National Congress, with its message of inter-ethnic African national unity. The famous acceptance speech of Pixley ka Isaka Seme, on being awarded a prestigious oratorical prize in 1906 in New York, pioneered an insight into a wider, uplifting identity.

'I am an African,' he declared, 'and I set my pride in my race over against a hostile public opinion.' The century ahead, he went on to predict, would be the harbinger of a 'regeneration of Africa' – 'a new and unique civilisation is soon to be added to the world'.[5]

A rich literature focusing on the challenges to African identity was already beginning to emerge. Apart from inspiring exemplars such as Sol Plaatje, Mweli Skota (editor of the *African Yearly Register*),[6] Soga, Rubusana, Bokwe, Fort Hare's own DDT Jabavu and ZK Matthews, and the brothers HIE and RRR Dhlomo, a vigorous black-owned press promoted knowledge of home-grown African literature. The likes of John Tengo Jabavu's *Imvo* and the ANC's *Abantu-Batho* in the Eastern Cape, *Ilanga* in Durban, and Selope Thema's *Bantu World* in Johannesburg regularly published past and current writers. Traditional bards were not neglected. This included the poetry of SM Mqhayi – famous for his lyrics for the anthem '*Nkosi Sikelel' iAfrika*' – as well as others ('*Ntsikana, Mafukuzela, Mnganga*'[7]) who composed in the mother tongue. Pan Africanist and other views from African Americans WEB Du Bois, Frederick Douglass, Marcus Garvey and Dr JEK Aggrey were also popularised in their pages. Speeches, too, were published in full. At the launch of the South African Native National Congress on 8 January 1912, Seme had eloquently called for black unity: 'We are one people,' he insisted. 'These divisions, these jealousies are the cause of all our troubles and of all our ignorance today.'[8]

For Oliver Tambo, the dilemma of negotiating identity – not to mention the variations of a more authoritarian or paternalistic style of Christianity than he was accustomed to – were still to be confronted. St Peter's had taught him and his fellow students a more holistic approach to spiritual and earthly life – unlike some churches, Victor Sifora said caustically, where 'you were invited to think in terms of the life hereafter – the life now was not your problem, that was the problem of the church'.[9]

From the start, the College was a church-driven project. The United Free Church of Scotland donated the land and the governing council represented the Anglican, Methodist and Presbyterian denominations (all of which financed their own students' hostels on campus), as well as the Department of Native Affairs. Supplemented by donations from the Administration of Basutoland and from the Transkei Bhunga, the South African government helped finance the teaching college and laboratories. Funds from the Students' Christian associations of the USA and Canada provided the building for the Students' Christian Union.

At first the College was poorly equipped – 'bare of comforts and full of hard work' – as the students were also employed in the manual labour of laying roads and gardens.[10] It was able to offer 'two oldish buildings' for about 20 students. The adjoining bungalow had to serve as a dining room as well as provide living quarters for the matron and the two female students. But the missionary workers adapted the resources while the students, according to Dr Alexander Kerr, the principal, cheerfully displayed 'the unconcern of the African in regard to what Europeans would consider to be the minimum of physical comfort, provided that their main objective, in this case education, was attained'.[11]

These fairly basic conditions lasted longer than strictly necessary, owing to Kerr's insistence that 'it was better to do without buildings than to allow inferior ones to be put up'.[12] ZK Matthews explained that Kerr 'might easily have done what other European administrators have done, and contented himself with the thought that inferior buildings were good enough for inferior Africans. Instead, he insisted that, brick for brick, Fort Hare had to be the peer of any college'.[13]

But by the time that Oliver Tambo arrived, Fort Hare boasted as fine a set of buildings as any historically 'white' university, and offered a matriculation course, to be followed by a choice of diplomas and degree courses. Kerr, affectionately described as a 'red-faced' Scotsman who wore thick glasses, was 'free of the racial attitudes common to the country'.[14] He had arrived as a young man in 1915 to help set it up. 'I was new to the country,' wrote Kerr half a century later during the apartheid era, 'quite unaware of the strength of racial tensions that even then existed.'[15] Before he had left Scotland for Fort Hare, he had been alarmed to read in a book on southern Africa the claim, 'on scientific grounds', that the brain of the African was incapable of growing, owing to 'the premature closure of the suture of the skull'.[16] Such were the pseudoscientific fallacies, he was to discover, that were used to justify the continuing exploitation of black people in South Africa.

Among Afrikaners, the education policy of the British missionaries was viewed as another imperialist attempt to create 'black Englishmen'. Their own defeat in the South African War, the treatment of Boer women and children in concentration camps and the subsequent suppression of the Boer culture and language in the schools during the Milner regime were still within bitter living memory. Better by far, many felt, if the different African 'tribes' were left to develop their own, separate identities.[17]

Fort Hare was frequently cited as an example of how the expectations of African students were raised unrealistically by providing an education they would not be able to apply in society. Indeed, the principal himself regretted the limitations imposed on Fort Hare students by its academic bias, and ascribed the cause for this restriction to the job colour bar imposed 'by the white man's fear that his standard of living would be undermined if low-paid African labour were employed':

'Missionaries have been blamed for giving [the African] an education which is merely bookish, but when they teach him such arts as building and carpentry, they find that their protégés are debarred from employment by the only persons with capital enough for undertaking contracts required for their services. As long as such a condition of affairs prevails, the education of the African is bound to have a bookish bias, and his field of employment to lie amongst the professions: ministers, teachers, doctors, lawyers, civil servants, journalists, the great majority being a band of labourers without the training or skill to qualify as artisans and form a middle class.'[18]

The College had produced its first two African graduates in 1924, when Edwin Ncwana had been awarded a Diploma of Arts, and Zachariah Keodirelang Matthews had taken his Bachelor of Arts degree. In the following year, Fort Hare College was constituted as a university college. The investment had proved to be a success. Kerr, reacting to 'the indifference or, in some cases, the actual hostility of the ordinary European to the education of the non-European and especially to that of the African', felt vindicated[19] and took a paternalistic pride in the achievement of their graduates.

'Any hesitation one might have had in regard to the innate ability or specific capacities of the African, about which various fallacies were current and seemingly deeply ingrained in the minds of ordinary [ie. white] citizens had become less tenable. We who were teaching them soon realised that we were in contact with a virile people who, in addition to the ordinary incentives to study, had an unspoiled enthusiasm for, and a profound faith in, education, a faith which sometimes had an element of pathos in it.'[20]

'Pathos' – because almost all would have to endure the humiliation of racism and economic exploitation in their future careers…[21]

Beda Hall, Oliver's residence, was the newest and perhaps most imposing residence on campus. Its original warden, Bishop Smythe, former Bishop of Lebombo, had had a highly successful tenure at the residence, deeply impressing students with his unpretentious lifestyle (as opposed, by implication, to some missionaries who, under pressure, sooner or later wavered in their commitment to the students' ultimate litmus-test, absence of racism). ZK Matthews wrote in his autobiography that 'Smythe was marked by his uniqueness as a European who not only opposed the racial customs of the country but actually lived by the precept of the brotherhood of man. He practised what he preached wherever he was, at home in the hostel or outside. He was not one of those Europeans willing to meet on a friendly footing with non-whites so long as no other Europeans were around'.[22]

Smythe thus set his particular stamp on the style of Beda Hall. According to Matthews, he insisted that cultural traditions could never be valued above human relationships: 'He pointedly welcomed members of all denominations as students in the hostel, especially Roman Catholics who had no hostel of their own. He also welcomed Indians, who were usually not Christians at all, but Hindus or Moslems.'[23]

Smythe bequeathed his open policy to his successor, Bishop Ferguson-Davie, who was warden during Oliver's time. 'A most pleasant old man,' recalled Tambo. The bishop's wife, a medical doctor, was also on the teaching staff. The warden's duties included spiritual guidance of the students, and he was expected to take his turn in conducting the College Sunday service and daily morning prayers.[24]

Oliver Tambo's unfailing routine of worship had continued, undiminished by academic achievements. Indeed, it was perhaps stimulated by his success; consistently throughout his life, prayer was an earnest and private ritual:

'After my encounter with evangelists of what was later called the Full Gospel Church at my home in or around 1930, my religious practice took on a new and more personalised character. I developed a liking for the early-morning Holy Communion service that would normally be held in a chapel, which, because it was early, attracted few people. Often I was the only one attending. But if there was no service, I went to the chapel anyway for prayers, if not in the morning, then at any time during the day... Being at Beda Hall provided me personally with the facility I had enjoyed both at Holy Cross Mission and at St Peter's Secondary School – that was the Chapel.'[25]

But Tambo's mission at Fort Hare was academic progress, and the 'first two or three days after our arrival, we were engaged in the business of sorting out our degree courses and deciding on the curriculum'. In his first lectures, he found that the lecturers seemed determined to stretch and test the students to their limits. They made an enduring impact on Tambo, who more than half a century later remembered these first impressions with precision and clarity.

'The first encounter with the Maths lecturer explained why we had been warned that no one had ever passed Maths... Bill Murdock, tall and broad shouldered, stooping slightly forward, with an aggressive booming voice, spoke English with a particularly strong accent that made it difficult to follow what he was saying. Nor did he wait until you did understand. He scrawled out words and figures on the blackboard, rubbing them out before you had copied them down in your notebook and racing down the blackboard again with his chalk. At the end of that first lesson, half of us had learnt nothing and decided that they could never learn anything and so they dropped Maths from their curriculum. The rest of us, including Joe Mokoena, Lancelot Gama, Sostenise Mokgokong, all from St Peter's, Rosettenville – Euclid Khomo – all of us stayed on and soon adapted to Bill Murdock's manner and style. For all the aggressiveness of his voice, he was full of jokes; he was also full of outbursts of temper, which cleared completely only a few minutes after. So we got to like him as a person, if his style did not endear Mathematics with some of us.'

Tambo, in fact, delighted in humour, and enjoyed observing people's foibles and eccentricities. He also became aware of the value of humour in capturing attention and interest in the classroom even when, in Bill Murdock's case, the teacher's raillery bordered on the uncivil. 'Bill Murdock was a terror,' commented ZK Matthews, 'but a good-humoured terror.'[26] 'For all that I felt about the way Bill Murdock handled Maths,' confirmed Tambo, 'he was always the subject of amused comment.' In fact, Tambo clearly remembered how, when a student provided an incorrect answer to a question Murdock had posed, the booming lecturer announced, 'You came to the wrong Fort!', implying that the unfortunate victim should rather have been 'enrolled' at Fort Beaufort, a small town to the west of Alice noted for its lunatic asylum.

In the meanwhile, Tambo soaked up all this new knowledge with enthusiasm; but his major frustration, he recalled, was his inability to follow up his interest in the humanities. 'I was deeply interested in Law, Philosophy, Sociology, Psychology, Anthropology. I had come across books on Economics, and various subjects of which I knew nothing. And which were there for the asking if only I could make the time; and I couldn't, because of the pressure of my science degree work.'

Nelson Mandela, a humanities student in the Methodist hostel of Wesley House, recalled that Oliver Tambo made his mark amongst his colleagues as one of the few science students who was politically articulate.

'He was outstanding even at that time in debates. He had a disciplined mind with a very good command of the language. A very clear thinker who always saw both sides of the problem; and he immediately was recognised by the students' body as one of the students' leaders. In fact one of our comments was the strangeness of BSc – Science – students, with such a good command of language and interest in things which went beyond the field of pure science. Unfortunately, although there were exceptions, the general trend at that time was that the science students were interested in their laboratories and the experiments and also that they found it difficult to express themselves on broad community issues. That perception may have been right or wrong, but that was the perception. And a man who could not be confined to those limits was Oliver Tambo.'[27]

Tambo also found intellectual stimulation in the company of old school friends, Congress Mbatha and Lancelot Gama. The three formed a band and called themselves 'The Syndicate'. It all began when the friends agreed that the meals in the dining hall were 'very meagre'. It was the policy of Fort Hare to keep the College fees as low as possible. The consequence of this attempt to remain within reach of as large a section of the black community as possible was that, by the principal's own admission, the 'diet had to be extremely simple and must have been monotonous'.[28] According to Tambo's recollection, 'For those of us who came from St Peter's there was virtually no supper, because what was called supper was four remarkably thin slices of bread, taken with a small cup of milk water, the water of which would be hot.'

The friends thus decided to take turns in collecting the slices of bread for the whole group and supplementing the meal with butter and jam, or tinned fish, which they bought from a café in Alice. 'The Syndicate,' explained Oliver Tambo, 'became an increasingly serious grouping that saw us through Fort Hare into the wider world, and its members were then bound by principles and considerations totally unrelated to what you eat in the evening. We were concerned with matters of life, matters of the future, our role in society.'

'JC Mbatha', recollected Lancelot Gama – by 1994, sole surviving member of The Syndicate – became a 'Principal of one of the secondary schools here and eventually he went to America, where he taught in one of the universities in America. He was quite a capable student'.[29] One of the founders of the ANC Youth League and a secretary of the Transvaal African Teachers' Association in the 1940s, Congress Mbatha (named after the ANC)[30] was to further his studies at the University of the Witwatersrand and eventually emigrated to North-Western and Cornell universities, where he wrote a number of studies on race and racism in South Africa. Lancelot Gama himself graduated with a Bachelor of Science degree and then went on to become a medical doctor. Although he did not become prominent in activist politics, Gama was to retain a lifelong contact and warm friendship with Tambo. More than 50 years later, he reflected on how the aims of The Syndicate had been successfully executed: 'We felt that we should keep together and work together for the good of life. We had pledged to help each other – it doesn't matter where. We must always help each other – we must always help each other – the six of us.'[31]

And so it proved to be, especially at crucial moments in the lives of the members in the years to come. This was an age cohort who, through their shared experiences, had bonded at boarding school – the institution that succeeded the extended family of the homestead and the rural community. Facing new challenges at the university and in the racially discriminating world beyond, they formed themselves into a kind of brotherhood for life, which provided emotional and even material support.

The group was later expanded with the addition of Joe Mokoena, the student who had surpassed Oliver in the matriculation examination and was eventually to succeed Murdock as Mathematics lecturer at Fort Hare. Two other St Peter's graduates also joined The Syndicate: Walter Gumbi and one Mofokeng, who was to become the first lecturer in Sesotho at Wits. 'He was an outstanding student too,' recorded Matthews. 'He got a first class, too, in Joint Board Examination with some distinction, also quiet and studious.'[32] The new members of The Syndicate, observed Oliver Tambo, 'fitted into this group very well'.

The Syndicate regularly discussed not only their assignments but also matters of moral philosophy and politics. Oliver, in particular, was loquacious and put a great deal of energy into winning a debate. 'He was very argumentative,' recalled ZK Matthews' son Joe: 'Mokoena was quiet, but Tambo was always involved in controversy and arguments and so on from the word "go".'[33]

Dr Gama recalled those all-night sessions: 'We used to study together sometimes right into the night. That's how we started being close together, because we used to sit down together and study and then, say about four o'clock in the morning, someone would go and make tea and coffee... We would test each other, and we would also study on our own, to work hard.'[34]

In his recollections of university life, Tambo also vividly remembered being particularly struck by two other prominent students, both of them the sons of chiefs: 'I had come to know and had become very friendly with two students of whom much was to be heard in later years. One was Kaizer Matanzima, and the other Nelson Mandela. Both had their homes in the Transkei and were roughly the same age; both tall and stately, born of royalty...

'Matanzima was a capable debater, his general inclination being to challenge the status quo. He was particularly fond of engaging issues that involved the constitution of the college, the regulations, and so on. He had a liking, quite clearly, for legal questions.

'Nelson Mandela, famous as an athlete and one of the foremost runners at Fort Hare, was always cautious and calculating in his statements on issues. He was highly respected and had a wide circle of friends at college...

'They were close relations, the one a nephew to the other, and both stayed at Wesley House. After leaving Fort Hare, both took up law studies, the one in the Transkei, the other in Johannesburg. Both qualified as lawyers. Both became involved in politics. And that is the point where their paths parted dramatically and irretrievably.'

The diverging fates of Mandela and Matanzima were to become, for Tambo, one of life's major morality plays, illustrating the catastrophe of shortsighted temptation – Matanzima was to become the first African leader to accept the offer by apartheid's architects of presiding over a 'self-governing homeland'. The consequence of ' independence' for Transkei was political separation from South Africa and moral disgrace. Economic interaction, though, continued to flourish in its customary, unequal fashion: migrant labourers continued to fortify the wealth of South Africa's mines, farms and industries at extremely low wages. From the time of its declaration of 'independence', Transkei's citizens were to become 'foreigners' in South Africa, harassed by the pass laws, and with even the few rights accorded to black 'South African' residents legally removed.

Tambo pronounced severe judgement on Matanzima's opportunistic decision: 'Kaizer Matanzima was to become a political disaster for the victims of what became known as apartheid, and was a great gift to the strategists for permanent European domination in South Africa. His contribution to the consolidation and survival of apartheid was to prove greater than that of any black leader.'

And pitted against Matanzima, the fallen patrician, was the conscious and long-term sacrifice of the nation's saviour, symbol of the ultimate salvation of all South Africans:

'Nelson Mandela, on the other hand, was to grow to become the pride of the nation, the man feared by the racist tyrants who ruled the black population in South Africa. Loved and followed by the vast majority of the people of South Africa, he was to become the most famous political prisoner in the world, honoured by countless awards of every kind by governments, political and labour organisations, educational institutions, local governments, cultural bodies, leading personalities and ordinary people across the globe. My friendship with him was to develop and mature into an enduring partnership that found firm expression in politics, law and life.'

The providing of intellectual training and skills for the sons (and sometimes daughters) of traditional rulers was a major consideration for Fort Hare, and a significant proportion of students was drawn from the African aristocracy. One of the most prominent royals was Seretse Khama, likeable and unassuming, who arrived at Beda Hall in Oliver's last year at Fort Hare, in 1942. 'He was not posing himself as if he is going to be king,' commented Lancelot Gama. 'He was just part of the student body; that is one of the things I liked about him. He never put his personality above anybody else.'[35] Khama, Chief of the Bamangwato of Bechuanaland, was under the guardianship of his uncle, the regent and classical scholar, Tshekedi Khama.

Almost all Fort Hare lecturers were white, but there were two African lecturers, 'very prominent and popular'. They presented the students with role models. Professor DDT Jabavu, son of prominent black editor John Tengo Jabavu, was in fact one of the founder staff members of Fort Hare, and one of some 60 African graduates with an 'overseas' university degree by the end of the 1920s.[36]

'Jocular and sociable and around 60 years of age, he was a man of the people. He held a degree in the Bachelor of Arts from the London University, which he insisted should always be distinguished from its South African equivalent, such as a BA from the University of South Africa, or Cape Town or any other university in South Africa. This was because he was the first African in South Africa to obtain a London University degree and was still the only one at the time of our studies at Fort Hare. The fuss about whether one held a London or South African degree arose from the fact that to qualify for a BA was very rare for Africans in the first instance, largely because they could not afford the cost of university education; and for Africans, this was not a government responsibility.'

One suspects that the implication that Fort Hare degrees were bound to be inferior to those obtained abroad bothered Tambo. Jabavu's more impressive achievements as an articulate though subtle critic of government discrimination and the initiator of the All-African Convention formed to protest against the 1936 Representation of Natives Act were not properly assimilated by Tambo at the time – Jabavu taught humanities, not science. To Oliver Tambo, Jabavu's own identity was primarily tied up with the College. And yet, many of Jabavu's interests coincided with Tambo's. As an educator, Jabavu loved teaching, but always looked beyond the classroom and promoted extra-curricular activities such as student debating societies and choirs. But Jabavu, in his fifties, belonged to another epoch, more optimistic about the eventual and full incorporation of the African elite into mainstream white society. The leadership of Tambo's generation – born after the 1913 Land Act, disenfranchised and growing up under the crass impact of urban areas acts, job colour bars, stricter pass laws and the Native Administration Act – were destined to become a tougher breed.

Bridging the gap between the two generations was ZK Matthews. Typical of many young students' image of their teachers, Tambo remembered Matthews – 'younger than Professor Jabavu but well into his fifties' – as much older than he actually was. At the time, Matthews was in his late thirties. Said Tambo, 'He held the honour of being the first student to graduate from Fort Hare, after which he obtained degrees from other universities overseas, including a law degree... He was of a less colourful mode than Professor Jabavu but had an equally friendly disposition. Matthews was profoundly intellectual and well informed. He exercised a tremendous influence among the students.'

Impressed by Matthews, Tambo longed to expand his intellectual outlook. 'It is unfortunate that I cannot do more subjects than these,' he wrote to the Goddards in October 1940. 'However, I intend to do subjects like Anthropology and Ethics as soon as I complete the BSc – that is, by private study.'[37]

Although deprived of the opportunity to study extra subjects, Oliver was nevertheless an active participant in extramural activities. He regularly attended the Musical, Science and Literary societies, and was vice-chairman of the Debating Society. He also played first-team soccer and cricket.[38] Mandela remembered first meeting Oliver on the soccer field: 'We played soccer – these things were organised according to hostels – and that is where I met him in 1939. He was a good footballer.' Mandela also recalled Tambo's impressive dexterity in stick fighting. 'And we were both members of the Students' Christian Association.'[39]

Prowess in sports, as in many universities, was an important social asset at Fort Hare, as was musical ability. Students formed themselves into musical groups, jazz bands or choirs, which regularly put on performances for the College and the community at large. The authorities, in fact, encouraged musical expression. In the 1920s, Alexander Kerr had undertaken an educational tour of the United States and had been particularly impressed by Fisk University in Nashville, Tennessee, 'built in part and made famous by its group of Jubilee singers', which 'seemed to us to be of the pattern we were likely to see being developed within a reasonable time, in South Africa'. Fisk University's non-racial staff, its links with the community on which it depended for support, and 'the contribution made by its students through their popularisation of folk music and spirituals, all seemed to align them with African students in South Africa'.[40] Kerr's vision, together with Jabavu's enthusiastic grooming and conducting of student choirs, thus created a high standard of choral activity at Fort Hare. Modern African music, whether jazz or choral, though largely influenced by Western culture, was already beginning to include indigenous idioms. Not so 'ballroom dancing', which was nevertheless considered a popular accomplishment by the aspiring young elite. Close friend Phyllis Ntantala recalled revelling in the attention she and Halley, her suitor at the time, attracted 'on that dance floor doing the waltz or the tango'. Halley was also 'a hot number for duets'.[41]

But serious-minded Oliver was less concerned with displaying his accomplishments to the opposite sex than with expressing his creativity through song. From his first year at Fort Hare, Oliver taught Sunday School. Part of his activity with the 10 little boys and girls included choral music. At Holy Cross, too, during one of his holidays there, he organised a choral event. He recalled the experience with obvious delight:

'I had arrived to find that Archdeacon Father Leary was retiring after many years of missionary work in Eastern Pondoland... I proposed a farewell concert in his honour. For the purpose, I formed a choir among the nurses of the Holy Cross Hospital, and was allowed to take over the school choir. I composed three songs for the occasion, one for the nurses and two for the school choir, and of course appointed myself conductor for both choirs. The school choir excelled itself, awakening from many years of slumber. Indeed for the first time that year, the Holy Cross Mission school choir took first place in the Annual Schools Singing Competitions.'

Miss Tanqueray, mistress at Holy Cross, writing to the Goddard sisters, also recorded the event. 'He was here for part of the vacation last Christmas,' she wrote, 'and seemed such a nice boy. He is still so keen on anything going forward, simple in his tastes – no side – and so jolly with everyone. He trained a choir for a concert and helped in some acting and showed considerable ability for teaching and training others.'[42]

Oliver also derived much fulfilment from his singing group at Fort Hare, the 'Beda Hall Double Quartet, a group of eight young men of our hostel who sing Negro Spirituals and Bantu Songs'.[43] The 'famous singers' who preceded him included Willie Nkomo, another future founder-member of the ANC Youth League and a medical doctor, and AC Jordan, the writer and linguist who subsequently returned to teach at Fort Hare and was then appointed to the African Languages Department at the University of Cape Town. In 1940, Jordan married Phyllis Ntantala. In later years, the couple were to become Oliver's warm friends; in exile, their son, Pallo, was to work closely with Tambo in the media, propaganda and culture department.

'During our day, the best singers were Miss Trieste Tsewu, later married to Joe Mokoena, himself a very keen singer... One senior student, Mr Bikitshe, put together a small college choir and Beda Hall formed a double quartet, which became pretty well known, and more than once broadcast spirituals over the

Grahamstown radio station. It travelled around the Alice area, holding concerts. Members of this group were Joe Mokoena, T Mbalo, Kobus Letlaka, [Apollo] Kironde [from Uganda], Sostenise Mokgokong, Velius Bam and myself.'

These broadcasts made considerable impact on their fellow students, and more than one of Tambo's peers remembered listening to the choir over the radio, with delight and admiration. Not that South African singers were unknown in the wider world – many black choirs had successfully undertaken tours in Europe and America since at least the late nineteenth century.[44] During Tambo's 30-year international sojourn, his love of musical expression was to emerge and indeed help harness the movement's genre of 'cultural' resistance.

A glimpse of Oliver Tambo's passion for the human voice was hinted at in his description of an experience which 'membership of a thousand choirs at St Peter's would never have given me'. It occurred on his way home from Fort Hare one holiday, when he had to stop overnight at King William's Town to wait for his train connection the following day.

'I heard there was to be a concert at a school nearby. I naturally took the opportunity to attend the concert. I sat among the audience and listened to what in my view was a wonderful rendering of the song, "The Sea and its Pearls", by the school choir. The Principal of the school was a Mr Magobiya and he was conducting the choir. At the end of the performance, to which I had listened, spellbound, I went up to Mr Magobiya and asked him how he managed to produce such beautiful voices, especially soprano voices. He said to me, "You should aim at producing a resonant, sonorous, rich voice" – three words that stuck in my mind and were to prove invaluable in after years.'

During another holiday break from Fort Hare, Tambo recalled an experience that was to have considerable bearing on his political attitudes. He had stopped over at Qumbu, in the Transkei, hometown of fellow Beda Hall resident, Pumele Mpumwana. It was June 1940, and the impact of the Second World War had reached even the most remote rural villages in South Africa. At school, Tambo remarked, he had heard of wars from his history teacher, Miss Tidmarsh at Holy Cross, who had lived through the previous war in England and shared with her class her growing concern of Germany's militarisation in the 1930s. 'At Fort Hare,' admitted Tambo, 'we did not feel the impact of the war until some of our lecturers were called up for service... Mr Davidson's absence, and the knowledge he was wearing a military uniform and carrying a gun somewhere, brought the war into closer focus and we followed it with keener interest.'

The students ardently followed the battle for democracy against fascism, which embodied both racism and dictatorship. Tambo recalled their eager pursuit of radio news over the progress of the war. Along with the others, he followed the Nazi invasion of the Maginot Line, which had previously protected France from foreign invasion, and was indignant at 'Hitler's contempt for International Law'. Tambo was stirred by Churchill's inspired call to mobilise the British people. In South Africa, said Tambo, 'the Smuts government had narrowly put the country on a war footing, but was also carrying on an intensive recruiting campaign among every section of the South African population including, notably, the Africans'. He was also well aware, from local popular memory, of the government's conduct towards black soldiers during the First World War in which Smuts, then too, had played a major role.

'During that war, hundreds of Africans danced their way to death on the decks of their ship known as the *Mendi* when they discovered that the ship was sinking in mid-ocean, after it was hit by the Germans and that there was no hope for them. They died most gallantly. That drama became a household story among the Africans, kept alive by the reality that although the war was won, far from improving, our conditions worsened. The persistent question, "What did the *Mendi* heroes die for?" had not been answered as General Smuts's men went around recruiting for the Second World War.'

In the early years of the Second World War, Prime Minister Smuts was particularly anxious to win the support of the Africans. His great fear, he confessed in Parliament, was that the Japanese might invade South Africa and be welcomed by the black population. At that time, Tambo was told of a meeting for 'chiefs, sub-chiefs, and all able-bodied men' called by the Bizana district magistrate and local Native Commissioner. In his retelling of this story, Tambo clearly delighted in the irony and the subtle metaphor of peasant discourse.

'Being the government official in charge of what we called "Native Affairs", he called for volunteers who were required to defend the country against Hitler of Germany, who wanted to take over the country and place it under German rule. He urged the people of Bizana to join up and defend their land. Native Commissioners were wont to treat Africans, especially peasants, like children; so when it suited them, the peasants too behaved like the children he believed them to be. In the present instance the Native Commissioner was asking the Africans to fight to defend land which they had been robbed of decades earlier. Land they no longer possessed. Land forcibly taken from them by the white government of South Africa. Why should they help the robbers keep the land? Therefore the reply they gave to the Native Commissioner's call was that they had never met this man Hitler. They demanded to know from him personally why he wanted their land. Only then would they decide whether to fight him or not. They therefore asked the Native Commissioner to write to Hitler to tell him to come to Bizana, so that the people could consider his claim. To a childish approach by the Native Commissioner, the people gave a childish reply. But the message was clear. No volunteers.'

At Qumbu in Pondoland, Tambo witnessed first-hand the practical lessons absorbed by ordinary people from their collective memory. It was 'an opportunity to be present at a recruiting meeting, related to a war that was to change much of the world'. Tambo dealt with the event at some length.

'While at Qumbu, we attended a meeting called by the Native Commissioner. He explained the purpose of the meeting. There was a war on, and the government wanted all able-bodied men to defend the country against the Germans. He emphasised that there was a threat from the Japanese. Those who joined would be given various assignments. Some would guard important installations such as water reservoirs, our station, bridges and so on. Others would be sent up to the north of the continent where fighting was going on and others would be deployed in other areas. Apart from considerations of the way they were let down after World War One, the people of Qumbu had a special grievance against the government which must have been shared by people in other districts.

'This emerged during question time. Two men stood up to ask questions. The first one wanted to know how the people guarding the installations would be armed, to which the Native Commissioner promptly replied that they would be armed each with a shield, a spear and a knobkerrie [or knob-stick]. The questioner went on. "And," he said, "how is the enemy expected to attack the installations? Would he be coming on vehicles, walking, or what?" The reply was that he would most likely come by air and drop bombs. To which the questioner commented, "So if I am there guarding a water reservoir and I see a plane approaching, I am expected to take my knobkerrie and fling it at the plane in an attempt to hit it and bring it down?" There was laughing among the people. The Commissioner did not comment.

'Another man stood up and asked how people being sent to North Africa would be armed; would they carry a shield, a spear and a knobkerrie? The Commissioner answered that for a person going to North Africa no arms would be provided in this country, but that when he is in North Africa he would be sent a pistol if he needed one. "And so," commented the questioner sarcastically, "if I am in North Africa and I see the enemy approaching, I am expected to write a letter to you that moment asking you to post to me my pistol so that I can defend myself against this approaching enemy?"'

Further exchanges illuminated for Tambo the bitterness of a people who had been disarmed through deceit. He recalled a conversation between two men seated next to him.

'[One man] was saying that they start by depriving us of our firearms and now they want us to join up and fight with knobkerries. "Never!" he said. I followed up the comment, and it appeared that sometime earlier on, the government had called on all those who possessed firearms to have them registered or licensed. Government officials had gone round the people explaining that this was just to regularise the possession of firearms by individuals. In fact, the intention was to enable the government to disarm the people completely; for some time later an order was issued calling for the handing in of all firearms, and by this time it was known who were in possession of firearms. There was no alternative but to surrender the weapons.'

But Qumbu was also the location that marked two other, unforgettable experiences in the life of Oliver Tambo. The first was the acquisition of a driver's licence, a rare and extremely valuable document for Africans, while the second was to dog Tambo for much of his life.

'We had arrived at Mpumwana's country home from East London. In the evening I was allocated one of the huts as my bedroom. In the middle of the night, I woke up, choking, suffocating, gasping desperately for breath. Something had happened to me. I was fighting for my life. I had to concentrate all my mental and physical energy in the struggle for breath. I had never had this experience and knew no one who had. Was there something wrong with that room? Was there some invisible thing in the room? What was it? I kept asking myself as night, pitch dark, dragged on interminably. There was no electric light, no lantern or candle or matches in the room. Throughout, my eyes were wide open, but I could see absolutely nothing. I was listening intently for the sound of a human voice, so that I could shout for help, but the only sound was the wheezing and buzzing in my chest as I battled for breath... I stared hard, my eyes rolling round and sweeping the walls, the floor, the roof, to find something whatever it was that had engineered this ferocious attack on me.'

The attack was, of course, asthma, though Tambo had never heard of the condition at the time, hence his speculation on a supernatural explanation. In the morning, he crawled out of the hut, where solicitous hands helped him to his feet and nursed him. After a few hours, he felt well enough to drag himself to Mpumwana's car, which he drove fitfully, stopping to rest every few minutes at the steering wheel. From the doctor in Umtata, Tambo learnt about the nature of his 'condition – not a disease – that medical science did not know why it occurred'.

Why had the attack come on so suddenly and unexpectedly? Perhaps the illness had not quite occurred without prior warning. Oliver's earlier bouts in the hospital with chronic chest and bronchial complaints may well have been not tuberculosis, as was initially suspected, but early signs of asthma which had become dormant during his adolescent period of rapid growth. Nevertheless, Oliver had undergone a stressful few years. Boarding school, long separations from home, the responsibility and anxiety of having to find his own funds for his education and, above all, the death of both his parents had taxed him emotionally and physically. He had developed an allergic disposition, particularly at the coast, where mites proliferated in the humid environment. The attack had come 'under cover of darkness,' Tambo commented wryly, 'while the unsuspecting victim was fast asleep'. It is at this time in the 24-hour cycle, according to medical experts, that physiological changes occur and an 'early morning dipping' takes place.[45] Later, Oliver recalled an incident on a stopover to Qumbu, which forebode the attack. 'The room in which we were accommodated,' he explained, 'was one of hundreds of temporary structures put up by individual families in a part of East London set aside for occupation by Africans, where these structures served the purposes of shelter pending the provision of better housing by the authorities.'

Since the upturn of the economy after the Depression, rapid urbanisation was overtaking the cities, and throughout South Africa the white town councils – with their measly budgets allocated to black residents – reflected the pervasive indifference to the housing needs of newcomers. Henceforth, squatter settlements were to become an increasingly common phenomenon, and Oliver was to witness the fruitful engagement of fellow activists, Walter Sisulu and Nelson Mandela, with squatters in Johannesburg. Many of the young, the aged and the vulnerable fell victim to the substandard living conditions in tin shacks. For Oliver, they were to have an unexpected side effect in that icy night in June.

'It was an extremely cold night and we were packed, about eight of us, into a small room, which could barely take an extra person. Because of the cold weather, the door had to be kept shut. Whatever window there was, had to be kept closed for the same reason. Someone was trying to light a primus stove in readiness for cooking as well as to heat up the room. She would pump the stove then light it and it would burn for a short while and then suddenly blow out, emitting huge, heavy fumes of gas which filled the room. Choking, I would leave the room and stand shivering in the bitter cold outside until I felt better after taking in some fresh air. I would then re-enter the room. This happened several times that night and for the first time I felt uneasy with my breathing. The fumes were affecting my chest, and that was the day we left for Transkei.'

The effects of Tambo's asthma were far-reaching. He rapidly lost his youthful roundness and became 'bony, groggy and strikingly lean'. In a letter to Bishop Ferguson-Davie from the medical officer at Holy Cross Hospital, Dr Rogers – who had seen Oliver after the attack while he was still on holiday – expressed concern over Oliver's weight – 127 lbs 2 oz (about 57 kilograms): 'I suggest that his weight might be taken at intervals, as he does not look a very strong boy.'[46] Tambo confirmed the sudden change in his physical condition:

'Before Qumbu, I participated in any sport, in particular soccer, cricket, athletics, tennis, boxing... By the time I returned to Fort Hare at the end of the June holidays, I had lost my capacity to play soccer, cricket, take part in athletics... I could not sprint beyond some 30 metres without provoking an asthma attack. In addition, for no apparent rhyme or reason, certainly no provocation on my part, I frequently came under violent attacks of asthma, which had a negative effect on my being and on my work generally, and which added to my frustration with mathematics. A poor Physics lecturer [who had replaced Mr Davidson while he was "up North"] served to make my second-year degree unduly heavy.'

Studious as the members of The Syndicate were, they did neverthless find solace in social relations with female students, who had been enrolled at the College since its inception. From the start, it seemed, it was African members of the Council who had insisted that the College grant women equal access. Alexander Kerr, accustomed to the male chauvinism of British academe, had not even considered the possibility of admitting women. Yet even before the founding ceremony had taken place, two applications were received from qualified women.

'When I ventured to surmise that these applications could not be entertained by the Council, I was startled by the vehemence with which their cause was pled by African members, and particularly by Mr J Tengo Jabavu, who declared that there was little point in educating young men if their future wives were unable to offer them the companionship and community of interest which only an educated woman could give. The argument was, of course, unanswerable, so with the best grace possible I promised to make some temporary arrangement which would allow these two women to be received. Thus Miss Laura Motebang from Basutoland and Miss Lily Msimang from Natal became the first women students at the South African Native College.'[47]

The enrolment of female students at Fort Hare nevertheless gradually increased, and space was found for them in the matron's living quarters. Later, recalled Phyllis Ntantala – who, at the early age of 15, had received a Bhunga scholarship to study for her matriculation at Fort Hare – the women were put up 'in makeshift cubicles attached to the Jabavu house' until the bungalow formerly occupied by Beda Hall students was vacated in the mid-1930s.[48] At the opening in 1941 of the new women's hostel, Elukhanyisweni ('the Home of Enlightenment'), Margaret Ballinger, parliamentary representative of an African constituency under the 1936 Native Representation Act, was invited to speak. Had it not been for that Act, she herself would not have been the parliamentary representative for Africans, she said. Some of the students were sceptical, but in her address, she demonstrated a sociological grasp of the situation, identifying the destructive effects of migrant labour, the subsequent strain on family life and hardship in the towns. 'Unfortunately,' she added, 'the majority of those who hold power are completely unaware of the nature of the situation.' The privileged few, she suggested, had a special duty to perform as mediators with the powerful, to remedy the situation:

'[A] very heavy burden falls upon educated Africans, that of helping their own people rise above their surroundings, and that of being their link with and their mouthpiece to the Europeans who ultimately control their destiny. On their lead will depend the re-inspiring of the home life of the depressed both in town and in country, for they can do what no European can do, see the home at all times and in all conditions and speak to the people as one of themselves.'

For Oliver Tambo, sitting in the audience, the obligation of the educated elite was obvious. These were duties that were bestowed on women, too.

The College was one of the few training centres for professional women, and not surprisingly, many Fort Hare romances led to marriage. One of the earliest was the match made by ZK Matthews and Frieda Bokwe. Matthews was a senior tutor at the College when he began to court Frieda, 'the most noisily vivacious of the girls in the group' and 'the daughter of one of the most distinguished and best-loved Africans of his generation, Reverend John Knox Bokwe'.[49] 'Actually,' Matthews elaborated, 'the idea of boys and girls pairing off was not popular with the Fort Hare authorities.

'Kerr used to say that he did not want to see the same boy and same girl together too much, for that sort of thing took young people's minds off the business at hand. But of course he may as well have tried to stop the grass from growing or the trees from coming into leaf. Boys and girls would hold their trysts under the trees along the Tyhumie River. Even Kerr, behind his Scottish crustiness, seemed to accept the banks of the Tyhumie as a place where his strictures did not apply... Boys and girls observed the restraints in their relationships much more so than in later years... There was still a conventionality by which most of us lived and were content to live.'

Courtship under watchful eyes at Fort Hare was like a delicately executed minuet – many intricate and formal steps had to be accomplished before a love affair could become public. African marriage, as in other societies, was not just a partnership of two individuals, but a manifest social compact between two extended families. At Fort Hare, though, the young people themselves made a number of matches, and the marriages of renowned academics AC Jordan to Phyllis Ntantala, and Joe Mokoena to Trieste Tsewu are testament to this. Monica Wilson, who in the mid-1940s was teaching at Fort Hare, observed:

'Those black Africans who first accepted education formed an elite throughout southern Africa. They knew one another, they intermarried even across language divisions, they served together on public bodies such as the African National Congress. They were prepared to make sacrifices to ensure the education of their children and Fort Hare was the focus of ambition. Graduation ceremonies were occasions of great gatherings and rejoicing, when relatives came from all over southern Africa. The Matthews family and the Bokwes were at the core of this network, with endless ramifications of kin claiming relationship... and both expecting and providing hospitality.'[50]

The elite, particularly in these early years, drew from a small pool. One has only to peruse TD Mweli Skota's *The African Yearly Register*[51] to realise how few there were in 1930. This was an elite still in the making. It was estimated that more than a third (32) were clergymen, 24 were chiefs and only nine were professional or white-collar workers.[52] But a rapid transformation was indeed taking place. While enlightened chiefs were still clearly valued among contemporaries (15 living chiefs were commended), the major criteria for inclusion more often embraced social service and education. Among the schools, Lovedale, Healdtown and St John's in Umtata had the highest social status – St Peter's was too new to have made an impact on the achievers of the 1920s. Membership of the ANC was frequently mentioned, as were epithets such as 'hard worker', 'good speaker', 'true gentleman' and 'true Christian'.[53] Dedication to the 'social, political, educational and religious welfare' of the community was regarded as 'progressive' and merited inclusion. There were also 'self-made' public figures – those who did not stem from the early Christianised families but nevertheless gained respect through their involvement in community and political activities. Accordingly, a number of early ANC and trade-union activists such as Letanka, Mvabaza, Mapikela and Plaatje in the latter category were included.

At Fort Hare, though, the majority of students were children of prominent Christians, a tiny proportion of the African population who had a future to which to look forward. Commented Oliver Tambo:

'During our matriculation years in Johannesburg (as must have been the case elsewhere in the country), Africans were justly proud of those of their people who managed to obtain degrees. In fact this achievement was every parent's wish for his or her son or daughter, and those few – and there were relatively few – who graduated were not only objects of admiration, but they themselves displayed a consciousness of being special in African society, not least because they could claim intellectual superiority over many members of the so-called superior master race. And so it was not unusual to see special meetings of graduates – gatherings, rather – whose main purpose was to display their [end of tape]... But the situation would change and by the time I left Fort Hare there would be more demanded of graduates than parading in their gowns. The last time that I would have need of my gown would be on my graduation day.'

Perhaps the confidence of this young elite, with its large, happy community life that was so much part of the College, is one clue to Tambo's relative detachment. Though a recipient of a Bhunga scholarship, he had had to gain it purely on merit, and not through kinship, as had most other Bhunga students. Unlike them, he was neither a member of the established 'school' elite, nor heir to a chieftainship. Indeed, Monica Wilson cited a pitifully short list of students from humble backgrounds who by the 1970s had successfully passed through the portals of Fort Hare. She specified Johannes Galilee Shembe, son of the 'all but illiterate' prophet Isaiah Shembe; DV Sekutshwa, 'son of an illiterate pagan'; and Oliver Tambo, who 'made the leap from an illiterate family in Eastern Pondoland, via the St Peter's school in Johannesburg and Fort Hare, to qualifying as an attorney and becoming international leader of the ANC'.[54]

But a fleeting snippet of information such as this, while sympathetic to the subject, somehow objectifies and distorts the identity and soul of a person. There was, of course, far more to Oliver's make-up than social reticence. As far as relations with the opposite sex, he felt he was not yet ready for any distraction from his earnest need to fulfil a pledge to his dead parents. Yet even a devout Oliver was capable of breaking out of the strict Victorian sexual morality prevalent at the time. It seems that he might have been involved in a conscious and apparently fleeting act of rebellion that occurred at the end of the frustrating year of 1940, a period of destabilising ill-health and academic setback. Asked whether Tambo had had girlfriends, Lancelot Gama recalled the two friends' avowed dedication to their studies:

'At St Peter's, both of us had no girlfriends. As a result, [it became] a joke. We didn't want to be concerning ourselves with girls, you see. So now what happened there, the first year in BSc, we did well. Then the second year for some reason, the professor was fed up with us, so he made it very difficult for people. So we got very low marks that year in June; for the first time, even Tambo for the first time got a low mark. We all went down to the forties. We were so fed up and said: "We are trying to keep ourselves not to run around with girls and so on, now here we are, we have done badly." So I was visiting a friend in the Transkei and, well, [Tambo] lived in the Transkei. So we were going to take the train together. So we said: "No, let us get girls now." I mean that was the first time we just went wild a bit... But I mean it was just for that moment. When we came back from the holidays, we concentrated again. We worked harder and well, after that we all did well, actually.'[55]

Precisely what 'going wild' actually entailed is hard to say, but unbridled sexual indulgence was uncharacteristic of Oliver, and he probably regretted his lapse. A few months later, he wrote to his benefactresses, the Misses Goddard. He described his period of setbacks, and confessed its consequences: 'The last two years have been much heavier than I had been led to anticipate. I seemed to encounter defeat at all fronts; difficulties arose beyond which I could not see. They cut me off from the world for over a year... Then as if to ensure my complete isolation, my studies became incredibly difficult. I was in utter darkness. Spiritually, I was only half alive.'[56]

Oliver's ideal, it seems, was for celibacy – he had had the living example of the CR brothers as his models. For him, then, there were to be no romances. But at home, he did enjoy at least cordial friendships with women in the neighbourhood. The two Nomtyala sisters, both school teachers, lived with their parents some 10 miles from Kantolo, and Oliver visited them regularly every vacation. At his schools, he recalled friendly rivalry with both boys and girls who competed with him academically. At Fort Hare, too, his friendships with women were contradictorily detached though warm. He recollected one set of women friends: 'At Elukhanyisweni, another group of three [like The Syndicate] became identifiable... [They] were obviously very close friends. One was Nomoto Bikitsha, later to become Dr Bikitsha, another was Phyllis, who got married and was Mrs Mziedume – she is unhappily now deceased – and a third one was Lorna, I forget her surname.'

They were, he claimed, 'highly respected women in the campus' though Lorna was 'a little inflammable and therefore to that extent unpredictable'. But Oliver's ambiguous message to women may well have communicated itself to these fellow students, and it seemed to nettle them: 'The thing about this group is that I became very close to it and this would not have been worth mentioning but for the fact that at some stage the three assumed a collective attitude of hostility towards me. I did not know what had gone wrong. They would not greet, they just froze up if they saw me approaching.'

Oliver's response was strategic, illustrating a typically intellectual rather than emotional approach. 'Unable to explain this strange conduct, I had decided I would behave as if nothing happened; whatever was worrying them was not worrying me, and I was not in the slightest affected by this attitude which I regarded as ridiculous,' Tambo explained. '[If] I met them, or any one of them, I greeted them as warmly and as cheerfully as I had always done, making clear however that I was expecting no response, and there was no response.'

After a week, the tactic paid off, and 'suddenly brightness returned from nowhere... I believe this wore them down and they decided to call off the demonstration, whatever its purpose and motivation had been'. Oliver never did try to discover what had actually initiated the coolness in their behaviour, preferring to treat the symptoms, rather than the cause. Friendship, rather than intimacy, was as much as he was prepared to give.

In the Christmas holidays of 1940, Oliver returned to Kantolo, where he immediately attended to his homestead duties by ploughing the mealie fields. That done, he checked in at Holy Cross Hospital for observation. At first, tuberculosis was diagnosed but, not long after he had returned to Fort Hare, he received a letter from Dr Drew, the hospital registrar, to say that the diagnosis had been an error. 'Good news indeed,' observed Tambo. '[But] there was more good news: James Davidson, our Physics lecturer, was back at Fort Hare and would surely see us through our final year.'

A bright future at Fort Hare seemed assured as Oliver Tambo returned to complete his final year for his Bachelor of Science degree. But 1941 also saw the first of the two significant events that he later identified as the 'starting point of my involvement in political life'. Until then, Tambo had taken a normal youthful interest in the affairs of society. 'We used to have discussions,' recalled Lancelot Gama, 'but those were just impromptu, with no definite lines of action, as any students would discuss in any university. It was not a solid organ going over it.'

Almost everyone supported the African National Congress as a matter of course. In contrast to the Communist Party, which since Eddie and Win Roux had pitched their tent on the slopes of Fort Hare in 1933 was actively enlisting students at Fort Hare – including their star recruit Govan Mbeki[57] – the ANC was passive, and relied on tradition. 'The ANC wasn't [recruiting]. You joined according to your feelings. Well, we felt the ANC as an organisation was started by our grandfathers. So we felt that we should support it.' Nevertheless there seemed to be a general agreement that the ANC 'was a bit slow'.[58]

Then the first of the events that marked Tambo's passage to politicisation occurred. 'Looking back,' he commented more than 40 years later, 'I can see quite clearly that if there was a single event that launched me on the road to ultimate involvement at the heart of South African politics – it was an assault on an African woman by her white employer in a kitchen in Fort Hare.'

Oddly, none of the informants whose lives as students it affected, seemed to have actually witnessed the incident. Tambo described the event: 'One day in September, the tranquil atmosphere of the Fort Hare campus was shattered when news spread that the college Boarding Master had brutally assaulted an African woman working under him in the kitchen. He had kicked and beaten her up, according to the reports.'

Lancelot Gama vaguely remembered the event in a similar vein: 'There was an African lady who was working in the kitchen and the gentleman who was in charge of the kitchen staff, a European gentleman; I think she made some mistakes somewhere, I don't know what had happened, anyway. Then he decided to hit her and kick her... That's what started the strike.'[59]

The official report of the principal and chairman, on the other hand, gave the following account:

'In September 1941, during the absence of the Principal, students demanded the dismissal of the Boarding Master of the Dining Hall because, as they alleged, he had "assaulted" a Native servant girl in the kitchen... The Executive of the Council (presided over by the Chairman of Council, the Vice-Chairman, the Chief Native Commissioner of the Ciskei, also attending) investigated the complaint against the Boarding Master and found that a young girl who was under notice of dismissal had carelessly, or wantonly, broken crockery in the kitchen in his presence and he had given her a slap, of which she complained to some students, magnifying it into a serious assault. The uncle of the girl, who is also employed at the Dining Hall, testified to the correctness of the Boarding Master's account of the triviality of the incident. The Executive, after careful enquiry, exonerated the Boarding Master from the charge of assault but censured him for striking the girl even though it was done under extreme provocation. To the regret of the Governing Council, the Boarding Master who had given six years' excellent service resigned at the end of the year.'[60]

The report is interesting in that it reflects the white South African mores of the time – not only does it differ in emphasis in its analysis of the incident from Tambo's and others, in which a blow in the face was deemed to be trivial, but also because of racial bias. Despite their commitment to the welfare of the students, the investigators of the university were all white men. The African employee (referred to, according to the manner of the time, as a 'servant girl') was deemed to be provocative, irresponsible and even mendacious. Her uncle, apparently the only African to be consulted in the enquiry, was a dependent employee, while the white Boarding Master, clearly guilty of an offence, was admonished with the utmost circumspection. Whatever the actual sequence of events, clearly for many students the affair became a symbol.

'I knew there were African women helping to prepare and serve our meals and I did not know the name of any of them or the name of the victim of the Boarding Master's outrage. I did not care to know, none of the students did. She was certainly someone's sister or mother or wife. Did the Boarding Master think that she was his slave, not a lady entitled to respect, like all other women? Would he have kicked and beaten up his sister or mother or wife? An agitated student body meeting in twos and threes and more were putting these questions to one another as they demanded immediate disciplinary action by authorities.'

The students of all the residences subsequently held an emergency meeting to discuss the affair. Unanimously, they condemned the assault, but differed on the most effective way of making a collective demand:

'Sharp differences arose... in considering what the student body on the one hand, and the college authorities on the other, should do about it, if anything. Two views stood on the extreme. The one, that the attention of authorities should be formally drawn to the incident, and the matter left to them to handle as they deemed fit. The other, that the boarding master should be subjected to instant justice by having his car set on fire, and suggestions along those lines. The proposal that was ultimately accepted by the majority – and which was reached after strenuous and heated debate – lay between these two extremes. It was that the authorities be called upon to dismiss the Boarding Master forthwith, and that the students take a protest action in the form of a boycott of lectures, whose duration would be determined by the authorities acting against the boarding master.'

The next morning, some of the students were taken aback to find that the boarding master's car had been damaged. 'This,' said Tambo, 'was seen in a very serious light by the majority of the students, and led to the debate having to be reopened, with many students expressing reluctance to be associated with what amounted to irresponsible conduct.'

He observed that there were two lessons to be learnt from going against the agreed decision: firstly, the group lost some of its supporters – 'some of the men and all seven women decided against participation in the strike'. Secondly, at times of high emotions, demagoguery was apt to emerge, and this was highly unreliable. 'It was noteworthy,' observed Tambo sardonically, 'that one of the men who had advocated harsh measures was one of the few who continued to attend lectures.' Tambo's strategic influence was evident in the 1941 boycott of classes. Conflating the stances, Lancelot Gama recalled that there was never any decision to cause injury or damage property: 'We just kept on striking and not going to classes. It was disciplined and it was through him that there was – in our language, we say *Manga-manga*. That means you couldn't go about being wild… And that was the discipline over all the students, and is the respect they had in him, almost all of them.'[61]

In his personal recollections, Tambo dealt with this strike – the prelude to the one he would lead a year later – in some detail. In the careful discussions, the detailed disputations on the most effective tactics, he immensely enjoyed exercising his natural proficiency in logical argument and strategy. For example:

'One of the questions which had risen seriously for this issue, and which affected whether we leave or stay, was the likelihood that the authorities would want to victimise supposed ring-leaders. We expected that already a witch-hunt had started, and the students were already concerned that any of them should be victimised as a result of action taken collectively by all of them. Indeed, part of the argument in favour of all of us leaving sought to address the question of victimisation. If we all left, there would be no question of victimisation. But of course that was no end of the matter, because if we all left, we were expelling ourselves. If we reapplied for readmission, it was still up to the authorities whom not to readmit.'

Mandela, who had been impressed by Tambo's skill in debating such issues, also remembered him as his counterpart in the student hierarchy: 'We were also elected at the Students' Representative Council at the end of 1940. I was among the six that were elected by the student body and then the rest represented their hostels. Oliver Tambo was a representative of the Anglican hostel.'[62]

The following year, 1942, Oliver was elected unanimously as the student head of Beda Hall and its committee. Students included in the committee were CM Kobus, who later became an attorney and a founding member of the Unity Movement, and Ntsu Mokhehle, who – after many decades in opposition – would become prime minister of Lesotho. The head of the committee was meant to act as a liaison between the warden and the students.

Tambo remembered this duty as 'wholly unburdensome' – relations among the residents were good, and between the committee and the warden there was a general spirit of cooperation. 'Occasionally, of course,' said Tambo, 'there were small hitches of no real consequence, which required that the warden should give explanations on matters of complaint to a meeting of students... and he was ever willing to do so.'

The warden, Bishop Ferguson-Davie, had come to Fort Hare on his retirement as Bishop of Singapore. He had also spent many years in India, setting up a hospital with his wife, who had had 'a brilliant medical career'.[63] At Beda Hall, by now an elderly man, he had no additional teaching duties and so had the time to pay full attention to his responsibilities. The year 1942 was to be his penultimate one at Fort Hare. On the whole, Tambo recalled the students 'felt affectionate towards the warden – they liked the old man'.

But he could, they found, become somewhat defensive at times. 'The Bishop did not believe that his views, once they were made, should be questioned or otherwise challenged,' Tambo recalled. 'Every so often, if I was debating an issue with him where we held different views, he would remind me that 50 years previously he would never question, or otherwise challenge the decision of his don in Oxford, England; and once he took this view, he expected that the matter would be seen by us as being over.'

Tambo remembered many examples 'really of little consequence – nuisance value, except that they resulted in a build-up of attitudes towards the warden' by students who were particularly sensitive to paternalism. And, to make matters worse, the Bishop – like so many accustomed to a hierarchical order – found clear, frank and reasoned arguments difficult to present. Whenever Oliver Tambo asked him to explain any of his decisions to the students, he would simply call a meeting, announce his decision, 'invariably say "Goodnight", then turn his back on the students, bang the door behind him, and in the meantime a forest of hands was in the air with so many students wanting to ask questions'.

The students' annoyance at the warden's responses should be seen also in the wider context of a world war currently being fought for democracy. But 'Democracy,' commented Ferguson-Davie, 'has affected the students in this and other Hostels. The interpretation which some apparently give to the idea was [sic] that the students should rule rather than the authorities.'[64]

It was towards the end of Oliver's final year at Fort Hare in 1942 that this difference of understanding was demonstrated, with significant consequences.

He had already obtained his BSc degree, graduating earlier that year. It remained only for him to acquire his Diploma in Higher Education. Shortly after his election as head of the hostel, Tambo launched a project involving the cooperation of the entire Anglican residence. But the outcome was to be as bewildering to the authorities as to the students, who had undertaken the task with enthusiasm and in good faith. It was not surprising that Tambo dwelt on the episode in some detail, as its consequences were to produce a turning point in his life.

'It struck me that Sundays were wasted days. People hung around, sat around; and I thought, why not rebuild the old tennis court, which would use up the weekends? And so, after broad consultations with the students, people agreed and decided to work on shifts to reconstruct the tennis court, digging up the ground and putting up the fence... We put the idea to the warden, and he was thrilled by it. And so the students were organised into teams, and I would wake up each team at 5.30 every morning and we would begin work on it, the tennis court. We had to go out to the countryside to collect the right type of soil – anthill soil for example – and got the warden's car. He met any expenses that occurred and the teamwork, the cooperation, was excellent.

'Around 9 September we completed the tennis court. We had it all lined up. We had bought, with the assistance of the warden, a new net, and it had been very well done. We then had a meeting to decide when and how to open the court. It was decided that there would be an opening on the following Sunday, in about a week's time. And we looked forward to this, everybody congratulating everybody else for a job of work well done. Until the tennis court had become unusable, Beda Hall students used to play, not only at Beda Hall but in previous hostels, which the students used to occupy before the extension.'

What followed was to amount to a misunderstanding that, despite a relatively more sophisticated approach of the Anglicans to rules of worship, neither the authorities nor the students were able to overcome. Tambo recalled how happy he had been to report to the warden, Bishop Smythe, that the mission had been accomplished with commitment and resourcefulness, and that the students proposed a grand opening of the tennis court the following Sunday. 'At [this] point,' remembered Tambo, 'he expressed shock and surprise that we should think of playing tennis on a Sunday. I was equally shocked and surprised to learn that at Beda Hall we could not play tennis on Sundays.'

As Anglicans, the students were, strictly speaking, within their rights to play on Sundays. 'It had always [been] allowed,' Tambo pointed out, 'until the tennis court got neglected.' Lancelot Gama's reasoning for the stricture was that 'there was a more-or-less Methodist atmosphere at Fort Hare'.[65] Certainly, the Bishop was clearly being sensitive to the principles of the other denominations. 'The Wardens at Fort Hare,' recorded the principal, 'presented an excellent example of the ecumenical spirit long before that term had become so frequent on the lips of churchmen.'[66] The Bishop had, in fact, consulted with wardens of the residences. 'In the interests of harmony and good order,' he concluded, 'I could not grant this request.' Tambo and other students, on the other hand, were not particularly sympathetic to this far-sighted spirit of reconciliation, especially as, after hard work and raised expectations, the decision came at their expense. There seemed to be a contradiction in the very structure of the College, with its inbuilt emphasis on separate denominations. If students were categorised according to finer points of theological differences, why suddenly make an issue of it? Once again, they discerned the heavy hand of paternalism. They could not accept the warden's reasoning that the Presbyterians and the Methodists did not play sports on Sundays. Tambo noted:

'And if we did, we would be subjecting them to a temptation to want to also play on Sundays, in breach of their faith. I was astounded. It was incredible! Every bit of his reasoning was wrong. With as much self-restraint as I could marshal I tried to dissuade him of this thinking, and said everything short of suggesting that he was being ridiculous, and even insulting, to members of other denominations. But the Bishop stood firm, and referred me to his experience with his don in Oxford. After months of hard work over the tennis court, this was a shattering anti-climax.'

Tambo asked the warden to meet the committee – and he agreed, but the meeting was not persuaded. Then, as always, the Bishop agreed to address the entire hostel. He 'carefully explained... the reasons for his decision',[67] then said goodnight and simply walked out, 'closing the door behind him'. 'As far as he was concerned,' said Tambo, 'that matter was also a closed matter. But it wasn't. The students were wild! Wild, above all, by the way he treated them. It was so provocative, so unnecessary. The Bishop was not dealing with a lot of youngsters, or schoolboys. It had not happened once, it had occurred too many times.'

Angry discussion followed. The meeting decided to embark on a campaign of non-cooperation: 'We would withhold voluntary services such as cleaning up, switching off lights, attending to various things, tasks which on a rotation basis were assigned to various students. The areas of activity affected by this decision were all listed out and they included playing sport as members of Beda Hall teams.'

It was agreed that, in the process, no regulations should be broken. But while the students were obliged to attend the church services, they were 'under no obligation to sing a hymn, say a psalm, or participate in any way in a service, beyond simply being there'. The official report stated that the students 'declined to abide by [the Bishop's] decision and proceeded to break down the customary discipline of the hostel by refusing to take part in inter-hostel sports and perform the customary student duties of the hostel, and by behaving in an irregular manner in Chapel'.[68]

'[For] about a week, the non-cooperation was observed,' Tambo recalled, 'and it had a most striking impact at the Chapel.' The Bishop sang the hymns alone; he was also obliged to respond to himself in the case of the psalms. 'We contended that no one was in breach of any rules,' explained Tambo. 'No one had a right to say whether one should sing, or say a psalm.'

The action had been going on for a number of days when, one afternoon, Professor Matthews asked to see Tambo. Matthews was a member of the Discipline Committee, together with lecturers Dent and Chapman, and the principal.[69] But because Kerr was away at the time of the 1942 strike, 'fulfilling a series of important engagements',[70] Matthews was elected to approach the student leaders. His son, VJ (Joe) Matthews, observed: 'Of course, [my father] was vital because of his links with the students. So they would probably listen to him, where they wouldn't listen to others, you know. And although he took a fairly conservative point of view regarding discipline by students, generally speaking he was quite a strict man himself and thought the people must do their education and go.'[71]

Tambo remembered Matthews from the strike of the previous year, when he unexpectedly turned up at a student meeting. 'In his intervention, he naturally advocated a return to lectures. He did not speak as representing the authorities as such, but it was clear he was putting forward the position of the authorities.'

As a social anthropologist, Matthews had not really got to know Oliver Tambo, but he knew that the young man was a Bhunga scholar. Joe Matthews recalled his father's pleasure on learning about Tambo's matriculation results:

'It was an unusual success story... It was always a nervous period when matric results came out as to how many students had got the exemption out of all the people who had applied to the college. And sometimes the results were very bad, and you'd find that very few people had got the exemption. Therefore that meant if Africans were too few, then the college made up by admitting Indians and Coloureds, and so on. So there was always this anxious period that so many people had applied and yet only a few would make it.

'But this particular year was exciting because you had Mokoena and Tambo. Not only exemptions, but also first classes and distinctions. So I remember my father was very excited about these students from St Peter's, and I suspect that my own interest in St Peter's started from the knowledge of this.'[72]

For Tambo, the meeting was one he welcomed:

'We met. He wanted to know what was happening at Beda Hall, what had gone wrong. And so I related to him how the problem started, referring to the general good relations between the students and the Warden, the occasional hitches and the way these were handled – the disputes that had arisen, the case of the invitation to women and similar instances in which the views of the students had been dismissed out of hand. And finally, of course, the tennis court issue. At the end of this account of developments, I asked where he thought we had gone wrong. He agreed with our positions the whole way, and made me believe that the Warden had gone wrong on quite a number of issues, indeed on all of them, including the question of playing on Sundays.'

At the same time, ZK Matthews tried to put across to Tambo what the principal designated as 'the main question… whether the Warden or the students were to determine what the rule of the hostel should be. On this question there was no room for discussion'.[73] But ZK's interpretation of the University's 'bottom line' was far more refined:

'[ZK's] problem was that this stalemate could go on indefinitely because, as he explained, it was always extremely difficult for the authority to give in without undermining its weight in relation to the future. It meant the authorities would tend to hold their ground once they had taken a decision, instead of revoking that decision under pressure. He asked whether he might meet my committee, which I welcomed, and we then agreed that I would discuss a convenient time with my committee and let him know the following day.'

But the reaction of the Beda Hall committee was 'swift and most decisive... this was not yet the time for him to intervene on this matter. When we sought his opinion, we would approach him'. Tambo himself, though, argued in favour of a meeting with Matthews.

'In my view, we lost nothing at all by hearing what he had to say. But the members of the committee were firm. It seemed to me that perhaps they had not been happy about his intervention during the 1941 college students' strike, and feared that one way or another he would influence our common action and introduce divisions which would ultimately lead to our having to call off our protest action without getting anything out of it beyond demonstrating a displeasure. Whatever may have been in the back of the minds of my colleagues, there was to be no meeting with Professor Matthews.'

Lancelot Gama recalled the meeting very clearly, particularly Tambo's all-important role: 'There is a speech he made. It is when we went on the last strike... He made an address to the whole student body. It was such a wonderful address that all the students just stood up and said: "Tambo has spoken!" and we all moved and acted accordingly.' And the following day Tambo met ZK and communicated the committee's decision. There was no question of watering down the decision of his constituency. 'As the Secretary of the Students' Representative Council, I had to take the responsibility for stating the students' case', he later explained to his friend, Father Trevor Huddleston. 'It was a small matter… but certain principles were involved, and anyway I had to put the case.'[74]

Matthews' response was shrewd and strategic. Although the students had contravened no rules, 'authority was authority,' said Tambo. '[And] they would not want to surrender to us without surrendering their authority.'

Matthews then suggested that the students might wish to appeal to another authority, the Archbishop of Cape Town, on the matter of the original dispute of playing tennis on Sundays. 'In the meantime, we should revert to normal.' This idea seemed to Tambo to be reasonable, and he agreed that this would be a helpful way out. 'We had no interest in sustaining this tension, and if an intervention could result in a resolution, we would be very happy.'

Tambo then went back to his room and drafted a letter to the Archbishop for the committee's consideration. 'But before we met as a committee... I received a note addressed to me by the Warden, asking me to see him at his office at ten to two that afternoon.'

And that was the last sentence recorded in Tambo's chronicle. Speaking into the tape recorder in his lodgings in Lusaka, Tambo put away the cassette, intending to continue the narrative at the next possible opportunity. But that chance never came. The year was 1988, and the pace of events was rapidly gathering momentum. The prospect of a negotiated settlement – a fresh initiative in ANC policy – was imminent. For Tambo, the priority was to prepare the world and the ANC constituency, both inside South Africa and in exile, for a major change in discourse. It was an undertaking that was to cost him his health and his physical autonomy. Significantly, in his memoirs he had covered the less public side of his life – his early years, the very foundation of the public and political person that, in 1942, he was on the verge of becoming.

What was the immediate outcome of the strike? In its presentation of the strike, the Fort Hare Calendar of 1944 described Ferguson-Davie's ultimatum to the students, probably first communicated to Tambo, to either comply with the warden's decision or be suspended. The students responded by signing their names to 'a peremptory letter to the Senate,' claimed the Calendar Report, 'demanding the reinstatement of the students "dismissed"'.[75] Ultimately, 45 of 66 were sent down for varying amounts of time. Seretse Khama was among those, but his guardian, Tshekedi Khama, eventually persuaded him to return.[76] All but 10 were readmitted after two or three weeks. Those excluded were not to be admitted in 1943.

Lancelot Gama, one of those excluded, recalled Tambo's sensitive consideration of the relative situations of all students concerned:

'You see, we had already got our degrees with Tambo, he was a BSc, I was a BSc. Now when we were expelled, the others had not yet written their exams. So we felt – I mean, you can see that Tambo was an understanding man – he felt that it would rob the students of their writing because of being expelled, and that means that they will not have their degrees. So he made an order that all those who want to write their examinations must remain. If they decide to go, they must decide on their own. They must not say they are being compelled by the strikers to go away. And quite a number of the students then remained to write their finals. I remember one of them said [his] father had passed away so he was going to be the breadwinner. So Tambo said, "No, remain."'[77]

But the University's opinion of the leadership was somewhat different:

'It is disconcerting to find senior students, some of whom are preparing for the teaching profession, averse to accepting the discipline of an educational institution and refusing to heed experienced counsel. It is disconcerting to find that members of a hostel that was erected by a Church in order to bring higher education within their reach should be so oblivious of the benefit received that they are prepared to acquiesce in conduct designed to make its working impossible... It is disconcerting to find that of the 25 students suspended for the term, 16 were in receipt of bursaries awarded by public bodies.'[78]

For Oliver's part, the authorities had encroached into the recesses of the soul. The pledge they demanded extended to their 'spiritual life and religious duties'.

'I asked the Warden for time to pray about this,' he told his friend Father Huddleston, to whom he could express his inner feelings, 'and I went to the Chapel for half an hour. I *knew* I could not sign that pledge... It demanded something from me that I could not give. It would have killed my religion stone dead – an agreement with God, written and signed? I could not do it!'[79]

He was expelled, added Huddleston, 'on the spot'. It seemed the end of Tambo's dreams, for who would ever employ him with such a record of insubordination? Deeply disturbed, yet seeing no way out, he wandered into Alice, where he walked around the streets for hours, thinking. At 11 o'clock that night, he crossed the bridge back to his residence and went straight to the chapel to pray. 'It was completely dark; completely empty; absolutely silent...

'But at the far end, near the Blessed Sacrament, there was a glow of light from the lamp that always burned there. I took that as a sign. That somewhere, however dark, there is always a light.'[80]

Not a month before the strike, the principal, Dr Alexander Kerr, had written Tambo a handsome reference. After listing the number of courses completed and his extramural activities, he went on to state that Tambo's 'character and conduct while at this College have been exemplary. Mr Tambo graduated BSc last year and has been taking the course for the University Education Diploma. He will make a sound teacher of mathematics or Physical Science. I recommend him cordially for employment in a secondary school'.[81]

But this commendation was overwhelmed by the inescapable fact of Oliver's being 'sent down' before the end of the academic year. Tambo recalled that, on returning to Kantolo after his expulsion, he applied for as many teaching positions as he could, always enclosing the reference on how he had come to leave Fort Hare. 'I knew,' said Tambo, 'that I was going to make a good teacher because the children liked me. It was wrong that we had been expelled... but when [prospective employers] read this statement, they wrote back and said "No, I am sorry, we have no position". All of them!'[82]

Despite his high and rare qualifications, Oliver Tambo was unemployed – and deeply embarrassed.

'There was no job in our part of the world. I couldn't continue staying among the people because I had been too long at school; and now people who had passed Standard 6, and then spent another three years doing a teachers' course, went out to teach. But in my case, I was [away for] three years, then two years, then five years. Then the BSc and the UED... Now I was back home – I didn't disclose the reason to the people at home. And now I was staying too long because letters were returning, turning me down.'[83]

Tambo was thus determined to find any paying job, and was forming a desperate resolution – 'I was prepared to work even as a gardener' – when, quite unexpectedly, he received a message that a letter had arrived from Johannesburg. Without telling the family, he 'rushed off to the post office', located in a store 'somewhere between Bizana and Ludeke'.

The letter was from St Peter's. At the last moment, the school had received a grant for an additional teaching post from the Transvaal Education Department. Oliver had, however, not applied to St Peter's for a post. 'Because St Peter's was my home; I never asked them for a job.' In any case, he added, 'I knew they had no money'.

But once again, providence had stepped in. 'I was the right person, at the right time.' The school offered him a teaching post as a Science and Higher Maths Master, to be taken up at Rosettenville from January 1943.

CHAPTER FIVE

The Trumpet Call

IN JANUARY 1943, Miss Tanqueray of the Holy Cross Mission School wrote to the Goddard sisters to express her disappointment in Oliver Tambo. That quiet, 'nice young man' had been 'sent down' from Fort Hare. She was perplexed and distressed, because 'he had always shown himself amenable to discipline'. Miss Tanqueray found it difficult to reconcile Oliver's old-world, rural courtesy, his steady, religious devotion and his rare, dazzling smile with the leaner, hard-line and unyielding student activist he seemed to have become. His expulsion, and his puzzling refusal to recant, dissipated the sisters' carefully saved financial contributions over the years, as well as Oliver's own hard work. It virtually negated his rare achievement as a Bachelor of Science. There was one consolation, though. Oliver had been offered the post of an 'ordinary' teacher (as opposed to a qualified position) with the CR Fathers at St Peter's – 'they will have the chance of showing him what discipline can do'. A little setback, his patrons mused, might in fact be quite a good thing for the young man. 'He has had an easy time up to now – money always at hand when he needed and no worries or anxieties as to means. Now he will have to work for his living and show his worth.'

A product of her race, class and culture, the dedicated missionary was quite oblivious of the anguish that Oliver had in fact experienced – in the cultural dislocation of a boarding school entirely alien to his family; his recurring anxiety over school fees, and the monumental loss of both his parents while still at school, a thousand miles away. Miss Tanqueray reflected a common assumption that suffering was the lot of Africans, particularly Christian Africans, who were breaking new ground. She was, nevertheless hopeful that Oliver would make good. He was 'still a very nice boy'. He was keen on his religion and demonstrated a wish to help his own people. She had observed how he had regularly spent his holidays at the family homestead 'ploughing or doing farm work, mending the huts and fences and always busy'. Oliver was not like the fine young college men 'who laze about and play with the girls instead of helping at their homes during their holidays'.[1]

Oliver did indeed arrive at St Peter's rather subdued, and feeling greatly indebted to the CR Fathers. His salary, which would otherwise have been a comfortable £250 a year, was now much reduced, and his plans for helping the family children with their education were similarly diminished. As a bachelor staff member, though, he was able to cut costs by living in the school residence as a house master. With St Peter's already his second 'home', he quickly settled into his new occupation as Mathematics and Physics master. A year earlier, when he had been practising as a student teacher, he had confirmed his own interest in teaching, indeed 'found considerable fulfilment'. The students had responded positively and the staff members who had sat in on his classes had, it seemed, also been impressed.

For Oliver Tambo, teaching went beyond a mere occupation – it was a vocation bestowed on him in trust, an opportunity to nurture and groom the next generation to fulfil a noble destiny. In his five years at St Peter's, he turned out to be one of the school's most well-loved teachers. Firstly, Tambo was conscientious. He scrupulously marked all the assignments and 'he really got to know our weaknesses individually', recalled Fertz Ngakane, who was taught by Tambo from 1942 – when he was a student teacher – onwards.[2] But his achievement lay also in his quiet confidence and calm manner, as well as his interactive and affirmative teaching methods. Two schoolboys who were first enrolled at St Peter's in 1943 both vividly recalled Oliver Tambo's teaching style.

One was Henry Makgothi (who was to become a senator in the first South African Government of National Unity in 1994); his father, a schoolteacher himself, had enlisted in the army and had gone 'up North' in 1941. The lonely boy had quickly attached himself to the considerate yet authoritative schoolmaster, and indeed became his devoted house monitor in the hostel – it was his special task to look after the master's room. Tambo, observed Makgothi, was his ideal: while a sensitive man of strong feeling, he displayed a tremendous humanity yet was 'severely logical and very scientific'.[3]

It was this combination that made Tambo a memorable and effective science teacher. Inspired by the literal meaning of education – 'to draw out' – Tambo would set up physical experiments and challenge the pupils to make their own observations, encouraging them to reach their own conclusions. 'With him, solving mathematical, scientific problems was always an adventure. He made you feel you were getting along and you would ultimately reach the solution.'[4] In the early 1940s this was an innovative approach, one he absorbed from the more progressive teachers at St Peter's and Fort Hare. Tambo was 'certainly one of the best teachers; and yet his style was just a style of his own'.[5]

Young Joe Matthews – who, as the son of ZK, Anthropology professor at Fort Hare, was familiar with the pedagogical methods and innovations of some of the lecturers there – suggested that Tambo's teaching methods were drawn from his professor of Physics. It was, Matthews recalled, 'a rather difficult style'. Tambo would challenge students by putting a geometrical proposition on the blackboard and inviting anyone in the class to come up and suggest solutions. Even when the students were wrong, as no doubt often happened, Tambo seemed to be genuinely excited in following their process of thinking.

'That was his big thing; to encourage people to think. And you see he taught people to be bold, not to be afraid of a problem because you thought you didn't know, or you are going to be wrong; because you were congratulated for making the effort and reasoning the thing out.'[6]

In his Science classes, having thoroughly aroused the students' interest in the problem, Tambo would then perform the experiment in the laboratory to test the solution.[7] The students were also intrigued by another innovative approach at the time, one which Tambo shared with the headmaster, Mr Darling. Tambo would set surprise tests, but would allow the class free access to their textbooks. Rumford Qwalela, future teacher and headmaster, recalled the excitement of these unexpected challenges: '"Test! Test! It's a test!" And even if you had the books, it is quite a job to find the reference and to get the information when you've got only 45 minutes to do the test... But it was a test of whether people had mastered the books... We really had fun; I mean, we had big fun.'[8]

And Vella Pillay, one of only a handful of Indian day scholars at St Peter's – in years to come, an economist for the ANC in exile – was another pupil who remembered Tambo as 'an outstanding teacher'.[9]

These favourable memories were, however, propagated by diligent students. Tambo could be severe (though invariably and logically correct) with backsliders. Obed Musi, a journalist at the time of Tambo's death in 1993, had only a brief memory of his Maths master in a fleeting obituary. 'I must admit quite frankly that I was his worst student and he did not hesitate to tell me so. He suggested that I go for subjects which did not require much logic – although he never told me which these were.'[10] Nor was Tambo's disapproval expressed merely verbally: 'He would count – he had a wonderful memory... "You have not done your work": one, two, three, four. Fifth time you have had it! Then you would get a hard punishment... corporal punishment. I would say he was the most feared because he could *klap* [hit] very hard... Otherwise he wasn't given to punishment. Flogging people no; but he believed in putting you straight.'[11]

Rural culture emphasised corporal chastisement. At home, Tambo went along with fairly stringent forms of discipline in the light of today's rather more liberal standards. Vuyiswa, Alan Tambo's daughter, specifically remembered, for example, how Oliver, home for the holidays, would send the children on an errand, say to fetch water or to plough the fields with the cows, and would then climb up a tree to see if the children were shirking.[12] Yet Tambo's sharp blows were accepted without too much resentment, largely because his warm interest and participatory style of instruction, combined with his status as a highly educated teacher, imparted an aura of unquestioned authority.

In 1945 the parents of Rumford Qwalela from the Lusikisiki district, inspired by Tambo's academic performance, sent their son to St Peter's. Rumford later became a teacher and regarded Tambo as a role model in his teaching methods, which he applied in later years in a managerial capacity. 'Give people an opportunity to solve the problem themselves,' he observed, 'and you get leadership qualities from among them.'[13] In 1993, Qwalela recalled the bygone ethos of St Peter's and contrasted it with the depreciated status of education since the school boycotts of the 1980s. 'In those days,' remarked Qwalela, 'the students were still very serious – they were diligent, they were ambitious. We were schooling under very popular figures; we were always wanting to mimic our teachers. I wanted to be like Brother T, as we called [Tambo] at school.'[14]

The appellation had monastic overtones. Both church and school occupations carried high status in African society.[15]

Oliver Tambo's encounters with the city as a schoolboy in the 1930s were a contrast to his experience of wartime Johannesburg in 1943. A professional man now, he became part of the small but densely woven network of Johannesburg's African elite. The threads of this social web incorporated bonds formed by kinship, clan and language, crisscrossed by education, occupation and service to the community.[16]

Huge numbers of people were moving from the countryside – the reserves as well as the white-owned farms – to the city, particularly during the late 1930s and forties. Among the newcomers were dozens of educated and professional Africans. Despite a disproportionate concentration on the Witwatersrand,[17] the occupational elites constituted only 2.7 per cent of the African population,[18] and – as with African Americans in the USA – middle-class professional men and women served as popular role models.[19] But because the majority were first-generation townspeople, their recent rural origins continued to modulate black urban society: the rural aristocracy continued to exert some influence in the city, and the 'home-boy' network continued to be a major support system, without which Johannesburg's impatient and often crass setting would be even more difficult to negotiate.

Both despite and because of these enormous drawbacks, a few black entrepreneurs were able to make their way in the racially discriminating inner-city jungle by offering services to a vulnerable community. Operating in the streets were micro businesses, such as the coffee carts that catered for black workers lacking dining facilities; photographers, who recorded the migrant's arrival for families back home; haircutters and herbalists, street salesmen and -women offering urban wares. To survive the assault of the pass laws and operate in the most accessible parts of the centre was itself a singular achievement, for any African would require exceptional enterprise to be able to secure an office in an area outside the black 'locations' or the freehold areas of Sophiatown or Alexandra Township. There were also all too few traders who, against all odds, actually rented premises downtown – traditional healers and one or two modest restaurants. And then there was the rare black pioneer who actually had an office in the city.

One such person was Walter Sisulu, an estate agent and a catalyst for his community.[20] It was through a kinship connection that Oliver Tambo met Xamela (Sisulu's clan name), the man who was to influence profoundly Tambo's political and professional career. Sisulu's colleague, Lymon Gama – the brother of Oliver's close school friend Lancelot Gama – was the secretary of a business association and a member of the ANC. He had taken an interest in his younger brother's accounts of the strikes at Fort Hare and formed the opinion that the students needed political direction. It was he who introduced the members of The Syndicate – Oliver, Lancelot and Congress Mbatha – to the city's political activists and intellectuals. Lionel Majombozi, for example, a former student leader at Fort Hare, was now a medical student at the University of the Witwatersrand. Through his ties of kinship, Mbatha had a further link with the group that was to found the ANC Youth League. William Nkomo, also an earlier St Peter's and Fort Hare graduate, was married to the sister of Congress Mbata. Subsequently, the two Syndicate members, Gama and Mbatha, brought Tambo to the office of Walter Sisulu.

In 1943 Walter Sisulu, with a partner Willie Thabete, ran a real estate business, Sitha Investments, in the central business district.[21] It had taken Sisulu the better part of 1939 and many letters to the authorities – including a petition to the Governor General himself – before the Johannesburg municipality permitted him to set up offices in town.[22] Consequently, Sisulu's office became 'a central meeting point for many, especially people who came from the Transkei'.[23] Sisulu himself was a remarkable man, and became an exemplar to the educated elite. He would also become a key influence on both Tambo and Mandela in initiating the political shifts of the African National Congress. Only

30 years old and with not much formal education, he had already had a range of life experiences. Unlike many of Johannesburg's African elite, including Oliver himself, he had direct knowledge of the black working-class experience.[24]

Sisulu had cordial relations with Lymon Gama. Like so many other black entrepreneurs (including Walter himself), Gama survived by operating a number of small enterprises simultaneously. He kept the books of colleagues and submitted their tax returns to the Receiver of Revenue. He also ran a fish-and-chips restaurant in Sophiatown, where he lived. In 1938, Lancelot Gama worked in the shop during his vacation, and so thoroughly enjoyed running the business for his brother that, at Lymon's urging, he nearly turned down his bursary to Fort Hare in order to join his brother in the business. But his friend Peter Raboroko was so incensed that Lancelot should even consider jeopardising his education for material gain that Lancelot was shamed into going ahead with his Bachelor of Science degree at Fort Hare.[25]

It was Lymon Gama who first told Walter Sisulu the story of the Fort Hare strike in 1941, naming Oliver Tambo as a leading student figure. Later that year, Sisulu met Nelson Mandela, who had also been 'sent down' from Fort Hare after a strike.

During the Fort Hare vacation, when Oliver had come up to Johannesburg to begin his six-week teaching practice at St Peter's, he learnt of the enormous interest there was in the Fort Hare strike. The protest action had been the first of its kind at Fort Hare – the element of race had political implications on a countrywide scale, and it became the subject of interest among parents as well as politicians. Many people who met Tambo and his colleagues were eager to know what had happened and whether, as a result of the strike, any students had been victimised by the authorities. One day, Tambo, Congress Mbatha and Lancelot Gama visited Sisulu's office. It was then, Tambo recalled, that he was introduced to the world of activists in Johannesburg. Those six weeks in January–February 1942 laid the foundations of a friendship between Oliver Tambo and Sisulu that was to deepen the following year.

Fort Hare archives reveal the spate of telegrams and letters of protest and enquiry sent by various institutions and organisations both to the University and to the ministers of Education and Native Affairs on the Beda Hall strike, as well as the ensuing flurry of correspondence by the authorities on the incident. The list, portraying a vibrant network of organised black civil society, included the Garment Workers' Union and unions from 14 industrial sectors as well as a number of political and civic organisations.[26] Of particular interest was the intervention of the Native Representative Council. All of this correspondence was dated October 1942, and reveals how rapidly a great number of organisations could communicate with each other and mobilise around a single, but indicative issue.[27] Fort Hare students were the pride of the black community, and while some parents voiced their disapproval at the way their children had imprudently jeopardised their futures,[28] there was also resentment that they should be treated in this drastic way.

Even mainstream university luminaries expressed their concern about the consequences of the Fort Hare judgment. Professor Hoernlé, vice-chancellor of the University of the Witwatersrand and the registrar of the University of South Africa, wrote to enquire about the wisdom of preventing, through expulsion, 50 potentially valuable and highly skilled personnel from making their full contribution to society.[29]

Black and left-wing newspapers, too, gave the event considerable publicity. It was not surprising, therefore, that Tambo encountered great interest when he arrived in Johannesburg. Oliver himself was very pleased to meet Dan Tloome, then secretary of the Council for Non-European Trade Unions, and thank him in person for his organisation's support. What impressed Tambo was that he was part of a group of energetic trade unionists who held regular public meetings in the community square of Alexandra Township and Sophiatown and outside Johannesburg's City Hall and on Market Square in Newtown. These activists included Dan Khoza and Self Mampuru[30] and many others, recalled Tambo, who 'turned out to be involved at the centre of the struggle against political, economic and social injustice in South Africa'.

All of these figures, though focusing on different aspects of the struggle – whether political, economic or social – were actively making contact with the grass roots, and attempting to organise them. 'It was this quality,' reflected Oliver Tambo, 'that drew me to them and them to me, for I had been involved at the centre of a student protest action against injustice which had political, economic and social implications.' His interaction with many of these activists was to make a decided contribution towards conceptualising the Youth League, in itself destined to pose new and urban challenges to organised political opposition.

On his return to Johannesburg in 1943, Oliver picked up his friendship with Sisulu, who invited him home. Sisulu's house was close to the Anglican church in Orlando West. Walter's mother, Alice – like Oliver – was a devout Christian. Very soon Oliver was a regular house guest on weekends, and the two would attend church together on Sunday mornings. Oliver also occasionally dropped in at the Bantu Men's Social Centre (BMSC), near the city centre. The BMSC afforded rare public space for Africans in Johannesburg. It was, in effect, a club 'to which we all belonged', said Walter Sisulu.[31] Lunch was served there for the few who could afford it, and young people passed their time playing billiards and sports, taking lessons in the Western pastime of tennis. The Centre was the meeting point for community, student and political organisations, branch meetings and cultural associations; musical concerts, choir competitions and plays also regularly featured on the BMSC calendar. Even Oliver's professional organisation, the Transvaal Teachers' Association, held its annual meetings at the BMSC, and Oliver's prize-winning school choir performed there. Both David Bopape,[32] the headmaster from Brakpan location, and Lancelot Gama recalled some memorable moments:

'[Oliver] was conducting a choir of St Peter's students and there was a song which he sang, "Emaqinene Ikhayalam". He sang it so beautifully with his students. He had terrific soprano gents, terrific basses and tenors... He took the first prize that year. But he sang so well in that song that everybody got out there and was going about in the streets saying; "Tambo has done it!" You can imagine people walking from Polly Street up and all of them saying, "Tambo has done it!"... You see, he interpreted that song so well.'[33]

Not long after his return to Johannesburg, Oliver was drawn into a select circle of regular visitors to the home of Dr AB Xuma, President of the ANC.[34] Xuma had been impressed by both young Tambo's academic achievements and his principled stand at Fort Hare. The respected ANC leader cultivated a group of young intellectuals whom he affectionately called 'The Graduates'. The group also included Joe Mokoena, Congress Mbatha, Willie Nkomo, Nelson Mandela and Walter Sisulu.

Mandela – handsome, tall and athletic – had been raised by the Regent of the Thembu near Umtata in the Eastern Cape. He had been educated at the Methodist missionary school of Healdtown and had then gone on to Fort Hare with a view to studying law. The year after Tambo's expulsion, Mandela too encountered some trouble. As an elected member of the Students' Representative Council, he had participated in a boycott of the University in protest against the quality of the food. When he was instructed to write a letter of apology, he had chosen to leave. Mandela had, as Tambo once commented, 'a natural air of authority'.[35] His charm and relaxed manner impressed Tambo. In a sense, Nelson was not unlike David Mankazana, Oliver's classmate to whom he had handed over the baton of head boy of St Peter's. Perhaps the friendship that developed was complementary, for in many ways Mandela was in fact the opposite of Tambo. Tambo's stature and demeanour were modest; he was inhibited and not comfortable with public attention, happy to work behind the scenes – in short, easily underestimated by the less observant. Mandela was generally seen as a 'show boy', while 'Tambo was considered the brainpower, the engine house,' remarked Peter Molotsi. 'Even then, [Mandela] had that reputation. This is Mandela, you see. You saw him and he was tall. And he greeted everybody. Mandela would do that. He would greet everybody, shake hands and pass, disappear. But Tambo was not in a hurry to any place. Mandela was always in a hurry for some other thing. Tambo was solid, just solid man, just solid man. That's OR. And so, that was the first impression. And it lasted for all the time, for all the time!'[36]

For his part, Mandela was somewhat in awe of the brilliant young man whose intellect was 'diamond-edged', he recalled,[37] and whose reputation had preceded his arrival in Johannesburg. Later in his life, Mandela confessed to having an uneasy feeling about his own intellectual ability – he realised that he needed to work very hard in order to distinguish himself intellectually. What both Tambo and Mandela had in common, despite the personality differences, was a solemn, lifelong commitment: each man recognised this in the other – although, of course, it was easier to discern in Tambo, whose delivery to his elected office and to his constituency at Fort Hare had been tested.

Like their colleagues, both men paid careful attention to their dress and were impeccably groomed. In the city, they wore suits at all times – the sartorial symbol of their class and status, which sent a clear message. It was a statement that defied attempts to infantilise black men and women, who were 'native girls' and 'boys' to whites. Black women were required to cover their hair (an almost universal acknowledgement of sexuality) with a *doek* (headscarf), while the uniform of male domestic and service workers, no matter how old, was the mandated short-sleeved tunic and shorts. The business suit was therefore an important part of the identity of the black professional. In the black teachers' protest march in 1944 (organised by fellow Youth Leaguer David Bopape), which Tambo supported as a member of the Transvaal African Teachers Association (TATA),[38] the members marched through the streets of Johannesburg in blankets – a graphic metaphor for their low salaries, only slightly higher than those of mineworkers such as the Basotho migrants who habitually wore blankets even in the city streets. Mandela, however, was fond of a statement bolder than his professional colleagues. His choice of suit and ties was more flamboyant, though always elegant. Tambo's style was understated, relying more (like his garden at school!) on immaculate neatness. Like their peers, the two men adopted the fashionable wartime hairstyle of the city – short-cropped with a parting, which performed a purely decorative rather than functional purpose for African hair.

According to Walter Sisulu, Oliver's attentive and thoughtful manner – 'you know Oliver's type: quiet and never saying anything unless it is necessary to say it' – made him 'the darling of Xuma'.[39] Tambo, too, was able to appreciate Xuma's resourcefulness in nurturing a new generation of young ANC stalwarts. In an interview with Africanist scholar Tom Karis years later, he acknowledged Xuma's instructive role:

'Take a person like Dr Xuma. He comes into an organisation which consists mainly of older, elderly people. There were few young people there. The main object, substance, is handled by elderly people, though younger people are there. He is in sight of everybody, young and old. What does he say to the young ones? I'm taking this as an example – as far as I know, and NEC work is concerned, Xuma would encourage the right people, to write letters, speeches for him. And he'd correct them – largely that. I did that. Nelson did that. Mji did that, the doctor, he wrote letters. You get the youth involved on drafting ANC policy statements.... They were Youth Leaguers, but they were also members of the ANC.'[40]

Xuma was also consciously helping to shape a new concept of leadership during this time, and this deeply impressed Tambo. He observed that Xuma did not tend to favour relatives or home-boys. Tambo himself, whom Xuma had singled out, had no important ethnic connections, nor was he a Xhosa-speaking aristocrat like Mandela. Xuma, observed Tambo, 'didn't look for a person related to someone of prominence, or someone who came from a particular place of birth. No. "Ordinary people" could be better than Nelson'.[41]

Dr Xuma was widely admired for his success in having turned around the ANC during his first term of office in the organisation. He had revived the ANC from its moribund state in the previous decade. Pixley ka Isaka Seme, who had ousted the communist-sympathiser president, Josiah Gumede, in the election of 1930, had not managed to bring together the loose and ramshackle organisation. Seme's emphasis had been on non-racial cooperation and constitutional change, but by 1935 – when white liberals were proving ineffective in preventing the Hertzog Bills, which made further inroads into the black franchise and rights to land – the ANC proved not to have the capacity to coordinate a nationwide response. DDT Jabavu, Xuma and Selope Thema then took the initiative, and in the pages of *Bantu World* called for a national convention 'of chiefs, leaders and representatives of all shades of political thought'.[42] The more than 400 delegates to the All-African Convention (AAC) included chiefs from most of the rural areas to church dignitaries, left-wing intellectuals from the Western Cape and ordinary people from all the provinces. They condemned the bills unanimously.

But the attempt to form a permanent umbrella body under which a variety of black organisations could shelter proved no more able than the ANC to impress the Hertzog government. Afterwards the ANC began to attempt a comeback. The ANC was still 'in the hearts of the people', argued many veterans,[43] and the new Native Representative Council – although opposed by the ANC as a government structure – was used by ANC sympathisers to provide resources and act as a mouthpiece for the organisation in their tours around the country.[44] Then in 1939, the South African government voted to join Britain in the war against fascism. New possibilities presented themselves. The following year, Xuma was elected to the presidency of the ANC by a majority of one. But he proved to be the man to meet the challenge. He had clear direction and decisiveness. He also had financial means, which was extremely useful for an organisation with only £491 in the bank.

Immediately Xuma was elected president of the ANC, he began to assert national authority over the provincial structures by establishing larger headquarters in Johannesburg. He insisted on a functioning central executive committee and he himself took over the administration of the Transvaal Congress. He tried to emphasise democratic administration by insisting that the treasurer and secretary be directly elected by conference rather than nominated by the president, as before. He also shifted the emphasis from the decision-making at the annual congress to year-round organisation. Xuma proved to be averse to mass demonstrations, but he nevertheless cultivated a policy of mass-based support by actively encouraging recruitment drives and report-back mechanisms from local branches to the provincial structures and then to national headquarters. From a paid-up membership in 1941 of a few hundred (it was never systematically assessed), the numbers swelled to 4 176 in 69 branches, excluding the Cape.[45]

When Oliver arrived in Johannesburg in January 1942, the political mood was optimistic. The rapid wartime expansion of the manufacturing industry ensured more jobs for even new unskilled arrivals from the white-owned farms and the reserves. The Minister of Native Affairs was assuring Africans that their grievances were legitimate and that they would be addressed after the war. He quoted the Allies' human rights document, the Atlantic Charter, as a reference point.[46] The Smit Commission, which was to report its findings in 1942, recommended that African trade unions be recognised and that pass laws be abolished. In that same year, Smuts himself vowed to arm every black person if the country should face a Japanese invasion. 'Segregation has fallen on evil days,' he declared. The 'Native' was carrying the country on his back, Smuts added, and was indispensable to an economy that all of South Africa shared.[47]

At the time of Oliver's first visit to Xuma's home, the doctor and a committee of ANC members (in particular Professor ZK Matthews plus a few who were also communists) were absorbed in designing a document they called *African Claims in South Africa.* As a response to the Atlantic Charter, it conveyed an African perspective on human rights. Oliver, as one of The Graduates, participated during informal discussions of the final stages of its preparation, and the *African Claims* document was finally adopted by the ANC at its annual conference in Bloemfontein in 1943. In its introduction, Xuma pointed out that the architects of the Atlantic Charter seemed to differ on whom the declaration was intended to protect. While Franklin D Roosevelt, President of the USA, wanted to apply the principles to all people throughout the world, Winston Churchill, prime minister of Britain, appeared to want to confine its application to the countries occupied by the Nazis in Europe. In South Africa, though, both the Prime Minister and the Minister of Native Affairs indicated that post-war society would apply the Charter to all South Africans. *Africans' Claims* was a response to the Atlantic Charter's focus on fighting 'territorial aggrandisement', which they interpreted as a rejection of imperialism in general.

The document was a resolute assertion by Africans of their equal status in the community of humankind. It detailed the fundamental human rights that were denied to Africans, most especially political, labour and full citizenship rights, including equal access to land, education, jobs, health and the law.

'The ANC was basing its programmes and actions not merely on the national only, but also on the international sphere; that it was asserting its right, not merely as the mouthpiece of the African people in South Africa, but also its right to a say in world affairs,' recalled Walter Sisulu in his prison biography decades later.[48]

Before it was published in its final form, Xuma sent a copy of the manifesto to Prime Minister Smuts. It, however, received a cold reception. 'Your study is evidently a propagandistic document,' replied the private secretary, turning down Xuma's request for an interview. The prime minister, he wrote, did not agree with the ANC's interpretation of the Atlantic Charter, nor with 'your effort to stretch its meaning so as to make it apply to all sorts of African problems and conditions'. 'The prime minister was pained to note,' he added, that Xuma had 'made no effort to recognise his government's efforts to improve African welfare'.[49]

This response was a heavy blow, though not entirely unexpected, and in a short space of time, the perspective and emphasis of African activists changed.

The year 1943 was to see general elections in South Africa. Jan Smuts was focusing at the hustings on 'European' (that is, white) unity in the face of the enemy. Coincidentally, in the constituency of Rosettenville – where Oliver lived at St Peter's – one of the few candidates in South Africa calling for universal suffrage was standing for elections. Betty du Toit, trade unionist and candidate for the Communist Party, was vainly attempting to persuade the white working-class district that class-consciousness was more likely to lead to an improvement of their lives than racism or Afrikaner nationalism.[50] Tambo no doubt would have seen the posters announcing Du Toit's pre-election meetings. As a disenfranchised black man with educational qualifications higher than 98 per cent of the white population, Oliver was excluded from participating in the election debate. In any case, he would have ignored the CPSA candidate's message – at the time, Tambo was not in sympathy with what was widely perceived as the 'ungodly' philosophy of communism and thus would have dismissed its arguments.

Like his friends, Oliver was indignant at Smuts's shoddy response to *African Claims*. Yet again, despite the ANC's courteous overtures to the state, the organisation had been rudely rebuffed. Since its inception, the ANC had received short shrift from those in power. To Tambo, it was indisputably clear that the movement had to turn to its own devices. Tambo often had discussions on this issue with Sisulu, Mandela and a circle of politically minded young intelligentsia such as the intellectually curious Willie Nkomo[51] and Lionel Majombozi – two medical students who eventually had to drop out of politics to complete their studies – as well as Anton Lembede and the insightful Ashby Peter Mda.

Tambo was familiar with the history of the ANC. For all its shortcomings, he argued that its most outstanding achievement was the bringing together of the various African nations under one umbrella. He was impressed that the ANC had organised and developed the tradition of African intellectual participation since the nineteenth century. These men and women had been concerned to use their Western skills to defend their oppressed people. But Tambo was determined to go further. Struck by the emerging activists of his generation, he was convinced that intellectuals should become activists themselves to agitate for national liberation. Together with Sisulu, Mandela and CPSA Youth Leaguers Dan Tloome and David Bopape, Tambo was in the forefront of urging the group to examine ways of reaching the masses directly.

One question they posed was whether the ANC was the most effective organisation to promote the changes they had begun to envisage. Like young intellectuals the world over, they were apt to hold night-long 'marathon discussions' on the burning issues of the day.[52] They would get together in the evenings after work or on the weekends at Sisulu's house, in his office or on occasion at the BMSC. They compared the ANC with the Industrial and Commercial Workers' Union (ICU), which had been more of a general movement than a trade union.

During the course of these discussions, the young political philosophers assessed the merits of the All-African Convention (AAC), which had emerged as a result of black outrage at the removal of the franchise from the Cape's African men in the 1936 Native Laws Amendment Act. The AAC had not managed to capture popular support – its boycott method seemed to the discussion group to emphasise a reactive rather than a mobilising tactic. Tambo noted how the ANC had endured 30 years of ups and downs, and that it had consistently survived any challenges to its paramount position in African politics. With Xuma as president, its future seemed assured. The thing to do, therefore, was to transform the movement from within. It was thus decided to form a 'ginger group' of younger members to revitalise African nationalism and prod the ANC into a more active grass-roots role. It was absolutely crucial, they determined, that the ANC should hold on to the best traditions of African democracy, never losing sight of collective leadership and consensus decision-making, on which unity, survival and the voice of the people were founded.

The notion of a national constituency of youth under the ANC was conceptualised by Tambo. One Saturday afternoon in 1943, Self Mampuru met Mbatha and Tambo at the BMSC to ask for their support for his candidature for the ANC presidency of the Transvaal. The two younger men suggested that an organised lobby be formed. It might be useful too, they said, to work out a programme of action that would express their aspirations. As it happened, Mampuru suddenly abandoned his campaign to join the more left-wing African Democratic Party (ADP). But the core group remained, and came up with some stimulating ideas. They 'decided that Congress needed the leaven of youth in any case', wrote Mbatha wryly, and so 'the idea of a Congress Youth League was mooted'[53] and the discussion groups began. The added urgency was that the ANC needed to move quickly to prevent the initiative from being siphoned off by its new (but relatively short-lived) rival, the ADP. But, as historians Robert Edgar and Luyanda ka Msumzi have observed, 'many catalysts contributed to the founding of the Youth League'.[54] This was an era of a world war, globalised through imperialism, whose cause was fought against racial persecution and for democracy. Its effect was to radicalise both the black youth and many of their elders. Numerous youth and student organisations had sprung up around the country – but what was needed now was a unifying, national organisation to make their voices heard.

The inspiration for developing the theoretical underpinning into a driving philosophy came from the brilliant young scholar, Anton Muziwake Lembede, who shared digs with AP Mda. Lembede, an articulate, intense young man with expressive eyes – 'highly strung, unlike Tambo. Tambo would be as cool as a cucumber in fire, not Lembede!'[55] – was articled to the illustrious past-ANC President, attorney Pixley ka Isaka Seme.[56]

Despite the progress made by Dr Xuma's more active intervention and his reaching out to the next generation, the movement seemed to the younger men to be moving too slowly – it was, they earnestly and sincerely reported to their president, in urgent need of a much more focused programme of action. The ANC, some said, was virtually moribund.[57] To their disappointment, Xuma's response to the idea of a youth league was not enthusiastic. 'We should think carefully about "Africa for the Africans",' he warned at a meeting shortly after the Youth League had been formally accepted in ANC structures, 'because we can make ourselves isolationists like the government we are opposing.' He also questioned the fact that they came with a manifesto. A manifesto implied, he said, that they had their own ideology.[58] Oliver himself, AP Mda observed, was cautious – he was not at the Easter Sunday inaugural meeting in 1944, but he had attended the important preliminary meeting in February.[59] Perhaps he was turning over in his mind how to marry his dual (or more) identities – in any event, it is likely that Tambo chose to attend church on that Holy Day.

While Tambo was embracing the stirring prospect of uplifting his people through political means, he never relinquished his religious devotions. He was pleased to see that the Anglican Church in this time of war was increasing its sensitivity to the oppression of black people. The Reverend Michael Scott drew attention to the plight of people in the townships by setting up residence himself in the shanty town of Tobruk and putting together a tin shack of a church there. The Bishop of Johannesburg, Geoffrey Clayton, too, was speaking out in the context of the crude racism of Hitler's nazism. In his sermons, Clayton critiqued the concept of the all-powerful state, sending the message that 'people are more important than things':

'From the Christian point of view, Man is an immortal soul and his most important interest is his relation to God. The State is not immortal.'[60] The value of each individual man, he preached, is 'quite independent of his race, class, or the State to which he belongs. And the One Divine event to which the whole of creation moves is not a Parliament of Man... It is rather a gathering together of all God's children, of all races, of all times, in the Body of Christ.'

It was therefore 'the duty of every Christian... to be on its guard against any possibility of the State's suppression of human worth'. Tambo was not uncomfortable with this interpretation of the Church and State, although it did not go far enough in addressing the situation in South Africa. It was not until he met Trevor Huddleston in 1943, though, that together, through day-to-day experience, they developed a more political explanation of the Church, and began to marry spiritual with political purpose.

'I remember as if it were yesterday,' Tambo wrote to Huddleston towards the end of his life, 'your arrival in racist South Africa, my motherland.' He recalled vividly a friend calling him at St Peter's: 'Bra T, this new priest that has arrived at St Cyprian's should prove to be just what our people need – a man who is prepared to work with the people – this might prove to be a worthy find.' 'You arrived,' wrote Tambo to Father Huddleston, 'armed with truth as your sword and integrity as your breastplate and ready to follow the Master to the cross if necessary.'[61]

The Community's provincial headquarters were at St Peter's, so Huddleston initially stayed there prior to his moving to Sophiatown. It was CR policy to live among one's flock, and Huddleston was a regular visitor to Rosettenville.

Father Huddleston, in his white cassock, cut a distinctive and sharply contrasting figure to Oliver Tambo. He was tall, fair, lean, long-limbed, with sharply chiselled features. But in his warmth of manner, his passionate nature, his profound, resolute commitment to his Church, his concern for social issues and his Christian humanism, Huddleston resonated strongly with Tambo. Two years older than Tambo, Huddleston had attended a High Anglican public school noted for its serious commitment to the Church. His schoolteacher described young Trevor as 'an average, charming, friendly prep school boy'. 'My confirmation was the beginning of what I can only describe as my real life,' recalled Huddleston years later. 'I could not have conceived the Christian life then as being possible outside that community. I cannot conceive it now.'[62]

Huddleston's indignation at the crassness and indifference of mainstream white society and his ability to articulate the problems meant that he forged a deep bond with the liberation struggle of South Africa. He became well known in the black community for his socially based sermons, which attracted people from other churches and other townships. Among the farflung worshippers was the young Adelaide Tsukhudu, a schoolgirl from Eastern Township on the other side of Johannesburg. Adelaide recalled a discussion at Orlando High after a school debate. 'They were telling us about Father Huddleston at school.' Huddleston's interdenominational sermon had impressed them all.

Regardless of whether one was Anglican or Methodist, 'your common purpose was worshipping God. Magdalene Marianne suggested we go and listen to his sermon in Sophiatown… Later, when I was courting with Oliver, I met him at a church rally in Wanderers Street, Union Grounds. Bishop Clayton had come from Cape Town to address the rally. Afterwards I saw him a lot.'[63]

In the process of exploring the spiritual landscape of the black community, Huddleston developed an activist outlook, one that was to work in tandem with Oliver Tambo both during his years in South Africa and, in later years, in the international arena of sanctions and boycotts. In Tambo's dual callings of Church and politics, Huddleston was to remain a key spiritual companion.

Years later Oliver Tambo wrote a tribute to Huddleston, recalling with much affection 'the people of Sophiatown and Newclare who never failed to notice and register your love for the children and the youth and your tireless efforts to advance progress in their chosen disciplines. A few examples are Hugh Masekela, Jonas Gwangwa, Archbishop Desmond Tutu, Archbishop Walter Makumbe, Reverend David Nape, and Dr Nthatho Motlana etc.'[64]

Father Huddleston, recalled Adelaide Tambo, 'became a religious model to Oliver. He conducted himself as a priest in a manner that Oliver would have liked to emulate, working among the people'.[65] He was an important influence in Tambo's decision to take up the ministry. He demonstrated – by example as well as through theology – how Christianity could resist the inhumanity of apartheid.[66] 'It has been the teaching of the Church,' Huddleston once preached to a packed Trades Hall of ANC delegates, 'that when government degenerates into tyranny... laws cease to be binding upon its subjects.'[67]

'I once said to Chief Luthuli,' recalled Tambo, 'that "The road to Freedom is long and hazardous – many used to drop out along the way. But I believe Father Huddleston will go with us to the end".' In a letter to Huddleston, Tambo evoked his friend's campaigns and 'numerous fights' in those early years – facing bulldozers in Sophiatown, the battle against the Bantu Education Act, 'the Congress of the People at which you received the "Isitwalandwe", our highest award – given to giants of our struggle and a giant you were – even then'.[68]

Huddleston himself was deeply struck by Oliver Tambo. In his momentous account of black urban life under apartheid – *Naught For Your Comfort*, which aroused widespread interest, selling 100 000 copies in 1949, its first year of publication – Huddleston offered a three-page biography of Tambo to illustrate the calibre of person the apartheid regime was treating with gross contempt. 'It seemed to me then and it seems to me now quite intolerable that the great mass of Christian people in South Africa should remain entirely unmoved when a man of Oliver's stature was victimised in this way.'[69] Huddleston's dedication demanded a special variety of passion and commitment, and profoundly moved Oliver. It was powerful enough to compete with his other vision – of service to his people on a political, secular terrain. His choice was to be decided ultimately more than a decade later.

In December 1943, the Youth League (YL) was formally accepted by the ANC congress in Botshabelo, Bloemfontein, and in the following September it held its official inauguration. A 'Trumpet Call' heralded its launch.

'The hour of youth has struck! As the forces of National Liberation gather momentum, the call to youth to close ranks in order to consolidate the National Unity Front becomes more urgent and imperative.

'1944 marks an epoch in the struggle of Black peoples of South Africa. A dramatic turning-point in the history of mankind, signalled by the global war now being waged, presents a clarion call to the youth of the Sub-Continent, to rally round the banner of the National Liberation Movement, so as to galvanise and vitalise the National Struggle.'

The Trumpet Call invited all youth from the province and its surrounds to attend a mass meeting at the BMSC. Speakers included Xuma and Thema, Dan Tloome on 'Youth and Trade Unionism' and 'Mr OR Thambo [sic]' on 'Our Congress Youth League'. The flyer ended with a final flourish: *African Youth! Do Not Miss This Opportunity! Come In Your Hundreds! The fault is not in our stars, But in ourselves that we are underlings.*[70] The end quotation, which emphasised the necessity for agency and self-reliance, employed the eloquence of Shakespeare and attested to their student and intellectual background.

Tambo was the last speaker at the meeting. He outlined the broad approach and development of the YL, and reported its formal acceptance by the ANC at its December congress. This meant that all Youth League members were automatically also members of the ANC, and they should see themselves as having a special role to play in strengthening and rejuvenating the mother body. The meeting was then followed by elections. Lembede was unanimously voted as first president of the Transvaal Youth League, AP Mda its vice-president and Tambo its first secretary. The three leading figures in this new and historic organisation constituted a formidable team.[71] The lucidly expressed minutes of the YL meetings in the years that followed bear testimony to Tambo's ability to communicate sometimes convoluted concepts and arguments with clarity and ease of understanding. New members were thus educated and reminded at every meeting of the vision and objectives of the YL.

Having critiqued the inertia of the ANC, it was incumbent on the YL to mobilise the youth on a national level. The constitution allowed for branches to be formed wherever 15 members or more were recruited. A key branch – and one of the largest – was at Fort Hare, which was chaired by Godfrey Pitje, an anthropology graduate student. Tambo also started a branch at St Peter's. Many of its adolescent recruits were to become senior members of the ANC in years to come – these included Duma Nokwe, Henry Makgothi, Joe Matthews, Andrew Mlangeni and Desmond Tutu.

The YL soon caused a stir in activist circles, and even the Young Communist League was excited by its formation. Ruth First, secretary of the Young Communist League at the time, soon wrote to the YL, hoping to recruit its members to their cause. Her overtures were, however, politely but firmly rejected.[72] A couple of years later, IB Tabata of the AAC (later to lead the Trotskyite Non-European Unity Movement (NEUM)) wrote to Mandela, warning him not to hitch the Youth League to the ANC. 'At every critical moment,' he cautioned, 'Congress has played into the hands of Government.' Examples he provided were the ANC's support of the Native Representative Council, thus refusing to support the AAC boycott of government bodies, and the 1947 Doctors' Pact between doctors Xuma, Dadoo and Naicker, which by their very existence excluded coloured representation in the alliance and, besides, were clinched with two members of the Communist Party. The 'opportunism' of the ANC, he argued, had allowed the CPSA to gain 'a foothold amongst the African people'.

'You and... the Youth League are talking with two voices at one and the same time,' he continued. 'As members of the Youth League, you speak the language of the modern intellectual – progressive, independent, rejecting inferiority. But as members of the African National Congress... you accept the theory of inferiority and trusteeship with all its political manifestations, eg. segregated institutions like the Native Representative Council, Advisory Boards, the Bhunga etc.'[73]

For the Youth League, however, both the CPSA and the NEUM had a fundamental Marxist characteristic they could not accept – their non-racial class analysis cut across the Africanist striving for the unity of African people. 'We are devoting our energies to the preparation of the greatest national struggle of all time, the struggle for national liberation,' replied Lembede to Ruth First. 'Our stupendous task is to organise, galvanise and consolidate the numerous African tribes into one homogenous nation.'[74]

Like Lembede, Tambo distrusted the dialectical materialism of Marxism, and was indeed, Walter Sisulu remembered, a 'sharp nationalist'.[75] But he had also had a different experience of diverse South Africans. Tambo was, therefore, quite comfortable with some white people. They had actively helped him – as benefactors, as teachers, as spiritual counsellors – and he was sensitive enough to acknowledge warmly their generosity. A tiny number were sufficiently forward thinking to grasp the need for a 'New Africa', and to anticipate a role for Tambo in it. In fact, Tambo's manner was so unfailingly courteous, thoughtful and discerning that his radicalism was quite unexpected. 'His gentle deportment,' said Ismail Meer, 'was deceptive.'[75] Walter Sisulu conceded that 'he was a refined person, yes. He would think of people as people, as human beings; but the spirit of nationalism is there! Which is not an antagonism to any particular section, but a desire to see of their own'.[76]

Oliver Tambo saw no reason for his militant ideas to impinge on his respect for people, regardless of colour. But his courtesy was not to be confused with his determination to help bring into being a united African nation, free of external intrusion or control. To his constituency, Tambo was quite capable of militant rhetoric. Writing in support of the YL's resolution to call for the resignation of the Native Representative Council, he declared: 'We have tolerated the partnership between "White Oppression" and "Black Treachery" for long enough. We shall square up accounts with the former in due course; we are dispensing with the latter forthwith.'[77]

Fiercely protective as the YL were of their own vision and their determination to 'Go it Alone', they were observing and borrowing relevant strategies and tactics of other organisations. They grasped, for example, the positive potential of the NEUM's boycott approach. For African people in particular, who had been stripped of so much – 'squeezed', Tambo wrote as the YL's secretary, 'out of the Land and into white Farms and Towns as cheap labour… discriminated against in industry', removed from the Common Voters' Roll to be organised 'into debating societies' – a conscious and systematic rejection of government subterfuges was an empowering option for the disempowered.

But nor (much as the YL resented the Communist Party of South Africa) could they help but wish to learn from the organisational skills of the communists. The 1940s was a good decade for the CPSA, especially as their membership and popularity increased dramatically during the war years. The Party had called for the arming of black soldiers and had run high-profile campaigns exposing profiteering on food shortages. Leading members had also revived the black labour movement, and through struggles in negotiations and work stoppages, black trade unions had – for the first time in history – made advances in real wage increases in shops and factories, which now relied on black workers while whites were fighting 'up North'.

But perhaps the Party's most successful coup for the politically aware was the 80 000-strong mineworkers' strike in 1946, which protested against falling wages and inferior food. JB Marks and Moses Kotane, members of both the CPSA and the ANC, led the African Mine Workers' Union. For a moment, the Youth League hesitated as to whether to support an event initiated by another organisation. Walter Sisulu was of the opinion that despite 'the situation that has been created, we must go in; but we must make it a success'.[79] The YL thus issued a flyer in support of the strike, emphasising its significance as 'a national struggle' rather than a class one.[80] And as a follow-up to the brutal crushing of the strike, in which at least 12 miners were killed and 324 wounded, the YL called for the immediate resignation of the entire NRC.

The YL were also galled to observe CPSA activity in communities. In 1941, David Bopape had led a 'stay-at-home' in the Brakpan Location in protest against the overbearing, crass racism of the location superintendent; in 1943, Schreiner Baduza had led a shanty-town movement in Alexandra, demanding housing for all. But the Party also made mistakes. They had snubbed James Mpanza, founder of the *Sofasonke* ('We shall all die together') movement, as a self-interested fraudster, thus missing the most significant and successful housing campaign of the decade. It was Sisulu, together with Lembede and Mandela of the YL, supported by the ANC, who became associated with the movement and benefited from the experience of working with the grass roots, inspiring YL members to become more involved in community activities.[81]

The other major show of resistance in 1946 also deeply imprinted itself on the minds of the YL leadership. The Passive Resistance Campaign was born out of protest against the Smuts government's 1943 'Pegging Act' – which forbade Indians to own property in so-called 'white' areas – and then the 1946 Asiatic Land Tenure Act, which restricted residential and trading rights. The latter was met with widespread indignation. The Transvaal and Natal Indian Congresses elected two radical leaders, medical doctors Yusuf Dadoo and GM Naicker, who organised a series of mass rallies in small and big towns in the two provinces. The two Indian congresses then embarked on a campaign of passive resistance to this most recent 'Ghetto Act'. Forming batches of 10, some 2000 Indian men and women – students, teachers, workers, doctors, lawyers, traders and sheltered housewives – volunteered to sleep in tents pitched on a piece of municipal property in Durban. As fast as each batch was arrested for trespassing, so another group arrived to camp overnight. Soon the 'Non-European' prisons were full; the policy was 'no defence, no fine', and most of the volunteers were sentenced to three to six weeks' imprisonment.

Although a practical application by the ANC of Gandhi's brilliant tactic of *satyagraha* was to materialise only six years later, the Passive Resistance Campaign itself was supported by the ANC, and Xuma and other leaders addressed a number of protest rallies. Youth League members were clearly struck by the mobilising power of civil disobedience. Through collective action, popular consciousness was radicalised. The 'ringleaders' – Dadoo and Naicker – were sentenced to six months' imprisonment, serving as important exemplars. More importantly, however, the campaign had helped alleviate the fear of prison that had come to be part of the struggle experience – it had been endured in a noble cause.[82]

The Passive Resistance Campaign did not succeed in getting the Acts rescinded; but it had an enormous impact on the public. In the following year, buoyed by the experience, Xuma, Dadoo and Naicker signed a pact that undertook to bring their organisations together in resisting racial discrimination. The leaders of the Transvaal Indian Congress (TIC) and Natal Indian Congress (NIC) had sensitised their constituencies to the tribulations of Africans, and convinced many that the interests of the Indian community could be better served by working with the ANC than continuing to curry favour with the white government. Ismail Meer, a leading figure among the Indian youth, recalled the 'hard talking' to Lembede, Tambo and others in the YL to present the strategy.[83] Tambo, Mandela and Sisulu had no problem accepting the principle that they could work with other groups provided each organisation retained its autonomy. Ultimately even Lembede, said Sisulu, accepted it – as long as the ANC led the move.[84] For his part, Tambo recalled that he had grown up 'with the feeling that Africans had no support from the West, but from Asian countries which sympathised with South Africa's problems – they had frequently sent messages of solidarity to ANC conferences'.[85]

But matters were not entirely smooth sailing for the new alliance. A sticking point came almost immediately afterwards, with their first joint battle. Anticipating the first post-war elections, a 'Votes For All' campaign was formulated. For strategic reasons, though, the YL could not afford to bring themselves to support it. 'We… were opposed, because the argument was that this tendency of these broad organisations was intended really to substitute the ANC,' explained Sisulu, and Mandela, who had agreed to help organise the campaign, thus stepped down.[86] More battles about the supremacy of the ANC, led relentlessly by the Youth League, were to come in the fifties and beyond.

In the meantime, the YL was preparing its tour de force – a Programme of Action that was to mark a turning point in the history and direction of the ANC. In addition to this blueprint of popular struggle, it had also crafted an African style of communal management. While Lembede and other architects of Africanism did not spell out in detail what the African tradition might be, its founders revived the African way of democratic decision-making. Collective leadership was emphasised, while thorough discussion would continue until consensus was reached. This meant that any achievement by one person was a cause for celebration by all. There was no room for the kind of individualism that looked after 'Number One', to the exclusion of the common good.

Movers and shakers in the YL in that radicalising decade, the forties, rapidly took senior positions within the mother body itself, imprinting on the movement a particular style of national popularisation. Walter Sisulu, elected as Secretary-General of the ANC in 1949, established broad consultation with the grass-roots members, inspiring those who succeeded him – including Tambo – to emulate him. Mandela, with his appeal and his art of public speaking, was to become a key organiser in the era of mass mobilisation and a national figure in the struggle. Anton Lembede, tragically, suffered a premature death, while AP Mda – who replaced Lembede – retired owing to ill health. Oliver Tambo, secretary of the Youth League, was to be unanimously elected on to the ANC National Executive and was to remain a key member until the end of his life.

As 1948 dawned, Oliver could look back on five momentous years. He had formed lifelong friendships; he had clarified for himself, both spiritually and politically, his path in life; he had committed himself to being part of the task of uniting and liberating the African nation. In the process, he had helped to define the role of his contemporary African intellectuals and leaders. The concept of Africanism, he suggested, was not of itself sufficient without a programme spelling out the necessary strategies, tactics and actions. His generation of young people, with their rural roots and their metropolitan adulthood, were either educated or had pertinent organisational experience – in larger numbers than ever before – well placed as intellectuals and 'organic intellectuals' to take the struggle forward.[87] They had no alternative, concluded Tambo, but to work as activists with the community and the black working-class movement. He had rapidly grasped that petitions, no matter how eloquent to the 'powers that be', were no longer satisfactory.[88]

CHAPTER SIX

'Holding a Snake by its Tail'

ON THE DAY THE RESULTS of the 1948 whites-only election were announced, Oliver Tambo was walking towards his office in Charter House, on the corner of Rissik and Anderson streets in Johannesburg's city centre. He was immaculately dressed in suit and tie. Suddenly, a white man accosted him, his face twisted with hatred. He worked his mouth, and then – without a word – spat in Tambo's face. Tambo walked away. He wiped off the spit with a snowy silk handkerchief. Forty years later, he still had the kerchief in his possession.[1]

For Tambo, this assault was a symbolic demonstration of the New Order – in itself, a more vicious offspring of South Africa's centuries-old policy of segregation. Unexpectedly, the complacent United Party had lost the election by a slender five-seat majority. Afrikaner nationalists were jubilant, spilling out into the streets, claiming the public space as a celebration of the birth of a new era. At every railway station from Cape Town to Pretoria, crowds of Afrikaner men and women were waiting to cheer and congratulate the new prime minister, Dr DF Malan. For black South Africans, the victory for Afrikaner nationalism seemed to endorse the licence to lord over black people even more openly and aggressively. The election ticket of the National Party had focused on *'die swart gevaar'* – 'the black peril'. In practice, it was rapidly brought home to blacks that there was to be no place for them in the 87 per cent of South African land that was officially proclaimed 'white', except as low-paid menial labourers.

Nevertheless, senior leaders of the ANC continued to dismiss the significance of the National Party victory. 'The Apartheid policy of the Nationalist [sic] Party is nothing new and should be nothing surprising to any honest and serious student of colour relations,' Xuma had announced a month before the elections. 'It is a mere elaboration, a natural and logical growth of the Union Native Policy with improvements and progressiveness by proposing the inclusion of Indians and Coloured people. It is, perhaps, to plagiarise the Union Prime Minister, General Smuts, a "Holism" in Union Non-European affairs.'[2]

In his autobiography, Chief Albert Luthuli later described the conventional wisdom among South Africa's black intelligentsia: 'For most of us Africans... the election seemed largely irrelevant. We had endured Botha, Hertzog and Smuts. It did not seem of much importance whether the whites gave us more

Smuts or switched to Malan. Our lot had grown steadily harder, and no election seemed likely to alter the direction in which we were being forced.'[3]

But Tambo was taking a more strategic perspective. Nelson Mandela clearly remembered Tambo's response: 'The victory was a shock... On election day, I attended a meeting with Oliver Tambo and several others. We barely discussed the question of a Nationalist government because we did not expect one. The meeting went on all night, and we emerged at dawn and found a newspaper vendor selling the *Rand Daily Mail*: the Nationalists had triumphed. I was stunned and dismayed, but Oliver took a more considered line. "I like this," he said. "I like this." I could not imagine why. He explained, "Now we will know exactly who our enemies are and where we stand."'[4]

It was this quality – of being able to prevent the mind from being clouded by emotions and to keep his eye on the struggle – that was beginning to make an impact on Tambo's friends and comrades. His circle was hardly a superficial crowd; the leading members of the Youth League were earnest in their stated task to work and organise in order to uplift and empower their people; and from the start, his colleagues appreciated Tambo's quiet proficiency. From the beginning, the calm young man who had come to Johannesburg with a radical reputation from Fort Hare impressed them. He was clearly a keen listener, though he seldom spoke. But it was only by degrees that his contemporaries discovered the extent and the value of Tambo's keen intellect.

Walter Sisulu once described how he was struck by a speech Tambo gave on the occasion of the formation of the white Congress of Democrats, spelling out the various reasons behind the strategy that they were considering, explaining and justifying its formation. It was a tricky moment, because his audience was simultaneously his own ANC constituency – more than a few of whom were uncertain of the wisdom of this new move – and some 200 whites, many of them communists or liberals, who had come to listen to arguments from the ANC executive on how they could help the struggle against apartheid.

'This speech of OR [Oliver Reginald] created a terrific impression on me,' explained Sisulu. 'I have no way of describing it. You take a thing by the tail. And you expose it. OR, in his artistic way of speaking, created a tremendous impression. Not only to me, but to the people who were there. Because he has a way – you take a snake by the tail and you are exposing its head.'[5]

Throughout the forties, Oliver Tambo had applied his mind to promoting an Africanist agenda. 'One of the things about him was that of national pride,' recalled Mandela.[6] Tambo continued to have problems with the Marxist class analysis of society. He was wary about working with non-African political groups in political campaigns, for fear of losing concentration on the independent development of Africans. More important, having committed himself to the ANC, and as a member of the executive committee of the ANC in the Transvaal, he was fully dedicated to its wellbeing. In their recollections of that period, both Walter Sisulu and Nelson Mandela recalled an event in 1948 that was something of a turning point in the relationship of the three comrades.

The intention behind the 'Votes For All' campaign, initiated prior to the elections by members of the Indian Congress and the Communist Party of South Africa, was to remind the general public of racial discrimination and to mobilise workers and liberal-minded whites as well as all men and women of colour. The meeting held at Johannesburg's Gandhi Hall attracted a multiracial audience of 300 to 400 people, and became something of a yardstick for future gatherings. 'It was my first experience where the overwhelming majority of the audience was black,' recalled Communist Party member Rusty Bernstein. 'For the first time, I saw the depth and richness of black political consciousness, which I had known existed but had never come against.'[7] Everyone should have the vote, argued the speakers, without educational or property qualifications or racial restrictions.

The ANC had been asked to join the campaign. Earlier, Mandela – as Master of Ceremonies at a banquet held to announce the 'Votes For All' campaign – had convened an event, but others in the YL, including Oliver Tambo, persuaded him to abandon it.[8] 'We were opposed,' Sisulu explained, 'because, the argument was that the tendency of these broad organisations is intended really to substitute the ANC.' They reminded each other about the consequences of the All-African Convention, which had attempted a broad alliance in opposition to the Natives Act of 1936. In the end, it had proved ineffective and had resulted in the sidelining of the ANC.[9]

When the Transvaal Executive of the ANC met, they considered how to respond. It decided, as a tactic, to 'prevent arrangements for this conference on the grounds that it was a communist initiative'.[10] Sisulu, Tambo and Mandela were mandated to communicate this at the next campaign meeting.

'Oliver and I kept to the decision of the Executive,' recalled Mandela, 'but Comrade Walter was persuaded by the arguments which were used, especially by eloquent speakers like Ismail Meer and JN Singh who were fellow students of mine at Wits [University] – very eloquent chaps.

'They were able to put up a very sound – and looking now with the help of hindsight – very sound and progressive views. And Comrade Walter now was persuaded by their argument [to support the campaign]. Whereas Oliver and I were keeping in mind the mandate that was given to us by our executive; we were so annoyed with Comrade Walter that as we walked down in Market Street – this meeting was almost just at the corner of Market and Diagonal streets, and we had to walk from there to Park Station to catch the train to Orlando – we left him behind and wouldn't talk to him at all!'[11]

Sisulu also vividly remembered the course of events. He recalled how impressed he was with their commitment and their analysis: 'I said, "No, I think it is clear that they are genuine, and therefore we must go ahead with that." Others were very angry... Oliver and Nelson were not talking to me any more – there were sharp differences on this. I was convinced; there is no motive behind an organisation like this. They mean what they say.' He recalled persuasive arguments by, in particular, Maulvi Cachalia and Ismail Meer. Afterwards, he remembered, laughing, how Nelson had accused him, saying sarcastically, 'Well, you became very friendly when Ismail praised you as a wise man!'[12]

The dispute continued when Mandela and Tambo confronted Transvaal ANC President CS Ramohanoe outside and they convinced him to make an alternative statement different from the resolution taken at the meeting. 'Absolutely wrong methods,' said Sisulu. It was necessary first to convince him and then take it back to the executive committee – 'not to isolate him and get him to sign. It looked like a bit of underhand work'.[13]

The point of the story, considered significant enough by both Mandela and Sisulu to relate, was that in the light of Tambo's subsequent strategically pragmatic behaviour, even at this early stage in his political career, he typically and consistently kept his focus on the interests of the ANC constituency. Looking back on the episode, one might argue from a Youth League perspective that Mandela had nearly lost sight, in the 'Votes for All' campaign, of the Youth League's goal of ensuring ANC leadership, while Sisulu was too quickly persuaded by the communists.

Both Sisulu and Mandela noted the consistently close attention Tambo gave to correct procedure in decision-making. In 1949, while still secretary of the Youth League, he sharply pulled up members who failed to adhere to the YL resolution to boycott the elections of black people in 'dummy' institutions. The leadership represented the men and women who mandated them to express their wishes; the democratic principle to maintain the collective integrity and legitimacy of the YL was key. 'The delegates at the Port Elizabeth Conference,' warned Tambo, 'who were at the time in their sound and sober senses and who were free to pass any resolution they pleased, decided by a democratic majority that these two elections [of the NRC and of white 'Native' representatives in Parliament] should be boycotted... From that decision there can be no retreat. Any attempt by any Cape Congressman, or any group of them, to temper or play hide and seek with the decisions of the Conference, will be interpreted as an open and naked betrayal of the people.'[14]

It would be incumbent on them, Tambo had argued, to take the discussion back to the provincial executive committee.

In that same year, Tambo and other members of the Youth League suffered a major blow. Anton Lembede, their seminal Africanist influence and inspiration, suddenly fell ill and died. 'His death was a great shock,' wrote Tambo in his own hand, some 20 years later. 'We knew he wasn't entirely healthy and had had an operation, something internal. When he went to the hospital at the end they operated on him but he died... Even the older men recognised Lembede's talent. He had a real reputation, including a professional reputation. If he had lived he would certainly have risen in the ANC and would maybe have become President-General.'[15]

As Tambo had foreseen, the ushering in of the apartheid regime in 1948 played right into the hands of the YL. Tambo himself was preparing to change his profession from teaching to law, and was studying by correspondence through the University of South Africa. Almost immediately after Malan formed his all-Afrikaner, all-male, white government, a spate of outright racist bills began to be prepared by members of the new cabinet and announced in the newspapers. These included a Suppression of Communism Act, a Population Registration Act to classify the 'race' of every individual in the country, a Group Areas Act to remove black people from working-class multiracial residential areas and to create ghettos, the tightening of pass laws for stricter social and labour control of blacks in the city, and so on... And already, the bureaucracy to administer this apartheid vision began to be enlarged, providing jobs for whites, and Afrikaners in particular. Clerks in the pass offices, labour bureaus and hospitals – insufferable as they had been before – were now even more openly arrogant and overbearing towards black people waiting in the endless queues.

The Youth League seized the opportunity. Tambo, as its secretary, responded with a long view: 'Today it is the Communist Party – tomorrow it will be the trade unions or the Indian Congress or our African National Congress', he prophesied. In a series of night-long sessions, the working committee – with Tambo as scribe – hammered out a Programme of Action, which they determined to put before the next ANC congress in Botshabelo, Bloemfontein. The programme selected tactics employed so effectively by other organisations in the preceding years – the civil disobedience of the Passive Resistance Campaign, strikes by the labour movement, mass action by the Communist

Party and indeed by grass-roots social crusades such as Mpanza's *Sofasonke* movement. The idea was, recalled Sisulu, that 'unless we are participating in a militant movement, we were not going to make any impression. We had come out against the petitions; we now wanted to demonstrate with the mass of the people. It was the only way out'.[16] The draft policy was sent to the branches at the 1948 conference, which then gave the Youth League executive a mandate to present it to the ANC. Tambo, together with Sisulu, AP Mda and Mandela, took the document to Xuma in Sophiatown. Their approach, they explained, was that they were not independent, but subject to everything that the ANC stood for. Then, on the eve of the conference, they presented him with their proposed Programme of Action – boycott of collaboration, of collaborationist institutions, and strikes.[17]

But Xuma was not comfortable with confrontational politics. He had already warned them not to isolate themselves from potential allies. He reminded his young hopefuls that his success at the United Nations had been assisted by the South African Indian Congress and the Indian government. The group, however, had already made a bold resolution to convey to Xuma that the Youth League would not support his re-election as president unless he himself advocated the Programme of Action, and in particular the boycott of advisory boards, Bhungas, local councils and the Native Representative Council at the next Congress.[18] Xuma was outraged at their impertinence. He felt that the Youth League was being somewhat callow and instrumental, and in a heated moment in the discussion he responded angrily: 'This is blackmail, which I am not prepared to accept. I have an independent mind; I am not going to be told by anybody what to do!'[19]

Prophetically, Xuma also warned them of the danger of their approach. It was tantamount, he felt, to 'offering the leadership of Congress for sale. It could open the way for opportunists, and even enemies of Congress, to take up the offer for the sake of a position'.[20] The group then began to look for an alternative candidate. Professor ZK Matthews was their first choice, but 'he was not ready at this time for the same reason – that the programme was too revolutionary', said Sisulu. And at the Bloemfontein congress they found that no other prospective candidate was prepared to support the boycott, so they waited to hear what Xuma would say in his presidential speech. The Conference itself had accepted the Programme of Action, but Xuma rejected the principle.[21] It was then, at the last minute, that Ntsu Mokehle (much later to become prime minister of Lesotho), accompanied by Tambo – the YL President AP Mda fell ill at the last minute – raced to the consulting rooms of the prestigious physician from the Free State, Dr James S Moroka.[22]

Dr Moroka was not well known to many of the youth. Those who knew him knew him by reputation only. As the great-grandson of the Tswana king, Morola, who had given military protection to the Voortrekkers in the 1830s, he was a member from a respected landed family and, like Xuma, had obtained his medical degree abroad, graduating at Edinburgh in 1918. He had acquired a reputation for militancy when he was part of the deputation to Hertzog to protest against the 1936 removal of African men from the Cape franchise. Unlike some of the others who wavered in their response to Hertzog's appeal to compromise, Moroka had stood firm. He was also known for his round denunciation of the NRC though, significantly, remaining a member for some time afterwards. But as a known veteran in the NRC, he was prepared to take a progressive line. 'OK, take Moroka,' they decided.[23]

Back at the congress, Xuma was shocked when the young medic, Diliza Mji, put forward a motion of no confidence in the president, and was supported by a sea of young hands. Moroka was then voted into the position of president. Ironically, when elections for the National Executive were in progress, Xuma supported the nomination of his favourite young man, Oliver Tambo. Ismail Meer, who subsequently heard about the proceedings, recalled that George Champion was said to have called out: 'Watch out, Xuma! These are the guys that are going to overthrow you!'[24] In the event, an overwhelming majority elected Xuma himself on to the Executive as an ordinary member, while Walter Sisulu was unexpectedly nominated by Lancelot Gama and accepted the position of Secretary-General, beating communist Dan Tloome by one vote. 'We were regarded as upstarts,' recalled Sisulu. 'There would be older people who would not be interested in supporting us at all because we are claiming we want to take over and all that.'[25] Youth Leaguers AP Mda, Dr James Njongwe from the Eastern Cape and Godfrey Pitje, an anthropologist from Fort Hare who was to join the Tambo and Mandela legal firm a few years later, were also elected on to the National Executive Committee (NEC). More than that, the influential Working Committee, which met regularly and more frequently than the NEC to direct campaigns and programmes, included Sisulu as Secretary-General of the ANC and Oliver Tambo as the secretary of the Youth League.

The Youth League's great coup, though, was the formal adoption of its Programme of Action by the ANC. Mda had worked himself to a point where he was jeopardising his health – touring the country, setting up branches and recruiting members for the YL, and organising transport for their attendance at the annual congress of the ANC. The programme presented to Congress, signed by David Bopape and GIM Mzamane, called for a council of action to implement the application of 'the following weapons: immediate and active boycott, strike, civil disobedience, non-cooperation and such other means as may bring about the accomplishment and realisation of our aspirations'. It focused on educational and economic institutions that would 'raise the standard of Africans' and promote industrial and commercial enterprises as well as 'a common education forum' in which 'intellectuals, peasants and workers [would] participate for the common good', providing large-scale overseas scholarships. It also undertook to 'unite the cultural with the educational and national struggle'.

Although an ambitious programme (and one deprived of Lembede's lyrical style), it was one that managed to sell itself to Congress. While it borrowed liberally from other organisations, including the Communist Party and the Unity Movement, it was advanced in many ways. It raised notions of self-help and independence, and linked the cultural to the political. The Programme of Action was, in many ways, a document that was able to stand up to the scrutiny of future generations and encourage them to scale further heights of Africanism. The Statement of Policy adopted at the annual meeting concluded that 'ultimately the people will be brought together by inspired leadership under the banner of African Nationalism with courage and determination'.[26]

From then on it was to be the YL's leadership that would dominate the ANC. Its emphasis on prioritising action to 'raise the standard of national consciousness' through popular participation was to mark the decade of the 1950s. In the process, it would alter permanently the balance of black opposition.

Earlier in 1949, Tambo had for the first time been called upon to act on a national level for the ANC. On an oppressively hot and humid January day in Durban's inner city an Indian trader struck a black child who had been caught shoplifting. Immediately fisticuffs broke out, and within a few minutes, angry onlookers began looting Indian stores. The incident exploded into a horrifying race riot in which 50 Indians and 87 black people were killed, many of the latter by police. Dozens more died later of injuries. Over a thousand were injured and thousands – mostly Indians[27] – were left homeless. The following day, the presidents of the ANC Natal and the Natal Indian Congress issued a joint statement. Xuma, as national president, hurried down and returned a few days later with a team to form part of the joint council – senior members Selby Msimang, JB Marks, Gana Makabeni, Moses Kotane and Oliver Tambo, who had come in his capacity as Acting Secretary for the ANC.

Following their discussions, the joint council reported that Natal ANC's George Champion and Natal Indian Congress member Ismail Meer had toured the riot area in an open loudspeaker van to address the people and appeal for calm. On 6 February, the council made a statement – a benchmark for the opposition organisations, observed Ismail Meer, for it was the first multiracial meeting held in Natal[28] – that pointed towards structural as well as racial inequities. Some of these were blatant forms of divide and rule. Against the background of the Doctors' Pact signed in 1947, 'The Government wanted to split the opposition to its apartheid policies,' declared MB Yengwa, an active Youth Leaguer in Natal and a friend of Tambo.[29] In the Cato Manor Location, for example, the government had given Indians preferential rights of land ownership. Indians were permitted to operate buses, to the exclusion of Africans, so that they had a monopoly over transport in parts of Durban. Similarly, Indians were given trading licences, and open resentment developed along racial lines. 'Basically, the Government was guilty of inciting Africans to rise against the Indians who were clearly not their opponents,' reflected Yengwa later.

The joint council made its report. 'This meeting is convinced,' it declared, 'that the fundamental and basic causes of the disturbances are traceable to the economic and social structure of the country, based on differential and discriminatory treatment of the various racial groups and the preaching in high places of racial hatred and intolerance.'[30]

Tambo was signatory to this statement, and Ismail Meer recalled with some satisfaction how the wheel had turned. 'Tambo came to Durban in the midst of these riots... and what had been opposed by the Youth League – to work together with the Indian community – here were the riots which caused them to change their mind.'[31] And indeed it was the first time that Tambo had been exposed directly to new political and sociological perspectives of the oppressed, and a growing awareness of the historical sufferings and the exploitation of Indians, also a colonised, marginalised people, whose origins in South Africa lay in semi-slave conditions as indentured labourers torn from their homeland. He was also disturbed to observe that the culture of racism had seeped into the consciousness of black people, as evidenced by the Durban riots. Tambo's first-hand experience of these distressing events was to begin to prise open a new outlook on the complexity of race relations, identity and struggle in South Africa.

Back home, having won a number of seats in the ANC's national structure at the year-end annual conference, the YL's next challenge was to secure the province of Transvaal. Communists had clearly packed the 1949 election. David Bopape and Elias Motsoaledi both clearly recalled how Bopape, on his way to the ANC meeting, had bumped into Motsoaledi in the street.

'This is an omen!' Bopape exclaimed. 'You absolutely must come with me to join the ANC. We must vote as many comrades as we can on to the executive.'[32]

And that, recalled Motsoaledi, was how he joined the ANC.[33]

The Youth League had noted these tactics by the communists.

'They had an irritating tendency of sectarianism, to the extent that they would choose their own man when there is going to be an election,' observed Walter Sisulu.[34]

But Ismail Meer, a member of the Communist Party, saw it differently: 'We sat down, we must join the Indian Congress, take over the leadership. Similarly, the ANC must have progressive leadership. And we want unity in action.'[35]

In 1946, Tambo, seconded by Mandela and Mda, had tried to outmanoeuvre the communists. They proposed a motion to disqualify from membership all those belonging to other organisations, but the proposal was heavily defeated.

Whenever they could, the YL tried to sabotage communist initiatives, and Tambo himself was no angel. In the upcoming 1950 elections for the Transvaal Executive, he was determined to prevent a repeat performance of the previous year's provincial executive, well represented by the Communist Party. As the president of the YL in the Transvaal, Tambo turned to his acting president.

'The communists want to capture the leadership of the ANC and we dare not allow it,' he told Godfrey Pitje.

Pitje recounted Tambo's tactic: 'The Transvaal ANC conference is called to sit in Springs. Springs at the time was one of the most important areas of the ANC… We get to the conference, [Tambo] is leading us, and we have some very heated discussions with the communists.'[36]

These communists included leading activists such as David Bopape, trade unionist Dan Tloome and the distinguished JB Marks, president of the African National Mine Workers' Union and leader of the 1946 miners' strike.

'Oliver assesses our position as not very strong and suggests that if there is an election, a communist is going to be elected to it, and all the influential positions in the Transvaal are going to be taken by them. We must not allow an election. So what do we do, Oliver? "You scream. You do anything that will make the comrades not to be elected." We were a disciplined group that respected its leadership! So we screamed and shouted, and jumped on tables – and we succeed in breaking up the conference, so that no election was held.'[37]

By this time, Tambo had left St Peter's and was serving his articles in tiny, partitioned premises in the National Mutual Buildings. In May 1948, he had been fortunate – for a black applicant – to have been accepted by Walter Sisulu's conveyancers, Max Kramer & Tuch.[38] In fact, over the years, Sisulu was responsible for the making of a number of black attorneys and advocates. He explained: 'It was my interest to begin with, that when I came across bright young men – and educated – I would have made the suggestion to take up law. Perhaps it is because there has been a tradition of law in the ANC itself, but also because of oppression. You found that the knowledge of law was very important in our struggle – an important weapon.'[39]

For Tambo, his late father's dearest wish for the independence of his children resonated powerfully in influencing his decision to move from teaching to law. But it was still extremely difficult for any black candidate to jump through the hoops. For instance, by 1948, Mandela had managed to get himself articled – also as a result of Sisulu's good contacts – but had had to wait a couple of years before the law firm where he worked consented to promote him from employee to articled clerk. There were indeed very few law firms who were interested in training black attorneys. The white legal profession was as racially discriminating as any other guild in South Africa, with an innate resentment of any member of the oppressed deigning to aspire to a status equal to him- or herself. In the late forties, only a tiny handful of lawyers, usually those at the bar, could be discerned to be sympathetic to black people in general and to their advancement. Most of these were communists – Louis Baker in Benoni, who worked with Mandela and Tambo, Roley Arenstein in Durban, Solly Sachs – but also included liberals such as Ruth Hayman and, of course, the most respected advocate of all, Abram Fischer – a man who was 'warm and friendly, as committed as Oliver'.[40] It was, however, noticeable – and indeed pointedly and publicly noted more than once by cabinet ministers in the apartheid government – that there seemed to be a preponderance of Jews who were 'trouble-makers'. Sisulu, who had a sensitive nose for sniffing out insincerity and paternalism, chose his lawyers carefully – even more so when he was soliciting articles for his friends. As Jews of that generation, they had witnessed the horrors of persecution and genocide in the Holocaust in Europe, and had themselves, in South Africa, experienced blatant anti-Semitism. Ralph Tuch believed these experiences sensitised many Jews to the iniquities of racism and oppression in South Africa. 'Max Kramer and myself, we came from a Jewish background,' explained Tuch. 'We were Jews. And, as Jews, we were treating even our menial employees... as human beings.'[41]

As far as racism against black people in the legal profession and the legal system, 'there was a lot of bias and prejudice. I saw it myself – it's a known fact. That was one of the reasons that the South African system didn't use the jury system'. Tuch also pointed out that Tambo, at the age of 31 in 1948, was at least eight years older than himself – and Tuch had qualified as an attorney in 1945. 'That's how it was in those days – [black people] couldn't find articles. They became attorneys when they were in their thirties.'[42] More than 40 years later, when Tambo returned to South Africa, he lunched with Tuch at the Johannesburg Sun. 'He embraced me, he had two bodyguards. In the course of the lunch, he said to his bodyguards, "If it wasn't for Mr Tuch and Mr Kramer, I would still be a teacher." In other words, I had given him the chance.'[43]

But Tambo had more than one attribute in his favour. Unlike Mandela, he already had a degree, and held a respectable post as the Mathematics master at a prestigious school. The qualification entitled him to be articled for only three years. Secondly, his modest manner and neat figure were unlikely to ring alarm bells. 'You know, his appearance is all humble,' commented Thomas Nkobi, who knew Tambo in the fifties. 'You'd think he is one of the ordinary people in the street.'[44] And Tuch also recalled his first and enduring image of Tambo – 'modest, moderate, softly spoken; a gentle person, so that often my white clientele who got to know him would have conversations with him'.[45] This was an occurrence worthy of note in the apartheid days. With a quiet dignity, Tambo had a way of making anyone, even white people, feel comfortable talking to him without needing to assert their dominance – it just did not seem necessary.

At the end of 1949 Max Kramer changed professions and Tuch moved with Tambo to join Solomon Kowalsky at Charter House. While many law firms practised segregation in their chambers – 'large firms [with] 10, 20, 30 partners (I won't mention names), which had separate receptions, separate lifts, separate rooms' – Tuch prided himself on never discriminating against his clients.[46] Sisulu had, as an estate agent, brought the firm a number of black clients from Sophiatown or Alexandra, the only two freehold townships in Johannesburg, and Tuch was well aware that they were members of the ANC.

But leaving teaching meant that Tambo also lost his accommodation at St Peter's. He thus moved in with his father's sister, Emma, who lived with her husband, the Reverend Weyi, in Wattville, Benoni. The simple, standard township house was 30 kilometres from Johannesburg, and Tambo had to catch an early-morning bus in time to take the crowded train in the blacks-only carriage, often standing all the way to Park Station in Johannesburg, then pace the brisk 20-minute walk to the firm's offices. 'I can't remember him ever taking a day off,' recalled Tuch. 'He was always there. And was always ready to work an extra hour or two at the end of the day. He was never in a hurry to look for 5 o'clock, to hear the 5 o'clock whistle. He would often work until six, half-past six. He was also painstaking in his preparation – unbelievable.'[47]

These were busy years for Tambo. While he was articled, he conscientiously maintained his positions as secretary of the Youth League, chairman of the Transvaal Youth League, and executive member of the ANC; he also attended meetings, contacted members, arranged venues, prepared agendas and kept up with the correspondence. As an articled clerk, he had to continue with his studies by correspondence with the University of South Africa in order to complete the required examinations within three years. But there was a further impediment. Without electricity in the township houses on the Rand, Tambo had to conduct his studies by candlelight.

At work, however, he was determined to learn as much as possible to master his new profession. The mathematician in him, the scientist perhaps more than the philosopher, needed to pay as much attention to the correct execution of detail as grasp the overall concept of the vocation. 'He always did his work in a very efficient manner,' testified Ralph Tuch.

'He made sure; he often asked if he was doing the right thing in the early days. He wanted to be satisfied with what he was doing, that he did nice work, work which he himself was a willing learner. Always ready to open a new file. And I fed him with files from time to time, work which he himself loved; [he] would speak to the client, he was able to read the documents. He would know how to prepare an agreement, what goes into an agreement, what goes into correspondence, apply the methods.'[48]

One of Tambo's first cases at Max Kramer & Tuch was a dispute among the Bafokeng over land rights in the Rustenburg district in the Western Transvaal. He had a good knowledge of customary law and brought the case to a successful conclusion. Said Tuch, 'I remember tribal chiefs coming into the office... Oliver was at the helm of this case – all the investigation. We had a counsel, of course, but he was doing the investigation; he was the link between the witnesses, the chief and the counsel – extremely conscientious. Whatever he did he would prepare well. He had a good legal brain... He could debate.'

With regard to his style, Tambo put his 'good legal brain' to good tactical use. 'Oliver had a very moderate approach,' observed Tuch. 'He would put over his argument in a cool, calm manner, whereas Nelson [Mandela] was more forceful. But nevertheless Oliver... impressed people simply by his quiet way and his approach – and it was always a moderate approach, with arguments well presented. He always kept his cool... He realised that he was treading on dangerous ground at that time, that there were hostile judicial officers.'[49]

And did Oliver Tambo have any weaknesses? 'I never had an argument with him,' declared Ralph Tuch. 'I know none of his faults.'

For the Youth League, all their irritations with the communists came to a head early in 1950, when the Communist Party managed to obtain the official agreement of the ANC through the less-than-strategic President Moroka to support their campaign. The CPSA's customary May Day venue at the Bantu Sports Ground at the bottom of Eloff Street made way for an innovative form of a general strike, organised not from the workplace but from the community, in protest against the planned Suppression of Communism Bill and other apartheid laws.[50] This tactic became known as the 'stayaway'.

The YL leadership was furious; it was claiming the black constituency as its own, as an oppressed majority – a black nation, not a colour-blind working class. The May Day stay-away campaign amounted, they felt, to playing second fiddle to a rival organisation. They were particularly irritated because they themselves had not yet had time to act on the ANC's resolution a couple of months earlier in adopting the Programme of Action, to call for 'a national stoppage of work for one day as a mark of protest against the reactionary policy of the Government'.[51] The communists had stolen the Nationalist tactic. Determined not to hand the communists publicity on a plate, the YL mobilised against the May Day stay-away. Tambo, with Mandela, Mda and other Youth Leaguers (though not Sisulu), handed out leaflets at stay-away meetings, heckling speakers and even manhandling them, urging the audience to ignore the campaign.

In the event, at least half the workers in Johannesburg as well as workers in the Eastern Cape heeded the 1950 May Day call. But the day was also marked by a major tragedy, when the police – witnessed by Mandela and Sisulu themselves – shot into a crowd of protesters at a meeting in Orlando. By the end of the day, 18 people had been killed and scores more wounded by the police in Orlando, Alexandra, in the township in Benoni, and in Sophiatown.[52]

Shaken by the consequences of peaceful protest, Walter Sisulu argued that the ANC leadership was lagging behind the masses. As Secretary-General, he was wearing another hat, as it were. It was his duty, he felt, to be non-sectarian, and to represent all the members in the organisation. So, although he was still a member of the Youth League, he withdrew from involving himself in the difficulties it had with the ANC.[53] His role was further enhanced by the fact that President Moroka had an extremely busy practice in another province and was not a member of the important 'hands-on' Working Committee.

In keeping with his mandate, Sisulu began to push for the ANC to seize the initiative by calling a joint meeting of opposition organisations. These included the SAIC, the African People's Organisation, the Council of Non-European

Trade Unions (CNETU) and the CPSA. Youth Leaguers in the National Executive had made the tactical leap, which justified the act of working with other organisations – provided that the ANC was leading the struggle. From then on, this principle was to become a consistent ANC axiom. The move was also a face-saving solution for those in the Youth League. It enabled them to work with and learn from the experience and concepts of activists in other organisations, activists whose commitment they were beginning to respect.

In trying to explain some of the underlying rationale, Sisulu later recalled how Lembede, himself always ready to learn, viewed the communists: 'A man who was strongly nationalistic, Lembede, who would oppose the communists from a philosophical point of view, as a Catholic and a strong nationalist, yet he preferred to work with the communists because of their militancy, and lack of militancy of the older leadership of the ANC.'[54]

The shock of witnessing police brutality on a peaceful audience, and the manifestation of large numbers of active supporters of the May Day campaign, caused Mandela and Tambo to revisit Walter Sisulu's stance. They recalled how, in 1946, when they tried to exclude members of the Communist Party from the ANC, they had aroused the ire of dedicated non-communists such as Xuma, Champion and Dr Molemo, treasurer of the ANC. 'Their argument,' recalled Mandela, 'was that the ANC is our parliament and we allow all political groups to be members... united only by our opposition to racial oppression.'[55]

They had also met impressive people like Moses Kotane, JB Marks and Yusuf Dadoo, as well as people like Ismail Meer and JN Singh. By then, Mandela had been co-opted on to the National Executive. The relationship between the Youth League and Xuma had ended badly, and Mandela had been brought on to replace Xuma, who had resigned after a few weeks. Xuma must have been especially wounded that the rejection of him had included Oliver Tambo, whose calm maturity he valued. A public correspondence ensued, initiated by Xuma's letter to Thema's *Bantu World*. Piqued by the YL's 'betrayal', Xuma had written a letter to the National Executive, criticising Moroka and suggesting that he was in fact an informer. 'Oliver,' said Sisulu, 'was very close with Dr Xuma [but he] took a very strong line. He actually said, "This dirty piece of paper must be removed from the files of the ANC." So strong was he, because I think he believed that Xuma had gone too far, and that there was no genuine complaint. Now that is an indication again of Oliver's character. His integrity – that he was disgusted by this letter.'[56]

The outcome of the ANC's constructive response to the May Day events was to form a coordinating committee consisting of representatives of the Communist Party, the Indian Congress, the ANC and the Youth League, including Moses Kotane, Yusuf Dadoo, Walter Sisulu and AP Mda respectively. June 26 was selected as a Day of Mourning and Protest, but the event received less of a response than the May Day strike, partly as a result of the short time available to mobilise – just over a month – but it was neverthless not without consequence. The ANC's annual report noted that there had been 'a complete stoppage of work at Port Elizabeth, Uitenhage, Durban, Ladysmith, Evaton and Alexandra Township'. There were also partial stoppages in Johannesburg and the Rand and other major centres. The stay-away in Durban resulted in a thousand dismissals, and Chief Walter Kumalo was victimised and charged for his open support of the protest. The Coordinating Committee had started a collection to assist Chief Kumalo. The Day of Mourning had cost the Committee £10,000. By the end of the year, it was still paying off the debt, grateful for the generosity of the Indian community and members and sympathisers of the Natal and Transvaal Indian congresses. But, as the ANC report observed, 'It must be taken into account that this was the first attempt at a political strike on a national scale by Non-European people of this country'.[57] In fact, the adjective 'Non-European' itself was an acknowledgement of the oppressed on a wider scale. The date was to be invoked, and was later to become historically meaningful. ANC veterans also remembered it for its significance. 'June 26 was the creation of what you call today the Alliance,' Sisulu pointed out. 'For the first time, we were joined in national action by decision, by agreement.'[58]

Aware of the potential the campaign had activated, the ANC National Executive (which, of course, included Oliver Tambo) initiated a planning meeting of the organisations that had participated in the Day of Mourning, as well as trade unionists such as Phillip Gosani, Dan Tloome, Gana Makabeni, JB Marks and James Phillips, who had been the president of the Council of Non-European Trade Unions during the miners' strike in 1946.[59] In July 1951 the meeting resolved to undertake a 'programme of direct action' to 'declare war' on oppressive laws by means of mass action. A Joint Planning Council was formed, and the Defiance Campaign was conceptualised. It was to be launched on 26 June 1952, the second anniversary of the Day of Mourning.

On 24 July 1951, Oliver Tambo completed his articles, passed his exams and qualified as an attorney.[60] During his period of service at Kowalsky & Tuch, Mandela had often visited him to share his lunch hour with his friend.[61] The two men, so remarkably in political harmony, not only shared their ideas on the burning political issues that were rapidly igniting popular consciousness, but often talked about their day-to-day experiences in law. It was crystal clear to both, that technically proficient as white attorneys might be, black clients were severely hampered in communicating their difficulties to them or understanding their behaviour and responses to disputes. Language was a barrier, even when good translators were at hand. White lawyers' lack of familiarity with African culture, tradition and values impeded communication and therefore the course of justice. Removing these obstacles by providing black legal representation might give black people an outside chance in the law courts.

Sometime before Tambo's articles had been served, Mandela asked Tambo if he would join him in forming a partnership. Mandela began his practice in 1951, a little before the Group Areas Act was passed. Even so, the main difficulty was overcoming the Urban Areas Act, which forbade any black professional operation in town without the permission of the Governor General. After a long and complicated process, and with the help of his white lawyer friends, Walter Sisulu had managed to receive permission for his estate agency a few years earlier. 'I don't think the lawyers, Mandela and Tambo, ever got permission. I don't think they did,' said Sisulu.[62]

But the inner city was the only accessible place to be, so Mandela found rooms in Chancellor House, which was owned by an Indian who was happy to have him as a tenant. The chambers were well placed opposite the Johannesburg Magistrate's Court. Within a few months, Tambo joined Mandela. 'Mandela & Tambo' read the huge inscription across the frosted window panes on the second floor, the gold-leaved letters 'standing out like a challenge' wrote Tambo more than a decade later.[63]

The partners agreed to accommodate their inter-related aims – to serve black people and communities both professionally and in the political struggle. 'We decided when we opened the partnership,' said Mandela, 'that Oliver would concentrate on the legal firm, and I was available for political work.'[64] But this division of labour soon became difficult to maintain, particularly after Mandela was banned in December 1951 under the Riotous Assemblies Act. Despite his relatively junior position in the ANC, he was rapidly gaining a high political profile, and the banning confined him to the district of Johannesburg. As a consequence, Tambo undertook more travelling in the course of handling cases. At the same time as Acting Secretary-General, he was steadily being pitch-forked into more work in the ANC, which also required travelling to attend national meetings.

In their chambers, however, the response from clients was immediate and gratifying. 'To reach our desks each morning, Nelson and I ran the gauntlet of patient queues of people overflowing from the chairs in the waiting room into the corridors,' Tambo wrote.

The range of cases spread from civil, criminal and political ones. Simply from the desperate men and women they encountered through their work, the attorneys rapidly gained an impression of the impact of a racist regime on black people. Even before the Draconian apartheid laws, prisons were teeming with those convicted of a range of misdemeanours, from violent crimes to petty transgressions of statutory regulations. Tambo said it best:

'To be unemployed is a crime because no African can for long evade arrest if his passbook does not carry the stamp of authorised and approved employment. To be landless can be a crime, and weekly we interviewed delegations of grizzled, weatherworn peasants from the countryside who came to tell us how many generations their families had worked a little piece of land from which they were now being ejected. To brew African beer, to drink it or to use the proceeds to supplement the meagre family income is a crime, and women who do so face heavy fines and jail terms. To cheek a white man can be a crime. To live in the "wrong" area – one declared White or Indian or Coloured – can be a crime for Africans...'[65]

The list of legal infringements was boundless. And, as the firm became known further afield, despondent men and women travelled long distances to reach Mandela & Tambo, the only black attorneys at the time, and possibly their last hope. 'They came from Natal, the Cape, the Free State and from the Northern Transvaal,' recalled Tambo, 'and of course many from Johannesburg and the areas next to Johannesburg.'[66] The work of the attorney was to apprise as much information as possible – 'in our offices or in prison'. On a trip from Umtata to Bizana in January 1993, Tambo remembered a group of villagers who had come from Mhlengana, not far from Umtata. 'They went all the way to find us in Johannesburg and tell us their case... They had travelled all the way from here to Johannesburg, although there were many attorneys here [in the Eastern Cape].'[67] But those attorneys were white attorneys. Trained and skilled as they were in the ways of the ruling class, the clients 'still believed that they would do better with us'.[68]

In the case of the Mhlengana clients, some peasant farmers – including the traditional leader – had been arrested for refusing to plough in accordance with government regulations. A great many more arrests were pending. 'The case was how they ploughed their fields; whether, for example, they went down the slope of the land or along the contours.' The case was successfully resolved.

Mandela & Tambo also dealt with a number of cases under the Bantu Authorities Act, where traditional leaders, in Rustenburg and Sekhukhuneland, for example, were threatened with deportation for identifying themselves with their people.[69] Struggles against the extension of passes to women, and against 'betterment schemes', which in many areas demanded a programme of cattle culling, were two important issues that won the support of the chiefs, or traditional leaders, despite the intolerable pressure on them to abide by the legislation imposed or entrenched according to apartheid policy.

With Mandela banned and confined to the Johannesburg district, Tambo endured long hours standing at bus stops and railway stations, and taking tedious journeys, particularly in the earlier years. When he had to take a morning train to get to his destination, he would not go home to Wattville. Instead, he would spend the night at the apartment of Mandela's friend Ismail Meer, at 13 Kholvad House, just a few streets away from Chancellor House. A young man, an activist with whom Mandela had in fact clashed during the May Day campaign in 1950, occupied the flat. His name was Ahmed Kathrada, and he was to be sentenced along with Mandela and others to life imprisonment in later years. Kathrada was a little shy and in awe of the polite attorney absorbed in his work. He remembered that Tambo would arrive, greet him courteously with a charming smile and then immediately settle down to his work, preparing the documents and papers for the next day's consultation, or go straight to bed. 'I didn't really get to know Oliver that well,' Kathrada confessed. 'He was not like Walter, or Nelson, who would make easy conversation.'[70]

Apartheid's immediate aim of limiting the number of black people in so-called 'white areas' – there were no cities or farm districts where blacks did not outnumber whites – led to the policy of 'influx control'. As a result, the pass system was tightened; the Group Areas Act was designed to begin a process of removals from residential areas according to race; the Population Registration Act used pseudo-scientific criteria to determine the 'race' of individuals; the planned Bantu Authorities Act resulted in the tighter control of traditional leaders. These and many more oppressive laws were being pushed through the whites-only Legislative Assembly. The opposition United Party, still reeling over their unexpected defeat – and in the wake of the death of Jan Smuts – could only feebly and half-heartedly object.

Mandela and Tambo soon saw the effect of these laws on the day-to-day lives of their clients – the criminalising of ordinary black men and women who were trying to go about their lives. Wrote Tambo, 'Our buff files carried thousands of these stories and if, when we started our law partnership, we had not been rebels against South African apartheid, our experiences in our offices would have remedied the deficiency.'[71]

It was so easy to infringe the pass laws, and the number of arrests escalated sharply. Men were stopped in the streets and hauled off if they did not have their documents at hand. Police would bang on doors in dawn raids, dragging men and women out of bed, to the terror of the children. The new government poured its resources into new departments, creating a vast white bureaucracy to administer the apartheid system. Tens of thousands of Afrikaners received jobs in the police force, and as bureaucrats, administrators, clerks and civil servants.

The result was that the legal structure similarly grew to prosecute the legislation that was rolling out of Parliament. As the decade proceeded, magistrates reached the point where they were literally rubber-stamping pass convictions, processing a dozen offences an hour. There was certainly no time to listen to hard-luck stories in mitigation. 'A clerk, a simple clerk,' reminisced Mandela, 'could change the character, the whole future of an individual.'[72] Section 10 of the Native Urban Areas Act decreed that any black man remaining in a 'white' area for longer than 72 hours without permission (stamped in his pass book) could be arrested. The pass also showed the area in which he had been born and whether he had worked for the same employer for more than 10 years. If a man failed to meet the required criteria – and there were many more – he would be 'endorsed out' of the area to a village or rural area where perhaps his parents had been born but which was entirely unknown to him. He would lose his job, his accommodation, his children's schooling, his family stability.

'Our legal practice brought us into contact with such suffering, and one of course had to develop a good relationship with the senior official in the Native Affairs Department – which was not easy because these departments are very corrupt... There were very honest and upright people, but the average official wanted to be bribed, to be given money in order to give a certificate for that person to look for a job. And we in politics could never do that.'[73]

Nevertheless, sometimes both Mandela and Tambo were able to reach out to clerks or court officials, approach them and appeal to their humanity, and their clients were saved from the fate intended for them by law.

In most cases, however, the partners found that there was a slim chance of winning their cases against an apartheid law because the law was very clear. In a judicial world where all the magistrates were white and the accused were black, the system was clearly intended to preserve white supremacy. On one occasion (after their practice had expanded) one of the junior partners, Arthur Lethele, had a nasty experience in the town of Welkom in the Orange Free State. 'I think he was physically thrown out of court,' disclosed Mendi Msimang, 'because they couldn't tolerate his manners of cross examination – [he was getting too 'cheeky'] for them.'[74]

In fact, as black attorneys, Mandela and Tambo often found the odds stacked against them. Sometimes ingenuity and social intelligence (which each partner had in his own individual way) were more effective than knowledge of the intricacies of the legislation. Race and racism were deeply embedded in the social fabric of South African life, particularly in the consciousness of both English- and Afrikaans-speaking whites. George Bizos, a young advocate who had been at law school with Mandela at Wits University, worked with the firm. A good storyteller, he remembered a tale that so typically illustrated the day-to-day complexities, the muddle and the avoidable distresses associated with the culture of white South Africa.[75]

It was a Saturday morning, Bizos recalled, when he received a call from Oliver Tambo. The desperate parents of a young convict had arrived from the Orange Free State. Their son was due to be executed the next day. Three people had committed the crime, but only two had been tried and sentenced. Their son had told them that the third had just arrived in the prison, and that he would be able to exonerate him. Tambo was asking George if it would be possible to apply for a stay of execution in view of this new development. There had been one or two successful stays of execution before, so there was reason to hope – though judges tended to be critical of lawyers giving false hope to the condemned.

'Unsure of my ground, I asked Oliver to come round and arranged for a typist. I phoned Sydney Kentridge [a senior advocate] and, with his sharp mind, he advised, in matters of life or death it wasn't for Oliver or [me] to decide, but to leave it to the judge.' As it was the weekend, they were required to contact the registrar to arrange for the judge to hear an urgent application and draw up a certificate of application. The two lawyers then drove over to Pretoria in Tambo's newly bought sedan, a second-hand Studebaker, Bizos remembered. They found Judge Quinton Whyte and a representative of the Minister of Justice. 'The presence of Oliver seemed to upset [Whyte]. Oliver, in the meantime, was quite relaxed; he was doing his job.'

Whyte then telephoned the duty judge, Judge Bekker, who asked them to meet him at his home, but Whyte pointed out to Bizos and Tambo that 'it wasn't usual for attorneys to be present at such an application'. While Tambo seemed to accept the slight, Bizos was silently indignant. He was convinced that Whyte had invented this 'legal practice' because of Oliver's colour. His experience of other cases indicated that Bekker would not have objected. 'Don't let Whyte get away with this,' George muttered. 'But Oliver in his quiet way said, "George, this is not a matter to stand on our rights – you go in and I'll stay in the car". This was typical of Oliver's strategic thinking,' added Bizos.

Inside the house, Bekker read the three-page petition. He wrestled with himself on whether to grant the order. He asked the accompanying representative of the Minister of Justice for his opinion, who then undertook not to hand over the warrant of execution to the sheriff until the conclusion of the other trial. Bekker was very relieved and offered George tea. Mrs Bekker came in with the tea and crumpets. 'I didn't have the courage to refuse,' admitted Bizos, and they chatted for 'a good half hour' before he left to give Oliver the result.

'Oliver was delighted, particularly for the parents. I told him the reason for the delay and apologised. Oliver touched my elbow and said it was not important. [But] the saddest part is that Judge Bekker and his wife wouldn't have minded!'

Some six months later, Tambo reported that he had spoken to the third prisoner but he had denied that he had anything to do with the crime. Ultimately, he too was found guilty and all three were finally executed.

In court, Tambo's style could be quite deceptive. Said Mendi Msimang: 'You know, Oliver Tambo was very humble. You'd think he was one of the ordinary people in the street. But let him stand in a court to grill a witness. He changed completely, not to say he was aggressive. No, he had a way of using the language effectively, to his advantage; never showed any signs of being angered by some direct remarks from the other side. And that thrilled people. [He never lost his cool], never; and very calculating. He made an impression not only amongst our people but also amongst the legal profession as a whole.'[76]

Lancelot Gama recalled learning from one of Tambo's articled clerks about a rare occasion when a magistrate went out of his way to commend Tambo for his well-prepared and -presented case. 'He was defending a person and the way he conducted his defence was so excellent that the magistrate praised him and said: "This is wonderful. This is the first time for me to see a lawyer presenting his case like this." He did not harangue the other chap, even if the other man had faults. When he penetrates, he asks nicely, "What about this and that?" Draws him out.'[77]

But Mandela cut a different figure in the courtroom. With his regal stature and his tailored suits, there was a 'hint of arrogance around him; which wasn't really arrogance, I think it was for him an instrument to hit at this system. To say, "Look, I am as equal with you as with anybody else in this courtroom. We speak the same language; we are addressing the same issues. I am not inferior to you."'[78]

Tambo had a bottom line, however. Albie Sachs (who later became a constitutional judge in post-apartheid South Africa) recalled a 'disgraceful' legal episode in the fifties when Tambo, in presenting his case at a preliminary hearing, was asked by the magistrate to sit at the section of the bar reserved for black lawyers. Tambo refused. He was threatened with contempt of court and the matter was adjourned until such time as he thought better of it. At the next hearing, he sent his clerk, Godfrey Pitje, to explain why he was not appearing in court. 'And that,' according to Sachs, 'was an example of [Tambo's] refusal to kowtow to apartheid, with a very strong dignity. While he would be as courteous to white people as he would to everybody else, he wouldn't kowtow.'[79]

But very often compromises were necessary to get their clients off, and deft footwork was required. In almost all of their cases, Mandela and Tambo were defence attorneys or arranging appeals. Mandela, for instance, recalled the number of coloured clients who had come to the firm because they had been classified as black under the race classification policy. The consequences were serious, not only because of the humiliation of the whole exercise, the loss of identity, sometimes loss of family support and, in the crudely mainstream culture of racism, loss of status. On an economic level, being black, as opposed to 'Coloured', meant lower wages, jobs limited largely to manual labour and – worst of all – the imperative to carry the hated pass.

The sheer, cumulative portrait of the bleakness of life under apartheid was emerging, and it further radicalised both Tambo and Mandela. As the mass campaigns stepped up, they increasingly took on cases of activists arrested for not carrying passes, for defiance, for demonstrations, for strikes and stayaways. For these arrests, the attorneys provided their services free of charge. George Bizos recalled that some of his white colleagues with a predominantly black practice seemed to resent the success of the firm, and would complain that Mandela & Tambo 'would use the "Afrika!" slogan'.[80] Mendi Msimang, who was articled by the firm and stayed on for years afterwards, recalled that there were also a number of criminal cases, such as murder, robbery and theft (for which the firm charged the full rates). Mandela recalled one particularly high-profile murder trial that rocked the black community. After a night of partying, the son of a highly respected black academic had irresponsibly let off a couple of shots in the car going home. One of the passengers, a fourth-year medical student, was killed, and the family took the case to Mandela & Tambo. The black community was indignant, and there was some pressure on the firm not to defend the reckless young man – despite the impeccable reputations of his illustrious father and grandfather, he was regarded as a *tsotsi*, a thug. 'But it was my duty as a lawyer to defend him,' commented Mandela. Ultimately, the charge was converted to manslaughter, and the young man received a suspended sentence.[81]

The heavy load of civil cases also helped to subsidise the heavy costs of the firm.[82] Many of these included the task of untangling customary marriages. 'Somebody marries a woman by customary rite. Then he decides to marry a woman by Christian rites. Who is the heir to the property that is left? All those problems affect us, and so you had a whole range of laws which brought you into contact with the real living conditions of the people.'[83]

Unexpectedly, civil cases included hundreds of divorces – a feature of society that may well have reflected the strains of urban life, the dramatic departure from tradition and the hardships presented by the migrant labour system. Many of the civil cases were also related to the hostile economic environment black people had to negotiate: people who were unable to pay their instalments, instant dismissals, assault in the workplace, forced removals, arbitrary arrests or beatings. In most cases, there was little in the law to protect the civil rights of blacks. The big picture that was taking shape was nothing less than a need for revolutionary transformation. The first step towards such a goal was the Defiance Campaign.

There is no doubt that the inspiration for the Defiance Campaign came from the Passive Resistance Campaign, which had so impressed the Youth League back in 1946. They had observed and learnt a great deal from the Indian experience. They had learnt that, ironically, passive resistance could become a proactive response to inequitable laws. They had noted the idea of volunteers. But, qualified Sisulu, it was not to be a carbon copy of the Gandhi-inspired campaigns. It had to be tailored to suit the needs of a mass black movement in the context of the apartheid era. 'We didn't really accept the "passive" aspect...' admitted Sisulu 'Ours was defying the laws of the country – actively, not passively. We wanted to show the big difference between the two. That is why we called it a "defiance", deliberately.'[84]

The plan, then, was to identify the six most rampant apartheid laws. Mandela and Tambo were in a position to identify from experience how the most pernicious of the laws affected the lives of ordinary men and women. Many of these laws and regulations had existed before but were now reintroduced in a more aggressive form. In fact, confining the campaign to six unjust laws was not that easy. The ANC's report to the NEC observed that Parliament had achieved 'a record session' that year. '[It] was outrageous for its concentration on the colour issue.' Apart from the creation of a Coloured Affairs Department (in addition to the Native Affairs Department), repressive legislation passed in the session for 1951 included a Separate Representation of Voters Act, a Bantu

Authorities Act, a Group Areas Act, a Prevention of Illegal Squatting Act and a proposed Native Consolidated Amendment Bill, which granted almost unlimited powers to the Minister of Native Affairs over the lives of black people.

The Suppression of Communism Act – it became clear – had a far wider reach than its stated definition. Once the communists were driven underground, it would surely be the turn of the ANC, given its confrontationist Programme of Action and the already enthusiastic response of hundreds of thousands of black people, especially in the towns, to the May Day and 26 June campaigns. The pass laws, it went without saying, had to be targeted, as well as the Group Areas Act, the Voters' Act, the Bantu Authorities Act, stock limitation (which had been a cause of profound anger among peasants throughout the country since its implementation in 1939)[85] and the Suppression of Communism Act.

The first task was officially to inform Prime Minister Malan that the Defiance Campaign would go ahead unless the government took steps to repeal these 'unjust laws which keep us in perpetual subjection and misery... *by no later than the 29th day of February, 1952*'. The ultimatum was signed by Moroka and Sisulu, informing Malan that the ANC had since 1912 'repeatedly pressed' the government to restore 'the inherent right of the African people to be directly represented in Parliament, Provincial and Municipal Councils'. The input of Marxists was also discernible. The letter pointed out the economic exploitation of Africans, who were used – with the aid of the unjust laws – to provide the system with 'a reservoir of cheap labour on the farms and the gold mines'.[86]

The reply was, however, little more than a contemptuous snub. It came from the prime minister's private secretary and – reprimanding them for addressing the letter directly to the Minister – disputed that the ANC represented black people. Furthermore, he claimed, its arguments were inherently flawed: the differences between white and black, he said, were 'permanent and not man made', therefore it was illogical that they should demand equal treatment. Nor had they understood that the laws to which they referred were 'protective laws', designed to 'train' them. They seemed not to understand, for example, that the betterment and stock limitation laws as well as the Bantu Authorities Act had been designed to protect the interests and land of the Bantu. The letter then went on to promise that the government would 'make full use of the machinery at its disposal to quell any disturbances', and deal firmly with those responsible for subversive incitement. It went on to conclude by urging the ANC to cooperate with apartheid's 'programme of goodwill' and 'work for the welfare of your people in a constructive way'.[87] Clearly, the gap between Afrikaner and African nationalism, as conceptualised by the party in power, was unbridgeable.

The National Action Committee – 'We [Moroka and Sisulu], Dadoo, Yusuf Cachalia, the Secretary and President of Indian Congress... and JB Marks' – immediately swung into action.[88] To mobilise the grass roots, it called for 10 000 volunteers to defy unjust laws, announcing Nelson Mandela as 'Volunteer-in-Chief'. The President and Secretary-General of the ANC, Moroka and Sisulu, as well as Mandela and the Indian Congress's Yusuf Cachalia toured the country, holding local meetings in town and countryside, explaining the purpose of the Campaign.

'We toured the country throughout South Africa, and met regional leaders and local leaders, discussed the whole project of the Defiance Campaign. How we saw it, how it was going to be, and what we expected local leaders to do. We went as far as Transkei. Met even the members of the Bhunga of the time.'[89]

In the following months, the pace picked up. Popular freedom songs were being composed and sung. In Zululand, the chant of '*Mthetho ka Malane us'phethe ka nzima*' ('Malan's laws are bringing us hard times')[90] could be heard; the 'thumbs-up' sign was increasingly flaunted; the call-and-response slogan, '*Afrika!*' – '*Mayibuye!*' ('May it be restored to us!') and the cry 'Freedom in our lifetime!' was being jubilantly chanted at meetings; the green-and-gold ANC uniform, adapted from church garb and speedily run up by dextrous township 'aunties', began to be proudly sported at marches and other gatherings. The myth, symbols and ideology of a modern black political movement were in the making.

The popular response was keen enough to alarm the government. In May, it attempted to 'decapitate' (to use Karis and Carter's word) the growing movement by banning 20 members of the Communist Party under the Suppression of Communism Act. Those affected included leading ANC members such as JB Marks, Moses Kotane, David Bopape and JN Ngwevela, chairman of the Western Cape Regional Committee.[91] White communists were also banned – including trade unionist Solly Sachs, who was now no longer a member of the CPSA. But this response by the government seemed to confirm for the organisers that they had analysed the legislation correctly and Marks, Kotane and Bopape went on to defy their bans by addressing the public in Defiance Campaign speeches. They were duly arrested and charged.

The primary launch of the Defiance Campaign was held at Mloteni Square in New Brighton, Port Elizabeth, where a vigorous campaign was being enthusiastically upheld by grass-roots support. Tambo and other representatives from the NEC were on the platform.[92] Tambo was still focused on guarding the interests of the ANC in this joint campaign. He was aware that the ANC in

Natal had called an emergency conference, anxious about feelings in the province in the wake of the 1949 Durban riots. After a day's debate, the region had voted overwhelmingly in favour of cooperating fully in the Campaign.[93] But at the Port Elizabeth meeting, Natal speaker MB Yengwa argued forcefully in favour of separating the organisations for the Campaign. It would take time to develop a joint leadership, he explained. The ANC had to be seen to be leading its own campaign – the NIC had its own offices and ample resources, whereas the ANC was operating from Yengwa's office. Always sensitive to grass-roots feelings, Tambo agreed with him and, buoyed by this understanding from national headquarters, Natal arranged that volunteers would be selected according to the laws they were defying. Where the curfew laws were targeted, for example, only Africans would defy; and where the law applied generally, volunteers from both the groups would be selected. 'I had a very good relationship with my fellow NIC leaders,' explained Yengwa later. 'What I was concerned about was the harm that would be caused by a precipitate unity between the various racial groups.'[94]

In the meantime, the New Brighton launch was exciting much international interest. 'We had calls from all over. We had everybody,' recalled Ismail Meer. 'We had the BBC, *The New York Times*, and all of them for the first time. So the BBC was Robert Stimpson. He had covered the transition from British rule to independence [in India] and he had come down here.'[95] For Tambo, this was his first taste of the potential power of the international media.

Another, much larger meeting was held in Durban, where the newly elected Natal president of the ANC, Chief Albert Luthuli, and the Natal Indian Congress president, Dr Monty Naicker, spoke and pledged themselves to the Campaign. Support had not been lightly taken. In a regional committee that consisted of elites – 'two businessmen, a conservative chief, a minister of religion, two professional men' – 'the idea of going to jail was rather a new idea for the executive committee'.[96] This was the second time that Tambo met Luthuli, and he was again impressed with the traditional leader's sincerity and integrity. After listening to everyone's opinion on the tactic of courting arrest ('and some said they were not in a position to risk their trading licences'), Chief Luthuli spoke last. 'I too am prepared to defy the law,' he stated in a sombre tone. 'This is a very solemn declaration which demands courage and God's guidance.'[97]

So it was that, on 26 June 1952, small batches of volunteers 'defied'. In Boksburg, respected veteran of the Passive Resistance Campaign, Nana Sita, and Walter Sisulu led their group of volunteers by entering the black 'location' without a permit. In Port Elizabeth, a batch used the whites-only entrance to the railway station. All were arrested. They were sentenced to a fine of £1. Despite the enthusiastic rallies, the Campaign spread slowly, but in the major centres as well as in the small towns in the Eastern Cape several thousands were arrested. Sentences varied from £7 to £10, or up to two months' imprisonment. By the end of the year, the total number of defiers arrested had exceeded 8 000, and 20 leaders had been sentenced to nine months' hard labour (later suspended) for 'statutory communism'.[98]

The Campaign was, however, marred by riots in New Brighton, Port Elizabeth, following yet another police shooting. Several people, including a white nun, were killed by an enraged crowd. Oliver Tambo was subsequently sent, along with the ANC's new full-time organiser, Titus Thomas Nkobi, to talk to the traumatised community. Said Nkobi of that meeting:

'Now I remember, when I went with him to Port Elizabeth to go and try and solve a very complicated case; a case where actually five of our people were killed – they were fighting amongst themselves... We met there from half-past seven to about half-past seven in the morning. The whole night... We were talking to our people, the branch of Kwazakhele. But [Tambo] convinced those people that it was proper for all of us to unite to understand one another when we want to solve a problem. We must listen to reason, not hot air. We must not think with our hearts, but we must think with our heads. When he left there, there was sobriety in the minds of the people.'[99]

But the aftermath of the riots shook the confidence of the volunteers, and while the leadership roundly condemned both the violence and the police, support from white liberals faded. The government also hit back. A new regulation was added to the unjust law of statutory communism already in force by making it illegal to protest against existing laws, imposing heavy sentences of hard labour and/or lashes. It also arrested and charged 20 leaders of the Campaign, including Moroka, Sisulu and the Volunteer-in-Chief, Mandela. The Working Committee took stock. Brawls with the police had resulted in shootings and deaths in four different parts of the country. The new laws, they decided, could only provoke the anger of people further, shifting opposition away from peaceful resistance and consequently spiralling out of control. The Campaign was finally called off. The political example had been made, they felt, despite the fact that they had been unable to have a single unjust law repealed. But a further disappointment was to come from within the ANC leadership itself. When the 20 were brought to trial, President Moroka seemed to lose his nerve in court, insisting that he hire his own defence lawyer, distancing himself from his comrades.

Despite these major setbacks, the Defiance Campaign, conducted in the year of two significant and contrasting anniversaries – 50 years since the founding of the ANC, and the tercentenary of the landing of Jan van Riebeeck and white settlers on the shores of the Cape – set a benchmark for the ANC. The public support for the organisation had far exceeded the number of volunteers or those arrested, and membership numbers increased dramatically. At one point, they exceeded 100 000. There were few black people in the cities who had not experienced imprisonment as a result of the poll tax or pass-law infringements. And on the land, stock limitation and the subordination of the chiefs to the government were quite clearly recognised as an attack on traditional leadership and the homestead cattle economy. The notion of the Defiance Campaign of turning the system on its head to invite arrest as a political act was a new and empowering concept for the public. 'The stigma associated with imprisonment had been removed,' Mandela reflected. 'From the Defiance Campaign onward, going to prison became a badge of honour among Africans.'[100]

Through the actual process of struggle, the participants found, the Campaign had created a new mood of black confidence and assertiveness. For Tambo, 'the Campaign uncovered and produced a large body of people of all races, in all parts of the world, who were sympathetic to the cause of the non-European people and of democracy'.[101] The Campaign had taught them, he said, that a plan for cooperation confined to black people only was limited. This was an emphatic shift from his public position not five years earlier about working with non-Africans. The Doctors' Pact had moved the Youth League along a path of alliance of the diverse black people. Through the Programme of Action and through direct, active struggle, the ANC had widened its horizons still further.

'In the absence of an organised body of European opinion openly and publicly proclaiming its opposition to the Government's racialist policies and supporting the Non-European cause, the political conflict was developing a dangerously black versus white complexion,' declared Tambo.[102]

But, that said, while the Defiance Campaign had succeeded in stepping up popular militancy, it was by no means revolutionary. The All-African Convention (which had earned the ire of the ANC, the Indian congresses and the CPSA, and had been excluded from attending as observers in the initial planning process) rejected the entire campaign, accusing the ANC of 'criminal irresponsibility' for organising an inadequately prepared campaign, 'unorganised, uncoordinated, with the resultant loss of life, arrests, dismissals and feelings of frustration and futility'.[103] The ANC, furthermore, had 'sold out' the people by calling for the repeal of a few laws without a long-term, planned overthrow of the entire system. It commented sarcastically:

'If only the Group Areas Act could be withdrawn and the Disenfranchisement Bill could be staved off; if only the Native Representative Council (NRC) could be enlarged and permitted to discuss policy... Then life could be normal again. We could go on having babies and burying them; we could go on filling the jails with Pass Law "offenders" and Poll Tax "defaulters"; we could go on being dragged out of bed in police raids for liquor offences or no offence at all; we could go on being chained by the farmers for fear of our sons and daughters escaping from slavery to the towns... We could do without self-respect, dignity and human rights as long as we can get [a farthing] per shift in the mines and 5 shillings a month on the farms!'[104]

While rejecting theories that were divorced from active engagement, the militant young leadership – Sisulu, Mandela, Mda and Tambo – were asking themselves, behind the scenes, some of the same questions: Had the campaign been adequately prepared? Should they have planned a follow-up in the event of a flop? Had the vision suffered from short-termism? What was the ultimate objective? Walter Sisulu intimated the faintest hint of their thinking in his statement in court during his trial in July 1952: 'Congress had endeavoured *by every constitutional means*', he stated, in the context of giving an outline of the history of the movement's half-century of resistance.[105]

In the meanwhile, political developments were taking place. After Chief Luthuli had been elected president of the ANC in Natal, and had been actively mobilising volunteers of the Defiance Campaign, the government summoned him to Pretoria and gave him an ultimatum – either he resign from the ANC or he foreswear his chieftaincy. Luthuli had no hesitation in refusing to give up either position. It was up to the government to take responsibility for removing him from his post as elected traditional leader of Groutville, a mission in Natal and the family's home. In November 1952, Luthuli was duly deposed, and replaced with an amenable substitute.

Tambo was very impressed with the way Luthuli handled the situation. Before responding to the ultimatum, Luthuli had called an *imbizo* of his counsel of about 50 – mostly cane farmers, with some teachers and administrators. They met on a little hill in the Groutville mission-school grounds near his home.

'He was a man committed to democratic discussion,' commented the ANC's regional secretary MB Yengwa, who had accompanied Luthuli to the *imbizo*. 'He did not want to influence the *amakholwa*'s minds at all. He merely placed the matter to be openly discussed; whilst personally I would have imparted my mind to the people.'[106] They deliberated for three hours before the meeting emerged with support for Luthuli. After the Youth League's experience with Moroka, Tambo was struck by the traditional leader's respect for participative democracy and accountability to his people – an inspirational demonstration that 'a chief is a chief by the people'.

Luthuli was a quietly impressive man. Articulate, warm, sociable, with a deep and contagious laugh, he was a devout Christian, a lay preacher, teacher, leader, and adviser to the African sugar farmers within the community. It was during his extensive experience as administrator, counsellor, mediator, adjudicator and business adviser that Luthuli encountered first-hand the 'predicament' of ordinary, rural African people.[107] 'Chieftainship had opened my eyes,' Luthuli wrote in his autobiography.[108] Thus it was that he was drawn to join the ANC.

Tambo was also struck by Luthuli's clear grasp of African Christianity. But, despite his old-world courtesy and respect, Luthuli's faith – like Tambo's – was unexpectedly militant rather than meek and mild. Luthuli combined, remembered Nkobi, 'the Zulu traditions and the modern intellectuals – African intellectuals'.[109] In Luthuli's reply (entitled, significantly, 'The Road to Freedom is via the Cross') to the charge that, as a chief, he was being disloyal to the state by his political activism, Luthuli reminded his accusers that a traditional leader did not belong to the state but 'is primarily a servant of his people. He is the voice of his people', paraphrasing the traditional African maxim, '*Nkosi ke nkosi ya Bantu*'. He asserted: 'Laws and conditions that tend to debase human personality – a God-given force – be they brought about by the state or other individuals, must be relentlessly opposed in the spirit of defiance shown by St Peter when he said to the rulers of his day, "Shall we obey God or man?"

'What must we do to meet this challenge of being spiritually if not physically destroyed as a people?' His answer revealed a holistic concept of the notion of what 'spiritual' meant. It meant, he said, asserting one's human dignity; and this could best be served by joining the ANC. Also, he advised: '... Develop in you the spirit of resisting anything that curbs or limits the development of your talents to their fullest capacity. [And] cultivate a sense of service and sacrifice without which Africans can never gain freedom. Freedom comes only to people who are prepared to pay dearly for it.'[110]

Luthuli's response, Tambo noted, was to equate the duty of the leader to his people with the actions of the ANC, which defended the dignity and wellbeing of an oppressed people. Given that the Campaign was 'a most legitimate and humane political pressure technique for a people denied all effective forms of constitutional striving,' he asserted, 'I saw no real conflict in my dual leadership of my people: leader of the Tribe as Chief and political leader in Congress'.[111]

It was, in fact, this workable syncretism that impressed and interested Tambo since the two first met in 1949. When the disappointment in Dr Moroka caused the younger kingmakers to look for an alternative, it was Tambo who motivated most strongly for the man who had proved himself to be ethical, courageous and able to grasp the political essentials. In December 1952, Luthuli was voted in as president of the ANC. He was to remain so until his death. And until the end of the decade, the two men, both Christians and non-communists, both lovers of eloquent language and the power of the word, were to spend increasing time working together as elected officers of the ANC.

One of Luthuli's characteristics took Tambo by surprise. He discovered that Luthuli set great store on the opinions of the somewhat abrasive and impatient communist, Moses Kotane. Tambo recalled that he himself had been interested in Kotane as far back as 1945 or 1946 – they supported the same soccer team! – at one of the annual conferences in Bloemfontein. Now, through Luthuli, his acquaintance with Kotane was renewed. Years later, Tambo admitted that Kotane played a significant role in changing his ideas about the desirability of communist involvement in the ANC.[112]

'It is significant,' noted Tambo, 'that Chief Luthuli, who was not a member of the Party, and not near to being a member, on difficult questions on which he wanted advice by-passed his officials and secretaries and sent for Moses as he discerned this loyalty in him. He knew Moses was 100 per cent a member of the Communist Party – in fact, its General Secretary – but he also knew him to be 100 per cent ANC, and this gave Luthuli great confidence in him.'[113]

Despite the good impression Moses Kotane left on Chief Luthuli, several years were to pass before Tambo was persuaded to work in the political arena with communists, and it was only after Luthuli was elected president that Tambo refined his attitude.

'For myself I am not a Communist,' explained Luthuli. 'The Congress stand is this: our primary concern is liberation, and we are not going to be side-tracked by ideological clashes and witch-hunts. Nobody in Congress may use the organisations to further any aims but those of Congress... [We] are cooperating in a defined area, in the cause of liberation.'[114]

This strategic shift by the ANC signified a widening in its conception of the movement. It was soon to lead to a further development; a small perhaps, but consequential step of drawing white democrats into the fold. During the Defiance Campaign, there were whites who wanted to volunteer but belonged to none of the organisations that had planned the Campaign. Eventually, the ANC was persuaded on the value of white participation in sending a message to South Africa and internationally on the universal abhorrence of apartheid.

The Campaign had been going a good few months when Patrick Duncan, son of the former Governor-General, and others were permitted to defy. These included several communists, such as trade unionist Betty du Toit, Frieda Levson and Percy Cohen, as well as other young radicals such as Albie Sachs, Hymie Rochman and Mary Butcher (Turok). Their motive was to indicate to the public that apartheid not only affected black people but all of entire society. Perhaps the message was too subtle, or more likely it aroused resentment among the mainstream white South African population, but the press played down their participation – except for liberal journalist Patrick Duncan.

Shortly after the Campaign was called off, sympathetic white South Africans again raised the question of support. A few had provided material support – Rica Hodgson, in particular, was a skilled fundraiser for the Campaign – but besides their access to resources and networks, the principle of multiracial alliances needed to be taken to its logical conclusion. In 1953, the ANC thus called a meeting of about 200 white activists, most of whom were either affiliated to the progressive veteran anti-apartheid soldiers from the Second World War who had formed the Springbok Legion or were liberals dissatisfied with the opposition United Party's acquiescence to the evolving programme of apartheid. Others were radicals who had, for the most part, been members of the now dissolved CPSA. The meeting was held one evening in Darragh Hall, adjoining St Mary's Cathedral in the Johannesburg city centre. Oliver Tambo, Bram Fischer and Walter Sisulu were on the platform, with Fischer in the chair.

Although the original transcript does not seem to have survived, Tambo's speech was memorable. Sisulu was struck by his argument, which for him was a dazzling unfolding towards the conclusion: 'Oliver, in his artistic way of speaking, created a tremendous impression – not only to me but to the people who were there.

'Tambo's address was delivered with great eloquence and charm. He explained the aims of the Defiance Campaign, and the way the African, Indian and coloured communities had responded to it. But where did white South Africans stand – especially those liberal and democratic white South Africans who opposed apartheid? If they remained silent and uninvolved while a struggle was under way to end unjust laws, those engaged in the struggle might well interpret their silence as collusion with racism and injustice. Their antagonism to the state could turn into anger against the white community as a whole. The Congresses opposed all racism, including black racism against whites. But they could not fight it alone. The time had come for those who sincerely shared the Congress aim of ending apartheid to take up their share of the burden.'[115]

The audience was clearly moved by the speech. One of the first to speak from the floor, Bernstein remembered, was from 'the liberal group', and suggested ways in which whites could lobby in their suburbs for amenities for blacks, for example parks where domestic workers could relax. After more input, Bernstein stood up. 'A park for nannies is a dismal and insulting response', he declared. 'We have been challenged to make a principled stand against apartheid and the status quo.' He went on to propose (as agreed beforehand by his group) that a Congress-aligned organisation be formed, so the chairperson, Bram Fischer, put the proposal to the vote. Less than half approved. The liberal camp had been offended and annoyed that Bernstein, a known communist, had taken the initiative – a clear indication to them that the communists had their own agenda. Soon after the meeting, those who had voted for Rusty's proposal got together and officially formed the Congress of Democrats (COD). Bram Fischer was elected chairperson, although it was not long before he was banned and forbidden to belong to any organisations except those pertaining to his profession. He was thus replaced by the trade unionist Piet Beyleveld – perhaps significantly, another Afrikaner.

The Congress of Democrats, a tiny organisation with never more than 200 members countrywide, was forever afterwards to be stereotyped a 'communist front'. In an article in the left-wing *New Age* newspaper, Oliver Tambo explained: 'In the absence of an organised body of European opinion openly and publicly proclaiming its opposition to the Government's racialist policies and supporting the Non-European cause, the political conflict was developing a dangerously Black versus White complexion. Such a situation no doubt suited the present Government, but it did not suit the ANC nor the movement for liberation, and had to be avoided.'[116]

For his part, the young quantity surveyor Ben Turok commented on the distinctive political identity associated with the Congress of Democrats. Official apartheid was cultivating increasing bigotry in mainstream white culture, even among those who might vote for the opposition United Party. Those whites who joined the COD, therefore, were in effect making a clear break with their communities and even their families, be they English- or Afrikaans-speaking, or drawn from more vulnerable immigrant communities.

'I was a rebel against my class, my race and my religion,' said Turok, 'and I didn't give a damn.'[117]

These whites were clearly not accountable to their community, and felt free to make as much noise as they dared. Their antics startled even the ANC itself – 'You were a wild young man, weren't you?' smiled Walter Sisulu at Turok when they met again after 30 years.[118]

The black leadership, on the other hand, had from experience a 'better sense of race relations, and how to overcome them', observed Turok. The tiny white group, therefore, fell back on themselves, forming their own community, organising their own social events, fundraising, multiracial parties and picnics and Christmas and New Year's Eve events for the comrades. And increasingly, in the nine years of its existence, young radical newcomers brought in energetic backup to support the ANC campaigns, attempting to inform and sensitise the whites about the rationale of the Congress movement, demonstrating unreserved support for the non-racial values of democracy and freedom. It was this end that Oliver Tambo had in mind when he was mandated to initiate the organisation.

He continued to acknowledge the existence of the Liberal Party, however. Formed in 1953 and extremely wary of the communists, they were attempting to draw white members into more active opposition by calling for a franchise for all, but to be qualified by education and property criteria. Attorney Jack Unterhalter, its secretary, recalled a protest meeting held in Sophiatown, which was broken up by ANC Youth League toughs. The next day 'Oliver came to see me in my chambers to apologise for the event'.[119]

The establishment of the COD also had repercussions in the black political community. Unreconstructed Africanists in the Youth League and the ANC tended to couch their criticism in anti-communist rather than race terms, though, and so made common cause with the Liberal Party, with far-reaching consequences. But it would be another five or six years before these matters would come to a head. When they did, Tambo articulately explained the ANC's non-racial policy. 'Who controls whom?' he asked in an interview published in *New Age*.[120] Turning an old Youth League theme on its head, he rather cleverly challenged those who rejected any sense of inferiority. They contradicted themselves, he alleged, if they feared domination by a '"white" organisation': 'Those Africans who believe, or have been influenced by the belief, that they are inferior or cannot hold their own against other groups are advised to keep out of any alliance with such groups and, prevention being better than cure, to refrain from joining the people in their active struggle for basic human rights.'[121]

Increasingly, as Acting Secretary-General for the ANC, as well as a member of the Working Committee and Transvaal President of the Youth League, Tambo found himself performing strategic administrative and organisational tasks. Sisulu was out in the field during the Defiance Campaign, and Tambo had been elected to head a team to redefine the ANC's constitution – the shift to a mass-based movement. Oliver Tambo was stretched to the limit. The usually crowded waiting room of Mandela & Tambo swelled with more patient and anxious men and women as the Defiance Campaign began to take off. So overwhelmed was the firm that Mendi Msimang who was a member of the ANC at Western Native Township branch, 'quite an active little branch' of the ANC, was roped in.[122]

Mendi had attended Roma University in Lesotho and was a member of the Youth League. He also worked voluntarily, on a part-time basis, in the little ANC office as secretary to Walter Sisulu. There was no money to pay him, but he considered himself lucky to be offered a share in the communal packet of chips with Walter, who himself very rarely received his monthly £5. (Walter's wife, Albertina, supported their growing family with her meagre black nurse's wage.) When the two were very hungry, Mendi remembered, they would drop in on the ever-hospitable Pahad family at Orient House, or find Ahmed Kathrada at 13 Kholvad House, where they might enjoy a spicy curry.

During the Defiance Campaign, Mendi became a volunteer. Walter – who had just returned from a visit to Chancellor House in Nelson's absence – saw the crowded waiting room and was aware that a number of the clients had come for legal help for friends or relatives who had been arrested for defying. Then he spotted the young man waiting to defy, and immediately plucked Mendi out of the queue and told him that his contribution to the Campaign was to be outside with Oliver, guarding the firm.

'I remember us dashing away with a lot of registration documents that night when it was surrounded by the police – very late at night, accosted by the police along the way. But it was very enterprising, very challenging.'

Mendi thus remained with the firm and, supervised by Tambo, was articled as a clerk. The office continued to be deluged by anxious people seeking legal help. 'With all the arrests, and all the demonstrations that were taking place around the country, it was extremely busy. And it became so popular, even among the people who were not in the movement at all.'[123] In the process, the waiting room became 'almost like a recruiting office. People began to understand what was going on. Here were these two black lawyers defending them'. Andrew Mlangeni, who had been a pupil of Tambo's at St Peter's, remembered a time when he was desperately looking for his younger brother, who had disappeared for a few days. Had he been arrested for a pass? Had he been accosted in the street and beaten up? 'We were looking for him high and low, we didn't know where to find him, whether he was dead or in one of the hospitals or one of the jails.'

He went to Mandela's office for help. Only a lawyer had the authority to scour prisons and police stations. He recalled his surprise when he found Oliver behind the desk. He had not realised that his old Maths master had become an attorney and had joined the increasingly famous Nelson Mandela.[124]

In the meantime, Tambo's conscientious and focused attention on the many and unanticipated tasks was in fact a godsend to the organisation. The ANC's 1950 report, drafted by Sisulu and initialled by Mandela, had expressed concern over the tendency towards 'a general negligence of duty on the part of the officials of Congress. Positions are used as positions of honour, there is no response to correspondence and instructions'.[125] It was also necessary for the national structure to give direction to the provinces. The Cape's Working Committee had also expressed concern: 'Letters are not acknowledged. Reports, if any, come slowly. Finances are not recorded properly... Decisions of grave importance are taken by branches and sometimes not reported to HQ...'[126]

The organisation had changed qualitatively. It was no longer simply an annual conference. Ruth First had observed that in between annual conferences, nothing would happen. Shortly before the next annual conference, people would begin to agitate – lobbying and caucusing to get their particular people voted into office. But now the ANC was becoming a mass-based organisation. Steered by the principles of the younger men holding national office – Sisulu, Mandela and, in particular, Tambo – it had work to do throughout the year. The conference was being transformed into a culmination of a year's work, where there were serious report-backs, and accountability was demanded for the decisions taken.

With Luthuli's accession and a clandestine trip by Sisulu in 1953 to Europe and China, Tambo worked more closely with the new president. Early in that year, though, the government took its revenge on Luthuli for his disobedience. It ensured Luthuli and his constituency would rue his choice as ANC President over a post as docile chief. He was banned from attending gatherings so he could neither attend meetings nor make speeches; and he was confined to his rural home district, which prevented him from visiting ANC branches.

Luthuli was, however, permitted to write speeches and make statements. These he would discuss, amend and hand to Tambo, who would then take them to the ANC headquarters to make public. Much like after Mandela's 1951 ban, Luthuli's banning increased Tambo's travelling on ANC business. It took days to get to Natal, but as the firm expanded, he was able to afford a second-hand car – the Studebaker George Bizos remembers and which probably made the work of the Special Branch easier in monitoring Tambo's whereabouts. Their police reports were building up. Tambo was becoming increasingly active. Politics was even impinging on his professional life – they were well aware, by watching who entered and left the building, and at what times, that the offices were also used for political purposes. They watched, and bided their time.

Ralph Tuch, who continued occasionally to do conveyancing for Mandela & Tambo, observed: 'After he qualified and became active in the movement, I said to [Tambo], "You are a young attorney; you're doing so well. You are getting yourself so involved in politics it's going to affect your future... Don't you think you should devote more time to your practice and less time to politics?"

'"Mr Tuch" – he always addressed me as Mr Tuch – "I've reached the stage at this time of my life when I can't make my own decisions. I am going with the current, and the current is carrying me with Nelson Mandela – side by side, next to me, and I feel I am just going with him."'

'That was my conversation with him,' said Tuch. 'He said, "It may affect my future, my practice, my family, but I can't help it. I'm going with the current."'[127]

Tambo's sense of purpose was to last all his life. Looking back on his youth, Tambo was able to trace a pattern leading towards a single outcome – 'it was meant to be'. His plans for the ministry, a stable family life, administering to the wellbeing of others, was not to take the form he had visualised. Instead, trusting 'in Providence',[128] he was being pulled in by the tide of the ANC's historical moment. And this 'moment' meant more tasks that steadily exposed him to the public. His hidden militancy was not only being revealed, but was seen to be expanding to grasp an engaging strategy – the liberation movement had no option but to embrace not only *all* the black oppressed, but to make use of the entire nation's most progressive resources, regardless of colour. At heart, this was a greater revolutionary proposition than a fenced-in Africanism. In the long run, it was to prove to be a greater threat to the apartheid state.

Bit by bit, coil by coil, Tambo was unfolding his personal narrative. The head of the creature he was dextrously wielding would soon be revealed. Tambo the devout, Tambo the equable, Tambo the courteous, gentle and discreet was exposing the true nature of the state's agenda.

Then, in 1954, two grey-suited men pushed their way up the stairs of Chancellor House. With the arrogance of their race and the power vested in the contents of their folder, they shouldered their way through the waiting room. The crowds hastily parted to allow them passage. They brushed past the desk of the office manager, Ruth Mompati, peremptorily burst into Tambo's office – and served him with his banning orders.

CHAPTER SEVEN

Negotiating Partnerships

OLIVER TAMBO'S CLOSEST FRIENDS AND COMRADES knew little about his relationships with the opposite sex. Walter Sisulu, for example, would not have dreamt, he said, of initiating a conversation about girlfriends, even though Tambo regularly stayed overnight at his home in Orlando West.[1] Indeed, Oliver was so much part of the Sisulu family that when Albertina Thethiwe married Walter and moved into the house, she was surprised to learn that Oliver and Nelson were not Sisulu kinsmen.[2]

Tambo was a private person and very discreet. By the age of 16, he had lost both his parents and, in faraway St Peter's, had turned to spiritual solace. He had many friends who valued his warmth and sensitivity, and these qualities endeared him to the extroverts, who tended to be more interested in expressing themselves than getting to know the innermost feelings of others. Oliver was never really intimate with his school mates. At a time when most adolescent boys were discovering the opposite sex, exchanging sexual ribaldry and bragging about their conquests, Oliver was not a great participator. His emotional and intellectual energies were focused on his studies. On Sunday afternoons, St Peter's boys were permitted to call on the girls' hostel, St Agnes, and 'we'd make proposals, have girl friends'. 'Do you know,' mused Victor Sifora, who was at St Peter's both as a scholar and a teacher at the same time as Tambo, 'I can't remember Oliver having a girlfriend at St Peter's.[3]

'I hope I am wrong. Not because he was religious, because there was nothing in his religion which was opposed to relationships with members of the other sex. You know, some of us would be attracted to a woman because she is beautiful and that could be enough, even stupid in class, it didn't matter. Tambo was critical. And with both male and female friends of Tambo, you had to be independent of thinking, of action. In fact, Tambo was attracted to persons and personalities who challenged him.'[4]

Compared with his colleagues Mandela and Sisulu, Tambo married relatively late – partly because, as the only professional man of his family, he was caught up with other obligations. He was paying for the education of a number of children – his younger sisters, his brother's children and the extended family in Kantolo. His nephew Tshepang was at the Maria Rachias school, his sisters

Constance and Gertrude at Inanda in Natal. Gertrude (and, later, Alan's daughter Vuyiswa) went on to King Edward Hospital to qualify as nurses. Oliver also helped support his eldest sister Lydia. He took a keen interest in the education of all the children, and went home whenever possible. Despite the relative luxury of St Peter's – with hot water, electricity and orderly, well-balanced meals – he loved to surprise the folk at home with an impromptu visit, bearing gifts, crayons, jotters and good things to eat. He loved the sound of his hut at night – the rustling of the wind in the thatched roof, the buzz of the insects and small animals as they jumped, whirred and hopped within earshot, and the fresh smells of dry grass and wood smoke. Perhaps most of all, he relished seeing his youngest mother, always smiling, always bearing up, an optimist who could make things happen. In later years, he would enchant the children when he arrived in his green Studebaker. While he was teaching, and also as an articled clerk, his entire salary went towards educational expenses. In fact, Tambo joked about how, on the day he received his cheque, he would put it under his pillow, 'just to own it for one night before it goes off'.[5]

The two most significant cultural influences on the life of Oliver Tambo seemed, in a personal as well as political way, to be in opposition: the traditional, patriarchal and unselfconsciously polygamous family (despite his Christian mother) into which he was born versus the monastic, celibate lifestyle of the Community of the Resurrection. Yet Tambo did not seem to be seriously torn – like so many others of his generation, he instinctively selected the cultural practices that could be best utilised, discarding or modifying the irrelevant. The tradition of defining one's identity through society, sharing resources, and helping each other – in short, *ubuntu* – persisted into urban life. If anything, the African culture of sociability, hospitality and sharing was even more crucial for survival in the hostile apartheid city. Again, Victorian intolerance of sex seemed irrelevant, even as their Christian hymns, apparel and religious symbols were accepted and employed.

In spite of his caution with women, Tambo did have girlfriends. There were at least two relationships before he met his wife, Adelaide – a nurse, Nomsa Shezi, at the Coronation Hospital, and another young woman called Rebecca.[6] There were others, too, but he was so caught up with his spiritual development, the great political adventure on which he had embarked, and the effort required to effect his switch in careers, that for more than a decade after arriving in Johannesburg, Tambo was not ready to consider a serious relationship. His emotional energy was channelled elsewhere. In his methodical way, he filed away the serious pursuit of a woman for an opportune time.

Mandela, on the other hand, was unselfconsciously a 'ladies' man' – he loved women, delighted in their company and enjoyed his conquests, without necessarily looking for long-term relationships. Tambo, somewhat vicariously, enjoyed his friend's success with women – Mandela was 'appealing to the women', he later wrote for an international audience, in describing Mandela's nature and his political qualities.[7] Walter Sisulu, on the other hand, was more experienced on the ground, in both traditional and urban culture, and more mature. He had been exposed to the kind of hardships and struggles that the two younger men thus far had only heard about, but were beginning to observe directly through their practice. Sisulu had waited until his thirties before marrying Albertina Thethiwe, an attractive, sensible woman with an acute social conscience. The harmony of the Sisulus' relationship was an inspiration to Walter's friends, and, according to Mandela – who, in many ways, yearned for security and affection – influenced him into marrying young.

Of all his contemporaries, Tambo was most intrigued with Anton Lembede's somewhat visionary approach to courtship. Indeed, Lembede's search for a wife was a demonstration to his colleagues, including Tambo, of the metaphor of the importance of national unity, even in the choice of a wife. Like Tambo, Lembede had a strong spiritual disposition and a lively respect for women. Tambo observed with interest the two major criteria Lembede had defined in his determined and somewhat philosophical search for a life partner. Lembede was very precise about his requirements. He wanted to find an educated woman, a wife who would be his equal and companion in every respect. Secondly, in his mission of nation-building, he wanted to start a family with a woman from a different linguistic background. 'He vowed that he wanted to meet and marry the most brilliant woman he could find, rather than confining himself to his own ethnic group,' wrote his biographers.[8]

It was at a Youth League event that Oliver Tambo first met his future wife. A new branch in Eastern Native Township, adjoining the white working-class suburb of George Goch in Johannesburg, was being launched.[9] In 1948, the human scale of the place, its proximity to the city centre, its convenient public transport, its modern amenities – electricity (not available in other townships), garbage collection and sanitation – and its relatively stable population endowed the township with a coherence and a sense of community. Eastern Township, as the locals called it, was the oldest municipal location, and the smallest. Like all other 'locations' on the Rand, it had its share of poverty, but there were also a few educated white-collar workers. This was not a freehold township. All the houses were originally 'subeconomic', brick-built two-roomed municipal constructions without doors, ceilings or a bathroom, with the kitchen included within the living room. Over the years, some tenants had added a veranda or an extra room, and later informal shacks sprang up in the back yards for subtenants or extended families. On the near horizon, mining shafts and the yellow mine dumps were visible, and residents were constantly sweeping away the film of fine white dust that seemed to cover everything. The boundary of the township was marked by a tall row of pine trees, which gave it some semblance of pleasantness. Sand roads doubled as playgrounds, and modest churches, one senior and two junior schools, a clinic, a square, a shop or two (including a 'Matlala' chemist), and lively outdoor informal trading completed the landscape.[10]

The launch of a Youth League branch in this small township, with its high proportion of unemployed *tsotsis* or gangsters (whom an urban anthropologist described as 'the most intelligent and adventurous' in the community),[11] was ambitious indeed. Many of the Eastern Township youth who were able to find jobs were working on the neighbouring mines. A few lucky ones had found employment as deliverymen or cleaners in the city, while a select few were commuting to high schools in the township of Orlando or in Sophiatown. The township's only senior school, the Matloporo senior community school, provided education for just over 300 13- to 16-year-olds, their classes divided into three language groups.

The signing up of a sufficient number of members to form a branch of the Youth League was thus a considerable achievement. As president of the YL, Oliver Tambo had been invited to be the keynote speaker, and the hall was packed. He outlined the vision and the aims of the YL and talked about the ways in which members could contribute towards its mission. Then a 17-year-old schoolgirl from Orlando High stood up. Young Adelaide Tsukhudu was confident, assertive and determined – she had been selected to be a speaker on this occasion. Young people had come from Pimville, Sophiatown and the East Rand to listen to Tambo. Nozipho Mabuza, her co-speaker, was intimidated, and at the last minute declined to come forward. But Adelaide forged ahead boldly. She had prepared her speech and she wanted to say it: 'I said that we needed our own people to represent us in Parliament so that they can take part in the laws that govern us. And I said it would be the same laws that would be affecting them and so they would make sure that we are not being sacrificed.'[12]

After the meeting, Tambo congratulated the steering committee. The two girls were significantly younger than the average YL member (in any case, heavily weighted in favour of men). Tambo was delighted at this new development and wanted to nurture the branch. He promised to keep in touch. He was also impressed at the courage of the schoolgirl who had so confidently addressed an audience of predominantly men – and so began a correspondence, one that would last for a number of years. Adelaide graduated from high school and then enrolled in a teaching hospital to train as a state-registered nurse.

Who was Adelaide Tsukhudu? What was her family background? Her parents originated from Lesotho; her father was a descendant of the house of Chief Moletsane, of the Bataung chieftaincy, her mother of the house of Hlalele, also of Taung. Around 1930, they left Lesotho because of the series of devastating droughts that contributed to the destruction of the economy of a country until then famed as the 'bread basket of southern Africa'. The family moved a number of times, crossing the Mohokare (Caledon) River into the Orange Free State in search of a living. Finally, just across the Vaal, they settled in Vereeniging's Top Location, where Mr Tsukhudu and his brothers found employment in a steel works. It was here that Matlala Adelaide Frances was born 18 July 1929. Like Johannesburg's Eastern Township, Top Location has since disappeared from the landscape. In the 1950s, deeming the village to be too close to white residential areas, and as part of the grand apartheid plan, the authorities removed the residents to the new township development of Sharpeville.

But long before that happened, Adelaide experienced an event that deeply disturbed her. It lingered in her memory, and was eventually to direct her towards a path of political activism. In 1939, she was seven years old. Her grandfather, whom she adored, lived with the family. A major strike in Vereeniging had resulted in a clash with the police and a white policeman had died. Hundreds of men were rounded up and imprisoned, and the police went on a blitz in the townships to see if they could pick up further 'agitators'. The residents of Top Location could hear the armoured Casspir rumbling through the streets during the night. At four o'clock in the morning, loud banging on the door awakened Adelaide. Policemen were demanding to see the men's passes. Adelaide's father and uncle had already left for work, but her grandfather was there. At the time, only black men – the women's turn was still to come – were required to carry a pass. The old man, who hardly ever ventured far from the house, had misplaced this important document. Grimly, the police hustled him outside, and – despite his sore and swollen feet – made him march the kilometre to the township square. What deeply upset the child was that the white policemen were mere youths, and they behaved in a callow and uncouth manner towards an aged person, who in African society would have been treated with respect if not reverence, regardless of the offence committed.

Although the policemen kept chasing her away, the distressed little girl followed the group until they reached the square, where other men had been lined up. Unemployed, they too had been home in the early hours of the morning. Adelaide remembered that her grandfather was so exhausted by the time they had reached the square that he sat down on the pavement, and when the pick-up van arrived, they ignored the old man, loading only the remaining complement of men. Adelaide ran home to tell her mother and they hired a taxi to take the old man home. 'I was so hurt,' recalled Adelaide, 'and I said to myself, "I'm going to get these white boys. When I'm grown up, I am going to get them. It doesn't matter what it takes."'[13]

Adelaide's parents enrolled their daughter at St Thomas's Primary School in Johannesburg. It was, of course, a mission school – there were few government schools for black children at the time. Those that existed were built by the community, following painstaking fundraising efforts, with additional funds made available by the provincial government, provided that the school followed the official syllabus. Adelaide's family were Methodists, but so successful and happy was the little girl at St Thomas's that within a few years she converted to Catholicism. In later years, Adelaide Tambo was still in accord with the Jesuit philosophy of early training. 'The most important part of any child's schooling is the primary school, because that is where you are nurtured; that's your foundation,' she maintained. 'Certainly, my morals in life later were influenced by the teachings I got at St Thomas's.'[14] By the time she had reached high school, Adelaide had established firm ideas of what was right or wrong.

'I could be assertive. I could say, it doesn't matter who says what, *that* I would not do.'

This early realisation of her self-worth and special identity was to guide her throughout her life. It was to be responsible for her exacting high standards – of herself and others – as well as for her eventual choice of a husband.

So that she could be nearer to her school, Adelaide was sent to stay with her aunt in Eastern Township, known to residents as George Goch. The little girl was extremely diligent and was determined to achieve the highest marks. After St Thomas's, she was awarded a scholarship to Orlando High, which offered science courses. But the memory of what had happened to her grandfather had not left her. One Sunday, while visiting her parents at Top Location, she attended an ANC meeting and tried to join the Youth League but was told that she was too young. At George Goch, she met Manusi, a member of the Youth League. He had organised a meeting of all the youth in the township. Adelaide told him that she wanted to join but again she was told that she was too young.

'[But], you know,' Manusi replied, 'we sometimes have confidential letters that we want to send to branches, and we need young people who can deliver them, especially during the weekends when you are not at school.'

And so Adelaide, working with a girl called Magdalene, would board the 'Ten Down' train on the weekend to deliver letters to members of the Youth League and other ANC members. They stopped at a number of the 10 stations on the 'Ten Down' line – Kroonstad, Meyerton, Springfield, Evaton – and, once, even went as far as Durban to deliver a letter to Anton Lembede.

Adelaide had not seen Oliver for a couple of years when an incident occurred at Adelaide's nursing residence in Pretoria. An outbreak of salmonella meant that the entire residence was up throughout the night with diarrhoea and vomiting. Inadequate food had often been an issue in black educational institutions, the cause of many student strikes. The student nurses thus called the Youth League to assist them in making representation to the hospital superintendent. Manusi and two others consequently came to advise them on a strategy, which involved careful caucusing before the interview, refusing to speak to the matron unless the superintendent was also present to listen to their grievances, and refusing to be called in singly. The outcome was that Adelaide and two colleagues were able to recruit 300 student nurses into the Youth League. The following Sunday, the three took the train to Johannesburg to deliver the enrolment fees.

Soon afterwards, Adelaide received a letter from Oliver asking her to attend a Youth League meeting at Lady Selborne Hospital. Some of her colleagues, who had been taught by Tambo, also went along. Tambo met them during the recess and treated them all to lunch. Afterwards he wrote again, thanking them for their contribution to the conference. At the end of the year, Adelaide passed her final nursing exams, and was thus too busy to answer. She then received a reproachful letter, to which she replied only briefly. After the exams, though, Adelaide and her two friends decided to visit Tambo in Johannesburg.

Young girls loved going to Johannesburg. What did they see in the streets of Egoli? Those were early days in the annals of apartheid, before it had asserted its overt control over black opposition, before, too, the era of rapid economic growth in the decade to come. Demolitions, although never at a standstill, were not yet rampant, and the urban landscape of the forties was virtually untouched. Mandela & Tambo, Attorneys at Law, was conveniently situated opposite the Magistrates' Court. The ANC offices in Macosa House, near the chambers of Mandela & Tambo, were yet to move into more expensive premises in Pritchard Street in the city centre as the ANC membership expanded. The offices of the Congress of Democrats, established in 1954, were also centrally situated at 100 Fox Street, while the trade-union federation SACTU and a number of trade union offices, such as the Garment Workers' Union, were available to city workers in Kerk and End streets. Strictly segregated Park Station, some 40 years before the black taxi industry was allowed to develop, vaunted long queues of black people every morning and evening.

Violent crime was rare in the city centre, but there were pickpockets aplenty. They, and pass offenders, regularly filled the *kwela-kwela* black police vans that wended their way up the hill to Hillbrow, which adjoined the Old Fort, notorious for having held hundreds of thousands of black and white prisoners.[15]

Although they were not welcome, black people were still visible in the city streets: workers, beggars and hawkers; women with babies on their backs sitting on the pavement, bringing to town their craft work such as crochet and basket ware, or large, shiny red and green apples and perfect oranges laid out for the white passing trade; 'delivery boys' (always white in the days of job reservation) cycling precariously between inconsiderate motor-car and truck drivers , transporting boxes and packages to a commercial or residential destination; shop and apartment cleaners in their uniformed shirts and shorts armed with brooms, mops and buckets; construction labourers repairing roads or laying new foundations for the ever-changing Johannesburg skyline (these workmen could often be seen and heard, moving and chanting in unison to coordinate and augment their collective strength); nannies in starched white uniforms, carrying white children, accompanying their 'madams' on a shopping trip.)

Occasionally, one saw a few better-dressed black white-collar office workers. Few as they were, their presence in the city was precarious, for apartheid legislation subscribed to the employment of semiskilled whites wherever possible. Clearly unwelcome unless they were 'serving the white man's needs', street vendors of traditional herbal medicines, and black 'coffee cart' caterers were being relentlessly hounded out of the inner city. Nevertheless, 'legitimately' employed blacks with their passbooks in order continued to remain visible in large numbers in the streets. At lunch time, with no cafeterias for black workers, hundreds of people would settle down on the pavements, eating half a loaf of bread, perhaps washed down by a carton of milk. Many could not afford even this simple meal, and would while away their hour playing dice or cards.

Whoever ventured into the city centre was taking great risks if their passes were not in order. Fortunately, as black women, Adelaide and her friends were not required to carry passes. The girls alighted at Park Station and walked the six or seven blocks to Anderson Street, and then turned right, towards Tambo's office at Kowalsky & Tuch. But before they reached Charter House, they saw Oliver crossing the street 'with some Indian friends. We just waved to him'.[16] But a few days later, Adelaide was thrilled to receive a letter from Tambo. He invited her to meet him in Johannesburg. On her next day off, they met in Sophiatown. From there, he took her to lunch at the Blue Lagoon, a multiracial restaurant in Albert Street. The Blue Lagoon was one of the last such establishments in the city.

'That's when the firm proposal really came. So I said: "No, I couldn't!"' And she explained why: 'Boyfriends tend to demand things I cannot give. And I am not prepared at the present moment to have a relationship.' Adelaide had had a number of unpleasant confrontations with young men, and was adamant in adhering to her standards. She was impressed, however, with Oliver's enlightened response.

'People should understand each other,' he said. 'We must know the truth about each other. If there are certain things that you can't do, you can't do those things. And whoever is going out with you should know those limits.'[17]

Adelaide said she needed time to think about it, and one Wednesday, Oliver paid her a surprise visit. She had just finished a shift and the two went for a stroll around Union Buildings. 'We spoke and thrashed everything out.' And, from then on, the two saw each other regularly.

Of course, Adelaide was attracted to Oliver. Not only was he good-looking and a highly respected professional in an exceptionally well-paid vocation, he was also religious like herself, and thus understood and appreciated her principles, responding to her demands with maturity and respect. She also shared his political commitment, and told him about her childhood experience that had propelled her into seeking out the Youth League at such a young age. They would have lively discussions. Adelaide was not too intimidated by this serious, laconic older man to initiate topics of conversation along her lines of interest. She was a good conversationalist, an entertaining storyteller. She often bought a magazine on psychology and would send it on to him when she had finished reading it. Oliver, in turn, would send her political newspapers. She shared with him the frustrations of being a black nurse when all the matrons were white. She talked about the shabby treatment of black patients, and how she sometimes got into trouble for protesting at the behaviour of the doctors and sisters. She described to him the heavy hours, inadequate working conditions and miserable pay of black nurses.

Oliver and Adelaide continued to see one another every week. They used public transport, and met in Sophiatown, or at friends' houses, or attended weekend meetings together. Or they might meet at Doornfontein Station and walk to the New Africa Café, where they would have tea and sticky buns – the pricier Blue Lagoon was reserved for special occasions. Occasionally the Reverend Weyi might lend Oliver his car if he did not need it for a special event such as a funeral, which in African circles took priority over any other appointment, work-related or otherwise. After Oliver joined Mandela as an attorney, his financial situation gradually improved, although his obligations to his extended family continued, indeed increased. In the meanwhile, Adelaide qualified and began working at Baragwanath Hospital in Johannesburg, near Orlando township. She moved into the Helping Hand Club, a hostel for young professional women in Jeppe, a multiracial suburb not far from the city centre.[18]

The relationship between Adelaide and Oliver was nevertheless characterised by a series of negotiations that took several years to conclude. One evening, Adelaide was leaving Baragwanath when she saw Oliver's car driving towards the entrance. Pleased, she waved and as he stopped, jumped into the front. Just at that moment, another nurse, whom she knew by sight, opened the back door and climbed in. Oliver was clearly embarrassed.

'Hello,' he said. 'I'm going to my office and I think you had better come with me. I've got a lot of filing to do.'

'Oh no! I'm not going to do filing,' replied Adelaide tartly. 'The *two of you*,' she said pointedly, 'had better drop me off at the Helping Hand Club.'

She was furious. Had she wasted her time being open and honest with a dishonest man?[19] Back at the Club, she phoned Solomon, an admirer and the young headmaster of a school in Johannesburg, who had often tried to ask her out. He immediately made a date with her for the following night. Adelaide dressed up – she still recalls the dress, and the tassel arranged at the back of her head. Solomon fetched her in his Citroën and, after a film at the Rio, a cinema at the bottom end of Market Street, they went on to dinner at the Blue Lagoon. But she felt terribly uncomfortable when she saw a group of Youth Leaguers at another table. A grinning Joe Molefe came over to say hello and to be introduced to her escort. Then another came, and another. Cheeks burning, Adelaide asked Solomon if they could leave, but as they walked towards his car, who should come driving down Von Weilligh Street? Oliver. He stopped the car and greeted them. Adelaide was carrying a packet of grapes and a box of chocolates her date had given her and Solomon held a bunch of flowers he had bought for her.

'Could I have a word with you?' asked Oliver. Solomon walked on while Oliver asked Adelaide to get into the car. Then he locked the doors and drove off.

'Stop, stop!' shouted Adelaide, 'I'm with that gentleman!'

'No,' Oliver said calmly, 'I want to us to go somewhere.' And he drove on. Adelaide, upset and angry, kept up a stony silence. Eventually they arrived at a wedding in Benoni, where a crowd of people pressed forward to greet them. Adelaide had no option but to interact with them. On the way home after the wedding, Oliver offered to take Adelaide to see her family as he was dealing with a case in Vereeniging on the Monday. Sulkily, she accepted.

The next morning, as her mother, Nono, opened the door, Adelaide burst into tears. 'Why is my child crying?' exclaimed Nono. 'Silly Nguni man!'[20]

She led her daughter to her bed, took off her shoes and hat, gave her two codeine tablets, and told her to sleep. When Adelaide awoke after a couple of hours, her mother had gone out and bought a 'pink piqué dress' – piqué, a new technology in textiles, was all the rage in the fifties. Adelaide got up, washed her face and put it on. Then she told her mother what had happened.

'Listen to me,' instructed her mother. 'A girl never asks a man about details. He is your boyfriend, not your husband. He is free to pick and choose whomever he wants. Remember that. You have one who wants to be your husband – if not, there will be somebody else.'[21]

Adelaide never spoke to Oliver about the episode. Soon afterwards, when she went to work in a hospital in Ladysmith (during which time she introduced Lancelot Gama – now a medical doctor – to his future wife, a nurse), she received a remorseful letter from Tambo. He was ashamed of what had happened, especially as her family had been so hospitable when he returned to take Adelaide home that evening. They had slaughtered a sheep, and the youngsters in the family had climbed the peach trees to pick them both fruit to take back with them. 'Am I worth their efforts?' he wondered in his letter. 'But this is all over now, and we must start on a new slate.' It was not long, then, before they agreed to marry, and set about planning the wedding.

Their vicissitudes were not over, however. Oliver and Adelaide had to overcome the reluctance of her family to give her away to an outsider – and then there was also the question of their differing religions.

'Have you met his people?' asked the family dubiously. The silent stranger was rapidly becoming known as one of South Africa's first black attorneys, but the Tsukhudus were wary of the 'Nguni man' with the ritually scarred face and Mpondo hairstyle. Nor was he tall, showy or glamorous, like Dr 'Boetie' Padi, the son of their good friends, into whose family they would have dearly loved their daughter to marry. 'He [Boetie] spoke the same language as I spoke.'

In fact, ethnic prejudice was not uncommon, even in metropolitan Johannesburg. At the time, Sesotho speakers predominated in the townships, and Xhosas had a reputation of 'being wily and deceitful'. Furthermore, most were migrant workers – their commitment was to their homesteads in the Eastern Cape. In Eastern Township, the derogatory term for Zulu and Xhosa speakers was *magantshega*, referring to the traditional leather apron worn by otherwise naked men to cover themselves.[22] Adelaide's grandmother, who had a keen mind, and was the only one in the family who understood her granddaughter's politics, warned Adelaide. 'Don't be *stupido*,' she cautioned her. 'You don't know where this one comes from. From my own experience, these people who come from that part of the world, what they do is come here and they marry our girls, then at some stage they just leave them and go back to their homes.'

'You are talking about mine workers,' responded Adelaide. 'I am talking about an educated man.'[23]

Yet her grandmother's warning was to prove ironic – in the years to come, Adelaide and her children were to see her husband at almost annual intervals.

The other contested issue in Oliver and Adelaide's courtship regarded their individual religious affiliation, and took some time to resolve. From the outset, Oliver had made it clear that he respected her faith, but Adelaide was nevertheless caught in a bind: the Church insisted that if she married in the Catholic Church, her children would have to be raised as Catholics. Oliver was bothered by this imposition: 'I can't decide on behalf of people who are not yet born,' he rejoined, nettled.[24]

Matters came to a head, though, when he decided to go into the ministry. The difficulty was that the wife of an Anglican minister would be expected to assist in counselling the Women's Union in the congregation – an important interactive role for the minister's wife – and thus belong to the same church as her husband. Adelaide was most upset at the thought that she would need to renounce her religion, and 'cried and cried'.[25] She told Oliver to 'look for somebody else'. She would have to give up the man she loved – this was the sacrifice she was being called upon to make for her God and her Church. To her surprise, her aunt and her cousins in George Goch were not impressed. Her cousin, Gladys Tuge, bluntly told her that she liked Oliver – he was tolerant, friendly and unpretentious despite his high professional status. 'Look, if you don't want to marry Oliver, say so. Don't keep making a string of excuses. It's becoming boring!' Adelaide's aunt also lost patience. 'You want to marry the man, yet you want to make the decisions. No, it is not done,' she declared. 'Not in our society. I don't know where you go and what people you meet, but in our society we don't do things like that.'[26]

Oliver made a special appointment to discuss the situation over a meal at the Blue Lagoon:

'I have been waiting for you all this time. I thought we loved each other enough to sympathise with each other's situation. I can't be a bachelor all my life. I want to join the ministry; I want to do many other things as well, but all these things are dependent on my marital status. There are things that you didn't want to do, and I had to meet you halfway. This might be bigger than these things, or perhaps less important. But it is my request that you do not marry anybody else. I want to marry you.'[27]

This was an honest appeal, but Adelaide was still in a quandary. But then the decision was made for her. She persuaded Oliver to meet Father Kelley, who ministered to her and whom she trusted to understand her dilemma. When they arrived, however, they found that Father Kelley had gone on leave to Ireland, so the couple met with a substitute priest. This priest's injunctions to Oliver, as a non-Catholic, seemed to be so patronising and bullying that Adelaide cut the meeting short. Oliver, having taken the trouble to get to the meeting, protested that he was interested in finding out more about the Catholic dogma. True to his nature, he was prepared to ignore personal slights and stay on until he had found out what he wanted to learn. Adelaide was struck by Oliver's generosity – for her sake, he had courteously put up with condescension and presumption. She determined there and then that they should have an Anglican wedding.

Oliver moved quickly. They drove to Rissik Street, where Oliver bought Adelaide a diamond ring. The next day, they held a ceremony to bless the ring, and the following Saturday, Oliver took Adelaide to Vereeniging to break the news to her family. Despite some initial reservation, her parents agreed to meet Oliver's people, and representatives of the Tambo family duly came to visit the family. Oliver gave them everything that was needed to conclude the arrangements for a marriage, and the negotiations began. But unexpectedly, the family asked for £300 for *lobola*[28] – an unheard-of amount in those days. The usual *lobola* for an educated city woman was in the region of £70–80. Oliver, though a successful attorney, did not make anything like as much money as he might have, because the firm defended many cases *pro Deo*. He had family obligations, and now he was about to undertake the responsibility of starting up a new home. Furthermore, as an ordained minister, which he expected to be soon, his income would shrink considerably. In the Anglican Church, as in others, a huge disparity existed between the stipends of African and white priests.[29]

Again, Adelaide took the initiative, stepping out of line with tradition. After church one Sunday, she sent her cousin Ellen on a picnic with Oliver, and then confronted her family at the lunch table. She announced firmly that she would marry Oliver with or without *lobola*. Her family were shocked and angry.

'How dare you! How much do you know about life to say you know better than anyone else? These are our traditions, and we will not be told what to do by you, young lady!' her uncle burst out.

The rest of the meal was eaten in silence. After Oliver and Ellen returned, Adelaide began to pack her things. Her grandmother came into the room, then left. Her mother came in nervously. She begged Adelaide not to be so rash as to marry in a magistrate's court. 'Don't disgrace me. I'll talk to your father and uncle so that we can come to some agreement.'[30]

And so, with *lobola* settled, the wedding date was fixed: 22 December 1956.

So, what was one to make of Oliver and Adelaide's relationship? Tambo's friends were struck by Adelaide's drive, her strong will. Yet, said Victor Sifora perceptively, Tambo was attracted to people who knew their minds. As soon as Tambo saw that one could take a stand, and defend it articulately, he would become interested in that person – 'male or female'. Sifora, who considered himself to be very close to Tambo, was at first puzzled by Oliver's choice of a girlfriend. Adelaide and Oliver seemed diametrically opposed.

'It was only after Tambo had fallen in love with Adelaide and ultimately married her that I looked at Adelaide a little more closely and realised that they complemented each other. In other words, whatever it was that was lacking in Tambo's personality, Adelaide supplied. They were stronger together than apart. Tambo apart was stubborn, argumentative, critical; he did not speak much. Adelaide could speak, you know.'[31]

It is interesting to note that, in the long run, it was Oliver whose values, where they mattered to him, won out. By his integrity, by his genuine respect for his partner's differences and for her identity, he wore away Adelaide's insecurities about her identity. In time, of her own accord, she began to defer to his wishes. Contrary to the preference of her family, she spurned the 'glamour boy' who was also a medical doctor and a member of her own people. In the end, too, Adelaide converted to the Anglican Church. And, in spite of her love of finery and luxuries – all too restricted in the bleakness of black South African life – she was prepared to curtail these to follow her husband into the low-paid ministry. This subtle but focused approach to relationships, whether personal or political, was a characteristic of Tambo that was to be manifested time and again throughout his years in exile.

Psychologists speak about a 'couple power', which complements and works in synergy.[32] In the case of Adelaide and Oliver, she recognised and embraced his mental power: the intelligence, perfectionism, ability and capability to become the leader and satisfy her need for status. Yet, beneath her flamboyance, there was something more spiritual – they were not as far apart as one would assume. In turn, Oliver recognised, perhaps subconsciously, that Adelaide could express on his behalf his own private ambition. For Oliver, ambition would always come second to the need for a greater vision – the liberation and upliftment of his people. Yet, in order to fulfil his dream, he needed to become something more than the average person – he needed to become a leader. Beneath a rather austere, polite, restrained man of God and of the people was an Oliver with a lively sense of humour, an exuberance, an aesthetic appreciation of fine objects and elegant clothes. In Oliver Tambo there existed, so to speak, a man with a big bright hat – only he could not wear it, so Adelaide wore it for him.

In political life, too, Tambo had spotted in Mandela a man who was 'a born leader'. As Tambo pointed out in his memoirs, he had always had 'an aversion to the limelight'. Being placed in the position of *primus inter pares*, to use his own words, was not for him.[33] His ambition and his energies were focused instead on scholarly excellence. In his memories of his school days, Tambo spent more time celebrating his academic success in the matriculation results than he did on turning down the position of head prefect at St Peter's. In the ANC, he preferred to work in a team, and to be able to employ his intellectual skills in a role of critical engagement. Tambo had already confessed to Ralph Tuch: 'I am going with the current; and the current is carrying me with Nelson Mandela.'[34] The metaphor was hardly one that extolled individualism.

In the meantime, apartheid legislation continued to cause consternation. In 1953, as the Defiance Campaign was ending, a Criminal Laws Amendment Act made it illegal to oppose a law by unlawful means once it had been passed – for example, in an illegal demonstration. This was intended to prevent any further mass civil disobedience. The penalty included 10 lashes, three years' jail and a fine of £300. The Public Safety Act, passed in the same year, allowed for the declaration of a State of Emergency, giving the government powers to arrest suspicious persons, without releasing their names for 30 days. The Reservation of Separate Amenities Act provided (after a legal challenge following the defiance of an African passenger who entered a 'white' waiting room) that separate facilities did not need to be 'substantially similar to or of the same character, standard, extent or quality' as those of any 'other race'.[35]

The year 1953 heralded an election, and the government was determined to put the leadership of black opposition out of action. A succession of bans included Walter Sisulu, Nelson Mandela and Chief Luthuli. Bans took various forms. Some opponents were 'banished' from their villages and sent to live in isolated rural areas; others were prohibited from entering factories, or educational institutions, which effectively rendered many unemployed. Bans included 'gagging' – their opinions and statements were not permitted to be broadcast or published – and they were forbidden to attend gatherings. A 'gathering' was defined as 'two or more people', which meant that a banned person was not permitted to talk to more than one person at a time or, in fact, be in the same room with more than one person.

Oliver Tambo was banned in 1954, but while forbidden to address meetings or attend gatherings, his banning order did not require him to resign from the ANC, so he continued to act as Secretary-General.

But, of all the crude, racially defined social engineering that was unrolling before black people, one of the most disturbing for Tambo was the Bantu Education Act. It seemed designed deliberately to withhold from black people the skills and technology of the twentieth century. 'This is the most evil Act of all,' Oliver told advocate Sidney Kentridge. He was clearly outraged. 'I fear for the future of our children, and for the generations of children to come.'[36]

Education had been the motor for Tambo's personal transformation. It had supplied him with the tools to challenge the ruling system and to fight back. It had enabled him to utilise the cultural weapons of the colonisers, turning them to his favour. As a successful teacher himself, he was already seeing the fruits of his own labours; his former students were making their mark for the advancement of black society in the Youth League and in their professions. Now, in the absence of the vote, of freedom of movement, of land and home ownership, and many other basic human rights, even this remaining, important medium of progress was to be cynically stood on its head.

The Bantu Education Act, which was also passed in 1953, decreed that all black education was to be separated from the Department of Education and transferred to the Department of Native Affairs. All non-government schools would lose their subsidies unless they complied and turned over their schools to the Department of Native Affairs. Flawed as black education had been before – and with only a third of the black school-going population able to attend school – the apartheid vision appalled black men and women with its malignant intent. In his motivation for passing the bill, Dr HF Verwoerd, Minister of Native Affairs, notoriously explained (denying, even in metaphor, the humanity of Africans): 'The Native must not be subject to a school system which draws him away from his own community, and misleads him by showing him the green pastures of European society in which he is not allowed to graze… I just want to remind the Honourable Members of Parliament that if the Native in South Africa is being taught to expect that he will lead his adult life under the policy of equal rights, he is making a big mistake.'[37]

In his view, a 'suitable' education for black students included firstly religion, a three-hour school day, with teachers working morning and afternoon shifts, and gardening and maintenance courses executed by practising on the school buildings and its grounds – an augmentation to the syllabus that certainly did not feature in the curriculum of white children. As Henry Makgothi, graduate of St Peter's and president of the Transvaal Youth League, noted, the syllabus provided for 'a smattering of English and Afrikaans in order to understand the commands of their bosses', but excluded History or Geography. The budget for the education of black children in 1951–2 was £7 5s. and 8d per pupil, compared with £43 8s. and 8d per white pupil. The gross disparity remained throughout the apartheid era.

The ANC viewed the new legislation as an act of conspiracy against the African people. The Act mocked the very notion of education – the one colonial resource which, despite its flaws, had inspired millions of mothers, fathers, grandparents and extended families to sacrifice hard-earned income, even to live in poverty for the advancement of their children. Education was the principal reason that so many women in the towns brewed beer illegally – risking fines, police and sexual harassment and imprisonment for a better future for their children. But now, 'Bantu Education' was to be manipulated to produce generations of black servants of apartheid.

There was confusion, though, within the ANC leadership on how to deal with this blow. The 1954 conference in Durban rejected the recommendation that schools throughout the country be boycotted for only a week – it favoured a permanent boycott. But ZK Matthews opposed this radical resolution. In his view, it was a foolhardy act of bravado by the Transvaal members of the NEC. Most prominent among these advocates of the militant approach was Oliver Tambo, who later wrote to Matthews that he himself had been a proponent of boycott 'from the beginning'.[38] Along with Trevor Huddleston, Tambo reacted unambiguously. Mandated by the NEC, he convened a national conference of a range of organisations in Port Elizabeth, which established a council called the African Education Movement. Whatever the tactical difficulties, the African community was united, in Tambo's words, in its condemnation of 'this tyrannical measure'.[39] Through the Church, all but one of the Anglican mission schools in Johannesburg were closed down on the day that the Act was promulgated – 1 April 1955. These included the Church of Christ the King in Sophiatown and St Peter's. Trevor Huddleston recalled the popular song sung by Sophiatown children at the time:

> There are two ways for Africa.
> One way leads to Congress,
> And one way to Verwoerd.
> Down with Bantu Education, down!
> Down with Bantu Education, down! [40]

On the Rand, 6 000 children boycotted school. The ANC NEC accepted in principle the formation of alternative schooling. But because the government forbade educational institutions that were not registered, the movement was obliged to form 'cultural clubs'. Textbooks, blackboards or other trappings of formal classrooms were forbidden. Teachers were renamed 'leaders', and knowledge was transmitted through songs, drama, poetry and even storytelling.

But the boycott tactic proved to be complicated. 'Events proved that a boycott of a temporary nature would have the correct strategy,' observed Walter Sisulu subsequently.[41] Not only did Verwoerd threaten to expel children who boycotted school but teachers were also dismissed. Indeed, during the boycotts, Verwoerd selectively retrenched 116 teachers because of the drop in numbers. It was not surprising, then, that many teachers were either obliged to continue with their government jobs, or openly oppose the boycott as irresponsible because it was simply serving to 'shift the burden of the struggle on the backs of our children'.[42] Nevertheless, there was a tremendous spirit behind the boycott. No measure, not even the pass laws, had such an impact on African people; the campaign affected all strata of society, in urban and rural areas – diverse peoples and schools – until new measures were introduced to prevent any private schools from operating. A Congress school was started in Fordsburg, with Alfred 'Hutch' Hutchinson, Henry 'Squire' Makgothi and Molly Fischer among the teaching staff under headmaster Michael Harmel. Students enrolled in the school included boys and girls who went on to become well-known political activists – the brothers Aziz and Essop Pahad, for example.

Some of the cultural clubs, though, were beyond the control of the ANC, Tambo observed. He sent a circular to 'all provincial secretaries', stating that the problem of Head Office was 'the complete lack of information as to the state of affairs in the different provinces or regions... Unless the state of affairs is attended to, we shall be faced with a chaotic situation within the organisation'.[43]

But the Working Committee continued to encourage the boycott, suggesting that parents act as they thought best according to their local circumstances. Evidently there lingered the hope that the protest movement might spread throughout the country and so oblige the government to amend or drop its plan. And while school boycotts also took place in the Eastern Cape, even in less central areas such as Peddie (Govan Mbeki's constituency) and Tsolo, as well as Port Elizabeth and in the Free State's Bethlehem, the tactics, reported Tambo to Congress in December 1955, resulted in 'sporadic, unrelated and ineffectual small incidents'.[44] Some boycotts were of short duration, in the nature of demonstrations rather than prolonged campaigns. But, as Tambo pointed out, 'an evil system of education... cannot be effectively attacked by means of sensational, dramatic campaigns of short duration'. In his report, Tambo examined ANC weaknesses – its tendency to rely on word of mouth, its failure to provide adequate literature and propaganda material, and an emphasis of the particular campaign rather than looking at the struggle holistically.

'Bantu Education is intended and calculated to undermine the entire liberatory struggle... To this extent the campaign against Bantu Education should not be handled in isolation from other campaigns as if it were something which has its own beginning and its own end. We must learn that... organisational preparedness does not happen overnight. It is the result of steady, even slow, patient, persistent work.

'The fight against Bantu Education must go on. We must build steadily, carrying the people with us, exposing the wickedness of the new Bantu Education syllabus and the way children are to be indoctrinated, achieving the boycott [by parents] of the school boards and committees, adapting the form of protest to the state of preparedness in the area and the local conditions there.'[45]

The Bantu Education campaign was beginning to reveal to the ANC leadership that black communities were not monolithic, and this was emphasised by the uneven and much-criticised resistance to the removal of black residents from the western areas of Johannesburg. The areas included Western Native Township and Newclare, though it was Sophiatown, the freehold, multiracial suburb adjoining white working-class Westdene, and Trevor Huddleston's parish, that attracted the most attention. It was to become the high-profile symbol of the iniquity of urban removals throughout the country.

Over the years, Sophiatown had become famous for its writers, journalists, artists, photographers and ministers. Everyone celebrated Sophiatown (sometimes over-romanticising it) through their writings, photographs and artwork. Huddleston's passionate witness of the day-to-day tragedies wrought on black people by apartheid policies in his book *Naught For Your Comfort*[46] brought

Sophiatown international attention. Can Themba, Todd Matshikiza, Bloke Modisane, Henry Nxumalo and Casey Motsisi drew vivid portraits of the vitality and turbulent creativity of 'Kofifi', as the locals called it – the shebeens, the *stokvels* (community savings clubs), the street music, the choirs, weddings and funerals, churches, schools, dirt roads, brick houses, shacks, the dense smoke from coal stoves, the *tsotsis,* the crime, the *kwela-kwela* police vans, the loud knock on the door, the danger in the night. Like other black 'locations', such as Tambo's Wattville in Benoni and Adelaide's Eastern Township or Top Location in Vereeniging, the élite, the workers and the 'lumpen proletariat' lived squashed together, sharing, cheek by jowl, their common experiences of racial oppression. The gap between the classes was never as great in the townships as the deep chasm that existed between white and black, whether working or middle class.

Nevertheless, there were differences, especially in the freehold area of Sophiatown. As the urban population grew, despite all attempts by the pass system to apply 'influx control', it was precisely the two freehold areas of Sophiatown and Alexandra that offered black newcomers the most protection. Both were among the earliest Johannesburg suburbs and had earned a certain measure of autonomy over their local affairs. In the process, a landlord class had developed. Living in the original brick houses, many of them pretty hard up themselves, the new 'landlords' managed to supplement their income by building shacks in their yards to let out to tenants. But this state of affairs was precisely what the apartheid state sought to halt.

Like the education portfolio, the government appropriated black local communities from city councils and transferred their provenance to the Native Affairs department. For Johannesburg's Western Areas, they earmarked a large piece of land adjoining Orlando. This they named Meadowlands, and prepared to move all black residents here. Once again, the ANC swung into action. They held protest meetings in the squares, holding up placards that read, *'Ons Dak Nie'* – 'We Won't Budge'. Indignant speakers spoke passionately about the move. 'Over our dead bodies!' they sloganeered. War images abounded, and Chief Luthuli called on the people to 'make the campaign the Waterloo of apartheid'.[47] There was even an instance of guerrilla theatre at the City Hall steps, where four men led by Robert Resha carried a coffin marked 'Sophiatown – RIP'. Expectations were running high. Dissident Africanists, critical of what they felt was mere rhetoric, indulged in some of their own. 'What is the use of calling on the people of Sophiatown to "resist" the removal "non-violently"? Since white domination is maintained by force of arms, it is only by superior force of arms that it can be overthrown.'[48]

Oliver Tambo was deeply involved in the campaign, although not in as public a manner as Huddleston or the Youth League. Leaflets and door-to-door canvassing were organised by 30 dedicated volunteers. Open-air meetings were held on Wednesday nights and Sundays and, as another leg to the campaign, the NEC called for a protest stay-away on 12 February, the day of the first removals. But the government, determined to make the Sophiatown removals apartheid's showcase for the elimination of 'black spots' in white areas, sharpened its tactics. Out of the blue, it announced just the day before that the removals would begin on 9 February. Lacking resources and fearing that the event would spiral into open confrontation, the Working Committee immediately made a statement, signed by Tambo, that the campaign – like all others – 'will be conducted in a disciplined and peaceful manner and the people are called upon to remain calm in the face of all provocation'.[49]

Early the next morning, in the pouring rain, Sophiatown heard the rumble of scores of military trucks come to collect the belongings of 150 families. Two thousand policemen provided back-up. Thanks to the volunteers, 40 families had packed their belongings the evening before and stored them at Christ the King. But the remaining families quietly loaded their furniture and boxes. By the end of the afternoon, the trucks were on their way to Meadowlands. Several blocks of dwellings – shanties, houses and huts – stood silent, smokeless, empty and dark, the symbol of great changes in the landscape to come. The 'resistance', overseen by Huddleston and Resha, seemed to have melted away. The very next day, bulldozers moved in to demolish the vacant dwellings. This proved to be the turning point. From then on, although it was not at once evident, the back of resistance to removals was broken.

What had gone wrong? Tambo, in his end-of-year report to Congress, put it down to two areas of confusion in the ANC. The one was 'the failure to indicate what type of action was to be taken and the creation of an impression in the propaganda campaign that the removal could have been stopped even in the face of military operation'. In other words the slogan 'We shall not move' meant that residents would have to be forcibly removed, but in a non-violent manner. The second problem had been, as Tambo recognised, 'the failure to recognise that the appeal to landlords could not be exactly the same as the one of the tenants. The tenants were in need of better houses, especially those who lived under bad conditions, and the minimum unity between the two groups was not achieved'.[50]

The ANC leadership had, in essence, captured the problem of the contradictions and vulnerability of class in black communities in Tambo's astute report to Congress in 1955. What he had not reported, though, was the stirring of vocal criticism of a group in the Transvaal structures – in the Transvaal Executive and the Transvaal Youth League.

Why was the ANC not leading? they asked. How could an important decision such as the boycott of schools be taken without putting effective organisational machinery in place? Why were they so ineffective on the morning of 9 February? 'Is Congress Yellow?' blared out the pages of *Drum*. The magazine interviewed Oliver Tambo for a response. Certain people had regarded Western Areas, he said, as 'an arena wherein they hoped to witness a clash between Government and Congress... According to them, Congress failed to turn up at the appointed hour; and the day, much to their disappointment, passed uneventful. And now Congress is required to account for its failure to entertain the spectators. The Congress is not in the position of a gladiator'.[51]

Instead, Tambo suggested, one needed to view the event more analytically. The correct question to ask was, why did the government suddenly find it necessary to avoid Saturday 12 February, the original date, and to mobilise 2 000 armed policemen in order to remove a mere 'handful of families'. The apartheid government feared Congress, he argued; by its very actions, the government had 'admitted the failure of apartheid and Verwoerdism and conceded the strength and unity of the men and women of all races who stand resolved to resist all forms of aggression on fundamental human rights'.

But there were two sticking points for the critics. The first was the weakness of organisation in the ANC, which Tambo admitted in his annual report to Congress, but not to *Drum*. A year earlier, Tambo had himself presented as part of the Acting Secretary-General's report, the principles of the 'M-plan', proposed by Mandela. In essence, this involved a system of communication and structures based on a cell system consisting of street committees or other 'small, manageable units' accountable separately to their branch committees.[52] The M-plan would lend itself to underground work when, inevitably, the ANC itself would be banned and forced to go underground.[53]

The other, a more deep-seated and long-term difference, was the issue of 'multiracialism', as it was called at the time, which was 'the strength and unity of men and women *of all races*', Tambo had said in a throwaway phrase. Uneasiness had already been expressed during the Defiance Campaign by Tambo himself and his close colleagues about collaborating with other organisations. Now, the Campaign's after-effects seemed to be taking the ANC further and further into alliances with non-African organisations – this at a time when campaigns were proving unable to halt the massive apartheid steamroller that was relentlessly flattening blacks' control over their lives. By 1955, non-African organisations included the white South African Congress of Democrats, formed under the patronage of Tambo, as well as the South African Coloured People's Congress (CPC). These organisations, as well as the South African Indian Congress, joined the new labour federation, the South African Congress of Trade Unions (SACTU), to become part of the Congress Alliance. In June, they all participated in the Congress of the People (COP) at Kliptown, Soweto. For the dissident voices, it was this event that brought matters to a head.

The idea of a 'Congress of the People' had been an imaginative suggestion by Professor ZK Matthews (whose analytical thinking had also played a significant role in the formulation of the *African Claims* in 1943) to involve the participation of the grass roots in fashioning a vision for a people's charter – a 'Charter of all the South African people for the things that they want to make their lives happy and free'.[54] At a follow-up meeting in Stanger on 21 March 1954, 40 delegates from opposition organisations squeezed into school desks to hear the proposal and respond – strictly speaking, the meeting was illegal, since Luthuli was banned from gatherings. Nevertheless, the event was a high-level meeting of all the congresses and amounted to, in the view of Rusty Bernstein, an unprecedented 'summit'. To mastermind the operation, a Working Committee was formed, chaired by Tambo (who replaced Sisulu after he was banned), with representatives for the SAIC (Yusuf Cachalia), the CPC (Adam Daniels), COD (Rusty Bernstein) and SACTU (Piet Beyleveld). Of course, in the ANC itself there was always the active support of the 'background boys' – those banned, senior leaders experienced in tactics and organisation. 'They would advise us,' said Thomas Nkobi, 'how to go about some of these things… [They] opened themselves to be used by the movement in any other way.[55]

'The combination of Luthuli and Tambo was one of the greatest assets… Let alone when the combination of Luthuli, Tambo, Sisulu and Mandela formed the real core; and at that time we [also] had people like Moses Kotane [and] JB Marks... All of them went to jail without exception; all of them went to jail. So that the ANC was really given a kind of real leadership in those days, among whom was Oliver Tambo.'[56]

Thomas Nkobi himself was to become another asset to the ANC. An ardent young full-time but unpaid national organising secretary of the ANC, his family – like that of Sisulu – relied on the earnings of his nursing wife. His father, too, was a reluctant helper.[57] The old man was disappointed that Thomas did not join him in the family business, but ultimately understood his son's burning need to commit himself to the struggle. While still a student, Thomas had been stirred by the 1944 Alexandra bus boycott and in later years was himself to organise, together with Alfred Nzo, the high-profile Alex bus boycott of 1957. He had also been jailed in 1952, during the Defiance Campaign, and since then had been actively involved in speaking around the country to explain and publicise the Freedom Charter.

In the meantime, other organisations were invited to send a representative to join the Working Committee, but in the end did not participate. The newly formed Liberal Party, in particular, was divided as to whether to participate in a planning committee alongside 'known' communists such as Rusty Bernstein. The United Party, the Dominion Party and the National Party did not even bother to reply.[58] The campaign called for a vanguard of volunteers to travel extensively around the country in order to ascertain the feelings of people in the villages, towns, farms, factories, hostels, churches and other community organisations – to attend to *stokvel* or burial society meetings, women's associations, sports organisations, and all ANC branches. The call was received with much enthusiasm and some 10 000 volunteers, drawing on the core that had been formed during the Defiance Campaign, set to work. A drafting committee determined that it was necessary to issue a leaflet to explain the mission of the campaign. 'Let Us Speak of Freedom' it urged in ringing tones, and explained the meaning of a Freedom Charter, and the preparations needed for a Congress of the People.

During the following 18 months, responses emerged out of large rallies, such as the one in Uitenhage, as well as meetings – big and small, study classes, street committees and house-to-house canvassing. The demands were to be sent in by the end of February in order to be formulated into a draft form of a Freedom Charter to be read to the Congress of the People. These demands arrived, slowly at first, but accelerating as the deadline drew nearer. They came in many languages; in boxes, on scraps of paper, on the backs of envelopes and questionnaires, in school exercise books. Some were one-liners, others wordy and obscure, a few written in essay form, outlining theoretical issues on economy and politics, and a few unclassifiable – 'Life too heavy', cried one.

At the same time, mammoth logistics, all conducted on a volunteer basis, had to be arranged. The site had to be chosen – one that was not controlled by white authorities: the dusty Kliptown field, adjoining the hardware store of a sympathetic Indian trader, had to be cleared and cleaned, electric power supplied, WCs erected, the platform constructed. Guides, marshals, stewards and waiters had to be coached. Donations needed to be collected and two days' food cooked. Overnight accommodation was required for the 2 000-plus delegates. Arranging a division of labour, all the ANC's alliance partners participated – the Women's League as well as the Youth League, the Indian Congress, the CPC and the COD were all directly involved in months of preparations (with women undertaking the traditional tasks of catering and preparing accommodation).

With barely a week to go, the Working Committee, which included Oliver Tambo, finally turned its attention to the Freedom Charter itself. They were faced with the thousands of bits of paper that had been thrown into an old cabin trunk. A team of volunteers was appointed, and together with Rusty Bernstein (who had in the meantime been banned and so was relieved of public duties) sorted out the demands into piles under categories such as 'land', 'education', 'votes', 'equality', and so on. Late one night the volunteers went home and Rusty was left to tackle the task. He went through all the piles again, made notes, and then set to work on a skeleton draft. Trying to rein in his own bias towards a socialist economy, Bernstein recalled, he aimed for a consensus. He liked to think he was balanced and objective when he identified the 10 final topics, 'each of which could be summarised in a single phrase such as: "The People Shall Govern" or "All Shall be Equal Before the Law."'[59] Adding a preamble and a call to action at the end, he then showed it to a few colleagues, made some amendments, and took the draft to the Working Committee. They approved it without change.

Ultimately, the Freedom Charter was the product of the Working Committee. While the leaflet was shown to the Joint Executive Council and to Congress, it was too late to make any changes because it had already been rushed to the printers. Perhaps, thinking it was simply a draft to be put to the COP for amendment, the document was not interrogated as thoroughly as it might have been; perhaps the all-consuming anxiety that the event itself should be carried out smoothly distracted the Committee – either way, the opening assertion in the preamble that 'South Africa belongs to all who live in it, black and white' was to cause long-lasting repercussions.

The event had brought nearly 3 000 elected delegates from around the country, with the audience itself reaching 7 000. Because he was forbidden to attend gatherings, Tambo watched from a hiding place in Stanley Lollan's house in 45–7 Beacon Road, Kliptown, which overlooked the square. By today's standards, the COP was a small gathering for a national event. Chief Luthuli, for example, had more than once drawn crowds of 10 000 people. But the long, expensive and arduous journey from all corners of the country to Kliptown had its consequences. For instance, many would-be delegates – especially those from the rural areas – were not able to find the fare to

RUSTY BERNSTEIN WROTE THE FREEDOM CHARTER.

Johannesburg. The police and the Special Branch, though, took the national gathering seriously. Besides the need to monitor and contain the event, for the Special Branch it was also an opportunity to identify more 'agitators' and gather evidence for a bigger picture of the resistance movement. The police contributed by harassing and intimidating delegates and would-be delegates at every turn. They held up buses, arrested those whose passes were not in order, and jailed some arbitrarily for the duration of the weekend. At the COP itself, police raids, the confiscation of all documents and signs – even those at the soup stands – stopped the meeting for hours. It delayed the discussion of the Charter, line by line, and eventually the meeting was forced to compress the responses to the document as a whole. It was dark by the time all motivations had been heard and a vote taken. Because of the numbers, the show of hands, the ululations and the shouts of acclaim persuaded the chairperson that the meeting had adopted the Freedom Charter by an overwhelming majority.

The outcome of the COP, many have since agreed, was a turning point. Members of the Working Committee concurred. 'For the first time, Congress activists had to learn to listen. From that process came a radical Freedom Charter, and the first outlines of a revolutionary new South Africa,' observed Bernstein about the process of popular participation.[60]

Of the Charter itself, Nelson Mandela wrote that it 'is more than a list of demands for democratic reforms. It is a revolutionary document precisely because the changes it envisages cannot be won without breaking up the economic and political set-up of present South Africa';[61] while Oliver Tambo, looking back at the year's events, reported that '[the] Freedom Charter has opened up a new chapter in the struggle of our people... Hitherto we have struggled sometimes together, sometimes separately against the pass laws, and Group Areas, against low wages, against Bantu education and removal schemes. With the adoption of the Charter, all struggles become one: the struggle for the aims of the Charter.'[62]

Luthuli, however, who was not able to attend the COP owing to his ban, was keeping his ear to the ground. He insisted that the Charter be taken to all the branches and that the ANC wait for their report-backs before endorsing it. A year later, the Freedom Charter was adopted formally by the ANC without amendments. Despite the failure to plan a follow-up campaign to publicise the Charter, thousands of copies were reprinted over the next few years, and the document became a popular reference point – 'our guide and organiser', to use Tambo's concept.[63] In the following four decades and beyond, the Freedom Charter was to become the foundation of the policy of the ANC, both inside and in exile, by which the movement stood or fell.

The Freedom Charter was also to cause a major lurch towards an attempt by Africanists to challenge the ANC's direction and reroute it back to the Programme of Action and a 'go-it-alone' policy. The dissident movement had been underground since the Defiance Campaign, when they supported the campaign in practice, but bided their time to see how the strategy would pan out. They were particularly suspicious of Walter Sisulu, whom they had thought of as their man in the position of Secretary-General, who led the breach into the resolute vision of a finely honed African nationalism. Sisulu was aware of their reservations.[64]

Opposition to the Congress Alliance came most vocally from the Youth League's Orlando branch. Its chairperson was fiery speaker Potlako Leballo, son of an Anglican minister from the bordering town of Mafeteng, in Lesotho. He had served 'up North' in the Second World War as a rebellious and adventurous teenager, and on his return taught for a few years before he left the profession because he found it restrictive on his political activism. He was an ardent supporter of Marcus Garvey's maxim, 'Africa for the Africans', and hero-worshipped AP Mda, the intellectual 'back-room boy' of Africanist philosophy. Leballo proved to be the epitome, as scholar Gail Gerhart pointed out, of the late Lembede's call to embrace nationalism 'with the fanaticism and bigotry of religion'.[65] A go-getter, along with other young nationalists, he helped to found *The Africanist*, a journal aiming to popularise African nationalism and agitate against multiracialism. Reacting to the Freedom Charter, Leballo and others argued that there was no role in the struggle for whites. All whites, he argued in *The Africanist*, 'sympathetic' or otherwise, were recipients of stolen goods, engaged in 'the maintenance and retention of the spoils passed on to them by their forefathers'.[66] It was particularly treacherous, therefore, to embrace the Freedom Charter with its opening salvo, 'The land belongs to all who live in it, black and white'.

'The truth is,' declared Leballo and Zeph Mothopeng, 'that the African people have been robbed by the European people.'[67] Hobnobbing with them was thus a corrupting activity that could only lead to the betrayal of one's own people.

Africanists were also particularly disturbed about the perceived intervention of the communists. Leballo criticised Walter Sisulu, Duma Nokwe and others for visiting communist China, further evidence of the perks that whites could dispense to blacks in order to indoctrinate them. Although the CPSA was banned, the Africanists knew – and rightly so – that communist members continued to be active, resourceful and influential. This was, to a certain extent, confirmed by Joe Slovo many years later: 'At that time, everything operated at two levels because, you know, there were the open structures; the ANC itself, the Congress of Democrats of which I was initially a member and elected to its executive, but then after the bannings could no longer take part. But most of the actual political initiatives were processed in sub rosa meetings, structures that continued to operate and give the guidance.'[68]

To the Africanists, too many of the clauses of the Freedom Charter smacked uncomfortably of communism. But for most of the ordinary people who supported the Charter, and even for much of the leadership, these clauses seemed to be mere, historically derived common sense.

'Let me be quite honest with you,' confessed Thomas Nkobi, who later himself joined the South African Communist Party (SACP), 'we didn't bother whether this thing was communistic or not… What we were interested in was that we must produce a government whose interest would be vested in the people. That's why we were thinking in terms of nationalisation, in case we take over... [We] thought it was a way in which we could empower our people. We could address some of the question of imbalances – the Nationalist Party, when they came into power, they used this question of nationalisation. They used it and they gave a lot of work to their own people. Today, they are a very powerful section in the economy and everywhere.'[69]

Other intellectuals in the ANC Youth League challenged the dissident voices, accusing them of 'chauvinism', 'isolationism' and 'racialist nationalism'. Recalling the dispute many years later, Sisulu distinguished between the 'ought' of the Africanists and the 'is' – the perceived reality by the 1950s – of the ANC:

'The PAC [regarded the Freedom Charter] as selling out the rights of the indigenous people. Whereas the Charter was expressing the truth of the situation, describing the actual position, which – whether you like it or not – is not going to change just by putting in very fancy paragraphs here and there. It was describing the situation: these people live here; we are fighting for a united non-racial democratic South Africa.'[70]

In May 1954 Leballo was expelled from the ANC and the Executive Committee of the Orlando branch of the Youth League was suspended. With fresh elections, Henry Makgothi was installed as chair. Leballo and his followers went on to challenge the ANC. Leballo was reinstated, then expelled again in an ongoing saga. Following Mda's advice, the Africanists formed a tight caucus within the movement and continued to raise the issue of a return by the ANC to the original Programme of Action at every opportunity.

Walter Sisulu confided: 'AP Mda is alleged to have said – warning those who were preparing to break to form a PAC – "Nobody goes out of the ANC and lives". In other words, if you try to go out of the ANC, you will be killed [politically] before [you succeed]. This was his reservation, and I think that is why he did not go all out [to challenge the ANC openly]. He, in fact, had reservations about the formation of the PAC... something that he thought was unwise.'[71]

It was the familiar ambiguity of the intellectual. Rather than lose the historical advantages of the mother body, the alternative was to change the ANC – and a few more years were to pass before Mda was no longer able to prevent an open schism from taking place.

The last five years of the 1950s proved to be as eventful as the first. Some campaigns, like the 'Azikwelwa' ('We will not ride') bus boycotts in Alexandra and Evaton, another freehold township not far from Vereeniging, were initiated by grass-roots communities themselves and left the ANC trailing behind, while other ANC initiatives enjoyed erratic support. The potato boycott campaign did, however, help to publicise the 'slave wages' and maltreatment – even murder – of farm labourers, particularly on the potato farms of the Eastern Transvaal. The ambitious but popular 'Pound-a-Day' Campaign of the South African Congress of Trade Unions; the boycott of consumer products – tinned foods and cigarettes – associated with the investments of apartheid's cabinet ministers; the ANC's discussions with white opposition political parties in an attempt to isolate the government; and even its intervention in the 1958 elections – with their slogan, 'The Nats Must Go!' – attested to the wide and broadening range of allies with whom the ANC was prepared to work in a United Front, assisted by their alliance partners, the Congress of Democrats, provided the ANC remained in a leading position in these campaigns. Of course, none of these projects succeeded in reversing any oppressive laws or preventing the promulgation of new ones. If anything, they exacerbated the government's determination to crush the ANC. But, despite some of the dubious tactical experiments and the leadership's incapacitation owing to bans and arrests, the campaigns nevertheless served to mobilise more people, and its popular support, even its membership, continued to grow.[72]

As before, Oliver Tambo was used to bail the ANC out of difficult situations. Thomas Nkobi, the first full-time national organiser of the movement, who often travelled with Tambo to attend meetings, recalled a number of occasions when Tambo was asked to explain to disgruntled people why a retreat might be necessary. He soon observed the impact Tambo made on audiences. They felt they had something to learn by listening to him. 'You would hear the dropping of a pin,' said Nkobi of when Tambo spoke. 'I remember one time they sent him to go and quell a sort of a riot in Sophiatown, after they called for a three-day stay-at-home. And after two days, our people saw that the people didn't really sort of accept this thing.'

This was probably the occasion when the three-day 'Nats Must Go!' protest and stay-away failed to resonate with the popular mood. The ANC thus decided to call off the campaign. Others, however, disagreed because retreat would result in a poor impression of the ANC. Said Nkobi, 'So we sent OR to Sophiatown to go and discuss with them, that at least we should retreat in an organised manner, rather than to retreat in a scattered way. At that meeting, he spoke to say that we are the people in a vehicle... waging a war. If you are a good general, you must see where your weaknesses are. In other words, if you need to withdraw, you must withdraw in order not to be scattered.'[73]

In this tumultuous era of protest and defiance, Tambo's low-key, calm style was highly persuasive. His effectiveness lay in his ability to appeal to intelligence and reason. He explained so clearly the need for shrewd tactics in a time of steadily hardening apartheid policy that the audience felt both exhilarated and empowered. Every meeting Tambo addressed seemed to be another lesson in political education.

Following the Congress of the People, perhaps the most dramatic display of popular participation was the work of the Women's League, which was able to mobilise thousands of women in a series of spirited campaigns involving women marching in protest to the offices of their local Native Commissioner. Then, in October 1955, 1 600 Transvaal women descended on Pretoria's Union Buildings to deliver their demands, including their concerns about a lack of social services, housing, schools and the threat of the extension of passes to women. Tambo drew two lessons for the ANC from the 1955 women's march. It illustrated, he said, 'how the people's daily needs can become the kernel of a united protest campaign' and recruit more people into the liberation movement. Secondly, he commented presciently on the need for men in Congress to 'fight constantly in every possible way those outmoded customs which make women inferior and by personal example must demonstrate their belief in the equality of all human beings, of both sexes'. He called on men to help emancipate women in the home, 'even relieving them of their many family and household burdens so that women may be given an opportunity of being politically active'.[74]

In the following year, this initial success was to inspire a massive, national protest march of women against passes. Up to 20 000 women were able to evade police vigilance by arriving at different times in groups of two or three

ABOVE *The Mountain of Knowledge. The metaphor of the summit as a pinnacle of noble inspiration was familiar to Oliver since schooldays.* (Margaret Glover, 1931)

ABOVE *The discourse of St Peter's, though well intentioned, was colonial – South Africa was conceived as consisting largely of 'Natives' and 'Europeans'.* (St Peter's)

ABOVE *The Standard 7 class at St Peter's, 1935, with the class mistress and headmaster, Mr Shearsmith. Oliver is in the front row, second from right.* (Community of the Resurrection)

ABOVE *Oliver (back row, right) poses with friends at Fort Hare, 1939.* (courtesy Dr Lancelot Gama)

ABOVE *Students at Fort Hare celebrate another identity, Rag Day, 1940. Oliver Tambo is on the left.* (Fort Hare Archive)

ABOVE *Oliver Tambo, Congress Mbata and Lancelot Gama, Fort Hare, 1940.* (courtesy Dr Lancelot Gama)

ABOVE *Oliver Reginald Tambo, Bachelor of Science, Fort Hare, 1941.* (courtesy Dr Lancelot Gama)

ABOVE *The Physics master at St Peter's, 1944. Tambo's firm but interactive teaching style made 'Bra T' a popular and respected master.* (Community of the Resurrection)

TOP *Attorney Oliver Tambo in his office at Mandela & Tambo, 1952.* (Jurgen Schadeberg)

ABOVE *Posing on the rooftop of Ahmed Kathrada's apartment, 1953.* (Herb Shore, courtesy Ahmed Kathrada)

LEFT *Young Adelaide Tsukhudu, 1947, around the time Oliver first met her.* (Tambo Family Album)

ABOVE *Wedding of Oliver Tambo to Adelaide Tsukhudu, December 1956. Next to the bride stand the Reverend and Mrs Weyi (née Tambo). Behind Oliver are Adelaide's cousins Nimrod and Gladys Tuge.* (Werner's Studio/Tambo Family Album)

ABOVE *Outside the Drill Hall, Johannesburg, during a recess in the Treason Trial, 1956. Joe Matthews (left), OR and Tennyson X Makiwane.* (Bailey's African History Archives)

ABOVE *Oliver Tambo addresses a rally in Alexandra Township, 1951.* (Bailey's African History Archives)

ABOVE *Africa Day Rally, Alexandra, April 1958. Tambo, in solidarity with his wife's clan, wore traditional Sotho costume, with its distinctive woven, conical hat. Flanking him are Alfred Nzo (left) and Duma Nokwe (right).* (Tony Seedat/Tambo Family Album)

ABOVE *Oliver Tambo is welcomed by supporters and admirers on his first visit to New York, October 1960.* (James Logan, New York)

CENTRE *Women, arrested during their protest against the impending imposition of passes, pose in the chambers of Mandela & Tambo. The Magistrates' Court may be seen through the rear window.* (Jurgen Schadeberg)

RIGHT *Chief Albert Mvumi Luthuli, President of the African National Congress, with his Deputy, Oliver Tambo, outside his home in Groutville, 1959.* (Alf Khumalo/Bailey's African History Archives)

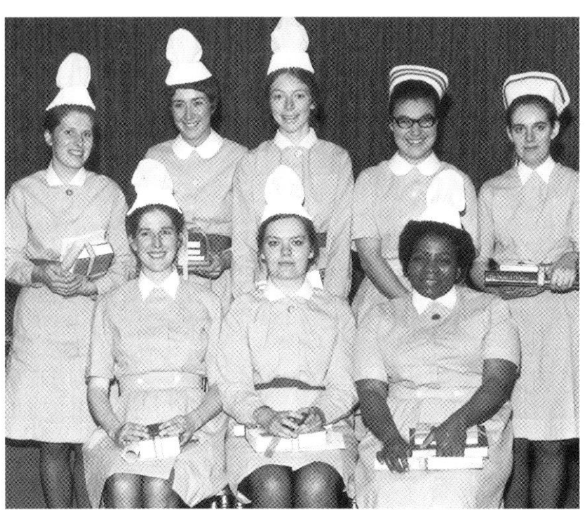

TOP LEFT *Botswana, April 1960. Oliver with Ronald Segal, who helped him – disguised as Segal's driver – cross the border into exile.* (Ken Montano)

ABOVE *Dali and Thembi, page boy and flower girl at the wedding, in London, of Ronald and Susan Segal.* (Tambo Family Album)

CENTRE *Oliver Tambo's arrival in Denmark, 1963. With him are the General Secretary and Executive Secretary of the Danish Social Democratic Party.* (courtesy Thabo Mbeki)

LEFT *Nursing Sister Adelaide Tambo with her colleagues at their graduation, Whittington Hospital, London, c.1968.* (Tambo Family Album) to walk through Union grounds, up the amphitheatre steps, and knock on Prime Minister Strijdom's door armed with over 100 000 petitions against passes for women. 'Our women are proving themselves brave and undaunted politicians,' Tambo commented. 'Yet they need special attention and training to assist them to become leaders of the people.[75] The Women's League is not just an auxiliary to the African National Congress,' he added, 'and we know that we cannot win liberation or build a strong movement without the participation of the women.'

Throughout the muddles and relative successes, Tambo's overall perspective continued to remain pertinent for conditions during the rest of the decade. In May 1955, he had written a frank appraisal to the Deputy President of the ANC, Wilson Z Conco. 'It seems to me,' he wrote, 'that the ANC is irretrievably committed to a bitter struggle – and maybe a long and eventful struggle in which there will be many losses and gains of varying magnitude.' This state of affairs, to Tambo's thinking, called for an intelligent pragmatism as far as tactical challenges were concerned.

'If any venture proves ill advised at any given time, the necessary readjustments in our tactics must be made. On the other hand, the mere fact that a particular campaign turns out to be beset with numerous difficulties is no reason, by itself, to justify a retreat, for, in the final analysis, the situation in South Africa today is such that alternative modes of struggle have been reduced to the barest minimum, and we shall not wait long for the day when only one method will be left to the oppressed people of this country.'[76]

Thinking ahead, Tambo was already articulating his awareness of the inevitability of the revolutionary path. Yet, it was in his nature to proceed methodically, giving all alternatives an honest try before such a drastic but probable conclusion to the struggle would be taken.

During the ferment of political activity, spiritual reconnaissance and personal courtship, Tambo continued to be the main working partner in his firm of attorneys. Each campaign brought its crop of activists who had been arrested and charged. In one fortnight alone, the women's resistance against passes provoked the authorities to arrest close on 2 000 black women, including several coloureds who protested in solidarity, charged with causing a public disturbance by taking part in illegal processions.[77] In fact, Oliver Tambo was called upon in several cases to defend those charged in a Johannesburg march, as well as rural women in the northwestern Transvaal, during the course of this campaign. Lilian Ngoyi's batch of volunteers was among the groups whom Tambo defended.

The forced removals from Johannesburg's Western Areas brought to court defiant youth, who if found guilty of a misdemeanour would be sent to labour camps that were being set up to provide white farmers with cheap labour. The removals went on to become a scourge throughout the country. Oliver Pelesane recalled clearly Tambo's professional presence in Klerksdorp in the context of removals in Jouberton Township, where he was called upon to defend a Mr Mokgatshani. As the demolition squad moved towards the outside walls of his house, Mokgatshani attacked and killed a demolisher. Defended by Tambo, he received a far lighter sentence than the death sentence that the accused would otherwise have received. Oliver Tambo's reputation was thus 'a legend amongst blacks', and Pelesane recalled a particular twist to the court case. While Tambo's car was parked outside the magistrate's court in Klerksdorp, a scaffold fell on it and damaged it. 'They were so afraid of him [that] they offered him a new car – this illustrates his legend and status. The idea of a black man defending a black person depended on his ability to annoy whites.'[78]

Tambo went on to conduct many cases defending victims of the apartheid legislation. Increasingly, the balance of the cases undertaken in the practice began to tip more heavily in favour of defences against apartheid laws. Bantu Education yielded a number of teachers who had been arrested for teaching children without the permission of the government. The women's march also netted hundreds of marchers whose unruly thumbs stuck out defiantly through the bars of the *kwela-kwela* police vans as they were carted off to prison. It was so easy to arrest a black man or woman. Vindictive policemen would routinely raid marked houses – or, indeed, any house – searching for a contravention of the law: illegal beer brewing, a missing signature in a passbook, suspicion of stolen goods, including any object or personal possession that looked 'too good' to be owned by a black person. In 1956, the ANC issued two flyers calling for meetings. 'Why Are We Treated Like Animals?' they asked in pain and anger.

Armed police invade our homes, drag us,
our mothers out of their beds almost naked,
beat them up, throw them in the troop carriers
and finally charge them for not having permits!
We must protest!
Every man, woman and child in Sophiatown...
Martindale... Newclare and Western Native Township

> *must join the mass deputation*
> to NEWLANDS POLICE STATION
> *To protest to the District Commandant of the Police*
> *against these daily police raids and brutality!*
> *PROTEST DAY. Saturday, 1st December, 1956.*

Every campaign netted the police thousands of *dompas* (passbook) miscreants or curfew breakers and, with the imposition of scores of bans, it was easy to tail marked men or women. Sooner or later, they would make a false move. Walter Sisulu himself was arrested for taking tea with a friend, and was sentenced to three months' imprisonment for breaking his ban and attending a gathering. Part of the daily schedule for the staff of Mandela & Tambo was the visit to the prisons and police stations, in Marshall Square, in the townships, or at The Fort, to gather statements in preparation for defence.

But, in tandem with his expanding workload, Tambo's political activities were becoming more and more demanding, despite his ban in 1954. His friend, the articulate Trevor Huddleston, had been so outraged at the persecution of an exceptionally fine man – and clearly not a communist to boot – that he was propelled to challenge the establishment in an article entitled, 'And the Church Sleeps On', printed in the British press and later in Johannesburg's *The Star*. In the piece, Huddleston used Tambo's life story, his character and commitment as a means of exposing the vile progression of apartheid, the disappointing indifference of the comfortable white population in South Africa, and the sorry impotence of the Church to protect the people. The article was the first of Huddleston's writings to receive national and international attention, and was to reinforce his resolution to continue his path of resistance, in passionate and moving form, against the abuses of apartheid and white supremacy.[79]

And all the while the apartheid regime was indeed sharpening its weapons against black opposition. In the same year as Tambo's banning, a significant chunk of the NEC was banned – including Chief Luthuli and Walter Sisulu, as well as Joe Matthews, president of the Youth League, and a number of members in ANC provincial positions in Natal, the Eastern and Western Cape and the Transvaal. By the mid-fifties, 50 per cent of the leaders had been banned, necessitating underground meetings.[80] But while Sisulu's ban forced him to resign formally from the ANC, Tambo was able to continue, working closely with Sisulu but being less available to follow his model of travelling around the country to maintain contact with the regions and the branches. Despite being constantly followed, closely watched at home in Wattville, shadowed in Johannesburg and even tailed to Pondoland, where the Special Branch arrived in Bizana to question his movements, Tambo was sufficiently adroit not to be caught out. His sister-in-law, Gladys Tuge, recalled how Tambo had once brought around his car to Eastern Township, where the family had a trading store. He parked the car outside the shop, borrowed the Tuge car, and disappeared for a week. The Special Branch could be seen regularly cruising down the road, checking out whether Tambo was still with his in-laws in the township. They never discovered his ruse.[81]

At the 1954 Congress, Tambo was elected Secretary-General. Much of his load entailed additional work to make up for restrictions placed on his colleagues, particularly Chief Luthuli. The issue of the continued backroom participation of banned people emerged as a further irritant for dissatisfied Africanists. It was another ploy, they felt, to perpetuate the existing leadership and thus keep out radical nationalists. Banned people worked behind the scenes, caucused and directed events, yet were not directly accountable to the electorate, they argued.

Yet, from the ANC perspective, the bannings led to an evolving tradition of collective leadership. Walter Sisulu, removed from official position, demanded a strategic approach. He continued to work clandestinely, continued with the correspondence and prepared a report for the NEC. He also attended underground NEC meetings. Tambo, now the Secretary-General, 'was a very busy lawyer and could not manage full-time organisational work', narrated Sisulu in his prison biography, and he himself continued in a full-time capacity as secretary underground.[82] Tambo had the right to use anything Walter produced, working in tandem with his friend and colleague, and using his own discretion in the drawing up of statements and reports. When Mandela was also banned, he too continued as Walter did, the effective head of the Transvaal region.

It was becoming clear that new devices were called for as the ANC began its partial slide underground. The leadership in the Transvaal discussed the changed state of affairs. They declared that banned leaders still carried their mandate from the movement, and decided that people should continue with their work as far as possible – in effect, they were to ignore the action of the government. Furthermore, Sisulu compiled a list of all the banned men and women members of the ANC. This list was then presented to Conference to allow people to express their views on the individuals. The result was that Conference unanimously endorsed them all. 'The leadership of the movement had acquired a very high degree of collective leadership; this had become a tradition within the movement,' suggested Sisulu.[83]

The collective also coopted other banned people, such as the articulate and newly elected president of the Youth League, Joe Matthews. In 1954, though banned, Matthews drew up the NEC report in consultation with others, in which the strategy of drawing the international community into the struggle was discussed. The approval of Conference was to have significant consequences for Tambo just a few years hence.

The year 1956 was a most eventful one for Oliver Tambo. It was a year in which the personal met the political. In March, South Africa bade farewell to Father Trevor Huddleston. His outspokenness, his increasingly close relationship with the ANC – the honour of *Isitlwalandwe* awarded to him for outstanding service to the nation or in a time of war along with Chief Luthuli and Doctor Yusuf Dadoo at the Congress of the People – and his flamboyant style perhaps all contributed to him being recalled to Mirfield. Huddleston had made his vows, and his duty was implicit obedience. Tambo, who had been waiting with keen anticipation to be ordained so that he could work on a spiritual level with his friend and mentor, was observed by Dr Jonathan Graham, a visitant from the Community of the Resurrection from Mirfield when the bombshell fell, to have wept when he heard the news.[84] He had offered himself as a priest to Father Huddleston. Now this was not to be. His offer was now to be considered by Bishop Ambrose Reeves.

Was his decision to seek ordination related to political persecution, or the difficulties in the law practice? he was once asked. 'It just came,' he said simply – it was a calling.[85] And so it was that Bishop Reeves accepted Tambo's ordination about a month before Oliver and Adelaide were due to be married.

The wedding date had been set for 22 December 1956, but in the early hours of the morning of 5 December, there was a knock on the door of Tambo's home in Wattville. Two plain-clothes officials from the Special Branch had come to arrest him on a charge of High Treason. En route, they picked up two more accused – trade unionist Cleopas Nzibande, who lived nearby, and the 'red' Methodist minister Douglas Thompson in Springs. By then it was late morning. They were driven along the familiar road to Johannesburg, past Gillooly's farm, through the white working-class suburbs of Bezhuidenhout's (Bez) Valley and Troyeville, along the streets lined with the high-rise apartments of Hillbrow and into Pretoria Street, stopping at the grim, brass-studded double doors of The Fort. Here, they were admitted into the 'Awaiting Trial Block', though Douglas Thompson was, of course, whisked off to the 'white' section. In one of two large rooms, Tambo found a handful of people, all from Johannesburg – Joe Matthews, Henry Makgothi, Paul Joseph, and others.

Nelson Mandela and Duma Nokwe (now the first black advocate at the Bar) were also there. As the morning progressed, more and more men arrived. (The women – they did not yet know how many – were locked up somewhere in The Fort's women's jail.) Some had been driven from other parts of the Transvaal, but the majority – some 140 prisoners from Natal and the Cape – had been ushered on to military planes and flown to Pretoria. With their somewhat sensational arrival, the communal prison rapidly filled up.

There was a sense of nervous excitement in the air. For many, the trial did not come as a complete surprise. Since the Congress of the People, in particular, bans, deportations, and raids on homes and offices affiliated to the ANC had escalated. At the COP itself, during laborious searches of the delegates, grim-faced policemen were asked what they were looking for. 'Evidence of treason,' they replied gruffly. In the Awaiting-Trial Block, joyful reunions and happy introductions were made. Individuals who had been only names before, admired for their courage and leadership, were now able to share their experiences in resistance. On that first day, Tambo and others noticed that Sisulu was missing. It was surprising, because ever since his visit to China, he had become a sinister bogeyman in the eyes of both the regime and the white press. It was only a week later that the early-morning knock came at No. 7372, Orlando.

'Have you arrived?' called Sisulu from his bedroom, in relief.[86]

While they waited for the lawyers to negotiate the terms of the trial, the accused organised themselves. They set up the NEC, the Action Committee, the Western Areas executive, the Bantu Education Commission; work needed to be done, and for the first time they were able to talk strategy, courtesy of the government. For fun, they formed the Accused Male Voices Choir, with Tambo conducting, and bridge teams. Outside, Rica Hodgson (whose husband, Jack, was one of the accused) and others set up a Treason Trial Defence Fund.

On the first day of the trial, all the accused were taken in a convoy of 'pick-up vans' to the Drill Hall adjoining Union Grounds in the city centre. As they alighted, they were greeted by a massive show of support – 'We Stand by Our Leaders!' waved scores of printed placards. Clearly, this was the beginning of another ANC mobilising campaign. The crowds cheered, sang, ululated and beat drums to welcome their heroes. Inside, not a single black spectator was admitted, but some broke through the police cordons to shout praises. The barn-like interior had been chosen as the venue to accommodate the 156 accused because of its size. As they filed in, it became evident that this was a multiracial, representative cross-section of the country's demography. The vast majority of the accused were black, but they also included 23 whites – in

South Africa's race-obsessed culture, this kind of statistic was noted. All the accused were affiliated in one way or another to the Congress Alliance. There were also four or five from the Africanist camp of the ANC.[87]

The inside of the Drill Hall had been fitted out as a courtroom, lined with hessian sacking, but the officials had forgotten to install loudspeakers and the preliminaries to the trial collapsed in chaos. The next day, they tried again. This time the accused were herded into a large hastily assembled enclosure bound by chicken-wire mesh. One wit among the accused found a sheet of paper and pinned it to the wire mesh – 'Dangerous animals! Do not feed'.[88] But the defence team, headed by the brilliant Vernon Berrangé, refused to consult with their clients under those conditions. Once again, the court adjourned. A short while later, the cage was dismantled, and the authorities agreed to reserve 50 seats for black spectators.

The trial proved to be an unexpected boon for the accused. For the first time, 156 key activists had been brought together. Many of the accused had been mere names to the others, but now they were able to share experiences, exchange political views and discuss long-term strategies and tactics. The accused identified themselves as proud delegates of their constituencies – blacks, whites, coloureds and Indians, workers, professionals, merchants, clerics, traditional leaders, communists and liberals. To be a treason trialist was a badge of honour conferred upon them by the apartheid state. The accused were brought together in The Fort and in Drill Hall during recess, over lunch and during adjournments. Ben Turok recalls his delight in having the opportunity to spend more time with leaders such as Moses Kotane and Nelson Mandela. It was also the first time that Turok met Tambo. He remembers him as being 'a very quiet person and, although he had a high status within the ANC it was not absolutely clear to us why, because he was so reserved.

'One thought he was rather aloof. He smiled readily enough and was cordial but either it was shyness or aloofness... He certainly wouldn't take initiatives in the way that Nelson would – or other leaders did – to get to know people, so one never really got to know him – even though we were sitting in the same hall for nine months'.[89]

But Oliver had personal problems. For starters, with both partners arrested, the law practice was running into difficulties. Mandela & Tambo had been 'busy, very busy,' he recalled, 'but our arrest... interrupted our work and we had to give our work to others'.[90] And then, too, there was the question of his impending marriage. The arrest for High Treason and his incarceration at The Fort was, to say the least, a serious disruption. Adelaide managed to visit her fiancé at The Fort – she was now working in the nearby Hillbrow Hospital –

but the question was, should they postpone the wedding date? They had no idea how long the prolonged negotiations would take before the accused were finally brought to trial. And, in any case, for High Treason there was no knowing whether they would be granted bail – in fact, if found guilty, the offence carried a death penalty. But Oliver was determined to be married, as planned, on 22 December.

'If necessary, we will be married at Number Four [the popular name given to the black section of The Fort],' he decided. 'I'll contact Mkwanazi [the taxi man] to transport Reverend Weyi and members of the family for the service.'[91]

As it happened, all the accused were released on bail, apartheid style, just two days before the wedding date – £250 for whites, £100 for Indians or coloureds and £50 for Africans. Just in time. Or was it? The next day, Oliver went to fetch Adelaide from the Helping Hand Club and also collected their two best men, Congress Mbatha and the Zulu lexicographer MB Yengwa (who was soon to have a 'Treason Trial' marriage himself).[92] Then they all drove to Vereeniging to pick up Adelaide's wedding dress and make final arrangements with the bride's family. After a celebratory dinner, they motored back. They were nearly in Johannesburg when the car in which they were travelling was spotted by ever-vigilant policemen – black passengers with a black driver inevitably meant trouble and had to be stopped. In the absence of night passes, they were all bundled into the pick-up. Oliver, who had an exemption pass, also climbed in. It was after midnight when they reached the police station, and 4am before they were released. And their wedding day had dawned...

From there, Adelaide was rushed to her aunt's place at George Goch to prepare for the ceremony at noon. The bride was, however, two hours late. After the ceremony, there was a small reception at the Methodist Church in Benoni. Agnes Weyi had managed to organise catering by the women of the church. When it came to the speeches, Godfrey Pitje spoke. 'We have a bridegroom,' he announced, 'who has been silenced at his own wedding. He has been struck dumb by the apartheid regime.' Oliver had wanted to speak, but Godfrey would not allow him to risk arrest – members of the Special Branch were watching the proceedings from a car parked outside the hall.

The wedding was a Western-style 'white wedding', but afterwards Adelaide had to comply with tradition and moved in with the Weyi in-laws – the parents and their sons – for six months. According to custom, she had to be taught how to cook, how to behave as a married woman, how to look after a child. Adelaide got on particularly well with the Reverend. During her apprenticeship as a *makoti*, she worked harder than she ever had in hospital. She was up at 5am, and although Mrs Weyi had domestic help, Adelaide was expected to undertake most of the work. 'I did not have tea time, lunch time. I was having this stream of ministers who were arriving from Krugersdorp, Klerksdorp and so on, and each time I had to prepare for all of them, baking for four o'clock tea, preparing dinner for the family and so on.'[93] Every morning, she was also expected to make coffee and to serve it to the men.

The Reverend saw the anomaly of it all – the two women, who liked each other well enough, were now beginning to become irritated with one another as a result of these rigidly applied roles. '*Malume* [Uncle],' he said, 'if you want to keep the peace between your wife and your relatives, the best thing is not to let your wife finish this six-month period they usually give to their daughter-in-law.' So it was that the Reverend, with insight and pragmatism, immediately found them a house – No. 2883 Maseko Street in Wattville. He handed the keys to Oliver. 'This is my son's house,' he said. It was the standard four-roomed municipal house – no inside doors, no plastering, no ceilings, no running water, no bathroom. It could never be theirs to own, but the young couple proceeded with improvements and planned to move in when they were done.

Reverend Weyi was delighted that Tambo had married. He had consistently urged him to marry Adelaide. 'He said that he doesn't want to die, him not married,' recalled Lancelot Gama. 'He wanted him settled.'[94] But very soon into Adelaide's period as a *makoti*, the entire family faced a terrible shock. One afternoon, sitting on his stoep, reading his Bible, the Reverend suffered a fatal heart attack. The Reverend's untimely death cast yet another pall over what should have been (but was not because of bail conditions) the honeymoon period. Adelaide stepped in to organise the huge funeral, for the Reverend had been both a respected and a loved minister.

In the weeks, months and years that followed, Adelaide and her sister-in-law subsequently became very close. Adelaide still bucked at subservience, however. One morning, she recalls, she was rushing to get ready for work – Oliver would take her to the hospital every morning – and left some of her toiletries in the bathroom.

Oliver called her: 'Look, you don't want all these people to have a bad impression about you.'

'What people?' asked Adelaide.

'My aunt is here. Do you really think that after we have gone they are not going to walk into our bedroom? And... they are definitely going to come into our bathroom to use it.'

'So I had to go back and tidy up. I felt very angry,'[95] explained Adelaide.

On the other hand, Tambo's own personal example was above reproach. 'Let me say,' conceded Adelaide, 'all my married life, I never made breakfast. He... could fry eggs very nicely and bacon and things like that... [He] always made breakfast before he went to the office.' He always made his bed, too – years of training in boarding schools had trained him to be at least as neat as Adelaide, the nurse. Later, as an early riser, he also tended to the babies. He tried to take seriously the speech he had made in 1955, when he had urged male members of the ANC to relieve women 'of their many family and household burdens'.[96]

During the recess, the trialists decided to throw the newlyweds a wedding party at the Taj Mahal in Braamfontein, Johannesburg. Adelaide recalled having to borrow Winnie Madikizela's graduation dress. 'Lilian Ngoyi organised it. James Hadebe was there. Oliver and Yengwa had been buddies for a long time. Self Letlape, Count Peterson were also there.'[97] The photographs show Oliver in fashionable groom attire, his hair closely cropped and evenly distributed with no parting – a fresh look for this most significant rite of passage, as well as a representation of a purifying and cleansing ritual after release from prison.

The Treason Trial proceeded in early 1957. But while the 156 accused sat through the year as the preliminary trial dragged on, all of them losing wages and income as a result, the protest campaigns continued. The leadership had been tied up, and so were unable to give direction. But the Treason Trial had given the ANC a boost in the black community. Where possible, the accused asserted their political identity, and they were able to make suggestions to the second tier of the Transvaal leadership that now came into its own – ANC organiser Thomas Nkobi, Mark Shope of SACTU, Alfred Nzo and others. The boycotts and stay-aways that followed asserted the power of black people as consumers as well as workers – no law could force people to board buses rather than walk or cycle, to smoke a particular brand of cigarettes, to eat a particular brand of tinned food, or consume potatoes instead of *pap*, the traditional maize porridge. The campaign amounted to a conscious conceptualisation of the importance of agency. 'The boycott is not a defensive weapon,' asserted the NEC's 1959 report. 'We are on the offensive and we are fighting on a battle field chosen by ourselves, based on our own strength.'[98]

During recesses in the trial, both Tambo and Mandela tried to catch up with the backlog at their practice. Tambo was also moving closer to his dream. Towards the end of 1957, he attended and spoke at a conference in Bloemfontein of the Interdenominational African Ministers Federation (IDAMF), which was called to discuss the 'grave national anxiety of the African people'.[99] The new legislation was unremitting. Verwoerd assured Parliament that he would apply the proposed Native Law Amendment Act 'with an iron hand' to ensure that Africans would, within five or ten years, cease to aspire to equality with whites and so undermine the government's apartheid policy. The new act outlawed mixed gatherings – social, political or religious. Most churches were intensely disturbed with the state's interference in the realm of worship. With what Tambo hoped was his imminent acceptance into the ministry, he wanted to make institutional links with church leaders and involve them in the struggle. Tambo was thus closely involved – indeed, highly influential – with the initiative chaired by Reeves' United Front, which drew 14 organisations, including the Black Sash, the Liberal Party and the congresses to combine against 'Nationalist tyranny'. As the future Reverend Tambo, Oliver anticipated continuing to act politically. In African society, there was no separation between religious and secular. Personal and social obligations required by ancestral decree were holistically linked, and an entire nation could be judged if these were defied. Huddleston, too, in the tradition of the Old Testament, where priests were constantly embroiled in politics, had acted unhesitatingly against transgressions of the laws of God. 'I believe,' Huddleston had always asserted, 'that the Christian is bound to act politically, wherever he may be.' This was a reversal of the established, modern theological convention. For him, and also for Tambo, the Christian's ultimate, most important mission was 'to protect from plunder: this most precious human treasure, the opportunity of love itself'.[100]

In December 1957, after a year on trial – during which the prosecuting team had revealed a mediocre argument and much ponderous evidence – charges were withdrawn against 61 of the accused, including both Luthuli and Tambo, the two top ANC officials. The decision seemed inexplicable to observers. If the state was trying to prove that the 'nationwide conspiracy' was a communist conspiracy, what of apartheid's broad, statutory definition of communism, which virtually included all extraparliamentary opposition? If the prosecutors' aim was to expose the ANC's plot to violently overthrow the state, why omit the organisation's two top leaders? The Defence was mystified. 'Mr Tambo was an attorney who practised in partnership with Mr Nelson Mandela. He, Mr Mandela, was also among the accused and he was committed for trial... How this selection was made remained a mystery.'[101] This seeming arbitrariness, 'the grab-bag nature of the arrests, the failure to put on trial major leaders such as Chief Luthuli and Oliver Tambo, and the presence of minor personalities among the 30 accused, we submitted, suggested that no conspiracy existed'.[102]

Another puzzle was that when proceedings began again in January 1959, charges against a further 65 were dropped. Only years later was a clue offered. It transpired that the extreme right-winger Oswald Pirow – Chief Prosecutor – was aiming to secure a conviction of the leading 'agitators'. After that, he intended to swoop down on the 'stooges'.[103] Clearly, he saw the two Christians, as well as Matthews and the others released, as the pawns of communists and rabble-rousers. That, however, left 30 facing charges of High Treason.

Pirow was not alone in his suspicion of communist conspiracy. In an article in *New Age*, Tambo tackled the Africanists, who had levelled the same accusation. In suspecting the ANC of being dominated by the whites in the COD, implied Tambo, the Africanists had not yet outgrown their 'inferiority complex'. They persisted in believing that Africans were not capable of holding their own against other groups. 'The ANC is not led by "inferiors",' he pointed out. 'It does not suffer from any nightmares about being controlled or dominated by any organisation; it is not subject to any such control or domination, and will not run away from the political struggle or from any group or organisation. On the contrary, it will continue to lead the movement for liberation against injustice and tyranny to freedom and democracy.'[104]

Ironically, the ANC received a number of applications from whites who wanted to join the ANC rather than the perceived communist-led Congress of Democrats. Both Patrick Duncan, the son of the Governor-General and well-known veteran of the Defiance Campaign, and Walter Felgate, future activist in the Inkatha Freedom Party (IFP), applied for direct membership.[105] In fact, the 1943 ANC Constitution was non-racial in the sense that it had stated that any adult could join. But since 1950 the ANC had decided not to allow non-Africans to join because of a negative rank-and-file perception of external domination.

In the meantime, Adelaide and Oliver continued to work. The law practice had suffered during the Treason Trial. After Tambo's acquittal, he worked hard to remedy the loss of clients, but the recovery was slow. Adelaide soon fell pregnant, and on 19 October, the couple's first child was born.

'Unto us a child was given', reminisced Oliver years later in a letter to his wife, ' – a child, but in many ways no ordinary child. Born wide awake and looking as if she was about to say something, she soon showed special endearments.'[106] After consulting with the family, they named her Thembi Gugulethu Nosnini, although her doting parents gave her many pet names, including Nini (after Oliver's mother), Manchu and Gugu. And then, less than two years later, on 1 March 1959, Adelaide gave birth to a boy. The labour was dramatic.

'You remember the drive in Gama's borrowed car to Pretoria; the blundering doctors and staff, the undignified attempt to hide the facts and the near damage they caused? [And] the hectic search for a name… [My] calling a special conference of Sophiatown Elders to ponder and deliberate on the complex problem of my son's name; their retiring to the densely populated suburb of Jo'burg and there conferring deep into the night; and their reappearance at my office the following morning, with faces beaming and radiating joy as their [sic] triumphantly announced the good tidings: "*His name shall be Thabo.*" This was the name his mother had found. And so he was Thabo.'[107]

But, like other African children, loving relatives and friends gave the infant a plethora of names, and the one that was eventually fixed on the little boy was Dalindlela [Dali], meaning 'to break new ground (for freedom)'.

Two years after the first arrests, the Treason Trial was still grinding on – and was to continue for more than two more years. In 1959, a not inconsequential minority of the ANC membership split away. It was Tambo who had the responsibility of presiding over the break. During the December Congress in 1957, Africanist delegates raised their criticisms yet again. They were not able to prevent the re-election of almost the entire NEC – 'We Stand by Our Leaders' won the day – but they had raised an issue concerning the irregular conduct of Transvaal's provincial elections, which had ended in heckling, jeering and such loud singing (mainly by ANC 'loyalist' youth objecting to Africanist candidates) that the proceedings were delayed and the elections postponed. This meant that the old provincial executive had therefore held on to their positions unconstitutionally. Accordingly, a date was set for a special conference to hold new elections at the Community Hall in Orlando. Eventually, the special meeting was combined with the annual congress the following December.

Adelaide Tambo, who was there, remembered it well. 'The little birdies said that the Pan-Africanists were coming to disrupt the Conference,' she recalled. Benjamin Pogrund, the sole white journalist and an Africanist sympathiser at the Conference, later verified the rumour. Wild ideas had been circulated at a caucus meeting of the Africanists – including the idea of kidnapping Luthuli, Tambo and Mandela – but wiser counsel prevailed. It was generally agreed, though, that violence was inevitable.[108] The Africanists believed that they would be physically attacked and were thus determined to defend themselves. It would require a highly skilled chairperson to contain the coming conflict and to prevent an open schism. The NEC appointed Tambo for the task.

On the day, Joe Molefe, Rosetten Nciba and others slipped in through the back entrance to ensure the best vantage point. At the back of the hall stood Leballo and Madzunya (both of whom had been expelled from the ANC a few months earlier) and other Africanist supporters, many of them carrying sticks.

'They are going to cause a ruction,' muttered Robert Resha, and he left.[109] The meeting, starting two hours late, began with the President's opening speech and was followed by long speeches from the floor. The next item on the agenda was the elections, but this was bogged down by endless wrangling on the composition of the Credentials Committee, whose task was to screen the delegates. Throughout, Tambo was calm and unhurried. As the chair, he was trying to send a placatory message. He even asked Robert Sobukwe to help count the votes from the floor, which he did, to the extreme annoyance of the Africanists. (Tambo had spent more than one evening talking to Sobukwe, with whom he had warm relations, trying to dissuade him from 'hard-line' Africanism – but to no avail.[110]) It was late at night before the voting for the Credentials Committee took place. The meeting was adjourned.

The next morning, people found the hall locked. Outside stood delegates from all over the Rand and other parts of the Transvaal,[111] as well as two busloads of Resha's 'volunteers' from Sophiatown armed with home-made weapons. It was then, Pogrund wrote, that Tambo's strategy became clear to him:

'He had spent Sunday assessing the Africanists' strength. On Sunday he simply made sure he had more thugs than they did... With everyone outside the hall, only the delegates who had passed the screening were allowed inside – about 200 of them from 80 branches... And that was the end. Tambo stood at the door. The Africanists moved off.'[112]

Tambo, though, saw things differently. This was when the Africanists threw away their last chance. 'Their designs failed,' he analysed, 'firstly because, for as long as was procedurally possible, they were allowed all the rights and privileges of accredited delegates and enjoyed the full protection of the chairman against impotent delegates; and secondly because when the critical moment came when the chairman had to order that they be forcibly taken out, the moment of violence for which they had prepared' was about to become a reality.[113]

Of Potlako Leballo's political behaviour, Tambo was particularly withering: 'The influential chairman of a small ANC local branch in Orlando East, he uses this branch to try and create anarchy and division on the Reef, including public opposition to an industrial action decided on at a conference of workers in Johannesburg, and defiance of disciplinary measures taken against him, again carrying his defiance to the point of near-anarchy.'[114] Egoistic behaviour to the point of divisiveness was for Tambo perhaps the greatest political transgression.

Pogrund, on the other hand, characterised Tambo as a 'fox'.[115] Be that as it may, with political and tactical skill and quiet authority, Tambo had managed to avoid the violence that some had feared and others anticipated with relish. Towards the end of the Congress, a letter was delivered to the platform. The letter, composed by Sobukwe but signed by Selby Ngendane, secretary of the Africanist caucus, was later read to the conference. It noted that the group had irreconcilable differences with the Kliptown Charter and had tried on numerous occasions to put their case 'peacefully and logically'.

'We have come to the parting of the ways,' it stated.

At the Congress, it had been met, it said, with murderous intent on the part of leadership. 'We are launching out on our own, as custodians of ANC policy as formulated in 1912, and pursued up to the time of the Congress Alliance.'[116]

The Africanists were claiming to be the true heirs to the African National Congress. But in future, Luthuli was to refer to the breakaway nationalist group as 'our far right'.[117] More than 10 years later, Tambo wrote a stinging criticism of the PAC, in which he accused it of being divisive and irresponsible. At the Transvaal annual provincial meeting, he said, they had 'brought to the conference a bogus delegation of armed thugs from a bogus branch with the obvious intention of violently disrupting the conference'.

The following April, in 1959, the Pan-Africanist Congress was formed, with Robert Sobukwe elected as president. It was a bitter conclusion to a long, drawn-out battle for the heart and mind of the ANC.

'But on a social basis, we all remained friends,' remarked Adelaide. 'There was a lot of teasing when we met. I used to say, "Sons of Africa, you have sold out the nation." Rosetten Nciba used to say, "Look, I have to come and talk to you and when I have finished you will leave Oliver Tambo in the Youth League and come and join the PAC!"'[118] On a personal level, their political differences were not permitted to interfere with long-standing friendships.

Oliver Tambo often went further. He had an unusually tolerant, Christian humanist approach. He could not spurn anyone, even his enemies. A startling example of this was, perhaps, after Thembi Tambo was born. Oliver and Adelaide held a party to give thanks for their daughter's birth. Gladys Tuge remembered the unexpected lesson she learnt from her brother-in-law. 'Everybody was there, even the [uninvited] Special Branch,' she recalled. 'They were most welcomed... And he was saying, these are my friends. We differ where we differ, but otherwise they are working. What do you expect, if they are told to go and write something about me, they have to. But, otherwise, they are human beings.'[119]

Certainly, while Luthuli observed the Congress proceedings in December, he seemed to feel that if Tambo had not managed to prevent the schism, nobody could have. In the months that followed, Luthuli made clear his high approval of Tambo. To his Secretary-General, he felt able to express his own concerns – about the Freedom Charter and the difficulties of Natal regionalism. He was relieved, too, that Tambo, who had been appointed to head the Constitution Commission, was able to balance provincial identity with the need for a central administrative efficiency. The Tambo Commission recommended that provincial identity be retained and local initiatives encouraged. It gave more constitutional recognition to the Women's and the Youth Leagues, and endorsed non-racialism as well as the Freedom Charter. The constitution, revised to reflect the ANC as a mass movement and adopted in 1957, came to be known as the 'Tambo Constitution'.[120] Walter Sisulu observed that Luthuli trusted Tambo and regarded him as a balanced political thinker. 'I think he would, on the other hand, be more suspicious about some of us. And he would think, well, this is my man. And I think that meant a great deal.'[121]

At the 1958 Congress elections, in the face of the serial bans on Luthuli, which confined him to the Stanger area, the new constitutional position of deputy president was filled by Tambo. Luthuli's public endorsement of Tambo made a deep impression on a young Jacob Zuma. In 1959, Tambo travelled to Durban to open a regional provincial conference. It was at a time of brief respite between bans, and Luthuli was also on the platform. Zuma recalled vividly Luthuli's comment after Tambo had spoken, explaining with great clarity the proposed national programme for the year. Even if he – Luthuli – and others in the leadership were to die, said Luthuli, there were young men like Oliver Tambo who were now ready to take over responsibility for the ANC.

'I believed in Luthuli, I loved him. He was the leader. For him to say so [this] to this other leader was an important thing to me.'[122]

Released from the Treason Trial, Tambo was able to resume his duties for Mandela & Tambo. Without his partner, though, the burden was heavy, particularly as an increasing number of victims of apartheid came forward. Campaigns continued. In his report in 1958, Tambo had spoken about the increasing numbers of mass trials emerging out of popular resistance. Besides the Treason Trial, these ranged from hundreds of women arrested for protesting against pass laws, dozens charged with incitement following the April stay-away during the whites-only elections, and the hundreds of peasants facing murder charges in the Sekhukhuneland uprising against chiefs perceived to be collaborating with the government as a result of the Bantu Authorities Act.

'[The] theatre of conflict is shifting to the law courts,' observed Tambo, 'in as much as effective mass demand or mass resistance to tyranny and fascism leads, almost inevitably, to mass arrests and prosecutions...'[123]

SACTU's Pound-a-Day campaign – although it, not surprisingly, failed to realise the demands of the workers (the official 'minimum' black worker's wage was 15s. and 7d a week) – proved to be very popular, drawing in the heartfelt support of crowds of women. It was their households that were struggling to make ends meet on the continuing miserable wages for blacks in the context of tightened job reservation; the increased poll tax for men and its extension to women; the strengthening of the pass laws and the extension of passes for themselves; the changing circumstances in their children's education; and the continuing exploitation of black labour both on farms and in factories. The campaign revived the image of the Congress Alliance in a highly visible way. (It was this and other campaigns that Tambo accused the PAC of vigorously opposing.) The potato boycott and the consumer boycott – although again having failed to achieve their demands – proved to be successful mobilising and public-relations exercises. And, added to the NEC's 1959 report, most likely penned by Tambo himself, 'When our local purchasing power is combined with that of sympathetic organisations overseas we [will] wield a devastating weapon'.[124] The report referred to the sterling work being undertaken in the United Kingdom by an *Isitwalandwe* ['Sir' or 'Lord'] of the ANC, Father Huddleston, who – together with Canon John Collins – formed the Anti-Apartheid Committee and was broadcasting Luthuli's bold call for full-scale international sanctions against trade, sport and cultural cooperation with South Africa and the boycott of its products. The publicity of the boycott exceeded the expectations of the organisation's leadership, and they began to prepare to follow up the notion of broadening the 'United Front' still further.

The NEC's annual report also identified the weaknesses that still beset the ANC. The wage campaign, it pointed out, had failed to be taken to the farms and compounds, whose workers were 'the most exploited group'. Administration and organisation continued to be uneven. They needed also to work among the peasants in the rural areas, and more work was needed to keep the Alliance united. But there were also limited achievements – for instance, the women's campaign against passes had resulted in the postponement of the fateful day when it should become a day-to-day reality for them.

Foiled by the publicity of the 1956 women's march, the government had shifted its attention to rural women, seeking to intimidate them far from the public eye. It sought – via the back door, so to speak – to create a *fait accompli* of women with passes. The response, with the help of ANC women, in particular, Lilian Ngoyi, who was in the NEC as well as president of the Women's League, contributed to a feeling of mutiny in the rural areas – in Sekhukhuneland, Pondoland and other areas – against increasing government attempts to usurp the role of traditional leaders as people's leaders. *Kgosi ke kgosi ka batho* was the maxim – 'a chief is a chief by the people'. Simmering resentment materialised in sporadic burning of huts, and the bitterness came to a head in May 1959, when nine people – perceived collaborators with the apartheid order in Sekhukhuneland – were killed, and Tambo was asked to defend them.[125]

As popular frustration spread, the authorities set out to track down the agitators. The fact was, though, that while the ANC had a rather loose network of supporters in the traditional leaders, it had not made much headway in the rural areas, partly because permission from the Department of Native Affairs to hold meetings was more often than not refused, but also because the leadership, though with rural roots, was urban-based.

Far more successful, since the 1940s, was the Communist Party, which had come to rural struggle via migrant workers in city hostels. They were the ones who joined the Party – Elias Motsoaledi, John Nkadimeng, David Bopape, John Phala and Flag Boshielo, all CPSA/SACP as well as ANC members. They were among the Bapedi leaders in political organisations, but there were others who retained more regular and emotional contacts with Sekhukhuneland.[126]

This was also the time of Mau Mau-inspired peasant uprisings, and the killing of some whites in Kenya. The attacks on 'collaborator' chiefs appeared to fearful observers to be a similar prelude to violent rural resistance in South Africa.

Tambo drove to Sekhukhuneland to speak to the growing number of accused, but the strains of the firm's shortage of legal resources, the increasing political pressures and tensions in the midst of the Treason Trial meant that he could not undertake the project as a whole, so Shulamith Muller, an experienced attorney and CPSA member, undertook the huge task. But that was not all Tambo had to deal with. Peasants were approaching the ANC with requests for arms to resist this onslaught on their traditions. The Sekhukhune revolt, as well as the later Pondo uprising, was ultimately to influence the movement in its consideration of taking up armed struggle two or three years later.

But the year 1959 proved to be eventful in other parts of the country too. Confrontations with the state were escalating, while strife in the movement itself was leading to irremediable cleavages. With the Treason Trial continuing to tie up most of the top leadership, it fell upon those remaining to pick up and carry the baton. In town and countryside, events were unfolding that necessitated the ANC to tail-end community confrontations, rather than guide them. Near Johannesburg, Everton Township, which was not receiving sufficient attention from the ANC, undertook a bitterly contested bus boycott. Further south, in Sharpeville, the ANC branch was struggling without national support to keep a coherent membership.[127] These were to become fruitful recuiting areas for the newly formed PAC.

Not long after the Sekhukhuneland uprisings, Tambo was called upon to assist as an attorney on another violent turn of events, this time a police massacre in South West Africa (now Namibia). On 10 December 1959 – Human Rights Day observed by the Congress Alliance throughout South Africa – police fired on a demonstration organised by the Ovamboland People's Organisation at Windhoek location, killing 13 and seriously wounding 32 others. A few days later, Oliver Tambo received an urgent message to take legal action to prevent the deportation from Windhoek within 72 hours of the four political leaders – Sam Nujoma and Nathan Mbaeva, president and secretary of the OPO (later SWAPO) respectively, and two leaders of the South West African National Union (SWANU). Ironically, but not surprisingly, the South African state dealt with protests against the violation of human rights by directly revoking even more human rights.

Tambo took the next available flight to Windhoek, but just as he stepped off the plane, two policemen and the Chief Bantu Affairs Commissioner accosted him. They informed him that as he did not have a permit to enter South West Africa, he was required to take the next plane back to Johannesburg. When Tambo pointed to many examples of permits not being required, they retorted that the waiver applied only to whites. 'Natives' required permits. Furthermore, they assured him, because of his political record, he would be refused a visa by the authorities. Despite legal arguments by Tambo, the officers were adamant, and even brought armed reinforcements to monitor him during his overnight stay at the airport until the next available plane. The only concession he could extract from them was to meet three of his clients – the fourth, Jacob Kuhangua, had already been arrested and was about to be moved. But early next morning, Tambo himself was deported back to South Africa.

A few days later, traditional leaders, chiefs Kutako and Samuel Witbooi, sent a letter of complaint to the Secretary-General of the United Nations.

'We find it very difficult,' they wrote, 'to have our cases defended in courts in South West Africa, where there are only white lawyers who are not keen at all to help Africans. For that reason, we asked Mr Oliver Tambo, a well-known African Lawyer from the Union of South Africa, who on his arrival by air from Johannesburg was not granted the necessary permit to enter South West Africa. In South West Africa, Africans have no lawyers to defend them.'[128]

While all these professional adventures were taking place, Tambo was also providing backing on the political front by calling on the ANC's international contacts. As Secretary-General (in cooperation with Walter Sisulu behind the scenes), he corresponded with a number of sympathisers abroad. He met visitors and journalists who were aware of the significance of the ANC. In 1954, he met Canon Collins of St Paul's Cathedral in London and founder of Christian Action, which aimed to draw Christians into agitating for peace in a Cold War climate. In 1952, Huddleston had written to Christian Action, asking for financial support in defending and assisting the families of volunteers in the Defiance Campaign. Collins had not hesitated. Through speeches, sermons and letters to the press, he raised £1 450 and sent it to the small committee, chaired by Alan Paton, the liberal and famous author of *Cry, the Beloved Country.* When they met Collins in person, both Tambo and Huddleston were impressed with the Canon's energy and commitment. For his part, the Canon was delighted with Huddleston, 'a wonderful person to meet', who showed him around a Sophiatown which was soon to be demolished. Huddleston urged Collins to consider launching a campaign to boycott South African sports and culture and publicise the evils of the Bantu Education Act. While there were indeed concerned whites, who helped him with a feeding scheme for African children, '70 per cent of our voluntary helpers are Jewish', he informed Collins.[129]

Oliver Tambo took Collins to meet Walter Sisulu and other members of the ANC at the office and, as Tambo drove him back to the home of Bishop Reeves, he opened up. He told Collins about his hopes of becoming ordained, but also of his discouragement at the timidity of the Church. There were, however, a very few white priests – Huddleston and Reeves among them – who gave him a small ray of hope. In his diary, Canon Collins described his impression of Tambo, to whom he felt especially drawn: 'A man of intelligence and dedication, without self-seeking and with an exceptionally warm and attractive personality: a truly Christian spirit.'[130] This was to be the first meeting in a close, warm and lifelong friendship that was to reap many benefits for the liberation movement.

Another visitor whom Tambo met was George Houser, a Methodist minister from New York and a friend of the African cause, and with whom he would form a warm friendship. In his correspondence with international figures, one of the most exciting for Tambo was the response he received from the famous African American baritone and political activist, Paul Robeson: 'I know that I am ever by your side... I am deeply proud that you are my brothers and sisters and nephews and nieces – that I sprang from your forebears. We come from a mighty, courageous people, creators of great civilisations... creators of new ways of life in our own time and in the future. We shall win our freedoms together. Our folk will have their place in the ranks of those shaping human destiny.'[131]

Robeson was proudly remembered by black South Africans for his 'thrilling' London speech in 1949 at the invitation of Krishna Menon (later India's delegate to the United Nations) and Yusuf Dadoo, who were opposing the UN's decision to grant South Africa a 'mandate' to administer South West Africa, the former German colony. Following Robeson's talk, the South African government banned the playing of all his records on radio. It was reminiscent, Robeson told the *Manchester Guardian*, of the time when the Nazi *gauleiter* of Norway banned his records during the war – 'But the Norwegian underground still played them right through the occupation'.[132] Later, he was to give another performance of spirituals at St Paul's Cathedral to a packed audience organised by Collins' Christian Action in aid of the Treason Trial.

Collins, it seems, proved to be a talented events manager. He held public appeals in a number of venues in London and other cities, placed full-page, discounted advertisements in *The Observer* and sent appeals, signed by famous names such as philosopher Bertrand Russell, writers Compton McKenzie and the South African Laurens van der Post and up-and-coming Labour Party politicians. The artist John Piper donated a Christmas card design. Huddleston's touch was also discerned in the international support facilitated by Christian Action. The jazz festival in the Royal Festival Hall attracted the likes of brass musicians Johnny Dankworth and Humphrey Lyttleton. Tickets were sold out.

In response to the publicity blitz, donations poured in by post, and the mammoth defence trial was able to grind on. The funds sent to Bishop Reeves were not only earmarked for the high costs of defence but also to assist with welfare for the dependants of the accused. At the end of June 1960, while the Treason Trial was still in progress, the London office of the International Defence and Aid Fund was able to record that it had raised £65,000, with an additional £75,000 for welfare in other parts of South Africa. This initiative was to lay the foundations for ongoing financial and activist support in the long, hard years that lay ahead for Oliver Tambo and the ANC.

In the meantime, in 1959, the ANC National Executive had also sent a memorandum to the United Nations to back up the call for international sanctions against South Africa's apartheid regime. The outcome was a great morale booster. Sixty-seven countries, including even the USA, condemned South Africa's racist policies. While the South African delegate boycotted the item on the agenda, Britain – South Africa's largest trading partner and co-Commonwealth member – opposed the motion, maintaining that South Africa's internal policies were their 'domestic affair'.

It was encouraging to see that independent Ghana, now a member of the UN, seemed to set a new tone to the community of nations – but there was still a long way to go. ES (Enuga) Reddy, a UN official and friend of the liberation movement from India, complained that 'every year, around October, the South African question would be discussed; people would make speeches and go home and nothing would happen. Next year, they'd come and make speeches again'.[133]

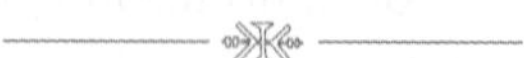

In 1959, young Swedish journalist Per Wästberg arrived in South Africa. A 'fabulous meeting' of the ANC in Johannesburg made an enduring impression on him – largely, it seems, because of the quality of speeches.[134] Oliver Tambo, Duma Nokwe and Lilian Ngoyi were on the platform. He specifically recalled Tambo's courtesy when he politely greeted Colonel Piet Simmel at the back, and then later towards a white member of the audience who asked if he could become a member of the ANC. The young man who made this request was Ronald Segal, talented editor of the opposition journal, *Africa South*. Segal recalled that Tambo looked extremely irritated, possibly because Segal had said he wanted to ask a question about 'Group Areas', and then proceeded to ask why the Congress Alliance had allowed itself to become a 'Group Area'. (He meant that, like the apartheid government, which segregated residential areas, the Congress Alliance had divided its organisations into separate racial groups.) Segal then flourished a pound note and offered to pay his ANC subscription well in advance.[135] Despite his discomfort at the unexpected question, Tambo thanked him for his interest and pointed out that the Congress of Democrats was a member of the Congress Alliance, and directed him to COD members in the audience. (This presence of mind and diplomatic response impressed Wästberg, and he remembered it when he met Tambo years later in exile.) Then, recalled Wästberg, the Security Police came in with their sniffer dogs: 'Lilian Ngoyi stood up, and Oliver, and they asked people to sing, and people sang a number of songs and "Nkosi Sikelele"; it was so touching. And then the hall was emptied, they were out in the streets and police rounded up a few people, questioning [them] and then let them go. They also [questioned] me.'

Less than two years were to pass before Wästberg met Tambo again, this time in his own country. Wästberg was to form the Scandinavian branch of the International Defence and Aid Fund, and become part of a team of warm supporters of the South African liberation movement after it was outlawed.

For the ANC, international relations also included the African continent. The annual reports to Congress increasingly included discussions of the beginnings of freedom – Ghana in 1957, and Nigerian and Tanzanian independence on the cards. The 1958 Pan African Congress in Ghana was the highlight of the decade. Africa Day was celebrated around the country in April 1958 and in the years that followed. In Alexandra, Tambo together with others – including his colleague, Duma Nokwe, who had been elected Secretary-General the previous year to replace Tambo, now the Deputy President – wore traditional Basotho dress. Afterwards, in exile, when Tony Seedat gave Tambo a photograph of him on the occasion, he treasured it, clipping a note to it, 'Historic photo – to be framed'. The ANC-organised event had been a way of sending a message that the Africanists did not have the monopoly of pride in Africa.

A few months after the ANC's 'bust up' with the Africanists, the Pan-Africanist Congress was officially launched in the Community Hall in Orlando. Significantly, the name was chosen to celebrate the dawning of a glorious new, independent African continent. As a defiant retort to the bad old history, the event took place on the April weekend of 'Van Riebeeck Day', a public holiday on which many white South Africans celebrated the arrival of the Dutch settlers with *volkspele* (Afrikaans folk dancing), sports and sunbathing. The new PAC unanimously elected Robert Sobukwe as president, with the fiery Potlako Leballo as the national secretary. Significantly, Alexandra's 'wild man'[136] Madzunya was not elected on to the executive committee. In the months that followed, Sobukwe did much to give direction towards refining the Africanist image. The group had often been popularly associated with fierce speeches and slogans such as 'Drive the white man back into the sea', but the bottom line was always that Africans must rule. Minorities, such as whites and Indians, would be welcome to stay, said Sobukwe, provided their sole loyalty was to Africa and they dropped any signs of racist arrogance. In a free Africa, if a largely black electorate elected a white candidate to Parliament, 'colour will count for nothing'.[137] But until then, the interests of whites and Indians, even those claiming to be sympathetic, were structurally opposed to the aspirations of native Africans.

Like the ANC, the new organisation began to plan a series of campaigns. The first, 'Call me mister', tried to raise the status consciousness of black men and women, who were routinely called by their first (always Western) 'Christian' names – or worse. Very few white employers even knew the surnames of their domestic servants and workers. The PAC urged supporters to demand that they be addressed properly. But the more familiar and even more urgent campaign, in the eyes of the PAC, was the one that had been on the ANC programme for an inexcusably long time, they felt – the pass laws. This had, in fact, been one of their chief criticisms against the ANC leadership; that the pass campaign was floundering. At the 1958 ANC Congress, there had been sharp questions as to why the phenomenal women's march in 1956 had not been followed up according to the Congress resolution of two years earlier.

At the 1958 Congress, Tambo had explained that it was naive to imagine that one campaign would succeed in eradicating the pass laws. The struggle was necessarily prolonged, 'now taking one form and now another. To hope that by striking one blow we would defeat the system would result in disillusionment'.[138] In the months that followed, the NEC thus worked on a strategic plan and the following year, Duma Nokwe, the new national secretary, unfolded the design for 'the second phase' of the anti-pass campaign – '26 June 1959–June 1960'.[139]

In a 12-point programme, Nokwe outlined the NEC's broadly based, holistic campaign, designed to build up resistance incrementally and inclusively over the entire country. Its plan was to draw in rural as well as urban demands in a series of widespread conferences, recruiting opponents of apartheid of 'all sections of the population', building up to a broad, united front. Participating organisations would include sports and cultural associations, churches, trade unions, and human rights, liberal and other associations. All these communications would culminate in nationwide demonstrations on Union Day in May 1960. This would be followed by a national 'All-in Conference'. If successful, the apartheid regime might well react negatively, and it was important to be prepared for any eventuality. 'We should be in a state of readiness for the banning of the organisation,' warned the NEC.[140]

At the very centre of the campaign would be the anti-pass protest. The launch of this was planned to take place on 31 March, the anniversary of the ANC's Transvaal protest against passes in 1919. From thenceforth, that day had come to be known as 'Anti-Pass Day'.[141]

This strategic programme received warm approval, and the preparations immediately began to take place. Branches in the Congress Alliance began recruiting drives to mobilise their members and supporters for a resounding national launch. One of these drives resulted in a march of thousands in the streets of Durban – Luthuli territory. The ANC executives were delighted at the popular response, and were optimistic that the 'second phase' was getting off to a good start. In fact, Tambo himself travelled to a number of key ANC strongholds to plan the preparations.

May Brutus recalled a secret meeting one night early in 1960 at her bungalow in Shell Street, Port Elizabeth. Her husband, Dennis, had asked her to prepare food for an unspecified number of people. Their home was a regular 'safe' venue, and May was used to cooking for the likes of Govan Mbeki, Raymond Mhlaba and Nelson Mandela. They arrived in ones and twos – 'you didn't realise there were so many... there might have been well over 50'.[142]

Suddenly, the news broke that the PAC had also organised an anti-pass campaign, and that its national protest was fixed for 10 days before the ANC's appointed day. At the PAC conference of December 19–20 (just a few days after the ANC Congress), Sobukwe had asked for a mandate to embark on such a campaign, and the move was unanimously approved. 'The movement is about to cross,' he promised prophetically, 'our historical Rubicon.'[143]

More than a decade later, Oliver Tambo would look back on the event, still indignant and mistrustful of the motives of the PAC. 'With typical disregard for united action,' he noted, 'the PAC had earlier sent, and published, a letter "inviting" the ANC to abandon the massive countrywide plans for action, and to join at very short notice an unplanned, hurried switch from a status campaign to an ill-prepared campaign which, but for the police bullets at Sharpeville, was doomed to fail... [It] was the massacre,' not the campaign, he argued, 'which drew attention to 21 March.'[144]

It seemed to Tambo and the entire ANC leadership that the PAC opportunistically and irresponsibly piggybacked the months of ANC preparation and propaganda for the benefit of their own campaign. 'They [entered] the field of direct competition with the ANC on the Passes, including the decision to jump in front of the ANC, ill-prepared and unprepared, with all the possibilities of confusing the masses and creating bloody chaos.'

But Tambo's intense irritation at the time rapidly changed to shock and horror when he learnt, through a radio news bulletin in the afternoon of 21 March, that 69 men, women and children had been shot dead at an anti-pass demonstration in Adelaide's home town of Sharpeville. The carnage of that horrific afternoon in 1960 would forever change the face of the liberation struggle and, indeed, the path it was to follow.

BOND ST OXFORD CIR
HOLBORN BANK
ALDGATE STRATFOR
FOREST GATE . ILFOR
25
VICTORIA
MLL 887

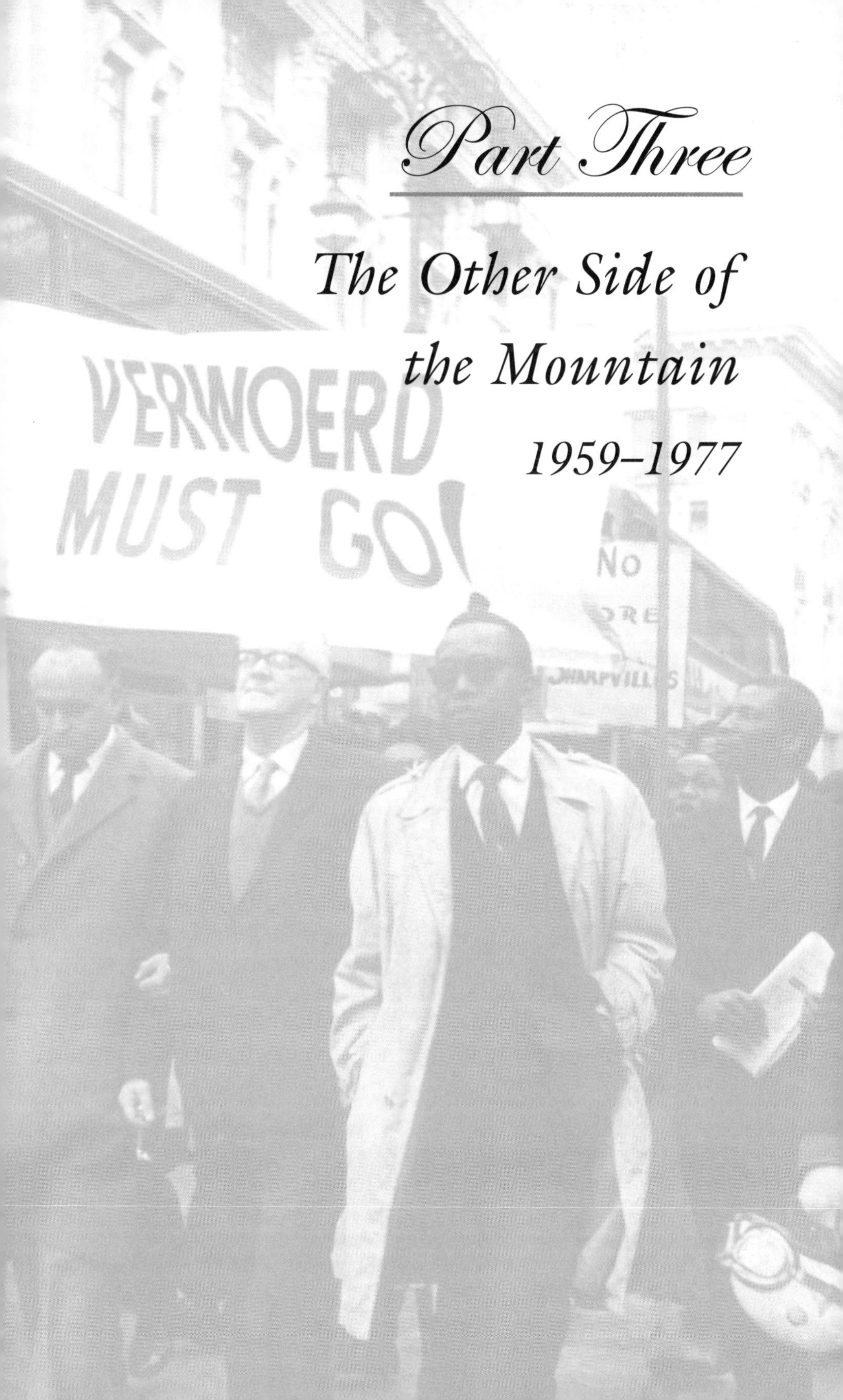

Part Three

The Other Side of the Mountain

1959–1977

CHAPTER EIGHT

Into the Wilderness

ONE EVENING IN APRIL 1958, Oliver Tambo had come home to his wife Adelaide and their baby in his little township house in Wattville and had said, 'The ANC wants us to leave the country as a family and tell the world what is happening here.'

He had just returned from an Africa Day rally in Alexandra Township, which was celebrating the Conference of Independent States being held in Accra at the same time. It had been a glorious autumn day; Tambo had donned a Basotho hat and blanket, the national costume of his wife's family. It symbolised the unity of the African nations, and was a considered retort to the Africanists threatening to break away over the first clause of the Freedom Charter – one of its most vocal and belligerent leaders was an Alex man. The event had been successful and exhilarating. Speakers exhorted workers to rally behind SACTU's 'Pound-a-Day' Campaign, which had indeed won the support of thousands of women, worn down by the miserably low wages of their men. Oddly, the very simplicity and boldness of the campaign's demand had expressed for working people an empowering agency, rather than an expectation of its immediate realisation. Alex leaders Alfred Nzo and Thomas Nkobi had organised it well. A few thousand had turned out in Alex's Freedom Square. Overflowing into the main street of modest shop fronts and the straggle of pre-war houses – their original styles misshapen by bumps and protrusions and lean-tos to accommodate the ever-growing population – the crowd struggled to hear the speeches amid the ululations, the 'Afrika!' salutes and the freedom songs. Oliver's ex-colleague and ex-pupil from St Peter's, advocate Duma Nokwe, who was soon to take over from him as Secretary-General, was with him, also in Basotho garb. Oliver was to be elected Deputy President of the ANC at its next conference, in the wake of yet another banning of Chief Luthuli. The crowd gave them both an overwhelming welcome.

In a caucus before the festivities, however, Oliver received word from Chief Luthuli, advising him to be prepared to leave South Africa in the event of the banning of the movement. When that occurred, the NEC anticipated, there would be widespread arrests, and the ANC would need an ambassador to carry abroad the message of its vision and solicit support for the movement.

Adelaide recalled their conversation that evening very clearly. 'I don't want to go with a small child,' she had responded in dismay. 'We have an ageing family. I don't want to come back to find that I have no relatives; that they have all died.'

Oliver suggested that they take a break before deciding, so they went to the cinema in the old location. Afterwards, they drove to the outskirts of the township. Oliver parked the car along a quiet stretch of road lined with dark wattle trees next to the veld. With the shadows of mine dumps looming above them, the two sat talking for a long while.

Tambo had already set into motion his application for the church ministry, an aspiration that had eluded him for many years. Now, at last, married and settled and with the Treason Trial behind him, the prize was within his grasp. The ANC had now disrupted his plans, but he accepted this turn of events philosophically. He reminded Adelaide of the words to an old song, 'You cannot refuse when you are being sent to do a mission.'

'We can't say no to the organisation,' he explained.[1]

It seemed that insofar as Oliver had received a calling, it was to take up the cause of the ANC and of his people.

The tragedy at Sharpeville had dramatically accelerated the plan for an external mission. In the rapidly unfolding events of the two or three days that followed, it became imperative that Tambo leave immediately, before he was picked up. It was also vital for the ANC to respond clearly – and politically – to the Sharpeville and Langa calamities. On the Saturday, Chief Luthuli publicly burnt his passbook, followed by other key leaders of the movement such as Walter Sisulu and Mark Shope of SACTU. A wave of pass-burning followed in ANC pockets throughout the country. Temporarily destabilised by the carnage, the Dutch Reformed Church condemned the pass system, which they now clearly saw as the cause of much suffering and anger among the black population. Cabinet minister Paul Sauer, who as Minister of Interior had been responsible for its administration, announced that the pass system would be abolished.

Three days after Sharpeville, Tambo received a telephone call from Ronald Segal, the editor of the liberal journal *Africa South*. Segal urged the ANC to seize the initiative, and reported that bands of 'young PAC toughs' were roaming the streets of Cape Town, threatening ANC leaders. They seemed to have taken over control of the city.[2] A mild Tambo was, however, noncommittal in his response to Segal's appeal. He recalled the young man's impetuous challenge to the ANC a year or two earlier, and was also mindful of the very real possibility that the telephone might be tapped – as they were both banned, just speaking to each other was inviting arrest. Tambo had nevertheless warmed to Segal even though his application for individual membership had been turned down. He had had the courage to make a public commitment to the ANC, and Tambo felt he could count on Segal's wholehearted assistance in the project now unfolding. The following day, Segal received a call, during which the unfamiliar voice asked him to make his way to a certain trade union office. Shrugging off the possibility that the message might be a trap set by the Security Police, Segal rushed over to the nearby building. There he found Oliver Tambo, smiling warmly and delighting in Segal's astonishment at finding him there, in Cape Town.

The articulate and successful youngest son of an upper middle-class family, Segal had access to his mother's chauffeur-driven Vauxhall. (His own car was too well known to the local police to risk using.) He proposed that Tambo and he drive north to the British Protectorate of Bechuanaland, the most suitable exit route, and one that did not require passports from South Africans. Tambo would drive, disguised as a chauffeur, while Ronald would pose as his employer. Then, once Tambo was under British protection, Ronald would drive himself back home to Cape Town. In the meantime, Walter Sisulu contacted Frene Ginwala, a young journalist residing in Rhodesia (Zimbabwe), and designated her to make follow-up arrangements once Tambo was out of the country.[3]

On 27 March, Oliver Tambo drove up with Ronald Segal to Johannesburg from Cape Town. He wore a white uniform, gloves and a driver's cap. There had been a tentative proposal that Arthur Lethele, a medical doctor and ANC leader in Kimberley, would accompany Tambo abroad. Despite the risk of being recognised, the two drove to Kimberley but were unable to locate Lethele, so they hastily drove on, nervous that they might be apprehended at each little *dorp* they passed through. South Africa was in turmoil. Cape Town's streets were facing the biggest ever march of migrant workers from the township of Langa to the City Hall, terrifying the white population, who feared that the dreaded 'Revolution' was finally upon them. The South African Defence Force, including its air force, was put on alert. Chief Luthuli had called for a nationwide general strike. In ANC townships, passbooks were burning.

Tambo dropped Segal at a cousin's house in one of Johannesburg's leafy northern suburbs. The plan had been to leave the country immediately, without going home. But, recalled Tambo, 'I could not bear not telling my wife, or attending to my files in the office.'[4] So he drove straight home to Wattville. It was a Saturday afternoon. Adelaide had just returned from her shift at the Non-European Hospital, irritated because she had not heard from her husband since he had left, allegedly to attend a court case. She saw an unfamiliar, shiny green Vauxhall stop outside the little house – and to her amazement Oliver stepped out, wearing a white uniform. After their embraces, Oliver related the latest, drastic turn of events. The ANC expected that the leadership would be rounded up imminently, and he had been instructed to leave as soon as possible. Adelaide found herself agreeing.

'I wasn't even thinking of jail, I was just thinking of the mission – that if he was not going, whatever mission he was going to perform, would fail. So I said, "Yes, you must go."'[5]

Nevertheless, she persuaded her husband to at least take leave of Bishop Reeves and Nelson. She pointed out that a news broadcast had announced that the police had been instructed not to ask people for passes or to harass them in any way. Tambo was sceptical but agreed to let Adelaide accompany him on these last errands. Then he scooped Dali up in his arms and put Thembi on his lap, and hugged them both. Adelaide went into the bedroom and packed a small navy-blue suitcase for Oliver. Then they left – it was to be more than 30 years before Oliver Tambo returned to his Wattville home.

Johannesburg city centre was buzzing with excitement. Africans were walking openly in the streets, taking advantage of their unaccustomed freedom, calling out greetings and telling each other that this could not last. The black cinemas, the Rio and the Good Hope, were packed with patrons. In Commissioner Street, Oliver and Adelaide met Arthur Lethele and his wife Mary.

'What are you still doing here?' Arthur asked Oliver.

'Come on, let's leave together,' Oliver countered.

He related to Arthur his search for him in Kimberley the day before. Arthur then called Mary aside and they spoke briefly.

'Go,' she said. Arthur was, however, hesitant, and then finally resolved to stay. Adelaide remembered Oliver 'grumbling to all the people there, "Why should I go, why don't you go?"' The following Tuesday, Lethele was rounded up, together with all the other ANC leadership, and was eventually deported to his birthplace in Lesotho (then Basutoland). A year later, in March 1961, he represented the ANC's South African delegation at the third All-African People's Conference in Cairo.

Late that night, Tambo dropped Adelaide at home, and then went off to his chambers. He worked on unfinished cases throughout the night and through the following day until 10pm, leaving written instructions for Mendi Msimang and Ruth Mompati. Just a few documents remained, and he took those with him. Then he stopped by the hospital to see Adelaide, to take final leave of her.[6]

It took Tambo and Segal three or four hours to reach Bechuanaland.[7] It became hotter and hotter as they neared the Tropic of Capricorn. As they approached the border, they decided to risk driving up to the legal frontier, and were relieved to encounter no trouble from a lone policeman with a register. They signed their names and drove on to the nearest town, Lobatse, six miles away, where they parked the car at three o'clock in the morning outside a local hotel. There they dozed and, later in the morning, drove to the office of the Commissioner and announced their intention to seek asylum in the Protectorate. While Segal carried a South African passport, Tambo did not have one, and had entered the Protectorate illegally. On their return to the hotel, they proceeded to book themselves in, but the young attendant, though sympathetic, seemed noncommittal. He told Segal that the hotel admitted only white guests.

But Seretse Khama, Oliver's old college friend who had left Fort Hare in support of the strike in 1942, was now the king, or 'paramount chief' in colonial parlance, albeit in an officially suspended capacity. Khama's marriage to Ruth, a white Englishwoman, in 1952 had caused an immense uproar in South Africa. Prime Minister DF Malan had refused to countenance Khama's natural succession to the throne of Bechuanaland, even though the marriage had gone down very well with the general populace in the Protectorate. Finally, though, the Khamas were permitted into Bechuanaland. Later, Khama renounced his claim to the throne, but was overwhelmingly voted in as prime minister once the Protectorate became independent.

Now, some five years after his return to his homeland, Khama instructed the Resident Commissioner to allow Tambo to stay at the hostel 'for visiting chiefs' three miles out of town. Despite holding the highest rank, Khama was powerless to insist that Tambo be allowed to stay at the hotel. Segregation, if not apartheid, still ruled as a matter of course in the colonial British Protectorates.

Ronald Segal thus drove Tambo to the hostel, and because no restaurant would serve Tambo, they had a lunch of biscuits and fruit. They then bade one another farewell and, wondering if he would ever see Tambo again, Segal set off back to Cape Town.

Twenty-four hours later Tambo, sitting on a straight-backed chair in the sun with his sleeves rolled up and working on his unfinished legal documents, was surprised but not displeased to see Ronald drive up again. Segal delivered his news. He had got as far as Johannesburg when the Security Police made their expected swoop in the early hours of the morning. Chief Luthuli, Walter Sisulu, Duma Nokwe, Joe Slovo and thousands more had been picked up, and a State of Emergency had been declared, which meant that legally their detention could last indefinitely. Verwoerd had repudiated Sauer's expression of regret and posted him off in disgrace to an embassy in Latin America. The prime minister had, furthermore, spoken to the Dutch Reformed Synod and had won them over too – it was imperative that, as Christians and Afrikaners, their commitment to maintaining the purity of the *volk* should not waver.

Segal had agonised and finally decided to return to Tambo to assist in any way he could. Oliver's response to Segal's news was firm – although it pained him that he could not be home to help strategise with his colleagues, what had happened was the very reason he had left South Africa. Under the circumstances, he could no longer expect instructions from his organisation – he must proceed to the post office to cable the United Nations. In his telegram, Tambo requested facilities to appear before the Security Council to explain the nature of the South African crisis. At the same time, Segal cabled Rosalynde Ainslee, the *Africa South* representative in London, to ask if she could make travel arrangements for Tambo and himself from Britain or an African country.

The pair were soon to discover that every missive that exchanged hands at the post office was relayed to South Africa. Soon after the despatch of the cable, minister Eric Louw announced in the House of Assembly that two of the country's most hostile instigators, Tambo and Segal, were in hiding in Bechuanaland, plotting to give evidence against South Africa at the United Nations.[8]

The day after the Minister's denunciation, Segal received a welter of calls from the press and began to parry their questions. It became clear to the press that Oliver Tambo was indeed in the Protectorate. One journalist, Joe Podbrey, correspondent for *The Rand Daily Mail*, related how his editor, Raymond Louw, sent him to Lobatse to interview Tambo. As an ex-serviceman and a member of the since banned Communist Party, Podbrey had met Tambo, Sisulu and Mandela at an emergency joint committee meeting a few months earlier. He had been deeply impressed with the three men.[9] So when Podbrey telephoned to propose an interview, Tambo readily agreed to meet him.

The day of the appointment dawned on a searing, dry Kalahari morning. Half an hour before the meeting at the Lobatse Hotel, Podbrey ordered an ice-cold beer. As he sat there, enjoying his drink in the coolly darkened room, he became aware of two safari-clad men conversing in Afrikaans. In a matter-of-fact way, the speaker mentioned Tambo's name – that he was in town, and that plans were well under way to seize him and shanghai him across the border. 'They apparently thought that nobody would understand them.' Podbrey quietly put down his beer and left to pre-empt Tambo's arrival. He walked down the street and saw Tambo approaching. The two conversed briefly, and then drove off in Podbrey's car. Tambo took the threat seriously. That evening, he made arrangements to sleep at the home of a farming friend of Podbrey's.

The decision, it seems, was a wise one. The story was corroborated by further, bizarre evidence from a different quarter. A day or two earlier, Adelaide, on duty at the Non-European Hospital in Johannesburg, had received an unexpected visit from an old school friend of Oliver's. At first, she did not recognise the man, as he had smeared his face and hands with white ointment, a traditional medicine believed to ward off evil. He told Adelaide that he was to visit Oliver the next day – would she like to send him anything? Embarrassed by the amusement of the white doctors and the raised eyebrows of the other nurses, Adelaide went down to a delicatessen and packed a basket of fruit and food. It later transpired that the man – who shall remain nameless – was accompanying two white men to Bechuanaland in order to kidnap Tambo. A nurse who knew Adelaide subsequently told her that she had seen the man in Lobatse with two white men: one was in a car and another was on horseback. The 'friend' was carrying a mask and chloroform. Apparently, the plan was for Oliver's supposed 'friend' to spend the night at the chiefs' hostel. Had he indeed intended to betray Tambo, he could have easily succeeded; Tambo later told Adelaide that this old school friend would have been the last man he would have suspected of treachery. Fortunately, Tambo had moved on before he could be tracked down.[10]

Although Tambo and Segal's saga of escape had so far been riddled with carelessness, both on their part and by the Security Police, Tambo was well aware of the dangers facing him. News had arrived that Frene Ginwala had called to say that the Indian Consul in Kenya was in the process of procuring travel documents for the refugees. Ros Ainslee, too, wrote to report that the newly independent government of Ghana was preparing passports for them. Good news – but clearly the implication was that there would necessarily be further waiting.

The sojourn in Lobatse was not only tedious and anxious, but it was also punctuated by the crude hostility of the white locals, many of whom were South Africans working in the territory. On one occasion, a large 'pasty-faced' bully walked up to Tambo, pushing him forcefully and repeatedly with the flat of his hand on the chest. 'Get out – we don't want your sort here,' until he was hustled away by less truculent individuals.[11] Segal was bothered by Tambo's failure to react to this sort of harassment, but Tambo's vision was, as always, fixed on his core business – the ANC mandate – and no tiresome incidents were to be allowed to disrupt his plans. More to the point, given the flagrant behaviour of the Security Police, Tambo was anxious to move on.

In the meantime, the presence of the fugitives from apartheid South Africa had elicited a flurry of correspondence between Britain and Bechuanaland. Earnest discussion on the 1881 Fugitive Offenders Act and the Extradition Act of 1870 considered whether the 'life or liberty' of Tambo 'would be in danger (on political grounds) or he would be exposed to persecution of such a kind and extent as to render life unsupportable if he were obliged to return'.[12] Bechuanaland's Attorney-General expressed a reluctance to condone the illegal entry because it might encourage 'more African refugees from the Union, some of whom are likely to be very undesirable'. In the UK, there was also some anxiety that Tambo intended to proceed 'to New York and hence to the United Nations' – indeed, Tambo had telegraphed a request to the United Nations' Secretary-General requesting permission to address the General Assembly. On the other hand, there were the wider implications of returning the refugees, with the likelihood that there might be protests from other Commonwealth countries. Report 595/2 pointed out that 'there is no such thing as extradition between two Commonwealth countries'. Perhaps it was the prime minister's response that clinched the decision. His personal assistant wrote, quoting Harold Macmillan's response to a report on the affair and South Africa's demand for the extradition of Tambo and Segal: 'I hope this means that in practice they would not go back. At any rate, not for a long time.'[13]

In Tambo's favour was a qualified if condescending approval of the way he had handled 'an incident at the hotel' – Bechuana intelligence was thorough, perhaps because there was not much else to occupy the office.

'Tambo has kept very much to himself,' commented the March report. 'Indeed he seems to be considerably more level-headed and retiring than Segal, an exhibitionist who clearly revels in the turn of events and is determined to extract as much drama from it as he can. Tambo on the other hand is worried and bewildered by events, and there is no evidence that he retains much of the initiative for further action.'

It was a typical revelation of British colonial attitudes and bigotry regarding both men – stereotyping the white man as the 'clever agitator' and the black man as lacking in understanding of the fast pace of changing events.

Nevertheless, Tambo himself was discomfited by Segal's disclosure to the press that the pair planned to cross into Southern Rhodesia. Segal's thinking was that Prime Minister Roy Welensky would be unlikely, in the glare of publicity, to return the fugitives to South Africa. Tambo decided, in the absence of further instructions, they should move as soon as possible. The next morning, they began the dusty drive to Francistown, 20 miles from the Rhodesian border.

But the pair were not the only fugitives from South Africa. Tambo had seen and spoken to trade unionist Dan Tloome in Lobatse, and had heard that Johannes Matlou was also in Bechuanaland, although he had not met him.

Tambo also became aware of the presence of Yusuf Dadoo in Francistown, which boasted an airstrip used primarily by the South African Chamber of Mines' recruiting corporation, WNELA, to transport migrant workers to the mining compounds. As the leader of the reconstituted Communist Party, Dadoo, too, had received instructions to leave South Africa. The new Communist Party in South Africa was working secretly underground, but the two organisations – the SACP and the ANC – were operating separately and there was no intention at that stage to work together on an escape route. Ultimately, it is not clear who facilitated the transport of the men, but Dadoo was, nevertheless, included in the travel plans.[14]

Yusuf Dadoo, who was to play an important role in the movement in exile, had been a radical student in India in the 1930s, and his dynamic leadership of the Passive Resistance Campaign in 1946 and his challenge to South Africa on an international platform had received wide publicity. Furthermore, he had taken a major initiative in cementing an alliance between the leaders of the ANC and the Indian organisations in Natal and the Transvaal. The accord became known as the Xuma-Dadoo-Naicker Pact – the Doctors' Pact. Dadoo was thus certainly an asset to anyone seeking the patronage of the Indian government.

It must have been more than three weeks since his arrival in Bechuanaland that Tambo, together with Segal and Dadoo, finally took off for Tanganyika in a small plane chartered by Frene from a boulder-strewn runway in remote Palapye. Their earlier attempt to leave via Southern Rhodesia (Zimbabwe) had been firmly intercepted by Cyril Segal, Ronald's brother, who lived in Bulawayo – Tambo's movements had become known and he was in danger. Further adventures were to follow their flight out of the Protectorate. In Nyasaland (Malawi), the plane was grounded for a night while a lawyer argued for the group's right of passage despite their lack of passports. It became evident that South African officials, assisted by informers monitoring their movements, were trying to have them extradited. On the third day, the fugitives at last landed in Dar es Salaam, Tanganyika, shortly to become the independent Tanzania.

An elated Frene Ginwala was at the airport to meet them. She took them immediately to meet Julius Nyerere, the leader of TANU, the party that was to govern Tanzania following independence. Nyerere, who years later vaguely remembered being called out of a central committee meeting to receive the political fugitives from South Africa, was not particularly struck by Tambo on that first occasion.[15] Like many others before and after him, he was to discover Tambo's subtle qualities imperceptibly but indelibly, over time. Nyerere did remember, though, receiving a message requesting him to intervene with the British governor not to deport the exiles back to South Africa. 'They wanted me to say, look, don't send these people back to South Africa. Let them stay here, or if they want to go through, they should go through.'[16]

Nyerere's influence proved powerful enough for permission to be granted at once and the following day, while the others remained in Dar, Tambo continued his journey. He had been invited to Tunisia by the General Secretary of the World Assembly Youth, David Wirmark, who was later to become a member of parliament for the Liberal Party in Sweden.[17] Wirmark recalled Tambo's 'fantastic speech... on the basis of non-violence, which was the ANC's policy at the time'.[18] Before Tambo left, he briefly met two other South Africans on the run: PAC members Nana Mahomo and Peter Molotsi. In their brief conversation, one of them mentioned that the interests of South African liberation should be coordinated abroad. They agreed to discuss this issue further at the first opportunity. Tambo had just enough time to ask Frene Ginwala to include them in her arrangements for travel documents – a thoughtful consideration that deeply impressed Frene, who had never met Tambo before.[19]

Tambo's gesture was not entirely disinterested, though. In the first place, it went without saying in black African circles that political differences should never interfere with personal relationships. In any case, the three men, far from home and united in the common oppression of both their organisations, were very pleased to see each other. In addition, Tambo may also have hoped to renew the opportunity to begin a process of reconciliation with the young PAC members. After all, the split had occurred just two years earlier; here was a chance to persuade them, eventually, to work within the mother body of the ANC.

But these considerations would have to wait for another opportunity. Tambo flew from Tanganyika through to Nairobi, where he was issued with travel documents courtesy of the Indian government. He then went through to Rome, where he caught a connecting flight back to the continent, to Tunisia. For the first time in his life, Tambo was exposed to the sheer cosmopolitanism of Africa. Here in the north, ebony blue-black men spoke fluent French and Italian, yet wore their own dress of vibrant textiles, design, colour and stitchwork. Colonised as most unmistakably were, they were also located in the nexus where Africa met the Mediterranean and the Levant, the cultural product of centuries of vigorous trade, war and religious transaction. This gave North Africans a wily ingeniousness, a sophistication surpassing Tambo's experience. His sojourn in Tunis, he recalled, brought home to him the magnitude of the change in his life.[20] He had now to reconstruct his identity in a world of new diversity. He was no longer simply a professional renowned and respected in his own community. He had to sell himself to an unknown audience as the full-time political dealer for the ANC. His instructions from his Executive Committee had been to act as 'roving ambassador' for the African National Congress. Now, in the context of the liberation movements in the continent, his movement lost its unique status; it became the SANC (the South African National Congress), for Zimbabwe also had an ANC.

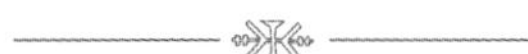

Tambo's speech at the International Youth Conference in Tunisia on South Africa's situation was the first address he was to deliver outside his country. The international audience knew little, if anything, about the background or circumstances of segregation and apartheid in a large colonial settler society. Tambo's chief task was to set up links with member states of the Organisation of African Unity (OAU). He, however, encountered scepticism among Africanists who were inclined to be critical of a multiracial movement whose policy was one of non-violence. Sharpeville had burst on to the world's consciousness: it was the PAC that had initiated the protest. 'With its slogan of "Africa for the Africans",' observed Aziz Pahad (who was later to become active in international relations), 'the PAC quickly captured the mood.'[21] For many, it seemed that the ANC, venerable and popular as it might be, was the old-fashioned movement of the past. To make headway, the oppressed should follow the direction of the PAC. Nevertheless, Tambo's composed, logical and articulate critique of apartheid, while lacking rhetorical flourish, could not fail to impress.

While Tambo was in Tunis, he was granted an audience with 'the old man of Tunis', President Habib Bourgiba, at which he was able to place the ANC in the context of the situation in South Africa and lay the foundations for future negotiations for assistance. He also saw the ambassador to Ghana, who immediately arranged for him to travel to Accra. Once there, Tambo was very pleased to see Tennyson Makiwane, also a treason trialist whom Oliver had known since their Youth League days. Makiwane had been sent by the SACP – which had reconstituted itself from the old, outlawed CPSA, and of which he was a member – to assist a small band of expatriates to begin operations abroad. As the correspondent for *New Age*, Makiwane was able to get around and make valuable contacts in Africa and Europe. Working with Tambo, he was to become a major figure in the panoply of exile figures in the ANC.

During his brief stay in Ghana, Tambo was also warmly received by Kwame Nkrumah, the prime minister of the newly independent state. Tambo's move into the African interior in 1960 had coincided with a major turning point in its history. Throughout the continent an atmosphere of celebration, optimism and determination reigned. The year 1960 was the one in which more African countries obtained their independence from colonialism than any other. The 17 new states included the former Belgian Congo (the Democratic Republic of Congo), 13 former French possessions such as Senegal, Cameroon, Côte d'Ivoire and Madagascar, and the British colony of Nigeria. It was a perception – an accurate one – that the decade to come was to see major winds blowing away cobwebs of submission and inferiority from even remote corners of oppressed colonies. There was also a determination to extend political independence to the entire continent. Kwame Nkrumah's almost biblical edict seemed clear: 'Seek ye first the political kingdom, and all things shall be added unto you.'[22] In that first heady decade, freedom was the immediate goal – the rest would almost certainly follow. The continent, as a terrain of intense international concern and manipulation in the shadow of the Cold War, was as yet only faintly discernible. Neocolonialism and the continuation of economic exploitation were struggles yet to be faced. In the meantime, the aim of Pan-Africanism, which Nkrumah himself revived from its origins at the turn of the century, was a vital goal in order to repair the devastated continent.[23]

Nkrumah was keenly interested to hear about recent events in South Africa, but expressed concern that there had been a split in the liberation movement. In Africa, he argued, there was no room for opposition groups among patriots. The African tradition of consensus needed to be revived and honoured. A union of the two liberation movements, he maintained, was both necessary to achieve success at home and appropriate for Pan-Africanism in the region. Nkrumah had already met the PAC members whose journey to Ghana had been facilitated by Tambo himself. Nana Mahomo and Peter Molotsi had left South Africa just before Sharpeville on a goodwill tour of Africa to promote and publicise their new movement. Molotsi remembered vividly the thrill of arriving in Accra, and being greeted with the words: '*Akwaba!* Welcome Home!' 'We had arrived at home,' he said, 'the home of "the Mecca of Pan Africanism".' [24]

Tambo, though in natural sympathy with the ideals of both unity in struggle and Pan-Africa, found himself in a difficult position. With the entire ANC leadership in jail or in hiding, there could be no immediate response from home. In Accra, accompanied by Makiwane, he decided in principle, however, to proceed with discussions with the PAC representatives in exile. This was the first of an ever-increasing number of situations in which Tambo was uneasily obliged to make decisions for which he felt he had not been given a mandate. In the meantime, as there was no time to thrash out the details, the group agreed to meet again as soon as possible.

It was now necessary to move on. Tambo was invited to attend a conference called by the Danish prime minister in Copenhagen on 1 May.[25] This was Tambo's first visit to northern Europe. May Day was Labour Day, and he addressed audiences in Copenhagen and Aarhus, outlining the recent history of South Africa and calling for trade-union help in the ANC's boycott call.[26]

'It is not the South African goods that are cheap,' he pointed out, 'but the forced labour of the Africans... The enemies of Africa are those devoted friends of apartheid and racial discrimination – governments, countries or concerns – which have trade agreements with South Africa.'[27]

Tambo's first visit to Scandinavia was to lead to valuable and on-going contacts in the future. From there, Tambo flew on to London. A group of South African activists there had in 1958 formed themselves into the 'South African Freedom Association' in order to alert the international labour and liberal community to SACTU's 'Pound-a-Day' wage strike. The Freedom Association involved such expatriates as the old trade unionist Solly Sachs, former secretary of the Garment Workers Union until he was banned, the moral support of writers such as Doris Lessing, Guy Rodd and Sylvester Stein, together with left-wing students from South Africa. Financial backing was difficult to obtain.

'We were battling,' recalled Mac Maharaj, one of the students there at the time: 'We had no money to buy tickets and there was no donor organisation. Literally, we were bumming lifts for Doc and Tennyson and OR.'[28]

Through previous experience of spiriting African trade unionists out of South Africa, however, they had 'learned how to work with British immigration'.

At the airport, Tambo was delighted to meet his old friend, Trevor Huddleston, now the Bishop of Stepney, and also to meet again John Collins, Canon at St Paul's Cathedral in the heart of London. Oliver managed to attend some of Bishop Huddleston's church services. With regard to personal and political developments, there was much to discuss and to share. Although Huddleston had become acutely involved with his working-class parish in London, he had continued to publicise the iniquities of apartheid in Britain, just as he had promised to do. Tambo stayed with John and Diana Collins, and his gratitude to them for their relaxed and warm hospitality was lifelong.[25] When Canon Collins died, more than 20 years later, Tambo rushed from Lusaka to Diana's side, saying, 'The eldest son must always come to bury his father. I regard myself as John's African eldest son' [30] – the Collinses had four sons of their own.

Despite his controversial ideas at the time, Canon Collins' intelligence, drive, dedication and personal charm had provided him with a prestigious position in the Anglican Church. His congregation included the royal family when they were in residence at Buckingham Palace and St James', and as a result drew public attention. He put the location of his parish to good use, for it was near Fleet Street, where the influential press was situated. Collins cultivated friendly relations with top journalists, regularly sending them copies of his sermons, with potential news items thoughtfully underlined.[31] With their assistance, he enhanced publicity for his projects. Amen Court, his manse, was an eighteenth-century house with a large basement that became the canon's offices. Diana's kitchen was an ideal place for frequently held meetings, invigorated by well-known figures in the artistic and publishing world such as JB Priestley, Victor Gollancz, and many others. There were also visitors of longer duration. A number of South African refugees spent their first days in England in Amen Court. Alfred Hutchinson and his wife Hazel, refugees from South Africa's Immorality Act as much as from political activism, were perhaps the first.[32] It was there that 'Hutch' began to write his book, *Road to Ghana*. Later, in gratitude, he sent his first royalties to Collins as a contribution to the Defence and Aid Fund, which Collins had set up. Later, Nkrumah assisted by offering to provide transport to fly South African refugees to England.

In the meantime, while in London Tambo held a second meeting with the PAC representatives, with Yusuf Dadoo (representative of the South African Indian Congress) and with Fanuel Kozanguizi, founder and leader of SWANU, the aspiring liberation movement from South West Africa. The intention was to bring together representatives of the liberation movements struggling against the stranglehold of the South African regime. The group drew up a preliminary document, sketching out their objective (to end white domination in South Africa), and a programme to achieve it. Their immediate aim, they agreed, should be to secure support from the UN for international economic sanctions, including the stoppage of oil supplies to South Africa. In addition, they should call for the transfer to the United Nations of the mandate granted to South Africa by the now defunct League of Nations in 1918 to govern South West Africa. This would be a first step towards the independence of Namibia. The group agreed, too, to agitate for international economic sanctions. Tentatively, the meeting agreed to name this new initiative the United Front (UF), but Tambo was cautiously determined not to accept anything officially until he had received approval from the ANC at home. In the meantime, offices should be set up in London. Krishna Menon, founder of the India League since his country's pre-independence days, and a personal friend of Dadoo's, offered the group premises. Nkrumah had guaranteed support in Accra. In addition, Cairo was another city in Africa able and likely to provide resources and support.

The United Front accorded well with the ANC's overall, inclusive approach. But Tambo was also aware, from personal experience, of the PAC's difficulties with communists. During the 1960 State of Emergency, the banned Communist Party of South Africa openly announced its existence, reconstituted as the South African Communist Party. A good number of the old members had decided not to work underground, but the great majority of the senior members came on board. These included JB Marks, Moses Kotane, Yusuf Dadoo, Michael Harmel, Ray Alexander and others. All intended to work closely with the ANC. In particular, the non-African members were also able to join Umkhonto we Sizwe (MK), which unlike the ANC, accepted membership across the demographic spectrum of South Africa. Tambo trusted that, under the present circumstances in exile and the agreed need to unite all anti-apartheid forces, the revived SACP would not put off the Africanists in the United Front.

Tambo's next task was to meet Colonel Gamal Abdel Nasser, Egypt's revolutionary nationalist leader, to enlist his backing for the United Front. This Nasser willingly agreed to do. Immediately afterwards, Tambo left for Addis Ababa to address the June conference. The United Front reconvened there. Tambo reported to the UF group on the success of his Egyptian mission, and the meeting agreed on the area representatives – Vusi Make of the PAC and Mzwai Piliso, a pharmacist and cousin of Makiwane's, who had qualified in England in the early 1950s, were sent to Cairo.[33] Tennyson Makiwane and Peter Molotsi were to open the Accra office, and Dadoo, Mahomo and Kozanguizi were to remain in London, with a desk for Tambo whenever he was in town. In that way, both the ANC and the PAC represented each office. The meeting also agreed that public mudslinging would defeat the objectives of the United Front and should therefore be disallowed. To prevent misunderstanding, all correspondence should be duplicated and sent to all the offices.

The conference in Addis Ababa was a major event as it was the first conference of heads of state in Africa, with representation from many parts of colonised Africa as well as progressive and non-aligned countries from beyond. A group of African countries – Morocco, Egypt, Tunisia, Guinea, Ghana, Liberia and Libya – commanded the proceedings. The South Africans had prepared a paper and presented it as a common position, to the enthusiasm of the delegates. The ensuing discussion helped develop some of the UF's ideas – that independent Africa's oil and transport facilities, shipping and air space should be included in the boycotts – and the conference adopted a formal resolution to that effect.[34] To have put the South African situation so centrally on the agenda was a great achievement for the Front. They hoped this augured well for its future.

For Tambo, there was an atmosphere of anticipation in Addis Ababa. This was Abyssinia, whose monarch, despite iron despotism, had by his very existence as the only surviving independent ruler in Africa inspired millions of black people throughout the Diaspora, from the Americas and the Caribbean through to the pockets of small black communities in Europe. In South Africa, a portrait of emperor Haile Selassie had hung in the homes of many Africans during Mussolini's attempted rape of that country. Now called Ethiopia, the ancient state was also the home of the earliest Christian church on the continent, from which had flowered Coptic art – the exquisite icons of lustrous-eyed saints, the intricately carved silver crucifixes and the holy talismans. Tambo was extremely moved by this native expression of Christianity. He was also at once excited and afflicted with homesickness to observe the long braided hairstyles of the Ethiopians, identical to those of the women back home in Pondoland.

Then it was back to London. In fact, Tambo was becoming familiar with an African activist's London. In Gower Street could be found the head office of the Committee of African Organisations, which had been providing facilities for the African Students' Association and the South African Freedom Association. Trafalgar Square, which adjoined South Africa House – a handsome Edwardian building occupied by the South African embassy – was a public rallying point for opponents of apartheid. Near the square, the India League kept offices at 31a John Adams Street, which it now offered to share with the United Front. Later, Kwame Nkrumah bought Africa Freedom House to accommodate all the African liberation movements. In addition, there were the Reverend Michael Scott's Africa Bureau and Canon Collins' Treason Trial Defence Fund.

Amen Court itself offered a valuable venue for recruiting patrons. In their South African support work, the Collinses and Huddleston had enlisted the sympathy of Labour and Liberal members of Parliament, including Barbara Castle, Hugh Gaitskell, Jeremy Thorpe and others, as well as a network of students and young professionals. The latter were not quite fugitives, but had left South Africa because of their opposition to apartheid or because, as 'non-whites', they were unable to continue their postgraduate studies in South Africa. Vella Pillay, Mac Maharaj, Ros Ainslee and Patrick van Rensburg were among this group. As non-Africans, they were not members of the ANC, but were nevertheless in strong sympathy with its ideals. Some were members of the SACP, although this was not necessarily generally known at the time. But this misgiving proved to be a stumbling block with the Labour Party until the group lobbied Michael Foot. They were also assisted by the arrival of Tennyson Makiwane – the Freedom Association had asked 'home' to send someone to help. When he arrived, Makiwane was introduced to Labour Party sympathisers, who took to him at once. It was through Makiwane that Conservative Lord Altringham also began to support the anti-apartheid impetus.[35] Despite initial hesitation, then, a group of disparate individuals and organisations began to work together to initiate boycott campaigns. During the farm-labour scandal, for example, they tried to publicise the significance of the potato boycott inside South Africa. In the same year, 1959, they set up the Anti-Apartheid Committee. In time, that committee was to grow into a 'Movement', greatly strengthened by the voluntary work of women in particular – Dorothy Robinson, Sonia Bunting, Frene Ginwala and Ethel de Kayser were among the early expatriates. In time, the Anti-Apartheid Movement was to become sufficiently clamorous to excite the implacable hatred of the South African government.

When Tambo was introduced to various activists in the UK, he emphasised the importance of maintaining its open image. He was particularly anxious for it not to become simply an organ of the ANC. He put it to ANC members in the organisation that they would need to consider whether to take a militant position, which would narrow the organisation, or not.[36] He advised against the former. The United Front was thus drawn into the activities – members of the Anti-Apartheid Committee claimed that, despite grievances expressed later by the PAC, they even-handedly invited ANC and PAC speakers to rallies.[37]

But anti-apartheid activities that year were not confined to Britain. Early in 1960, even before Sharpeville, the Swedish journalist and writer Per Wästberg, who had visited South Africa in 1953, had taken steps to start an anti-apartheid movement in Sweden. Immediately after Sharpeville, Wästberg initiated a fund-raising appeal, signed by bishops – 'even the conservative bishops signed' – members of parliament, and the prime minister himself, to form a Swedish Defence and Aid Fund.[38] Wästberg had heard of the efforts of Huddleston and Collins to support South African liberation, and towards the end of 1960 he went to London to collaborate with British supporters. It was during this visit that he met Tambo, who remembered him from his visit to South Africa. They were to meet frequently at Amen Court over the following two decades. Wästberg worked closely with the British Defence and Aid Fund, spending a month every year with the Collinses. He would see Oliver 'because he was constantly visiting there,' recalled Wästberg. 'He just knocked on the door without phoning, and he went into the kitchen if we were having breakfast or afternoon tea. He sat at the fireplace in winter and discussed things; he was extremely relaxed with John Collins. I mean, they really loved each other.'[39] Wästberg's organisation was to work in tandem with the British counterpart.

With the United Front, the Anti-Apartheid Committee launched a crusade. In the wake of Sharpeville, they renewed a month-long boycott against South African products with speakers and banners in Trafalgar Square. Britain was South Africa's most valued customer for fruit, wool and wine and, therefore, important to South Africa's economy – as a member of the Commonwealth, it enjoyed numerous trade benefits. The campaign was then extended to a call for South Africa's expulsion from the Commonwealth, whose composition was beginning to change – India and Ghana had new representation, Tanganyika was about to achieve independence and the liberation of other British colonies such as Jamaica, Kenya and Nigeria was on the cards. Tambo and other UF members spoke to Nyerere on the issue, who vowed that if South Africa was not expelled by the time Tanganyika became independent, his country would withdraw from the Commonwealth. In Britain, the Anti-Apartheid Committee organised a 72-hour vigil outside the Commonwealth. Again, Tambo urged the organisers never to allow the organisation to become an extension of the ANC but to work with the British – 'a very important foresight', commented Abdul Minty, who came to London from Liverpool, at Tambo's behest, to help develop the Anti-Apartheid Movement.[40] Assisted by Barbara Castle, they were able to recruit prominent people – actors, actresses, writers and parliamentarians – to stand for an hour or more in protest at South Africa's membership. With pressure and response of this kind, the issue of South Africa's membership looked set to be on the agenda for the Commonwealth's next meeting.

Soon after the Addis Ababa meeting, the United Front made a follow-up in the UN. Tambo, as the most senior and accomplished member of the group, was chosen to make the presentation in New York in October. The address was a joint statement by Tambo and Vusi Make, and referred to the referendum by white South Africa a few days earlier, by which a majority of 7 000 had voted in favour of a republic. Clearly, said the statement, the apartheid regime was determined not to be swayed in its programme. The extension of passes for women was going ahead and the establishment of Bantustans was continuing. 'The massacres of Windhoek, of Sharpeville, and now of Pondoland, are evidence of an attitude of contempt for human life, world opinion, and the United Nations Charter.' It would only be by the firmest measures – in short, economic sanctions – that rampart apartheid could be brought to a halt.[41]

The campaign had some impact inside South Africa, too. Verwoerd, always the astute politician, was preparing to pull the rug from under the feet of the black members of the Commonwealth. With the majority of white voters now fully behind him, his party launched a counter-campaign. In the press and on radio,

Afrikaners were reminded of their struggles to overthrow British imperialism – no other country had the right to tell them what to do, or how to conduct their own affairs. It was a theme that was to be repeated throughout the international debates and dialogues on apartheid for the following 30 years.

As soon as Oliver had arrived in London, he contacted Adelaide. He had also sent her messages from Botswana. He was now able to telephone her twice – despite the telephone being tapped – and she received letters from him. Then, in June, a Labour Party member of the House of Lords, Sir Frederick Allen Jones, came to see her at the hospital in Johannesburg. He had a message from Oliver. She was to prepare to leave with the children for Swaziland, where an aeroplane would pick them up and fly them to Ghana. She was to wait for further details. Two weeks later, a farmer from Swaziland, Oliver Tedley, appeared in the nurses' sitting room. He had come to fetch Adelaide and the children. They were to be ready that evening. Adelaide was to remove all her jewellery, put on a headscarf and disguise herself as a Swazi peasant woman.

'When we get to the Swazi border,' Tedley instructed, 'you don't speak English very well. You work for me, your name is Martha Mokoni and these are your children who were in hospital in Johannesburg and we went to collect them.'

Adelaide tried but failed to reach Godfrey Pitje, who was running the Mandela & Tambo office – Mendi Msimang and Ruth Mompati had, by then, left the country to join the underground – and then left for home, packing all she could carry. Tedley arrived. They left late and drove until five in the morning.

Mbabane already had a fair share of South African refugees, mostly COD members in hiding during the State of Emergency – Ruth First, the Rosenbergs and Melville Fletcher, among others. They had managed to escape the mass detentions and were attempting to operate from the Protectorate. There was thus no room for Adelaide and the children in the ANC-occupied apartments downtown, so she moved into an isolated house a few miles away 'in the wilderness', which was sheltering more South Africans – Ruth Makiwane (Tennyson's wife), Piet Beyleveld and Jack Hodgson. And there she stayed for six frustrating weeks. The plane that was meant to rescue her was shot down into the Congo River – 'it was the time of Lumumba'.[42] Adelaide felt trapped and dependent on others for money and transport to Mbabane, where she needed to go for food supplies and to telephone her family. Finally, her patience exhausted, she sent a telegram to Oliver that she wanted to return home. Tambo hastily cabled back, asking her to hold on. Shortly afterwards, Adelaide heard that Nkrumah was sending a plane to Botswana to transport South African refugees. Adelaide and the children left for Botswana, where they put up at a London Mission house. Their arrival, just three months after Tambo's much-publicised sojourn there, caused a stir in the community. Seretse Khama visited, and brought the gift of a sheep; the future foreign minister took them home for lunch; and the new ANC representative, Mr Sello, was at her disposal with his car. Nevertheless, it was an anxious time, having to feed and care for two toddlers – Thembi was just two-and-a-half now, and Dali nearly 18 months old. One morning, Adelaide sent a telegram to Lancelot Gama, saying that she was out of money. By the time she returned to her room, she found a message informing her that the money had already arrived – another example of the solidarity of The Syndicate, so romantically conceived all those years ago at St Peter's.

The plane finally arrived after Adelaide had been in Botswana for nearly three weeks. She remembers the white women at the post office asking her to sell them her smart clothes – she had taken so much luggage that she would need to leave much of it behind. She refused, packing them in cardboard boxes tied with string; but she shared out the babies' excess clothing among the needy. Then they caught the plane, finally landing in Accra – hot and steamy, and thronged with people moving easily in the streets, exquisitely dressed in traditional Ghanaian attire. But Oliver was not there.

'I think that's the one time when my spirit sank.'

He had sent a compatriot to meet her – George Chaane, who was teaching there, was to help Adelaide leave for London. She also met again young Peter Molotsi of the PAC, who had also been assigned to help Ruth Makiwane. Tennyson, her husband, was away with the task of finding offices for the United Front.[43] In the meantime, Oliver had left a firm instruction with Chaane. Adelaide was not to buy any clothes in Ghana – they were very expensive – 'either for yourself or the children. Wait until you are in London'. But Oliver had also asked Chaane to give Adelaide whatever she needed and promised that he would reimburse him. Warily, Chaane told Adelaide, 'I've got limitations, so I can't provide much. What I can't provide, I'll let you know.' So Adelaide confined her purchases to suitcases.

A week later, Adelaide and the children finally arrived in London by Air Ghana. The tickets had been sent by the combined efforts of the Anti-Apartheid Committee and Canon Collins. And, at last, Oliver was waiting to meet them. That night was a culmination of months of anxiety, uncertainty, overwork and stress: 'The night we arrived Oliver had an asthma attack and he was due to leave in two days' time for the United Nations... I had not seen him for about six months. We got to London on 15 September in 1960.'[44]

It was a clear signal of the pattern of things to come in their marriage. Not only was Oliver due to leave as soon as they arrived, compromising his health for urgent meetings, but accommodation still needed to be found.

'Oliver was living with the fathers. He had no flat. He had asked James Phillips [a trade unionist who left South Africa in 1953] to accommodate us. It was myself, the two children and Oliver, and we had a room the size of this little place and there was one single bed. And I just missed home! I felt, it doesn't matter, apartheid or what, home is best. Oliver… was ill for seven days and then he had to go to the UN to petition there. He was still not well when he left.'

While he was away, the family moved into a small flat in Cholmeley Park, found by the young London expatriates. Almost immediately, Adelaide found a job at St George's Hospital. For the next three decades, she was to provide the movement's London lodgings and be the family breadwinner – the ANC had large expenses and no money to spare. In a sense, Adelaide herself was doing pioneering work, laying the foundations for an ANC reception infrastructure.

'I did tell you about the arrangement we had before we got married, about how we are going to carry out things and that one of us would have to do full-time politics and the other one would do part-time politics and earn a living for the entire family. So when we first went to live in London, we lived in a flat in Cholmeley Park. The International Defence and Aid were then paying for us, a flat which was £7 a week, and at that time was a lot of money. I then had to take a job because the children needed to be looked after,' explains Adelaide.

'While at the Royal Northern Hospital. I had to go to the Unmarried Mothers Association. I took one of the unmarried mothers, Cynthia, and she lived with us and I worked on night duty. She was with them during the night and took them to a nursery in the morning. So I saw them before they went to the nursery and when they came back. As years went by, Cynthia had to leave – she got a letter from her mother in the West Indies to ask her to come back home. That was the beginning of my problem. I then had to lock the children in every evening when I was going on duty and come back to them in the morning. I had to instruct them not to open the door to anybody even if it was someone they knew. It turned out that people went there and the children refused to open the door.'

Oliver was to travel extensively over the following 30 years, and would send her a few pounds every now and then, saved from limited personal expenses budgeted to him by the ANC. Adelaide was to see her husband fitfully; at times, a year or more went by before they met up again. She, too, like the wives of migrants back home, was to be obliged to adjust her life, and forage for resources. The early sojourners in London recalled the rota they devised to baby-sit Thembi and Dali when Adelaide was on night shift at the hospital.

In the meantime, Oliver Tambo's movements began to accelerate. Looking back, he was able to recall only fleeting impressions. He received many requests to address meetings, both in the UK and beyond, and built up networks for the ANC. He travelled to China and to the United Nations to put the South African case before world delegates. He was also able to address gatherings in New York, despite the restriction imposed on him by the USA government ban to within a 25-mile radius of the United Nations building. Warm support came, in those first days, from only a small band of Americans.

'He went to Mrs Peggy Delaney [at] 70 Lassaly Street, Brooklyn,' recalled Adelaide. 'He met people like Peter and Cora Weiss; there is a man called Kerina. He is a Namibian and is married to an American. Mrs Delaney came later and spent a holiday with us in London.'[45]

Many organisations and a number of countries were eager to offer Tambo all-expenses-paid invitations. Letters from the USA arrived from Mary-Louise Hooper, who had performed secretarial work for Luthuli and, as a result, had been hounded out of South Africa in the 1950s. She was now managing the South African Defense Fund in San Francisco. Other US correspondents included the Episcopal Churchmen for South Africa in New York and the American Friends Service Committee in Pennsylvania, and a request from the National Association for the Advancement of Coloured People asked Tambo to address their Minnesota convention. The organisation was 'keenly interested in the struggle in South Africa and in the fine work done by the ANC'.[46]

From the United Kingdom and Ireland Tambo received invitations from the universities of Oxford and Dublin. In Oxford, the Church Union wanted Tambo to address the university's Summer School on the theme of 'The Moral and Social Problems of a Multi-Racial Society'. On 18 May, *The Irish Times* reported that 'Mr Oliver Tambo, one of the few Bantu leaders to escape arrest' talked about the 'tyranny of the passes to maintain white supremacy'. Tambo also observed that it was not possible to enslave people without damaging one's own character. It also reported Tambo's conclusion: 'A solution could only come from the outside'[47] – he was, of course, referring to sanctions.

Then, in April 1961, while lobbying delegates to the UN, Tambo was invited to speak on Africa Freedom Day, together with other African liberation leaders and African-American writer James Baldwin and South African performers Miriam Makeba and the Dinizulu Dancers. The programme was 'a sell-out'.[48]

So it was that, through Oliver Tambo's articulate and personable style, the ANC looked set to gain the acceptance of the Western world. But within the space of a few hectic months, Tambo's world was once again to be overturned by a sea change in the strategy of the liberation struggle.

CHAPTER NINE

Reinventing the ANC

THE YEAR 1961 PROVED A WATERSHED for the ANC. Its president, Chief Albert Luthuli, was awarded the Nobel Peace Prize and, in that same year, the movement turned to armed struggle. For Oliver Tambo, leader of the ANC's Mission in Exile, it was the start of an unanticipated, prolonged journey towards recasting, rebuilding and reconceptualising the African National Congress. It would now become necessary to legitimise the seemingly contradictory arenas of both peaceful protest and armed struggle.

Tambo's task, assigned by the National Executive Committee of the ANC, had been to head the movement's diplomatic mission to communicate to the world the black experience inside apartheid South Africa, and so mobilise international support. This required an adjusted representation of the ANC identity to reach new and diverse international audiences in the West, and the Eastern Bloc, as well as post-colonial and the still colonised part of Africa.

The initial aim was to project both the political image of the ANC as well as a conception of its leadership, 'the most visible members of an entire community'.[1] In October 1962, a consultative meeting chaired by Govan Mbeki was held in Lobatse to confirm Tambo's mandate from the ANC's NEC at home and in exile and to confront its dilemmas. Tambo was delighted to see Walter Sisulu again, who was operating underground and had slipped out of the country for 36 hours. The 50 delegates from home and abroad, including representatives from the Congress Alliance – Yusuf Dadoo from the SAIC and Moses Mabhida from SACTU, for example – had an emotional reunion.[2] It had been 18 months since Tambo had first arrived there as a refugee. Much had transpired since then.

But scarcely a year passed before events rapidly overtook the mandate, and Tambo had to 'busk' his way into an alternative but recognisable image for the movement. With the formation of the ANC's armed wing, Umkhonto we Sizwe ('the Spear of the Nation'), the emphasis shifted to a careful explanation of how violence had become unavoidable as a last resort in the face of unrelenting, brutal oppression. With memories of the Second World War still painfully recent, the ANC was able to communicate a comparison of apartheid with Nazism, which resonated with Europeans.[3] At the same time, the armed struggle was introduced as a carefully selected and orderly sequence of targets designed to avoid the loss of life. The ANC saw itself as a disciplined liberation movement, eschewing terrorism in the pursuit of a legitimately moral goal: in defence of a nation wrongfully attacked and dispossessed, its people crudely oppressed and exploited. Tambo himself, trained since childhood in the moral discourse of Christianity, had as a politician frequently to cross the lines between the religious and the secular worlds. In doing so, he developed an amalgam of the two arenas, for he felt profoundly the ability of the moral or religious discourse 'to touch that place in the human heart where we know right from wrong'.[4] It was this heartfelt conviction, that he was sanctioning a great cause, that was to persuade so many international observers to support the ANC even after it had literally declared war on apartheid. The concept of a 'just war', expounded most systematically by St Thomas Aquinas in the fifteenth century and revived in the twentieth century prior to the Second World War and then again as the Vietnam War flared up, were of particular value for the ANC. The principles evolving from these debates were held to be five: the cause had to be just – that is, the war was retaliating against a wrong already committed. It had to be declared by a proper authority – in the case of the ANC, a body representative of the popular will; it had to possess the right intention, and be motivated by the conviction of reasonable success. Finally, it had to be committed to minimising destruction – the only method for securing guarantees of no future reprisals.[5] The ANC, 'under the guidance of Oliver Tambo', was in the forefront of exploring the reconciliation of religious and Christian principles with an armed struggle, and argued that their cause fulfilled these criteria.[6]

By 1963, a significant proportion of leading ANC members had moved out of South Africa. Exile was now a metaphor by which its visible presence implicitly expressed a powerful, ongoing critique of the apartheid nation-state, sending messages both to the oppressed at home and to sympathisers abroad. While the reasons for the exodus might have been obvious to the refugees, it was important that they should have a voice – to explain to the world, and to those at home, the meaning and legitimacy of exile. As more and more of the ANC's internal leadership were arrested and imprisoned, exile had to be coherently projected as an alternative blueprint. Tambo was concerned to remind the world that prison and exile were the two sides of oppression. But if exile was allowed to continue for too long, it risked becoming a paradox: inducing alienation from home and from its underground political culture, increasingly unable to speak on behalf of those silenced voices. (And indeed, in the decades that followed, the interrupted lines of communication with 'home' were to become longer, sometimes leading to political gaffes and serious errors.)[7] But back in 1961, who could predict the long haul of the struggle? At that juncture, overwhelmed by rapidly unfolding events at home, Tambo was obliged to tackle the challenges strategically but reactively, step by step, so that exiles would carry the struggle further than they otherwise could have done at home.

Tambo's first task was to redefine the role of exile and create a new repertoire, to re-evaluate and relegitimise the ANC's concept and methodology of liberation, as well as the roles of race and class in the struggle. With political rivals vying for authenticity and African voices critiquing the ANC's multiracial alliance, it became an ongoing struggle to focus on who was to control the discourse.[8]

Tambo had also to renegotiate the structures and culture of politics in exile. Throughout his 30 years of expatriation, Tambo displayed a consistent anxiety to follow correct procedures. As head of the Mission in Exile, it was Tambo's mandated role to articulate this new experience – once again, putting his Western education at the service of the oppressed people of South Africa. Effectively, despite the ANC's culture of collective leadership, it was Tambo who was to become both 'prime minister' and CEO of a steadily growing international operation. In addition to heading MK's armed forces, finding them accommodation in military training camps and plotting the war of liberation, Tambo and his team had to manage fundraising; set up distribution centres for food, pocket money and clothing; initiate the restructuring of decision-making bodies; create service departments in education, health, foreign affairs, welfare and culture for both the cadres and the 'civilians'; establish ANC offices around the world; identify members for skills-development and capacity-building in preparation for the ANC as a governing party in a free South Africa; support and nurture the ANC's public relations and communications departments; and constantly search for ways of keeping in touch with the comrades in the townships at home and those incarcerated in prisons.

The unavailability of the elected NEC called for new forms of legitimacy and decision-making. From this time onward, Tambo had to negotiate his way around a culture of politics in exile – a particularly difficult task for one who had been so conscientious about the democratic procedures of the ANC structures while it had still been legal in the fifties – and cultivate new forms of authority. Tambo chose to emphasise and foster the ANC's traditional consensus decision-making. It fell to him, assisted by his key advisers, such as JB Marks, to dovetail the democratic centralism of its Marxist ally, the SACP, with a consensus process that would unite rather than separate members into winners and losers within the movement. Procedures in exile had now to be negotiated by the exiled ANC in its own right – in the words of exiled writer, Ngugi Wa Thiong'o, 'in the anguished ambiguity of an embryonic diaspora community'.[9]

Tambo's intelligent use of consensus ensured that it was not of an artificial kind in which people kept silent because of tacit pressure from above, but a subtle drawing out of opinions. But because opinions, especially in the diverse experiences of exile were not always uniform, Tambo's skill lay in pulling these opinions together in an exercise of collective ownership. His wisdom, unlike some of his comrades, particularly those in the SACP, which espoused an unqualified, 'scientific', 'Stalinist' ideology, lay in an understanding that, in the words of William Gumede, 'Consensus is not [always] the perfect kind, where everyone sings in unison, but a more agreeable *a capella* where disparate voices chime in an extended social dialogue.'[10]

But the ANC's strategic shift also resulted in a further complexity – the steady widening of the composition of the movement, bringing with it a spread of ideological tendencies. This turning point for the ANC was to have profound repercussions in the movement's international and internal relations for decades to come.

During 1960/61, various ANC supporters in the UK and Sweden, encouraged by Tambo, began to lobby the Nobel Peace Prize Committee for the recognition of Chief Albert Luthuli's unceasing and peaceful efforts to persuade the South African government to negotiate social change. In 1952, the ANC had launched the non-violent Defiance Campaign, which had been inspired by Mahatma Gandhi's principles of *Satyagraha*. Under Chief Luthuli's leadership of the ANC, the Freedom Charter envisioned a society in which all could live in harmony. The stay-aways and the bus boycotts had all been attempts to express peaceful protest effectively. Such deaths as had occurred in these campaigns had been almost without exception initiated by the police; the massacre at Sharpeville was but a culmination of this trend.

Following Sharpeville, Luthuli had also made a special appeal to the white community in his speech, 'Freedom is the Apex'. Using the metaphor of the mountain, and the efforts needed to reach its peak, he reassured them of the sincerity of his people. He referred them to the Freedom Charter, the vision of a democratic, nonracial society, shining at the pinnacle.

'I personally believe that here in South Africa, with all our diversities of colour and race, we will show the world a new pattern for democracy. I think there is a challenge to us in South Africa to set a new example for the world. Let us not sidestep that task.'[11]

All these factors, as well as Chief Luthuli's own track record, thus influenced the Nobel selection board to receive with favour the applications of the anti-apartheid committees in Britain and Sweden. Tambo, too, had maintained the contact he had made with Liberal Party MP David Wirmark (whom he had met during the Youth Conference in Tunis), Swedish journalist and writer Per Wästberg, whom he had first met in South Africa, and other Scandinavians – they recalled his quiet assurance in dealing with the ANC's policy of non-violence at the time, and were very favourably impressed.[12]

The award to Luthuli had immense symbolic significance. It gave the ANC international prominence, but the South African government was, of course, furious – firstly, because it honoured an organisation that they had banned. Secondly, they were obliged to give Luthuli permission to leave the country – to refuse a passport to the Chief, himself banned and therefore restricted in his movements, would earn the scorn and ridicule of the Western world. Clearly, the award of the Nobel Peace Prize was a calculated censure of the apartheid regime. Resentfully, the Minister of the Interior granted Luthuli a limited travel document – a passport was 'a privilege, not a right'. The Chief and Mrs Luthuli were thus permitted barely a week away. In Stockholm, the formal ceremony, the courtesies, the ritual, the mark of respect and the acceptance speech were all part of a discourse with which an African chief is familiar. Luthuli's speech – thoughtful, reflective and morally impeccable – was received with acclaim.

'[The] Award is a democratic declaration of solidarity with those who fight to widen the area of liberty in my part of the world. As such, it is the sort of gesture which gives me and millions who think as I do, tremendous encouragement... This Award could not be for me alone,' he said, linking it to his broadest constituency, 'nor for just South Africa, but for Africa as a whole. Africa presently is most deeply torn with strife and most bitterly stricken with racial conflict. How strange, then, it is that a man of Africa should be here to receive an Award given for service to the cause of peace and brotherhood.' But, he warned, hinting at things to come, 'peace and revolution make uneasy bed-fellows. There can be no peace until the forces of oppression are overthrown'.

Throughout the visit Oliver Tambo was beside him. The message was plain for all to see: despite the collective leadership of the ANC, Tambo was Luthuli's formal representative in the world at large. The two men naturally had much to discuss. During the State of Emergency in South Africa, more than 1 000 people had been detained or arrested and Mandela had gone underground. Tambo was also anxious to hear more details about Pondoland, whose peasants had risen up in arms against the Bantu Authorities system and its appropriation of traditional leaders, cattle dipping, and additional birth and death taxes. They particularly unleashed their anger against chiefs collaborating with the apartheid state rather than lose their stipends. Chiefs' huts had been burnt, and some people were even killed. At a large gathering called to present grievances to paramount chief Botha Sigcau at Ngqusa Hill, armed police fired into the crowd, killing at least 11 people and wounding dozens more. Hundreds of Pondos went into hiding in the mountains, embarking on prolonged guerrilla warfare against collaborators. A number of the community leaders had been taken. Tambo heard that one of Bizana's most active ANC members, Lumford Anderson Ganyile, had been banished to a deserted area in far-off Sekhukhuneland.[13] In Tambo's own homeland, opposition was taking the form of violent resistance reminiscent of the conflict in Sekhukhuneland in the late 1950s, when Tambo himself had been called upon as an attorney to defend villagers charged with the murder of chiefs collaborating with the Bantu Authorities system.[14]

Luthuli knew, and was concerned, about the intense debates over the proposed shift in ANC strategy to armed resistance. Earlier in the year, a clandestine meeting had taken place in Natal.[15] The ANC and the other Congresses, as well as the SACP, were represented, and the earnest discussions lasted for two days. Chief Luthuli had grave misgivings about the ANC's shift from the policy of passive resistance to a strategy of violence, and wavered more than once in the discussion meetings.[16] He had, of course, demonstrated his outrage by publicly burning his passbook after Sharpeville, but he could not in all honesty accept the change. Subsequently, however, Luthuli stated that he understood why people embarked on an armed struggle. 'When my son decides to sleep with a girl,' he explained to Moses Kotane, 'he does not ask for my permission, but just does it. It is only afterwards, when the girl is pregnant and the parents make a case, that he brings his troubles home.'[17] Though he himself would not countenance armed struggle, he could not condemn anyone who could no longer tolerate the conditions at home. Maulvi Cachalia, of the Indian Congress, and his brother Yusuf, both leading figures in the 1946 Passive Resistance Campaign, which had profoundly impressed and influenced the Youth League, and the 1952 Defiance Campaign, also opposed the move.

The resolution, when it came, was a compromise, but one that smoothed over some of the contradictions inherent in the Alliance. The new body, Umkhonto we Sizwe (MK), would embark on 'armed struggle' and, nominally at least, would be separate from the ANC – 'a necessary fiction', commented SACP member Joe Slovo.[18] MK would also welcome members from all races. In practice, this meant that whites could join MK through their membership of the SACP. The deliberate ambiguity of the origins of Umkhonto gave the ANC several advantages, most notably ostensible legal cover, as it did not publicly announce the policy of armed struggle. The ANC's NEC adopted the tactic of formally endorsing a Working Committee – their idea was that a military movement, while separate from the ANC, would nevertheless be linked to it and come under its formal control. Mandela, who had been the most persistent and persuasive proponent for such a move, was mandated to form the Committee, 'and would not be subject to the mother organisation'.[19]

The actions of Umkhonto we Sizwe, once made public, could not be attributed to people who were found to be members of either the SACP or the ANC,[20] though this did not for a moment stop the South African regime from harassing and detaining members of the Alliance. The tactic was politically important, though, as the ANC was able to retain its traditional African racial composition yet maintain access to its members for mobilising and recruiting.

Tambo was well aware of the discussions going on inside South Africa and was neither disturbed nor surprised by the turn of events. In 1953, the Executive had considered armed struggle and had opted for peaceful tactics not, he said, because they were pacifists, but 'because it was politically wise'.[21] Some 20 years earlier, Tambo – as a student – had supported the war against Hitler and fascism, despite the South African government's sorry record of the treatment of black soldiers. In exile, too, the discourse among the sympathisers of the liberation struggle increasingly turned to guerrilla warfare. The liberation war was perceived to be gaining ground in Algeria, particularly after it began its strategy of sabotage and bomb attacks on the sizeable settler population. In Cuba, Fidel Castro's small band of revolutionaries invaded their country in a rickety old boat and successfully toppled a corrupt regime. African states were expressing, in the words of Joe Matthews, 'surprise that we thought non-violence could work in South Africa'.[22] And, at home, the PAC had launched Poqo, a rural-based resistance movement that was executing terrorist attacks on white civilians. There was also a small group of white intellectuals who formed a National Committee of Liberation (later renamed the African Resistance Movement), which initiated a series of sabotage attacks until the organisation was smashed a few years later. Pressure was thus mounting for the use of armed struggle.

Officially, however, the ANC continued to present a non-violent face, and Tambo was obliged to fence around the ambiguity of the situation. His pragmatism was exemplified by his comment in an interview that the ANC did not want to say that they believed in violence – they preferred to prepare for it.[23] Nevertheless, in early May, Tambo alluded to the ANC's change in strategy when he made a speech in London, warning the South African government that if it used force to crush the planned stayaway, 'it would be the last time the ANC would talk of peace'.[24]

Still, during this concealed period of transition, Tambo was not privy to all the developments. The SACP, for example, had as early as June 1961 already decided to go ahead with armed resistance, and its members were beginning to receive military training. Although Tambo was in close touch with some of the young activists in London, they did not reveal to him their membership of the Communist Party, or why one of them – Mac Maharaj – slipped out of the UK without reporting to Tambo. However, as Maharaj was not a member of the ANC, Tambo chose not to raise the matter with the young man's friends and comrades.[25]

On 16 December 1961 a sequence of bomb attacks on government installations was detonated in different provinces of South Africa. Thus the armed struggle was officially launched. MK distributed its manifesto, offering a moral explanation for its actions. 'The people's patience is not endless,' it declared. 'The time comes in the life of any nation when there remain only two choices – submit or fight. That time has now come in South Africa.'[26]

It now became necessary for its leaders to communicate with the outside world; Tambo must be properly briefed, and moral and material support solicited for the struggle. The high command mandated Nelson Mandela, who had already been clandestinely travelling around South Africa for 10 months, to go abroad to explain to the External Mission the strategic shift of the ANC. In January 1962, Tambo received a letter from 'Wamba', which had twice been forwarded. It informed Tambo that 'Wamba' and 'Bakwe' (Bakwe was a Tswana name that Tambo would almost certainly associate with Joe Matthews, whose mother's maiden name was Bokwe) would be attending the forthcoming conference in Addis. 'Hope to be in Dar 13/14th inst.' advised the letter. 'Sending photos for travel papers. A family chat before the Conference is absolutely essential... It has not been possible to advise Jimmy [Julius Nyerere] of our arrival in Dar and hope you will be able to attend to it.'[27]

Frene Ginwala, who had helped Tambo to find asylum in Africa in 1960 and was now a journalist based in Dar es Salaam, was increasingly occupied with organising routes and travel documents for refugees.[28] Some of these early arrivals included MK volunteers, and it was her task to process their applications, although their photographs did not match the names ascribed to them. Often, she would see familiar faces in the passport-sized photographs, but, she said, for security reasons she would deliberately not speculate as to who they might be.[29] One evening, she received a visit from Tambo.

'Where is Nelson?' he asked anxiously. Frene took out a box of photographs, which she kept mixed with family documents. Sure enough, there was Mandela's passport photograph, which meant that he was probably on his way. She remembers sitting in a car with Tambo, waiting for the bus to arrive from the Tunduru border post. Nobody arrived. After a few days of vigil, Tambo left for London, in case Mandela had made his way straight there. But before he left he gave her instructions that if Mandela arrived in Tanzania, his visit was not to be public – he was 'buried' deep underground. She was simply to arrange a meeting for him with Julius Nyerere.

Shortly afterwards, Frene received a telephone message from the commissioner at Mbeya: Would she be able to authenticate two ANC people who had arrived from South Africa?

'Put them on the line,' she replied.

The voice on the other end was that of Joe Matthews, who was now domiciled in Basotholand (Lesotho), and had identified a safe route for refugees to Tanzania. He did not say who the other person was. Frene immediately gave the commissioner the go-ahead. Shortly afterwards, a towering figure, heavily built and wearing a conical grass Basotho hat and large mosquito boots loomed on her doorstep. It was, of course, Nelson Mandela – wearing a disguise.

Tambo soon joined his friend. Mandela related entertaining stories of his escape and described the covert hospitality he had received from Seretse Khama. But it wasn't long before he got to the point. He told Tambo that he had been particularly anxious to explain to him in person the process by which the decision had been reached to form MK in October 1961. The two men's close bond has been described romantically as a biblical 'David and Jonathan relationship'.[30] For Mandela, it was essential – both personally and politically – to discuss with his closest comrade this major change of strategy, explain his own involvement in it and secure Tambo's wholehearted support. He knew that once he obtained his partner's accord, Tambo would never waver in the pursuit of the new policy. Mandela sketched out the events leading to the decision. The May strike in 1961 was marked both by the partial response by black workers in some areas and the state's massive military build-up and repression. The ANC leadership – Walter Sisulu, Duma Nokwe, Mandela – as well as the SACTU[31] leadership, chose to interpret the stayaway as an illustration of disillusionment by their followers. The movement's traditional weapons of protest, they claimed, were no longer adequate.[32] It seemed to them that it was imperative that the leadership be seen to be providing clear and active direction. For many nights, the leadership discussed and carefully assessed the extent to which conditions for armed struggle were favourable. Popular response to armed struggle, Mandela was confident, was widespread. The physical terrain on which war was to be waged also had to be considered, including securing friendly neighbouring borders; and the international context of support had to be encouraged. With regard to the latter, an 'underground railway' was already established, thanks to Seretse Khama's willingness to take some risks, to transport MK recruits to be trained outside South Africa in guerrilla operations.[33] In these last respects, Tambo's role was to be crucial. Mandela had come to join him in ascertaining the level of assistance African and other sympathetic countries could offer.

Mandela was particularly anxious to clarify for Tambo his reasons for the decision to collaborate with SACP recruits. The Communist Party had operated underground for a decade and was experienced in clandestine activism. Many had also acquired military skills in the Second World War and had the relevant professional training – Jack Hodgson, Rusty Bernstein, Wolfie Kodesh, Ivan Schermbrucker and Joe Slovo, for example, had served 'up North' (in North Africa and the Mediterranean during the War), while younger recruits like Denis Goldberg and Ben Turok, who were assisting in the manufacture of explosives, were professional men with technical qualifications. And in the same way that Tambo himself had made an honest attempt to get the United Front going, argued Mandela, this historical moment required the liberation movement to pool all its creative forces into a consolidated effort. He reported, too, that the High Command had established regional commands to cover the main centres. Recruits numbered almost 250 people, including whites.

On receiving the mandate to head the High Command, Mandela had proceeded to merge the SACP squad with the new one formed by Congress Alliance members. The new organisation received its own identity, distinct from the ANC, and had been named Umkhonto we Sizwe. The first group of the new squad was being prepared to receive six months' military training in China, and a second group, consisting of 32 young workers recruited by SACTU members, was in the process of formation.[34] All these recruits were to return home after their training, where they would in turn train others and so help mobilise on a large scale inside the country. Sabotage was then to be undertaken by selected units. Mandela's role of political mobilisation was to continue alongside the armed struggle. Clearly, popular support and organisation would always be paramount. But because the South African state was powerfully armed, ruthless and had the support of the vast bulk of the whites, it was vital that the movement indicate to the people a sharp break with the impediments of the past and display a willingness to consider drastic steps.

Tambo had no problem with Mandela's outline of the decisions taken. He had been aware of the debates on armed struggle for months and, in any case, he himself had been exposed to the sentiments expressed in the African continent. Misgivings about working with the communists were dispelled when Tambo heard that the ANC leadership had overwhelmingly accepted this working relationship, as it had done so pragmatically before. The shift for Tambo politically was therefore, according to Joe Matthews – for many years his personal assistant – 'not a major psychological switch'.[35]

Tambo and Mandela then worked out a programme for the External Mission in the new circumstances. The pair were to canvas support for the armed struggle in Africa. Personnel reinforcements for the follow-up were on their way – Robert Resha, who had headed the anti-Bantu Education campaign from Sophiatown, was one of them. Tambo was to correlate external facilities with developments at home. He was also to concentrate on obtaining both neighbouring and diplomatic support. Tambo had clearly made a good impression in Sweden, both during and after his visit there at the time of the Nobel award to Chief Luthuli. He had developed friendships with key members in both political parties in that country. There was, of course, his friendship with David Wirmark,[36] and he had also met Olof Palme, a member of Parliament and rising young star of the Social Democrats. But with these friends, the ANC would have difficulties with the switch to armed struggle; it would thus be Tambo's task to reconcile them to the necessity for this change. He would need to persuade them to continue with their support for ANC activities in ways other than military.

Tambo, in turn, gave Mandela an account of the United Front – the working alliance between the Pan-African Congress and the ANC in exile. The UF had achieved some major gains – most notably the exclusion of South Africa from the Commonwealth, and a high-profile appearance in the United Nations. The strain of a unity imposed by convenience and the desire of African leaders such as Nkrumah and Nasser, rather than principle, was beginning to show. True, the distances and the uneven representation in the UF offices had resulted in communication difficulties. Tambo had been irritated to learn of a separate PAC office in London, while the ANC had scrupulously refrained from presenting any of their initiatives as exclusively their own; the Dar es Salaam office, for example, had started off as a United Front venue. In Ghana, the radio programme, the *Voice of Africa*, had launched a series of attacks on the ANC, breaking with the original agreement not to criticise fellow members of the UF. Tambo could only explain this divergence as the anxiety of the fledgling PAC, banned so soon after its formation, to promote itself. Compared with the respected and established ANC, the breakaway group was at a disadvantage, and it seemed that Peter Raboroko, who had instigated the broadsides, wanted to draw attention to the PAC by embracing a more militant rhetoric.

Inside South Africa, the PAC had withdrawn from the All-in Conference held before the May stayaway.[37] According to Tambo, the UF meeting in London in September/October 1961 'reviewed the situation' and the members agreed to communicate with their respective organisations at home. At the United Nations in New York, Tambo received word that Mzwai Piliso in Cairo had received a message from home 'stating that the United Front had served its purpose'. The PAC had publicly opposed the stayaway in May 1961:

'What happened to Congress Alliance leaders with Emergency? Where are they now? They have already started to run... We, the PAC, have, as you know, broken away from the Congress Alliance because their leaders are such *cowards*... The PAC *do* [sic] *not support Congress Alliance* with their present move to a National Convention. We do not want our people to become *Russian* slaves as the *Congress Alliance* do.'[38]

When Tambo returned to London, he saw the communiqué to Piliso but did not release it because (as always, punctiliously following the correct procedure) he wanted to put it to the next UF meeting. Then Mandela arrived. Tambo, in keeping with prudent habits, was inclined not to tackle the PAC publicly, but to wait to see how things would develop. When Mandela addressed the Addis Ababa conference, he – on Tambo's advice – did not refer to the rift that was clearly on the cards. This was despite a leaflet attacking the ANC, distributed by Philip Kgosana (the young leader of the Langa march to Cape Town nearly two years earlier, who was now at odds with another faction of the PAC).

Observing a fair amount of prejudice against the ANC – and again following Tambo's counsel – Mandela's speech focused instead on a description and history of the ANC, and the need for organised support in the battle against apartheid. At this conference, the Pan-African Freedom Movement of East, Central and Southern Africa (PAFMECSA) was formed. Its constitution was committed to non-violence, Pan-Africanism, and to setting up a Freedom Fund to aid the liberation movements.

Mandela and Tambo went on to visit a number of other countries in North Africa. The two friends and partners were delighted to be together again. In Algeria, Mandela underwent a period of training before he proceeded to London. The group of South African activists who had founded the Anti-Apartheid Movement was able to arrange meetings for Mandela with 'top people', including Hugh Gaitskell, newspaperman Lord Astor and a few embassies.[39] By now, his presence outside of South Africa had become known, and journalists were eager to interview him.

'Armed struggle,' he told them, 'is only one weapon – we must use many different tactics. There is a role for passive resistance, for the churches, for liberals.' Mandela saw armed struggle as a weapon, he said, not so much to overthrow the state as to force it to negotiate. It was also an important way of boosting morale at home.[40] Yet, Mandela confessed privately to Colin Legum, a South African-born journalist and a friend, 'I dread going back and telling Chief [Luthuli] I'm now committed to armed struggle.'[41]

In London, Mandela also had a long talk with Adelaide. An important part of his visit there, he later revealed, was to discuss with her the supportive role she would need to play.[42] Tambo's role was about to change, drastically affecting his lifestyle. He was no longer to be the ANC's diplomat at large, with headquarters in London. It would now be necessary to raise funds for military support in Africa, the East and the West, organise military training outside South Africa for recruits, and run and maintain military camps stationed in various African countries. He would seldom spend much time at home with his family. It was vital that Adelaide, as Tambo's partner, understand and assist during the new and difficult phase the ANC was entering.[43]

For Adelaide, the news came as a thunderbolt. She had managed to find work as a nurse because Oliver would be receiving only a small allowance from the ANC. But she had expected him to at least be domiciled in London. Mandela's visit was to be a turning point. It was clear that Tambo's role had in an instant been transformed from diplomat to all-embracing revolutionary. With extremely limited funds, it was also clear that Adelaide would need to be the family breadwinner and, in effect, a single parent. The metamorphosis was to divide the couple not only geographically, but also impose an ideological strain on their relationship – while Adelaide had to raise her children in a sophisticated metropolitan environment, sending them to more well-resourced middle-class schools that could assist her in childcare, Oliver's role as a revolutionary was to take precedence over his original mandate to head an international diplomatic mission for the ANC. This sharp division of roles was to haunt their marriage for more than a quarter of a century.

Having completed his discussions with key contacts, Mandela took leave of the members of the External Mission and returned home. As a sign of things to come, so caught up was Tambo with the urgency of the new role of the ANC in exile and indeed his own managing of it, that he omitted to take formal leave of his wife. His remorse regarding this oversight was expressed in an 11-page letter to Adelaide in reply to hers, which he received a few weeks later in Dar es Salaam, and indicates how overwhelmed he felt at this personal and political moment.

'I wish to apologise most sincerely, Delie, about leaving home without saying goodbye to you... we were getting late and I was worrying about all sorts of things related to Wamba's security... It was wrong of me not to think of you and part properly... You have borne the brunt of our burdens, single-handed, and in this life of hardship, of physical and mental strain, I have featured only as an aggravating factor – a source of added grief and spiritual distress, a corrupting influence although my guilt consisted of acts of omission – the things I omitted to do and say...

'At the moment of writing, I feel the sense of failure so strongly that I cannot undertake anything or promise anything save to pray while I breathe – to pray for you, Delie, for Dudulani, for Dali, for Nini and for Sis Lydia, the five people who are closest to my life and whose names form part of my prayers anywhere at any time, on any day.'[44]

Adelaide was 'deeply touched' by her husband's letter.

'My love,' she replied, 'for a long time I have been misjudging you and piling one grievance on another against you whilst you were innocently unaware and, worst of all, I could have easily acted in a way that I could only have regretted afterwards.'

Instead, after Mendi Msimang had moved out to his own place in Unity House, she had undertaken a frenzy of cathartic activity. She painted the walls and doors of her flat with the help of a young South African, Elijah, who was staying with the family, but doing most of the work by far. Then she washed all the blankets and curtains and, on the fourth day of this marathon clean-up, the carpets in the lounge and the entrance hall. On the next day, she wrote, she was in bed from exhaustion and flu, unable to do the children's laundry.

'How stupid. My only consolation is the flat is, in any way, nice and clean.' But, she assured Oliver, 'you are and always will remain my husband and the father of my children and my prayers are that God should be with you in all that you do and guide you accordingly. I know you are overworked and working very hard for the love of our dear people and country, and I shall always be on your side, for better or for worse, as I promised the Bishop on our wedding day.'[45]

The exchange was to define the parameters of their marriage, and from then on, Adelaide more or less resigned herself to a relatively less proactive contribution to the struggle as a supportive partner and proficient, virtually single mother – as millions of South African women have been both before and after her.[46]

Meanwhile, immediately on Tambo's return to Dar, where he stayed in Ruth and Tennyson Makiwane's apartment, Joe Matthews arrived with a message from the NEC 'with a hot problem from the South'.[47] Matthews also brought a number of other items from the NEC to be discussed, and for Tambo the next few days were taken up with ongoing meetings with Matthews and James Hadebe. Plans needed to be made for the External Mission to acquire an official mandate from the NEC to the Mission in Exile to represent armed struggle to the outside world, to dispel any further ambiguities on ANC policy.

As for Mandela, his life too was soon to be dramatically overturned. And it was to be the last time he would see Tambo for close on 30 years.[48] Three weeks after his return home, in August 1962, Nelson Mandela was arrested in a roadblock outside Howick, Natal. He was returning from a report-back to Chief Luthuli and had been exposed, it seems, by CIA agents.[49] Mandela was charged for incitement and leaving the country illegally, and was sentenced to five years in prison. The arrest was a major blow to the movement, but not mortal. Socialist and African countries had promised support, and the High Command felt confident that their cadres would be able to put all available resources to good use. At home, there was an eager response by hundreds of young people to the call to take up arms. In Tambo's correspondence files, for example, a letter dated March 1962 came from Z Ngalo, E Qono and H Fazzie, advising of their arrival in Tanganyika and asking for assistance. 'Our greatest ambition is known to you.'[50] Frene Ginwala attested to the growing number of would-be trainees who applied for papers. In the 18 months following its launch, MK sent more than 100 recruits out of the country for military training.[51]

Oliver Tambo continued to cultivate a network in the sphere of international conferences and to encourage the formation of support groups. Basically, he was the leader of what was still merely the external mission of the ANC. He soon found, as he expected, that the friends he had made on the basis of a non-violent policy of resistance were not prepared to support an armed struggle. This called for a careful presentation of the ANC. Tambo explained, in his considered and methodical way, the history of the movement, emphasising the responsibility that the South African regime itself carried for the slide towards a possibly bloody civil war. He described the ANC's many patient efforts over the years to reach the country's rulers through petitions, carefully worded letters, requests for appointments, passive resistance campaigns, boycotts, mass mobilisation and mass campaigns. Each attempt had been met with further violence and oppression. He quoted from Luthuli's statement in 1952 on his dismissal by the government from his position as the elected chief of the Abase-Makolweni: 'Who will deny that 30 years of my life have been spent knocking in vain, patiently, moderately and modestly at a closed and barred door? What have been the fruits of my moderation?'[52]

He also quoted the MK proclamation: '[We] have always sought to achieve liberation without bloodshed', and 'we hope even at this late hour, that our first actions will awaken everyone to a realization of the disastrous situation to which the Nationalist Party policy is leading'.[53] MK had also emphasised that, while the acts of sabotage were intended to send a graphic message to the people and its oppressors that the nature of the struggle had changed, their operations were specifically designed to avoid the taking of life.

The apartheid regime was now embarking on an increased reign of oppression. During 1962, the South African government launched a process of extending its already considerable powers. The new 'Sabotage Act', defined very broadly, carried the death penalty, with a minimum five-year sentence. Bannings and house arrests were increased, and opponents in rural areas or in the townships were 'banished' to isolated rural districts far away from their own communities. The tiny Congress of Democrats, which had gamely tried to take up the baton as a surviving legal organisation by distributing pamphlets and conducting public protests, was also banned. Many of its members were detained. The Security Police, under the baleful eye of the Minister of Justice, John Balthazar Vorster, were promoted to special Secret Service status and entrusted with the tasks of infiltrating the ANC and extracting information. In response to the launch of MK, the Nationalist government tightened measures for the 90-day detention law of 1963, by which anyone could be picked up and held without access to lawyers. Under this widely used law, torture was more frequent, and eventually became routine.

In the meantime, MK was retaliating. Mandela's successor after his arrest was Port Elizabeth activist Raymond Mhlaba, SACTU trade unionist, leading figure in the Defiance Campaign in Port Elizabeth and Treason Trialist. Immediately after Sharpeville, Mhlaba had gone underground. He was slipping in and out of the country, and had been trained in China. Walter Sisulu and other leaders also went into hiding. On 26 June 1963, Freedom Charter Day, Sisulu broadcast a message to the people over a radio transmitter in Johannesburg. It was reminiscent of the resistance manoeuvres of the partisans in the Second World War and had been set up by comrade veterans. It was becoming clear that there was no hope of getting anywhere without intensifying and changing the character of armed activity. MK began to embark on a stage of preparing for classical guerrilla warfare. The hundred or so cadres had concluded their training in China, absorbing the tactic of the 'war of the flea', and were ready and eager for action. Some members of MK prepared a plan, which they named 'Operation Mayibuye' – perhaps best translated as 'Operation

Restore'.[54] 'Mayibuye', part of the ANC slogan, evoked the passionate cry for the restoration of the land.

'Armed to the teeth,' declared the draft, 'the white state... has presented the people with only one choice and that is its overthrow by force and violence. It can now truly be said that very little, if any, scope exists for the smashing of white supremacy other than by means of mass revolutionary action, the main content of which is armed resistance leading to victory by military means.'[55]

But not all the leadership accepted the wisdom of this strategy. 'There are conflicting accounts of Operation Mayibuye,' pointed out Pallo Jordan. 'Rusty Bernstein says it was still under discussion; others say it was a hare-brained scheme cooked up by non-Africans; others claim it was authored by Joe Slovo.'[56] Slovo himself claimed that the plan went to the High Command. It contained, he said, 'rather euphoric expectations at that stage about what help Africa could give to help us go into the second phase of our armed activity which we envisaged as guerrilla warfare... So there was a plan to sort of combine general political mobilisation and intensify organisation in all the regions and those regions were specifically targeted to be the kind of bases from which guerrillas could operate.'[57]

A parallel process was envisaged by which general political mobilisation would be combined with intensified political organisation in all the regions. 'The time for small thinking is over,' argued the document, 'because history leaves us no choice.'[58]

In May 1963, Joe Slovo asked the Central Committee of the SACP if he could leave the country to discuss an MK High Command proposal of Operation Mayibuye with Tambo and the Mission in Exile. JB Marks, who was sent on a separate project to report to the Mission in Exile, accompanied him. Taking the underground route, they arrived in Dar es Salaam, where Tambo had established exile structures. Slovo met Oliver in the Palace Hotel and presented the draft document of Operation Mayibuye, which outlined a plan to move from sabotage to guerrilla warfare. The document argued that a widespread conviction was prevalent and that the road to victory was through force. It followed, therefore, that a general uprising could be sparked off, as in Cuba, 'by organised and well-prepared guerrilla operations during which the course of the masses will be drawn in and armed'. Slovo explained the plan: to train and equip several thousand guerrillas 'in all aspects of military operation' abroad and then return in platoons, by air or ship, in four pre-selected areas – Port Elizabeth, Port Shepstone, the northwestern Transvaal on the borders of Botswana and the Limpopo, and the Northern Cape – to join and arm prepared bands of the local population. The key to success was the political, underground mobilisation and 'if every member now prepares to make unlimited sacrifice for the achievement of our goal'.[59] The movement would approach African governments – Algeria and Ghana – to see what could be done to help the specific project of getting the guerrillas back home. They held extremely high expectations of PAFMECSA's contributions to finance the liberation armies in southern Africa and envisaged – perhaps romantically – the possibility of the cadres being parachuted back into South Africa.

'There was a complete sort of unrealistic assessment of what had happened in the rest of Africa and what the capacity was of these newly independent states,' commented Slovo in hindsight years later.[60] And indeed a number of the Rivonia underground members – Walter Sisulu, Rusty Bernstein, 'Kathy' Kathrada and, in particular, Moses Kotane – were quite dubious about the plan. They criticised it because it was 'an easy way out', foregrounding the military over and above the political struggle.[61] On the other hand, Govan Mbeki, one of the authors of the document, and Nelson Mandela both supported the project.

But if Slovo had been at all uncertain about Tambo's reaction to the plan, he must have been delighted with his response. As far as Tambo was concerned, the Draconian legislation at home had put the resistance on a war footing. Less than a generation earlier, the partisans in Europe, assisted by the armies of friendly states, had conquered the might of the Nazi army. The document warned that the liberation movement should prepare themselves for a protracted war. Perhaps, too, knowing that Mandela backed the plan may have assisted him to look favourably on Operation Mayibuye.

'I don't know if you have ever been with OR at a meeting where he really becomes passionate and excited,' recalled Joe Slovo. 'He had the most remarkable eyes. His eyes used to just physically dart from one side to the other as you were looking at him and you could see he was terribly taken up with excitement... [He] was sitting there reading this document and his eyes started darting and... I have never seen him do that before or since. He actually got out of his chair and did a dance round the room. It seemed to everyone at that stage that, you know, we were now in business. That now there were possibilities and serious plans for beginning to meet the other side – on its own ground.'[62]

Marks and Slovo planned to return to South Africa with messages from the External Mission and to report their findings to the High Command. But before this could happen, disaster struck.

In July 1963, the bulk of the top leadership of the High Command and some members of its support formations were arrested in a swoop on a farmhouse in Rivonia, on the outskirts of Johannesburg. Those who had gathered together in Rivonia included Walter Sisulu, Elias Motsoaledi, Raymond Mhlaba, Govan Mbeki, Andrew Mlangeni, Ahmed Kathrada, Denis Goldberg, Rusty Bernstein, Bob Hepple and James Kantor. Other arrests were to follow. The already imprisoned Nelson Mandela, who was charged with leading the planned insurrection, headed the list of the accused. In the rounding up of scores of known members of the ANC and its affiliates, no charges needed to be made. They were simply kept incommunicado for an indefinite period. Unprepared for the ruthless interrogation methods the Security Police were learning from the French and Portuguese secret police in the suppression of resistance movements in their colonies, a few detainees cracked and, from the information they provided, the state was able to mop up any further attempts to revive the leadership. After the Rivonia Trial was concluded, its highly respected defence advocate, Bram Fischer, went underground in a last endeavour to sustain the internal base. But a few months later he, too, was exposed, arrested and sentenced to life imprisonment.[63] Wilton Mkwayi, who had taken over the leadership of MK, was also taken a few months later. 'We have broken the back of the ANC,' boasted JB Vorster, the Minister of Justice, allaying white fears. Indeed, that seemed to be the feeling of the movement too. Slovo spoke of 'the destruction of the whole movement and the demoralisation which swept throughout the country because there was nothing left for practical purposes...'[64]

There were, however, those who managed to escape capture; hundreds now 'skipped' the country. They took with them a message to the External Mission that the responsibility of leading the movement now fell on them.[65] Until the reconstituting of the ANC leadership by due process could took place at home, the external mission would be obliged to take decisions on behalf of the entire organisation. The MK High Command would need to be reconstructed in exile. The training, the camps, the military strategies and the return of the cadres would henceforth be coordinated from outside. Tambo, who after the arrival of Adelaide and the children, had set up his base in London – until then an appropriate centre for running an international campaign – had now moved his headquarters to Tanzania, which had offered land for training camps and an office for the ANC in Dar es Salaam.

For Tambo, it was to be the beginning of decades of separation from his family. After some exploration of possible countries of domicile in Africa, Adelaide decided to stay in the UK. To follow Oliver around, she felt, would be a security risk for both him and his family.[66] He would always need to stay in safe houses, and be inaccessible to her for long periods. Besides, she could earn a better salary in the UK. Trevor Huddleston, commenting on this decision, chose to see it as a vote of confidence by Tambo in the UK: 'I do think again that he chose to leave Adelaide and the children in England because he had a great affection for England. And he had a great affection for England because he was educated by English missionaries, you know – however paternalistic they may have been.'[67]

For the ANC, the urgent and immediate task was to put every skill at its disposal into saving the lives of their comrades. For Tambo, especially, the news of Rivonia was shattering. He had always regarded himself as Mandela's lieutenant, the caretaker to his leadership.[68] Tambo's 'aversion for the limelight' since his schooldays had not diminished.[69]

Since Mandela's arrest in 1962, the burden of continuing the struggle without access to his partner's and Walter Sisulu's counsel had been heavy. Still, at that time the ANC (as well as the PAC) believed that revolution would come within just a few years; Mandela would be released, the comrades reassured each other, before he served the full length of his sentence. But now the accused faced the death sentence. The vindictive behaviour of the South African authorities, particularly in the light of the recently launched MK, gave Tambo no reason to suppose that those indicted would receive a lesser sentence.

Tambo's immediate task was to approach the United Nations – while the Eastern Bloc could assist financially, only South Africa's trading partners could apply pressure on the apartheid system where it hurt most – in its burgeoning economy. Tambo's speech on the first day that the Rivonia accused were put on trial was passionate and memorable. He outlined the iniquities of apartheid, emphasising its structural violence – amounting to 'genocide masquerading under the guise of a civilised dispensation of justice' – and reassuringly contrasted this to the vision of the inclusive, non-racial African humanism of the ANC. He quoted the Freedom Charter – 'South Africa belongs to all who live in it' – a drastic concession, he acknowledged, on the part of the oppressed. He quoted South Africa's endangered leaders: 'I detest racialism because I regard it a barbaric thing whether it comes from a black man or a white man', Mandela had declared in his 1962 trial, and in his statement, Walter Sisulu had declared, 'The fundamental principle in our struggle is equal rights for all in our country, and that all people who have made South Africa their home, by birth or adoption, irrespective of colour or creed, are entitled to these rights.'

Tambo also invoked the incarcerated leader of the PAC, Robert Sobukwe, 'who after serving for a period of three years, is still in detention indefinitely – perhaps for the rest of his life unless we do something in the meantime, which we hope to be able to do'. [Sobukwe] said, '"Freedom of the Africans can only be established when the African group comes into its own. Freedom of the Africans means freedom for everyone, including Europeans in this country"'.[70]

Tambo did not directly mention armed struggle. But in his conclusion he spoke firmly about the ANC's determination to fight back: 'If the UN finds any real difficulties, we are bound, most naturally, to explore every other avenue that is open to us, whatever that is, to strengthen ourselves in every way that is conceivable. There is no question from our point of view of postponing anything. Apartheid has outlived its time in the world and most certainly in Africa.'

Tambo's passionate plea received a standing ovation. 'I think that is one of his greatest speeches he made to the Security Council in 1964,' said Joe Matthews. 'Of course, it occurred in the emotional aftermath of the Rivonia arrests.'[71] There were many who were convinced that the positive response it generated played a major role in influencing the outcome of the sentence – life instead of death.

While the Rivonia trialists were incarcerated on Robben Island,[72] Tambo issued a press statement from Dar es Salaam: 'Nelson Mandela, Walter Sisulu, Govan Mbeki, Ahmed Kathrada, Raymond Mhlaba, Andrew Mlangeni, Denis Goldberg and Elias Motsoaledi were today sentenced to life imprisonment in the Rivonia Trial which since last year, has been the focal point of world attention. The judge in the trial has done his duty to the white government which appointed him. The Rivonia leaders have done their duty to South Africa and all its people. They have done their duty to Africa and the world. Those who opposed evil have been put away by the evildoers.'

Tambo presented the sentence as historic. It seemed to justify perfectly the reason for the ANC's strategic shift on moral grounds. '[S]ince in South Africa moderation and reason leads only to Verwoerd's death cells and torture chambers, then moderation and reason must take leave of the South African situation... We salute the heroes of Rivonia. Their imprisonment is not the end of the liberation struggle or of resistance to tyranny; it is the beginning of a new and decisive phase.' But it was a phase, he warned prophetically, 'that will embroil the continent of Africa and destroy the foundations of international peace'.[73]

With the arrest and life sentence of MK commander Wilton Mkwayi, it now fell upon Tambo, as leader of the Mission in Exile, to take on the leadership of MK. 'It appeared,' reflected Tambo years later, 'as if the guns of MK had been silenced for all time... the only cohesive organised force of our revolution that remained at the time was the comrades who had been sent out of the country to train in politics and in the art of modern warfare.'[74]

Tambo's approaches were met with some sympathy, particularly from the Scandinavian countries, which indicated that they were open to giving aid, providing it was for humanitarian purposes only. This qualified offer was not inconsequential; Tambo had a growing number of ANC non-combatant refugees to support. They required feeding, clothing and non-military training. He also had to equip and run offices in various parts of Africa. But this earmarked aid also complicated Tambo's task. One of the consequences was that MK was obliged to turn to the Soviet Union and other socialist countries.

Perhaps significantly, it was as late as 1963 – some time after the shift to armed struggle, and after Mandela's arrest – that Tambo first visited the USSR, on his way to and from a visit to Beijing marking the anniversary of the People's Republic of China.[75] Years later he recalled how he 'was in no hurry to visit Moscow'.[76] His priority had been to procure support for MK from the West.

It had become patently clear, though, that material support for armed struggle would not be forthcoming from the sympathisers in Africa, or from the West. The independent African states and PAFMECSA's Liberation Committee, though warmly supportive, were unable to summon up the resources, while the Western countries baulked at providing direct assistance to armed struggle. The financial support given to the ANC from Africa was limited. In the first five years of the OAU's existence, the ANC received £35,000. Subsequent amounts were severely decreased – in 1967/8, for example, instead of the promised US$80,000, the movement received just US$3,940.[77] Very few resources were available. 'We were shipped out of countries because of our stand in Angola. [ANC members] were living in terrible conditions, we were living in camps. Those were difficult years,' confirmed Aziz Pahad, at that time a young ANC member studying in the UK.[78] It was virtually only the Eastern Bloc that provided training and education and a modicum of food, clothing and arms.

There had been earlier visits by ANC members to Moscow – as members of the reconstituted SACP, they were 'wearing two hats'. National chairman Yusuf Dadoo, who had escaped from Bechuanaland on the same plane as Tambo in 1960, soon afterwards visited Moscow, accompanied by other Party members who were also in the ANC. The second visit included ANC and Party member Joe Matthews. (The others were Michael Harmel and Vella Pillay.) In October 1961, on Dadoo's third visit to Moscow, he waited for Moses Kotane to leave South Africa illegally to join him for the Communist Party of the Soviet Union (CPSU) conference. Kotane was visiting Moscow after the absence of a quarter of a century.[79] He intended to return to South Africa, but events at home overtook his plans. The SACP created a special subcommittee with the aim of finding the means to train cadres in sabotage operations. In the Soviet Union, the SACP had a party-to-party relationship with the CPSU. The outcome of the SACP's request for further funding to support the armed struggle was positive. An additional grant was immediately made available to increase the initial amount for the SACP from US$50,000 in 1961 to US$112,445 in 1962.

Tambo arrived in Moscow, significantly, accompanied by Kotane (Luthuli's favourite communist and the ANC's Treasurer-General), and was offered respectful hospitality. He was particularly concerned to secure funding and training facilities for the ANC in its own right, and reported that the South African government's unduly repressive response to Umkhonto's limited sabotage was a clear indication that urgent changes were needed. The ANC leadership, which had done its utmost to avoid a destructive racial civil war, had now accepted the necessity for guerrilla warfare. At the same time, Tambo stressed, it was crucial to continue with both political propaganda inside South Africa and the international campaign to isolate South Africa politically and economically.[80]

The CPSUnion immediately made available £300,000, a considerable sum in 1964. In addition, military training was increased. It quickly became evident that countries within the socialist bloc were the only ones with means to support the MK armed struggle.

Once the Eastern Bloc was engaged, more careful diplomacy was needed by Tambo to ensure the independence of the ANC. Although some independent African countries were, at first, not happy with the ANC's alliance with the SACP, many understood precisely its situation. Julius Nyerere of Tanzania, who found his country in a similar situation when he was fundraising after independence, explained: 'I said to the Americans, "if you want to support us, support us. But you don't support us; so when we take arms from the Soviet Union or China – and at that time, really, it was China – don't be surprised, because you are not giving any support at all. This does not mean that we are aligned to the Soviet bloc. But the Soviet bloc is helping us, so we will take their aid, but this does not mean that therefore we want to be satellites of the Soviet Union". I took that position all the time.'[81]

And Oliver Tambo, he said, took that approach as well, although possibly the Soviet rather than the Chinese link was more difficult for the ANC.

'I knew the link he had with the Communist Party here [i.e. in South Africa] and because of that link therefore a different kind of link with the Soviet Union than say we had, because that was an ideological link which is not the same kind of link as my link with them or my link with China. We got on well, but a practical thing – I was not a Marxist and especially with the Soviet Union they wrote me off completely. Fine. I accepted that. So it was a different kind of thing, and I understood Oliver's position, it was because of the alliance with the Communist party here, and the Communist Party had an ideological link with the Communist Party of the Soviet Union, fine. This I did accept.'[82]

Tambo thus had to work considerably harder than Nyerere to reassure the Western countries. Firstly, Tambo's representatives reached an agreement that any funding should be supplied directly to MK, and not via the SACP. But this was not always sufficient to mollify the Western powers. For many years to come, the ANC's warmest and most liberal supporters in the West worried about the extent of the SACP's influence. Endless speculation on who in the National Executive Committee might also be communists, the problem of primary accountability and uneasy notions about Stalinist manipulation of the direction of the struggle was never far from the surface of any European or US analysis.

In addition, further difficulties ensued. As well as disturbing the West by accepting assistance from the Soviet bloc, the ANC also seemed to close the door on China, as the two powers were locked in the Sino-Soviet Dispute for hegemony over world socialism. Tambo had had a warm reception during his visit to Beijing in 1963, and had had a personal audience with Chou en Lai, who acknowledged that strategies had to be adapted to the different circumstances in each country. But on his way back, Tambo stopped over again in Moscow to close a firm deal on funding. It would be over a decade before he returned to China. Close to the end of his life, Tambo expressed puzzlement as to why the ANC had to be lumped with the SACP even by China. He might have been questioning tacit pressure from the SACP, or the Chinese ultimatum to choose between the two socialist powers – one felt it was probably the latter.[83] Either way, these were contradictions that would have repercussions for a long time to come.

The policy of armed struggle was to prove to be difficult, capricious and extremely complicated. The inevitably closer working relationship with the SACP led to repercussions in the ANC's internal political programme and ultimately to changes in the structure of the organisation and in the movement's international relations. From time to time, its value was challenged. Throughout MK's 30 years of existence, Tambo's concern was to maintain the ANC's image of 'the moral high ground', with the minimising of non-violence as the preferred option.

The 'moral high ground' included pointing out the immorality of South Africa's most successful trading partners and challenging the West to hit out hard against the apartheid regime. Tambo's message conveyed that armed struggle was not the sole option, and indeed might be reduced if economic and political sanctions were employed. 'There was another reason we thought of sanctions,' was his sensitive explanation to the General Assembly in 1963. 'We do not believe in violence. We do not think that anybody believes in it. We do not want it; nobody wants it. We did not think of invoking the world to invade South Africa.'[85]

In 1963 and 1964, following the launch of MK, which had occurred barely six months before the arrest of Mandela, Tambo made a number of high-profile speeches to present the ANC to the world. The most prominent had been the presentation made to the United Nations' Special Political Committee of the General Assembly in October 1963, after which the General Assembly passed Resolution XVIII of 11 October 1963, requesting the South African government to 'abandon the arbitrary trial now in progress and forthwith to grant unconditional release to all political prisoners'. A United Nations Special Committee on Apartheid was set up. Tambo made follow-up comments on subsequent resolutions of this committee.

Then, in March 1964, Tambo delivered a statement, 'Make Accomplices of Apartheid Account for Their Conduct', in which he called for vigorous sanctions against breakers of the boycott to the apartheid state. He was quite specific, underscoring by implication the military menace of the apartheid economy itself: 'We propose that a blacklist of companies such as De Beers Limited, African Explosives and Chemical Industries and others that collaborate with the South African government in the manufacture of ammunition in the country should be compiled. Members of this Organisation should be called upon to sever relations with these companies.'[86]

After the Rivonia sentence, Tambo called a consultative conference – in Lusaka on 8 January 1965 – of the ANC representatives from all their international offices. With half the senior leadership in prison and the president out of action in Groutville, the Mission in Exile had to establish a working organ of the ANC and take responsibility for the organisation as best they could.

'Now it might sound like an obvious decision,' commented Joe Matthews, 'but when you have an organisation like the ANC, you see people would again say, "But you are self-appointed, you haven't been elected by the conference of the ANC."

'And we had to say, "Now look, man, these are the realities of the situation that faces us. The most we can have outside the country is the consultative conferences, we can't call a regular conference in terms of the constitution, but we will consult our people as widely as possible, but we will have to take a decision on the question of leadership otherwise the organisation will disintegrate." So we took that as the first decision.'[87]

Since the apartheid onslaught in the 1950s, the ANC had had to respond creatively to the system of banning orders, arrests and other restrictions – Walter Sisulu, 'named' communists and other elected leaders who were fingered by the state had dextrously continued their political work regardless.[88] The constituted NEC in exile included the available NEC members constitutionally elected in 1959 – Deputy President Tambo, General Secretary Duma Nokwe, JB Marks, Moses Kotane – supplemented by the newly elected, former full-time national organiser Thomas Nkobi, plus Joe Modise, Tennyson Makiwane and Themba Qota (aka Alfred Kgokong). To this team were co-opted Alfred Nzo, Robert Resha and Johnny Makatini.[89]

It was also an adroit tactic for Oliver Tambo and the ANC to swerve somewhat from the culture of collective leadership to build up Mandela as the charismatic personification of the South African struggle. Mandela's stirring speech from the dock resonated throughout the world. Soon afterwards, the ANC, assisted by Ruth First, had compiled a book of Mandela's speeches to which Tambo had written the introduction, explaining Mandela's relevance to the continuing struggle.

'As a man, Nelson Mandela is passionate, emotional, sensitive, quickly stung to bitterness and retaliation by insult and patronage. He has a natural air of authority. He cannot help magnetizing a crowd: he is commanding with a tall, handsome bearing; trusts and is trusted by the youth, for their impatience reflects his own; appealing to women. He is dedicated and fearless. He is the born mass leader.'[90]

Pointedly, Tambo also linked Mandela to the ANC's calls for sanctions: 'Mandela and his close friend and co-leader Walter Sisulu were perhaps the fastest to get to grips with the harsh realities of the African struggle against the most powerful adversary in Africa: a highly industrialised, well-armed State manned by a fanatical group of White men determined to defend their privilege and their prejudice, and aided by the complicity of American, British, West German, and Japanese investment in the most profitable system of oppression on the continent. Nelson was *a key figure* in thinking, planning, and devising new tactics.'[91]

Tambo went on to trace and reinforce the making of a Mandela legend of revolution and romance – the M-plan,[92] the call for a nationwide stayaway 'in the name of Nelson Mandela', and his decision to go underground, giving up his wife and family, his profession and his liberty.

'Here,' wrote Tambo, 'began the legend of the Black Pimpernel. He lived in hiding, meeting only his closest political associates, travelling around the country in disguise, popping up here to lead and advise, disappearing again when the hunt got too hot.'

Betrayed, he was caught. He narrowly escaped the death sentence. 'Nelson Mandela is on Robben Island today. His inspiration lives on in the heart of every African patriot. He is the symbol of the self-sacrificing leadership our struggle has thrown up and our people need. He is unrelenting, yet capable of flexibility and delicate judgement. He is an outstanding individual, but he knows that he derives his strength from the great masses of people who make up the freedom struggle in our country.'[93]

From then on, the image of Mandela grew steadily in stature, and was to become a major weapon in globalising the struggle against apartheid.

In the meantime, Tambo and the ANC worked patiently and strategically – at first with civil society in the West – the churches, NGOs and communities. Their publicity and support provided the ANC's other major weapons in the struggle – sanctions and boycotts. To them, the ANC often played down the armed option until such time as their governments could be won over. Tambo pointed out that the ANC had refrained from calling on foreign powers to march on the apartheid regime, as some other beleaguered liberation movements in Africa were inclined to do. What he did not reveal just yet, though, was the series of meetings in Moscow, and the warm response that the ANC had received from a number of socialist countries in Eastern Europe.

There followed a turbulent quarter of a century of conducting complex, multifaceted struggles on many different fronts – dealing with setbacks and demoralisation in the military camps; managing contradictions internally and exploiting them externally; holding together an exile organisation of multifarious ideological tendencies; educating and training rebellious and traumatised young refugees; enduring informers and massacres; reviving the decisive presence of the ANC as the leader of the revolution back home; and exerting the sheer hard slog of always maintaining the 'moral high ground' before the world. All this and more was to occur before Tambo and his team were able to draw in the West in taking effective economic action as part of a holistic strategy capable of bringing down the apartheid system.

The turn to armed struggle thus firmly shifted the locus of the ANC, the national liberation movement. In its early exile years, it had endeavoured to build its key alliance partner with the Pan-African Congress and reaffirm its identity as a dedicated African organisation – albeit a broad, inclusive one. Yet the imperatives of guerrilla warfare pushed the movement, again, towards working more closely with the South African Communist Party.

'One of the consequences,' remarked Joe Matthews, 'was that you had to move sharply to the left and get aid now from the Soviet Union and other socialist countries which would be prepared to support an armed struggle.'[94] Umkhonto we Sizwe was to become the structure through which the SACP's non-racial membership could influence the strategy and direction of national liberation. In the years to come, more and more MK cadres, as well as a significant portion of the senior leadership of the ANC itself, joined the SACP. They saw no contradiction in belonging to two organisations. In fact, they firmly believed that true liberation would only occur once both visions – that of national liberation as well as the socialist revolution – had been realised.

The rapidly growing stream of refugees arriving in Dar es Salaam and London confirmed the legitimacy and authority of the exile movement. To these exiles, the pain of separation, the sense of an altered significance, the restructuring of meaning to guard against the 'pointlessness' of exile had to be acknowledged and articulated. Tambo's role was to voice these feelings in accessible language, spelling out the significance of the ANC not only as a defence, but also as the express inspiration for exile, a guard against integration with the host countries. Over the years, Tambo was able to represent the state of exile to most ANC expatriates – with some chilling exceptions – as a kind of 'liberated space'.[95]

In the following decades, the ANC landscape was thus to be characterised by constant relocations and new renderings of nuance, emphasis and structure. The unavailability of the elected NEC after Rivonia, the tension between security and democracy, the crafting of processes of decision-making in a vastly new context bred in the ANC structures a further dextrous adaptability to almost any unanticipated sequence of events. Oliver Tambo was to emerge as the central figure in managing this process.

CHAPTER TEN

The Freedom Train

I read in the papers about the
Freedom Train.
I heard on the radio about the
Freedom Train.
I seen folks talkin' about the
Freedom Train.
Lord, I been a-waitin' for the
Freedom Train.[1]

IN THE SOUVENIR ISSUE OF *DAWN* IN 1987, Chris Hani was quoted as saying that 'our plan was to build bridges, a Ho Chi Min train to South Africa'. But escape from bondage was not always by train. Freedom seekers crossed the border by car, bus or cart – most also trudged many kilometres on foot. Almost always, they journeyed in secret. They crawled in the veld, hid in the tall grass or among the bushes, they scaled wire fences in the dark of night, they braved wild animals and vicious watchdogs, they sheltered from the police in safe houses and in remote, hospitable villages. They moved along age-old routes mapped out in past millennia by their Stone Age ancestors migrating northwards, then traversing south again, across the Limpopo River, and back towards their roots.

Since the nineteenth century, when European colonisers carved up the region into spheres of interest, economic migrants crossed the border from north to south in search of jobs – the colonisers' arbitrarily drawn borders, splitting up chiefdoms and disturbing traditional habits, otherwise held little meaning for them. Kinsmen, with a shared culture and values, and speaking familiar languages, lived on both sides of the Limpopo and across the Gariep (or 'Orange') and Mohokare (or 'Caledon') rivers. To become a migrant worker in the industrialised south was often an unavoidable response to the traumatic events of the loss of land and independence.

Now, in the 1960s, men and women were taking these ancient routes for another kind of survival. Often, it was a political assignment commissioned by the community or the movement, be it the African National Congress, the Pan

Africanist Congress or the Non-European Unity Movement, or simply by traumatised and determined individuals, driven by a vision of a liberated world. A significant number of these political travellers had recent ties with the region – some, like James Chirwa, Michael Dingake, Fish Keitsing and others, had been born outside South Africa, while others, such as Thomas Nkobi and Joe Matthews, were the children of immigrants to settler South Africa.[2]

To escape South Africa was to find a safer home in order to prepare for the return. Crossing the border seemed less like exile to the dispossessed of land and freedom. Besides, over and above legally sanctioned oppression, activists were imprisoned, placed under house arrest, banned or banished to remote rural areas. Increasingly, after the two liberation movements were outlawed, the South African Security Police were making use of torture.

Thomas Nkobi, the ANC's national organiser soon became a target the Security Police. He had been followed and arrested in the Orange Free State, during the State of Emergency after Sharpeville, when he had been trying to contact and organise members into Mandela's underground M-Plan of street-committee-based cell units.[3] What happened next was a haunting experience. The Security Police beat him up, and then took him to the roof of the headquarters of the Security Branch.

'See this tranquillity?' asked his interrogator aggressively. 'All the Natives are fast asleep, and you are coming from Johannesburg to come and poison them here.'

'I could see the whole of Bloemfontein,' recalled Nkobi, 'the lights and the glamour, the galaxy of night. And then he took his revolver. He hit me on the head. He said, "Now look, I can shoot you and throw you down and say [that] the Native was running away from custody."' And, to illustrate his point, he hit Nkobi on the head with his revolver. 'I fell where I was standing.'

Nkobi regained consciousness at the police station. He was held incommunicado – neither his family nor his comrades knew where he was – 'I thought I was gone' – but, ironically, it was a white policeman who saved him. He walked into Nkobi's cell soon after he had been taken there.

'They are going to kill you,' he warned. But Nkobi was resigned to his fate. 'It doesn't matter; they have killed so many people.'

'Give me a name of somebody you know, so that you can alert your people that you are in jail.'

Nkobi, suspicious, sent him away. After 29 days, the white man returned. This time Nkobi gave him the name of Reverend Thanqa in Bloemfontein. Thanqa contacted lawyers, who invoked habeas corpus, a law that required the accused to be presented in court after 48 hours. Nkobi was thus taken to court and charged with distributing illegal leaflets. The policeman's intervention had saved his life. Nkobi then 'skipped' the border to join the Mission in Exile.

'This fellow, before I left the police station, said: "Please, when you are ruling, you must remember me."'[4]

It was, in fact, cases like this that led the National Party government to devise ways of overcoming the 48-hour law. Within the following two years, Minister of Justice JB Vorster was able to pass through Parliament a series of laws that permitted long periods of detention without trial. Torture became a regular means of extracting information, and ANC and PAC members across the board suffered brutal treatment, both physical and psychological, as a result. The number of fatalities in detention subsequently increased. In 1963 SACTU detainee and alleged MK cadre Looksmart Ngudle was found hanging in a Pretoria cell, a thousand miles away from home.[5] A year later, Babla Saloojee fell to his death from the seventh floor of the interrogation room of Security Police headquarters in Johannesburg, The Grays. Others received jail sentences under the Sabotage Act, which permitted a death sentence. In the Eastern Cape, another unionist, Washington Bongco, and MK members, golden-voiced Vuyisile Mini as well as Wilson Khayingo and Zinakhile Mkhaba, were executed in 1964.[6]

After Mandela's trip abroad and the promise of support from independent African countries, MK instructed activists to leave clandestinely – authorities were not to know that they had left the country – to undergo military training. This ensured a return ticket to fight the apartheid system. In June 1962, as part of the Operation Mayibuye plan, senior ANC members Wilton Mkwayi, Joe Gqabi and Andrew Mlangeni, under Raymond Mhlaba's command, had been sent abroad for training in China.[7] The plan was to launch a guerrilla struggle by selected combatants who would be trained and then re-infiltrated back home in four key rural areas. When Mandela was arrested, Mhlaba took the reins and by 1964, at the time of the Rivonia Trial, the MK High Command had overseen over 190 acts of sabotage without loss of a single life.[8]

In the next few years the numbers of recruits leaving the country increased steadily. The journey to freedom was circuitous, arduous and dangerous. Dozens were arrested, charged and imprisoned before they had even reached the border. One who was caught was Jacob Zuma, a young worker in Durban, Natal. In June 1963, he arranged to 'disappear' for six months, hoping to return after a six-month military course. 'But, unfortunately we got arrested near the Botswana borders in the Zeerust area.'[9] About 50 hopefuls were arrested and held under the new 90-day detention law. By means of torture, the state managed to produce an alarming number of state witnesses. The remainder, including Zuma, were finally charged for conspiracy and sabotage, receiving a 10-year sentence on Robben Island.[10]

Others were, however, apprehended on the other side of the border. On one occasion, a group of MK volunteers were apprehended by British colonial authorities before they were able to board the Livingstone–Dar es Salaam train. They were subsequently deported to South Africa, where they were horribly tortured. All except one, who turned state witness, were eventually tried, and received long sentences.[11]

The early batches of volunteers for military training from the Eastern Cape, Natal and the Western Cape would arrive in Johannesburg by train via Krugersdorp, surviving pass searches and other dangers posed by the apartheid system. From a base in Alex, Joe Modise (who would become the first Minister of Defence in a democratic South Africa) organised safe houses for them, whence they and others were then smuggled to the border by car either to Francistown or, when this was too dangerous, to Mafikeng or Zeerust, and from there on foot to Lobatse. Subsequently, hundreds of refugees made their way via the 'underground train'. The 'train' took different routes. At first, hired lorries transported the recruits across the veld to Kazangula, the junction of the Northern and Southern Rhodesian, Namibian and Bechuanaland borders. From Bechuanaland to Rhodesia, they travelled across the Zambezi by ferry, hiding in the bushes by day. Mark Shope, General Secretary of SACTU, and Johnny Makathini, later to become prominent in the diplomatic world, led the first two such batches and endured many adventures.

As the neighbouring countries were not independent, black travellers had to be careful to avoid arrest. Archie Sibeko related how, in a train bound for Northern Rhodesia (Zambia), the South Africans, who could be spotted by their lighter complexions, borrowed infants from local passengers and held them in their arms.[12] But arousing suspicions nevertheless, the groups were obliged to alight at the station before their destination and walk 50 kilometres to Livingstone in the dark. In several instances, the groups were arrested, but were saved by the intervention of the liberation movement of the United People's Independence Party (UNIP), which managed to organise cars to transport them to Tunduma, the border post adjoining Tanganyika. There they were again dropped; they walked across the bush and were then picked up again in 'no-man's land' and taken to Tanganyika, where they were instructed to proceed to the immigration office to report their arrival. From there, they drove to Mbeya, the first big town in Tanganyika, and thence to Dar es Salaam.

It had taken the first contingent nearly two months of a wandering and hunted existence to reach their destination.

The long, arduous trek had also required intensive preparation, cooperation and solidarity from a wide range of comrades at home as well as sympathisers across several borders. The variety of unanticipated escapades necessitated emergency contingencies. After the second group, which included Thabo Mbeki, was detained and deported (fortunately, back to Bechuanaland and not South Africa), aircraft were chartered, at considerable expense for the movement, to fly recruits to Dar es Salaam. But South African intelligence forces soon picked up this information and demanded that the British authorities inform them of all flights and passenger lists in the British Protectorates – Bechuanaland, Basutoland (Lesotho) and Swaziland – as well as the two Rhodesias (Zambia and Zimbabwe). On one occasion, South African Intelligence received advance notice of a plane preparing to transport an MK group, and sabotaged it. As a result, the road to Kazangula again became the freedom train's main, long and risky route. After arriving there – usually in groups of 30 to 35 – and following a faint track through the bush, then crossing the Zambezi by ferry, recruits finally reached Livingstone, where again the local branch of Kenneth Kaunda's UNIP assisted them. Northern Rhodesia continued to remain hostile territory until the independence of Zambia in 1965.

In 1964, Dar es Salaam – the chief city in the newly independent Tanzania – was a sleepy, sprawling, humid port, its main road fringed with palm trees and the verandas of shops and colonial hotels. Julius Nyerere was now the country's prime minister, and one of the first steps he took for his oppressed brothers and sisters in the colonies of Africa was to provide facilities for all credible liberation movements to set up their headquarters in his territory.[13] He was even-handed in his hospitality. With regard to the South Africans, he regretted that the United Front had foundered, but gave both the ANC and the PAC offices from which to work. Tambo thus set up the ANC's headquarters there. With not a single country next door to South Africa that was really independent, there was no nearer base. Tanzania was the closest MK could get to the South African border, and provided MK's major station on the route to the north.

After the Rivonia arrests, the little community of exiles expanded rapidly. Those who made it to Dar were processed into the 'camps' – in reality, a couple of houses on the outskirts of the town. In October, 11 individuals left for Nairobi by plane, and then went on to Juba (southern Sudan) in hired taxis along a rutted road, then on to Khartoum by boat down the Nile, and finally by train to Cairo and Morocco. Some 20 others got to Addis Ababa, also via Nairobi.[14] The OAU members had also set up a training camp for the liberation movements in Algiers.

In Dar, administrative staff in the ANC office – a long, narrow room partitioned into sections – grew significantly. Newcomers included awaiting-trial escapees from Rivonia, Mosie Moola and Abdul Jasset – Moola was producing a news digest called *Spotlight on South Africa*. Two leading SACP/ANC veterans of the struggle, JB Marks and Moses Kotane, with whom Tambo had long political discussions on the nature of the Congress Alliance in exile, were part of an interim executive committee. Their open-mindedness struck Tambo. Kotane, in particular, it seems, turned over in his mind whether the Communist Party itself should be subsumed into the service of the immediate needs of the national liberation movement. The role of the Party had, of course, been thoroughly aired before its relaunch underground 10 years earlier, but now, it appeared, the ANC's turn to armed struggle warranted a review. The SACP had developed a theory of South Africa as 'a special type of colonialism', in which black South Africans were simultaneously oppressed and exploited as a race. Class differences such as existed in the black community were insignificant compared with their treatment as a still-colonised people within the apartheid system. The Party had opted, therefore, to throw its weight behind the national liberation movement. Its members felt that the SACP continued to have a role, both in its ability to provide the ANC with a theory of society, of a political theory of liberation, as well as to offer a non-racial organisational home in the context of the PAC's Africanist offensive. In line with general revolutionary thinking at the time, once the ANC adopted MK and armed struggle, it went along with an anti-imperialist strategy of insurrection – the apartheid regime would never willingly renounce, let alone share, its power.[15] The broad-ranging views and international experience of JB Marks and Moses Kotane, as seen through African eyes, impacted on Tambo and opened up for him vistas for the way forward. Tambo had, therefore, expressly requested that Kotane be sent out to assist him and the Mission in Exile.

Tambo was making a point of finding out more about Marxism and the vision and practice of the SACP. When he was in England, for instance, he would motor with Michael Harmel, SACP General-Secretary, to visit Mannie and Babette Brown (a COD couple who went into exile after helping to organise the escape of four Rivonia trialists), who now lived near Epping Forest, for Sunday afternoon tea. During the hour-long drive, he would discuss political philosophy with Harmel (once lauded as 'the Lenin of our movement'),[16] and the SACP's concepts of 'the national question' and 'colonialism of a special type'.[17]

And then there was Tambo's friend, Moses Kotane. Renowned for his intellectual creativity, Moses Kotane's meaningful communication with Chief Luthuli was an illustration of his ability to look after the interests of both the ANC and the Communist Party without compromising either organisation. Indeed, he was able to link them syncretically by combining his support for African nationalism with his commitment to an egalitarian society – he was, in short an *African* communist. In fact, Ben Turok, who went into hiding with Kotane for five months during 1961, considered Kotane to be 'far and away the most important figure in the South African movement for decades… as a political theorist and policy-maker'.

'He was head and shoulders above anybody else. I mean Harmel *was* very good in terms of strategy and learning and Lenin… But Moses was the leader. And all the people around him were small boys, actually. [He was] way, way ahead in terms of calibre, insight, wisdom, understanding of situations and careful decisions.'[18]

In the meantime, Tennyson Makiwane, Duma Nokwe ('one of the ANC's ablest politicians,' remarked Tambo)[19] and Mendi Msimang (formerly from the chambers of Mandela & Tambo) were charged with setting up the office, and younger members such as James Hadebe, Reg September and Eleanor Kasrils provided back-up services. Until Tambo arrived, recalled Eleanor Kasrils, the pace of the office day was leisurely and easy-going. They would arrive at 9.30 or 10am, have a cup of tea, take time off for lunch, close early in the afternoon and stroll around the town or down to the beach. Often, they would visit the offices of other liberation groups. Frelimo were nearby, with Zapu and Zanu offices also in the vicinity.[20] Personal relations among the liberation groups were good in those early years: 'There was a very good atmosphere actually,' recalled Eleanor Kasrils fondly.[21]

After supper, with not much to do, the comrades would spend the night sociably at the New Africa Hotel, a cosmopolitan hangout, which was later to be declared out of bounds because of the security risk of informers. JB Marks, a gifted storyteller, was often seen surrounded by attentive young listeners, bonding with them, holding the floor with Marxist theory and humorous tales of the struggle in the thirties, forties and fifties in South Africa.[22] A tall pint of beer – a '*tuska*' – cost a shilling and was considered money well-spent, particularly to the city-slicker South Africans from Sophiatown and Soweto, whose township experience associated entertainment with a shebeen culture.

Tambo was now leading both the ANC and MK. He arrived in Dar to take up his post and, a few days later, called a meeting of all office staff. He looked at his watch, tapped it and said sternly, 'From now on everybody will be in at

8 o'clock in the morning', his canny eyes making contact with each staff member one by one, as he used to do in class at St Peter's. The effect was instantaneous. The staff were uncomfortably aware of Tambo's severe gaze if they walked through the door even five minutes late. Oliver Tambo himself was in the office at six o'clock every morning, attending to paperwork and correspondence before seeing new arrivals and arranging for their training programmes – the comrades could hardly baulk at his request.[23]

Tambo was not so fortunate in controlling their leisure hours, however. His teetotalism, while impressive to many, was hardly to be emulated. Tambo was to find that the convivial pastime of drinking was almost essential to stressed exiles separated from their families and communities. Thrown into a new milieu, with the prospect of moving on very soon, they had only their political vision to sustain them. In later years, alcohol was to become a tangible problem, and Tambo lost a number of his most valuable lieutenants to liquor.

By contrast, Tambo suppressed his own tensions, sublimating his yearnings to provide direction by instruction and example. He behaved in his customary, impeccably disciplined way. He was considerate in his habits, neat and modest in his day-to-day needs. He stayed at the nearby guesthouse, which was shared by all the office workers. He cooked when it was his turn (though, later, students waiting to be placed in colleges and universities were given the task of preparing the meals – with rather unappetising results). He slept on a mattress on the floor when accommodation became crowded. Tambo worked unceasingly, usually until well after midnight at the office, and tried as much as possible to help the office workers improve their skills. When Mosie Moola asked him, as he often did, to write an editorial for *Spotlight*, he could never turn down the request, despite the restrictions on his time.[24]

Tambo worried about the welfare of every ANC member and kept abreast of news from home. 'Comrade OR Tambo… kept in touch with us, visiting every morning to see how we were,' recalled Archie Sibeko about the early period. 'He had time to give us individual attention, which we needed in a foreign country.'[25] Even when the numbers grew, Tambo continued to visit the expanding settlements and offices now spreading elsewhere. 'OR was always ready to listen to problems and to try to help. No one was unimportant to him.'

It was at his instigation that arrivals give themselves new first and second names, to protect the families left behind. Tambo suggested that they decide carefully, selecting names that might be known by their people back home – if they were to die in exile, their *noms de guerre* would be recognised only by them. Sibeko, for example, took the names of his two sons, left behind in Cape Town – Zola Nqaba.[26]

Refugees who arrived from South Africa were struck by Tambo's modest and unpretentious manner. 'We were inspired by him,' recalled Chris Hani, who arrived in Dar in the latter part of 1963. 'He would come to see us whenever he had time, to discuss with us and to listen to us – [to] what we thought were insignificant experiences; we never thought they were important.'[27] To the 'young lions', Tambo represented a different kind of role model. He was the respected teacher and guide, but combined knowledge with a honed militancy. While the traditional, manly virtues of physical prowess and courage were very relevant to these soldiers, they also had altruistic ideals. Despite Tambo's relatively slight physique and unassuming manner, his self-discipline, his incisive and cultivated intellect, his calm control, and above all his dedicated commitment pointed to highly prized qualities. Tambo was also one of the surviving, accessible founders of the Youth League. His generation, by their clarity of purpose and militancy, had transformed the ANC, both by personal example and in its tactics, and actually managed to engage the white government.

'As youngsters, these were our idols, these were our heroes,' explained Chris Hani. 'We admired people like Tambo because we saw in them a different type of intelligentsia – an intelligentsia which is selfless, which is not just concerned about making money, creating a comfortable situation for themselves, but an intelligentsia which had lots of time for the struggle of the oppressed people of South Africa. We admired [the way] they [had] used their legal knowledge to alleviate the judicial persecution of the blacks through the pass laws, through Bantu Authorities, or the Group Areas.'[28]

Using the keen responsiveness of the young men, Tambo would encourage them to read books in the 'library' set up in the office to inform their political discussions and expand their intellectual horizons.

But while Tambo was always 'kindly',[29] his administrative colleagues recalled his austere, almost tight manner. He seldom smiled. 'OR was a strict taskmaster. He could be intimidating,' recalled Ronnie Kasrils. 'He was more formal in those early days.'[30] The absence of Mandela and Sisulu clearly affected him deeply. Despite the collective nature of the Executive, his was the responsibility – and he felt it profoundly – of working for their release.

The immediate task, however, was to provide for a growing exile population. This was a time of material deprivation for the ANC community. There was not enough money to pay for anything but the most basic amenities. Besides bananas and mangoes, which were plentiful and cheap, food was scarce. At first, MK's most willing supporters were from the Eastern Bloc. The ANC relied on shipments from the Soviet Union and the German Democratic Republic (and later from Sweden), for tinned and dried food, as well as bales of basic clothing.

In a letter to Adelaide, Tambo wrote: 'We are pulling hard and working hard on half-empty stomachs. *We trousers sezabaukulu.*[31] I cannot remember when last I had a full meal. And then of course we are working at a forced pace. Sleeping 11.30 or 12pm and up at 6 am. But everybody is keeping cheerful – hoping and hoping.'[32]

As a direct result of the deprivation they suffered, a few of those permanently stationed at Dar became ill. The ANC managed to find the money to send them for nutritious charity meals at Luther House. Eleanor Kasrils, pregnant and suffering from malaria, was diagnosed with malnutrition and anaemia. Two other comrades, the brothers Obed and John Motsabi, were diagnosed with diabetes and the three were treated in a special unit at the hospital in Dar. Clothes also arrived by boat in boxes from the German Democratic Republic. To economise further, the salaries of the ANC officials were cut from £7 a week to £2, though board and lodging were now provided.

Added to Tambo's responsibilities was also the worry of the survival of his own family in London. Though he always controlled these concerns beneath an upbeat exterior, physical and psychological wounds were apt to surface from time to time. The physical environment in Dar was an additional irritation. The chicken coop in the yard of what Tambo termed his 'mini-residence', coupled with the lack of curtains, the low altitude and the humidity of Dar es Salaam, all conspired to ward off much respite from his asthma. Through most of his years in exile, Tambo tended to suffer attacks on stressful occasions, which put him out of action more than once. His personal assistant, Joe Matthews, recalled an occasion in about 1966, of Tambo gasping for breath in a Rome hotel, as he prepared himself for an important meeting with sympathisers to the cause. In this instance, the alarmed Matthews packed Tambo off to England for emergency treatment.[33]

Despite his frequent travels, Tambo seldom saw his family. Since the ANC's turn to armed struggle, major adjustments had to be made. Adelaide came to accept the long separations from her husband, wryly recalling her grandmother's warning not to marry him, as Xhosas were migrant workers who seldom saw their wives and children. It soon became clear that Oliver was not going to be able to supplement her earnings as the family breadwinner. In fact, in the early years, Adelaide was more likely to send her husband clothes and even cash, than vice versa.

'How nice of you to send me some money,' Tambo wrote to his wife in July 1965. 'As soon as I received it I went off to have lunch, even though it was slightly too early for lunch. I happened to be rather hungry that morning.'[34]

This was not surprising, since he always left home too early in the morning to have breakfast.

Intellectually and politically, Adelaide had accepted and supported her husband's decision to accept his new role in the armed struggle and his subsequent relocation to Tanzania. Mandela's private conversation with her had confirmed her commitment.

'I have been tempted to move to Africa and live with my husband,' she once commented. 'But what would be the sense? As soon as the enemy knew of his whereabouts and the fact that he moved predictably from point A to point B, he would be the assassins' target.'[35]

Barely a week after Adelaide's arrival in London, Tambo had left the country to address the United Nations, then to relocate the ANC in Tanzania. Her search for a job and accommodation (ANC comrades helped her in this respect), her encounters with more sophisticated forms of race prejudice, foreign culture and customs, all contributed to the stress and strain of settling her small children into a new and alien country. She recalled with pain and anger the smirking when people saw her carrying her baby on her back.[36] During their first 10 years in exile, the Tambo family would have hardly more than three or four days together in six months.[37]

Meanwhile, in Dar es Salaam, the ANC community continued to grow. They had been obliged to abandon the guesthouse and move a few miles out of town, to two houses, which they named Luthuli House and Mandela House. Nyerere had donated these houses, or 'camps', as the ANC called them, to a number of liberation movements. The Frelimo 'camp' was nearby. These modest dwellings had to squeeze in an elastic number of lodgers, including those waiting to depart for military training or education courses in other countries in Africa or in Eastern Europe. Before long, heavy traffic operations had to be organised from East Africa to a military college in Odessa, which was selected, partly because of its relatively mild climate (for the Soviet Union), in which the African cadres could receive their training. One recruit, Zeph Mokgetla, still in his teens and thrilled about having been chosen to undergo military training, had worked hard to persuade his seniors of his commitment to the struggle. He recalled his 'culture shock' when he was introduced to his fellow trainees, 'and standing out among the group there, grinning at me, was this white guy – Ronnie Kasrils! Who the hell was he? What did he think he was doing there?'

It was Zeph's first important lesson about the ANC and also, he recalled, about Tambo and the others – 'they showed us the wider picture, a united South Africa rising above the differences'.[38]

But even before the recruits reached their Soviet destination, Tambo made a point of continuing their education and training. He was also acutely conscious of their eagerness to start operations, and the need to keep their vision alive. He regularly visited the camps, talking to the young cadres about their experiences in the countries where they had trained. He discussed their courses, and also briefed them on what had been happening in South Africa during their absence – the Rivonia arrests, the conviction of the leaders, the tactics being explored on how to get back home to help rebuild the organisation – and asked them for their own opinions. He would present the camp itself as an opportunity for learning and personal development. 'Think of Kongwa as the University of Life,' he would urge them.[39]

'We were ordinary cadres, we were not important names,' reminisced Chris Hani, 'but Tambo wanted us to feel an important part of the organisation.'[40]

Some very promising men had passed through Tanzania on their way to be trained in the Eastern Bloc countries, and many had only rudimentary experience. Some, like Joe Modise, Chris Hani and Ronald Kasrils, had operated on a relatively small scale, throwing Molotov cocktails, cutting telephone cables and the like in South Africa. Hani and Kasrils both left Dar in 1964 to train in the Soviet Union, and returned a year later. Tambo chose these two men, with markedly contrasting backgrounds – the black mission-raised Catholic from the rural Transkei village of Cofimvaba, and the white Jewish '*boykie*' from Johannesburg's inner city of Yeoville – to work on a text-book of military theory for South African cadres. Kasrils was 'an enthusiast', said Mac Maharaj, who worked intensively underground with him. 'That's what's good about him – he's a real fuckin' enthusiast!'[41]

The thinking in this period, swayed by the arguments of Regis Debray and Che Guevara and Mao Ze Dong's doctrine of the War of the Flea, was that the forces would return to South Africa to mobilise in the rural areas.[42] The uprisings in chiefdoms in Sekhukhuneland and Pondoland had strengthened the conviction that the nature of oppression was such that the mass of the peasantry would readily respond to a call for armed confrontation. And, indeed, in a few areas traditional rulers themselves were initiating age cohorts of young men to become warriors and then sending them on to join the military struggle.[43]

The first intakes by MK were sent to the OAU countries that had offered to provide training. Ethiopia, Morocco and Egypt were some of the destinations, but despite their generosity, the Soviet Union had the resources to offer supplementary courses, together with political education and suitable accom-modation for military training. In any case, after Rivonia, the reception structures inside South Africa, which would have organised hiding places and equipment, had been smashed. On, therefore, to the Soviet Union for further training for 9 to 12 months. Their training was mainly guerrilla warfare – sabotage, explosives, weapons, political education and the organisation of military units.[44] By 1965, about 500 ANC members had undergone training in Odessa in the Soviet Union. The ANC had between 800 and 1 000 people based in MK camps in Tanzania or on training courses in Czechoslovakia, Odessa in the Soviet Union or in China (until the Sino-Soviet split cut off relations with China for some years).[45]

In 1965, MK set up a proper camp in Kongwa. Tambo had negotiated with the Liberation Committee of the OAU and the Tanzanian government for the use of land that included a disused railway station south of Dar es Salaam near Dodoma. The cadres set up tents and began to build the infrastructure for a military camp of the ANC. For the young servicemen, particularly those who grew up in the townships, this was also the beginning of an essential lesson in self-help and community development, an attribute that was also the driving force behind the Tanzanian Ujamaa programme. The camp was provided with basic infrastructure, and the OAU organised food supplies, but at the same time, the cadres were learning to build, cultivate the land and raise chickens and pigs for sustenance. In the process, they mastered new skills. When inspecting the camps, Tambo admired the armouries, the pitched tents, the brick wall and the tilled soil. He scrutinised the recreational facilities and cheered the football, volleyball and table-tennis matchesthey laid on for him. Encouraged by Tambo to develop the cadres' education, and fired by the Marxist vision of integrating intellectual knowledge with manual and physical labour, commanders arranged courses on political education and revolutionary theory for the young cadres. And they were ready and impatient to test these skills in the open bush on their way home.

But this goal was not so easy to attain. Unlike Frelimo and the Zimbabwean movements, their country's borders were not next door. How was MK to cross the 2 000-kilometre divide of hostile territory? And then, too, there was the more ambiguous image of the ANC, whose leader was not a military man, nor a permanent fixture in the camps. For at least some of the time, Tambo lived the lifestyle of the diplomat and broker, negotiating on an international level for resources for his movement. It said a great deal for his personal style that Tambo was able to retain the affection of the cadres, despite their chafing at some of the other leaders.

Tambo's role was all the more onerous because this was a time of much experimentation, often of working in the dark, divorced from the guidance of the broader collective. Furthermore, events had overtaken the struggle. There was an uneasy feeling that 'somehow the movement had been dragged into a new phase without adequate consultation, without adequate preparation'.[46] Operation Mayibuye's plan was boldly ambitious and called for at least 7 000 highly trained soldiers to launch a guerrilla plan.[47] It was being applied, post-Rivonia, without formal sanction because it seemed to make sense in the circumstances. But back home structures were being denuded of their most creative and vigorous leadership. SACTU, which had escaped being outlawed – although its key officers were banned – lost almost all its top organisers to MK. Those remaining in South Africa worried that the underground would not be able to recover from the capture of the High Command at Rivonia. The thorough mopping up by the Security Police of the organisational capacity of MK, the ANC and the SACP left virtually the only functioning components stuck in exile, unable to return.[48]

Tambo and his community in Dar essentially had to 'busk' their way forward. Tambo was reluctant to let his comrades try to make their way back home through the bush without properly prepared underground structures to receive them. However, in consultation with the MK operatives, Tambo was exploring more ordered ways home, so that the cadres could apply their hard-won training. He was already talking to Kenneth Kaunda, leader of UNIP. The MK was also working on a plan with ZAPU, the liberation movement in Southern Rhodesia, to devise further strategic moves.

In 1965 Zambia had become independent and, responding to Kaunda's invitation, Tambo prepared to transfer the ANC's headquarters to Lusaka, the Zambian capital. The move entailed an additional office, extra staff and more work for Tambo. His tasks increasingly included educating and grooming competent administrators and instructing them on correct procedure. Shortage of funds continued to tax the ANC and harass the office managers. In a letter to Thomas Nkobi, Tambo urged strict budgeting, suggesting 'a permanent economy commission to help spread the responsibility to members, sympathisers and friends'. He suggested that problems be addressed in monthly reports 'per couriers', rather than wait for a grand conference.

'Raise every problem,' he exhorted Nkobi, 'make suggestions; put forward criticisms in every sphere of activity. This is not a privilege you are entitled to enjoy – it is a duty you are bound to carry out... You are at the front line and have a welter of delicate problems which you dare not shelve.'

Then typically, narrowing the gap between teacher and student, he concluded with mild, affectionate humour: 'Show this to Gcwanini,' he wrote, 'but don't show him the next line: (When last did you have a haircut?) Bye-bye, Tom. Regards to *all. Maatla!* OR.'[49]

Great new opportunities were opened up by the move to Zambia. Its borders were only a country away from South Africa, and the new circumstances demanded a bold manoeuvre. The MK command entrusted to Joe Modise and Chris Hani the task of beginning the process of the reconnaissance of routes into South Africa. They began to work with Akim Ndhlovu and other Soviet-trained colleagues in ZAPU, who were preparing to penetrate Rhodesia. Rather than accept majority rule, white-supremacist Rhodesia's prime minister Ian Smith had defied the United Kingdom and had, in late 1965, unilaterally declared independence. South Africa was supporting the Smith regime to withstand international sanctions. Clearly, there was a basis for cooperation between the two resistance movements.

'Rhodesia is an indivisible part of Southern Africa, hence the predictable involvement of South Africa in the battles which our Freedom Fighters are waging stubbornly and courageously in the bushes of Matabaleland,' wrote Tambo to his friend in the United Nations, ES Reddy. 'Soon the whole area, and I repeat, the *whole* area of Southern Africa, will be caught up in the crisis.'[50]

Tambo and James Chikerema of ZAPU then held a press conference to announce a military alliance. This was followed by a plan to assist the ZAPU forces to begin their guerrilla war inside Rhodesia, which would also provide a future underground transit 'train' for MK into South Africa. The team undertook reconnaissance operations; they swam across the river, noting what animals were in the area, which people crossed the river, mapping the riverbanks and about eight kilometres beyond. The joint logistics team planned the numbers of cadres required, their particular skills, ammunition, food, equipment and identity documents. Intelligence reports indicated that there was an increased South African presence operating alongside Smith's troops in Rhodesia.[51] All the reports were forwarded to the political heads – in the ANC's case, Oliver Tambo. The two groups were to march together as far as the Wankie Game Reserve, after which they would separate. The ZAPU column would move east to base itself inside Rhodesia and commence guerrilla warfare. The MK group was to head back to South Africa via Botswana through a corner of Rhodesia.

Commuting between Dar es Salaam and Lusaka, Tambo was an integral part of the discussions. It was the duty of the organisers to report to him, and he became intensely involved in the military strategy of preparing for the trained combatants to penetrate South Africa. 'He would be involved in the smallest details,' recalled Chris Hani, who was appointed to lead the main body of troops heading towards South Africa. Tambo accompanied the group a number of times in their reconnaissance of the Zambezi River, sleeping in the open veld with them the night before 'D-Day'.[52]

For those chosen for this first detachment, a great and historic honour had been bestowed upon them. They had undergone years of military, physical and political preparation, and at last they would make their way home and assist in training recruits and thus help to regenerate the damaged underground structures. Tambo named it the 'Luthuli Detachment', following the mystifying death in July 1967 of the president, whose body was found, run over by a train, on a railway line near his home in Groutville. It was 'a train which no African driver was permitted to drive,' noted Tambo bitterly.[53] 'His widow does not accept that he was struck by a train. Neither do we.'[54] A month thereafter, Tambo assembled the troops. In preparation for the crossing, they sacrificed two oxen – to ask for the blessing of the ancestors – and threw some meat to the crocodiles.[55] Early in the morning, Tambo rose with the men and delivered a farewell address. He stood on the high-cliffed banks of the river, gazing for a long time as they crossed the Zambezi: some 50 MK cadres, together with a band of about 30 ZAPU guerrilla fighters, setting off on their long and perilous journey.

The corps never reached South Africa. After some time in the bush, they were intercepted and fought a number of battles.[56] The '*mgwenya*', as these first-generation fighters under the command of Charles Ngwenya (*nom de guerre* John Dube) came to be known in later years, inflicted losses on the Rhodesian troops, capturing weapons and food supplies. They were able to inflict 'several nasty reverses', admitted the founder of Rhodesia's Selous Scouts.[57] The enemy retreated and requested assistance from the South African Defence Force. Archie Sibeko, who fought in Wankie, noted that South Africans were fighting on both sides of this battle. He took pride that the MK – 'a well-disciplined, well-officered army, under firm political control', showed the enemy 'for the first time this century – the determination of our people, and their toughness when properly trained, organised and armed'.[58] ANC historian Mzala noted with pride that 'for the first time since 1906, the time of Bambatha in Natal, the colonial forces of South Africa were met with fire-power from the oppressed community'.[59]

But mistakes had indeed been made. It seemed that there had not been enough political work undertaken by ZAPU among the black population of then-Rhodesia to prepare receiving structures for the guerrillas, despite the careful training in the USSR on this crucial aspect of guerrilla warfare.[60] Nor had the guerrillas known that there was no water to be had on the Zambezi Escarpment. Later, ZAPU's George Nyandoro spelt out the lessons they had learnt from this costly mistake. They should not have sent easily identifiable uniformed troops into the country, nor should they have sought shelter in caves and forests, because when they were discovered they could not evade the enemy. They had failed to mingle with the populace, 'like fish in water'. 'They had violated the cardinal rule of guerrilla warfare.'[61]

These difficulties were made known to the leadership only later. In August, Tambo and Chikerema issued a joint statement, reporting that 'furious fighting' had taken place in the Wankie area, the scene of the 'most daring battles ever fought between the Freedom Fighters and the white oppressors' army in Rhodesia'.[62] The Wankie excursion marked another shift towards a more openly guerrilla discourse. For the apartheid regime, the incursion upped the stakes significantly, to the point where civilians were called upon to involve themselves. The enemy had acknowledged MK's shift to guerrilla warfare. Afterwards Tambo commented that 'in 1967, when we were involved in Wankie, the commissioner of police at the time called on farmers in the Northern Transvaal to arm themselves and to report any terrorists that they saw around. If the farmers are going to be outposts of the police, and make themselves part of the army, then we can't pretend they are civilians'.[63]

Yet with Tambo, the accent always had a moral inflection. Albie Sachs, a young lawyer, writer and member of the Congress of Democrats, who had been detained and tortured by sleep deprivation in 1963 and again in 1966, recalled the somewhat incongruous setting of a Quaker Friends' venue in London for an MK solidarity meeting chaired by Tambo. Wankie was the first, and immensely significant, military campaign for ANC members. To know that the MK had guns and were fighting back generated a powerful symbolic and psychological effect. An audience of several hundred attended the meeting to hear Tambo's briefing.

'Our comrades were in action,' he reported. 'Five of the enemy were killed.'

There was enthusiastic applause. Then someone at the back called out, 'But that's murder!'

Tambo stopped, thought for a moment, and then replied quietly and evenly, 'Yes, that is murder'. The deliberate taking of human life was always murder, he acknowledged, whatever the circumstances. Then, turning the accusation on its head, he added, 'That is what we have been driven to.'[64]

The military gains, in any case, were temporary. South African police and helicopters quickly reinforced the Rhodesian army, and further battles ensued. Hani's group ran short of supplies and lost communication with the rear. They also lost 10 to 12 men, although they believed that they had killed 20 or 30 of the enemy. But with their presence exposed, they could not survive much longer, and decided to proceed to Botswana. Their arrival there, however, created an international embarrassment. Despite its membership of the Organisation of African Unity and its sympathy for the ANC, Botswana was obliged to imprison the trespassers.

Looking back on this experience many years later, Chris Hani concluded: 'The pressures were just too powerful. The neighbour [South Africa] was actually demanding that we should be handed over. And one must say, we admired the fact that Seretse Khama's government refused to hand us over; and instead, after serving those few years, they sent us back to Lusaka. An important experience.'[65]

The outcome of Wankie was also to make a historic impact on the movement itself. Clearly, the expedition had failed to get the troops back home – a few who reached the border were captured by the SADF, and at least one, boasted South African Police General Stadler, 'turned' to become an early 'Askari'.[66] But the setback was a valuable lesson, the movement consoled itself, and in any case infiltration was necessarily a longer-term project. Wankie had drawn the first blood; it had provided MK with valuable experience: MK had actually engaged the Rhodesians as well as the SADF and inflicted damage on the enemy.[67] This first incursion, they fully expected, was but the start of the gathering force of the cadres who would invade the borders of South Africa. Five other raids were in fact mounted; three more with ZAPU forces, in which MK lost a number of valuable members, and two small joint campaigns with Frelimo. In all these cases, the goal had been to find a route back into South Africa. But in every instance, not a single MK guerrilla succeeded in firing a shot in South Africa. The freedom train was derailed on every return trip.

Historically, Wankie came to symbolise the problem that was increasingly to bedevil the ANC's armed wing. Despite repeated attempts to return home in large numbers, this was never achieved and, as the Supreme Commander of Umkhonto we Sizwe, Oliver Tambo was answerable for this failure. In addition, the lack of success bred additional dissatisfactions, and Tambo, as Acting President, came under the harsh glare of criticism.

CHAPTER ELEVEN

Mapping the Way Forward

In 1969, Chris Hani, 'Hempe', 'Mgiza' and four others were released after two years in prison in Botswana.[1] Angry and feeling betrayed by the ANC's failure to rescue them, they 'blew our tops'.[2] They furiously demanded from the leadership why they had been allowed to rot for so long, and what MK had been doing in the interim to get cadres back into South Africa. Said Hani, 'I felt that we did not get proper support, a proper follow-up. And I didn't think that when we came back there was an interest in our experience, and what we had done, and what was the next step... We were in that state of limbo, state of suspense; and I and others could not stomach it.'[3]

And they were not alone. Many of the MK had become disillusioned with the lack of progress in returning home, and blamed the style of the leadership of the ANC. The officers in charge of the camps were accused of 'brutality, arrogance, militarism'.[4] At Kongwa, for example, the camp commander would take morning inspection of the troops in his dressing gown. At times, he would follow the cadres in their early morning roadwork in a Land Rover. 'We could hear the clink of glass, and a peep into the vehicle revealed a bottle of whisky. This at 5.30am.'[5] There had also been outrage at the cover-up of the rape of a woman cadre by a visiting NEC member.[6] Some township recruits were unversed in fairly standard military discipline and rebelled, and a number of disaffected young cadres absconded. Others were antagonised by the gap between leadership and the rank and file, and resentful of the harsh punishments imposed on them. They accused the leadership of 'corruption and mismanagement' – one angry cadre testified to Tambo himself that camp leaders had 'revealed things to prostitutes', one even being 'in love with an air hostess from SA'.[7] Another cadre, who had absconded, reported that while some cadres were dressed in rags – 'I had one leg to my trousers, and that came up to my knee, and no seat at all!' – they suspected that clothes and provisions sent from foreign countries were being funnelled to the People's Bazaar in Dar, where 'the leadership was doing a thriving business'.[8] A disaffected deserter also reported that 'undisciplined' members such as Themba Mqota and Ambrose Makiwane were wheeling and dealing, using the organisation to obtain travelling tickets from embassies. They would move about without Tambo's knowledge.[9]

In fact, Tambo himself did not escape censure either. He was accused of leniency, especially towards selected comrades. 'Many times [he] promised mistakes would be rectified. I can find nothing which has been rectified,' complained one, while another testified, 'in 1964 there was a complaint that the External Mission was dominated by Cape comrades. The President came. He explained, admitted, but did nothing about it'.[10] And 'if the AP [Acting President] does not favour you, you have had it', complained yet another.[11]

Much of the testimony was indeed worrying and clearly needed swift intervention. But the grievances went much further than the outburst of the seven rebels emerging from Botswana's prisons. Underlying the anger was the deep unease that the struggle, after almost a decade in exile, had failed. A number of cadres who testified in Tambo's enquiry questioned the Wankie and Sipolilo campaigns. Why was MK sidetracked in the Rhodesian bush? The leaders who had launched the strategy 'think they are clever. People were sent to abattoirs in Rhodesia to earn a name for the ANC and funds for their people'.

'We have lost the struggle; we must admit defeat,' said one disconsolately.

'We cannot say fighting in Rhodesia is any benefit for our struggle.'[12] It was hard to accept that all the incursions attempting to reach home had failed.

'I have a wound unlikely to be healed during my lifetime,' lamented one Mokoena. 'Which way is our struggle going? I appeal to you: do away with the present headquarters and form one which will guide the people.'

The leadership, it appeared to these complainants, had lost focus; they had forgotten the true purpose of the Mission in Exile. Tambo himself was seen as part of the 'globetrotting' and conference-going activities that seemed to be sapping the energy of the movement.[13] He and the other leaders were deeply involved in international work, which – it seemed – was unreasonably demanding. It was the ongoing pressure of survival, replied Joe Matthews to a document sent to head office, to conduct negotiations around 'training in various countries; collecting weapons, obtaining funds; persuading governments to allow camps in their countries which took years to achieve; to getting governments to agree to arms being brought into their countries and to allow them to be used for training; to go through the excruciatingly painful job of begging for all kinds of governments and organisations for what appear to any revolutionary simple and obvious requests'.[14]

Nevertheless, accompanying all the hard work, all the petitioning and the cajoling, and the stress of rejection, was also the diplomats' world of air travel, comfortable accommodation, and cocktails.

Oliver Tambo was acutely aware of the criticisms. His notebook carefully summarised an enquiry into these complaints, and he paid special attention to accusations against himself, scrupulously underlining significant points.[15] In 1968, writing to Adelaide to urge her to take a break from years of work in London's hospitals, he wrote: 'It does so happen that among some of the youth here – and this is understandable if one puts oneself in their shoes – there is a great deal of bitterness which feeds on the accusation that "the leaders have taken care of their families who are well supplied in funds, whereas our families and our children at home have been left to fend for themselves".'[16]

But he also spellt out his justification for inviting Adelaide to visit. 'I do not think that this is any reason why one should avoid meeting one's family whenever possible. If the leaders are looking after their families and no one else, or at the expense of others they claim to be leading, then of course this is wrong and people are perfectly correct in raising an outcry about it. For our errors we must be prepared to take criticism. But wild accusations and political absurdities should not deter us from doing a correct thing... No one's funds are being used. Wild accusations will be in the air for a time, but they cannot survive the facts of honesty and integrity.'[17]

Joe Matthews, too, was determined to correct misperceptions: 'ANC leadership can hardly be described as living the life of an "elite" as compared with other members, including MK... Conditions under which our top leadership such as Tambo, Kotane, Marks and other leaders are living ought to fill members of the Congress movement with absolute shame if they had any conscience.'[18]

Tambo lived under constant pressure and stress. 'There is an interminable chase after time,' he wrote, around 1968, to Adelaide, 'hours, mornings, afternoons, weeks, months: each has its own demand and its own ultimatum: so-and-so must happen by 12 noon; this or that at 2.15pm, this and that must be disposed of today; we have only this week to do it in – a cable, a trunk call, "Awe must leave today". And so it goes on like a running brook.'[19] The pace not infrequently resulted in bouts of burnout, often in the form of asthma attacks. In a letter to Adelaide in 1968 – a stressful and discouraging time – Tambo wrote from Dar es Salaam: 'Just arrived here, forced out of Morogoro by continuous chest attacks, which successfully prevented me doing any work whatever. Some mysterious thing I am allergic to there which has defied a whole week's treatment.'[20]

Joe Matthews recalled a two-day delay in a hotel room in Rome on such an occasion. Tambo was also briefly hospitalised on a couple of occasions, under strict medical supervision, in the GDR and also in the famous Barvikha Sanatorium in the Soviet Union. In the opinion of medical advisers, Tambo had not taken off enough time to recuperate effectively. Such was the emotional consequence of an existence, reminiscent in some ways of the life of the radical Trinidadian, CLR James – 'characterised', according to his biographer, 'by constant relocations and several ideological refashionings'.[21] But in this period of adjustment to new tactics and strategies, Tambo was equipped better than most to the major personal reorientation in the active shift to armed struggle. He was able, as he had done in the past, to adapt, to draw on what was most relevant from the different cultures that he had had to master in his childhood and youth – but not without cost to his health.

In the meantime, though, there was also the worrying perception – 'a correct perception', according to Joe Slovo [22] – that the leadership had 'failed to even begin to tackle the question of recreating the political structures within the country'.[23] Two of the 'pillars of struggle', the underground and the mass base, were non-existent. African students studying in the West were also disillusioned by the ANC's apparent failure. 'After the Revolution, Tambo will be the first to go,' declared a self-assured young Marxist, referring to the SACP's 'two-stage' theory of revolution. There was a 'deep-going malaise such as we have never known before', wrote Ben Turok from Tanzania. No effort had been made, said Turok, to keep the membership informed of the military campaigns, the conferences, or discussions around the immense difficulties surrounding the exile movement.[24] There had also been too little evidence of democracy, or of accountability of the leaders to the members. Specifically, Turok's criticisms were directed at the office in Dar es Salaam and the military camps. Apart from an endemic drinking problem, officials had shown 'the most appalling contempt' for the men in the army. 'Our men in Mandela camp live in squalor. They sleep on the floor on thin mats, their building is in disrepair and there is evidence of gross neglect... At present, it is a slum.' Furthermore, the wider membership had been left in ignorance of theoretical and political developments.

'There have been no reports back from conferences, no formal reports on the fighting in Zimbabwe, no discussion on the difficulties around us. Instead, we are faced by bureaucracy, heavily entrenched in office, hostile to questions and tight-lipped in the extreme.'

Expressing concern that an elite seemed to be emerging, Turok observed that 'too many of our people are no longer concerned with the problems of the struggle but rather with those of adjustment to life in exile'.[25]

But it was the memorandum of Chris Hani et al. that had blown the lid off the organisation. They had hit out at the gross contrast between the political and military wings of the ANC. Duma Nokwe, as Secretary-General of the ANC, had asked the seven to put their criticisms in writing.[26] The memo singled out Duma Nokwe and Joe Modise in their handling of the camps, and Moses Kotane, the Treasurer-General, for failing to give primacy to the internal base. They also accused Tambo of failing to adhere to democratic principles, and of continuing to 'keep his own men in position'.[27]

It was perhaps not surprising that Kotane and Nokwe, both on the Central Committee of the SACP, were at the receiving end of the criticisms. Both were forceful in expressing their opinions. 'Moses [Kotane] would erupt and lead the debate and push a point of view – similarly with a man like Nokwe.'[28]

Kotane, who had done extensive fundraising in independent African countries and in Eastern Europe, had also been a stern and conscientious treasurer. He was miserly about handing out hard-won funds, to the resentment of some of the younger members.[29] At the time of the release of the memorandum, Kotane had suffered a stroke and was being treated in a hospital in Moscow. Tambo, who had an enormous affection for Kotane – and respect for his integrity – was affronted by the *ad hominem* attack. He immediately called a meeting of all members and MK troops in the vicinity of Lusaka. In 'an emotional speech', he expressed his indignation that so dedicated a leader should have been slandered.[30] The memorandum, too, incensed many of the other leaders.

'I think people generally were not used to being criticised,' reflected Chris Hani. 'They thought that we are going to just applaud everything they did and say hallelujah... And some of them wanted us to get punished; and we were punished, in the sense that for some time we were left in the cold.'

The seven authors of the memorandum were, in fact, suspended. 'But again it was the intelligent leadership of Tambo that again brought us together, and we came back. He had no inferiority complex,' added Hani.[31] 'He never felt that he was being abused or his dignity was being impugned, or he was being attacked, and his leadership being questioned or challenged.'

Tambo, in fact, was not at that time necessarily regarded as the top leader. He was one among equals in a culture of collective leadership, one that had been affirmed by the Youth League itself.

'He wasn't seen as the natural heir... he was more the diplomatic representative, chief of the Mission,' commented Ben Turok.[32]

Nor was he overly conscious of having an exalted status. 'I can recall an ANC party in Dar es Salaam, at a small house somewhere in the townships,' reflected Ben Turok, 'and M... was at the door, blind drunk. Oliver arrived and M grabbed him by the tie and shook him. I thought Oliver would [discipline him], in front of the Frelimo leadership, AZAPU -- they were all there. Oliver sort of pushed him away, broke away. I thought he would discipline M. And

I really hoped he would; I thought it called for serious discipline. But he didn't... He did nothing; he let it pass.'[33]

It was a typical illustration of Tambo's obliviousness of status, but 'he was not really defending his personality – he was not into the personality cult'.[34]

Tambo was particularly disturbed by the memorandum of Hani et al. because it was a reflection of the low morale that was clearly developing in the camps. The movement clearly needed a shake-up – so much evidence of disappointment, anger and division had been expressed. In the collective leadership were individuals who had behaved badly. How was one to restructure the movement and constructively assess its progress and challenges? Tambo held discussions with colleagues in several cities, listening to their opinions on the problems facing the movement and the way forward. As had been the ANC custom at home, his conversations went beyond the paid-up membership to include an ad hoc co-option of former Congress Alliance members.[35]

For Tambo, this step was clearly urgent. The seven rebels had opened a can of worms. They had deeply angered many in the leadership – some even demanded that the young men be court-martialled and executed for treason. A divisive crisis was developing in the ANC. Apart from the sharp criticisms of the lack of movement both inside and outside South Africa, frustration was breeding a self-destructive tendency. Resentments were also beginning to surface in the London office, which coincided with racial identity. Some members felt that non-African communists were dominating the ANC. This was aggravated by the fact that known communists, who could not be members of the ANC and who were also strong personalities – like Joe Slovo, Yusuf Dadoo, Michael Harmel and Ruth First – had been declared prohibited immigrants in Tanzania and had consequently been obliged to operate from Europe. Coloured members, too, it seemed, felt beleaguered. In 1969 Tambo wrote to his wife in response to a comment she had made: 'Yes, I think Reg [September] is a good administrator. I hope he will remain assured of our full support for his work despite attacks, whispers and other acts and moves which have the effect of creating obstacles for him.'[36]

The ANC had already suffered the loss – a political blow – of the Coloured People's Congress, which was dissolved, and some of the remaining activists relocated themselves in the PAC. This move included the ANC London office's Lionel Morrison,[37] who alleged that the ANC, by insisting on the multiracial Congress Alliance (as opposed to the PAC's non-racialism since its decision to accept committed Africans of all colours), was in fact a racially influenced organisation. George Peake and Barney Desai also joined the organisation.

But the immediate challenges of exile were a reflection of the bigger picture of the 'global offensive of imperialism', as Tambo put it.[38] War was raging in Vietnam and Indo-China; the Six-Day War in the Middle East had resulted in further Palestinian territory being annexed by Israel; Greece, Spain and Portugal languished under dictatorships. Large tracts of Africa were still colonised. The USA was actively undermining democratic movements in South America, notably Chile. And government endorsed a National Security Memorandum 39, which proposed that the 'only hope' for black people in South Africa would be to develop 'closer relations with the white-dominated States'.[39]

As for the situation at home, 'grand apartheid' was reaching the pinnacle of its power. Vorster's Draconian laws seemed to have crushed resistance once and for all. From the ANC structures, as Joe Slovo gloomily remarked, there was 'the silence of the grave'.[40] But this was not quite true. Continuing detentions, followed by the trial of 'The Twenty-Two' in 1970, including Winnie Mandela, pointed to underground ANC activity. By and large, though, the ANC had become exoticised. Popular culture tended to rely on liberation to descend from outside – and clearly this was not happening. White South Africa rested assured that all that was left of the ANC were 'a few sad exiles out of touch with home'.[41] Indeed, in South Africa it was the new movement of Black Consciousness that was attracting attention. A black student caucus led by Steven Biko had walked out of the National Union of Students to form their own South African Students' Organisation. Influenced by both the USA's Black Power movement and Francophone Africa's *negritude* movement, they declared that Black was Beautiful, and called for an end to their dependency on white liberals and multiracial alliances – a clear jab at the ANC.

On the African continent, the OAU was growing impatient with the lack of progress by the liberation movements of South Africa. The armed struggle seemed to have been a deplorable failure. The notion at the beginning of the decade – that revolution was around the corner – made the liberation movements look ridiculous as the decade neared its end. The reputation of the ANC appeared to be in limbo.

But, generally, the disappointment of the OAU also embraced the PAC. Some quarters had pinned their hopes on them for an early resolution to apartheid, but internal squabbling was ravaging the struggle here too. Since the break-up of the United Front in February 1962, relations between the ANC and PAC had reached an all-time low. There was the accusation that the

PAC's support for the anti-SACTU Federation of Free African Trade Unions of South Africa (FOFATUSA) had been sponsored by the USA's CIA.[42] Tambo and other ANC leaders were particularly repulsed by the current acting president/national secretary of the PAC, PK Leballo, who had succeeded in beating back and expelling his rivals, including fellow founder members such as Peter Raboroko, Nana Mahomo and Peter Molotsi. Leballo, it seemed to them, was at best a 'loose cannon', prepared to use any tactics in order to attract attention to himself. In 1963, Leballo divulged secret information at a press conference held in Maseru, as a result of which, according to Leballo himself, 10 000 PAC members faced long-term imprisonment.

'If he had wanted to destroy the PAC he could not have thought up a better plan. Thanks to this announcement, made nearly 10 years ago, PAC President Sobukwe is still without his freedom of movement, association or action,' commented Tambo acidly.[43]

To top all these concerns, 14 African states, headed by Zambia's Kenneth Kaunda, were preparing to do the unthinkable – to negotiate with the apartheid system – and this without even so much as consulting the liberation movements. In early April 1969 the Lusaka Manifesto, endorsed by the OAU and adopted by the United Nations, offered to drop their sanctions against the South African regime provided that the government accepted the 'principles of human equality and dignity'. In historical fairness to the protagonists of the document, the rampant conservative context of the Western powers should be taken into account.[44] A Republican administration reigned in Washington, in league with the Tory government in Britain. Tambo's notes revealed his indignation at Houphouet-Boigny's smooth rationalisations. 'Apartheid,' opined the president of the Côte d'Ivoire, 'falls within the domestic jurisdiction of South Africa and will not be eliminated by force. After so many years of silence, a South African leader has made an overture. Let us seize this opportunity. Mr Vorster has promised to receive us on a footing of equality.'[45]

Tambo's response was to spell out firmly the ANC's approach of using the power of the black majority 'to win economic power for the people'. For that purpose the ANC was committed to 'preventing the balkanisation and dismemberment of our people... whose unity is essential'. In point form, he sketched out his reasons for the necessity for continuing armed struggle. The South African regime's stratagem was, as Tambo saw it, 'introducing dialogue and discussion across the colour line, granting higher wages here and there, permitting skilled and semi-skilled jobs here and there, the promise of Bantustan independence – all these are tactics designed to relieve, to lift internal and external pressures while as far as possible, leaving apartheid intact'.[46]

Tambo used his customary lateral approach to view the setback as a window of opportunity. The fact that the South African regime had been obliged to approach independent African states represented a significant victory for the ANC, he argued, for it proved the effectiveness of their tactics.

'If we are correct in the view that change on the part of the [government] is taking place as a result of our tactics, methods and strategy, then our reactions to this change should be to try and maximise it by intensifying the pressures on all fronts, by multiplying the causes of change so as to increase to the maximum both the depth and the extent of the change. It is precisely in the course of the change itself that we must mount a new offensive.'

Typically though (and also prophetically), even in his most determined arguments, Tambo allowed a loophole of logical pragmatism: 'It is only when our tactics can, at a given historical phase, produce no further changes that we should change the tactics.'[47]

What was particularly galling to Tambo was that Houphouet-Boigny was simplistically echoing Kaunda's humanism. During the exchanges, the South Africans 'will grow to see that we are human,' suggested the Ivory Coast leader. 'Such a realisation might begin to erode apartheid'. But he restrained himself, for Kaunda was generously keeping the ANC in Zambia. Tambo realised that Kaunda, to a certain extent like Khama in Botswana, was dependent on South Africa economically and traded in South African goods. He recognised, too, an additional factor forcing Kaunda to clasp South Africa. Zambia had problems with the Ian Smith regime in Rhodesia; Kaunda needed to play South Africa against Rhodesia in order to ensure that the economy did not suffer the long-term effects of the blockade that Zambia, with the support of the international community, had imposed on Rhodesia. Kaunda was not unaware of the effect on the ANC; he appreciated particularly Tambo's diplomatic handling of the Manifesto, and regarded highly what he termed Tambo's 'grasp of the realities'.[48] As a result, Kaunda himself claimed, relations between the ANC and the Zambian state were not jeopardised.[49]

'This was one of the qualities of OR,' confirmed Chris Hani. 'OR developed very strong relations, personal relations, with Kaunda, and many leaders in Africa. He was actually so well respected continentally that I think we survived as a movement [because of] his logical analysis of the situation; his presentation of problems; and his avoidance, even of confrontational situations with the leaders of these countries, where sometimes they had acted heavily against us.'[50]

With this overview, following intelligent listening and groundwork, Tambo chose not to discipline the seven authors of the memorandum directly, but to call for a consultative conference to be held as soon as possible to examine problems raised within the movement. Its purpose would be to redefine or re-examine the role of the movement in relation to the internal structures, and its strategy and tactics in dealing with the way forward. The outcome was to be a reorganising of the ANC Mission in Exile.

This was a bold move. Despite several conferences in exile, Tambo had argued that the ANC had not given the external wing a mandate to hold elections. Now he sent word via his secret route (possibly in a diplomatic bag or by a sympathetic warder)[51] to Robben Island that a consultative, decision-making event was not only vital, but also overdue. In due course, Tambo received a reply agreeing to the conference. It now remained for him to find the means to bring together the ANC in exile from various corners of the world to Morogoro, its military headquarters.

A Preparatory Committee invested months of intensive preparation in the conference. Funds had to be raised for this expensive event, documents circulated to all the centres. The Preparatory Committee solicited and received all documents and feedback and, informed by them, prepared an agenda. Tambo's idea was that the major problems should be examined constructively before the conference, 'so that, when we come to this conference it is not for the purpose of firing rockets at one another, because the rockets would have been fired in these documents in the course of the pre-conference deliberations and we would be assembling at this conference to discuss the proposed and concrete answers to the situation'.[52]

He conceived the preparations as 'a great campaign of discussions of our problems, of analyses of our situation, for weaknesses and shortcomings, of proposals, of an attempt to give answers, a determined effort to move forward and desist from marking time'.

And indeed contributions to the debate 'poured in… from comrades in Asia, in Europe, in Africa', although 'not all were received in time'. For Tambo's part, he felt confident of handling the situation, because in many respects, it was 'politics and nothing else, and I can deal with it quite effectively if it comes my way'.[53] As far as genuine grievances, there were those who were being 'very helpful because they are critical about things and raise issues'.

Finally, at the end of April 1969, a broad representation of about 700 delegates of the ANC in exile gathered at Morogoro for the Consultative Conference, the first since Lobatse, 1962. Delegates from MK and the camps, from units in the UK, East Germany, the USSR, India, and the offices in Algeria, Egypt, Zambia and Tanzania, as well as the Indian and Coloured People's Congresses – over 70 delegates in all were assembled, including 11 non-Africans, who were invited as representatives of the broader Congress alliance.[54]

Chaired by JB Marks, the conference began with Tambo's presidential address. There had been changes since the last conference, said Tambo. The ANC had lost its President-General, and the armed struggle had been put to the test on the battlefield.

'In the course of that we have lost some of the great sons of our country. Since that time, we have seen problems for our struggle mounting; mounting primarily because we were engaging the enemy in armed struggle... Despite the heroic actions of our youth in the battlefield, we have watched and seen a growing situation in our ranks which spells doom for the future of our struggle unless it receives our determined and devoted attention.'[55]

Tambo was at pains to encourage an open atmosphere of free discussion. This was a consultative conference, he said, and suggested that as it was focusing on the movement's internal situation, what he had to say should be received not so much as a presidential address from above, but 'an address by OR, the fighter for freedom, to fellow fighters for freedom about matters that are of immediate concern to all of us today'.

The documents received and distributed contained, he said, 'in many cases hard, solid and even bitter talking... In some cases, comrades had ideas that some of us felt were driving us into great difficulties. But they were entitled to express those great difficulties... I don't know whether there is anything that has been left unsaid. But if there is, we welcome it here'.[56]

The National Executive Committee then delivered a report. Its intention was to situate the present internal difficulties in the context of the liberation struggle at that particular historical moment. It gave a political analysis of South Africa's spectacular economic growth since the beginning of the decade. The 1960s had become the high noon of the apartheid regime. Black opposition, including trade unions, had been successfully crushed. The apartheid regime was now able to prosecute its profitable programme. Its success was based on the intensification of the exploitation of black labour. Thousands of people from the urban areas were being shifted to the rural Bantustans, which in effect consigned them to reservoirs of labour. The NEC reserved special censure for the first 'independent Bantu homeland', the Transkei (strictly speaking, it was pronounced formally 'independent' by Pretoria only in 1975), which included in its boundaries Tambo's own province of Pondoland.[57] The proposed prime minister of the Transkei was Chief Kaizer Matanzima, a fellow student of both Tambo and Mandela (and, in fact, Mandela's nephew) at Fort Hare. Despite the fact that his party had garnered only a third of the few votes cast, Matanzima had agreed to the South African government's proposal for an independent black state. In return, a small class of elites received 'high-sounding titles, salaries, ministerial houses, trading and business opportunities' that constituted, in the eyes of the NEC, 'the basis of a comprador, collaborator class'.[58] The NEC also noted the dramatic escalation of military expenditure in South Africa. The state now imposed long-term periods of military conscription for every white male over the age of 18. In part, this was an acknowledgement of the effectiveness, however limited, of MK insurgency. It was also evidence that South Africa was 'the main bulwark and fortress of... imperialism' in its 'desperate attempt to stem the anti-colonialist revolution'. The murder of Eduardo Mondlane of Frelimo was an example of the tactics of assassinations and the fomenting of 'splits and desertions in the ranks of the liberation movements... [T]hey bribe spies, informers and traitors to try to wreck the liberation movements'.[59]

The conference went on to examine the most substantial document submitted, the ANC's strategy and tactics based on a paper prepared mainly by Joe Slovo with Duma Nokwe, Joe Matthews and Reggie September.[60] The document embraced many of the grievances expressed by the preparatory statements before the conference; it also surveyed the achievements of the ANC – how, despite the setbacks, MK had in fact engaged with the enemy and inflicted deep psychological wounds on the 'myth of white superiority'. The report noted the 'mounting terror and repression at home' and the shift of the burden of leadership almost entirely on the External Mission. All these stresses had, however, resulted in 'weaknesses in the structures, emphases and style of work of the movement, which urgently called for correction'.[61] With the collapse of the old alliance machinery, a dangerous chasm was opening up between the leadership and the rank and file. The latter were left in the dark, resulting in resentment, divisions and a lack of integration between the political and the military structures.

The discussion was then opened to the floor. There followed 'days of open, frank and democratic discussion'.[62] Names were named, and fingers were pointed at some of the most senior officials. 'There was some straight talking,' recalled Chris Hani.[63] To most though, criticisms of the leadership and its structure tacitly excluded Tambo: his ingrained habit of staying out of polemics, of reserving judgement, of speaking only after great consideration, tended to recede his image in the thick of turmoil. Consequently, observed Joe Slovo, Tambo 'wasn't the target, it was people around him who were targets'.[64]

Tambo was, in the meanwhile, listening intently and making notes. JB Marks, who was chairing the meeting, allowed free expression. But the general condemnation began to escalate and took a new personal turn. 'Why is it,' somebody asked astutely, 'that whenever we ask a question, only Comrade OR answers? Is this a one-man operation or what?'[65]

When the call came for nominations for the election of a new executive, one of the delegates 'made a clumsy input'.[66] Tambo interpreted this as a personal rejection. He quietly laid down his pen. Slovo recalled that, suddenly, Tambo stood up – 'and this was the moment of the greatest drama' – and announced his resignation and immediately walked out of the conference.[67]

Tambo returned to the house where he was lodged. He went into his room and stayed there, reflecting, perhaps praying. Back at the meeting there was dismay. This turn of events was entirely unexpected. Of the whole leadership, Tambo would be the last to indulge in theatrical displays or calculated tantrums. Small groups gathered to discuss the implications. Abruptly, the conference was forced to address the immediate issue, which directly impinged on the direction the movement wanted to take in the future, and the image it wanted to project. The ANC's collective leadership had tended to place Tambo, in the minds of its members, as the first among equals. Since Chief Luthuli's death, Tambo had continued in his old capacity of Deputy President, a post created in 1959, and one to which he had been elected to act on behalf of the heavily circumscribed and banned Luthuli, where necessary. Without an officially sanctioned announcement on the late president's successor, the ANC was formally leaderless. Now, the delegates were forced to consider the matter of the succession, so long delayed. Sharp talking was followed by introspection.

The nationalists saw that the loss of Tambo might lessen their leverage, which was already threatened by the dominance of highly respected Marxist senior leaders in the ANC. To those who were members of the SACP there came the realisation (if they did not have it before) that Tambo was the only credible figure who could protect the image of the ANC in a Cold War world. Of all the senior leaders, he was the only known non-communist outside prison.

'Internationally, here was a man who was well respected and known as leader of the ANC,' commented Thami Mhlambiso, the ANC's UN delegate.[68] He had built up transcontinental support; he had been elected by the movement at home before its banning; he had personally been chosen by the NEC under Chief Luthuli to carry the flame abroad; he was a legitimate leader of the ANC as far as all the followers of the different tendencies within the movement were concerned; and he had the general acceptance of the cadres.

At last, after six or seven hours, JB Marks was commissioned to approach Tambo and, after a couple of hours, he returned with him. It was an emotional moment. Tambo explained, with feeling and a scrupulous concern not to be misunderstood, the reasons for his actions. He wished to be the facilitator, not the obstacle, to the strengthening of a united ANC.

'I was not taking a precipitous decision,' he is reputed to have said, 'but I thought that the leadership was not really understood by the ordinary people. I wanted to relieve myself of the responsibility of president to get down and reach to the masses.'[69]

He had resigned – indeed the entire executive had resigned before the conference had begun. It was now necessary to elect a new chairperson and a new National Executive. A vote was thus taken. Tambo was unanimously re-elected. Speaker after speaker rose, with moist eyes, to detail Tambo's role and welcome his return. When the smaller, leaner National Executive Council was elected, the entire committee was new, except for Tambo. Significantly, Chris Hani was one of the new members of the restructured NEC.

At the end, Joe Slovo began by saying, 'what happened today is that we lost a great president – and gained an even better one'.[70]

In the course of this drama, important decisions were made. The effect of the conference was to kick-start the means by which the anger of the cadres was converted into a political force – although this process took several years. The Hani memo itself was not addressed directly, but in his conclusion on behalf of the NEC, Tambo remarked that 'many are the mistakes committed by the heroic revolutionaries who give a monopoly to the subjective factor and who confuse their readiness with the readiness of others'.[71]

The ANC's strategy was recast into providing a greater balance between the political and the military. The internal base, which had been neglected since the trials earlier in the decade, had to be revived, and special emphasis, it was agreed, had to be placed on the working class. The leadership was restructured; a potentially powerful Revolutionary Council (RC), also chaired by Tambo, supplemented the more compact NEC, now reduced from 20 members to 8, which would make it more accessible for regular meetings. The RC, with 20 members, was mandated to develop both the military struggle, which should defer to the political imperative, and the underground base inside. The committee's design was meant to ensure that it would be fully involved in planning as well as in activities. The multiracial RC included Yusuf Dadoo, who was very popular with MK cadres. 'He was like an old-fashioned revolutionary. He would give an old-fashioned 1930s militant style, and people liked it, and they felt an integrity there.'[72] Reg September and Joe Slovo were the two other non-Africans in the Council. Previously, these three had been consulted from time to time, but as outsiders they had found themselves in a difficult position, without mandate or accountability. The RC, now an elected body, was the corrective step.

More significant was the vision that it implied for the ANC's period in exile. It was a rejection of the pressure by the West and Africa itself for a compromise with South Africa – to negotiate in conditions of weakness would have meant capitulation. The theme of the conference, then, was that there would be 'no middle road'.[73] It consciously affirmed the revolutionary line, while explicitly establishing the civilian, political control of its armed wing – with Tambo as the Commander in Chief. But Kongwa was to be closed, pending restructuring, and the cadres sent abroad for further education.[74] Indeed, 'the movement must reject all manifestations of militarism,' concluded Tambo, 'which separates armed people's struggle from its political context'.[75] Indeed the struggle was a holistic, 'indivisible theatre of war' with 'interlocking and interweaving of international, African and southern African developments which play on our situation'.[76]

Another closely argued resolution was passed, one that was opposed, ironically, by a number of white SACP members who feared that it paid insufficient attention to the strength of African nationalism. The membership (though not the National Executive) of the ANC was thrown open to all, regardless of race. Tambo summarised the outcome of the discussion at Morogoro:

'The formula that was adopted was this. All patriots who support the Freedom Charter… and the policy of our movement could become members of the External Mission. There was no urgency about people at home then, because they were underground anyway… That was the formula that was created; so therefore, non-Africans can perform any duties and fill any positions, except on the national executive committee.'[77]

To change the composition of the NEC, all agreed, would need the agreement of those inside.

Albie Sachs, who had not attended the conference, commented later on the awkward consequences of the formerly multiracial (as opposed to a non-racial) policy in an international setting: 'It made less and less sense. You can't have four organisations in the underground. Can you imagine four separate undergrounds? In London we had an ANC office. Imagine if you are telling the English people, here is the ANC, there is the Coloured People's Congress, there is the Indian Congress, there is the Congress of Democrats. And you are fighting apartheid. You just couldn't.'[78]

Tambo, procedurally correct as he always was, had no problems with the decision. He maintained firstly that the ANC constitution was not racially exclusive, even though in practice it had confined its membership to Africans; and secondly, that before he left South Africa the NEC had accepted in principle the opening of membership to the ANC in exile, and that it was permissible to work towards that end.[79]

'So the Morogoro conference reviewed that situation. The general consensus was that the time had now come to open the membership. But then it was necessary to consult the leadership which had taken this position [in 1959].'[80]

The 'formula that was adopted', he elaborated, was that 'all patriots who support the Freedom Charter and the policy of our movement could become members of the External Mission'. They could fill any posts within the ANC structures bar the NEC, which had been elected by the ANC at home and required consultation with the leadership at home to change.[81] (Interestingly, on Robben Island, the decision had been taken to operate only one organisation, one allegiance to which all Congress Alliance and SACP prisoners belonged, and that was the ANC.) In the meantime, to harness the strategic and mobilising talents of leading members of other national groups, the Revolutionary Council, which included Yusuf Dadoo, Joe Slovo, Reggie September and Joe Matthews, and was chaired by Tambo, was to interact with the NEC.

This last decision was to have major repercussions after the conference – some of the nationalists feared that the resolution, combined with the powers of the new Revolutionary Council, would shift autonomy away from the African members of the movement. Tambo, as always highly sensitive to subtexts, sensed a measure of disappointment, and he was concerned to remind all the members of the importance of consensus and accepting the majority feeling. He defended the right of the conferences of the external mission to make the changes.

'It is by force of circumstances that we are meeting at Morogoro and not in the Trade Hall or in Port Elizabeth or Uitenhage or in Stanger or at the Social Centre in Bloemfontein. It is by force of circumstances.' This was a conference of the African National Congress 'by its members who are on their way back home even if they take 6 or 10 years to do so'.[82] Tambo and the movement's other strategists concluded that a long-term, incremental, multistaged and disciplined guerrilla campaign had to be supported by both mass-based political activity and external support.

In his closing address, Tambo summed up the mood of sober determination. 'These are the orders to our people, to our youth, our army, to every soldier. These are the orders to our leaders,' he announced. United and coherent action was paramount. Savouring the dramatic rhetoric of the embattled revolutionary, he declaimed with prescience: 'The order that comes from the Conference is, "close ranks". Be vigilant, comrades. The enemy is vigilant. Beware the wedge driver! Men who creep from ear to ear, driving wedges among us; who go around creating splits and divisions. Beware the wedge driver! Watch his poisonous tongue!'[83]

Tambo emerged from Morogoro with increased stature. Since the death of Luthuli, he had, as elected Deputy President, become the *de facto* head. Tambo himself insisted that the position of president would be filled only when the ANC, both inside and in exile, was able to elect one.[84] In the years to come, even after he was formally elected president, following the direct intervention of the Robben Island prisoners, Tambo continued to refer to himself and the ANC leadership in exile as 'the current custodians of the... oppressed people, and the democratic forces of our country'.[85]

Oliver Tambo's leadership – low-key, unpretentious, almost diffident – had formerly been accepted, but not consciously proclaimed by the membership. It had almost been taken for granted. Now, they confirmed 'by acclamation'[86] his rank as acting president. Tambo bore the title not only through the legitimate process of election by the ANC before its unbanning, but through the reaffirmation of the remoulded ANC, the movement which now took on an international and revolutionary status. At the conclusion of the conference, Tambo held up before its members a global image:

'We of South Africa have taken charge of a sector that is vital to the success of the struggle against imperialism. The whole of the revolutionary forces of the world look upon us to play our role in this struggle. Our international duty is clear. Let us march against the enemy!'[87]

The Morogoro Conference, many agreed, was a 'turning point'.[88] The movement in exile had bonded through a process of problem-solving. It had now been restructured so that it could fulfil its necessary purpose as 'a proper instrument for organising and leading a revolutionary struggle'.[89] The most important outcome of the conference, reflected Tambo in later years, was the reorientation of the movement 'towards the prosecution and intensification of our struggle inside South Africa, the restoration and reinforcement of unity within our own ranks and the integration of all revolutionaries within the ranks of the External Mission of the ANC'. It also set out to achieve 'the proper balance between our internal and our international struggle, with the internal being primary'.[90] In short, it reasserted the ANC's primary policy of inclusiveness, unity and holistic strategy. By foregrounding the political, it provided a 'roadmap' that indicated the direction the struggle was to take, no matter how prolonged the journey. The lessons learnt from the hard experiences of the first generation of MK combatants were to pave the way for the fruitful incorporation of the next Soweto Black Consciousness generation.

In less than 10 years, Oliver Tambo had twice steered the exiled ANC and its collective leadership towards a review of its direction and its strategies. At the beginning of the decade, when the ANC formally announced its armed struggle to the international constituency, he engaged with its moral base. In the process, he had succeeded in bringing to the movement loyal supporters of its cause, both from the West and the Eastern Bloc. In order to achieve this, a reinterpretation of the past had become necessary. To Western politicians, the history of the ANC's patient but futile attempts to reach both the segregationist and the apartheid governments over a period of half a century was understood to be the reason for its conversion to armed struggle. To the East and the non-aligned, the national liberation movement was gearing itself for a titanic revolutionary struggle.

In a world context of Vietnam and anti-colonialist struggles, even as guerrilla warfare remained indisputably the foremost means of insurrection, the easy confidence in its execution in South Africa faded during the course of the decade. The revolutionary rupture, to be sparked by the advent of MK insurgents into the countryside, had yet to materialise. It had become once again necessary to re-evaluate the ANC by reassessing its past. Its culture of collective leadership helped to explain the reasons for the ANC's endurance. However, a perception persisted that the 'real' ANC leadership was at home, incarcerated on Robben Island. The Morogoro Conference and the election of a new National Executive went some way towards legitimising the headquarters in Lusaka, particularly after word was received from Robben Island approving the process and the results.

But once again, as with every strategic shift in the ANC, losses would be incurred, and costs would need to be calculated. This process was to become an ongoing operation throughout the exile period, during which time Tambo, chairing the most important structures, the NEC and the RC, would constantly need to re-evaluate the ANC and reassess its strategies in terms of shifting realities. The contradictions within the movement, as a broad umbrella under which many sheltered from hostile winds, would need very skilful negotiating to keep it from being blown away in its long and difficult climb towards the summit of freedom.

CHAPTER TWELVE

The Winding Path

IN 1976, A SMALL BREAKAWAY GROUP of the ANC launched a blistering attack on Oliver Tambo. 'It is now more than 15 years since Oliver Reginald Tambo left South Africa and established the ANC "Mission Abroad" for purposes of preparing for guerrilla warfare inside South Africa,' they charged. 'Yet Tambo has nothing to show for all the material support that the outside world has given him. Not a shot has been fired in defence of the defenceless Black people of South Africa. These are the direct results of surrendering the leadership of the ANC to the Slovos of the SACP. The judgement of history will be that Tambo sold his soul to the SACP white leadership and in the process betrayed the struggle of the African people of South Africa.'[1]

The resolutions at the Morogoro Conference of 1969, the first major gathering of the ANC outside of South Africa, though passed unanimously, resulted in considerable disquiet: the answers they provided generated new problems, exposing fault lines along the way forward. While some of the structural problems within the organisation seemed to have been settled, unresolved contradictions surfaced. These were problems and contestations that seemed to crop up every generation – questions of class, nationalism and ethnicity that affected the strategy of struggle. It fell upon Tambo, as Acting President, to deal with these perennial issues at this lowest point in his exile years.

An immediate cause of dissatisfaction arose out of the reshuffling of the NEC. Some of those senior members who were dropped from the NEC also failed to be re-elected onto the Central Committee of the South African Communist Party. This had occurred just as non-African Party members were receiving official recognition by the ANC for their contribution to the struggle over many years. SACP members had been responsible for the *Strategy and Tactics* document, which had been passed without dissent at the conference. Before Morogoro, the Party hierarchy, led by Moses Kotane and JB Marks, supported by Joe Matthews, Flag Boshielo, Ben Turok and others, had advocated the opening up of ANC membership to all races (although some black and white SACP members, including Brian Bunting, Joe Slovo and Ray Simons, opposed this view).[2] They had also urged a radical restructuring of the ANC-SACP alliance, recommending a clean sweep of the old Executive. These decisions were passed as resolutions at the conference. It was easy to see why some of those ousted from the old National Executive Committee should view themselves as victims of a conspiracy. In fact, not only was the bulk of the former NEC dropped after Morogoro, but those holding senior positions in some of the military camps were also suspended. As the months went by, a pressure group began to emerge, objecting to both the opening up of the ANC membership to non-Africans, and the acceptance of the *Strategy and Tactics* document. The leading dissenters to the Morogoro resolutions identified themselves as 'African Nationalists'; they became known as the 'Gang of Eight', a play on the Gang of Four, dissidents gaining notoriety in China at the time.

The long-standing debate over race, class, ethnicity and nationalism was once again in the air. Its roots lay in the two-fold nature of the anti-apartheid struggle: on one hand, a struggle against the colonial order and, on the other, a struggle for hegemony among the oppressed. Throughout the black diaspora, ideas inspired by Franz Fanon, Malcolm X, Aimé Cesaire and others were fuelling the rise of a Black Power movement. The special nature of the South African colonial order, with its large non-African population, made their role a central issue. In 1970, Tambo penned a 10-page letter to an unnamed nationalist, detailing precisely his own thinking on the relationship between class and nationalism.

'All Africans,' he argued, regardless of whether they were co-opted into the apartheid system or were living comfortable middle-class lives or were resigned to discrimination, were 'victims of white rule whether they are resisting or not'. As for whites in the struggle, 'as a group they are no force. They are individuals who have chosen their places on the side of the Blacks in the Black vs White conflict'. While they were not 'black' in colour, 'in so far as we represent the struggle as assuming a Black vs White character, then they are part of the blacks. The distinction I would make is that a white man must identify completely, to a degree which makes his skin colour irrelevant'.[3]

Tambo's notion of nationalism revealed that his attention to race was as keen as ever. His post-Morogoro concept of African nationalism, though, had undergone modification. It now embraced a wider, more inclusive and non-racial definition. Although 'non-Africans' were not permitted to serve the ANC's National Executive, by admitting members of all races into the ANC itself, Morogoro had otherwise shaken off the multiracial alliance structure so frequently criticised by the PAC and other Africanists.

At first, Tambo, as a respected founder of the ANC Youth League and sharply conscious of racism, was seen by the 'African nationalists' as a potential ally.

Based mainly in London, and led by 'TX' (Tennyson Xola Makiwane), they requested that Tambo call a meeting at the home of Thami Mhlambiso to listen to their grievances.[4] At least 10 ANC Africans attended.[5] They were particularly unhappy, they confessed, about the opening of the ANC membership to all races. The London office was a case in point, where they maintained the 'African image' had been supplanted. The chief representative there had been Raymond Mazisi Kunene, but after the conference there was a reshuffling, and Reg September had now been appointed the new representative.

'People were complaining that, look, when people from home come and visit the office, they don't see the Africans,' recalled Mhlambiso, 'and most of the people at the meeting felt they were being pushed into the background.'[6] Strong egos abounded in London. The exile community there was described by one Africa-based ANC member as a 'snake's nest... gossipy and backbiting'.[7] Exiles included members of the SACP, whose absolutist and confident judgements often discomfited followers and non-followers alike. There were also other complaints: 23 cadres in Lusaka had been suspended; questions were raised over corruption – the 'pickpockets' – in Lusaka. Notwithstanding the hopeful note on which the Morogoro Conference had ended, there was, they insisted, a crisis in the movement.[8]

The meeting lasted for two days. Tambo acknowledged some of the points that were raised and promised to discuss these concerns with the National Executive. It was then agreed that a conference should be held to discuss the matter further with an enlarged executive, with as many of the members of the NEC as possible and, as a result, a consultative conference was held in Lusaka later in the year.

'And I must say,' commented Thami Mhlambiso about Tambo, 'all the problems were faced squarely. I mean there was no dodging or ducking of issues, and whenever there was disagreement we tried to iron out those differences.'[9]

A national secretariat was then appointed by Tambo to explore these issues. Nevertheless, Tambo's perspective was more in keeping with the ANC's inclusive approach: 'We must not allow ourselves to forget that our influence in London was maintained by non-members (Europeans and Indians) when we were either not there or were not sufficiently strong to hold our own ground,' he once wrote to Adelaide. 'I think it would be a mistake to cast these people aside now that our boys have decided to enter the battlefield.'[10]

Tambo attempted to raise the issue of race, in relation to what he called 'the weapon of unity', in his New Year message to the External Mission in 1971. Unity was precisely the weapon that the apartheid regime had sought to smash through its policies. 'The colour bars and job reservations, the Bantustans, the

Coloured and Indian Councils, the group areas and the ethnic groupings, the Fort Hares and Turfloops, the Matanzimas, Bandas and Houphouet-Boignys – all these are a grab at the weapon of unity,' he reminded his members.

In 1972, the External Mission expanded. New offices were opened up in Sweden, the United States, Canada and others, and a number of the men who had expressed their concerns at the London meeting were appointed to the new posts. Tennyson Makiwane already held a new post in London as Deputy Director of External Affairs. Thami Mhlambiso was assigned to the United Nations in New York. Among the military men, Ambrose Makiwane was relocated from Kongwa camp to the office in Cairo; and Tambo appointed Robert Resha to chair the National Secretariat.

The other objection at the London meeting had been the perceived 'hijacking' of the ANC by the SACP. The *Strategy and Tactics* document, they charged, though circulated and discussed for some time before the conference, was adopted without formally putting the document itself to the vote at the actual conference. The setting up of the Revolutionary Council, which was originally appointed as a 'home-go' committee, was also viewed with suspicion. The RC was potentially as influential as the NEC, and it seemed to them that the new structure was the product of well-orchestrated SACP caucusing before the conference. There was an uneasy perception that non-Africans might come to dominate the leadership of the Party; this was all the more disturbing now that the new structure gave non-African communists more influence in the ANC. Spokespersons at the meeting distinguished between African SACP members who were sensitive to the national question, such as Moses Kotane and JB Marks, and those who were under the influence of whites – the Slovos, Carneson, 'middle-class whites', they alleged, had no mass base.

Because of his own political history, Tambo was able to appreciate the fears of the nationalists of an ideological takeover by the communists. To demonstrate his understanding of their anxieties, Tambo looked favourably upon a project proposed by Johnny Makathini, which aimed to deflect the interventionist role of left-wing whites in black politics.[11] In this context, Tambo agreed to the formation of an alternative organisation within the ANC alliance, distinct from the SACP, aimed at focusing white members' support work on their own community in South Africa.

It seemed the right moment for a leftist challenge to Soviet-oriented communist parties the world over. The students' ideological revolt, inspired by the writings of Herbert Marcuse, had begun in Frankfurt, Germany, in

1968, spread to Paris and other European cities, crossed the Channel to the United Kingdom and then traversed the Atlantic, making a deep impact on an American youth already radicalised by the Civil Rights Movement and the anti-Vietnam war campaign. These initiatives dovetailed with the New Left, which had its origins in the post-Hungary 1956 split from the Communist Party in the UK.[12] The movement embraced a Marxist class analysis of society while rejecting the Stalinism of the USSR and its satellite countries. Naturally, the SACP, which had looked to the USSR since its inception for inspiration, guidance and support, was uncomfortable with the New Left.

Makathini, based in North Africa, had developed contacts with French radicals. Like Tambo, he gave priority to an open, pragmatic strategy that would harness all those opposed to apartheid. In Africa, Makathini had initiated relationships with 'unfashionable' states such as Côte d'Ivoire, Gabon, Senegal and Zaire, despite the reactionary nature of some of these regimes.

'Johnny ended up with all sorts of diplomatic bed mates, which worked to the advantage of the ANC,' commented Neo Moikangoa, one of Tambo's personal assistants, who knew Makathini well.[13]

And so it was that one wintry night in 1972, Oliver Tambo hurried under the shelter of an umbrella through the streets of Paris to a certain Left Bank café to meet the key figure in this project, Breyten Breytenbach.[14] Eloquent, romantic and extremely talented, the well-known Afrikaner poet lived in exile. His Vietnamese wife, Yolande, had years before been refused an entry permit into apartheid South Africa (although more recently he had been permitted to visit South Africa with Yolande, as special dispensation from the apartheid authorities to grace an Afrikaans cultural event).[15] Breytenbach (once a Stellenbosch flatmate of Marius Schoon, COD member who had served 12 years in prison for attempted sabotage) was offering to recruit and mobilise intelligentsia, particularly radical Afrikaner thinkers, artists and writers, to resist the apartheid system from within. His key argument was that as oppressors, whites were deeply alienated. To illustrate the message, Breytenbach gave the analogy of the lion-tamer and the stool. The lion saw no distinction between the stool, or the whip, or the lion-tamer. White South Africans were, by definition, part of the oppressive machinery, and only by recognising the leadership of the liberation struggle could they come to terms with their alienation.[16]

Briefed by Johnny Makathini, Tambo was given a rundown of the activist poet's achievements. Together with artists and intellectuals in the café society of Paris, Breytenbach was one of the founders of Atlas, the anti-apartheid organisation operating in France and the Netherlands. Atlas saw its mission as a direct action group involving European and South African radicals. In Holland, they persuaded the dockers in Rotterdam to refuse to unload South African cargo, and exposed tobacco smuggling as well as sanctions-busting schemes in the Netherlands. Atlas was also involved in exposing sanctions-busting oil deals to Rhodesia. In Paris, when the South African Embassy moved location, at Breytenbach's behest a number of French Trotskyites hijacked the transit van and stole all the documents to do with the French-South African deal on Mirage aircraft.

On the night of the Paris rendezvous, Breytenbach proposed to deliver to Tambo an amalgamation of Atlas with a specifically South African-based Okhela – a white, New Left alternative to the South African Communist Party – operating within the ambit of the ANC. It was important, argued Breytenbach, that white people be seen to be supporting the ANC in a nationalist perspective. Breytenbach's record of achievements was in a very sensitive realm, but his proposal was in keeping with the ANC's inclusive approach and its new membership policy. Tambo indicated that he thought the proposal was a good idea and accepted it, on condition that the project be kept under close wraps.

Soon afterwards, the Okhela made its first move. Makathini, however, was later to remind them that they had undertaken their first assignment against his wishes. Makathini, some believed, backtracked because he understood that Tambo, having encountered determined opposition by the SACP members on the Executive, was not going to support Okhela.[17] The ANC perception was that the talented Johnny had moved too quickly, pre-empting a proper mandate from the ANC.[18] Be that as it may, Breytenbach travelled to South Africa in disguise as one Christian Galaska, accompanied by an Okhela colleague, Barend Schuytema, from the Netherlands. Breytenbach's aim was to make contact with the local left intelligentsia through Gerry Maré, a young Afrikaner activist in Natal, in order to offer educational and military support. Maré, though, rejected what he regarded as an adventurist proposal. Breytenbach then travelled around the country, trying to identify recruits among student leaders.

'As I understand it, a lot of them were very keen, in a romantic sense. And also with Black Consciousness at the time, there was this sort of searching for a path. It was totally disorganised, unstructured,' commented a one-time Okhela member.[19]

The detentions of a number of student activists followed and in the ensuing trial the entire plot was blown out of the water.[20] Breytenbach himself, embittered by the absence of the ANC's political back-up, recanted – 'grovelled', by his own admission – in a painful show trial and received a nine-year sentence.[21] And when he finally emerged from prison, he rejected the ANC and, apparently, even offered his services to the Security Police to infiltrate the SACP.[22]

'The [Special Branch] of course graciously served that up to the media', commented Pallo Jordan wryly.[23]

Okhela lasted only a year or two longer.[24] Ultimately, the remaining activists of the organisation realised that 'in the real world to do anything you have to recognise the ANC... To fight against them you might set up some some small outfit, but you are not going to get anywhere'.[25]

Clearly, though, the dissatisfaction of activists from all directions indicated that the ground was fertile for political entrepreneurship. For the Group of Eight, Tambo was not moving quickly enough in advancing their demand to reverse the Morogoro resolutions. In fact, the steps he had already taken to meet their grievances and anxieties had backfired. The Executive Committee, who saw no particular reason for the existence of an additional structure, had dissolved the national secretariat. And then there was the embarrassment of the Okhela debacle, which was revealed to ANC members only when Breytenbach was put on trial.

More disturbingly, Tambo had to deal with a wave of complaints about the new positions granted abroad. Following the Morogoro Conference, Tambo had appointed Alfred Nzo to head a commission to examine grievances. What emerged was a disquieting degree of 'tribalism' or, as Tambo preferred to call it, 'provincialism'. The testimony of indignant comrades gave clear evidence of this trend. With greater or lesser diplomacy, witness after witness outlined the grievances of the victims in the camps, who perceived the reshuffling of the offenders to other positions as reward rather than chastisement, and this because they were, like Tambo himself, 'Cape men'. The relocation of Xhosa-speaking instigators such as Chris Hani and Ambrose Makiwane seemed to them to be clear evidence of Tambo's bias in favour of 'home boys'.

'Some comrades think you are acting for your tribe. Others think not,' attested one witness. Others were less tactful: 'Comrade OR has over the years indulged in this sort of practice.'

In a later meeting with a group of Transvalers, Tambo met with even darker accusations of blackmail. 'What have you done which prevents you expelling [a Xhosa-speaking culprit]?'[26]

Tensions had also built up between the followers of Chris Hani and Joe Modise, and by 1972, despite the resolutions at Morogoro, these had still not been resolved. Urban Transvalers were described as 'thugs organised by Modise to destroy his enemies' – possibly a reference to Modise's youthful career as a gang leader in Sophiatown.[27] 'Cape men' seemed to be unwilling to accept Modise's authority – 'Joe is the commander of Sothos'.

In the notes jotted down by Oliver Tambo himself, he emphasised the complaints that were of most concern to him: 'Previously, we hear a comrade has done this or that; he must be reprimanded. Later he is again in another [different] position. This has meant offence is rewarded with positions... '[There] is bias in the organisation in favour of a group who seems always to be given positions... Many times, [the President] promised that mistakes would be rectified. I can find nothing which has been rectified... [The president] promised to deal with the case of the 7 [Hani and others who issued the memo], but no sign that anything had been done... I can't blame anyone who says [the president] is favouring one side. I appeal to [the President] to rectify mistakes.'

The ethnic factor seemed to be further compounded by class differences.[28] For historical reasons, the Cape men were better educated and had acquired professional qualifications. As a result, they had gained ascendancy in the ANC. But some had also revealed themselves to be arrogant and unwilling to accept the leadership of lesser-educated comrades.

'Some of us are just there for the spade work', protested one complainant.

The leaders seemed to be out of touch with the experiences of their grass-roots members. Tambo's personal notes also revealed criticism of leaders, who were perceived to have become so comfortable in their positions that their revolutionary ardour had been dampened. A London friend described the atmosphere among disgruntled members.

'One of the criticisms was that when OR comes into the country, you could hardly meet him because he is taken here and there, surrounded by these white groups and so and so. But the last people to see him were the African members who wanted to meet him.'[29]

Another censure was the house in which Tambo was living. After 15 years of working double shifts in hospitals, the determined Adelaide had saved some money and drawn on anti-apartheid organisations to assist her family and scrape together the deposit of a comfortable house in the upper middle-class suburb of Muswell Hill. This move may have caused embarrassment to Oliver, but as an absentee husband and father, he felt he had forfeited the right to interfere. The outcome, though, was that this residential upgrading of his family politically undermined him.

'So many of our boys and girls who struggle were really living under very bad conditions all over the place,' explained Fertz Ngakane, while not necessarily agreeing with the criticism. 'And it does not speak well to find that the leader is living in comparative affluence... OR's children happened to have been in very expensive public schools.'[30]

In the camps, too, creeping disaffection was expressed. 'I find differences from top to us,' declared one of the witnesses (as transcribed by Tambo in his notebook). 'Why are we staying in one place and never moving forward home? This is because leaders are living with families, receiving salaries; their wives are employed. It seems leaders are dedicated only as long as they continue to receive these salaries... Only those who have their wives here are paid. Those whose wives are at home are not paid.'[31]

The Wankie misfortune thus continued to be perceived by some to be a cynical exercise to promote the image of the leadership while the foot soldiers were sacrificed in the process, and it fell to Tambo not only to respond to personal accusations, but also – although he belonged to the ethnic group that dominated the leadership – to be the conciliator. But to the end of his days, Tambo steadfastly refused to acknowledge, at least publicly, that ethnicity had any influence on decisions in the ANC. After all, the movement's entire *raison d'être* at its formation had been to unite all black groups throughout the country. 'What is called tribalism is one of the reasons that kept us apart. If you wanted to do anything, you had to show you were all suffering the same thing,' he explained.[32]

Tambo believed, however, that ethnicity had stayed alive in the minds of people because of the territorial and cultural differences that had existed since precolonial times. He illustrated the way in which, in apartheid South Africa, these differences were perpetuated, both by the ruling class and the media, as well as in popular culture.[33]

'It's an ongoing thing... Take in Johannesburg. We all get employed by the same body and are paid in the same manner. The wages are the same. We knock off the same time. There's no tribalism in that. And yet two people will quarrel, then the issue becomes "you're a Xhosa, I'm a Sotho, and that's why we're quarrelling". The reason for quarrelling has nothing to do with tribe... It's an excuse people look for to explain disagreements.'[34]

Regional differences, or 'provincialism', Oliver Tambo conceded, did however influence material conditions and therefore perceptions, but whether tangible differences were based on ethnicity or material conditions, the ANC was determined to minimise them.

Under the heading, 'Disparity', Tambo recorded in his 1970/1 notebook: 'This meeting considers it essential, and accordingly instructs the NEC, to investigate and take steps to eliminate the disparity and inequalities between cadres in the leadership and those in the rank and file, as reflected in the practice and basis of payment of allowances to the one category of cadres and the provision of general maintenance for the other.'[35]

Tambo held a joint meeting with the Revolutionary Council, the President-in-Council and the CPO to discuss the restructuring of personnel. He called it the 'Operation de Move-On' (reminiscent of the 'café de move on' at home – the coffee cart in the streets of Johannesburg that had to be easily transported in an emergency, for the police might descend on it at any time and close down the entire operation). But in the reshuffle of personnel, however unfortunate and in whatever form, Tambo had to acknowledge ethnic susceptibilities. He restructured command lines in order to increase accountability to the main structures and the top leadership. In his notebook, he wrote: 'NB. *All Army* personnel, all MK members, all ANC members [are to] move...' – all, that is, except the 'Transvaler' Joe Modise, who was to remain as Commander-in-Chief. To those who commented on Modise's regional and cultural origins, Tambo was firmly dismissive: 'No! People say all kinds of things about us. Modise is a very capable man. There's no one to put in his place. Someone who says he should be removed is talking rubbish!'[36]

Nevertheless, despite his rejection of ethnicity in the ANC, Tambo had 'virtually handpicked a new leadership... in a pluralistic way,' observed Albie Sachs. 'Balancing out older/younger [and] to some extent rural/urban, although it always had a very strong urban bias; Johnny Makathini, representing certainly non-communist at times anti-communist positions, linking up with people in America and representing a certain style on the one hand, and people like Yusuf Dadoo at a later stage on the other, in the Revolutionary Council, representing a totally different tradition. Joe Slovo representing the SACP and, important in relation to MK, balancing out the MK people with the political work, the international work.'[37] And, in addition, it might have been added, Tambo chose with an eye to ethnic and provincial backgrounds. He hoped that these measures would reassure the MK as well as those who were not 'Cape men'.

But many of the 'Cape men' themselves were not happy. They were suspicious of the motives of the 'white-led SACP' and came out openly in a racially based critique: 'Slovo is busy projecting himself as the *military* expert for the ANC. Dadoo is used as the voice of the minority interests whilst effectively having taken over the ANC leadership, Reggie September and Alex La Guma play the same roles... Those who were present at Morogoro in 1969 have now seen the grave mistake they made in accepting the Morogoro Resolutions.'[38]

In 1975, frustrated and disappointed in Tambo, eight of the dissenters took the decision to break away – their complaints had been heard and addressed, but insufficient steps had been taken to give them a stronghold in the organisation. Their sense of belonging and leadership in the organisation had not been forthcoming.[39] They chose the occasion of the unveiling of the tombstone of Robert Resha, a veteran of the Sophiatown struggle, the ANC representative in Nigeria, communist and nationalist, and frequent companion of Oliver Tambo in their various diplomatic missions and fund-raising efforts. Ambrose Makiwane launched an abrasive attack on the ANC leadership.

'The ANC has been hijacked by non-Africans,' Makiwane declared. 'Our strategy and tactics are in the hands [of] and dominated by a small clique of non-Africans. This is the result of the disastrous Morogoro Consultative Conference of 1969 which opened membership of the ANC to non-Africans. At this conference, Robbie [Resha] opposed this on the grounds that, that was a violation of the policy of the ANC.'[40]

Makiwane called for 'fundamental changes in the manner in which the ANC operates abroad'. He did not mention the leadership itself, but spelt out the nationalists' perspective: 'South Africa is an African country. The African is the most oppressed. He suffers the worst deprivation and exploitation. This is not being racialist, it is a fact; it is an objective reality.'

Tambo was indignant, not at the argument, but at what he considered to be the appropriation of Resha's memory, and smuggled a report to the Island – to his closest friends and comrades to whom he could express himself unconstrained by the fear of political backlash: 'What they claimed had happened at the Conference of 1969 was a palpable untruth,' he wrote, 'and they knew it.

'To their shame, they used the honoured Robert Resha in his grave, to do what he has never done and never would do, namely, to try and destroy the ANC. In all the chicanery, I have known throughout my involvement in the ANC, there is nothing to compare with the way Themba Mqota and Ambrose Makiwane used Robert Resha – against his silenced will, when he could no longer say "No!" And in the result, at the very moment when people all over the world and in South Africa were paying homage to his great service, he was suddenly projected by this group as the leading crusader in the service of counter-revolution, anti-ANC, anti-coloured, anti-Indian, anti-white, anti-communist. The crusade by the Mqota group never had any chance of destroying the ANC, but the great image of Robbie was severely marred in the process.'[41]

Resha, like Duma Nokwe, had been involved in discussions among Africans on nationalism. He opposed the opening of ANC membership but would never have consented, Tambo was adamant, to expose internal discussions in this way.[42]

'Robert Resha's name was desecrated as if he were supporting something to which he was opposed to throughout his whole life and service to his people, his country and his organisation,' wrote Tambo. 'This they did deliberately because they thought that Robert Resha was silent, but he is not.'[43]

Members of the SACP were equally outraged. Duma Nokwe, who himself had not been re-elected to the NEC, swore then and there to have the eight leading dissenters ousted.[44]

'He went back to Lusaka,' recalled Albie Sachs, 'and said: "These people are not ANC. They are against ANC."'[45]

Among the younger intellectuals, a great deal of passionate debate was also taking place, with concern about the impact it was having on the ANC as a whole. The strategy, they reasoned, appeared to have been to target Tambo as the person holding together the 'left' grouping and the nationalists, so that narrow nationalists alone could emerge as the ANC. Ultimately, it was the younger people, including Thabo Mbeki, Mavuso Msimang, Chris Hani and others, who argued that the movement could not take this continual factional activity.[46] Ironically, Joe Slovo – one of their main targets – argued unsuccessfully for their right to be heard.[47] Tambo himself made several attempts to meet their concerns. To the High Command on Robben Island, he recounted:

'It would be wrong to say there has been no cause for criticism directed at the way certain sectors, levels and contingents of our broad movement were carrying on. There have been instances of frustrating insensitivity to the strategic and tactical demands of our situation. On the other hand, we have had a series of representative meetings or conferences in which there was frank criticism and self-criticism, and all of which were by common agreement, very successful. The most important of these was the Morogoro Conference, and another in Lusaka in 1971.'[48]

The conference of 1971, reported Tambo later, raised the differences that had emerged since Morogoro, and reaffirmed the decisions, strategies and tactics adopted in 1969. It suggested, though, that members of the Group of Eight be given specific tasks, acknowledging their experience and seniority.[49] But despite attempts to placate them, the Group seemed determined to dismantle the post-Morogoro structures, at the risk of severely impairing the cohesiveness of the entire movement.

At the following ANC Executive meeting, the eight were summarily expelled.

'[But] it wasn't OR who led to this conclusion,' argued Thabo Mbeki, 'because he felt that reason would ultimately prevail.'[50]

At the meeting, Tambo sketched out his thinking. He was openly critical of the conduct of the UK faction but, in the interests of preventing a split, counselled further work with the dissenters. But the level of indignation overrode his arguments and although Oliver Tambo voted against their summary expulsion,[51] he abided by the majority resolution of the NEC to expel the eight. The decision was one of the few that did not follow a process of decision by consensus. Uncharacteristically, Tambo allowed their expulsion to go ahead unprocedurally. They were not given a hearing, nor the opportunity to defend themselves.[52] The first that Tennyson Makiwane heard of the move, he claimed, was on Radio South Africa.[53] Retrospectively, Tambo blamed himself for not being more scrupulously correct during the process.

'It could have been dealt with differently,' he admitted years later. 'These people were never asked to explain why they'd said those things. They were never charged... But the matter having been decided, I assumed the position of the Executive.'[54]

Once again, his priority was damage control. But to his critics, Tambo's rare blunder seemed to confirm the suspicion that he was under the thumb of the SACP. For Tambo, this unhappy experience also proved to be a lesson. In later years he was to become more assertive: on occasions of unresolved consensus, he was to communicate more effectively his own will by virtue of his status as the leader acting in the interests of the movement as a whole.[55]

In the event, some of the group, including Ambrose Makiwane and Pascal Ngakane, rejoined the ANC after its return home at the movement's invitation, largely a result of the personal contacts Tambo maintained with some of them.

'This was not a personal fight,' Thabo Mbeki asserted. 'OR... would keep a space open to see if they would come back. He would talk quite frankly, straight, and challenge them to speak openly, to take a rational position and respond to whatever might have been the cause of the tension and conflict.'[56]

By his own admission, Tambo had been disturbed at this unprecedented turn of events. 'Three of these chaps, he happened to like very much', observed Moikangoa, who was to become Tambo's personal assistant, and whose comments expressed a widespread and enduring interpretation of Tambo's feelings about the affair.[57]

To his closest comrades, Tambo mourned the loss of 'many bright and talented promising cadres of our movement, including Ambrose Makiwane'.[58] 'He was very, very fond of TX [Tennyson Makiwane], the way he was always fond of bright people', pointed out Moikangoa, 'and he was very fond of Themba Mqota, who was known as Alfred Kgokong at that time. And if OR had a blind side it related to the way he could completely trust a person. He had political confidence in these comrades, and would practically leave things that way – for instance, he had confidence in Johnny [Makathini], confidence in Thabo, confidence in any number of people, where he would say, "Who is in that delegation that's going to this place?" – and someone would say, "No, Johnny is in there". Then he would say: "No, that's fine. They will handle it."'

Tambo was grieved by the loss of the eight men, maintained Moikangoa. As with Sobukwe, for whom Tambo had had an affection,[59] 'he saw them as wasted because, as far as he was concerned, they were supposed to be inside the movement, where their talents would have full play to the benefit of the movement'.[60] At the same time, the Group of Eight enjoyed suprisingly little support from the ANC rank and file. According to Albie Sachs, 'this was not only because their politics did not ring true (particularly their attacks on OR) – they just weren't active, ever since being disgraced. Although they spent most of their time in London, they did no solid work, were held in contempt by MK cadres and spent all their time plotting'.[61]

Tambo was now at a low point. The disappointment of middle-level and rank-and-file cadres in the military still rang in his ears, while in their statement following the expulsion, the eight attacked the 'corrupted and co-opted section of the ANC leadership', 'the abandonment of elective procedures, the accountability and renewal of leadership'. They made a point of singling out Tambo, censuring him for his 'duplicity': 'Tambo has failed to make public pronouncements as Head of the ANC, instead, in private gatherings he says different things to different people, depending on who and where they are.'[62]

In the context of the heady guerrilla victories in Angola and Mozambique, they revisited the military failures of MK: 'Tambo, his hand always clutching a passport, always on the point of flying off somewhere, makes a remarkable contrast to a leader like Machel, who during the struggle was seen always having a gun slung over his shoulder, leading his men into the fight.'

Tambo's quiet, unassertive style sometimes exacted a personal price. A couple of years after the expulsion, Thami Mhlambiso, who had been posted to the USA, was replaced by the talented Johnny Makathini. Mhlambiso felt that his association with the eight was the cause of his demotion, and recalled a pointed and hostile comment by one member of the executive. He decided to discuss his situation with Tambo, one of whose 'blue-eyed boys' he had thought himself to be.[63] Tambo promised to set aside some time to consider Mhlambiso's case. Instead, shortly afterwards Mhlambiso received a cable from the Secretary-General via ES Reddy (a valued friend in the United Nations but not a member of the ANC) advising Mhlambiso that his representation in North America was terminated forthwith. He was to report to Dar es Salaam for further instructions. Mhlambiso, hurt and apprehensive, did not follow these orders and instead took a post in the United Nations' Department of Public Information.

He was deeply wounded by Tambo's silence during the whole affair, but tried to analyse and understand Tambo's delicate situation. Ultimately, 'when it came to making a decision, OR sided with the old guard', he said.[64] But then again, he conceded, the dissenters themselves had failed on their side, 'to take the initiative... you either apply yourself fully or you can't be effective'. Nor had they offered sufficient support to Tambo. 'They knew what the situation was... When you heard people talk about certain things... you felt some just [had] an axe to grind and some of them were just power hungry.'[65] A close friend of Mhlambiso's, never a member of the ANC and more in tune with Black Consciousness, was angry with Tambo for his 'failure to give moral personal support' over the matter.[66] Mhlambiso recalled Tambo's perspective of leadership, and the pragmatism that inevitably accompanied it. Tambo saw his role as leader to hold the movement together – not to take sides, but to chart a course that would be beneficial to all.

'People must understand you to be many things to many people,' Tambo had once told Mhlambiso. This approach made it extremely difficult to pinpoint Tambo's position.

'Would you say Oliver was Marxist? [Was he] a member of the Communist Party or wasn't he? You wouldn't be sure. You would have to dig a lot. A lot of people believed he wasn't, he was a devout Christian... Others said he is a loyal nationalist... At the time, when you are thinking of what was going on in all the political formations in London, you had to be quite a leader to be able to survive and continue.'[67]

Tambo had considered the full implications to the movement of the demands of the eight, who, NEC members contended, had not presented a well-argued intellectual position.[68] The group had their own axes to grind because they were also among those who were dropped from leadership levels. Some of them had been in the Party, Joe Slovo pointed out. With this background, despite (and because of) his personal friendship with all of the eight, Tambo had had to weigh up particularly carefully their requirements against what their target, the SACP, had to offer. Once the Group of Eight realised that Tambo was not going to risk splitting the movement wide open, they attacked him personally and openly compared him unfavourably with Mandela.

'It is our considered view that Oliver Tambo has clearly betrayed the sacred trust and mandate given him by the ANC to head the External Mission... His conduct has been a betrayal of colleagues languishing in jail like Nelson Mandela, whose hopes of leaving Robben Island lie in the successful prosecution of the struggle. No, the truth must be said as it is, that this man – that Oliver Tambo – is unfit to lead a revolutionary struggle.'[69]

But individual members of the Executive swiftly and hotly denied the charges. So, more formally, did the SACP, which had been accused of being white-led and usurping the ANC. In due course, the leadership on Robben Island also distanced itself from the eight. Wilton Mkwayi and Elias Motsoaledi had received several letters of complaint from Themba Mqota.[70] He was particularly derogatory about Tambo, as well as Ruth Mompati, who was a member of the NEC, and asked the High Organ to intervene. Mkwayi and Motsoaledi were asked to attend a High Organ meeting.[71] Discussions were raised about the question of the presidency. Years had passed since the death of Chief Luthuli, but with the escalating contestation by the Group of Eight, to choose a new president seemed divisive and was postponed. Tambo himself insisted that it would be unconstitutional to choose a president without an election of representatives both inside and outside the country.

On Robben Island, the issue was also raised, some pointing out that Mandela was head of the High Organ and it therefore followed that he should become President of the ANC.[72] Such a move they argued, would be highly symbolic – it would unite the movement and resound throughout the world. Tambo could then continue to act as Deputy President, as he had done since his election to that office in 1959. But another group on the Island disagreed strongly with this romantic notion. They argued that it would be absurd for a prisoner to try to run the movement.[73] But, as Walter Sisulu remarked, 'We formed a very formidable team because we knew each other so well, what the other was thinking.'[74] The same applied to the 'Class of 44', as the founders of the Youth League were popularly called. In prison or in exile, the bond between Tambo, Mandela and Sisulu, in particular, was never permitted to be strained.

Some time in 1975, a visitor from one of the official international bodies permitted to check on prisoners brought the news that the Mission in Exile had appointed Mandela as President of the ANC.

'But Madiba never wanted this,' commented Ahmed Kathrada. 'It was a policy decision on Robben Island that prisoners cannot make policy. Ever since Rivonia, we had all agreed that we were to give no instructions to outside.'[75]

Messages were sent out reiterating this decision, but these were not received until Mac Maharaj, released in 1976, left the country the next year for Lusaka.

Incriminations in some Western countries, in particular, contributed to the ANC's negative image. In the eyes of even some sympathisers, the ANC was 'stolid [and] deadly dull'.[76] A sense of unease infused the branches – nothing seemed to be happening. The image of Tambo was conflated with the ills of the movement. 'There was generally an atmosphere that we are not going to get anywhere; a lot of people felt that,' recalled Joe Slovo. 'And of course when you are in that kind of mood then it's easy to find targets; and one of the obvious targets is the leader of the organisation.' Tambo's visit in around 1973 to an American university – where he was thought to have made a somewhat lacklustre speech – provoked Ali Mazrui's question, in private, to some South African students: 'What has the ANC done to the ANC – or what has Tambo done to the ANC?'[77] It is true that Tambo's quiet style did not make an immediate impact in the USA, where image and charisma counted for so much. Nor did he have quite the same status or image of an uncontested, highly charismatic individual leader such as existed at the time in Cuba, in Frelimo or in Vietnam. He was still merely the Acting President in an organisation that emphasised collective responsibility. He was to remain in this indeterminate state for 10 years after Luthuli's death.[78]

It was a climate in which many in the ANC 'had a bit of an anti-leadership approach' – in the revolutionary tradition, the masses counted, though they would somehow make an exception for OR – perhaps because he himself was an 'anti-leader' leader![79] Tambo was thus caught between the strident demands of the nationalists to reverse major decisions at Morogoro, the low morale in the MK camps, the most recent high-profile failures to penetrate the home base, and the angry accusations of tribalism and favouritism in the granting of positions to 'home boys'. In the context of the self-destructive fractures of the PAC, Tambo faced a potentially fatal fragmentation. Certainly, as the Group of Eight began to attack him personally, some got the feeling that they were planning to choose a leader from among themselves.

But attacks were also being launched from outside. Gleeful press bulletins from South Africa reported Tambo's imminent resignation amid job offers ranging from Attorney General in Tanzania to a United Nations post with the Organisation of African Unity.[80] It seemed imperative to stabilise the ANC with an unequivocal decision to elect a president. In a smuggled letter to the Island in about 1976, Tambo spelt out his concerns. He wrote about 'an issue… which it seemed could only be resolved to my satisfaction at the expense of unity within our ranks and the united world support the ANC enjoys. It is the issue of a successor in office to our late President-General, AJ Luthuli'.[81]

The number of alterations in the draft letter indicated Tambo's difficulty in raising a delicate subject, but he set out the two problems that arose following the death of Chief Luthuli and his succession as Acting President:

'(a) The process or procedure by which an authentic incumbent of the office of President-General could be elected, given that the bulk of the membership was in South Africa and unable to meet, and that those outside South Africa, who could meet, were only a small fraction of the membership and that a President-General of the ANC assumes leadership of our people in general and is not a president only of members who happen to be outside South Africa. The problem was therefore, at least, how to ascertain the will of the people in the country as to who should succeed Chief AJ.

'(b) The choice of successor. Perhaps because I had been acting in a way ever since 1958 or 1960, the question of coming to grips with and solving this matter was not felt to be an urgency. My own position was that the situation should be regularised. I contended that the President-General of the ANC should continue to have a Deputy President-General outside the country.'[82]

Tambo's sensitive communication made it quite clear that Mandela was the people's choice. 'It would... be easy to measure the consensus of the masses in the country as to who should be the President-General and the whole movement would be guided, appropriately, by such a consensus. None of us outside here have any doubt as to what that consensus is... [But] what has been the matter of doubt is the wisdom of imposing on an imprisoned leader responsibility for the conduct of an armed struggle. While he cannot very well take decisions about the struggle, his assigned role would most likely remove any possibility of his release, which we are all campaigning for.'

The international context, Tambo went on to point out, also demanded a decision. Mozambique and Angola had recently achieved their independence, and friendly governments were in power. In the region, a group of Frontline States of Southern Africa had been formed, which gave the ANC liberation movements a status that placed them on a par with the presidents of independent states. But the ANC was at a disadvantage as its leader was the only Acting President among presidents of the liberation movements. These included the presidents of SWAPO, ZAPU and ZANU. The outcome was 'a tendency to relegate the South African situation to the background as something to be attended to some time in the remote future.

'The world public, in general, assumed that NR [Nelson Rolihlahla] was the president and we found it unnecessary to correct the impression, because we always made it clear that our national leaders (mine included) are on Robben Island, serving life imprisonment.'[83]

Tambo then went on to report that the National Executive Committee, at a meeting he had not attended, had taken the decision to select him President of the ANC. When he rejoined the meeting, he was 'astounded'.

'A heated argument ensued in which I challenged the right of the meeting to elect a president of the ANC. This issue was not finalised at this meeting and was raised again at a subsequent NEC meeting held in Luanda, where it became clear that I had no support whatsoever among the members. It remains a burden on my mind that I am the first and only President of the ANC to be elected by the NEC without a mandate from the available membership.'

Tambo's letter had a powerful effect. 'He saw the necessity for his position to be bolstered by that position,' recalled Maharaj. 'He was very clear that it had to be Nelson and Walter that is consulted, and that this friendship must never break. And this is exactly the mirror of Madiba because Madiba would not make a move without OR.'[84]

'In Tambo, you had a completely selfless man,' contended Joe Matthews, 'who had no personal ambitions or love of positions and so on; because Mandela was also his friend, he never tried to stop us from this campaign of making Madiba the big figure.'[85]

Soon after Maharaj was released in 1976, he was sent on to Lusaka with a message from the High Command.

'There is only one ANC,' was Nelson Mandela's communiqué, 'and that is the ANC, which has its head office in Lusaka, and whose president is OT.'[86]

The episode of the Group of Eight had clearly shaken the movement. But it had also coerced the ANC into examining more carefully the nature of its own relationship with the SACP. The Party was indeed a formidable ally, and the ANC had to be extremely skilful in riding this tiger – and who better than the adroit diplomat, the astute non-communist, Oliver Tambo, to undertake the charge. To be sure, the ANC had lost potentially valuable support through its strategic alliance with the SACP – the Cold War had, in effect, been delivered right to its very doorstep. Tambo had, for example, supported Duma Nokwe's ostentatious statement of support for the Soviet Union during its incursion on Czechoslovakia in 1968, but it did not sit well with Tambo. He admired the genuine commitment and sacrifices made by many comrades, and above all, their dedication to what he termed 'humanity', or *ubuntu*. And although the materialist philosophy of communists was at odds with Tambo's own Christianity, it was their vision of an egalitarian society, which valued people above property, that he found both inspiring and powerful, conferring an added meaning to the ANC's rather more general version of African nationalism.[87] Oliver Tambo shared with Mandela, Sisulu and others, both a respect and warm appreciation for the almost unique commitment displayed by the SACP.

'For many decades,' Mandela had pointed out in the Rivonia Trial, non-African communists 'were the only political group who were prepared to treat

Africans as human beings and their equals; who were prepared to eat with us; talk with us; live with us and work with us.'[88]

On the occasion of the ANC's sixtieth birthday in 1972, Tambo made a point of honouring the SACP's General-Secretary, Moses Mabhida, for his 'absolute loyalty' to the ANC: 'Our alliance is a living organism that has grown out of struggle,' he testified.[89]

But how powerful were the SACP members within the ANC? The Party had certainly grown in stature since the shift from mass movement to armed struggle in the liberation movement, and its underground experience, revolutionary theory and association with a world power had given it an edge. The USSR and the states within its orbit agreed to – and were in a position to deliver – financial, material and educational support for armed struggle, though the Soviet Union insisted that the assistance would have been forthcoming anyway. After all, 'no less assistance was provided to peoples' struggles in other countries where communist parties did not exist, for example, in Namibia'.[90] Nevertheless, the cooperation between the SACP and ANC was an important factor for the Soviet decision-makers.[91]

Tambo had himself undergone a political journey that had begun in the early 1950s, with the Defiance Campaign, of learning to work with anti-apartheid communists, and then becoming more intimate with the impressive minds of JB Marks and Moses Kotane and the disciplined commitment of many others after the advent of armed struggle.

For Tambo, the alliance with the SACP was a purposeful strategy. In his speech of July 1981 on the occasion of the Party's sixtieth anniversary, Tambo underlined the nature of the relationship between the SACP and the ANC. It was 'not an accident of history', he declared, nor was it 'a natural and inevitable development'.[92] Neither was assistance from the Soviet Union to the South African liberation struggle an accident. There was a long historical relationship (if sometimes contested) between the ANC and the CPSA. There were roots to its continuation in exile, now reaffirmed by material and moral assistance not forthcoming from elsewhere.

The SACP recruited a number of talented members of the ANC, and Marxist analysis permeated the movement. But the SACP's culture of discipline and tight security created a problem of perception – while the known, senior figures were disproportionately non-African, the bulk of the membership was indeed African. There was a suspicion that members secretly caucused before important ANC meetings in order to influence direction and vote their own members into power, although many vigorously denied that this was a practice in the SACP.

'It didn't operate in that way,' insisted Joe Slovo. 'I am not saying there weren't individual communists who used, and even still use, their position to try to advance sectional interests. I am sure that did happen from time to time, but certainly it wasn't the overall approach of the Party. I mean, we would have destroyed ourselves if we would have done that and certainly OR would never have accepted it. He wouldn't have stood for it.'[93]

Ben Turok confirmed this interpretation: 'We had a very mature approach to the way to work in a mass movement; that was: never force through a decision; no entryism – you never voted for a communist, you voted on merit. We were extremely careful, leaning over backwards never to offend.'[94]

Other SACP members claimed that the ANC also learnt to broaden its vision of the liberation movement through the SACP. As the first non-racial political organisation in South Africa, 'the Party shaped our non-sectarian approach to the struggle in South Africa,' observed Chris Hani.[95]

'It is often claimed by our detractors that the ANC's association with the SACP means that the ANC is being influenced by the SACP. That is not our experience,' commented Tambo a few years later. 'Our experience is that the two influence each other. Ours is not merely a paper alliance created at conference tables and formalised through the signing of documents and representing only an agreement of leaders... Ours is a living organism that has grown out of struggle. We have built it out of our common experiences.'[96]

The SACP was, arguably, as influenced by the demands of African nationalism as it was by Marxism-Leninism. This was the critique consistently put forward by the Unity Movement, which distrusted nationalism itself.

But there were others within the ANC itself who also deeply distrusted the role of the SACP in the movement. Sections of the senior and middle-level, who were not members of the SACP – as well as those who were not necessarily nationalists so much as neo-Marxists or Maoists – wanted the ANC to distance itself from the Soviet rendering of socialism.[97]

Breyten Breytenbach, who was friendly with some of the Eight, accused Tambo of being the SACP's 'useful idiot'. The indictment was greeted with outrage by those closest to Tambo. Tambo – highly intelligent, subtle and strategic – was his own man, but, conceded Albie Sachs, it was possibly true that he 'didn't have that robust conviction and ability to take swift decisions that would impact heavily on the lives of others.

'He would be willing to try radical new ideas, but his way of doing it was very much just to let it mature. Let people imbibe it, take it on, and get used to it; enrich it and develop it. If he felt membership was firmly against it, he would leave it... He would wait until its time came, and people took it as their own.'

The disadvantage of this approach was the length of time it took to reach a decision, and Tambo's concern not to simply confront members outright. 'He would be rather reluctant to take steps to reprimand and discipline people. Always understanding the problems and difficulties of person's lives and all the rest,' said Sachs. 'But in the end he wouldn't duck.'[98]

'Essentially there was no way of manipulating OR,' asserted Joe Slovo. 'Anybody who ever attended a meeting of the Revolutionary Council or the leadership structures outside, the whole of this period at the time, would be aware that at the end of the day it was OR's assessment, taking into account – and because he was a great democrat – the thinking expressed at this meeting. And he was perhaps one of the greatest listeners that I have come across... who had the talent and the capacity at the end maybe of a three-day session of the Revolutionary Council or an extended meeting of the NEC at which some of us were invited, to summarise the discussion and point the way in the most brilliant fashion in a way which kept us together, which took into account the differing views. He had the talent there that I have never seen equalled by any other person in the movement. I mean they were just gems of summary; because he would sit for three days, sometimes not taking part in the discussion at all, just making notes; and come back the next day, and then spend two hours saying; "Right, these are the issues, this is what has been said, these are the tendencies," and so on. By the end of it we felt, there is the concept. He pulled it, always pulled everything together.'[99]

Tambo's more subtle, strategic approach was not lost on the more perceptive of the younger generation. 'Watch how OR handles himself at meetings,' Thabo Mbeki advised Joe Slovo after the latter had been elected General-Secretary of the SACP – 'how he rarely speaks at the beginning of a discussion.'[100] Tambo's approach was to allow everyone a voice before he himself spoke.

But for those who were anxious to push their line, or impatient to reach rapid conclusions, Tambo's style could be misinterpreted. As Albie Sachs observed: 'Going for consensus rather than majority rule meant that you speak a little bit longer; you don't have this fierce thing of majorities and minorities, and the minority winning over some people and becoming a majority. It's a kind of core set of values and approach, and then you bring in the people. You arrive at something that gives everybody a little bit of something – and certainly a chance to be heard.'[101]

Tambo seemed not to live up to the expectations of those with a lesser sense of strategy and nuance, who expected a leader to be authoritative, if not autocratic. They did not see that Tambo's priority was to hold the movement together;

and he did this, observed Mac Maharaj, 'partly... by fudging issues. Because if he didn't fudge [them], he would not have held the movement together'. Tambo 'developed a knack of... picking some aspect of what you have said and stitching it together in a different way, but leaving everybody feeling that you had made the decision'. Tambo's style was one of pragmatic crisis management.[102]

Tambo's task in preventing the fragmentation of the movement taught him to become a skilful balancer of tendencies. In the context of the anti-imperialist struggles in Vietnam and Africa, Tambo realised that the exploration of Marxist-Leninism had become very popular. Dialectical materialism appealed to the MK youth, particularly as it offered a coherent explanation of society and conflict.

'Congress had no theory of social change other than the struggle for power,' argued the respected activist and professor, Jack Simons, one of the cadres' most popular teachers.[103] Tambo, trained as a scientist, displayed a natural caution towards what seemed to him extravagant claims by Marxists to be 'scientific socialists', yet he appreciated the theoretical and analytical skills that the SACP brought to the movement. The *Strategy and Tactics* document, for example, commissioned by Tambo, had been put together by communists, and was useful in pinpointing the weaknesses of the movement and giving direction. Its declaration that 'the main content of the present stage of the South African revolution is the national liberation of... the African people' was reminiscent of the SACP's two-stage theory of revolution.[104] SACP member Chris Hani singled out what was for him the principal achievement of the Morogoro Conference: that 'the ANC began to say the working class is the backbone of the struggle – of course, working with other classes and strata'.[105]

The ANC, as a national liberation movement, was a multiclass movement in which a range of classes had come together – the middle, the working and (to a lesser extent) the peasant classes – against a common enemy. Despite the alliance with the SACP, the 'national question' demanded that class cleavages be downplayed. This made eminent sense during the struggle against the common enemy of apartheid. But repeatedly, tensions between race and class analyses inevitably arose. The Group of Eight specifically accused 'Tambo's ANC' of 'a thinly disguised sectarian attempt to substitute a class approach for the national approach to our struggle'.[106]

But the ANC was not only a multiclass movement – it was also a multiracial movement. The race question was a more difficult one to deal with, for downplaying race in a sharply racially divided society such as South Africa was a more exacting task – to marginalise race in the struggle against apartheid seemed like evading the central issue, and the challenge of the Group of Eight could have been a serious threat to the ANC.

Tambo saw the balancing of class and race issues as a necessary condition for the success of the broad inclusive nature of a national liberation movement. At the same time, this umbrella movement also had to allow expression to both class and race struggles. Anyone who persisted in excluding either the one or the other, would themselves eventually be excluded. In his notebook on the mid-seventies, Tambo wrote: 'Widespread emphasis on importance of workers' struggle this and ensuing years. Yes. Correct. But the criticism directed at the Labour movement is that of Utopians passing simple judgements where sages would prefer balance.'[107]

A balance, that is, between struggles of class and race, the employed and unemployed, urban and rural. Tambo clearly accepted the SACP argument on the value of class but never for one moment overlooked the national struggle. 'For tactical purposes, colour analysis remains valid and there is national opposition of the blacks despite few new black recruits to the bourgeoisie', he noted.[108]

The expulsion of ideologists was to occur only once more, nearly a decade later, when a group of class analysts within the ANC wanted to eclipse race. To block either race or class was to court division and destruction. At all costs, Tambo worked to avoid such a consequence. Personal friendships, family comforts, private reservations – all had to be relinquished for the sake of holding the movement together. That, for Tambo, was the bottom line.

CHAPTER THIRTEEN

The Search for the Road Home

HOW TO GET HOME AGAIN – that had been the chief purpose of exiles who had risked all to leave South Africa. Their fervent aim had been to acquire the expertise to mobilise more effectively: to continue the struggle inside the country, to rebuild the underground and set in motion guerrilla warfare against the apartheid regime. The ANC's interactive cry itself evoked this vision: 'Let it be restored to us!' '*Mayibuye!*' was the prompting call, to which the respondents would passionately answer, '*Afrika!*'

Yet for many years, the long-awaited return of the exiles, come to pick up the fallen spear, was no closer to realisation. For the common people, a virtual iron curtain had clanged shut, shrouding the vision and the voices of those who were determined to smash apartheid. This screen obscured the political prisoners on Robben Island. But resourcefulness prevailed, and no matter how irregular, links between the political prisoners and the exile leaders were sustained.

Perhaps not surprisingly, considering the challenges facing the movement as a whole, many of the debates encountered outside had their parallels on Robben Island. At around the same time the External Mission of the ANC was experiencing differences, the political prisoners on Robben Island were also having 'hot' disagreements over strategies and tactics. These included discussions on how best to represent all the members of the Congress Alliance in prison; how to maintain unity in the context of other liberation organisations on Robben Island; awkward questions around leadership following the death of Chief Luthuli; and heated debates on the most strategic line of approach on the Bantustans. In time, these issues eventually made their way outside, just as the arguments of the Group of Eight in due course reached the prisoners. For the ANC in exile, the 'road home' most definitely included a dialogue with Robben Island.

There were at least eight different strategies to re-establish structured links inside the country. The first, the most ongoing and central, was dialogue with Robben Island; the second, the elusive attempt to establish a military presence inside the country, particularly in the 'homelands' and rural areas; and the third, to establish a political presence. And there were others.

The question of the Bantustans occupied the minds of the ANC prisoners for many years. Some were inclined to consider political solutions – including optimistic attempts to dissuade the government-appointed or sanctioned 'chiefs' from accepting apartheid's phoney 'independence' (young Chief Buthelezi was an example of an ethnic leader who might be able to beat the system by playing a double game), while some advocated working with the Bantustan opposition parties; still others sharply insisted on a total boycott of the system.

For the Mission in Exile, fine distinctions in strategic approaches did not sit comfortably with MK's pressing need to infiltrate cadres into the country's most receptive rural areas.

'The greatest single objective necessity of the South African situation today,' wrote Oliver Tambo in his notebook in 1971, 'is an effective ANC presence and direction inside the country.'[1]

Since the formation of the Revolutionary Council (RC) at the Morogoro Consultative Conference in 1969, he was pleased to note, the task of rebuilding the organisation inside had begun, and machinery had been set up to develop political structures at home. Despite police vigilance, a series of leaflet bombs had been successfully distributed in a number of cities. For Tambo, the campaign demonstrated 'indisputable evidence of the existence of the ANC inside and outside South Africa'.[2]

One of the significant decisions at Morogoro had been taken to confirm the ANC's holistic approach. The conference had resolved to do away with the parallel structures of the political and military wings of the movement in which the two threads did not intersect. It was more difficult to turn this intention into reality, however. The long distances home confounded the question of returning across hostile territory. South Africa was surrounded by a broad *cordon sanitaire* of colonial or economically dependent states on its borders. The inability of the Wankie and Sipolilo incursions to get cadres home demonstrated the difficulties of penetrating this barrier. But Tambo knew that the way home was an ongoing process, rather than any single dramatic 'Big Bang' event. The plan was to continue to infiltrate MK cadres into the most receptive rural areas adjacent to the borders of South Africa.

It had, after all, been rural resistance to the 1951 Bantu Authorities Act that had put armed struggle on the agenda. The transfer of the chiefs' accountability from the people to the apartheid government had resurrected the centuries-old, simmering anger over the dispossession of the land. The Zoutpansberg and Zeerust areas, Sekhukhuneland, Natal, as well as Pondoland, were all affected. In exile, Tambo's speeches to the ANC regularly invoked ancestral chiefs who had resisted the desecration of colonialism.

During the 1900s, homestead economies were further battered by commercial agriculture and an increased demand for migrant labour. Pass laws were being applied more ruthlessly and 'surplus' people were forcibly moved to rural camps such as Limehill, Dimbaza, Onverwacht and Sada. Apartheid's determined attempt to clear the cities of those black people who were deemed not productive to the white economy aggravated overcrowding on the land, reducing rural productivity to below subsistence levels. As late as 1976, the Minister of Bantu Administration and Development was continuing to reiterate apartheid dictates:

'All Bantu persons in the white area, whether they were born there or not, remain members of their respective nations. In other words, the fact that they work here does not make them members of the white nation – they remain Zulu, Tswana, Venda and so on. The basis on which the Bantu is present in the white areas is to sell their labour here and for nothing else.'[3]

As a result, the reserves were, in the words of Ben Turok in his analysis of the strategic problems facing the ANC,[4] becoming 'rural slums ruled by indifferent officials using the harshest of regulations'. The function of the Bantustans, it was clear, was to stockpile labour managed through pass laws and the migrant labour system. The land struggles of the 1950s were still fresh in the memories of the External Mission and the struggle was 'a people's struggle for land, for control of territory and administration,' Tambo wrote.[5]

But they were also well aware that ever since the leadership had shifted predominantly to the urban, educated elite, the rural constituency eluded the ANC. Now here again was an opportunity to mobilise the peasantry.

'The rural areas are a priority', wrote Tambo, summing up the feeling of the Revolutionary Council. With less policing in the countryside and the still coherent but disaffected communities there, it might be 'easier to reach the masses and more difficult for the enemy to have a presence'. By contrast, armed actions in the urban areas would have to be limited to 'basically armed propaganda; can't grow beyond doing protest actions'.[6]

But again, both town and countryside were locked into the migrant labour system – yet it was just this contradiction of the apartheid system that created great potential for revolutionary consciousness to be spread from the cities to the countryside by workers returning home to their villages. During the women's pass campaigns in the 1950s, such a political message had been carried home powerfully in Zeerust, with notable consequences.

'Keep it going in the cities while you organise in the rural areas,' had been Tambo's advice in his summing up of an RC discussion. 'Open up in the rural areas with rural men. Surround the cities. Urban struggle has never led to the seizure of power' – at least, 'never of its own'.[7]

It seemed to the Revolutionary Council that the Bantustan, or 'homeland', system had created a situation against which peasants would not need much more than practical encouragement to respond to a call to arms. According to the 'detonator' thesis (which the RC criticised but did not seem to be able to free itself from in practice), once the arrival of MK became known on the ground, resistance against the apartheid oppressors would spontaneously swell up from below and rapidly spread across the length and breadth of the land.

There were immense difficulties, though. Tambo listed the obstacles: the lack of facilities from neighbouring countries; the ad hoc improvisation and underground preparations needed; the need at home for much more propaganda and rural guerrilla development; the uneven development in the urban areas, and the shortage of ordinance and finance.[8]

It was conceded that liberation would take much longer than had previously been hoped, especially as South Africa's neighbours were still struggling for their own freedom against colonisation. The RC began to plan several operations to get their cadres back home. The key points of entry, they agreed, would be the areas that had developed a tradition of resistance to apartheid – the north and the Eastern Cape were more accessible because they bordered neighbouring states or the Indian Ocean. In the first case, land incursions would once again be attempted; in the latter, a bold sea invasion was being formulated.

Flag Boshielo, who had always manifested a pioneering spirit, led one of the earliest post-Morogoro expeditions and had headed the first Johannesburg unit in the Defiance Campaign in 1952.[9] In the 1940s, young Boshielo had migrated from Sekhukhuneland, found work in Johannesburg as a gardener and joined the Communist Party and the ANC. In the course of his political work, through his 'home-boy' networks in the white suburbs and the hostels, he helped to found Sebatakgomo – the rural Sekhukhune resistance movement. Boshielo went into exile in the early sixties and was part of the cadreship that had set up camp at Kongwa and planned the Wankie campaign. Frustrated by the failure to cross the border, in 1970 Boshielo led another small contingent to cross Rhodesia to reach Sekhukhuneland and organise underground units there. But he and his companions were ambushed and killed crossing the Zambezi River, and it was years before their families knew what had happened to them.[10]

Further attempts to infiltrate South Africa were made at the border posts, with varying results – James April, a Wankie *mgwenya*, managed to slip through using forged papers, but was eventually caught in Durban. Another detachment led by Josiah Jele (30 years later, the South African ambassador to the UN) attempted to infiltrate via the Nyasa province in Mozambique. After six weeks under the protection of Frelimo fighters, Jele and his group began to move further south, but were ambushed and barely managed to return to their base. Another group spent five weeks in the Kabo-Delgado province but had to abandon their expedition. The ANC concluded that 'to pass to South Africa through Mozambique was an impossible task'.[11]

Sea invasions were another possibility, which would have the element of surprise as an added advantage. Parts of the east coast fell into 'homeland', rural areas that were not directly policed by the South African government. The northern coast of Natal, once the terrain of resistance against British colonialism, was targeted as a possible site for such an operation. In 1968/9 the ANC women's leader Dorothy Nyembe and 11 other MK guerrillas were arrested, tried and sentenced to long periods of imprisonment. Nyembe received 15 years for 'harbouring terrorists'.

In 1972, MK approved a project, code-named 'Operation J', to land highly trained cadres on the east coast of South Africa. Two left-wing internationalists unknown to the apartheid intelligence, Alex Moumbaris and Sean Hosey, were briefed to courier information through to South Africa. The plan was executed under Tambo's authority. Together with comrades inside, they would provide transportation, contact local peasants and begin organising a military force that would be ready to meet the MK force due to land on the Transkei coast. It was an ambitious project, involving landing craft and the secret flotation of weaponry, as well as careful step-by-step preparations with the aid of Soviet admirals and generals. An old cargo ship, the *Aventura*, was bought in the Mediterranean and sailed round to Somalia, where the 25 MK guerrillas were waiting to embark. But the project encountered difficulties from the beginning. First, the captain and then the crew proved to be unreliable and had to be replaced. Eventually, the boat's engine, repaired before departure, broke down too.

Tambo's response to the whole venture startled his comrades. Joe Slovo, deeply involved in the preparations, recalled the story in detail. One evening before the departure date, the planning group received a request from Tambo.

'I remember sitting in Moscow with admirals and generals from the Soviet armed forces who were helping us in this... [We] had spent four, five days. Chris [Hani] was there – Dadoo was there as well... Mabhida – and we then had finished all our consultations, all the complications about radio contact – of course, we had sent people inside the country to be on the beaches and so on and so forth. It was really a very sophisticated project which we had with the people who knew what they were doing... We eventually finished all these consultations, we had our dinner and OR said that he wants a special meeting now. And he said he hadn't slept the night before because the whole process was to begin within a day or two…

'He had been seriously thinking about whether he has the right to give a go-ahead of this plan unless he is part of it. And he said that he wants to be part of the landing party. He wants to be part of the landing party!... [The] landing was going to be in an area very near to his home, as one of the landing points, and he says he wants to go now to Mogadishu to join the group that is already there and to land with them, and to lead them.

'And we were astonished by this. And we all of course said, "You know, at this point in time to risk you on what we can't be 100 per cent certain, it could go wrong." And we said, "On no account."

'You know, it's the first time and the last time that I have ever seen [such a response] – he broke down and he wept. Tears were just streaming. It was phenomenal, it was absolutely so genuine. He couldn't expect others to risk their lives because this was the real, first big thing, and he is the leader; and he feels you've got to be there; and he tried to talk us into accepting that because this was his area. It was Pondoland, you see, and he knew the place; he would be able to play a positive role and, in addition, if things did go wrong it wasn't just the leader sending other people.

'And this, I think, more than anything, is an indication of what OR was about... It was absolutely from his soul. It is difficult to recreate this sort of passion with which he raised this point. And he was angry for days with what had been decided.'[12]

Tambo's intimate knowledge of the territory seemed to coincide perfectly with his longing to return home and participate directly in the struggle. Subsequent to the rejection of his proposal, throughout the continuing planned incursions into rural areas in years to come, Tambo expressed doubt about simple reliance on maps as against prior experience of the terrain:

'Start off with no experience, no contact, no knowledge of political set up, enemy depositories. We start off with a map? *Not again*,' he wrote in his notebook. 'Can you open up a guerrilla region? *No*. Can we wait for development of internal policy? *No*.'

There were alternatives, though. Far better, he insisted, to identify local comrades before embarking on a new project: 'Send one, two or possibly three people for a short reconnaissance in terrain for two/three weeks. Examine whether bigger group can survive.'[13]

The small advance group selected, wrote Oliver Tambo, should be regarded 'first and foremost' as 'politically conscious, politically trained persons, under the political direction of a political commissar'. Anyone who was to be selected for such reconnaissance work should take age and occupation into account, as well as fill Tambo's criteria of having a knowledge of the operational area, the language, local politics and individual contacts. In fact, Tambo felt that he, himself, was an ideal candidate for Operation J.

As it happened, Tambo would not have succeeded in landing in his beloved countryside. One of the guerrillas was apprehended and, under severe torture, revealed the whereabouts of his comrades. Moumbaris was identified even before he entered South Africa at the Botswana border, while Hosey walked into a trap set by the Special Branch. The commander of the operation, Lemmy Booi, and *mgwenya* Justice Mpanza were also arrested. They received 15 years. Moumbaris, it was revealed during his trial, had been slipping in and out of South Africa since 1967, transporting literature and materials for the movement, and had once even managed to unfurl an ANC banner from a building in Durban.[14] In 1979, he was again to make sensational news when, together with two other white political prisoners, Tim Jenkins and Stephen Lee, he escaped from Pretoria Central Prison and successfully made his way to France. Tambo held a press conference to welcome them to Lusaka, confirming during this time of contestation the value of non-racial resources.

'The ANC has in its ranks people who are fighting together across the race and colour line, and who sacrifice together in that struggle.'[15]

In the meantime, the evidence was that something indeed seemed to be stirring inside the country. After the assassination by Demetrio Tsafendas of Prime Minister HF Verwoerd, the intellectual 'architect' of apartheid, his successor JB Vorster kept his old portfolio as Minister of Police. 'We are no longer dealing with Red ideology,' he warned the white parliament, 'but with Red arms.'[16]

The sixties had seen game attempts to revive the underground, but Bram Fischer in the Transvaal and the lawyer Griffiths Mxenge in Natal had been apprehended and sentenced to long terms of imprisonment. Mxenge was released in 1969 and, undeterred, began again slowly and carefully to rebuild underground structures in Natal. In the Transvaal, Mandela's wife Winnie organised members of the ANC who had remained behind to produce and distribute leaflets about the movement, but they were arrested, betrayed by a police informer who had infiltrated Winnie's circle. Those arrested included SACTU trade unionists Samson Ndou, Lawrence and Rita Ndzanga, Joyce Sikhakhane and Solomon Pholoto – 22 in all. In a two-year ordeal from May 1969, they were detained, tortured, tried (in what was known as the Trial of the Twenty-Two), acquitted and then redetained under Vorster's new Terrorism Act and the Suppression of Communism Act.[17]

The public was learning of the ANC mainly through newspaper reports of the detentions and trials of those caught or those who gave evidence as 'turned' state witnesses. Ironically, both despite these failures and because of their publicity, popular propaganda for the ANC was filtering down to grass roots.

Two SACP members of the Revolutionary Council based in London – Yusuf Dadoo and Joe Slovo – helped to generate more political activity inside. Despite the focus of the ANC on armed struggle, the exclusion of many of its non-African members from the continent forced them to concentrate on means other than military in contacting home. In a sense, London was closer to South Africa than Tanzania because of greater traffic to and from South Africa, and its easier access to the many South African students studying in Europe. A crop of young white activists such as Raymond Suttner, Jeremy Cronin, Tim Jenkins, Stephen Lee, David and Sue Rabkin and Tony Holiday were recruited and, through the SACP, trained by Ronnie Kasrils.[18] These recruits were instructed to avoid any legal or semilegal oppositional work. The Party decided to take advantage of these favourable factors and attempt to create limited structures that could begin to publish underground literature, leaflet bombs, comic books and other items of propaganda. The Moumbaris banner and others, such as that unfurled outside Johannesburg's Rissik Street post office announcing 'ANC Lives', were public indications of the presence of the ANC.[19]

In 1971, Tambo wrote: 'The improved contact we have been able to make with our people inside, following the formation of the RC and its machinery, the series of leaflets distributed successfully despite police vigilance, the indisputable evidence of the existence of the ANC inside and outside South Africa, despite the racist government's offensive to destroy it – all these have not only helped sustain the morale of the masses of the people, but have also encouraged them to engage in open, unrestrained political attacks against the ruling regime, such as have not been experienced since the early sixties. This is true with regard to non-white workers, peasants, the youth and intellectuals, clerics, etc. The result is that a state of political ferment prevails among the oppressed masses and has produced conflicts and divisions within the white ruling class. A situation thus exists in South Africa that offers great possibilities for building a powerful underground political movement and of which every possible advantage must be taken.'[20]

The context in which activists risked their freedom – and lives – continued to deteriorate. The Terrorism Act allowed suspects to be held incommunicado indefinitely. Tortures and deaths in detention became routine. The news of this mounting brutality inside apartheid's prisons haunted Tambo.

'We who are free to eat and sleep at will, to write, to speak, to travel as we please,' he exhorted all South Africans outside the country, 'we who are free to make or break a revolution, let us use our comparative freedom... for rallying to the banners of the ANC and consolidating our ranks when danger threatens.'[21]

A few weeks later in 1971, Ahmed Timol, caught in a roadblock with a packet of ANC leaflets, was thrown out of the tenth-floor window of an interrogation room. Many more deaths followed. Underground activity, whose task it was to unlock mass struggle, was becoming increasingly dangerous and difficult.

'The underground activist is a social outcast isolated in his network of close associates,' wrote Ben Turok in 1974. 'Contact between ruler and ruler is broken and the activists are consequently subjected to even more extreme forms of repression, including torture and detention, to enable the police to break into the underground network.'[22]

Tambo was convinced, though, that conditions on the ground could sustain resistance. Up to the early 1970s, while the South African apartheid economy was expanding, the gap between black and white workers marginally narrowed. During this time, the black working class grew correspondingly and the growing manufacturing industry was becoming increasingly dependent on cheap labour. The economic tide began to turn when the international price of oil increased dramatically. Inflation swelled as a result, leading to a squeeze on profits in the gold mines and the factories, and the barely subsistent wages of black workers were sorely affected. In 1973, a relatively spontaneous general strike by 100 000 black workers hit Durban's industry. The immediate cause was the rejection by workers of the new Bantu Regulation Amendment Act, which attempted to impose factory-based liaison committees instead of trade unions on African workers. Certain informal organisations such as the student-based Wages Commission at the University of Natal and the Black Consciousness Movement may have influenced the strike,[23] but unbeknown to these activist-academics was the input of covert SACTU sympathisers such as Beksise Nxasana, one of the founders of the influential *South African Labour Bulletin*, who also acted as translator of *Isisebenzi*, a workers' news sheet produced by the new worker organisations.[24] At least eight others, including Harry Gwala and William Khanyile who were subsequently detained, were part of the underground that had links with SACTU.[25] Chris Hani, who was deployed to Lesotho in 1975, said meetings with various trade unionists had been taking place since 1973.

'But our approach was that, whatever, we must form one federation in South Africa. We should bring together, weld together, all these tendencies.'[26]

'Once again, the African Workers are coming to the fore as a great force to be reckoned with,' reported SACTU excitedly to Tambo and the NEC in 1974. In its analysis, the report saw the demands put forward by the workers as markedly new in the history of African trade-union struggles: 'The workers show a qualitative change in their political awareness – and this needs to be developed. It is here where not only SACTU but the whole machinery of the Liberation Movement must concentrate their efforts. A way must be found to create political cells in the factories, apart from shop stewards.'[27]

But one of the major drawbacks was the lack of skilled organisers. 'I [probably Moses Mabhida] think the time has come for the ANC to appeal to African teachers and intellectuals to begin to associate themselves with the struggle of our people. Teachers must help in the drafting of letters and memos on behalf of those African trade unionists who did not get sufficient education. I believe the fault in this regard is with us in the liberation movement.'[28]

Once again, this was a pointer towards the deficiencies of placing the armed struggle centre stage without preparing the political ground. In the event, the ANC's inadequacy allowed mostly white radical students, influenced by the New Left movement, to become the proactive force in the democratic labour movement – a pressure group that was suspicious of SACTU (which they saw as allowing the trade unions to become subservient to the ANC and thus losing the opportunity to lead workers into class struggle after the ANC was banned). As a result, the strategy of many of the new worker organisations was to forswear direct confrontation with the apartheid system in favour of challenging the bosses exclusively in the workplace, on both economic issues and for the empowerment of trade unions. Political confrontations were premature, they argued pragmatically, until worker organisations grew strong enough to take on the state.

The labour movement continued to grow rapidly throughout the seventies. In the background, attempting to permeate the infant unions in Natal, were ANC members such as the union organiser Zodwa Skosana and ex-Robben Islanders Judson Khuzwayo and Jacob Zuma, who had been released in 1973. In addition, the latter were also setting up an underground transport and courier route from Natal to Swaziland.

Possibilities also surfaced on the educational front. Naturally, conditions in schools, colleges and universities were of particular interest to Oliver Tambo. The birth of the South African Students' Organisation (SASO) was marked by the breakaway in 1965 of a group of black students led by Steve Biko, who was also a member of the liberal Students' Christian Movement. Tambo noted the event with interest. He was, of course, aware of black student clashes with university administrations and police in the early 1970s and how these had foiled the idea of apartheid strategists that black consciousness was consistent with their grand plan. Acknowledging their mistake, the government banned Steve Biko, Barney Pityana (a Christian activist who was part of a growing network of church members wanting to explore the decolonisation of Christianity and help shape social change through black theology) and other leaders in 1972.

Many of the activities that emerged in the 1970s aroused the deep hostility of the state, and in 1973 a commission was appointed to probe into the affairs of the University Christian Movement, the National Union of South African Students, the Christian Institute and the South African Institute of Race Relations. Perhaps intelligence had picked up the fact that a couple of years earlier, Tambo had personally proposed 'that the NEC takes steps to keep all South African students outside South Africa fully informed on the trends and developments in the political situation in our country.

'The establishment of the South African Students' Organisation, whose main aims are to unite all Black students to project the true image and dignity of the Black man, and to assert the right and ability of the Black man to lead wherein the past he followed white leadership, is a welcome and necessary trend in the situation prevailing in our country.'[29]

'This was the sort of thing that [the ANC] had encouraged all the time – student activism,' observed Lindelwe Mabandla, a former leader in SASO at the University of the North.[30] 'In other words, they didn't wait until they saw that SASO was now successful, and then made a beeline for the leadership. I think that is something that they continuously tried to develop.'

While Steve Biko himself, according to Bridgitte Mabandla (also a SASO member), was determined to retain the independence of the organisation, 'he was quite firm in his idea that this is not simply a kind of stepchild of the PAC – it is a students' movement and it is not within the space of these organisations'. Nevertheless Biko 'had enormous respect for the ANC leadership outside as well as those who were inside. In fact, there were many, many occasions where there were interactions between Steve and a number of ANC people inside the country'.

Oliver Tambo was equally encouraging of white NUSAS students' opposition activities in the universities of Cape Town and the Witwatersrand at the time. 'NUSAS research: good. Would like to get some of them doing our research. Where are any reports by them?' And on hearing of their work on wages and removals, he wrote, 'Can we have some?'[31]

Whenever possible, Tambo would make a point of meeting anyone coming out of South Africa, showing personal interest and concern. Sometimes he would surprise newcomers by knowing a lot more about them than they had imagined.[32] He would question comrades about conditions at home. Tambo was, as many confirmed, 'a particularly solicitous leader'.[33] When Jacob Zuma met Tambo three years after his release from prison in 1973, he briefed Tambo in Maputo. It was, said Zuma, an exhaustive report on 'what we had been doing inside the country, the structures that I had established, even how I left Swaziland [and got] back into the country without anybody knowing... quite a detailed briefing I gave, because I thought this is the man who ought to know his organisation in and out... He gave me also a very thorough briefing... From him I got a very clear insight of what was happening, and how he had gone through'.[34]

This approach, Tambo felt, was far more fruitful than risking the lives of cadres dispatched to South Africa for reconnoitring purposes. When, in an RC meeting, it was suggested that they 'send someone in for a short trip', Tambo responded, 'No, better that someone comes out to ask questions and get policy guidance.'[35]

The early to mid-seventies saw a considerable flow of students from the country as a result of SASO strikes and the punitive responses at Turfloop and other apartheid 'bush colleges', as anti-apartheid activists dismissively called them. The students fled to neighbouring states such as Botswana, Lesotho and Swaziland. But older people represented the ANC's forward area structures, and there was a growing feeling in the leadership that they would need younger cadres to relate to these BC-oriented students. Lindelwe and Bridgitte Mabandla were working under cover in Botswana, while Thabo Mbeki, Albert Dhlomo and Jacob Zuma (who made frequent trips in and out of South Africa) were posted to Swaziland. Other ex-prisoners reactivating the underground included Harry Gwala (released in 1972), Judson Khuzwayo and Jacob Zuma (released in 1973) and Shadrack Maphumulo (released in 1974) in Natal. In the Transvaal were Joe Gqabi (released in 1975) and Martin Ramokgadi (also released in 1973).[36] The Natal cell was developing contacts with the emerging labour movement and was fully expecting a blow-up to occur in the unions there.[37] This expectation was not surprising – in 1974 alone there were 194 'illegal strikes' involving almost 39 000 African workers, reported the Minister of Labour to Parliament. There were 'no lawful strikes' in that year, he added.[38]

Overtly, the political pace was accelerating. News of South Africa's abortive raid on Angola, and MK support for the elected MPLA, though suppressed at home, spread by mouth as well as through leaflets smuggled into the country. White supremacy, it seemed, was being challenged throughout the continent.

'Nothing can hide the fact that White South Africa is in irreversible crisis,' proclaimed the ANC message. 'Vorster thought he could send his army into Angola and place his stooges in power, but the MPLA thrashed him in battle and sent his White soldiers and stooges flying.'[39]

The overthrow of the dictatorship in Portugal in 1974 had led almost immediately to the independence of Angola and Mozambique, opening up new potentially friendly frontline states from which the ANC could operate. With the establishment of the new government of Frelimo in an independent Mozambique, the mood inside South Africa was exultant. Jittery, the apartheid regime was determined to send a clear message. When SASO and the BPC called for pro-Frelimo rallies nationwide, arrests of these organisations' leaders followed shortly afterwards. Charged with promoting racial hostility, at the end of a long trial, the accused received five- and six-year sentences and were promptly despatched to Robben Island. In 1975, a number of white students were detained as a result of Breytenbach's illegal entry into South Africa. In that same year, Raymond Suttner, then a university lecturer at the University of Natal, Durban, and two students were charged, after suffering grotesque torture, under the Suppression of Communism Act.[40] At the end of the year, four NUSAS students and a lecturer were arrested and charged for calling for the release of political prisoners.[41] The following year the other two underground cells of white intellectual activists, trained by Kasrils, were busted. They were discovered to have been distributing thousands of leaflets and letters by way of bucket bombs at railway stations and bus stops. They were detained, tortured, tried and sentenced to 7 to 10 years' imprisonment.

'[A] new generation of young revolutionaries, embracing all races, is beginning to take to the political battlefield,' Tambo informed an extended consultative meeting of the NEC in 1975. 'The demand for the release of the people's leaders from imprisonment has taken firm root in the country.'[42]

In early 1976, ANC and SACTU cadre Joseph Mdluli was arrested in Durban. Three days later, he was dead. He had suffered 'extensive bruising, a fractured thyroid, fractured ribs and brain haemorrhage'.[43] Another 18 people were to die in detention in the next 20 months. Steve Biko was one of these victims.[44] In May, six ex-Robben Island prisoners, including Harry Gwala, were accused under the Terrorism Act of recruiting people to join the ANC or to undergo military training abroad.[45] They were tried in Pietermaritzburg. A similar trial against S Ndebele, P Tshabalala and T Mashamba (for attempting to recruit) played itself out in Turfloop in the north, while five men in the Transkei were sentenced from two to four years under the Suppression of Communism Act.[46] In Pretoria, 12 men were charged under the Terrorism and

Internal Security Act, and in Randburg and Cape Town dozens were apprehended, tried and sentenced. Through the 'snowball' effect of torture, this led to more names and even more detentions. In the Eastern Cape there were also three trials involving PAC members, but it was the ANC by far that dominated the political courts. The Minister of Justice, Jimmy Kruger, boasted that the remnants of the internal ANC were now crushed. Nevertheless, the trials proceeded in packed courts. The image of the ANC thus became increasingly prominent, especially in the minds of would-be activists.

Clearly, political expectations among the oppressed were rising. Tambo asked his Executive in 1975, 'Do we belong to the past? Are we properly marching with the time?' He recalled how, at the time of the formation of MK, ANC leaders had had to consider the possibility that unless they acted swiftly other forces could capture the moment. The emerging situation 'could be used by somebody else, who would ignite the fire'.[47]

Meanwhile, in Swaziland the authorities, leaned on by South Africa, detained and expelled the ANC representatives to Maputo. Tambo was planning to replace them when the situation in Soweto schools flared up. Since Tambo's departure and the internal rupture with the ANC, the calculated exclusion of black children from the field of knowledge had bred an entire new generation of Bantu Education offspring. Conditions in black schools had deteriorated significantly. By 1975, the state was spending R42 per year for every black school-going child, while each white child received R591 of the state's resources.[48] Black teacher training colleges – authoritarian and dogmatic – were often staffed by unmotivated white lecturers, who turned out inadequately prepared and underqualified teachers. Under the Bantu Education system, black teachers continued to be grossly underpaid – in 1975 a black female secondary-school teacher, for example, was earning the equivalent of an unskilled worker's wage at R108 per month.[49] The most talented and committed teachers had already begun their wholesale exodus from the profession since the introduction of Bantu Education in the 1950s. In 1961, 36.3 per cent of secondary- and high-school teachers had university degrees; by 1974, this figure had dropped to 1.56 per cent.[50] Classrooms were shamefully overcrowded, and it was common for teachers to work double shifts in a day. Phefeni Secondary, from which the June 16 protests originated, had a teacher-pupil ratio of 1:300 for some subjects.[51] The most basic school equipment was often absent, while commissioned school textbooks were carefully vetted for their ideological content. Methodologically, Bantu Education relied on rote learning, which actively hindered the skills of critical thinking. In many township schools, it was common knowledge that quisling teachers were bribed to spy on their colleagues. Teachers who became too much of a nuisance – such as Victor Wessels in Cape Town – were dismissed or transferred to some isolated village to neutralise them.[52]

Although its influence was not widespread in the schools, the Black Consciousness Movement (BCM) was beginning to make an impact on young people disenchanted with the 'apolitical and ineffective' social organisations among the youth.[53] A schools organisation, the African Students' Movement, had developed in Soweto in the late sixties around issues such as a campaign for Student Representative Councils, a demand for less high-handed control by the teaching and administrative staff, and a call for more serious attention to academic subjects. In 1972, this student organisation changed its name to the South African Students' Movement (SASM), in acknowledgement that there was a need to form an alliance with other black students. It began to work with the Black Community Project to promote self-help programmes – small-scale literacy campaigns, building schools, clinics and community centres, and co-operative bulk buying. The BCM (much like the ANC 'go-it-alone' Youth League a generation earlier) advocated psychological independence from whites: 'Black man, you are on your own', they admonished. In 1972 Onkgopotse Tiro, a past president of the Students' Representative Council at the blacks-only Turfloop University in the Northern Transvaal, was expelled for attacking, in a speech at a student assembly, the discriminatory education and apartheid system – an event reminiscent of Robert Sobukwe's speech at Fort Hare. A boycott of lectures followed and the university was closed. The boycott spread. (A few years later, Tiro was killed by a parcel bomb in Botswana.)

'We are talking of the mid-seventies, a period of very high repression,' recalled Ngoako Ramathlodi, a student at Turfloop in 1976. 'The regime was in total control, there was no doubt about it: their rule held sway, organisations were banned but, you see, a very interesting thing was – and this does not come out in the history of South Africa as clearly as it should – that the form of protest shifted from political activism to the arts in that period… the period just before '76; what had become the most popular form of political expression in townships was drama and poetry.'[54]

Poets and playwrights, artists, actors and writers, like Mothobi Mutloatse, Ingwapele Madingwane, Matsemela Manaka, Jacky Seroke, Thami Nyele, Wally Serote, Achmed Dangor, and Gibson Kente (whose play, *How Long?* was being performed before packed audiences in the townships) and many others, were to make their mark in the eventful years that followed.[55]

'[The] message they were putting across was very powerful. It changed a lot of people. And people would pay to go and see those dramas. People would pay to go and listen to poets reading their poetry.'[56]

Increasingly, students were becoming aware of the bigger picture of the oppression and exploitation of black people. In September 1973 black and white students protested across the country against the Anglo-American Corporation after 152 mineworkers were killed in a clash with the police. In the wider region, in addition to the independence of Mozambique and Angola, the liberation struggles in Zimbabwe and Namibia were intensifying. And as the first intake of 1960s' Robben Island prisoners were released, some young intellectuals were becoming exposed to seasoned political activists. Undeterred by the risks, they joined the ANC underground.

Then tragedy struck the people of Soweto. Protests had been building up for two or three months prior to 16 June 1976. An ad hoc organising committee, headed by Tsietsie Mashinini of SASM at Morris Isaacson High School, planned a march to the Orlando police station to protest against the imposition of Afrikaans-medium instruction in some of their subjects. On the day, thousands of children gathered in the streets, converging on Orlando West Junior Secondary. They were in a jovial mood, shouting slogans, waving placards and singing 'Nkosi Sikelel' iAfrika'. As they passed other schools, they called on pupils to join them. At mid-morning, 10 vans filled with white and black policemen drew up. They were armed and carried megaphones, which they made no attempt to use. Suddenly, a white policeman strode up and fired tear gas into the crowd. Angrily, some students began to throw stones. Then three shots rang out. A child crumpled in the dust. The throng began to scatter in all directions. Others were paralysed with fear. Then the police dogs charged and the students were galvanised into action. They stoned one of the dogs and it died. For the rest of the day, children moved in groups throughout Soweto. Some took the wounded to hospital, others marched to the buildings of the West Rand Administration Board and set fire to it and to police vehicles. Their anger was fanning out against other aspects of government oppression. They broke into bottle stores, seized the liquor on the shelves and poured it into the gutters. 'We can no longer tolerate seeing our fathers' pay-packet emptied in shebeens,' they said.[57] They built barricades, highjacked bakery vans, set them alight and distributed the bread to bystanders. Police reinforcements spread out in large numbers, shooting with submachine guns and rifles into crowds. Bodies lay scattered in the streets. On a wall facing the main road, Orlando High School students, undeterred, painted the ANC slogan – 'Victory is Certain!' And 'Orlando MPLA'.

School students had for years walked past the homes of absent heroes, now incarcerated on Robben Island, or those driven into exile, where they were said to be training in military camps to return to liberate their people. The publication of any documentation or information about banned organisations or individuals was forbidden. But oral history and popular memory survived. Passing schoolchildren attending Phefeni Junior Secondary, or Morris Isaacson and other schools in the neighbourhood, were able to point out the homes of Walter Sisulu and Nelson Mandela and others in Orlando.[58] These men were an enduring, silent testimony to the younger generation. Their wives and families still lived there.

Around 1974/5, political prisoners who received 10-year sentences during the Rivonia upheavals were being released. A number of young people made it their concern, however risky, to discuss political history and principles with these veterans and other known activists such as Lawrence and Rita Ndzanga.[59]

The newborn communications between students and the banned organisations were still fragile, and the ANC was entirely unprepared for the far-reaching and historic event on 16 June, manifestly equal to Sharpeville. If anything, it was immediately apparent that this was a phenomenon even more dramatic – Pallo Jordan spoke about 'the sort of veldfire effect of the mass uprisings'.[60] It spread from centre to centre to centre in a matter of a few weeks, in some cases days. 'This was unlike anything one had seen in the past,' Jordan observed. 'In the past what had happened would be that the key urban centres would come out on strike – that was what one had seen in the 1950s and '60s – two days, three days, one day or whatever, key centres would come out and that would be the form that the demonstration would take. Occasionally associated with such events there might be scattered incidents of street fighting here, there but it wasn't a sort of national pattern. In 1976, we saw this as a pattern in almost every major urban area and even in a number of the smaller ones as well.'[61]

On 19 June, for example, the students of Turfloop began a stayaway. The university authorities called in government forces, and a serious confrontation followed. Ramathlodi maintained that it was on that day that he was 'initiated almost fully into political activism'. At least two students died, thrown from upper-floor windows.

'The helicopters were flying. It was like a battlefield, except that one side was armed, the other had stones. Of course the university was closed temporarily, and then I came back home. I came to Tembisa. When I arrived here, I found that the township was smouldering in fire. People were dying, so we joined the battles in the township… you know '76 never really stopped. It continued.'[62]

Throughout the country, hundreds of young people were detained and tortured – including many of the SASM leadership – in an attempt to root out the shadowy figures behind what the authorities were certain was an orchestrated conspiracy.

But this was not quite the case. The truth was less tangible. MK's attempts to reach home had been focused on the rural terrain. Despite the 15 years of intensive, training abroad, no secretly trained urban guerrillas were ready to spring into action in the townships at this historic moment. On the contrary, by the end of July 1976 the ANC had organised charter planes to accommodate several hundred young people from within South Africa and place them in either MK or (for the minority who preferred to continue their academic studies) in training institutions in Africa or overseas.

On the other hand, even the ANC was not able to grasp the extent of its own penetration in the communities, and the widening climate of political consciousness it had helped to build. Pallo Jordan, who became involved in the ANC propaganda machinery after 1976, was aware of some stirrings:

'I think many of [ANC members] don't realise that that whole period – '72 to '76 and even after – there had been a continuing dialogue with individuals, leading figures in the Black Consciousness Movement, which had assisted in beginning to build some sort of infrastructure.

'Now, of course, the thing about the Black Consciousness Movement was that it was mainly located in the universities, not very much in the communities, even less so in trade unions. But, at the same time, too, the self-mobilisation of the working class made possible the establishment of core groups in various parts of the country to do trade union work, which assisted in the whole process. Many of these were experienced unionists and that, in turn of course, fed the underground with working-class cadres. But the core groups were, I think, the important seedbeds for the future wave of underground recruits, activists and others, and played, I think, a very, very important role in this period in terms of providing political training and experience to the sort of cadreship who, I think, came into their own in the period after '76, when the mass democratic movement now actually began to consolidate itself.'

But for observers both inside and outside the ANC, June 16 was 'a missed opportunity'.[63] In the event, the handful of ANC underground operatives – comprising 'perhaps 50 formal units, totalling perhaps 200 people'[64] – was able to make some headway in the weeks and months that followed. Joe Gqabi's clandestine visitors, for example, increased dramatically in number. If not in practice, at least in propaganda, the MK was reaching ordinary people. Young people had heard about MK, and leaflets were now calling them to arms. Thousands left home to join the armed struggle. Others, driven out of school, wanted to further their education. Fifteen months later, the United Nations Commission for Refugees reported that 3 000 South African student refugees were seeking refuge in southern African states. The Nigerian government, Lesotho and some of the socialist countries also provided scholarships. In the latter case, the ANC, it was known, provided access to these resources and dreams. The Freedom Train was stoking up its old engines again to transport the 'June 16 Detachment' to their destination.

In 1976, Totsi Memela, a student representative at Diepkloof, was in her tenth year of schooling. One of the witnesses to the events on 16 June, she left for Swaziland the following year to continue her education and was officially recruited into the ANC. In time, she was also able to take a degree at the university. Totsi became a courier for the movement, skipping in and out of South Africa with crucial information, and was among those fortunate enough never to be caught.[65] Tony 'Gabs' Msimang, who was eventually to become a driver and bodyguard for Tambo, was another recruit. Gabs was only 15 years old in 1976 and lived in Mamelodi, a township that serviced white Pretoria. The youngest of six, Gabs's role model was his eldest brother Dennis, who, despite his working-class background, had managed to enrol at Fort Hare and was studying economics there. He had himself been involved in a student strike just prior to the Soweto uprising, and urged his younger brother to support the protest movement. On the day that Gabs joined a march to denounce the events in Soweto, he saw his closest friend shot dead by the police, and vowed to consecrate the death of his friend by becoming active in student resistance. He helped to plan a commemoration of June 16 the following year. He and his friends risked their lives painting murals and placing placards on street corners at night, slipping into the shadows as police cars prowled the dirt roads. Gabs attended school irregularly, alternating the morning and afternoon sessions to avoid being detained. But the police, determined to track down the organisers of the commemoration, were catching up with them.

'They were out hunting for us,' said Gabs, so he got in touch with the grandfather of one his schoolfriends, 'Mkhulu' Madukana, who was in the underground. 'I told him that I wanted to leave. So this old man said that he can give me a hint, provided I am serious. He asked me how many of us wanted to go. So I told him four. He said to me: "Don't bring those other three here. You should be the only one coming here and I'll be telling you what to do, where to go, whom to contact. So that they shouldn't know me, in case you get arrested."'[66]

Eventually, three of the youths took the Mozambique route via Swaziland and in Maputo were billeted to a refugee camp, which they shared with Namibians and Zimbabweans. After a week, the ANC arrived and began to interview them and check their reports and biographies. Ultimately, Gabs and his friends were sent for training to an Angolan camp. None of the three was to return home before liberation – Audrey was accidentally shot in the Kashito camp in Angola, while Ben was killed in a motor accident in Lusaka. Gabs was eventually transferred to the ANC's Security Department, where he became a driver to the president and also guarded NEC meetings in Lusaka.[67]

June 16 had upset the MK theory that the urban terrain was not suitable for insurrection. Within days of the uprising, Tambo's message linked the slain and jailed children to past martyrs and to the struggle for national liberation.

'It is writ large in the unknown hundreds of others who have died at the hands of successive apartheid regimes… It encompasses all the millions who have perished at the point of a gun or under the whip of a white farmer; those who have been recklessly sacrificed in the search for gold in the bowels of the earth; those who have been starved to death while they were still infants or diseased prematurely into their graves. The history of the colonisation of our people is a history written in the blood of these black millions. The colonial system of apartheid was born dripping with the blood of our people.'[68]

In a direct 'message to the people of South Africa' beamed into the country via Radio Freedom in August, and also distributed by the underground inside South Africa, Tambo likened the children's campaign to armed struggle: 'Demonstrations and acts of resistance in Soweto and other parts of the country are therefore not riots by anti-social elements but blows for the liberation by an oppressed people… Our youth have raised this struggle to new heights. They have enriched our revolution. The struggle continues… There can be no going back.'[69]

The Soweto uprising shocked the Revolutionary Council into some restructuring. By then, Moses Mabhida had succeeded Joe Matthews as secretary, with Thabo Mbeki as assistant secretary in charge of administration. An 'Operations Unit', headed by Joe Modise with Joe Slovo as deputy, was formed and charged with giving emphasis to military work. Tambo, along with the entire leadership, was disturbed at the movement's lack of readiness to seize the historic moment for which the schoolchildren had unwittingly sacrificed their lives. Taking stock a few years later, Tambo praised the role – however limited – of ANC activists inside the country.

'We had not sufficiently recovered to take full advantage of the situation that crystallised from the events of 16 June 1976. Organisationally, we were too weak. We had few active ANC units inside the country. We had no military presence to speak of. The communication links between ourselves outside the country and the masses of our people were still too slow and weak to meet the situation such as was posed by the Soweto Uprising.'[70]

In August 1976, Tambo was able to be in London, where he arranged to meet Pallo Jordan, the son of his late friend, AC Jordan, who, after leaving the University of Cape Town in 1965, had become professor of African Studies at the University of Wisconsin in the USA. Pallo, a post-graduate student, had himself been forced out of the US for his anti-Vietnam war activities. Tambo had been impressed with young Jordan's work in starting, with others, a small publication directed mainly at South Africans, especially black students studying abroad. The intention was, said Pallo Jordan, to 'find the ways and means of linking up with the home fountains'. The journal was one route of establishing contact with students, 'and then perhaps drawing them into ANC structures, hopefully being able to use them as a jumping off point for building networks inside the country'.[71]

Tambo thus recruited Pallo Jordan to serve on the propaganda portfolio, and he was posted to Luanda to develop Radio Freedom, which had been set up by Duma Nokwe, who was now ill and, as it turned out, did not have long to live. The new propaganda team produced a memorandum outlining their strategy.

'We recognised,' said Jordan, 'that radio was a very important medium; what we said was that radio offers the movement the rare opportunity of holding what can in fact be a mass meeting inside the country at least once a day, if you did it right.'[72]

They saw propaganda occupying several layers. In the case of Radio Freedom, on which Tambo often spoke, the message could be openly ANC because it was broadcast from outside the country; but there were also 'non-overt' forms of propaganda.

'We said that the space can be occupied in various ways. What you've got to do is first of all test the space. The T-shirt, stickers, bumper stickers, the poster, various items of clothing, buttons and all these are propaganda media which are used for all sorts of purposes, especially in advanced capitalist countries.' Certain messages began to be sported.

'And all this, you see, because the items are either big or small you could then adapt them for overt and for covert [purposes]. For instance, stickers; if you make a sticker the size that can stick in someone's hands, they pull off a piece of paper and, walking around, stick it on a piece of pole and continue walking and no one knows you did it or who did it. People will then just see it after that, even stuck on the window – [there are] lots of things you can do with that. At the same time, you could make the same long sticker and stick it on the back of the bumper of one car, and everywhere where the car goes, that message is taken.'

The central themes were not necessarily recognisable as ANC slogans, but put out a message that was 'consonant with the ANC', like T-shirts declaring 'The people shall govern' (the Freedom Charter was not banned). And when the *Government Gazette* declared certain articles banned, the ANC knew that the messages were getting through and that people were responding.

'I think we were the first to use items of clothing as media, arising out of that memorandum,' reflected Jordan. 'This must have started in '77/78.' In the eighties, as the struggle intensified, Radio Freedom was to become a crucial mobilising medium, a tradition that went all the way back to 1963, when Walter Sisulu had broadcast his underground messages from Lilliesleaf Farm in Rivonia.

In the meantime, there was no let-up by the South African regime. In September 1977, the public was stunned by the news of the death of Steven Biko. Tambo had been searching for inside leadership among the black opposition. After the Soweto uprising, the Azanian People's Organisation (AZAPO) grew to new prominence, and the ANC had made a point of developing contacts with the leaders of the new Black Consciousness Movement (BCM).

'Our aim,' reported Tambo later, 'was to establish close fraternal relations with this movement and encourage it to grow, but as the instrument of the mass mobilisation of our people into struggle', thus 'frustrating the scheme to build up a so-called Third Force'.[73]

Among a number of impressive young men and women, Biko was perhaps the most charismatic. His book, *I Write What I Like*, was articulate, thoughtful and influential among community intellectuals. It advocated a conscious self-empowerment and pride in being black, a philosophy very reminiscent of the outlook of the Youth League's founders 30 years previously.[74]

In 1973, Biko was banned and, two years later, apprehended together with fellow activist Peter Jones, in a carefully planned roadblock set up by the Security Police. They had received intelligence (probably, the ANC would later deduce, from two white undercover operatives posing as students)[75] that the two BC leaders were preparing to slip across the border to meet Oliver Tambo. Indeed, according to Jones, for the previous three years Biko had been 'leading talks as a major catalyst' to reconcile the two liberation movements.[76]

'We had by 1976,' reported Tambo subsequently, 'arrived at the point where the time had come for us to meet that leading representative of the BCM, the late Steve Biko.' Biko and his colleagues had arrived at their agreed positions, elaborated Tambo: that the ANC was the leader of the revolution; that the BCM would focus on mass mobilisation; that it would work according to the ANC's broad strategy, and that a meeting should take place between the leadership of the Black People's Convention and the ANC.[77] Unfortunately, the meeting arranged for 1976 was too risky and another was arranged for the following year. In the meantime, Barney Pityana, another BC contact, was arrested, and before Biko could meet with the ANC, he too was apprehended.

The possibility of a united black opposition, combining the two exiled movements as well as a new generation of black intellectuals organising themselves throughout the country aroused the fear and fury of the Security Police. Minister Kruger was later to assert that 'the Black Consciousness Movement... has turned into the black power movement which has been infiltrated by members of the ANC'. Detained under Section 6 of the Terrorism Act, Biko and Jones were held at the infamous regional headquarters of the Security Police in Port Elizabeth, where people 'had the curious habit,' said Tambo sarcastically, 'of falling down the stairwell near the interrogation room on the sixth floor'.[78] After being hung from window rails by their shackles for a few days, the two men were separated and, within a month, Biko was dead. He had been held for 20 days, naked and chained, in solitary confinement. During an interrogation session, he was struck with a blow to the head serious enough for even his hardened interrogators to call the district surgeon. The surgeon, and later his senior, signed certifications asserting that no signs of abnormality were evident. A few days later, unconscious and foaming at the mouth, Biko was transported, still naked, 1 200 kilometres in the back of a van to Pretoria. Once there, he was dumped on the floor of the prison hospital, where he died. Two days later, Jimmy Kruger, Minister of Justice, refused to acknowledge any responsibility for Biko's savage murder.

'I am not glad and I am not sorry about Mr Biko,' he told a National Party congress to applause. 'His death leaves me cold.'[79] This callous boast reverberated around the world and the resultant indignation was to lead to even more widespread condemnation of apartheid. Steven Biko's death was to be another turning point in the history of apartheid.

For the ANC and for Tambo, Biko's death was a direct setback. 'The brutal murder of Steve Biko,' lamented Tambo, 'is the act of a clique, dehumanised by the practice of its own outlook and policies, and doubly dehumanised.' For Tambo, the greatest indictment on any person or system was the accusation of inhumanity.

'But the great thing about the mode of murder of Biko,' he continued, 'as revealed in the inquest, is that it tells the public of the murder in which our people have met their deaths in Vorster's prisons: scores of Soweto children were arrested during 1976, killed in prison, and carried by helicopter to mass graves.

'Scores of workers similarly brutally murdered,' Tambo went on, 'died as a result of a hunger strike, fell from a chair broke his ribs and died, hanged himself, jumped from a window to his death, died from natural causes, heart failure, hit his head against a wall and damaged his brain – all there... We knew Jimmy Kruger was lying, as he had done before, when he told the public how Biko died. What we did not know was the incredible degree of brutality he was concealing. Now we know that even respectable members of the medical profession have been parties to the deception. Their certificates of death are dictated by the Bureau of State Security (BOSS). Those who allegedly committed suicide by jumping out of windows were most probably thrown out as corpses. We have some idea of what happened to Wellington, Looksmart, Timol.'[80]

(Years later, the ANC realised that the brutality against Steve Biko in detention 'can be partly explained by the fact that he had made moves towards contact with the ANC and was on the verge of a historic meeting with OR Tambo'.[81])

A torrent of bannings followed, which included BCM and labour leaders, and the ANC in exile was quick to communicate with 'home'. It began to produce a 'more subtle form of propaganda', commented Pallo Jordan. For example, 'a bumper sticker that said: "Ban apartheid not people." Which, I mean, anyone could use. It wasn't seen as ANC and anyone could be saying that. But it was injecting a certain mood into the country.'[82] But propaganda messages through novel uses of the media tended to reach the towns rather than the countryside.

Particularly since the collapse of the *Aventura* expedition, Tambo himself displayed a resistance to ill-prepared, romantic expeditions in the rural areas. He continued to express his unease at the less than meticulous rural incursions. In his reports, he kept detailed inventories. In Sekhukhuneland, for example, the Sebata Kgomo movement was relatively successful and was managing to recruit for MK. A young local, Elleck Nchabeleng, son of a released Robben Islander, recalled his excitement at meeting 'the first guerrillas. [They] came with some equipment, AKs, scorpions, Tokerov pistols, and an FI. With two others from our discussion group, we organised a meeting place on the banks of the Oliphants River. We held discussions explaining the history of South Africa, why there is a need for the armed struggle and why people should take up arms and fight. Then they asked us whether we were interested in joining MK... So we joined MK on the banks of the Oliphants River'.[83]

Tambo confirmed this encounter in his notes in 1977. AK47s, rounds, makarovs, mines and other weapons had been despatched to the Northern Transvaal.[84] But the outcome became evident a year later when it was reported that about a third of the weapons had been 'seized by the enemy'.[85]

Furthermore, the reports of 1976 to 1978 revealed steady losses through deaths, arrests, torture and exposure by spies.

'What have we achieved in the rural areas, in fact? We've exposed some Sebatakgomo activists – 20 reconnaissances,' wrote Tambo, troubled. The problem lay in insufficient direction and coordination with the 'political machinery', as Tambo called it – one of the 'four pillars in the struggle'. At an NEC meeting, Tambo expressed his concern that workers and peasants, 'those very strata which in the strategic concepts of the ANC were always regarded as the decisive moving force of the revolution' were glaringly under represented. He refused to believe, he said, 'that they were not in the camps because they were cowards or not interested in their own liberation. No, this situation could be explained by the fact that the ANC leadership was not being proactive; while building up Umkhonto, the movement was relying mostly on the people who were coming out of the country rather than on its own recruitment needs'.

'We never paid attention to training leaders,' added Mac Maharaj. 'We assumed activists could be leaders without training – a huge gap.'[86] Some of the movement's organic intellectuals were studying Gramsci's categorisation of supporters, activists, cadres, and leaders in the organisation. In their quest for reviving the underground, Kasrils, Slovo and others turned to the international communist community – for example, Moumbaris and Hosey – to kick-start the underground at home.

With the paucity of ANC members living freely in the townships, Tambo's approach to opponents of the system was flexible and open-minded. A few years after the expulsion of the Group of Eight, Tambo continued to remain pragmatic on the issue of theory and practice. Reports he was receiving about the emerging labour movement from inside seemed to be confirming 'important questions of a proper approach to our struggle at both the theoretical and the political... But it is at the theoretical level,' he continued, 'that they make the greatest contribution. We shall need to avoid any tendency to lift our struggle into conceptual levels where the people are expected, as the NEUM expected them, to learn from lectures rather than from struggle at the mass, grass-roots level. The enemy's crimes against the people are a sufficient provocation to mass action, aimed at destroying the system... Our people must not at this stage – when we are so far from victory – be divided into socialists and non-socialists.

We cannot fight and defeat the enemy that way. The process of education must go on, the people must be educated, but we must not try to force the pace in a way which makes it an issue whether some accept the ANC or not'.[87]

Tambo's practice had always been to make contact with as many community leaders as possible. Now, with Steve Biko murdered, he continued to comb them for potential. The problem was, contended some members of the RC, that many of them were 'not providing realistic political leadership'. They were 'prevented by the system – blocked by internal conflicts'.[88] Leaders mentioned in this category included bishops Manus Buthelezi and Desmond Tutu, ex-Youth Leaguer and medical doctor Nthatho Motlana, and journalist Percy Qoboza. Tambo himself worried that there seemed to be 'no effective X-ian challenge to System'. Even among political opponents, 'AZAPO, the Committee of Ten, etc.', there seemed to be 'no search for a pattern for the future, or a strategy to reach it', to which Tambo emphasised, in parenthesis, '(The ANC should do that)'.[89]

The Committee of Ten had been formed by a group of Soweto community leaders, including Winnie Mandela and Nthatho Motlana. While Tambo observed the 'pathos of grown-up men fighting a general election in a ward in Soweto for membership of a toy government', he was puzzled by Motlana's counter-strategy of demanding an independent Soweto, for that seemed to him to amount to nothing more than 'an urban Bantustan'. Botha's more sophisticated strategy had been to 'take [the] ground from under Motlana's feet by giving what C/10 [Committee of Ten] asked for – semi-autonomy in Soweto'.[90] Nevertheless, 'we do not expect people like DT, NM and PQ to behave like revolutionaries,' Tambo wrote.[91]

'To castigate them because they are not measuring up to revolutionary standards would be wrong. They are people of some influence. It is this attribute we must exploit – put their influence behind and in support of our struggle, even if not in support of the ANC as such. We must not turn them into enemies. If they are enemies, we can surely neutralise them – they and the ANC have plenty in common.'[92]

Tambo was keeping track of resistance from all quarters, including white opposition. He noted in his diary, for example, the imprisonment for contempt of court of two white women, 'Ilona and Jackie' – Ilona Kleinschmidt and Jackie Bosman – who had refused to incriminate Winnie Mandela after they had visited her in Brandfort, where she had been banished and forbidden to receive visitors. Tambo also took a keen interest in NUSAS politics. Beyers Naudé of the Christian Institute had contacted him, through the auspices of Walter Felgate, on one of the latter's trips to the UK.[93] Both in Lusaka and in London,

Tambo would from time to time meet past friends from inside who, because of their cooperation with the apartheid regime, were permitted to travel abroad. Despite political differences, Tambo exchanged courtesies with his black brethren. In the same way as he had routinely kept in touch socially with PAC leaders such as Nana Mahomo and others, attending weddings, funerals and other social gatherings whenever he had the opportunity, so did he consent to receive more politically dubious visitors. For traditional as well as tactical reasons, Tambo kept the lines of communication open to all. Like Mandela, he was constantly on the alert for possible political openings for the ANC.

'Prevent the balkanisation and dismemberment of our people – resist the destruction of a Black national group whose unity is essential... Hence Bantustan independence, whatever it turns out to be, is meaningful only if it is a stepping stone to the conquest of power in South Africa,' he noted.[94]

Kaizer Matanzima, old colleague at Fort Hare and 'Chief Minister' of the Transkei Bantustan, was one such guest. Men such as he who had consented to take positions in the apartheid structures (in marked contrast to Chief Luthuli) defended their stance by arguing they were not only shoring up the endangered, traditional authority of chiefhood, but could use the space granted to them by the system to protect their subjects in the city. Considered by many to be intelligent, wily, haughty and proud, Matanzima attacked British colonialism, white liberals, communists and the PAC. But he seemed to refrain from criticising the ANC explicitly – Nelson Mandela, by Thembu custom, was his uncle.

In 1972, Chief Matanzima visited London as part of the South African government's drive to legitimise the Bantustan system. Shortly after his return home, the Holy Cross Mission School was astounded when a large black limousine swung into its driveway. The paramount chief's bodyguard stepped out, bearing a handsomely wrapped box, a gift for one of the schoolmasters, a Mr Mngeyane, from Oliver Tambo, his old school friend. 'It was a hat – a Battersby hat from London.' As the news spread, 'we were all thrilled', recalled Tambo's one-time pupil at St Peter's, Rumford Qwalela, at the time a senior education officer in the Transkei.[95] The gesture was a message, a communication of solidarity to all at home, a symbol of Tambo's reaching across the years to his early life, across time and culture, from the international metropolis and a locus of the liberation struggle, to his home, and to the remote mission station in Flagstaff, Pondoland.

During the brief stay of Matanzima, Buthelezi and Mangope in London, Tambo and other South Africans met with them. It is not clear whether any significant discussion took place, but on his return, Matanzima indicated a new purport. He was losing patience with the South African regime's failure to accede to his demands for the consolidation of the Transkei lands, and expressed publicly an entente cordiale with his rival, Mangosuthu Gatsha Buthelezi. The following year, a 'summit' meeting of six homeland leaders was held in Umtata. 'We want one nation,' declared Matanzima, in a reversal of his previous, somewhat Xhosa-chauvinist stance 'and not weak tribal groups divided along ethnic lines.'[96] This was a pan-South Africanism more akin to the African National Congress, though moderated by federalism – the summit approved the principle of a federation of states in southern Africa, which would be non-racial. Resolutions were also called for the consolidation of homeland territories and the scrapping of laws that restricted the movements of black South Africans. The English press hailed this as a significant step forward. Was this the beginning of a new anti-apartheid base? Alarmed, the regime moved swiftly to pre-empt any further damage. This proved to be not too taxing. Firstly, Pretoria firmly held onto the purse strings. Patronage was a political tool, which homeland chiefs, as patrons themselves, understood only too well. Within a few months of the summit, Matanzima led his party into voting unanimously to begin negotiations for independence – without consulting his five colleagues, the other homeland leaders. By 1976, the South African government triumphantly announced the Transkei as its first, fully independent homeland; Matanzima had dropped the demand for additional, consolidating territories.

Tambo's brush with Matanzima was not his only contact with homeland leaders. Other riders of Bantustan tigers, such as Phatudi and Mangope, were similarly lured by the vision of long-term independence combined with power and self-interest. The enemy had isolated them, noted Tambo. They had chosen to play along with a paternalistic 'superficial political analysis'; they had accepted 'toys to play with'.[97] Tambo had a personal relationship with Lucas Mangope, whom he had taught at St Peter's. In London with other visiting homeland leaders, Mangope seemed pleased to see his old Maths teacher. Tambo invited him home to Muswell Hill and Mangope agreed to go. Before the appointed time, however, Mrs Mangope called and offered her apologies – the cost for the 'Chief Minister' of a Bantustan in the pay of the South African regime was prohibitive.

Far more significant, and with far greater potential, was the delicate footwork needed to spar with the enigmatic Gatsha Mangosuthu Buthelezi, who was playing a skilful game with the South African regime. By declining the invitation to independence, Buthelezi showed himself to be shrewder and more courageous than the other homeland leaders. The son of King Solomon's sister, he had grown up with a keen sensitivity to the shabby treatment meted out to his royal uncle by the South African government. Solomon had responded to the removal of his dignity by finding refuge in alcohol, which allowed him at times to behave provocatively and utter statements that would have been considered insolent by the white ruling class had he been sober. It is from this background that the young Buthelezi emerged – manipulating his position as a traditional ruler with the vulnerability that all blacks endured in a racist society. This was a time of intense social dislocation, particularly for migrant workers. The rural villages were almost completely dependent on their low wages. The apartheid system had succeeded in streamlining the Bantustans as reserves of labour. Ironically, Buthelezi too was anxious to ensure that these migrants should not become culturally urbanised in the PWV (Gauteng) or some other faraway city centre, but that they retain their loyalty to their kinfolk and to their chiefdom. By keeping the government on a string, Buthelezi was thus able to buy time. Eventually the South African government was obliged to revise its legislation and KwaZulu became a 'Territorial Authority', with Buthelezi as Chief Minister.

To many ANC members, including non-Zulus, Buthelezi had demonstrated how brilliantly he could outsmart the system. Perhaps it was possible that this strategy could be used by the ANC in alliance with Buthelezi, who after all had been a member of the Youth League and, in fact, had been expelled from Fort Hare for his activism. Like Tambo, Buthelezi was known to be a genuine admirer of Chief Albert Luthuli, and since 1973 had cooperated with the ANC in helping to set up the Luthuli Memorial Foundation, headed by Nat Masemola, to raise funds for bursaries for exiled South African students.[98] Through Luthuli, in the ANC's Durban offices and at Fort Hare, he and Tambo had met in the 1950s.[99] The two men had subsequent social encounters in the 1950s, and after the banning of the ANC, Buthelezi continued to associate himself with Luthuli – at the unveiling of the memorial stone of the Chief at Groutville, Buthelezi made the principal speech.

In 1963, Buthelezi visited London. This was a time when South Africans were likely to be penalised for visiting the ANC leadership, but 'I couldn't resist going to visit the Tambos', confessed Buthelezi.[100] Tambo was concerned, though, that Buthelezi should not expose himself politically. He himself understood, as a highly educated, accomplished professional belonging to the oppressed, the strategy of 'acting right', to be unthreatening in thorny situations, to show a maximum affability and minimum arrogance – these were qualities Tambo had internalised, yet they did not compromise his integrity in any way. He had taught himself to negotiate a balancing act that required enormous self-control.

'Mr Tambo was a bit unclear about [the visit], as the place was bristling, he said, with BOSS agents.' In fact, Tambo gave Buthelezi 'a pound or two' to visit the South African Embassy in Trafalgar Square 'just to keep the balance'. 'He was a very responsible man,' said Buthelezi. Tambo was keenly aware of the ambiguous game in which Buthelezi was enmeshed. He was familiar with the tactics of ambiguity of the oppressed, and accepted its necessity. According to Adelaide, the ANC arranged for Buthelezi to stay at the Strand Hotel, and she remembers taking him and his wife to meet Dr Mungai Njoroge, a future cabinet minister in the soon-to-be independent Kenya, as well as other old Fort Hare colleagues from Kenya.[101] Evidently, however, the South African government took a dim view of Buthelezi's insubordination, for on his return they withdrew his passport.

But the Chief's famed skill for ambiguity continued to beguile not only Tambo but a range of fascinated observers across the political spectrum. In 1971, for example, at the inauguration of the KwaZulu Territorial Authority, Buthelezi made a play for the national stage in Soweto when he criticised ethnic categorisation. 'Whites are united by their colour; this is what we should do.' Radical changes were needed, he insisted. But characteristically, he kept his options open by expressing hope for change through dialogue.[102] For the ANC, interesting ironies were revealed. In 1972, the South African regime compromised with Buthelezi by declaring KwaZulu a 'self-governing territory'. This meant that Buthelezi would be able to utilise many of the benefits of independence without being formally defined as such.

In that same year, Buthelezi's passport was restored to him, and he formed part of the publicity tour of four chiefs to Europe and the USA to legitimise the homelands system. In London, despite the reservations of many ANC members, an enthusiastic Dr Wilson (Willie) Zami Conco held a large reception party for Chief Buthelezi at his home. Only Zulus were invited – Tambo was out of the country. As Buthelezi entered the house, all the guests dropped to their knees and raised traditional sticks in salute to their chief.

'Being Zulu is something special,' explained a Zulu-speaking member of the ANC, perhaps in defence of his comrades' disapproval. '[But] how do you explain yourself, then, as a member of the ANC?' Tswana-speaking Oxford graduate Seretse Choabe is said to have retorted.[103]

In 1973, when the Luthuli Foundation was launched to raise funds for the further education of young South Africans, Buthelezi was approached while he was in London, and asked to introduce the Luthuli Foundation in South Africa – it was both a wish to bring him on board the ANC vessel and also to diversify the image of the Foundation. Trustees should not be loaded with ANC names, noted the ANC's NEC minutes – writers Breyten Breytenbach and Alex La Guma, and SACTU's John Gaetswe were suggested as trustees. It was agreed that Tambo, the executive manager Nat Masemola and Chris Hani be mandated to go to London to finalise the trustees. Eventually, the trustees chosen were Archbishop Huddleston, developmentalist Gunnar Myrdal, Mary-Louise Hooper, Dr Willie Conco, Bailey, Nat Masemola and P Mbata. Buthelezi was not in the final list. As always, inclusiveness also delivered pitfalls. Concern was expressed with regard to the Luthuli Foundation's involvement with Buthelezi, 'a tribal leader'. Criticism was also levelled at the danger of subsidising Bantu Education schools. The Trust, it was said, should reflect the Luthuli Foundation as national, and not provincial, for Luthuli was a national leader. Research should promote the history of the African people, their cultural heritage, journals with poems, and literature.[104]

Tambo was not, however, the only opponent to dally with Buthelezi; the chief's way with words attracted many intelligent participants. He had a warm relationship with the courageous anti-apartheid clergyman Beyers Naudé, and Alan Paton remained his admirer to the end – Buthelezi, Paton stoutly maintained, would be 'no stooge'.[105] In 1973, soon after the Durban strikes, sympathetic to the emergent labour movement (though assuring employers that trade unions should be developed as a 'machinery for negotiation'), Buthelezi consented to become the chancellor of the newly created Institute of Industrial Education, initiated by the banned political philosopher, Rick Turner (assassinated by the regime five years later).[106]

In that same year, Buthelezi travelled abroad. Financed by the USA, he breakfasted with Richard Nixon in Washington, was warmly received by African leaders such as Julius Nyerere and Kenneth Kaunda, and attended a conference in Addis Ababa. On his way to the conference, he met Oliver Tambo in Nairobi, where they had a long conversation, lasting through the night. Again, Buthelezi found Tambo to be cautious – 'I would say almost too cautious'. Buthelezi had been invited to participate in the debates at Addis, but Tambo was reluctant to share a platform with him.

'He said the Americans were being mischievous because they knew I was against sanctions myself, and that the ANC was in favour of sanctions; and he said that they wanted us to clash there. And he didn't attend the lecture.'[107]

Buthelezi did not seem immune to Tambo's arguments, though: at Addis he apparently refrained from distancing himself from international sanctions against South Africa, as he had planned to do.[108] But on his return to South Africa, Buthelezi faced a different audience – he was able to report, he announced, that he had facilitated Prime Minister Vorster's policy of detente in Africa.

Despite these ploys, Buthelezi himself would have preferred to move away from his dependence on the Bantustan system and, from time to time, his radical accents would alarm his patrons. Buthelezi recalled that once, on meeting Tambo secretly in Malawi during the anniversary celebrations of the country's independence, the ANC leader warned him to 'soft-pedal' his message. 'He said that Nelson was in jail. Who is there in South Africa to look after you if the regime does something to you? Slow down!'[109]

But Buthelezi, it seemed, entertained ambitious aspirations to national leadership. While not abandoning Zulu rhetoric at home, to BC supporters he claimed that the forceful nationalism forged by Shaka was the historical forerunner of black consciousness. Buthelezi demonstrated his ability to combine in his discourse a variety of popular elements. Furthermore, under the cloak of a dormant cultural body, Inkatha ka Zulu (Council of Zulus), founded by the Zulu aristocracy in the early twenties, Buthelezi was able to extract the blessing of the ANC to reinvoke the movement, internally and legally. Tambo later confirmed that he had indeed given his blessing to this strategy:[110] 'Being itself illegal,' wrote Tambo, 'the ANC encourages the people to form legal organisations and use them to advance the cause of liberation.'[111]

Tambo's pragmatism conceded that these organisations could not be expected to 'embrace the ANC strategy in its entirety and expect to avoid being likewise declared illegal. Therefore, it is not calling on the people to establish what would in all but name be the ANC'.[112]

An additional influence may have been his visit in 1978 to Vietnam, where the National United Front in that country had managed to build up an impressive mass resistance movement by not losing sight of the main objective. 'Policy vis-à-vis the NUF,' noted Tambo in his diary, 'define who is the enemy, who the ally – actual and potential. This policy should be enunciated on every possible occasion.'[113]

The ANC had been encouraged by the example set by King Sabata Dalindyebo of the Thembu in the Transkei, 'one of the stalwarts who, for so long,' said Tambo in a tribute, 'held high the banner of genuine national liberation in one of [the Bantustans, the Transkei], an outstanding leader of our people.'[114]

It was in that context that Tambo maintained regular contact with Buthelezi, and indeed was instrumental in encouraging Gatsha Buthelezi to create the Inkatha Freedom Party. The ANC saw it as a base, as a means of mass mobilisation using the cover of the Bantustans. 'In the course of our discussions with him, we agreed,' reported Tambo, 'that this would also necessitate the formation of a mass organisation in the Bantustan that he headed. Inkatha originated from this agreement.'[115]

In 1975, Inkatha ye Nkululeko ye Sizwe (Inkatha Freedom of the Nation) was revived as a 'cultural movement'. The modification in its new name hinted at a political dimension. Inkatha boldly adopted the ANC colours of black, green and gold, as well as 'Nkosi Sikelel' iAfrika', the anthem composed by Enoch Sontonga in 1897, and first popularised by the ANC.

With the active cooperation of the chiefs and headmen, Inkatha's largely rural membership grew rapidly – by 1976 the organisation claimed 100 000 members. Institutionalised patronage enabled it to acquire the membership also of traders, teachers and civil servants, dependent on the KwaZulu administration for their livelihood. Buthelezi, with his claim bearing a multifaceted heritage, was further authenticated when he accompanied Mrs Luthuli to Maseru, Lesotho, to receive an OAU award on behalf of her late husband. It was clear to observers, however, that the homeland leader was a surprise guest. ANC members based in Lesotho had grave reservations about the chief. They suspected that he was making political capital by associating himself with the widow of their acclaimed leader.

Further afield, too, there were elements within the ANC who were uneasy about the movement's flirtation with a government-paid chief, no matter how astute he seemed to be. Buthelezi had demonstrated his skill in manoeuvring the politics of dependence by using the space Pretoria allowed him,[116] but by the same token, Buthelezi was beholden to Pretoria. Having decided – encouraged by his royal mother and also, he claimed, by Sisulu and Mandela[117] – to claim his chiefly legacy and use his position to manipulate the system, he would necessarily in the last analysis be obliged to act in his own interests. There were many who presumed this would be an inevitable consequence. On one notable occasion, after Buthelezi had divulged to a Langa township audience that he had met Oliver Tambo, Dr Nthato Motlana rejected this claim, saying that 'Tambo could not meet with traitors'.[118] This attack on Buthelezi, followed by the unmannerly reception accorded to him by university students in his own chiefdom, as well as his ejection at the funeral of Robert Sobukwe, deeply wounded him. 'Some people were attacking me in the name of the ANC. Relations between [Tambo] and me were cordial. I was corresponding with Mr Mandela and Mr Tambo. But these people here, who were much smaller people than Mr Mandela and Mr Tambo, were sniping at me.'[119]

Within the ANC, there were many who would have no truck with the NEC's degree of pragmatism. It was one of the reproaches of the Group of Eight that Tambo's relationship with Buthelezi compromised the movement. It smacked of 'duplicity', they charged.[120] But Tambo, in communication with Mandela, and with his keen appreciation of political nuance, aspired to influence the homeland leaders into rejecting 'independence'. He defended his approach, particularly with regard to homeland leaders who were still sitting on the fence.

'We are too purist politically,' he observed in his notebook (perhaps bearing in mind the discussion on Bantustan strategies coming from the Island), 'also orthodox; we run, like a train, on fixed rails, inflexible. We wear thick blinkers, we can barely hear what someone is saying. As a movement, we are not prepared to be original. We are conformists as reliable as robots when in working order.'[121]

Yet, while taking into account the chief's constraints, Tambo was by no means uncritical of Buthelezi. He analysed the Inkatha constitution and Buthelezi's speech at the launch of the new status of KwaZulu as a Self-governing Territory. Buthelezi declared that the time had come for dialogue. With one eye on his Pretoria monitors, he evoked 'in particular' the struggle of Afrikaners, 'who had also shed blood and lost lives to gain independence'.

'Why do you condemn violence, then?' wondered Tambo in his notebook.[122] He noted with exasperation, yet some amusement, Buthelezi's colourful, bellicose warnings to his rivals in the name of liberation: 'When Inkatha speaks, the people speak... Send the scrawny cockerels scattering in every direction'; and 'so-called leaders who have no constituencies must be rough-handled out of the way so that the people can march onwards towards victory'.

Tambo rebutted Buthelezi's opposition of sanctions by invoking common heroes of struggle, Luthuli and Mandela, who had first advocated this strategy. Buthelezi had more than once made a point of attempting to disassociate the 'internal' ANC from the External Mission. Invoking the 'internal' ANC as the legal, non-violent movement before it was banned, he distanced himself from the external wing of the ANC. He '[wished] them well in the path they have now chosen in their wisdom', to which Tambo asked, with prescience: 'Inkatha plainly declares itself to be an instrument of Liberation'; but how did it see itself in relation to ANC, 'the instrument of liberation'? The indivisible ANC alone, insisted Tambo, could claim the long lineage of struggle for the African nation as a whole: 'A "Liberation movement" is no cheap label,' he wrote pointedly. 'The phrase carries a revolutionary context. To use it as you do is to denigrate the struggle, to deprive it of content and substance.'

Tambo was still prepared, however, to highlight those sentiments of the Inkatha leader that were more in harmony with the visions of the ANC. When Buthelezi avowed that 'history does not permit sectional leaders to create their own stamping grounds. All responsible leadership is faced with national questions' above 'personal edification... Our oppression has gone on for so long because we allowed [division]', Tambo responded with '*Right!* Right. Now let's stop the bickering'. 'Enemy [is] not Inkatha but Nats,' he emphasised.

As a fellow oppressed black leader, Tambo's own experience of two cultures and two unequal power structures imbued him with an acute understanding of the tactics of ambiguity and circumvention. He understood the necessity of juggling contradictions in order to survive; he appreciated the strategies of the dependent and the vulnerable. Like women in strictly patriarchal societies, African political trailblazers were obliged to develop a watchful, compliant and strategic mode which, in general, avoided threatening or confronting directly those in power. At the same time, they had an alternative discourse which their own constituencies had no trouble decoding. While Tambo had long since abandoned any pretence at accommodating the ruling class, his concern to protect the emotional younger man touched Buthelezi. It fostered in him a strong wish to take the heroic course, but in such a way that personal sacrifice could be avoided. On Tambo's part, he hoped to mentor Buthelezi, highly intelligent and keenly sensitive, to utilise legal space so as to open up opportunities for the ANC's separate underground activity.

From time to time Tambo and Buthelezi kept in touch through emissaries – Thabo Mbeki on behalf of the ANC, and Inkatha's Walter Felgate and Gibson Thula during visits to London, the Netherlands, Switzerland and Sweden.[123] What struck Buthelezi most during these external visits was the widespread good reputation of Tambo and the resultant power that emanated from it. When Buthelezi wanted to start a newspaper, *The Nation*, he approached SIDA, a Swedish organisation, for funding. It soon became clear that 'unless Tambo nods, they won't accept [the proposal]'.[124] Despite Buthelezi's successful entree into the White House (where ANC leaders were *persona non grata*), it was still an advantage for Inkatha's international image to be on the right side of the ANC. At the same time, Buthelezi was also acutely aware of the need to build up Inkatha's legitimacy with black people at home. A working relationship with the ANC might cede its internal base to Inkatha.

In October 1979, a two-and-a-half-day formal meeting between the executives of Inkatha and the ANC took place in London. Tambo was struck by the size of Buthelezi's delegation. Inkatha's 17 delegates included the entire KwaZulu cabinet, representatives of the women's and youth brigades, as well as the enigmatic Walter Felgate, who it was later speculated, kept in touch with the South African regime's intelligence service, the Bureau of State Security, during the course of this visit.[125] The ANC team included Alfred Nzo, Thomas Nkobi, Johnny Makathini, Cap Zungu, Thabo Mbeki and MB Yengwa. At Tambo's suggestion, Bishop Alpheus Zulu from the Inkatha commission chaired the meeting. In his welcome, Tambo commenced on a positive note. Buthelezi, he said, had achieved 'an impressive record of projecting the ANC while walking on a tightrope...[126] We come with no fixation,' he reassured the gathering. 'We have a duty to our people and their future; to their leaders past, present and future; to the fallen heroes, to AJ Luthuli.'

Throughout the meeting, courtesy and affability prevailed. According to Buthelezi, 'the meeting had wide-ranging discussions about how we could strategise together'.[127] When Buthelezi spoke, two issues were put on the table for discussion. The first was a motivation for why Inkatha was the ideal organisation to 'keep the ANC alive'. The emphasis was on the leaders being outside South Africa and, therefore, unable to organise on the ground. The alternative black opposition organisations, Buthelezi maintained, were suspect. Who, he wondered, funded WASA or AZAPO or COSAS?[128] Buthelezi could not understand some of the individuals and organisations, such as Obed Mbatha of AZAPO, and COSAS – 'funded by the CIA' – which associated themselves with the ANC. 'Is the ANC all things to all people?' he asked pointedly.[129] All these organisations amounted to nothing, he assured the ANC delegation, because they had a negligible following. Why, after intensive publicity, the BCM had only been able to muster 450 people at their rally! Inkatha, on the other hand, compared with the ANC's 100 000 signed-up members at the height of its popularity in the 1950s, could claim 300 000. ('What is the 300 000 doing?' Tambo wondered later in his notebook.)

Inkatha was in a position to build the ANC image inside the country. But in return, the ANC should support and defend Inkatha. Buthelezi had been offended and angered by the attack on him by Motlana and claimed that there had been a plot to kill him (a fact that Bishop Tutu himself later confirmed). Buthelezi mentioned the incident several times, and wanted the ANC to define its attitude to Inkatha. A civil war situation was building up, he warned. The ANC should make a public statement against Motlana. Buthelezi also made it clear that he wanted the public blessing of the ANC in order to obtain recognition from the international community. For Tambo, this latter demand seemed to be in conflict with Buthelezi's determination that there should be a division in the movement between the internal and the external, and that Inkatha would lead the movement inside.

Buthelezi wanted to pick up the ANC's old call for a national convention. He disagreed with both armed struggle and sanctions as tactics for social change. At the meeting, he suggested that he initiate diplomatic exchanges to explore the preconditions needed for the ANC to hold discussions with the PW Botha regime. 'We were groping for ways of anything I could do in the set-up here, to synchronise with what they were doing,' he explained.[130]

Tambo was concerned to clarify the tricky way forward by outlining bottom-line yet strategic principles. They should ask themselves what had changed and what was changing. Tambo jotted down some points for Buthelezi:

'Don't get involved. Don't be a broker: be on the side of the people. We are not asking to see PW at all. He has not said he wants to see us. Therefore your move will be a diversion – a lot of talks which can have no meaning except as something for the papers. We don't want the ANC to be dragged into that kind of thing. It would be chasing a desert mirage.' After all, 'What has PW done to suggest that he's worth seeing?'[131]

As for other opposition organisations, Tambo explained that the ANC wanted to encourage them too. Indeed, 'among oppressors there is unity, and no quarrelling; but the Press they control fills its columns with news and comment which pictures Africans and Blacks at one another's throats.

'Those who see this internal war as a duty they owe to themselves are rendering dutiful service to white domination and to no one else. Who is the enemy of the people? Let's get on with the business of fighting him – from wherever we are, with whatever we have. The process of our struggle will itself deal with our secondary enemies – the spies, agents, stooges, collaborators. There are self-confessed... traitors who have closed ranks with and are part of the enemy. But we must not place in the category of traitors those who do not in fact belong there.'[132]

The meeting ended as it had begun, cordially, and with the understanding that what had transpired would remain 'under wraps', as Buthelezi put it. Tambo undertook to report the substance of the meeting to his NEC and to get back to Buthelezi in December.

But the two leaders were never to meet again. The following week, the *Sunday Times*' Suzanne Vos, later to become a leading Inkatha Freedom Party official and eventually one of its Members of Parliament, interviewed Buthelezi and published a report on the 'secret' Inkatha meeting with the ANC. Tambo was astounded. He waited for an explanation from Buthelezi. It never came.

Some 14 years later, in a discussion this author had on ANC relations with Inkatha, Tambo suggested that should I ever procure an interview with Chief Buthelezi, I was to try to find out why he had broken the agreement between the two parties.[133] When I interviewed Buthelezi in 1994, he responded to the question that the idea that the affair could have been kept secret was 'very naive', indeed 'impossible'.

'As I got off the plane,' he explained, 'there was a young Afrikaner who was apparently representing *Die Burger*, I think. He was asking me – I don't know how – all the papers in South Africa had said that I was secretly going to London... There were some young people, leaders I had brought with me, like Musa Zondi, who was the leader of the youth, and some women and so on; I thought that as South Africa operates, there was no way I would subject these young men to questions by hiding that I had gone there. There could have been a BOSS agent, that chap from the press... but the substance of what was discussed has never been revealed, up to now.'[134]

On the ANC's part, it seemed that Buthelezi was not prepared to participate in a project he could not himself control – a man 'on a tightrope' could not afford to take chances. This was clearly signalled by the *Sunday Times* interview. But the meeting itself had revealed additional information about Inkatha. By insisting that PW Botha and Piet Koornhof were 'good men', the delegates had displayed, from the perspective of the ANC, a low political consciousness. Tambo set down somewhat hard-hitting follow-up tasks for the ANC after this debacle: 'It was very important to set the record straight, consolidate our following by correcting any muddled impressions and reiterate a firm comprehensive political line [on] strategy'.[135]

Publicly, Tambo was obliged to issue a denial: 'It has come to our notice that the issue of the Johannesburg *Sunday Times* of 4 November 1979 carries an article that there has recently been a secret meeting in London between representatives of the African National Congress and Inkatha. There has been no secret meeting.'[136]

The ambiguity in Tambo's denial lay in the adjective 'secret', since Buthelezi had broken their pledge. Tambo went on to deny the implications made by the report, of having met Buthelezi: 'The said article also raises other points that are likely to give the impression that the African National Congress has abandoned some of its most fundamental positions. We hereby wish to affirm with all the authority at our command that such an implication is without any foundation whatsoever... [There] can be no meaningful negotiations between [ourselves] and the fascist and militarist regime of Prime Minister Botha and Magnus Malan.'

Going on to reaffirm the ANC's holistic policy, he explained: 'The strategic objective that we pursue is the seizure of power by the people and the use of that power to build a united democratic, non-racial and peace-loving South Africa as visualised by the Freedom Charter. Our situation dictates that we must use all means and methods to achieve this objective, including legal and illegal ones, combining both the political and the military. The masses of the oppressed black people constitute the principal and central instrument of change – the forces charged with the task of carrying through the struggle in all its forms.'[137]

A few months later, on the ANC's Freedom Day, the Secretary-General of the ANC, Alfred Nzo, launched a scathing attack on Buthelezi. Tambo himself also criticised Inkatha in later years. 'When all is said and done, [Buthelezi] is the leader of a homeland, and that means that you are collaborating in the homeland policy,' he told a Dutch newspaper. 'His statements are also contradictory. Sometimes he is for and sometimes against a boycott of South Africa. It has also emerged gradually that he is not popular with the black population.' Tambo also quoted an opinion poll in South Africa, which found that '40 per cent would vote for the ANC in free parliamentary elections and only 21 per cent for Inkatha. We are by far the largest resistance movement in South Africa and are supported by church movements, youth organisations, trade unions, coloureds and even white students. From this poll, you can quite safely draw the conclusion that people are beginning to think more and more along the lines of the ANC'.[138]

But it was Nzo's attack that brought 'the parting of the ways', according to Buthelezi. 'After that, it was just vitriol after vitriol.' From then on, relations with the ANC, both inside and outside South Africa, deteriorated rapidly. Yet, despite the hostilities, Buthelezi insisted that he continued to reflect fondly on Tambo. When Tambo suffered his stroke in 1989, Buthelezi sent flowers. He had wanted to visit him personally, but under the highly charged circumstances, felt he could not do so. He deeply regretted the loss of Tambo to the ANC leadership. Tambo alone, he felt, despite Mandela's obvious qualities, had the potential to negotiate a solution to the impasse between the two organisations and so prevent the bloodshed that followed the unbanning of the ANC.

Where did the ANC go wrong in its analysis of the direction given to resistance in rural Natal? 'In a way, [Buthelezi] is our fault,' confessed Tambo later. 'We have not done and are not doing sufficient political work among the millions of our people who have been condemned to the Bantustans. The artificial boundaries purporting to fence them off from the rest of our country do not make them any less a vital and integral part of the popular masses fighting for national liberation and social emancipation of our country.'[139]

'We were instrumental in encouraging Gatsha Buthelezi to create the Inkatha Freedom Party. We saw it as a base, as a means of mass mobilisation using the cover of the Bantustans', confirmed Mac Maharaj. 'But instead of putting our cadres into it at all levels and guiding them, we left it in the hands of Gatsha Buthelezi,' he conceded. 'That was a big mistake... Because, of course, the IFP was brought into being not just by talking to Gatsha Buthelezi but by talking to a lot of other people who went into the formation of Inkatha. But they were just left with no lines of communications, no guidance, no exchange.'[140]

It was not as if the lines had not been set up. Senior members of the external mission were slipping in and out of South Africa and its neighbouring countries. Jacob Zuma and Judson Khuzwayo, for example, had received instructions, probably from Moses Mabhida, secretary of the Revolutionary Council, to recruit members in Natal and send them out. Thabo Mbeki, his assistant secretary, was based first in Botswana and then Swaziland.

'Once Thabo was removed from the scene in Swaziland,' recalled Maharaj, 'and Zuma and them had to flee, the assumption was made that the same guidance would be given by the Zumas, now based in Maputo; but it didn't work out that way... Home had those arrests in 1975 – the Jo Mati group in Port Elizabeth, the trade unionists who got killed in Cape Town, the Pretoria Twelve trial, the Harry Gwala trial. That smashed these networks... The weakness was that we did not exercise that guidance.'[141]

The ANC and Tambo himself interpreted the turn of events as a realisation by Buthelezi that, while the ANC was banned, he had tremendous freedom to build up his own party, which would otherwise be tremendously curtailed if he were going to be loyal to the ANC.[142]

In the meantime, communications with Robben Island continued. Jacob Zuma was, over the years, one of hundreds of comrades to bring news to Tambo.

'I briefed OR extensively about Robben Island, which had its own dynamics, including the contradictions that had arisen among ourselves there at a political level... I had views on Robben Island and indicated to him where other comrades thought my views were wrong. So I was as objective as anything because I wanted him to understand.'[143]

Tambo was particularly affected by news of the Island, and wrote to sympathise with the differences that caused ideological tensions for a while. 'The knowledge that these two colleagues [Mandela and Sisulu] were sitting in prison was like an absolute imperative in his life,' observed Mac Maharaj, a prisoner who himself developed elaborate and ingenious forms of communication.[144]

In their regular debates, the Robben Island prisoners came to the conclusion there was a critical need to do mass political work, both in the legal as well as the illegal spheres.[145] They had managed to get topical books about Vietnam, critiques by Noam Chomsky and other literature smuggled in.

'And these stimulated a vicious debate… about apartheid structures. Do we utilise them or don't we? Was the tactic of boycotting… a correct tactic? The whole Inkatha debate and Gatsha Buthelezi – having gone through all those debates, a number of us were very clear that political work was critical.'[146]

Always conscious that the elected executive of the ANC inside the country were on Robben Island, Tambo would not make major decisions without consulting them. He sent accounts in code form, and in one of the surviving draft letters Tambo reported on the progress of 'sports clubs'.

'One such,' he wrote to Mandela via Adelaide, 'is the Zwelonke Federation, which every club wants to join. But the federation insists splinter clubs are unacceptable, where an association is already a member of the federation, it is not allowed. This is because it has been found that some association leaders quarrel with whole sections of their members. They then parcel out these members into separate clubs, isolate them and make them apply for affiliation with Zwelonke. The leaders of the association have everything to gain from this arrangement and nothing to lose. Zwelonke opposes it, and says splinter clubs will not be recognised. What I am sure will happen, however, is that some members of the Federation, certainly the oldest and more powerful ones who can dispense with everybody else, will arrange private informal bilateral games with new clubs. The Muyamana group of clubs has quite a few who are under the strong influence of old well-established members of the Federation, and who would like-wise have off-the-record fixtures with new groups.'[147]

Robben Island, in turn, also kept Tambo in touch with the progress of opposition movements. From Island 'graduates', he learnt that talented BC leaders such as 'Terror' Lekota, Popo Molefe and Eric Molobi had been recruited. In the context of the disintegration of the Portuguese colonies in Africa – in Mozambique, Angola and Guinea Bissau – 'we saw ourselves being part of the unfolding drama,' explained Popo Molefe. 'We saw apartheid, now, also being in the throes of its collapse.'

Tambo himself received BC converts in Lusaka. Lindelwe and Bridgitte Mabandla, activists as students at the University of the North and in Durban, where Lindelwe was a history teacher in the early seventies, had both been banned in 1975 and banished to the Transkei town of Tsolo. The couple then 'skipped' the country and settled in Botswana, where Lindelwe eventually became headmaster of a school there. Secretly, however, both had decided to join the ANC. Why the ANC, rather than the PAC, whose Africanist philosophy might have appealed more to Black Consciousness?

'We did not think that the PAC had sound political principles,' replied Lindelwe Mabandla. 'We had been debating this issue for a long time, and to us the most attractive thing about the ANC, apart from its inclusiveness, was its democratic base and the fact that it allowed participation. And more than that, its principles to us were very sound and were not far removed from the things that we have been saying in SASO. It talked about empowerment of people, it talked about democratisation of strictures and emancipation; all of the things that we thought were crucial in this country. For us that was a natural home, a natural development of political thinking and this represented an advanced position in political terms of the notions that we had started to articulate with Steve Biko in the early years – in the early seventies.'[148]

Eric Molobi, converted to the ANC a few years later on Robben Island, confirmed this perception. As an affiliate of the Black Consciousness Movement, Molobi, along with others in the BCM, had the idea that their role was to unite 'the mother bodies', the ANC and PAC. But on the Island they discovered how profoundly the two organisations differed in style, strategy and ideology. They observed how, as the June 16 batch of prisoners streamed in, the ANC seized the moment and recruited aggressively in large numbers. Although Molobi and others were initially taken aback at this rather pushy approach, they were also impressed by the movement's superior organisation. Around that time, he said, they also began to find the PAC's political notions somewhat crude and undeveloped. The PAC assertion that whites were 'inherently racist' seemed a contradiction to the young BC members, for it implied a biological, rather than a socially constructed affliction. Then again, the PAC's deep suspicion of the 'white-dominated SACP' was offset by the ANC's greater access to resources. They heard favourable stories of MK cadres who had been trained in the USSR and the GDR. For Molobi, personally, any prejudging of the Communist Party was mitigated when he learnt from Ahmed Kathrada and other Party members that his own esteemed father, a gentle but reserved and austere lay preacher, had been an SACP man himself. Mr Molobi had never revealed this to his son, although he had clearly sympathised with Eric's political activities and had been proud of him. And the presence of MK on the Island was further evidence that the armed struggle was functioning, even if – it was becoming increasingly clear – informers, who were responsible for a crippling proportion of arrests, infiltrated it. The PAC, on the other hand – or so it seemed to the young BC members – was rather too complacent and was failing to take the initiative.

Outside the country, too, it was the ANC that had bagged a much larger number of the 1976 exiled students. 'The youngsters came to see us in our offices, and asked us if we would be able to train them and send them home within six months,' recalled Victor Mayekiso, who was then a representative of the PAC in Botswana, 'but then the next thing I heard was that they had joined the ANC camps.'[149]

Ngoako Ramathlodi, whose group of literary friends formed themselves into a secret cell based on what they had read about the Mau-Mau oath-taking in Kenya, crossed the border in December 1977 to Botswana.

'Everyone was BC,' Ramathlodi said, 'but we knew there were bigger things elsewhere. But I suspect that if I had been called by the PAC, that time, I would possibly have been equally happy.'[150] It was just that the ANC had 'reached us first'. While the ANC was not quite ready to develop insurrection inside, Tambo's Mission in Exile had unified machinery outside, ready to receive young people seeking to become freedom fighters. Among its resources were a functional logistical capacity, a conceptually developed strategy of combining different forms of struggle with a shared understanding that politics were in command, and an all-embracing revolutionary nationalism as the driving force. The resolution of the crisis that had led to, and followed on from, the Morogoro Conference meant that the ANC was a relatively cohesive and unified striking force with the capacity to absorb, integrate and deepen the political consciousness of the BC generation who poured over the borders.

As one of the new intakes, Ngoako Ramathlodi underwent an intensive course in Botswana on underground work and propaganda, and when he returned to campus in the new year, his cell began to set up ANC 'machinery' (a cluster of cells, ready to receive instructions from ANC operatives). ANC slogans began to appear on campus – 'Umkhonto we Sizwe is here' and 'The ANC Lives', in black, yellow and green.

But for thousands of young people, it seemed no longer possible to survive inside South Africa, and they clamoured to be sent for military training. For Tambo and the other leadership, it was quite clear that a substantial intake into the military camps would present logistical, if not political problems. They urged the young recruits to consider first furthering their studies – education, too, was a weapon in the struggle, as the 1976 intake themselves had demonstrated. They would also receive political education and training in the process.

Unexpectedly, like Mao's metaphor of a single spark setting the bush alight, leading to liberated rural zones, here it was the children of urban workers, escaping to the 'liberated zones' of Africa, seeking to return and fight in the towns. By their exit, a synergy between the Mission in Exile, the community at home, the underground and the military was set in motion.

O.R. Tambo
We salute you

Part Four

Towards the Apex of Freedom

1978–1993

CHAPTER FOURTEEN

Family in Exile

WHEN ADELAIDE TSUKHUDU HAD broken the news to her family that she intended to marry Oliver Tambo, they were dismayed and had tried to persuade her rather to take the tall, good-looking young man in their neighbourhood. Adelaide was, however, set on the quiet, unassuming Mpondo attorney, highly respected in political circles and an 'educated man'. How ironic then that, once in exile not four years after her marriage, Adelaide was to be lucky if she saw her husband more than a few days a year.

For many South Africans in the liberation movement, exile had taken on an ironically familiar metaphor. For some, the migrant labour experience and the exclusion of blacks from productive life in the city had been a brutal preparation for the indefinite, long-term migration and homelessness of political exile. By the 1960s, when the first small wave of exiles left the country, migrant labour had already profoundly affected traditional culture in South Africa. In time, as the land was less and less able to provide sustenance to their families, migrants needed to spend more and more working time in the city. The deeply rooted African tradition of the extended family was beginning to show signs of unravelling. The longer workers stayed on in town as migrants, the more their hard-earned money was spent on meagre luxuries, on drinks at the shebeens on the weekends, and on temporary partners. 'Town wives', or *nyati*, and even town children became common. Some, therefore, had to divide their pay packet between two families.

It was thus a wry twist of fate that exiles should experience migrant labour all over again in another quintessential form. Their political and military activism laboured for the absent, extended family of the nation. How much more destabilising was this rupture when there was no way of knowing when the banished migrant would return.

As Tambo wrote, 'There is no difference between forced removals from land and forcible removal from citizenship – which is why the denationalisation is an aspect of the implementation of the apartheid policy. Of course, even without the legislation that created the homelands and used to effect denationalisation, Africans were in any case treated as foreigners in their motherland, South Africa'.[1]

The double irony of the ANC in exile was that the escape from dispossession and homelessness, both real and symbolic, imposed on black people by apartheid in the land of their birth, was now duplicated by the anguish and predicament of exile experienced by Tambo and many others committed to the national liberation movement.

'The family [the ANC] is in sound condition,' reported Oliver Tambo to the High Command on Robben Island – 'full of energy and working in unison, and with measurable effect both at home and abroad. As a family among families, ours is accorded a position of seniority and respect by friend and foe, a position it has earned by deeds acknowledged by those even whose business it is to show up the family's faults.'

The redefining of the nation as a family of brothers and sisters, for whose welfare all were responsible, was to bring added heartache to many, though it was also to deliver a strange, sometimes rich alternate life and meaning to the most dedicated members of the ANC.

After the first shock and relief of having fled successfully from oppression, imprisonment and constant danger at home, a sense of loss began to settle over the exiles. Family, community and landscape, language and personal identity – all seemed gone. A 'psychological deportation' had taken place.[2] Anxiety about those left behind, rumours, tormenting memories and anguished tales of the increasing brutality of apartheid wore at the consciences of many.

And these feelings jostled with new challenges and new adjustments. As the exile movement grew, people were increasingly deployed further away from the ANC headquarters in Dar es Salaam or Lusaka. Military training sent cadres first to North Africa and then across the seas to Eastern Europe. As Tambo's fund-raising efforts began to be realised, diplomats and administrators opened up new offices in Europe, in North America, in Cuba. Many ANC exiles spoke with pain of the difficulties of living in a foreign country, and often too of their bewilderment and experience of the more subtle and sophisticated forms of racism and silences in Western culture.[3] Even in Canada, one of the more welcoming and enlightened societies, well-meaning comments were stereotypical and hurtful; Africa was seen as a place of disadvantage and lack of opportunities. 'People do not realise that you might not have opportunities, but you do have capabilities.'[4]

All the more important, then, were the little ANC communities that drew sustenance from each other, by sharing and participating in shaping policies and programmes. Moeletsi Mbeki, son of Govan and Epainette Mbeki, and a journalist who travelled frequently, spoke of the importance of arriving in a new country and being able to find an ANC office, attend the branch meetings, congregate with comrades and communicate in his mother tongue.[5] For ANC members, their liberation movement was their extended family of brothers and sisters in the struggle. Experiences, community, vision and the justification for their situation provided the basis of a discourse that resonated with exiles.

Tambo's own wife and children were also in exile, but far removed from him. His emotional energies thus radiated out to embrace and empower all the members of the ANC, in particular the children and women in the movement. There were, of course, racial, ethnic, cultural, class and ideological differences within the ANC, but Tambo worked hard to craft an imagined community, bonded by its shared Mission in Exile to wipe apartheid off the face of the earth and free South Africa for a united, democratic and non-racial society.

In his mandated position as head of the Mission in Exile, Tambo was acutely aware of his responsibility to sustain and keep together the ANC in the context of its dislocation. He had been rudely alerted to the divisions caused by the dissatisfaction of the Group of Eight in the early seventies.[6] This unfortunate episode brought home to Tambo the imperative of maintaining unity. He observed anxiously the danger of deflecting the energy of the movement into self-defeating, internecine conflict, such as was occurring in a number of exiled liberation movements in Africa and South America at the time. It was Tambo's conscious duty to protect and nurture his vastly extended family.

Tambo's character itself was a product not only of his parents' care, but also of his homestead culture. As a member of a large, polygamous family, he had had to share not only his mother with many others, but his father with his other mothers, uncles, aunts, siblings and kinfolk. Unlike most middle-class children reared in a nuclear family structure, the young Oliver had had to sacrifice some of his own ego, his own sense of identity. But at the same time, having access to other mothers, aunts, uncles and older brothers and sisters provided at least some compensation. The child's growing sense of self was tied up with his extended family, with his neighbours and with his community. The day-to-day lifestyle, and hence the value system, was one of sharing.

In Oliver Tambo's case, this sense of obligation was magnified. Over the years, his concept of 'the community' was to grow, little by little but steadily, along with his increasing exposure to that wider world of his childhood, beyond the Engeli Mountains. His sense of personal responsibility for the welfare of the community continued to grow – until it reached a point where the identification of his kinfolk, and his obligation to them, expanded to include all African people, indeed all the oppressed and exploited of South Africa.

In exile, Tambo's role was to maintain the coherence of the movement. To guard against the 'pointlessness' of exile, he responded tacitly to the pain of separation, the sense of insignificance and the restructuring of meaning. He worked with these feelings to find tangible expression of the ANC as an inspiration and the motor of liberation, translating it into accessible language. He worked actively to avoid the sense of alienation of the ANC External Mission from their environment, or from the movement at home. As leader of the mission, Tambo's antidote to the condition of exile – living 'as if everything around you is temporary and perhaps trivial'[7] – was constantly to remind the ANC of the purpose of the struggle.[8]

In notes prepared for a meeting, Tambo wrote, 'Our situation is complex and tough... [It] is weakest under conditions of exile which impose an ever increasing strain on morale. This strain is always aggravated by remoteness from the scene of conflict. What does unite people in action is action against the enemy.'[9]

On a more subliminal level, he worked to refashion nuances, emphases, symbols and heritage, to instil in disparate and far-flung communities a sense of belonging.

The expatriates would indulge, over drinks, in nights of story-telling – tales of childhood adventures, family and home, memories of apartheid's slights, insults and physical battering, turning points and political awakenings, stories from the different parts of *ekhaya* ('home') helped to maintain connections with the variety of backgrounds that made up the ANC membership.

Stories about the leadership – exemplars on Robben Island, in history and outside – were also significant in forming a shared, collective narrative for the ANC in exile. Even tales told by Tambo, related in snatched interludes at airports or during taxi rides, were circulated. Jacob Zuma, attempting to recall the essence of the man, remembered Tambo's gently humorous anecdotes.

'It used to be very few occasions where he'll relax and talk about things. Now I liked telling stories and I used to tell him stories as well and the times I remember in London. [When] we were meeting Chester Crocker, we were also meeting the British Foreign Secretary on the same day and we had to travel to different areas in a car and he was telling me stories, which he used to do, because I used to tell him stories about [Zuma's village of] Nkandla, about everything.'[10]

Zuma recalled the tales of Tambo's childhood in Pondoland and his unforgettable first impressions of Johannesburg, arriving by train as a 14-year-old with his close friend, Robert Sonqishe.

These were the stories that circulated and, at times, they even came full circle. Tselane Tambo, born in exile, had all too few memories of her father. Through the stories of him told by visitors to their London home, she was able to piece together an identity of him. Years later, after liberation, old comrades who had been in exile during their formative youth were still bonded by their common experiences, and back home now, still swapped stories in Gauteng's suburban pubs, including tales of 'Comrade OR' and memories of their exile days.[11]

As Edward Said once observed about the long-term condition of exile, ANC members fended off a sense of homelessness by fashioning 'a community of language, culture and customs'.[12] Words like *ekhaya* (home), *mgwenya* (veteran fighters), 'frying' or 'dicing' (the bartering of ANC clothes and supplies rationed to members for goods or money) echoed their shared experiences.

Special names of affection and respect for the leaders, over and above the *noms de guerre* adopted for security reasons, were generally used throughout the exile community, drawing from the tradition in African political circles at home, when the intelligentsia during the forties and fifties came to be known affectionately by their initials. 'ZK Matthews was known as ZK,' Pallo Jordan observed, 'as were WB Ngakane (Pascal and Lionel's father) called WB, AC Jordan known as AC, IB Tabata known as IB, etc. This was true of the PAC as it was of the ANC. Leballo, for example, was called PK by his colleagues'.[13] In exile, rather than being addressed by their official titles in the movement such as 'Acting President' (later 'President'), Tambo became known as 'Comrade OR' – after the initials of his first two names, Oliver Reginald – or 'Chief'. Joe Slovo was JS, Dadoo, 'Doc' and Nkobi, 'TT' (Thomas Titus) or 'TG' (Nkobi was the Treasurer-General), and Nzo, 'SG' (Secretary-General). 'OR's more intimate names among comrades were names like "Bones" – Tambo means "bone"; or "Bra B". OR was aware of these nicknames, and in fact surprised NEC members once by referring to himself by one of them,' remembers Pallo Jordan.[14] There was also more than one 'Joe' in the leadership – Joe Modise, Joe Nhlanhla, Joe Jele and Joe Slovo were known by their initials: 'JM', 'JN', 'JJ' and 'JS' respectively.

Many jokes did the rounds and served to bond the scattered exiles. There was the true story of the BC rercuit in the camps in Angola who learnt that one should say 'the racists' instead of stereotyping all whites. He ended up pointing to Joe Slovo as an example of a 'good racist'. Slovo himself was well known for his political jokes. One of these was: 'Whenever I'm asked when the revolution will come to South Africa, I always say "In three years' time..."'

'Oh, how so?'

'Well, in 1960, the PAC told us that 1963 would be The Year of Liberation – after three years – and, frankly, I see no reason to question their decision now!'

Oliver Tambo, too, loved a good laugh and had a well-developed sense of fun. But on a more profound level, his speeches invoked a panoply of heroes and martyrs, historical and geographical landmarks, the founding fathers and mothers to bond his family in exile. The list was broad and representative – they were not simply confined to the military, but men and women who demonstrated the wide range of contributions they had made to the struggle. On MK's tenth anniversary, Tambo asked:

'Is the *oath* we took of any meaning and substance to those who swore to fight until freedom is won? We must unite and follow in the footsteps of our martyrs – in the footsteps of the men who fell in the frontline in South Africa and Zimbabwe and in other countries.' It was the day after the death in detention of Ahmed Timol. There were other martyrs, too, who he named for everyone to honour – Molefe, Mini, Khayinga, Mkaba, Bongco, Solwandle, Saloojee, Imam Haroun, Paul Petersen, Patrick Molaoa, Florence Matemola, Alpheus Madiba and Caleb Mayekiso.[15]

It was the custom for Tambo to give a speech every year on 8 January, the anniversary of the ANC's founding meeting in 1912. From 1980, the ANC embarked on a mobilising exercise (an innovation by Thabo Mbeki), one that also affirmed ANC identity by selecting a theme for the coming year – The Year of the Charter (1980), or The Year of the Women (1984), or The Year of the Cadre (1985), for example. Every speech delivered on 8 January was embedded in ANC heritage, and presented the movement as the custodians of a proud history of struggle. The speech was customarily written by Thabo Mbeki. The year 1980 was to prove highly effective, and particularly captured the imagination of the youth. From that year onwards, Tambo would announce the ANC's theme and focus for the coming year in his anniversary speech.

The ANC was far from monolithic, and the choice of theme for the year, the interpretation and content of each speech, was often debated and contested. The 'correct' analysis of the situation, the strategies and tactics needed for the immediate way forward, and the motivation for what would resonate most powerfully with the growing numbers of listeners back home were of vital significance. It was Oliver Tambo's task to provide considered guidance to ANC thinking, imparting coherence to what became a highly symbolic and powerful site of struggle.

In the context of a powerfully bonded, political culture, exiled members made a conscious effort to experience and get to know local society as intensely as possible without integrating in a way that dampened their passion for home. Although many held jobs outside the movement as teachers, lawyers, doctors, lecturers, journalists, or in semiskilled work, thousands were financially dependent on the ANC. These included students for whom the ANC had found placements in universities in the socialist bloc and in western European countries and the USA. And then, of course, there were the full-time political and military cadres for whom the ANC raised funds to provide for them and their families. But there were no salaries as such.

Apart from the military personnel, most officials stationed in ANC offices around the world. The majority were working in African cities and towns such as Lusaka, Dar es Salaam, Manzini in Swaziland, Roma in Lesotho and later Maputo, with the largest number located in the ANC's head office in Lusaka. 'There was a strong sense of community and trust. We had a belief in people,' recalled James Stuart (real name Hermanus Loots) wistfully. 'In a sense, our lives as ANC were almost unreal, unaffected by battles raging outside, [and we were] sheltered from local politics.'[16]

Money was not part of the mind-set of that older generation. Apart from their very modest monthly allowance (one or two beers or a packet of cigarettes), they could sometimes look forward to the 'departure fee' of 20 Zambian shillings granted to those who were going abroad on official business. Once, in this regard, Stuart recalled Tambo's unworldly generosity. They were both waiting to leave Lusaka for a conference. The plane was delayed for several hours, and late into the night Tambo noticed that Stuart had spent his 'departure fee' at the pub. He searched all his pockets for some time, and finally found his untouched 20 shillings, which he then handed over to Stuart.[17]

Icons and role models are standard mobilising devices to revolutionaries and, in exile, these become crucial in providing tangible links to the cause. In the ANC, after two decades of patiently building up the identity of the exile mission, that person was Oliver Tambo. Jacob Zuma's description of the anxious audience in the waiting room of the head office in Lusaka echoes scenes in the chambers of Mandela & Tambo in the 1950s: 'There was always a queue because everybody, either affected by his department, or whatever, ended up with him.'[18]

Tambo himself had internalised perfectionism, and his work ethic had brought him both respect and applause. These were qualities that he sought to transfer to the ANC members with whom he came into contact. In fact, at the Lusaka office, Stuart recalled how 'we all tried to emulate OR's person – his uprightness, his integrity, his intellectual and political ability. Yet he would listen to people's smallest problems. He would listen, and talk. Often he would go and see people, just to chat.'[19]

In this context, it was Tambo who fashioned a new metaphor of exile, presenting it as a kind of 'liberated space',[20] for it reinforced a sense of agency for the movement, giving scope to explore new tactics and acquire new skills for its ultimate goal. He succeeded in fashioning a sense of community out of these far-flung exiles. Tambo was a kind of 'non-iconic icon': polite, business-like, unassuming and concerned. He made modesty respectable, even something to be emulated. 'He showed,' reflected Albie Sachs, 'that you could lead just by listening. Whoever you were – and the range was immense – you felt you had a special bond, that you were a favourite of his.'

Exile meant separation for very long periods – between couples, and between parents and children. Many marriages fell victim to the strain, and families were ruptured. Mzwai Piliso, who spent years training cadres in the military camps, remembered going to England to see his wife after three years.

'I knocked at the door. The children came. "Yes?" I just looked at them. I didn't say anything. And the older one, after about five minutes, jumped at me and says, "Daddy!"

'The younger one goes in, I don't know where he had gone to, and when he comes out he says, no, that is not my daddy. He was four. When I last saw him he was about a year [old]. He was not four years. "That is not my daddy." That was because the mother had a photograph of me with a huge beard, and he went and looked at that. Came and looked at me: This man has no beard, therefore he can't be my father. But by the end of the week, I was already Daddy also. That is the problem with many of us.'[21]

Nevertheless, a surprising number of marriages did survive the trial of separation. Piliso's explanation was that 'the men were pricked by their consciences that they didn't look after their wives and children, and that the wives had a difficult time raising the family... Fortunately, almost all wives were members of the ANC, and many of them had been in the ANC for a very long time'.[22]

In many cases, marriages remained nominally intact, with both partners continuing to be active parents – again reminiscent of the practical arrangements back home of many family homesteads interrupted by migration.

The children of political activists inside South Africa continued to suffer the uncertainties and anxieties that followed a parent's detention, arrest or disappearance. But at home, there was almost always a strong and supportive community structure. In exile, family connections were more deeply eroded. After the uprising in Soweto and other parts of South Africa in 1976, more and more young people went into exile and into the ANC, and it was this group in particular that absorbed much of Tambo's emotional energy. In the military training camps and in the ANC's Solomon Mahlangu Freedom College, he and other senior members became intensely conscious of their duties to act

ABOVE *Addis Ababa, 1962. Tambo and Nelson Mandela attended the Organisation of African Union conference. Mandela had slipped out of South Africa to give advance warning to the Mission in Exile of the decision to turn to armed struggle.* (Mayibuye Centre)

ABOVE *Freedom Day, 26 June 1968. Oliver Tambo addresses a rally of the Anti-Apartheid Movement in Trafalgar Square, London. Tambo paid great attention to 'people-to-people diplomacy'. Eventually, popular opposition in the USA and UK obliged their governments to impose sanctions on apartheid South Africa.* (*Sunday Times*)

ABOVE *Oliver Tambo arrives in Dar es Salaam, 1960. In the doorway is Frene Ginwala, who was able to arrange a travel permit for Tambo, courtesy of the government of India.* (Bailey's African History Archives)

ABOVE *The Luthuli Detachment trains for MK's first military attempt to cross back into South Africa via Rhodesia in 1987. Tambo, as Supreme Commander, accompanied the soldiers to the banks of the Zambezi River, watching over them as they swam across.* (Mayibuye Centre)

TOP LEFT *Tselane Tambo, photographed in 1972, on a rare occasion when both her parents were able to fetch her from school.* (Tambo Family Album)

TOP RIGHT *Trevor Huddleston, Bishop of Masisi, champion of children and lifelong friend of OR, at St Cyprian's, 1967.* (Tambo Family Album)

ABOVE *OR, accompanied by Thabo Mbeki, meets with USSR President Gorbachev, 1986. In the early years the Socialist Bloc were the only countries to actively support the armed struggle taken up by the ANC. Their solidarity alienated many Western countries from the ANC, however.* (Mayibuye Centre)

LEFT *OR discusses the United Nations exhibition on apartheid with UN officials and the UN representative ES Reddy. Accompanying him are (from left) Joel Netshitenze and Thabo Mbeki.* (Mayibuye Centre)

CENTRE *Sweden's prime minister, Olof Palme, enjoyed a warm personal relationship with OR. Here they attend the opening of the Swedish People's Parliament Against Apartheid in February 1986. Less than two weeks later, Palme was gunned down in Stockholm.* (Tambo Family Album)

BELOW *OR leads a delegation to The Hague, hosted by the Netherlands in 1977. In attendance were, from left, Henry Makgothi, Alfred Nzo, Thomas Nkobi and Tambo.* (Tambo Family Album)

ABOVE *Oliver Tambo addresses the Harare International Convention, held in 1987 to focus on the plight of children in neighbouring South Africa.* (Tambo Family Album)

RIGHT *ANC President Oliver Tambo mourns the massacre of 42 comrades and Basotho civilians at Maseru, capital of Lesotho, after a military attack by the South African Defence Force, 1982.* (Tambo Family Album)

ABOVE *A reunion of the Rivonia accused at a clinic in Sweden in 1990. Standing (from left) are Thabo Mbeki, Joe Nhlanhla, Govan Mbeki, Raymond Mhlaba, Tambo, Andrew Mlangeni, Walter Sisulu, Wilton Mkwayi, Joe Slovo and Henry Makgothi. Seated are Alfred Nzo, Albertina Sisulu and Elias Motsoaledi.* (ANC Commemorative Card No. 2)

LEFT *OR visits an Umkhonto we Sizwe camp in Angola, 1993. He was ceremoniously presented with civilian clothes during the demobilisation process prior to going home.* (Tambo Family Album)

LEFT *OR was the keynote speaker at New York's Riverside Church in 1986, on the occasion of the commemoration of the assassination of Sweden's prime minister Olof Palme. Also on the platform were representatives of the Riverside Church Disarmament Program, the UN and Sweden as well as Jesse Jackson, US politician and activist.* (John Goodwin, courtesy United Methodist Board of Global Ministries)

ABOVE *Comrade OR Tambo, home again at his sister's house in Kantolo (traditionally 'Nkantolo'), gazing upon the Engeli Mountains, January 1993.* (courtesy Luli Callinicos)

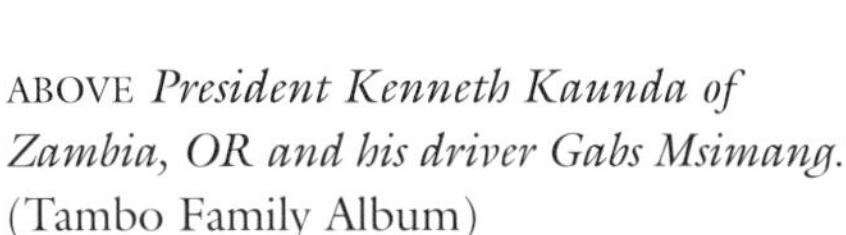

ABOVE *President Kenneth Kaunda of Zambia, OR and his driver Gabs Msimang.* (Tambo Family Album)

CENTRE, RIGHT *Reunited after 28 years, Nelson Mandela and OR, London, 1990.* (ANC Commemorative Card)

RIGHT *Walter Sisulu, the USA's Andrew Young and OR at the conference hosted by the ANC to thank the international community for its support, Crown Mines, Johannesburg, February 1993.* (Tambo Family Album)

ABOVE *After treatment in Stockholm for his stroke, Oliver Tambo returned to his home in London, 1990. A joyous reception, led by the ANC's Amandla choir, awaited him.* (Tambo Family Album)

ABOVE *The Tambo family gathers at the unveiling of Oliver Tambo's tombstone in Wattville, Ekurhuleni. From left, Thembi Tambo (partly obscured), Dr Adelaide Tambo, Maxine Tselane Tambo, Dali and Rachel Tambo, and Lindiwe Mabuza, South Africa's High Commissioner to the UK.* (Tambo Family Album)

in *loco parentis.* Tambo was also anxious to give as much as he could to the motherless children in exile, hundreds of whom arrived at ANC offices, traumatised, hungry, exhausted and parentless.[23]

Tambo had to deal with hundreds of disturbed young people. He was in a unique position in that he was occasionally present at debriefing sessions with newcomers and, in his talks with ANC members around the world, was exposed not only to the guilt felt by parents but also to the suffering of children. It was his clear duty to look after these children. They needed loving care, healing, guidance and education. Childcare was foregrounded as a conscious, deliberate priority. Jane Dumasi, a professional, exiled nurse, acknowledged that 'the ANC was very cooperative'. 'Even now I haven't found any problem in my work, because whatever we need for the children the ANC says children are the first preference,'[24] she explained.

Mzwai Piliso, who had set up the camps in Angola, described his attempt to be a father figure to the newly arrived youngsters, many of whom were very young and undeveloped, until then still dependent on their mothers.

'[They] had to go out and all of a sudden become men... And I was saying to them, "I think what you need to do is to pretend, play, that you are five years older than you are". They were so young, so tender. A person had to wake up in the morning, decide and fend for himself what he is going to wear. It was not much choice. It was military wear, but he is going to come to the lines with a dirty uniform and he is going to be told, "Go back!" And, therefore, each time he takes out the uniform, he needs to wash it. Some of them had never washed a handkerchief.'

He recalled how 'most of those in Angola don't call me comrade; they say *Tata* (Daddy). And I encouraged them because they needed a Tata... If there were problems, it would be difficult to go to a Commander, but it would be easy to go to Tata and say I have this problem – even the women, to a point where they had no qualms, and they would discuss anything with me. And I was ready to discuss it with them. So that in fact I think the numbers that [suffered] mental breakdowns were not as many as ought to [have been]'.[25]

Tambo was especially aware of the MK cadres in the camps – largely young men with a small fraction of women, isolated after their military training and short of day-to-day resources. His visits were, wherever possible – either at induction or graduation ceremonies – warm and supportive. He would take them seriously, giving reports and updates on the situation in South Africa and abroad. Perceived as the man who was working to make things happen, Tambo's unassuming and unpretentious style was received with much affection and immense respect.

Ironically, Tambo, 'father of the nation' during the exile period, was seldom there for his own children. After the ANC's embrace of armed struggle and Tambo's move to Tanzania, it had been decided between he and Adelaide that she would remain in London, where she could earn a living wage. Then, with the move to Zambia after its independence, Tambo obliquely raised the possibility that Adelaide might come to Africa.[26]

'I always felt it would be excellent if you visit Zambia,' he wrote to her in 1969. 'You would find many old friends here, including Betty Kaunda and crowds of South Africans. You would also see the country and meet Zambians and get to know something about the schooling possibilities of staying and working here.' But, he added, 'it might also give you a tatste of the sort of burdens I am bearing in my irrevocable determination to do what to many seems impossible – to make South Africa an independent African state ruled by the majority of its black, brown and white people, and not a patch of black and white stains.'

But his letter failed to convince her. 'There was no way I could have stayed in Lusaka because there was a price on Oliver's head,' declared Adelaide flatly.[27]

As marriage partners, the relationship of Adelaide and Oliver remained long distance, conducted by irregular but affectionate letters.

'I never knew when I'd see him and the only communication we had were his letters. He was travelling, but could not come to London all the time. He would go from Kenya to the USA or something like that... So it was very difficult to make any communication except by letter. It would be posted in Tanzania. Nothing was safe those days. Most of the letters reached him when he was in Tanzania but when he was in Zambia, he did not get all the letters.'[28]

But the long separations did not diminish their commitment to each other: 'You are never there when I phone! Why are you dashing around so much? Are you taking good care of the leg? I suspect that you are over-working as usual,' Tambi scolded his wife affectionately. 'You must *stop it*! Do you hear?'[29]

As in any marriage, there were times when they quarrelled – at a distance, though, retorts were suspended for weeks, even months. Like many couples, they did not always agree on priorities in the distribution of income and expenditure. In one letter, Tambo expressed his exasperation with expensive public schools that catered for upper-class families, yet not necessarily delivering what he called 'a good education'. 'They are not even teaching proper manners, let alone the 3 Rs. The English school system completely baffles me,' he continued ruefully.

'For example, as you told me today, they make children learn sewing. This is fine. The subject is compulsory. Why this should be is not very clear to me. But when they insist that *we* must buy a whole sewing machine for a child who is never going to be a dressmaker, then I fail to see the point...

'Then you have another absurdity. The school decides to have a play. Fine! So it needs costumes for the actors. But then the parents must buy costumes... Why? What on earth is our child going to do with this costume after the play has been performed? Surely the school should buy it and use it every year?'[30]

Adelaide's determination to send the children to public schools of high repute had, of course, reverberated on Tambo. The dissidents had used Tambo's children's schooling and Adelaide's house in Muswell Hill to make unfavourable comparisons with the lifestyles of leaders of other African liberation movements. The fact that Tambo was seldom able to enjoy the relative comforts of a London suburban home was immaterial – the image had been painted. But the device failed to damage his personal integrity. Pallo Jordan once commented that the final nail in the coffin of the Group of Eight was that they had criticised Tambo personally – the NEC, and Duma Nokwe in particular, had been fiercely protective of their much-loved chairperson. He, of all people, was perceived as having the highest integrity.

For Tambo's part, his approach was more complex, the delivery of a virtually unspoken pact, which not many of his friends – even his closest religious friends – could quite accept. Fertz Ngakane, a close family friend in London, explained:

'You see, OR... could never have made those contacts with the various people throughout the world if the problem of his at home had not been solved. And he would never have had peace of mind to work, to do the demanding type of work if there was a lot of dissension really... Unless he could make his wife happy about this, he could not do the work he was doing. It was to me a very small price to pay for the type of man he was and the type of work he was doing... I wanted to bring the point about her strong side. She is a very strong woman and I think Tambo, in this respect, could not have had a better support from a wife than Adelaide. Very well informed, very, very informed. And she can make a strong point herself about what she feels strongly about. So, in that way, she is quite a lady. I know she likes [pomp and ceremony]. But that is a small price to pay. Some people like that... And I have never really worried, because to me it is a very superficial thing.'[31]

Adelaide's style was effusive and affectionate. 'Impulsive, spontaneous, and generous... She would rather spend all she had than count her pennies like a poor person,' commented Albie Sachs. Not necessarily given to heavy political discourse, she would see things in people in a practical and direct way.

Ironically, like the migrant labour system in South Africa, the long absences of the father resulted in many family decisions being made, despite the patriarchal system, by the wife: 'I missed him terribly and thought of him a lot and sought his advice on everything – *except the children's education*.'[32]

Over the years, then, the long separations trained both partners to fashion their own way of living apart. Some who saw more of Tambo in Lusaka assumed that he and Adelaide had drifted apart, each living their own lives. Certainly, there were times when Tambo clearly could not cope with his wife's expectations, and sometimes a letter from Adelaide lay unopened on his desk for days. He dreaded opening it. Nevertheless, despite their difficulties and occasional resentments, they remained steadfastly committed to each other. Asked about the years of loneliness, Adelaide recalled many trying times. She spoke about 'people trying to ruin it all; men trying to come and propose. It also made them hate you because you have rejected them, and they start labelling you with this and that: "This woman who likes upper class."'[33]

Tambo's affectionate nature and Adelaide's unflagging pride in her husband's qualities and achievements sustained their deep commitment to their marriage vows, but it fell upon Adelaide to support the children both emotionally and financially. In this she was determined to provide them with the best, displaying the same drive and resolution to strive for equal resources and opportunities that had propelled her into activism in her youth, and which Tambo had found so attractive. Adelaide was once described as 'single-minded, stoical and friendly but defensive'.[34] She not only worked double shifts to improve her income, but also worked to raise further funds for her children's education.[35]

Because she worked such long hours – 'between 12 and 20 hours a day' at Whittington Hospital, as well as a district nurse with an agency – she did not see enough of the children and felt constantly anxious and guilty about leaving them alone. Whenever she could, particularly in the youngest child Tselane's early years, she would enlist the help of London ANC members, such as May Brutus, Stephanie Kemp, Eleanor Kasrils and ANC students studying in London, for baby-sitting. Adelaide had a knack for organising people and making them see their assistance as a contribution to the broader cause. But there were many times when she had to leave her children alone during her night shifts.

Of course, Adelaide was also involved in ANC politics. She would occasionally attend branch meetings, and became an effective public speaker. She was articulate, and commanded the attention of her audience. On one memorable occasion, after the fire, she made a dramatic impact in a beautiful traditional gown, walking slowly and with great dignity with the aid of a walking stick to denounce in ringing tones the divisive behaviour of the dissident Group of Eight.[36]

As 'first lady' of the movement, she was as conscious of her obligations as she was of her status. From time to time, Adelaide looked after others besides her children. Refugees, students, children of ANC members from home or in exile, illustrious visitors from all parts of the world – many could recall days or evenings, even weeks spent at Adelaide's house in Muswell Hill. Sometimes, students and other young people would stay for months until they were placed in an educational institution, or were deployed elsewhere in the movement.

'The kids got into difficulty at school and I was the only person they could come to. Their parents were in jail on Robben Island. They ran away to go to Lusaka, then they were sent abroad, wherever scholarships were for them to carry on with their education. A lot of them came to see me. [At one point] we were 16 altogether. The kids were good. They washed up the dishes; I did the cooking. I did the laundry and they helped with the ironing. We never had the same amount of people all the time; it was varying at different times. Some of the girls doing nursing would get difficulties through the hospitals where they were working, they would leave their jobs and they would come and stay, and some would be on holiday from the hospital and would come and stay...'[37]

They were, after all, members of the extended ANC family. The South African system of 'home-boys and -girls', whereby any clan member or neighbour from one's village would spontaneously be made welcome in the city for as long as he or she needed hospitality, was thus extended throughout the world.

One night, while Adelaide was on night duty and the children were alone in the house, something shocking galvanised her into taking further action. A Peeping Tom had scaled the wall and spied on Thembi, lying in bed in her room on the first floor. The 12-year-old child was terrified, and for months afterwards was afraid to be left in the house at night without adult protection. Adelaide immediately contacted John and Diana Collins, the British Defence and Aid Fund and other funders, and managed to place her children in boarding schools. The fees were high, and the funders were ambivalent about doling out money for expensive public schools. But Adelaide was unblinkingly adamant. Her children needed care and, effectively a single parent, she was not able to give it. She needed peace of mind.

Adelaide Tambo fought fiercely to give her children the very best education. 'I'd seen how the British regarded their children's education in South Africa and I was damned if my children would have anything but the best in this country. Besides, discipline was what I wanted for my children – they were going to need it.'[38]

Once, young Dali was upset by an ugly racial incident at boarding school, and telephoned his mother in tears. Furious, Adelaide called the headmaster and the next morning went straight from her night shift to the school. She arrived in time for the morning assembly, marched up to the platform and sat down to witness a public apology from the headmaster and an exposition on the destructive nature of racism. The event meant a lot to the 12-year-old boy, a black child in a subliminally race-conscious society, which made subtle discrimination all the more difficult to confront. The Tambo children's confidence was boosted by their mother's determination and protection.

When Tambo passed through London during term time, he would not find his children at home. But even when he did, he would not always be able to offer them the full attention they needed. His visits, few as they were, were fleeting and distracted, and he was invariably accompanied by an entourage. The London office, too, almost always paid anxious visits, documents and agendas in hand, while ordinary members, sniffing out his presence, eagerly dropped by.

Dali Tambo once spoke – in an interview as a young man in London – about the shadowy image the children had of their father.[39] They knew he was somehow important – 'the big meetings they would have in my mother's flat, and uncles and aunts constantly coming in' – yet, strangely, there was never enough money, unlike the parents of their friends at the prestigious public schools they attended. Students and important-looking men, including well-known British figures, visited their home. Thabo Mbeki was often a house guest, indeed he was seen as an 'older brother' to the children, talking to them about the ANC, its objectives and their father's role in the movement. As they grew older and began to comprehend their father's occupation, they began to feel inadequate. Why was Dali not like the sons of Govan Mbeki or Walter Sisulu, Adelaide would sometimes ask in exasperation. But they, as pointed out by Dali, were born into a very different situation.

'I didn't feel I was British,' confided Dali Tambo. 'I felt you could only be British if you were white.'[40] Yet they could not be South African either. 'Since early childhood, [I was] out in a nunnery and then a prep school and a public school, how would I be a Zwelakhe Sisulu or a Thabo Mbeki? Culturally, I was a little black Englishman [Laughs] ... When you sit in a room with your parents, even at 20 or 21, you just feel, why am I the only person who doesn't understand what they're talking about?'[41]

For the older children, there came a time when they remembered returning home from school and realising that they could no longer understand Xhosa.

Of course, Tambo was pained that he saw so little of his children, though he put on a show of delight that they had grown or matured so much since he had last seen them. Adelaide recalled how he used songs to create a link between himself and his children during his absences. When Thembi was little, he composed a song especially for her in Sotho and English, which she learnt and delighted in singing.[42]

But lacking the day-to-day, incremental relationship that certainly for Tambo would have brought depth and understanding of these special young individuals, he often tried to reach them through humour and story-telling. As they grew older, he would try to extend his time with them by finding ways of combining working time in another country with a holiday with his children. In that way, he was also able to give his wife a rare break. Thembi recalled four holidays with their father. Much as they wanted to be with him, these holidays were not much fun. She recalled, once, despite their guided tours of Moscow or Berlin and friendly adults, spending long hours in hotels while their father attended meetings. She also remembered being offered money by their hosts so that they could buy souvenirs, but their father forbade them to accept any handouts – they had been given an allowance, and they should budget accordingly.

But the children also remembered their father's sense of fun, and his gentleness. Once, when the three came home after an outing with him, they sat him down and promised to bring him 'something very special' to drink. Amid much noise and giggling behind the closed door of the kitchen, they concocted a mixture of fruit juice, tomato sauce and washing-up liquid. Tambo drank it all up, playing along with their game, smiling in seeming pleasure at the 'delicious drink' that his children had prepared for him.[43] They adored the irony of his response – the joke was on them!

When political realisation came, all three children became anxious about their father. They became aware that his life was in constant danger. Thembi Tambo recalled that in their prayers, they would ask God that their father be permitted to die at home.[44] Yet they knew that he would never retire, not until liberation had come. Every time Tambo departed from his London home, Adelaide recalled, the children inevitably cried, were grizzly, and impossibly demanding.

'One time Oliver came back and I had a tiff with him about the children. What happened was that every time he came for about two days, when he goes, I have to struggle. The children cry, they want him and so on.

'Then for those two days when he is there, the children don't even have time because the politicians come to see him. He can't have a meal with them because when I cook lunch and these people are here and are sitting with him. It became very irritating. So I said: "Don't come. If you do come, why don't you go to a hotel and then stay there? These people can come and see you there and the children and I can come and see you there."'

Tambo did not reply, but when he returned to Lusaka, he wrote to her. Adelaide remembered the substance of his letter: 'I understood what you have said and I understand the difficulties. But the people in Robben Island don't come to see their children even for 30 minutes. So when I get a day or two, I am most grateful. I do agree that I don't have time to sit with the children, to play with them or encourage them. That is the way things are going to be for as long as we are in a political struggle.'

'I think that I replied to that letter. I did not want to break Oliver's spirit saying that we are living through difficult times and that I haven't got endless energy. I said that I am sorry about what I have said. Since we left home everything has been on my shoulders; besides that there are other people's children, too, who were coming to stay with me until they got settled.'[45]

Tambo himself, in fact, had very little money and hardly ever spent his ANC allowance of £2 a week on himself, saving what he could for birthday and Christmas gifts for the children. Diana Collins recalled how once her husband, Canon John Collins, insisted on giving to his reluctant and slightly embarrassed friend money to buy gifts for his children. In his letters to his wife, Tambo on more than one occasion wrote to thank his wife for clothing and a gift of homemade fruitcakes and other delicacies.

A few years after the Peeping Tom incident, the family suffered yet another trauma. The house caught fire one night while Thembi and Adelaide were upstairs. Dali and Tselane were away at boarding school, but coincidentally, Oliver was at home and had gone out to find a repairman to attend to a gas leak downstairs in the kitchen. Seeing the smoke rising from the floor and under the door, Adelaide hastily knotted some sheets together to enable her to jump through the window. But the reef knot broke and when she landed on the ground below, she suffered multiple fractures to her legs and hip. The alarm was raised and Thembi was rescued, shocked but unhurt. Shortly afterwards, Oliver returned and Adelaide was rushed to hospital, where, avoiding amputation, her bones were pieced together with metal screws. The day after her 13-hour operation, Adelaide, however, went into secondary shock, convinced that her husband and children were dead, and was given injections to tranquillise her. It took five days before she was able to recall what had happened. For Tambo, the contradictions between his duties as a family man and a political leader of a movement in exile had been cruelly tested.

'Oliver came in to say that, "Look, I'm not going to go until I am certain that your condition has improved and although I do not live here I still have a duty to protect you and I'll be here until I'm satisfied that you can go." But things were pressing, and again the movement took precedence. He was there for the next week and then had to go and appear at the UN and he left.'[46]

For a long time, Adelaide had to give up nursing. Tambo sent help whenever he could. Ruth Mompati came to London to help clean up the burnt shell of the house, scrubbing the walls, rescuing furniture not already ruined beyond repair by fire or water, and helping with the housekeeping and cooking. Adelaide remained on crutches for quite some time, and afterwards walked with difficulty. In the long term, through self-medication, she was able to avoid further drastic surgery, but for the rest of her life the accident continued to affect her health, contributing to the rheumatoid arthritis and the diabetic condition she later developed.

Without work, Adelaide needed funds, and so she set about applying for financial assistance. The [British] Defence and Aid Fund gave £500, and Adelaide wrote to the local government of Haringay, 'to tell them that I had had the accident, that I was the bread winner of the family, and that Oliver was in the struggle'.[47] Adelaide was not embarrassed to assert her claims, and did not hesitate to apply to the broader community, including the British welfare system, for help. According to her values, humanity, reciprocity and acknowledgement of the sacrifices endured by her and her children in the struggle against apartheid were to be expected from any caring society.

This was a value system shared by the movement. The ANC's attitude to all children was 'Every child is my child'. Indeed those who did not have their own children with them loved to visit the crèches and the college.

'You know, when men see children and they don't have children around they become very much interested in children,' commented Gertrude Shope. 'They would come and take them and play around with them. And sometimes, it would bring up very, very sad occasions.'[48]

It seems ironic, then, that a culture universally known for its love of children should have produced, in its political movement, children who felt neglected and abandoned – until one recalls the widely felt sense of responsibility the entire community was supposed to carry for all of its children. Political activists, migrant workers, ailing or gestating mothers, all tended to take solace in the belief that their children would be cared for by the extended family, which after all embraced the entire community. It was this attitude, and the assurance that the movement would take care of their families, that helped sustain the political prisoners on Robben Island. Even before he was imprisoned, Govan Mbeki, for instance, as an African and a communist, was able to feel that the 'family' would look after his children. Fertz Ngakane, headmaster of an elementary school in London, confirmed this transfer of traditional culture into the political sphere.

'If a woman lost her husband, she was never left on her own, because she was now part of the family – and was looked after by the family. Her children were looked after by the family. So, in that respect, socialism and communism were sort of almost blending. Communism perhaps is a higher form of socialism, perhaps, I don't know. But, as far as I am concerned, it has the basic principles that I agree with: socialism.'[49]

Still, despite the ANC's collective culture, the ache in many a parent's heart would not go away. 'The hardest thing,' recalled Ruth Mompati sadly, 'I missed the childhood of my children.'[50]

Gloria, the daughter of a senior member of the ANC, recalled some of the pain that she felt when she realised, at the age of 14, that she had to share her father with the movement. Having left her mother at home, she and her brother and sister were extremely thrilled to be reunited with their father after a separation of more than a decade. So, desperately missing her mother, she clung to her father.

'I used to ask my dad for things when he came back in the evening, "Can I have this and that? Can I?… because we had left all our clothes and our things in South Africa. He used to give me small things like sweets. But one day, he spoke to me, saying, "All these children who are here are my children. I think you should stop asking me for little things, because when I buy sweets I must buy for all of them. And if I give to you, it's not nice for those who don't have anybody who they can ask for things."

'From that day I... I just closed myself up, and told myself that I no longer have a father. I thought that maybe my dad doesn't like me any more. He's much more in love with his cause than with us, his children.'[51]

Gloria's father had had, of course, the noblest of intentions. Like Tambo and colleagues of his generation, all children of the ANC were their responsibility, so no blood relative could make special claims. Penuel Maduna, an activist who had had to leave home precipitately after a bomb blast at a police station in Johannesburg, was studying law in Swaziland. He met Tambo in 1983 and, from then on, felt that he was being 'treated like his own son – he encouraged and took a close interest in my progress'.[52]

Neo Moikangoa, one of Tambo's personal assistants, once described an astonishing encounter during a heated conversation with Tambo. It was on an occasion when a group of Tambo's staff was urging him to allow his biography to be written. Tambo had already refused a number of times, but they would not allow the issue to rest. He suddenly raised his eyes and fixed each one of them with a cold, steely glare. 'What have I done?' he asked (an African adage in a time of distress) with suppressed fury. This was an unprecedented response from the usually warm, accessible leader. Shocked, they beat a hasty retreat from his office. Displeased, Tambo stood up and left the room too.

'I followed him out, I was very close to him, I also used to take liberties with him. I said to him: "I don't like the way you dealt with the comrades in there because you were rather like a bully; because you just fixed everyone of us with a stare and didn't explain why you didn't want us to continue with this thing, and you sort of enjoyed our retreat." And then OR said to me: "You know, I have just noticed something – that you are really like your father."

'I said to him, "You know my father?"

'And he laughed at me and said: "Your father was my first cousin."

'I said to him; "You are not serious!" He proved to me that he was. And then he said to me: "Don't think that gives you permission to take liberties with me, I'll put you in your place."'[53]

For adult exiles fortunate enough to have their children with them, particularly if they were residing in non-African countries, it was a struggle to pass on to their children an understanding of their cultural roots, facing what they saw as a losing battle against the erosion of the mother tongue.

But many also suffered a sense of loss, anxiety and guilt themselves, especially if this stemmed from the death of a parent back 'home'. For adult children in exile, this meant that there was no funeral, no closure. One of the most painful memories of exile for Barbara Masekela was her inability to attend her mother's funeral – she had not seen her mother for 20 years. Similarly, the Ndlovu sisters recalled an unanticipated pain. As defiant schoolgirls in 1976, they had stolen out of their Soweto home one night, leaving their mother behind to wonder what had become of them, and to agonise over their safety. A few years later, she died of a heart attack. The sisters had been in the camps; they had never been able to contact her directly, but expected to be allowed to send a message to her once they graduated from training. In a culture that values in particular the spiritual importance of the presence of loved ones and friends at funerals, to assist the deceased to make the crossing to the other side, absence was extremely difficult to bear.

Phyllis Altman, working for the International Defence and Aid Fund in London, recalled Tambo's own family loss: 'When his [youngest] mother died, he came to London and set up a memorial service for his mother, which I went to. He was waiting at the door as we all came in and I told him my mother had died in South Africa and I hadn't seen her, and that I was pleased that I could go to the service. Anyway, when we left he was again standing at the door to say goodbye, and to my astonishment I flung my arms round him and wept. And he said, it was very hard when a mother dies, but when she dies and you can't be there, it is worse. He was a very gentle and good and kind man.'[54]

There are, however, many stories of grief, guilt and heartache at not being able to say goodbye to loved ones not seen for years on end – it was 'a part of our living self brought to an eternal standstill', as Tambo so earnestly put it in his letter to Adelaide upon the loss of the aunt who raised her. Yet, as leader of the ANC, he was not able to be there for his wife at this time of mourning; he could only offer £40 – 'all I have' – which he had saved for Christmas and was able to send for funeral expenses.[55]

When Tambo's beloved (youngest) mother died, he kept in his collection of papers all the condolences he received. He grieved for this last parent, but the process of being orphaned had begun long ago when, as an adolescent schoolboy in faraway Johannesburg, geographically and culturally cut off from his family, he had received two telegrams within the space of a year, bringing bad news. Now this procedure was complete. Many more miles and ideologies away, over the mountains and generations later, in the last two decades of his life, at a time when one begins to veer back to one's roots, he had become truly an orphan. This was at the same time as his passionate plea – and astounding tears – to be part of Operation J to invade the Pondoland coast, and was some indication of his longing, his homesickness and his heartache.

About his own life, he had once written to Adelaide: 'I believe I have a fascinating story to tell… Nor is it all about political meetings.'[56] And indeed, he longed to find the time to revisit and record his pre-political life. Once, on an undated scrap of paper, during a lull at one such political meeting, Tambo was impelled to record a dream – or was it a daydream? – that had deeply affected him. 'I must record the dream while it is fresh in my mind and before I get ready for some work – our day is so short and there is so much to do!'[57]

It was a rare occasion when Tambo would ever allow himself to express his innermost personal feelings, or step out of his political persona. The dream was intimate, graphically detailed, and imbued with a nostalgia that transported him to the very roots of his heritage. The memory represented 'a hundred years, according to the people in my dream', he wrote.

'At first it consisted of my mother. With her nearby, my world was complete, self-sufficient in every way, and perfect. Then I noticed my father and my elder sister. The fowls, a dog and various objects at the back of the round house and along the walls. We lived in this house, ate there, slept there. I became quite familiar with this world: near the centre a pillar supporting the roof; near the pillar a round place where fire was made and the cooking done; the doorway, and at the back of the house, opposite the doorway various other objects on the floor, along the walls and hanging from the walls.'

But for Tambo, the dream served as a metaphor for his early, now overwhelmed identity: 'Gradually, imperceptibly, like dawn creeping in, my world was widening... With my mother, father, sister and myself in this house there seemed nothing missing. Outside, there were other round houses. My world grew to include my senior mother and other brothers and sisters and also my paternal grandfather and grandmother, and uncles.'

Discovery brought rewards, yet inevitably a sense of uncertainty, perhaps loss, that accompanied it. 'Soon, I was part of a wider community, a wider world of family groupings, all in the same pattern as mine, groups of round houses dotted across the land as far as the eye could see. I grew to be proud of my father, of my home and family. But who were we? And where was all this?'

Tambo's exploration of his own development as 'a human being' was quite clearly linked with that 'wider community', which was the ANC, and the movement's search for an identity within the 'wider world of family groupings'. The questions he asked, 'Who were we?' and 'Where were we?', could only be answered through the process of collective struggle. One recalls Tambo's affection and approval, in his recollections of his youth in the village, of the collective work parties, or *izindima,* where the community shared the more burdensome labour of ploughing the land at the beginning of the season, or harvesting the crops towards the end. At the end of their hard work, the entire community would enjoy a party. The women of the homestead that had been helped would prepare meat and drink. And so, through participation, a common meal was created. In politics, a memory of that tradition was kept alive. Personal fulfilment was accessed through the vision of the fulfilment of the community as a whole.

Commitment meant a willingness to suspend personal freedom and individual pleasures if necessary. Officials of the ANC, from Oliver Tambo at the top to the foot soldiers on the ground, were not paid salaries in the normal way. Aaccommodation was arranged by the movement itself. Once pledged to the ANC and undertaking assignments for the movement, members became part of the ANC family. They were even obliged to obtain permission to marry. Parents often placed their children in the crèches and the college of the ANC in Tanzania, and had to request permission to be allowed to live permanently with their children.[58]

In his role as father, there were times when Tambo intervened in personal lives with regard to drinking. Over the years, some senior members, including NEC members, found themselves in difficulties and had to go to sanatoria to 'dry out'. Some of Tambo's most talented lieutenants died prematurely from an excess of alcohol, succumbing to stress and liquor, and the loss of focus – the strains of a life in exile: 'Bernie cannot control his fear. And he is dead scared. And his retreat in the process, when he's gripped with fear, is liquor.'[59]

Tambo seemed to understand its solace. 'I can't smell alcohol,' he would sometimes remind them smilingly, in the face of fatuous behaviour. It was his way of being simultaneously reassuring, yet hinting at the dangers of liquor if allowed to go unchecked. Neo Moikangoa recalled how Tambo prevented him from sliding down that slippery slope: 'At one point, I really misused the bottle and after the death of Duma [Nokwe], [Tambo] sat on my back until I stopped and he was so effective that [now] I don't even miss liquor. There is liquor all over me where I live, where I operate and I don't miss it and it's because of him.'[60]

Moikangoa also described how Tambo acted as father to young adults. 'He would actually make me feel guilty. He would say to me: "You know, amongst all my children, you are the one I feel least free to let loose because I am not sure you will not get into trouble in the very next step you take away from me."'

Tambo would, though, nurture their moral and intellectual progress with charm, humour and intelligence. 'The worst feeling you could get was that you have let down OR. I mean, we were so fond of him, we used him as a yardstick against which to measure ourselves and each time we did something he disapproved of, it was like you slipped a few rungs; it was not the nicest thing. And... he wouldn't spend 30 minutes scolding you. It would take him about a minute, a very incisive covering of all bases and there was absolutely no room for a response. We learnt to do that to people as well.'[61]

Penuel Maduna, another who owed much of his political upbringing to Tambo, remarked that Tambo was 'like an old-fashioned rural school headmaster'.[62] In style perhaps, but not in content, for Maduna himself went on to say that Tambo 'was always the father, the teacher, the spiritual leader, the lawyer. His mind perceptive and incisive... a man of foresight'.

But how did Tambo get through to this generation of young intellectuals?

'Joe Nhlanhla, Thabo, Pallo, Chris, Mac, Sisulu, me. He would find us wherever we were and would actually sit down with you and sound you out on various issues. First he would find out "What are you working on right now?" And then you would throw everything out and then he would say: "How is it going, how do you see things?" And a discussion would get going, and he was drawing you out all the time and guiding you at the same time, and he left you with the feeling that this man takes me seriously, you know, there must be something to me after all.

'He just genuinely liked to be with young people. That's when he would actually become a young person himself; he would tease us about things which were important to you: how is your girlfriend, where are you going to drink tonight, are there any parties around here? Why am I not invited to these parties, and sometimes he'd just show up at the party which was supposed to be secret because somebody had betrayed us to him at the time when there weren't supposed to be parties. He would just show up there, people would start disappearing like that. But in order to lure them back, he would walk up to them and say: "Where can I get a drink?"'[63]

Above all, Tambo preferred to teach by example. Looking ahead to the time when the people of South Africa would be free of apartheid and the majority would take their rightful place in the running of the country, in the economy and in government, Tambo was particularly keen to nurture a generation inculcated with the practical skills for such responsible positions. He himself personified the old-fashioned virtues of discipline, punctuality and sobriety. He would pay careful attention to detail; he would always finish a job he had started. And, leading by example, he would expect others to do the same. Thabo Mbeki, one of that younger generation mentored by Tambo, gained an insight into how Tambo functioned intellectually.

'Here you had a person,' Mbeki commented, 'who could deal with both the concrete and the abstract, the specific, the particular and the general, between tactics and strategy.'[64] He 'understood very well the interconnection between the two; the way these two categories influenced each other... how the particular would influence the general, and how in turn the general would determine the particularities'.

'[Tambo] was an intellectual – a person of rational thought, of reason – a person who behaved, who governed his conduct very much according to an understanding of these concepts.

'What many of the comrades were bothered about was "why is he attending to so much detail? Once a general position has been established, we can attend to these details". But he thought differently... He knew that you couldn't stay merely on the general plane and forget about the particulars, because of the possibility that you could be wrong about the general – because you didn't understand sufficiently the particular. And you might very well be wrong about the specifics if you did not understand about the general.'[65]

Tambo demonstrated that discipline and high standards of intellectual application were required for a commitment of the intelligentsia to the liberation movement. Thabo Mbeki recalled Tambo's overall communication to his interns and his team:

'Working with OR as closely as we did, you learn the sorts of things I have been talking about... You've got to understand that change does not come of its own – it requires human beings. People must apply themselves; you've got to work at it. You've got to understand that. You are in an organisation, fine –

but you have a personal obligation... *You've* got to act, precisely because you are part of that organisation.'[66]

Mbeki also recalled other lessons by example, teaching the youth not to lose sight of the major focus of the ANC's mission.

'When I got to Lusaka we stayed in a house, a farmhouse. There were no beds and no mattresses. OR stayed in the same house. There were a whole number of us – Chris [Hani], Mavuso Msimang, myself, other people, OR. We were all staying there and we would, as in a prison, roll out a blanket on the floor when we wanted to sleep and a blanket on top of you, another blanket rolled up to be a pillow. We stayed with him like that. Which was fine. He had no problem with it because it was not an issue, of the comfort... Because in the end what was driving him was this particular vision; and the rest was incidental, including where he slept, and how he slept and so on. No sense of "I lead this organisation, therefore I need to sleep on a bed with a mattress"; whereas "we don't have the means; all that we can afford at this moment is this house and this blanket and this floor". So I think all of us who came directly under the leadership of Oliver Tambo in the way all of us did, would have picked up all of those things: about work, about no airs, no behaviour or sentiment, which says I am a big person and therefore the rest must respond to me in a particular way. All of those things we would have picked up from Oliver Tambo.'[67]

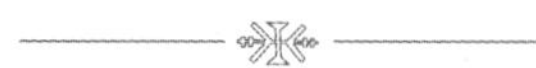

In the early years in London, educationist activists from back home – Robert Resha, Tennyson Makiwane and Fertz Ngakane – were appointed to set up a scholarship committee for young refugees from South Africa. In time, the Luthuli Memorial Foundation was able to acquire a number of scholarships for thousands of men and women in the ANC worldwide throughout the exile period and also to encourage and sponsor a chair of African Studies at an influential university.

One young ANC scholarship student was Sipho Pityana, who had left South Africa after his detention in 1982 and, with the help of the ANC, was able to study at Roma University in Lesotho. By then, 'OR was a household name'. With a group of 'ANC loyal intellectuals', such as Michael Lapsley, Tito Mboweni, Ngoako Ramathlodi, they would regularly 'interrogate the complexities of OR's statements'. Pityana recalled with a thrill the moment he first met Tambo at an ANC bazaar in London in 1983. Someone must have pointed out the young man to Tambo, for 'OR walked up to me and embraced me. I felt greatly valued and affirmed'.

For Pityana, the act became a symbolic 'embrace by the movement'. What inspired him, and many others, he said, was the link that Tambo made between the ANC's 'moral high ground' and victory. Hard tasks lay ahead, but Tambo, in his meetings with students, made it clear that he was prepared to entertain creative thinking. It was remarkable, reflected Pityana, to observe 'the ways in which OR managed and channelled the different strands'.

On one occasion in 1987, Pityana taped a session Tambo held with graduate students and other ANC members in London. The event was a briefing on the context of the rapid escalation of events inside South Africa and internationally. Tambo spoke for nearly two hours, holding the audience enthralled. He shared with the members the issues repeatedly raised at the number of meetings the ANC was having with state representatives, the corporate world in the West, and businesspeople from South Africa (despite PW Botha's denunciations and threats). Tambo's articulate, warmly accessible style, his clarity of thought and his reasoned presentation of the ANC's complex and difficult, yet clearly principled strategy and tactics deeply impressed his audience. In a time of rapid transition in the nature of the struggle, which disturbed many who feared that the ANC might be 'selling out' by agreeing to talks with the enemy, he was able to communicate the big picture, yet at the same time answer in detail the particulars contained in each question. His fine intellect, uncommonly nuanced insights and obvious integrity radiated into dark corners.

Tambo's extemporary talk in London was a *tour de force*. It was rare that he was in a situation that permitted him to give a public speech that was not pre-written, and the audience was deeply impressed by his ability to consider all alternatives with equal consideration, one at a time, of all aspects of the tactics required in considering the contradictions of, say, whether to modify, confirm or lift the cultural boycott. He carefully laid out all the considerations, providing an overview of the implications to all those who might be affected. The outcome of that talk was that there were many in the audience, including the *cognoscenti*, who renewed their efforts to strengthen the ANC and give it greater visibility in the UK.[68]

Drawing from a band of younger speech writers, Tambo mentored them not only in the craft of political speech writing, but also in the very art of politics itself. As Thabo Mbeki (who was to emerge as the president's major speech writer) reminisced: 'He would say, "Well, you know there is this conference, a conference against apartheid in Amsterdam", or some place. And you would get a sense what the conference is trying to achieve; the level of education about your audience in terms of their understanding about the South African situation; level of commitment; are these our friends; are these hostile people – whatever. So that you would know how to fashion the speech… Once we were done – I'm saying the general direction, about where we were going: who was the speech intended for – then we would sit down and then draft the speech.'[69]

Once the speech was drafted, and he was satisfied with the content and message, the process would not be over. Tambo would then interrogate the draft in detail, scrutinising the grammar, the construction of sentences, and the meaning of every word – 'sometimes we would spend an hour just debating one word in a speech', recalled Mbeki, one of the speech writers.

'And part of the reason for that,' Mbeki expained, 'was that it's that level of precision which he thought was necessary… Once he uttered a particular word, it had to communicate what he meant it to communicate. We couldn't allow for a situation in which it would be read *differently* from what he intended to say… We had to be very precise about what you had to convey. That was important in itself… If you got the *particulars*, as represented by these words – if you got the particulars wrong, then you got the general wrong.'[70]

Those privileged to be chosen to attempt to write his speeches would learn valuable political lessons. From one of his notebooks, we find a comment on someone's draft speech, a lesson in the art of shrewd diplomacy and face-saving from which revolutionaries were not exempt:

'We should not rejoice at having forced them to do what we want. We do not have to celebrate their defeat. "Imperialists have at last succumbed to the pressures..." Bad thing to say in the middle of a struggle, calculated to make them resist us. We would rather they did not resist: our tactics must aim at stopping them from fighting us – make them neutrals of necessity. Is it a question of their being "class enemies"? Do we want to raise that issue now at this stage of our struggle, in this particular form?'

Neo Moikangoa elaborated on how Tambo never lost sight of the essential political project. While encouraging the young man to explore Marxist political theory, he also listened carefully when Moikangoa expounded on what he had learnt. 'Fine,' Tambo cautioned, 'but don't paint yourself into a corner. Say what needs to be done; you don't strengthen your case by insulting someone... You burn all your bridges, and one day you are going to have to talk to these people or their successors or descendants.'

Tambo had the facility, Moikangoa said, 'to look through a person and ideological labels... and establish contacts with the persons themselves'. He tended to avoid ideological or value-laden debates because he did not want to alienate any of the tendencies in the ANC. Nevertheless, he was a good listener. He also asked pointed questions on what Moikangoa had been reading. But always he came back to the bottom line – what was best for the movement.

'I hope that this stuff is not going to land you in a position where you find it difficult to work with people who do not share your convictions,' he once said. 'Because you must always remember that the ANC is the Parliament of the People, and that it is the home of any number of political positions which are opposed to apartheid. So, don't paralyse your ability to communicate effectively in that Parliament, by rigidifying your ideological and political position.'[71]

Throughout Tambo's political career, his special skill as a teacher remained one of his most valuable assets. He preferred to emphasise education as a foundation for political activism, although he was obliged to accept the determination of many of the post-1976 intake to undergo military training before they finished high school. As Bridgitte Mabandla explained:

'Most of the young people who came in wanted to go and fight, and I know that efforts were made for those who came in, for example, through Lusaka. There was a place [for them to study] and a number were being discouraged from going into the military but going to school. And they actually refused and wanted to go to the camps... It is these young people who Tambo then met, and he said that they must be sent back to school. He actually said that we had to... abide by the standards that are set in the convention on the rights of the child. He was a great advocate of that. And then also it was a tradition for OR to come for special children's days, so he was really concerned about the children in the camps.'[72]

Many children, though, wanted to further their education from the outset. 'Kids were sent to Guinea, Egypt – African countries; quite a lot in Nigeria, coming to Cuba,' explained John Pampallis, an ANC educationist for more than a decade. 'I think it soon became clear that if the ANC was actually going to keep these students within an ANC community abroad, it was going to have to have some place where it can bring them together.'[73] The ANC thus took a decision to establish a school that could offer the education that had been denied these child refugees, and Tambo and his diplomatic team set about raising funds and finding resources.

Immediately after the 16 June uprising in 1976, Oliver Tambo called on the international community for assistance. The ANC approached the regional government in Morogoro in Tanzania for a grant of land and when the central government learnt of the application, it donated an abandoned sisal estate at Mazimbu (the school was afterwards simply called 'Mazimbu' by the South Africans), where the school was eventually established. UNESCO granted the first funding, giving equal amounts to the ANC and the PAC, who were also planning to start a school near Bagamoya in Tanzania.

The ANC school was named after Solomon Mahlangu, the young 1976 MK cadre who with Mondy Motloung had infiltrated back into South Africa, but had been caught after an attack in a warehouse in Goch Street, in the inner city of Johannesburg, in which a man had been killed. Both men were detained and tortured. Motloung suffered brain damage and was institutionalised, while Mahlangu was tried and eventually sentenced to death and executed. He sang freedom songs up to his last moments. The Mahlangu tribute seemed to be a fitting acknowledgement of the sense of injustice and the willingness of the youth of his generation to make a supreme sacrifice for the liberty of the people.

'Someone like OR has to deal with millions of things – to do with struggle, international struggle, the function of the organisation,' Thabo Mbeki observed.[74] All Tambo could do in the circumstances was to mandate a reliable and experienced cadre to head the school. But whenever he had the opportunity while in Tanzania, he was keenly interested in dropping in on Mazimbu, and did not fail to attend the special events focusing on children's rights, either at Mazimbu or in the military camps.

Over and above questions of progressive pedagogy and methodology for young revolutionaries, the school faced a number of difficult challenges. The post-1976 intake included children from a wide variety of educational backgrounds: 'I am telling you we had 14-year-olds. During the repressions of '84 and '89, we had quite a number coming from Natal; homeless children, literally. And, I mean, they almost disrupted Mazimbu because they came in with a South African culture of defiance and they were studying with Nonkululeko [Mabandla's daughter], who were the regulars. So there was that problem, and we had to address it also.'[75]

But even in the relative safety of an ANC sanctuary, young people were not always able to realise their dreams. With the rush of intakes, the ANC tried frantically to place the young people with scholarships. They sometimes had to wait for months, even years before promised international support was realised.

During this anxious time, many new arrivals became aware of Tambo's active role in securing resources for them. The respect with which Tambo was held was well captured by Pampallis. 'In all my years out there,' said Pampallis, 'everybody was generally criticised for one thing or another, especially the leadership. But the one person you never heard anybody criticise is OR. Maybe in the last little while before we came, things were getting, well, tumultuous in exile, but he and Chris Hani are two people who, for a lot of that time, seemed to be above criticism – and then later Chris came into some kind of criticism from some particular MK people.'[76]

Much as Tambo, as leader of the Mission in Exile, performed the part of mentor, role model and father figure for the growing number of members younger than himself, he was becoming aware increasingly of the particular need to empower the women members of the ANC.

'OR was seen, and very highly by all, as a father figure, even if he was still acting as president then,' commented Gertrude Shope, who for many years headed the ANC Women's Section. 'And, in fact, let me say that not only the ANC people but even the Zambian government and parties, whenever they had their very big occasions, their occasions would be incomplete without him going to say one or two words. But at the same time, OR [took the trouble] in that even the young women who had problems went to him to go and discuss their personal problems with him. Now, to us they were – you know, he was too busy for such things. But, somehow, in one way or another, he always had time for them. He was that type of a person.'[77]

But what was the position of women in the ANC? In theory, the ANC policy promoted sharing, regardless of gender. Women's roles and women's rights in the ANC had a long history of struggle, but had also never directly confronted patriarchy. Rather, it had been conducted very strategically. The struggle to end apartheid was always the priority, and the women sought to insert themselves more centrally in that mission. In the 1950s, women had not only been active in the mass campaigns, but had taken the initiative to march, spectacularly, against passes in 1956. The event had also been a demonstration by the women, as Ida Mtwana had declared in ringing tones at the time of the campaign, of their right to march 'side by side' with the men.[78]

The vision for the communities set up in Mazimbu, at the Solomon Mahlangu Freedom College, and at the orientation centre for young South African newcomers at Dakawa, both in Tanzania, was to build a culture free from racism, sexism and inequality, a living community that would be a model for the new South Africa.[79] In this different environment, the constraints of traditional patriarchy eased. Gertrude Shope, for example, described how gradually an awareness of unequal treatment of the young men and women 'in pregnancy' developed:

'We felt that we should help these children because if they were at home, one would go to her aunt's place or to her sister or whatever. So we felt that to make up for that, we should discuss with the organisation that in Mazimbu... there should be some buildings put up specifically for young girls who fell expectant and we got a very good cooperation from the treasury and the other officials and there was this place which we called the Kate Molale Centre [named after Kate Molale, who was killed in a car accident in Tanzania]...

'They would leave Angola to go there because conditions would be much better there than in a camp, for instance, where they would be looked after health-wise, the food; they wouldn't be subjected to a rough life in a camp where you'd have to go and jump and run and do everything else. So, these women would stay there until they had their babies.'[80]

The girls were vulnerable, being so young. They were not ready for parenting and needed guidance to prepare them for taking on new responsibilities. 'They in fact did go ahead and have their children,' said Shope. 'And one would understand that maybe that was security for themselves, someone to love.'[81]

But the Women's Section soon realised that the girls were being penalised in their education and training by having to leave the camps if they fell pregnant.

'And the young woman would have to leave school because she is going to be expectant and of course the young man would carry on with his studies and by the time [the woman] has a baby, he is now ready for university. And we felt that was very, very unfair. If any young man makes a young woman pregnant, knowing that he is interfering with the smooth running of her schoolwork, he must also be let out of school. So again we discussed with the authorities; we had regular meetings with [the NEC] actually to make these suggestions.'[82]

But gender was broadly subsumed by the national struggle. In exile, it was especially the women who worked 'incredibly hard'[83] to develop a welfare system for the movement. They set up crèches, clinics, schools, and the distribution of food and clothing. In order to set up sustainable projects, they also had to raise funds (with the support of Oliver Tambo, the ANC's supreme fundraiser). The sphere of reproduction was of course traditionally the concern of women, but in exile, in the absence of formal employment, with the majority of cadres in training or in camps, it was even more vital for survival.[84]

The effect, though, was to reinforce the traditional role of women in exile, particularly where host countries, even those newly liberated from colonialism, maintained a comfortable male culture of patriarchy, while male comrades were apt to congratulate themselves and the ANC on their progressive gender relations. Albie Sachs, himself an active feminist, observed:

'The status of women in the ANC was far from brilliant. And you knew it was bad when you would get members, often fairly senior members of the ANC, saying, "We have got no problem about women's rights in the ANC, everybody is equal...". There were problems inside the organisation, problems in terms of the whole vision of the nature of the struggle, and the future of women in South Africa. The issue was taken up by people in what was then called the Women's Section. At one stage, the Women's Section was really like an auxiliary organisation. Their role was just to mobilise women into the struggle behind the men. But certainly by the seventies many voices were being heard saying that we are comrades, we are patriots, we are in the struggle, we want full equal rights in a meaningful sense, inside the organisation and outside.'[85]

A subtle discrimination demanded that women should over-perform to prove themselves. In the military camps, women were simultaneously and contradictorily cushioned from military rigours, and disempowered by this protective attitude. They tended to be excluded from military and even intelligence issues, or deployment inside the country. Then there was the strain of being outnumbered, which skewed power relations and complicated gender relationships. 'We were demobilised by menstruation and pregnancy,' concluded Thenjiwe Mthintso. 'There were never more than five women who made it militarily. OR was one of the few of his generation who was sensitive to gender. But he was constrained by his culture, although he tried to overcome it.'[86]

Tambo's priority was to bring all on board, and empower them. His keen antennae did not require many stimulants to communicate the need to send a clear message to all the members, both men and women, that women needed acknowledgement, capacity-building and encouragement for the overall health of the movement itself.

In 1981, at a conference in Luanda, Tambo delivered a keynote speech that was to become famous and inspirational in the ANC, especially for women. It has been quoted many times, particularly because he presented gender relationships in the movement as a challenge for both men and women.

'Women in the ANC should stop behaving as if there is no place for them above the level of certain categories of involvement. They have a duty to liberate us men from antique concepts and attitudes about the place and role of women in society and the development and direction of our revolutionary struggle.'[87]

'That [speech] was often referred to by leaders of the Women's Section,' commented Albie Sachs, 'particularly those one might call African feminist, in support of their claims for a stronger position for women inside the organisation. The Women's Section, as far as I could understand, always felt very close to OR; that he was aware that this was another section of the nation. It had particular problems and felt particular forms of oppression and exclusion and marginalisation. And I think if there was one thing he hated it was marginalisation. Everybody had to count and be involved.'[88]

But aside from the speech, with its warmth and humour, Tambo's personality itself exuded a sense of caring and comfort. 'A man who has no woman in him is dangerous,' Mazisi Kunene, activist poet, who spent many years at the ANC London mission, once observed.[89]

Tambo's self-representation as a nurturer, an understanding and sympathetic listener, communicated an almost non-gendered image – 'almost' because in the latter years of exile he was also widely seen within the ANC as the provider and the affectionate, approachable father figure. Certainly in the minds of many of his supporters Tambo also had the reputation of an ascetic. Tambo's simple lifestyle in Dar es Salaam and the camps, his indifference to personal possessions, were often mentioned and admired. And, like Gandhi, his image perhaps combined the most admirable of both male and female qualities.

Said Gertrude Shope, 'He was a very, very warm somebody, a very simple somebody, what I would call the typical example of an educated man, of a learned man... Because, you know, the more the people get education, the simpler they become.'[90]

Tambo's intellect, his revolutionary commitment to MK were indeed beyond question – these were generally admired as male qualities. Yet Tambo did not have a macho image. 'Everybody felt safe in his hands,' observed Jacob Zuma.[91] Some of Tambo's most loved qualities were the 'feminine' ones – nurturing, gentle, sensitive. His ability to listen genuinely to people's problems, no matter how seemingly mundane, made an impact of wisdom beyond his years.

Drawing on his patriarchal, polygamous cultural background, and probably because of his own reflective nature, Tambo had always been conscious of the crucial role of women in the homestead economy. He had, in fact, developed an immense admiration for the women in his own homestead – their good-humoured, uncomplaining, unremitting hard work, their productivity, their vitality, their creative strategies of survival and their nurturing role. With most of the men away from home for much of the time, the labour of the women had excited his appreciation of what women could quietly achieve. But he observed, too, in that Luanda speech, how many women in exile lacked the confidence to contribute fully and creatively towards the movement. He attributed their lack of consciousness to the way men in the ANC treated women – as being there to serve.

Conservatism, of course, also existed among the women themselves. Firstly, they were apt to prioritise the national struggle at their own expense. Small ANC communities in exile were, at times, both comforting and defensive. Sometimes they cut themselves off, like migrant workers, emotionally and culturally, from their hosts. Almost every small community throughout the world seeks to control its members, and in the ANC enclaves, women – revolutionary women – were often expected to comport themselves in a traditional way. Despite the ideological influences of either socialist or Western feminism, women were expected to commit themselves to a partner and defer to him. This habit was difficult to resist. Exile was thus lonely, increasing the need for a partner. There was, too, 'the contradiction of the desire for children – in an abnormal situation'.[92] It was difficult to resist the strong desire to bear the children of the man one loved.

There is also evidence of resistance to women on a professional level. Bridgitte Mabandla had a special memory of Tambo's fatherly support:

'When I joined the legal department I had very serious difficulties with the men. I was the only woman, and they treated me quite shabbily, and OR helped us to grow and, in fact, helped us to learn to work together. They tried to discredit me; they left me out initially, when I first joined them, out of a number of activities. I mean, there was this particular incident where there was a committee that had been set up to evaluate departments and OR came to look at the legal department. He met them at some place. They didn't fetch me – we had a car that used to fetch departmental members.'[93]

By the time she had made her own way to the office, the meeting was over, so she confronted Tambo. She was quite emotional and almost in tears: 'OR, what did you think when you didn't see me? I am a member of the department.'

'OR was surprised: "I asked and I was told that you had gone to Ethiopia."

'I said: "No, but I leave in the evening and I wanted to be part of the evaluation committee because I have things to say and I wanted to say them in front of my co-members."

'OR just listened to me. I was quite emotional and I just spoke my mind out.

'Thereafter, in fact, OR called Zola Skweyiya. Zola was so nervous, Zola is my best friend today, we work so well together; we are so close, but it is thanks to OR – he made us grow... He had us look at ourselves... OR listened to me... He wasn't soft with me; he said, "You ought to understand that [there is] prejudice against women."

'He said to me, "You are not here by mistake. It was considered; of course, you did offer yourself, but you need to apply yourself with the consciousness that there is prejudice. We are going to tackle this thing. I apologise that you were not present." I did accept the explanation...

'All I know is that after that incident I know that that was the very last time that we had problems working together. We started growing together. When we came into South Africa, we were a team. We came in, we set up the land commission, the regional and local government department. We worked.'[94]

Years later, when it transpired that women were being abused in Lusaka, Tambo commissioned a Code of Conduct. Once on the ANC's legal commission,

Bridgitte Mabandla immediately noticed how Tambo 'was champion of the recognition of the rights of women; respect for their position where people have actually contracted as partners... He did say that he is concerned that we must make sure that we stamp out any forms of abuse of relationships, in the family where children are abused or women are abused. He was very mindful of weaknesses in his movement.'

Mabandla observed that these abuses were exacerbated by the context of stressful living in exile. 'People assumed new bad habits such as alcohol abuse as well as smoking a lot. In fact, somebody made a study of people in liberation movements and said they smoke heavily and, yes, in the ANC in particular, there were incidents where people were broken up because of infidelities which arose out of separation of families, like where people are deployed separately. The man is sent to the forward areas – in other words, to infiltrate South Africa – and the woman is left behind. So we have had those incidents. They are reported. It destabilised family lives.'[95]

With regard to the abuse of women, traditional methods of discipline were devised to reprimand the miscreants from within the community. 'I remember many, many cases,' commented Lindelwe Mabandla. 'I sat at that kind of tribunal where there were many cases of abuse of women; domestic. The ANC did try to regulate that kind of abuse. There was a kind of a punishment, obviously there were certain guidelines where a person, for example, had beaten up his wife; there were certain things that were opened to us to implement, like a person would not be allowed to do certain things. Those were public.'[96]

Public exposure of the perpetrators, particularly in closely knit communities, was a humiliating punishment. It was a powerful method (if not necessarily wholly adequate) that was to be used years later in post-apartheid's Truth and Reconciliation Commission.

'Even if he denied whatever it is, the fact is that the community would know that this is what so and so had done and this is what the committee had suggested as punishment and it was carried out.'[97]

Thenjiwe Mthintso had similar memories. A highly talented young woman who had been a pioneer of the Black Consciousness Movement in the Eastern Cape, and had worked with Steve Biko in his community centre, Thenjiwe had been detained and tortured, and had gone into exile. After liberation, when she was considering standing for election as Deputy Secretary-General in the ANC in 1997, she 'missed OR – and Chris (Hani)'; she missed their advice, their strategic thinking. And she particularly missed OR's approval when she was elected. In the radically altered conditions of post-apartheid South Africa, the ANC was the ruling party in government, but its Revolutionary Council without Tambo's leadership made an unfavourable comparison for Mthintso. 'The membership still has to make leaders of us,' she observed in 1998. 'We have to learn to listen, as OR used to. Now, a balance between centralism and democracy is needed. OR managed both.' While the ANC still held onto its tradition of consultation, it was not enough.

'Participation is needed. OR had the opportunity to interact and dialogue with the world, and this enriched his perspective. Madiba's identity is as a chief; he holds onto his views – it's a different style. The point where Madiba puts his foot down can put you in a spot personally. OR had more patience.'

Of course, Tambo had other female fans. Lindiwe Mabuza, whom Tambo had humorously reproached in his Luanda speech for at first turning down his appointment as the ANC representative in Sweden, spoke lyrically about the reverence Tambo elicited. Mabuza was an academic schooled in the USA, acquiring her Masters degree in African Studies at Ohio, and had experienced the civil rights movement, the tumult over the Vietnam War, and the women's movement. Mabuza was also a poet whose work was eliciting warm interest among South African exiles. She had been a firm supporter of Black Consciousness, but had left to join the ANC because she had realised that 'the ANC represented the full picture, not just a stage in the struggle'. But a major factor for Lindiwe Mabuza's fervent commitment to the movement was also 'the quality of leadership', in particular Oliver Tambo's 'elegant leadership', and his 'simplicity'. 'You get spoiled,' she observed, 'because you know what is the best.'[98]

Despite the admiration of so many female comrades, Tambo's inherent sense of duty and discretion did not, however, provide much opportunity for salacious conjecture. His evenly distributed warmth and physical contact, walking hand-in-hand, African-style, with both men and women, was never discerned to be suggestive. An attractive and sophisticated young female ANC member, the secretary of the Regional Politico Committee, recalled, eyes shining with pride at the memory, visiting the Morogoro pig farm in Tambo's entourage. Tambo, who had never met her before, looked at her quizzically. He smiled and took her by the hand, 'and together, hand-in-hand, we walked through the pig shit'. When she was asked whether she felt he had been flirting with her, she was shocked by the question. Despite her experience of male innuendo, it had never occurred to her that Tambo's reaching out to her was anything but affectionate, platonic comradeship.

Nevertheless, not all the leadership was above reproach. A number of younger women in exile broke new ground in questioning the role of women in the movement, and also the conducting of power relations in the sexual behaviour of their leaders. They took up the feminist argument that the 'personal is political'. In at least two instances, they campaigned against patriarchal exploitative behaviour. For example, a Robben Islander, imprisoned for 10 years and released in 1974, kept his undertaking to marry his fiancée, but simultaneously began a serious relationship with another woman. Both his wife and lover bore him children around the same time. Once in exile, his wife's unhappiness became known and the caucus of younger women comrades censured him. In another case, a senior member in the NEC was blamed for being responsible, David and Bathsheba-like, for the posting to another country of the husband of a young wife with whom he was having an affair. These matters were raised at branch meetings,[99] and provided examples of unequal power relations between senior members and heroes in the movement, exploiting vulnerable younger women and undermining the respect to which female comrades were entitled. In the camps, too, it was revealed that those in senior positions were exploiting women cadres. The consequence was the women's diminution on many levels. Women thus chosen were 'given special treatment and they tend to reject the authority of their immediate commanders', reported the Stuart Commission, appointed by Tambo to investigate abuses in the camps. 'There is a widespread belief that women are sex objects and that they do not develop politically and militarily.'[100]

There was talk also among rival movements of the unfair advantage male ANC members had over others in exile, owing to their relatively more abundant resources. The ANC team under Tambo had worked hard to provide for their members. Under the *mphando* system, the provisions supplied to all members – mostly sent by the Scandinavian countries, the USSR and the GDR – were largely in kind: food, clothes, and even a small tobacco ration, with a minute cash allowance. By Tanzanian standards, the ANC members were thus comfortably off, even privileged, and some of these provisions could be 'diced' or 'fried' to local people for cash. Access to local women by ANC members was envied and resented by relatively less well-endowed liberation movements, such as the PAC, which was also located in Tanzania.

For many exiles, their commitment to South Africa's liberation precluded serious relationships with local women. Their affairs tended to go no further than short-term sexual liaisons, leading to sometimes problematic and exploitative relationships.[101] A decade after ANC cadres returned to South Africa, dozens of wives, children, widows, orphans and lovers were still stranded at Mazimbu, unacknowledged by their partners and fathers, or their South African families.[102]

As the years went by without sign of material progress towards liberation, a steady adherence to the local ANC often became restricting, and required some measure of endurance. Many comrades in exile recalled how it was Tambo who provided the movement's narrative. He it was who unremittingly insisted, repeatedly, articulately and persuasively, that 'Victory is Certain!' in his public speeches; in the movement's publication *Sechaba*; when he spoke to the cadres in the camps; to the scholars at the Solomon Mahlangu Freedom College; at branch meetings as an honoured guest – the 'logic of history' and the national liberation movement itself made this an inevitable consequence. It was a slogan that Tambo repeated immediately following 16 June 1976: 'We are entering a very difficult period in our history. Many more people will be called upon to make the supreme sacrifice. The enemy himself will throw in everything he has in order to ensure our destruction. Victory however is certain.'[103]

The harshness, the brutality, the inhumanity of apartheid, together with the gathering strength and numbers of the multifaceted liberation movement ensured that there could be only one outcome. The slogan that came out of this reasoning was eagerly popularised inside South Africa in 1976, through to the eighties, and married to songs and slogans already in use.

> Victory is Certain!
> *Amandla Ngawethu!*
> *Maatla ke a rona!*
> Power to the People!

For Tambo, in all his multiple dealings with the 'four pillars of the struggle' – the international, military, political and underground arenas – what mattered most was keeping the ANC together. To achieve that holistic endeavour, messages of inclusiveness were constantly disseminated.

First, Tambo tried to make himself available whenever possible – excessively so, some felt.[104] He made time to listen to the problems people brought to him, in the chiefly tradition.

'Here you have a man like your leader, like your father, like your real comrade, who if a cadre was going into the country, he talked to the cadre as if he was going with him. And if a cadre came back to report, he would listen and almost be part of that cadre's experiences... He had time to listen, even to cadres coming from inside the country... I began to look at him, and he always reminded me of Chief Luthuli, who at the young age and when I began to be political, I realised that he was a symbol of unity in the ANC. He will be able to sift the right things from what you are saying and also help you on the wrong things that you are saying. So, no one would say "OR belongs to me" or "he listens to me". He belonged to all of us, he listened to all of us.'[105]

Tambo would, however, also consistently remind members, verbally and by example, of the core values of the ANC, citing the Freedom Charter. He was, for instance, warmly supportive of biracial unions. 'Let the children marry,' he affectionately urged Ann and Bob Seidman, American comrades who had worked for years in independent Africa, and whose 18-year-old daughter Neva and young Zeph Mokgetla fell in love. And then of course, the Tambos' eldest daughter, Thembi, married the British banker Martin Kingston in 1981. True to his unpredictable schedule, Tambo only just managed to attend the wedding, and make a speech.

The ANC's non-racial message was a defining identity, one that had survived the early years of Africanist hostility in post-colonial Africa. More than formal membership, its message signalled an inclusiveness appreciated by many comrades. Trade unionist, communist and activist Violet Weinberg, who with her husband Eli Weinberg left South Africa after the Soweto uprisings, recalled how honoured she had felt when, at a meeting in Dar es Salaam, Tambo had spotted her in the audience and singled her out to sit next to him on the platform.[106]

Tambo was careful to go out of his way to make white supporters feel included and appreciated. After apartheid operatives assassinated Ruth First in 1982, Tambo received a letter from Ronald Segal, who wrote to him with a problem. He wanted to start a Trust in her memory, and had encountered resistance from an ANC representative in Sweden who felt that others had also fallen victim to assassination and asked why a white woman should be singled out for special commemoration. Tambo replied:

'My dear Ronald, I've written to you officially about the Trust. I make no reference to the race question because anyone who thinks in race terms about Ruth is committing an outrage on a whole lot of us and can only be grossly misrepresenting the ANC.'[107]

The construction of the public image of a leader, even in a culture of collective leadership in which no individual was meant to be singled out above others, was inseparable from the necessity to be an ANC exemplar. Nevertheless, despite Tambo's sharp mind and finely honed political skills, his unassuming style could also be misleading – often to his own detriment. In the USA, Republican President Ronald Reagan's Secretary of State George Schultz, not particularly prepared to be impressed with the ANC, confided to his lieutenant Chester Crocker that he 'wasn't overwhelmed' with Tambo when he finally met him in 1986: 'I mean, he had no way of drawing any conclusions about Oliver Tambo as a personality or a leader, but he could listen to what he was told, and he wasn't overwhelmed.'[108]

In fact, Tambo's gentlemanly deportment often doubly offended those whose image of him was of a calculating terrorist. He did not conform to their stereotype, and therefore posed a threat that he might be a devious, Machiavellian character. The Schultz meeting notwithstanding, this perception tended to be only until people met him. The ANC treasurer observed how many conservative politicians warmed towards Tambo after they had met him. One example he cited was UK Foreign Minister Lynda Chalker's defence of Tambo to her fellow Tories in Parliament.[109]

Rusty Bernstein, who had known Tambo since the fifties and had been active in the liberation movement for even longer, ascribed the coherence of the ANC to Tambo: 'OR was one of those who set the tone, he was the one with the diplomatic skills to hold all the other conflicting elements... together and to keep them in one go. If Kotane had been left in charge of the thing, unquestionably there would have been splits over his sheer abrasiveness and abruptness and short-temperedness on occasions when he thought people were either wrong, or being dishonest. Tambo has been the perfect diplomat.'[110]

And it was as part of that diplomacy and the unity he sought to encompass that Tambo emphasised the importance of 'morale'. 'Morale' was an important concept in ANC exile discourse. As the tension escalated in the military camps and ANC offices, Tambo increasingly coupled the ANC's need for strategy and honest hard work with the historical inevitability of the downfall of apartheid.

'Make-believe and show arrangements can only increase our problems, however attractive their external appearance... A united front of external militants, which has its base and source of inspiration in the battlefield, cannot permit of adventurists and impressionists, of slogan-shouting pseudo-revolutionaries who happen to write well, speak well, mix well.'[111]

But what of Tambo's inner life? There were times when he had to take the walls down and be alone. Tambo's isolation, despite his outgoing persona, was partly the inevitable loneliness of a leader, even in a collective culture such as the ANC's: a private man who by and large expressed his inner self through his spiritual resources. He kept this crucially important source of sustenance to himself, as a private concern, lest it prove to be divisive in the movement. No matter how gruelling his schedule, he would find time to pray, and whenever possible, attend church – sometimes in the early hours of the morning before the day's work began. Joe Matthews, who was his personal assistant in the sixties, observed Tambo's daily prayers, and the need – far too seldom – to take stock of himself.

'He would go to Mirfield [Community of the Resurrection headquarters] whenever he didn't feel good about himself.' But were these moral issues, marital relations? In his marriage, with its inevitable ups and downs, Tambo had, from the very beginning, shared with Adelaide a spiritual commitment. Whenever they encountered difficulties, they would seek solutions in prayer. Each time before parting, they would pray for strength and fidelity to their common commitment as parents and marriage partners, for fortitude, understanding and faith.[112]

As the years and then the first decade went by, Oliver Tambo began to realise that his private, preferred occupation as spiritual leader was never to be. Nevertheless, his faith was a crucial part of Tambo's ability to balance the intellect with the soul, and the ANC benefited enormously from this capacity. Neo Moikangoa onserved that Tambo was able to interact with a number of ideological positions, systems of belief and value.

'He had a towering intellect, but it was an intellect which is prevented from becoming the perfect dispassionate and disembodied machine by his Christian values. I haven't seen anybody actually more Christian than Oliver Tambo, and it was a very bread-and-butter type of Christianity. He believed in the sanctity of life – both human and non-human – in the brotherhood of humanity and which is very strongly opposed to what I call injustices and indecency in the generic sense. So that in the end, in the political arena, the human being was his first love... Because of the type of mind he had, he was able to peel away ideological, value accretions from any individual, and see [him or her] ultimately as an individual.'

Tambo would look beneath the communist, anti-communist or atheist and observe the human being and assess the intrinsic worth of the individual. His African humanism taught him 'that there was something in all of us that can be appealed to in the name of decency and in the name of justice'.[113]

In order to prioritise the movement, Tambo suppressed important facets of his nature. His own natural creativity and love of arts and culture were set aside. Instead, Tambo sublimated his urge for creative performance by acknowledging the value of the cultural and symbolic terrain of the struggle.

The diversity of those in exile, for Oliver Tambo, was also a metaphor for the cultural diversity within South Africa itself. 'Through struggle, we are cultivating a sense of common nationhood, embracing the entire people, wherein various cultural strains are seen as components of a united people's national culture.'[114]

'The apartheid enemy tries to separate us into ancient "tribal" entities and pretends to be concerned about the preservation of our cultural heritage,' Tambo explained in an interview. 'We are one people with a rich cultural heritage which manifests itself in many variations. Our task is not to preserve our culture in its antique forms but to build on it and let it grow to assume a national character, the better to become a component of all evolving world culture. In this context, oral literature, dance, etc., become elemental parts of the national culture – a people's possession rather than a simple means of tribal identification.'[115]

The ANC's cultural desk and its popular 'Amandla' musical ensemble became an important dimension in mobilising both the international community and the membership itself. 'I think perhaps one of his strengths is that he is a lover of the arts,' commented Mzwai Piliso.

'He is a musician, a writer, he loves poetry, he loves culture generally, and he always encouraged the ANC externally to develop these things. And he has always been in the forefront in the development of these things... And whenever he comes to Angola, he would visit the [ANC cultural ensemble], he would ask them to perform for him.'[116]

But such occasions could only be small indulgences – the struggle was a Herculean, multifaceted task, embracing every aspect of life. Mac Maharaj, himself a full-time revolutionary, portrayed (perhaps projected) Tambo as 'a thoroughly political animal. He was like the Lenin who loved chess, music, but who then says in the heat of battle, "All that thing is over". Lenin put it extremely; he said, "When I listen to music it makes me become soft. So I stopped listening to music, I have no time for chess, for relaxation." OR had nothing left. You could not get him to read a novel. Anything you gave him, [he would ask] "Is it directly relevant to the struggle?" He had no time for anything else. He was totally immersed...'[117]

In the best of Christian, as well as African fashion Tambo seemed to see his responsibilities in reaching all South Africans. In exile, despite his strong rebuke of the PAC, he would not turn his back on them in times of need:

'You know the PAC used to quarrel and expel one another. One time they split, the biggest split they had, and the splinter group came to the ANC to say, "Our children are starving."'

Without hesitation, Tambo called together his team in Tanzania.

'Look,' he said, 'it doesn't matter if it is PAC. Those are our children. I suggest that we assist them immediately. Let them be sent to our stores.'

That same evening, he followed up on his instructions. Were the children given food? 'Did you give them money to buy vegetables and meat? No? Please do; we agreed that they must be given everything. We should do everything for them.'[118]

Tambo's style of leadership also reflected the traditional culture of consensus.

'I would say he would take a little bit of the Chief, the traditional leader, but the benign chief,' observed Albie Sachs, '– the benign traditional leader, the good one, who listened. And every meeting in that sense would be something of a *lekgotla*, where everybody comes in, everybody has a chance to be heard, and it is very democratic. You go for consensus rather than for majority rule.'[119]

For Jacob Zuma, what was 'amazing' was 'the leadership that Tambo put across – a leadership that made him to be respected by all in his leadership. In his time, thorough as he was, in terms of discussing issues, we developed a culture in the ANC leadership of actually taking decision by consensus. Now, that was due to OR's calibre and quality and understanding. He never allowed discussions to be haphazard and to take decisions that we were not all clear about... By the time you reached a decision, you all had agreed. If you had views, different views, you had time to put them across or to test them.'[120]

Penuel Maduna made a similar observation. 'OR would never express a viewpoint,' he commented. 'In discussions there were no holds barred. He liberated the personality. You were all equals in a debate.'[121]

Within his community, a traditional leader should always be nonpartisan. If someone acted out of turn, Tambo would try to find out why.[122]

As a leader, said Neo Moikangoa, Tambo 'would never allow himself to be enslaved to any circular political position and was just able to walk around any political position, rise above it and look at it from below and therefore be able to deal with that position and the individuals who subscribe to it.'[123]

An important role of the traditional leader is to provide for the people. From the beginning, as coordinator of the Mission in Exile, there was an immediate and urgent pressure provided for the material and spiritual care of young cadres. 'He [Tambo] was the key. He would go begging,' said Mac Maharaj. Mzwai Piliso confirmed this.

'I don't think there is an honest ANC person who can say that after about 1970 they ever starved, they didn't have shelter, they didn't have clothing. What we didn't have at a certain time was cash to give to people and those who had nothing to do and were sold to liquor and promiscuity, sold their clothes and food and were seen not to have clothes and things like those. But the movement had always endeavoured to give clothing, it may be second-hand clothing, every six months at least there was an allocation. But some people were given that allocation today, and by tomorrow they had sold it all.'[124]

Fundraising took up a large proportion of Tambo's diplomatic activity. A number of his letters to his wife provide directions on how gifts of clothes should be distributed among ANC members. One of his letters to Adelaide neatly balances his obligations:

'In this lonely world, I looked back and saw you with my mind's eye, carrying on your unaided shoulders, like a giant, a mountain of complex problems... The redeeming feature in all this is the nobility of the cause that takes us through dark months... I failed, after trying desperately, to get coats for the children who were facing a bitter winter with insufficient clothes and no coats. But it all proved hopeless. Things have become very hard now – all round... I hope you and the children are well and having something to eat.'[125]

Tambo, in fact, paid enormous tribute to his wife's role in the movement, and Adelaide, deprived by the movement of her husband, claimed her position as consort of the leader. At times, her interventions were inconvenient to the ANC's London office. People grumbled that Adelaide made long and expensive telephone calls, and that she gave interviews to the press 'speaking for the ANC' without a mandate. 'Your name is very important', they would lecture her, to her irritation, considering that she gave so much to the ANC herself.

And so it was that Adelaide, who was so admired for her consistency, her fidelity and her unshakable pride in her husband and children, found that her own identity was frequently overshadowed by the demands of the collective culture of the ANC.

As the years went by, the leader also had to provide for mental and physical healing. A hospital was established at Mazimbu, and was staffed by medical men and women from the international community. To counter those who had succumbed to anxiety, stress and despondency, the ANC was able to set up the Raymond Mhlaba Rehabilitation Centre, named after the Port Elizabeth Defiance Campaign leader and Robben Island prisoner. Section 1 was for the mentally ill – a tragic sequence for the pursued, the exiled, the ex-prisoners, the tortured, the shell-shocked, the unbearably homesick – while the other was set aside for those guilty of misbehaviour, yet considered capable of rehabilitation.

Tambo himself was not without the threat of assassination, or the stress of loneliness. 'Over the years, we met in all these hotels where he was isolated,' Lisbet Palme, widow of the assassinated prime minister of Sweden, recalled. 'I thought about it, for he had to live in such stress and isolation. When he did his travelling he always had to be guarded as he was always in danger... Nelson Mandela was almost more safe in prison than Oliver Tambo was out there, working for the task and the ideas of a free, democratic non-racist society.'[126]

As a result, Tambo moved from one safe house to another in Lusaka – an unsettling lifestyle that led to considerable personal strain, a strain that was only expressed years later, when he spoke of it to his doctor in Sweden.[127] OR probably had to draw on all his spiritual resources to keep himself emotionally stable. Stress also had the effect of encouraging paranoia, hence less tolerance of unconventional behaviour. In this context, the power of ANC security inevitably increased.[128]

On a personal level, it seemed Tambo was one of the few who stood firm against debilitating temptations. It was he who worked so hard to rehabilitate those who had succumbed, only sometimes with success. After the crisis in Morogoro, followed by the wounds inflicted by the Group of Eight, and in a context of ominous restiveness in the camps, Tambo emerged as the *only* man to lead the movement back home, and to freedom.

'OR is sitting in all these things', recounted Maharaj as the political tension escalated in the early 1980s. 'By this time the camps are bursting at their seams. And there is no way that the work can be done without delegating. There is this flood of people coming from outside, from inside the country, and our international work has now gone to a spin, and the only man holding the ANC together is really OR. Because, whatever the mistakes that the movement has made, Uncle JB is dead, Kotane is dead, Dadoo is in London, [X] is finished, [Y] and [Z] have been rescued from alcoholism and reinstated… and there are no bright sparks, no authority. But OR's life with the men in Kongwa, OR's being at the river when Wankie took place, OR's being in the bush with the chaps in Zambia and his very simplicity and style, have won him substantial support and he is holding together... But then he has troublesome people like [A] and all; sniping away in the hills, but what is patently clear is that his leadership has been established, amongst the men in the camps and internationally. And in the African context, he has created relationships with the African leaders. That balancing act, I don't know if Madiba could have done that, quite frankly. Because Madiba, when he makes up his mind, he becomes hot-headed and he just goes. Once he has decided that this is nonsense, I don't know whether he would have been able to court the Western community [and] the African leaders with the same doggedness and patience and then having to balance the men.'[129]

Through his carefully crafted style, Oliver Tambo did indeed achieve a 'giant triumph' in holding the ANC family together; but with it came a price to his family and also to the hidden recesses of his private dreams. But in the context of the greater sacrifices of those families of the hanged, the tortured, the incarcerated 'in Vorster's dungeons',[130] the bulk of Tambo's emotional energy was directed at holding together the movement. As the most difficult, final years of the struggle brought bomb attacks, assassinations, infiltration and paranoia, his great challenge was to retain the trust and coherence of the far larger, inclusive 'family of the nation', the ANC.

CHAPTER FIFTEEN

'Shishita' – Sweeping the Path

THE POST-'76 ERA BROUGHT NEW OPPORTUNITIES and dramatic predicaments. Tambo had observed, as early as 1968, that the ANC's exile status had forced upon the liberation movement 'a gap'. The important task, he reflected, was to maintain strong and durable lines of communication between the leaders inside and outside. 'It is to be expected that these lines of communication constitute one of the main targets of attack by the enemy,' he added.[1]

And this prediction did indeed come true. As the fortunes of the ANC surged forward – following political revival and activism with the re-emergence of the democratic labour movement and the school uprisings – the apartheid regime stepped up its programme of infiltrating state agents into the movement in exile. Along with hundreds of young men and women of the Soweto generation who applied for membership of the ANC, they burrowed their way into the very nucleus of the struggle itself – the military camps, whose primary purpose was to prepare the liberation army to return home to continue the struggle through guerrilla warfare. This penetration not only shook the stability of the movement, but also threatened to erode its very foundation – its value system – and was to have repercussions for many years to come.

The damage inflicted was hidden at first: a worm in the bud, revealed only with the unfolding of time.

In 1977, PW Botha introduced a White Paper for Defence. It outlined a 'total national strategy at the highest level' in order to counter resistance and crush the liberation movements. Apartheid's new prime minister revealed an 'interdependent, coordinated action in all fields military, psychological, economic, political, sociological, technological, diplomatic, ideological, cultural etc.' The project was to launch a period of increasingly sophisticated covert operations coupled with barbaric and illegal methods of torture, murder, intimidation and defamation, disinformation, attacks on neighbouring countries, the use of surrogates to commit massacres, and so on. A paper written by an official of the South African Defence Force (SADF) in 1977 sketched out their counterinsurgency methods – a panoply of what inadequately came to be known as 'dirty tricks', and which were used against the ANC in particular and other effective opponents of the apartheid system. The programme included recruiting agents positioned in strategic places such as in the media and in exile structures, setting up the special elite forces, destabilisation units, 'stratkom' (Strategic Communications) operations and the use of 'false flag' operations – those seemingly coming from within the movement but in reality undertaken on the instructions of the enemy's security forces. Its aim was to 'discredit the liberation movement in the eyes of sympathisers'.

Intelligence services, it suggested, 'can also create some havoc by the supply of false information, particularly the type to create mistrust. Thus the leader of the insurgency could be made to appear as a police informer'. The article also detailed ways that could 'sap confidence and morale... creating distrust between the insurgency and its suppliers'.[2] These could include doctoring food, mixing petrol in the paraffin for lamps, and tampering with medical supplies and arms.

In September of that year, 1977, some 500 cadres were hospitalised for food poisoning in the Novo Catengue camp in Angola. No one died, but it caused great disruption and did indeed dent the morale of cadres and administrators. The event came to be known as 'Black September'.

Novo Catengue was one of MK's largest and most successful camps. Commissar Mark Shope, a SACTU leader, had been very keen on political education. Tambo had encouraged this approach in all the camps. A deeper understanding of the liberation movement, its history, context and theory of struggle laid down firmer foundations for the security of MK. The expansion of knowledge and the cultivation of critical thinking that rested on fundamental values such as those enunciated in the Freedom Charter were, therefore, an asset, not a threat. Wolfie Kodesh, who ran an international campaign to deliver more books to camp libraries, recalled an example of Oliver Tambo's broader concept of education:

'On this particular occasion, I had visited the USSR embassy in Dar and there they were, giving out a lot of literature: Marxist literature, Little Lenin Library stuff and Marx, Engels, heavy literature and so on. And I got bundles of it...'

Tambo looked over the material and asked for a wider range of reading matter 'for the children' (as they were called in the camps).

'I said, "Well, look, I've got all this... What do you think?"'

'No, no, by all means take it,' Tambo reassured Kodesh. 'It doesn't matter, you know – they'll read and formulate their own ideas. But, they must read. They mustn't just hear about things. They must read what it's all about when they talk about Marxism and all the rest of it... I would also like them to get other literature as well, so that there is a balance of the reading matter.'[3]

After political instructor Ronnie Kasrils was deployed to Novo Catengue[4] and then back to London to undertake underground work, Tambo suggested that the camp request Jack Simons, the brilliant retired Professor of Sociology at the University of Zambia and formerly a popular radical lecturer in African Government and Law at the University of Cape Town, to run a course on the history and theory of the National Democratic Revolution for MK recruits at Novo Catengue.

Oliver Tambo was concerned not only to use education as a weapon in the struggle, but also to build an intelligentsia within the army itself, as well as throughout the movement. History and political theory were particularly important in developing political cadres. Their key task on their return was to wage a disciplined and informed guerrilla operation, which would recruit and guide the community in which they found themselves. A grasp of the strategy of liberation as a whole was crucial to the success of this process.

In the ANC's concept of 'the four pillars of struggle', Morogoro had confirmed that the armed struggle could not stray from the political in the holistic strategy of the ANC.

Tambo, who often stayed with Jack and Ray Simons when he was in Lusaka, became close to them, enjoying many discussions with these revolutionary and activist intellectuals. Ray, who had arrived in South Africa from Latvia in 1928, was a well-known trade union veteran and a member of the Communist Party of South Africa, while Jack – also in the CPSA – had written a treatise on colonial legislation regarding black women. Together, Jack and Ray Simons had also written a path-breaking book on class and colour in South Africa.[5]

Jack spent two periods at Novo Catengue – in 1977–78, following the large intake of 1976 arrivals, and then again from December 1978 to March 1979. His students – including Chris Hani, Peter Mayibuye (Joel Netshitenzhe), and writer and historian Mzala – remembered his theory of political education, the quality of his teaching and his interactive methodology. The emphasis on political instruction startled Cuban instructors, who were focusing on preparing the cadres for military combat.[6] MK 'didn't just lay emphasis on producing and reproducing guerrilla fighters…,' commented Hani. 'Our feeling was that they must organise people politically, and the people, if you like, would become the forest and the caves and the camouflage of the incipient guerrilla movement'.[7]

The resulting synergy worked positively, and 'if we achieved a lot now, it's because – despite setbacks and errors – that was our strategy'.[8] Novo Catengue acquired the reputation of having developed a model People's Army, where political training and development was impressive, where the cadres themselves were involved in solving problems and where discipline was 'constructive'.[9]

In the meantime, the ANC was developing its own counter-intelligence. Since 1976, an MK security apparatus had been briefed to screen recruits. Its other main brief was to gather intelligence in order to defend the ANC. In 1979 word came from home that Novo Catengue would be attacked. Counter-intelligence was able to obtain prior information of the attack, particularly as SWAPO's Cassinga camp had been attacked earlier and 200 people massacred.

In Novo Catengue, 500 cadres had, night after night, hidden in the culverts formed by the nearby Benguela railway line.

'When they were bombing the camp, we were looking at them,' chuckled Mzwai Piliso, who headed the intelligence and security unit.[10] From then on, though, the security department increased its vigilance and powers, becoming known as 'Mbokodo', or 'grinding stone'.

But the South African National Intelligence Service (NIS), too, was steadily building up a programme of destabilisation of the movement.

'Ja,' confirmed operative Riaan Labuschagne, 'NIS was effective in a lot of ways; we wrapped up Zimbabwe agent-wise, so every cadre who crossed the border we knew about.'[11]

Since the Novo Catengue camp had been destroyed by the SADF attack in 1979 with a precision that clearly indicated an inside informer, the vision of a People's Army was damaged. In 1981, cadre Ndunga (code name 'Joel Mahlatini') was caught smoking dagga. He was so severely beaten that he died a few hours later. A shaken leadership, including Tambo himself, visited all the camps. They called for an investigation into the death and indiscipline incidents. It transpired that there were infiltrators in their midst.

It was discovered that the camp commander, Kenneth Mahamba, who had ordered the beating, was an undercover agent for the South African government. He had been recruited in 1976 and had been so well trained that he rose in the ranks of MK to achieve a highly responsible position. He and other agents had been to blame for the poisoning at Novo Catengue in 1977. They also passed on information that led to the 1979 SADF attack on the camp.[12]

Some 20 agents were uncovered. They had worked their way into top positions in various departments, including the Treasury Department, the Youth Headquarters and in the camps. Others had been placed in useful positions in neighbouring countries. Oshkosh Khumalo, for example, was a protocol officer in Zambia, clearing ANC personnel travelling to, through and from Zambia.[13] Some operatives worked for foreign intelligence services that cooperated with the regime, and were able to supply information about the location of military installations, residences of senior ANC personnel and the Solomon Mahlangu Freedom College. Their information led directly to many arrests and murders.

'The previous system turned our young ones into murderers', mourned a witness in the Truth and Reconciliation Commission, many years later.[14] This was the case in exile as well as at home. Other operatives in junior positions were instructed to stir up discontent in the camps, culminating in what the ANC later described as a 'rash of bizarre incidents of indiscipline'.[15]

Between late 1983 and 1985 there were two mutinies. In the first, a group of cadres demanded to be deployed to the home front. When this was not forthcoming, they refused to be disarmed and fired shots into the night. The incident was dealt with 'politically' and seemed to blow over. But increasingly, there were a growing number of incidents of indiscipline. These included pilfering or sabotaging supplies, smoking dagga, rape and even murder – in the camps and in neighbouring villages. Part of the problem was a difference between the generations. Mature soldiers had imbibed the lessons of political patience through experience and an understanding of strategy and tactics in their long-term mission. The young intakes were impatient, the disillusioned victims of Bantu Education; they were unschooled in politics or revolutionary theory or ANC history and had not necessarily internalised organisational discipline. They were too young to have been trained and disciplined in the politics of the labour movement, in civil organisations or in the underground. The '76 generation had also learnt that their elders were not necessarily wiser, and the status of teachers, once esteemed by black society, meant nothing to them. This was a township world that older commanders had not experienced, and they were perplexed at the unruliness and impertinence of the youngsters.

Many of 'the new crop', commented Zola Skweyiya, 'had no politics... [The] only thing they wanted was a gun, and as far as the ANC [was concerned], the act of carrying a gun was political, and as such, they had to be politicised first'.[16]

After the mutiny in 1983/1984, Tambo appointed the Stuart Commission to investigate. A disturbing picture emerged. It was not easy to untangle the relationship between camp dangers – mutiny and enemy infiltration. James Stuart convened a team who visited all military camps in Angola and interviewed 'practically all the occupants', including all 33 cadres detained in Luanda Maximum Security Prison as well as the senior personnel of the military.[17]

The events reflected 'the frightening situation into which our organisation, the ANC and MK has sunk in the People's Republic of Angola', warned the Commission's report. 'It is clear that since 1979 there had been a gradual development of an explosive situation which finally erupted in December 1983.'

The background to the story gives a vivid sense of the build-up of misunderstanding, suspicion, defiance and increased antisocial behaviour in the army at the time. Early in 1983 Tambo had visited camps to explain that one of their Angolan allies, FAPLA, together with Soviet Union technicians assisting in the area, had appealed for reinforcements against the opposing UNITA army, backed by South Africa. As UNITA was only 40 kilometres away from the MK camp in Malanga, its own security was threatened. The combat experience would be valuable, Tambo explained, and deployment would not detract from MK's main theatre – inside the country. Anyone participating in the 'LCB' – Luta Contra Bandidos[18] – would immediately be recalled, he reassured troops, if the 'forward machineries' required him or her to be deployed inside South Africa.

The response to the president was warm and enthusiastic, and very soon the northern camps – Quibashe (or 'Quibaxe') and Pango, as well as Caxito and Luanda – were depleted. And the cadres did indeed gain experience. They participated in mine-defusing, laying ambushes and patrolling duties.[19] But the situation changed when operations were extended to cross the Kwanza River to attack UNITA in their own stronghold. Chris Hani opposed the scheme; MK troops did not know the terrain, he argued; no proper reconnaissance had been carried out and there were no reliable maps. Neither did they know the enemy, their weapons or the extent of their reinforcements. But after Hani left the area, Commander Lennox was instructed to cross the river. From there, cadres were separated into small groups and placed in FAPLA units all around the area. The cadres discovered that many of the other troops were inadequately trained – some had been in this crisis situation for only two weeks – and at least once had to march for three days without food, in the absence of reconnaissance.

On 26 December, one of the units fell into an ambush in which five MK cadres were killed, while the other LCB soldiers ran away. The survivors had to return to take the mutilated and dead bodies of their comrades back to the camp. They were convinced that they had been led into the ambush.

In the same month, Angolan troops requested further reinforcements to take a defensive position in the village of Cangadala, in the Malanga Province. A total of 104 MK cadres regrouped to assist, but they made it clear that they would not prepare their positions before FAPLA moved out. Once installed, their duties included patrolling. But discipline had broken down. Some went into the village to get drunk, incidents of dagga smoking increased, and a number failed to sleep in their positions. Lennox was sent to locate the problems, and held a three-day meeting with the soldiers. Some were suspicious of the entire operation – the Eastern Front was a diversion, they were convinced, and wanted to know why there were no operations inside South Africa.

At the camp of Musafa, where other MK soldiers were stationed, grievances were similar. The commander there also reported random shooting under false pretexts. Some losses had occurred – a comrade had been blown up by a UNITA mine, a trainee at the LCB Caculama camp had been 'punished' and died on release. But after Lennox left, unauthorised shooting in the air continued, and indeed the practice was adopted by a few in the village itself.

'We are doing this to draw attention to our demands,' they said.

Eventually about 60 cadres were removed from Cangadala, Cacuso and Musafa and were returned to Viana in Luanda. Another 40 left for Luanda without permission. Discipline had clearly broken down. When the first group arrived at Viana, they refused to surrender their arms, as was customary. They needed them, they argued, 'for self-protection from the Security Department men'. The second group followed suit. To add to the tension, a cadre who was reportedly 'mentally unstable' and was having epileptic episodes was detained in a container in the camp. After several days of incarceration, he died. It was rumoured that his body was found 'riddled with bullets'. In an atmosphere of defiance – despite the appointment of an Interim Administration – order rapidly declined. Livestock was slaughtered without permission, arms were openly brandished and drinking and dagga-smoking became commonplace.

The military sent a committee to iron out the difficulties. At a meeting at Viana, a 'Committee of Ten' was elected from the soldiers to work out an agenda and to prepare discussions with the Regional Command. The Committee represented the cultural ensemble 'Amandla' as well as the Women's Section in Angola and the Department of Information and Propaganda. On their agenda were a call for a national consultative conference; the return home to continue the armed struggle; increased contact with the leadership; evacuees to be returned to Viana Camp; improvement of camp conditions and medical supplies; and an application to disband the Security Department.

But on the morning of the scheduled meeting, a FAPLA unit arrived to disarm the camp. The camp inmates were, at first, under the impression that they were being invaded by UNITA troops, and a confrontation followed. There was a brief exchange of fire and an MK soldier was killed. In Luanda on the same morning, the Security Department arrived at the radio unit's flat to disarm the personnel there. The ensuing scuffle, when one of the radio unit staff tried to resist with a hand grenade, resulted in two deaths. At the end of the day, the Committee of Ten and others were arrested and transported to the maximum-security Camp 32 in Luanda, there to languish for up to four years.

The Security Department was convinced that there had been a conspiracy within the movement to subvert the organisation. Angolan camps were 'riddled' with 'suspects', the Commission confirmed, and there were those, including members of the Committee of Ten, who had a record of divisive regionalism.

It had long been Oliver Tambo's feeling that many young enemy agents had not willingly betrayed their people, but had been forced into infiltrating the ANC through torture, or to protect their families, or as a trade-off for long sentences. Indeed, there were many who felt safe after humane handling, who confessed as much to the ANC and subsequently became committed comrades.

The Stuart Commission found that Angola had become the 'dumping ground' for 'enemy agents, suspects, malcontents and undisciplined elements' – all were sent to the camps in Angola to have discipline instilled in them. Some of the suspects were deployed as cooks, medical officers and even commissars.[20] In that regard, the Commission commented, it was grossly unfair that so-called suspects had to live under a cloud, their cases not investigated for many years.

'For those amongst them who are innocent, life must be real hell,' noted the Commission, 'and it's a sad commentary on the efficiency of the Security Department (and the internal structures of our movement) that this should be so.'

For enemy agents, the opposite was true. The poor conditions and general life of the camps cultivated fertile ground for them. With a lack of transparency on policy, most cadres suffered from psychological deprivation, waiting year after year to be deployed to the home front. There was also a fear of punishment, which became increasingly common in camps. 'Our lengthy stay and conditions in [the camps] has made some of us to lose all sense of human feeling, lose complete touch with humanity,' stated one respondent to the Commission.

'Usually there is no further contact with their previous machineries,' remarked the Commission. 'Most believe they will never leave the camps again and a sense of frustration, desperation and anarchy sets in.' The Commission agreed that under such conditions it was 'practically impossible for cadres to survive (politically, morally and psychologically) in the camps for several years'.[21]

The Commission found that an elitism had developed that separated the administration from the rank and file – in diet, accommodation, even access to cigarettes and liquor. Even female cadres were perceived by complainants as having become 'sex objects' who did 'not develop politically and militarily'. Mismanagement and victimisation were rife; problems and mistakes continued without resolution. Bureaucracy was now overtaking the discourse of the camps. 'In many cases, autocratic centralism has replaced democratic centralism... Cadres believe it has become impossible to see the leadership because of bureaucratic manoeuvrings', stated the report.

On top of this, the disciplinary problems (drunkenness and dagga-smoking affected behaviour and exposed the movement to risks) and antisocial behaviour in villages (including sexual molestation) embarrassed the movement in relation to their Angolan hosts. Camp equipment was also known to be sold in the villages. Punishment, though, seemed to be aimed at demoralising and humiliating offenders rather than correcting and building. Offenders were locked up for days in metal goods containers without light or air; forced to stay in swamps every night for weeks, carrying sacks full of soil; beaten, and tied to a tree for 24 hours. The Commission found that at least five people had died of ill treatment and several had committed suicide. Others had deserted.

The long list of ailments also arose largely from the poor camp conditions. Because of lack of medical care and medication, malaria was rampant, and there were cases of asthma, skin diseases, mental illness – nervous breakdowns and even psychotic episodes[22] – as well as bronchitis, tuberculosis and kidney disorders. There was a shortage of clothes, boots, tents and even soap. Recreation equipment was rare, and radios, libraries and transport were lacking. Cultural programmes – much less a development and education policy – were poorly planned. As a result, morale was low and relationships also reached a low point.

What had become increasingly obvious was that basic necessities were often distributed under a patronage system dispensed by the Security Department, which monopolised control of the military. The Stuart Commission found that the Security Department, whose leaders had come from MK, had 'become totally isolated and alienated from the general cadreship'. Their 'power and privileges, their lifestyles, their image and method of work' notoriously placed them above those living in the camps.

The Commission made several pointed suggestions. It recommended, firstly, that a consultative conference be called, as had been done during the post-Wankie crisis in 1968/9. More specifically, it recommended that the National Commissar and several other senior officers be redeployed. The Commission also called for the abolition of privileges, the setting up of a code of conduct, a policy on cadre and commander development, and more frequent visits by the leadership to update the cadres on development on all fronts.

But then another mutiny erupted. This time it was at Pango, and the rebels employed machine guns and heavy weapons and killed the camp commanders and other cadres. Eight men were subsequently tried and sentenced to death, although Tambo later commuted the sentences.[23]

The NEC received the news and the Commission's findings with consternation. Tambo asked if any of the committee would visit Camp 32, where some of the cadres were imprisoned. (The NEC decided that it would not be appropriate for the president to visit problem spots before the second in line had done so.)[24] Gertrude Shope, head of the Women's Section, volunteered and duly took the trip with Chris Hani. Shope was taken aback at what she saw. Escaped and recaptured cadres were held as prisoners, dressed only in underpants. In interviews, one by one they voiced their grievances. Shope ordered that all prisoners be given proper clothes, and that ill treatment stop immediately.[25] (This visit was not sufficient to uncover the worst conditions at the detention camp, however. It later transpired that systematic violence and torture were used to extract information, 'at any cost', in the words of Mzwai Piliso.[26])

On her return to head office, Shope delivered her report to the NEC, and they then implemented some of the Stuart Commission's recommendations. One of the commissioners, Sizakele Sigxashe, replaced the senior security officer who had been looking into the details of the mutiny. Mzwai Piliso, head of the Security Department, was redeployed and, in time, had to answer to four commissions for his methods of interrogation. But, he maintained, even in hindsight, 'All that is important is not my skin. What is important to me is the skin of the young people under me... So I say to them, if there is anybody to answer, come to me. And I still say so to this day. Not those young people – because if anything happened in the camp, I knew... And after I had dealt with the person who did whatsoever it was, I took the responsibility.'[27]

The Commission's brief had, however, not included the investigation of conditions at Quatro, a detention camp set up in 1979 by Mzwai Piliso, and named after Section Four of Johannesburg's notorious Fort. It was only later that the extent of the treatment of the inmates at Quatro – administered by the Security Department – came to be revealed. Tambo responded after his first visit there: it was, he said ruefully, 'one camp the ANC could do without'.[28]

Mwezi Twala, a dissident incarcerated in Quatro, recalled with some bitterness how the security had taken control of Tambo's visits to the camps.

'OR used to queue up for his food like any other soldier, and wash his own plate... Later this was all to change in the name of security; Tambo would receive special treatment and special food, as would the camp administration...'[29]

But for the leadership, while the disillusionment and the appalling behaviour of some in charge of the camps were extremely disturbing, there was another, even more sinister phenomenon. It had become increasingly clear to the ANC that there were informers in its midst. It had begun, the Intelligence Department realised, with the substantial early intake of the 1976 recruits.

At that stage, the ANC had no efficient screening system to verify the biographies of potential recruits. With hindsight, it was not surprising that agents were being swept in with the many eager youngsters; hundreds of young people had been detained and tortured. A few had succumbed. They joined the ranks of the 'Askaris' – the Kenyan word for soldiers in colonial times – who had been 'turned' after capture and torture. Others were seasoned cadres who were kidnapped, taken across the border into South Africa and tortured.

'September [nom de guerre] was one of us, who defected and became an Askari,' reflected Farouk Timol, working in the Intelligence Department of the ANC. 'There was a lot of information that he diverted.'[30]

Once they had betrayed the movement, there was no return, and the regime was able to develop a destabilising programme using collaborators in a variety of ways. A number were deployed to the camps, where they were instructed to embark on specific projects, such as poisoning the food, sabotaging equipment, and generally using camp hardships to stir up discontent. They were able to provide information about the location of bases, the names of key individuals in MK and the whereabouts of ANC premises. It was such intelligence that led to the massacres, ambushes and assassinations and to the arrest, torture and imprisonment of cadres, as well as the destruction of the Novo Catengue camp.

For Chris Hani, senior member of the National Command, 'the mutiny actually was a crystallisation or a culmination of systematic infiltration of the ANC by skilled and well-trained enemy agents.

'They exploited the grievances of the people because life in exile was very difficult... When we defeated the mutiny, it is true that the ANC had to set up a tribunal and some people were sentenced to death for having killed some of our outstanding officers. I remember that a big number had been sentenced to death, but OR intervened – together with the leadership, of course – to stop those executions and save some of those people who were very young and gullible. Even those who were actually sentenced to death were kept in a rehabilitation centre. The ANC never carried out those executions.'[31]

All those arrested were afforded legal representation. Lawyers such as Penuel Maduna, Zola Skweyiya and later Matthews Phosa defended those charged.

'It was very exciting, you know,' remarked Maduna, 'injecting justice in very difficult conditions and saying that even those who were real enemies of our people, who had killed people, were entitled to be heard by the tribunal – and they were heard and assisted. A lot of them were rehabilitated subsequently.'[32]

The tribunal heard many cases, and handed down many death sentences. At least 34 were executed before the ANC outlawed the death penalty in 1985 (confirmed by the Kabwe Conference).[33]

Throughout this time, Tambo's visits to the camps were welcomed by cadres. 'OR had the most retentive memory for detail,' recalled Jonas Gwangwa, a leader in MK's cultural wing, Amandla. 'He knew everybody's names.'

They knew that they would receive an up-to-date and informative briefing from the highest source, and that they were encouraged to ask questions. In the wake of the Nkomati Accord, both the camps and the high school erupted in demands that they be permitted to go home to take up arms. Tambo spoke to the soldiers, painting the bigger picture, in which diplomacy, the underground, as well as preparing for guerrilla warfare at home had to be balanced.

Every talk given by Tambo was a lesson in political education and in strategy and tactics. 'Let us pledge ourselves never to allow MK to be emasculated', he cautioned the cadres on the 25th anniversary of Umkhonto we Sizwe.[34]

Every visit was also an opportunity to demonstrate the camp's musical and sporting accomplishments. Tambo loved to conduct the choirs, and often suggested songs with a political message such as 'Uboni' (praising the horse), giving them new arrangements. The song, 'Tambo, get all the boys from Angola', gave reasons why cadres could not go home.[35] The role of arts in the camps, even with the shortage of food and clothes, served to cheer and reassure. The fact that there were no more mutinies, some believed, owed a great deal to Tambo's 'democratic behaviour' and attempt to make time for everybody.[36]

In order to situate the harsh responses of the authorities to the indiscipline of some of the cadres, one needs to take the context into account. In 1982 alone, a letter bomb doctored by South African agents killed Ruth First in Maputo; it was discovered that two ANC members in Lusaka were in fact enemy agents, and in December the SADF raided Maseru, killing 42 people, including 12 Basotho civilians. The Minister of Justice, Jimmy Kruger's public boast that 'of every ten who cross the border to join the ANC, five are mine' unnerved the movement and sowed distrust – 'one's bunkmate could be a plant', commented the Motsuenyane Commission Report about the feeling at the time.[37]

Both the ANC's Security and Intelligence departments were further distressed to uncover a plot to overthrow the leadership of Oliver Tambo.[38] Once a man turned up in Lusaka and asked to stay with Mr and Mrs Kaupepe, whose home was one of Tambo's 'safe houses'. Later it became clear that the guest was a spy. He was taken to Angola, where he was grilled, and confessed that he had been sent by South Africa's Bureau of State Security (BOSS).[39]

Tambo's secret movements from one 'safe house' to another, usually late at night, heightened the levels of stress and tension. For the leadership, these revelations were a serious worry. Focus inevitably fell on the inadequacies of the National Security Council and its departments. They redoubled their efforts to identify the traitors in their midst, and set up a counter-intelligence operation that uncovered a number of spies. The ANC cadreship named the operation 'Shishita', an Angolan word meaning 'to sweep (out of the house)'.[40]

It was in this period, in the early to mid-1980s, that a gripping apprehension set in. Zealous methods of investigation and punishment were enforced that often proved to be out of proportion to the offences committed. Was the sometimes antisocial behaviour of youthful miscreants in reality deeply sinister? The outcome could be a matter of life or death.

Identifying undercover agents was made more complex by the fact that some agents in the camps were in senior positions, which enabled them to make accusations and intensify the sense of paranoia. Beatings and torture to extract information, in the absence of evidence, escalated and, in some cases, those detained were innocent of the accusations of spying – some were 'either falsely implicated, or had merely shown signs of ill-discipline' – and many were ultimately released.[41] But there were nevertheless at least two cases in which innocent people were falsely accused and executed, and in the years between 1980 and 1984, at least 28 ANC members were executed.[42]

The number of executions of even proven operatives disturbed Tambo. Piliso, called 'Tata' by the younger cadres, was a strict disciplinarian who had become hardened in the face of the dangers and his responsibility for the security of the ANC and of Tambo himself, and he began to condone the tortures. He recalled his exasperation with Tambo's response to the escalation of sinister developments, even while he admired Tambo's integrity. Tambo had been 'very angry' at the destruction of Novo Catengue. But his 'sense of democracy', said Piliso, impeded investigations. 'For him, even security had to work democratically.'[43]

'For instance,' Piliso elaborated, 'if you caught somebody for perpetrating terrible acts against the ANC or the people, if you had proof, you couldn't act against those people according to him, unless you reported and [Tambo] took the final decision – which I think was a good thing, because some of us could have chopped many heads... OR [was] full of the idea of justice.'[44]

'Most of the detentions happened after huge calamities within the ANC, like raids, and at that time the security would be more active in terms of vigilance. So otherwise it was much more liberal as liberation movements go. We had a security system but... one didn't get a sense that they really went on wild witch hunts packing in people.'[45]

Part of the problem was the generation gap. Between the mid-sixties and mid-seventies, there had been few intakes, and there were not enough experienced personnel to administer the growing number of departments. Its effect was to create, in the words of Joe Slovo, 'a log-jam at the leadership level'.[46] Most of the Politico-Military Council (PMC) were doubling up in other committees.

'I'm on the PMC,' explained Joe Slovo by way of example. 'The commander of the army is on the PMC, and he's on the Military Head Quarters (MHQ). Chris [Hani] is on the PMC and the MHQ.'[47] He might have added the multiple roles of many others – Mzwai Piliso, in charge of all the camps in

Angola, was also the head of the National Security Council, which oversaw subdepartments such as the Security Department.[48] In that instance, the dual roles of intelligence gathering and discipline led to confusion. The result was that investigators, accusers, judges and retaliators all came from the same department. And because of security considerations in a fraught context, key decisions often had to be taken without the individuals responsible for them.

'You take the military headquarters,' elucidated Slovo. 'If it was sitting and doing only what headquarters normally do – and they've got an army and camps and they are with the people – they are planning campaigns; there's a ministry of defence behind them, supplying the necessities and so forth.

'But it can't happen in our situation. The result is that people like the commander and chief of staff, instead of having all their time taken up with actual planning and implementation of military operations, have to rush to the camps, deal with logistics, go to OAU meetings, deal with supplies, visit the Soviet Union… meet Front Line States, [and] counterparts in the military sphere.'[49]

The president himself, increasingly caught up in sensitive diplomatic work,[50] was not available to apprise himself directly of the situation in both the camps and with the details of intelligence findings. Nor was he able to obtain clarity from those in charge in the Security Department, who earnestly showed him evidence of many a conspiracy, indeed backed up by the losses incurred by the movement. He had delegated this crucial work to trusted lieutenants and had to trust them to acquit themselves with integrity. Nevertheless, as Supreme Commander of MK, Tambo took ultimate responsibility.

'We could not have foreseen that this was going to happen. Perhaps commanders who were closest might have, but ultimately this was entirely a matter of hindsight,' reflected Thabo Mbeki. 'Matters like this were not endemic to the movement, so I don't know what one would have expected Oliver Tambo to do… The reality is that one is dealing with an exceedingly complex situation… It couldn't be expected that he would have such detailed information.'[51]

There was also the structural weakness of the parallel identities of the political and the military. The different experiences between these two spheres, particularly in exile, sometimes led to contradictory perceptions. Military struggle imposed its own culture, including a stricter approach to discipline, obedience and an increased awareness of the immediacy of sacrifice. In exile, the environment in which a leadership had to operate and the responsibility that it had to carry out imposed its own urban mode of life, with access to technology that was vastly different from the one in the bush. As early as the 1960s, this had led to a feeling among some cadres that the lifestyle of leaders in the political and diplomatic sphere reduced their revolutionary fervour. The 'softer' life reduced the pressure on political leaders to get home, they felt, and undermined the urgency with which many vital tasks were tackled. These perceptions came to the fore particularly when frustration over the slow progress of the armed struggle, together with deprivation in the camps, came to a head. The outcome was sometimes also a questioning of the very values of the struggle. When the circumstances of the non-military came to be regarded by the rank and file as the plums of status, or as evidence of double standards, an inevitable feeling of alienation from leadership resulted.

This disaffection was not, however, expressed by the majority of cadres. Thousands, while frustrated and deprived, accepted the logistics of the situation and also the good faith of the movement. Remarkably, Supreme Commander Tambo was not blamed for the rising tensions, which was an indication of his perceptive leadership. He emphasised the importance of briefing the cadres and supplying them with ongoing political information where security permitted.

Rashid (Aboobaker Ismail), who became head of Special Operations, recalled how 'OR would come and talk to us as commanders, and say, "We expect you to do the following: these are the problems... Can you explain what is happening? What do you do in your training situation, [and] why?" One got a general sense that there was a lot of planning taking place. Somehow, the resources for MK were being found. We always knew that MK was the priority; that if there was any call upon anything, MK would get it – over and above everything else.'[52]

Tambo's respect for the cadres' need to be treated as intelligent adults was rewarded with genuine popularity. 'Of the senior leadership, he was the most regular visitor to the camps from 1977 to 1984,' observed Pallo Jordan (who was detained, in Quatro, for six weeks for criticising the Security Department).[53]

Joe Slovo once asked Ronald Segal if he could not 'speak to OR about using his time more economically'. He and OR had visited a camp together and spent an enormous amount of time listening to seemingly trivial complaints. Segal duly relayed the reprimand, to which Tambo retorted, 'You are the one who is always complaining that African leaders are becoming more remote!'[54]

'OR was... very keen in knowing what was happening, wanting to know at every stage what is going on,' commented Rashid. 'One always felt a tremendous presence when he came to the camp. For the cadres it was a big occasion when the leadership came to talk to them about what was going on inside the country. But when OR came, the camp would be buzzing. You could feel the electricity. There was a tremendous lull and everybody wants to get close to him. He would talk to cadres about the problems. One never felt that he talked to people from up above. You felt that he was a person you stood in awe of, but at the same time a person who really cared about the lives of the cadres.'[55]

For Tambo, it was crucial that a democratic process confirm the drastic changes that clearly needed to take place. A consultative conference was imperative. Bigger than Morogoro, 16 long years earlier, this one involved scores of branches worldwide, camp delegations and even emissaries from home. The event finally took place at Kabwe in Zambia in 1985, the largest ANC conference thus far, with 250 ANC delegates. The question of grievances and military discipline was discussed in a special commission – 'precisely to deal with the question of human rights within the organisation', commented the four commissioned to investigate the death of one of the Quatro inmates, an MK soldier of long standing, Thami Zulu, shortly after his release from detention.[56]

'Delegate after delegate stressed that the viciousness of apartheid in no way justified viciousness on our part. On the contrary, we are fighting for justice and respect for life, and respect for life must exist inside our ranks.'

Conference approved many reforms and provided for restructuring to enable further legal processes to tackle problems. These included stricter monitoring by the president of the death penalty, which Tambo in particular would have preferred to see abolished (as it was soon afterwards). Convinced of the legitimacy of their cause, the ANC replaced Quatro with a rehabilitation camp that emphasised re-education rather than retribution. Tambo argued that many of the cadres would come to understand the ANC's noble vision and aims.

'It is a sort of political way of winning over hearts and minds,' explained Chris Hani. 'The regime uses its resources to corrupt people by offering them money, by offering them bribes. We win hearts and minds by showing the nobility of our struggle, by telling them that victory is inevitable.'[57]

And indeed, a number of informers, particularly lesser-trained agents who had been sent en masse to act as a smokescreen for the sophisticated undercover agents, were rehabilitated and deployed in various positions.[58] 'I wouldn't like to mention their names and embarrass some of them,' said Penuel Maduna.[59]

An additional structure designed to separate the prosecutors from the judges was the People's Tribunal, appointed to try those accused of working for the enemy. It was in principle against the death sentence, which was reserved for only the most acute cases. Although it had its operational limitations, it became a pointer towards reflecting the values of the society it was attempting to shape.

The Conference also endorsed an Officer of Justice and a National Review Board, which responded to the findings of the People's Tribunal. It too was to be guided by the Code of Conduct commissioned by Tambo.

In a conversation with Tambo as to why the Code was necessary, Albie Sachs recalled that Tambo had told him that the ANC statutes were silent on certain issues of procedure and detention.[60]

Sachs also recalled vividly his own confident response: '"Well," I said, "of course, whatever we do, we can't use torture"; to which Tambo quietly replied, "We do use torture". He said it very calmly and quietly. I got such a shock.'

When it was finally formulated, the Code of Conduct was guided by the Freedom Charter – 'all shall be equal before the law', 'no one shall be imprisoned, deported or restricted without a fair trial', 'imprisonment... shall aim at re-education, not vengeance'. 'Our justice,' the Code pointed out, 'must be fair, humane, honest, comradely, democratic, accessible, popular, equal for all members and dedicated to serving the interests of the people as a whole.'

Those suspected of having committed 'grave crimes' had rights. All normal or reasonable forms of investigation were permitted in the course of investigation, but torture, whether physical or psychological, or any form of cruel, inhuman or degrading treatment of a detainee was forbidden. The Code also pointed out that suspects were innocent until proved guilty, and that enemy agents had the right – according to the international Geneva Convention that Tambo had signed on behalf of the ANC in 1980 – to be treated as prisoners of war.

The dramatic increase in the escalation of the internal struggle had brought new needs and also more dangers, and clearly capacity had to be further reinforced. Before Botha's 'Total Onslaught', a detention camp had not existed.[61] Following Kabwe, an Internal Political Committee was set up to strengthen Political Headquarters. The military was extended and personnel redeployed. A Provisional Directorate of Intelligence and Security was created to manage the National Security Council, and to clarify the command structures in Angola. The Council would be accountable to Tambo's President's Committee.

The abuses were greatly reduced as a result of these measures, but it took some time for them to be halted altogether. The ANC's records, though not entirely accurate, showed that at least three convicted informers were executed after the death penalty was stopped. As raids, assassinations and massacres continued, it was difficult to stem the atmosphere of anxiety, suspicion and fear. Mbokodo leaders felt justified in continuing their methods of interrogation to save the movement from destruction. Suspects continued to be detained for years on end, and some continued to be subjected to beatings and torture and/or kept in inhuman conditions of confinement. The idea of rehabilitation was lost in the process. The Officer of Justice, Zola Skweyiya, for example, was firmly kept out of Angola, being denied an entry visa – as a non-military person – into a war zone until Oliver Tambo intervened and visited Quatro himself in 1987. The outcome was an immediate change of leadership in that department in 1987.[62] In the meantime, contact with the Review Board, too, was minimal and the chairman of the tribunal had very little interaction with the Officer of Justice. It took many months before resources and personnel were put in place to enable the new structures to function as mandated. Despite the Code of Conduct, the reforms and the restructuring, enforcement, monitoring and supervisory powers were lacking – 'the machinery,' concluded the Motsuenyane Commission, 'was unable to stop abuses of human rights, which continued'.[63]

There were some senior leaders, though, who insisted that executions and torture were necessary for the survival of the movement. In 1996, General Andrew Masondo, who had been National Commissar, in giving evidence to the Truth and Reconciliation Commission, was adamant on this point:

'We were at war,' he said. 'We executed [enemy agents] and I wouldn't make an apology. We were at war.... There might be times when I will use third degree in spite of the fact that it is not policy.'[64]

But why did it take so long for the leadership to intervene? In practice, 'this was not an OR problem,' explained Thabo Mbeki. 'Someone like OR has to deal with millions of things – to do with struggle, international struggle, function of organisation. The information about abuses came to the leadership quite late because it was dealt with by the military structure, including intelligence.'[65] It seemed clear that the old, parallel bodies, which were supposed to balance the military committee with the political committee had failed to prioritise the political trajectory, as envisioned by the Morogoro Conference in 1969. The military was clearly proceeding along its own lines, and its security had acquired immense powers. During the eighties, as the struggle intensified on all fronts, Tambo was not able to maintain direct contact with the camps. As Thabo Mbeki pointed out, the military had its structures of responsibility. Tambo relied on the military and political and the accountability of Intelligence and all the other bodies to report to him and the NEC, as they were mandated to do. Added to which there was Oliver Tambo's characteristic of investigating methodically before making major decisions.

'OR disliked quick conclusions with insufficient preparation,' confirmed Mazisi Kunene. 'He was more cautious in sensitive matters.'[66]

'There was trust,' commented Thenjiwe Mthintso. 'There was democracy, there was unity, there was loyalty.' At the same time, 'there was indecisiveness about these things'.[67] But 'it was not a negative indecisiveness', Mthintso said.

'Let me weigh,' Tambo would respond to difficulties. 'What are they saying? Let me hear more, let me hear more.'

'It was within OR to actually approach certain leaders and say to them they must not stand for election. But he didn't, because there's always this trust in these comrades. And also, really caring for the comrades that perhaps it would have been seen as dumping them,' added Thenjiwe Mthintso.

Chris Hani, who had himself reported abuses to Tambo, gave his analysis of the situation: 'Tambo himself knows that we have clashed on this issue. I thought he moved slowly… I said that there was a need to move quickly, to put a stop to what we saw as abuses in the camps, to what we saw as incorrect methods of interrogation and handling of suspects and agents.

'But OR is a person who wants to study a phenomenon first, who does not want to make rash judgements, because I think he would like any judgement to stand the test of time. He has a mind which says, "Let me get all the sides of this story." He appointed a number of commissions, and we must also put ourselves in his position. It was easy for me; I was not President of the ANC, to say "Act immediately. I know there are rogues in the Security Department".

'But OR was saying, "Look, I have lost men and women as a result of the activities of agents; I have to account to the people of South Africa, what I did about their children." As a movement, what measures were taken to protect our cadres from elimination? You must remember that lots of cadres died because of information given to the Security Police, of leaks and everything. Comrades were intercepted, killed at roadblocks. They were entering the country. Ultimately, the person to answer is the head of the organisation. So OR could not be brash like me and Pallo Jordan and others.'[68]

And indeed, the Security Department saved a number of ANC lives on many occasions when they intercepted the enemy – the bombing of Novo Catengue was a case in point. As the raids and massacres and assassinations continued, in Mozambique, in Swaziland, in Lusaka, in Harare, in Botswana, in Paris and London, resulting in the deaths of targeted individuals and hundreds of ANC members and civilians of the host countries, and with clear evidence of a 'third force' gathering strength, the enormity and moral and political complexity of the situation confronted Tambo.

'The task,' commented Pallo Jordan, whose outspokenness had caused him to be detained by Mbokodo, 'of someone whose job it is to defend the movement against assaults and attacks by the enemy is not an easy one… If your responsibility is that, you are in a sense in a no-win situation.'[69]

Tambo had begun to put checks and balances in place as soon as he discerned possible problems – the year after the first SADF attack revealed there were enemy agents in their midst, he took the initiative of signing the Geneva Convention in 1980, thus maintaining the moral high ground. On the occasion of the signing, Tambo affirmed: 'We have always defined the enemy in terms of a system of domination and not of a people or a race. In contrast, the South African regime has displayed a shameless and ruthless disregard for all the norms of humanity... It is the conviction of the African National Congress of South Africa that international rules protecting the dignity of human beings must be upheld at all times. Therefore, and for humanitarian reasons, the African National Congress of South Africa hereby declares that, in the conduct of the struggle against apartheid and racism and for self-determination in South Africa, it intends to respect and be guided by the general principles of international humanitarian law applicable in armed conflicts.'[70]

When the Declaration in itself did not prevent the abuse of suspects and dissidents in a climate of acute anxiety, fear and paranoia, Tambo commissioned the movement's finest minds to research and produce a Code of Conduct. In addition, he set in motion the updating of the ANC's constitution, which he himself had been at the helm of revising in 1958. Naturally, in a discourse of challenging apartheid as a 'crime against humanity', as defined by the United Nations itself, it was not surprising that human rights played a central role in the new constitution.

The ANC Constitution, the Code of Conduct and setting up checks and balances in the structures received democratic ratification by the Kabwe Conference. Although change and improvement came about incrementally rather than swiftly and dramatically, Tambo took steady, systematic and procedural steps to protect the movement and, as importantly, its values, while ensuring that it did not suffer another damaging rift among its most loyal but zealous members. Consistent with his principles, he rehabilitated them through careful deployment. The process was lengthy, but the outcome was to contain a profoundly destructive prospect.

Tambo wanted more than simply to stop the abusers by presidential *diktat*. He wanted the issue to be seen as political, the movement as a whole to take a principled stand and proper institutional arrangements to prevent reoccurrence.

'One reason we have a strong Bill of Rights today,' commented Judge Albie Sachs in 2004, 'was the painful lesson of those who ran Quatro: that even people with an honourable record of defending a good cause can execute power in an abusive and inhuman way.'[71]

As Thabo Mbeki observed: 'That matter [of abuses] would have to come up through the structures for us to deal with it. As in the end it did.'[72]

CHAPTER SIXTEEN

Indima *Diplomacy – Acre by Acre*

THOMAS NKOBI, THE ANC'S ONLY FULL-TIME NATIONAL ORGANISER in the 1950s and subsequently the Treasurer-General of the ANC in Exile, once commented that Oliver Tambo, while Secretary-General of the ANC, was nicknamed 'Sekindima' by his comrades. *Indima*, in the Nguni languages, denoted a strategic, methodical way of ploughing.

'If you are ploughing a field, you don't just go ploughing,' explained Nkobi. 'There is a point where you start... That's why we called him "Sekindima" – because of the way he discusses things.'[1] Rather like smearing a floor with dung, one must begin from a strategically chosen point to avoid painting oneself into a corner.

Wilton Mkwayi remembered the precise event that earned Tambo this name: 'It was during the stay-at-home of '58... The late Sehale in Sophiatown was saying, "We must stay away forever till we are free." So OR says, "You know, you come from Rustenburg. You have a piece of land there. When you are ploughing it, you always take an acre at a time. You plough it. You take another acre. That is *sekindima* – one by one. You can't say now this strike must go forever until we are free. What are we going to eat?"'[2]

The image was an attractive one, particularly as Tambo's systematic and careful approach was so recognisable and distinctive. But, like all metaphors, it has limitations. With a visible field, no matter how uneven, rocky or even partially obscured, one is able to assess the terrain as a whole and develop a strategy of operation. In exile, Tambo was venturing into uncharted territory. He could not foresee the dimensions or the topography that lay before him. The length of time the task would take was not a given, nor were the changing conditions in which Tambo's team, the ANC, would operate. Indeed, strategies and tactics came under revision almost from the beginning. Tambo and his team had at an early stage been obliged to reinvent – or rather, represent – the movement in order to accommodate the altered circumstances of armed struggle and, a few months later, the arrest of virtually the entire internal leadership of the ANC.

The ANC's vision, spelt out in the Freedom Charter, was the attainment of a non-racial, democratic South Africa, envisaging 'a mixed economy'. The racial inclusiveness of the Freedom Charter was a bottom line to which Tambo and the ANC clung, regardless of the cost in material or political terms. The strategy rested on a holistic plan based on 'four pillars': mass mobilisation at home, organising the underground, the armed struggle, and international support and sanctions. Then in 1969, the congress at Morogoro revised the strategy and tactics of the ANC. It aimed to empower the armed struggle while at the same time ensure that the military was subordinate to the political programme. In particular, there was to be a special focus on internal dynamics. According to the ANC's holistic plan, this embraced the movement's very important strategy of building international consensus against apartheid.

Traditionally, formal diplomacy cultivates relationships between sovereign states. From its inception, the ANC undertook diplomatic initiatives to communicate with state officials. In 1912, its leadership petitioned the new South African government to try to pre-empt the 1913 Land Act, which served to advance the dispossession of black people. In 1914, it sent a delegation to Great Britain to urge extending the old 'qualified' Cape franchise to all South Africans. In 1918, at the end of the First World War, Congress sent a delegation to Paris in an attempt to influence the Peace Congress at Versailles – again, without results. Petitions to South African prime ministers and cabinet ministers continued into the 1920s and 1930s.

The failure of this form of diplomacy, of course, led to a reaction by the newly formed Youth League in 1944. Even so, when Walter Sisulu was elected into the ANC leadership position as Secretary-General, he informed Prime Minister Malan directly of the movement's intention to undertake the Defiance Campaign – an act of diplomacy that put the ANC on an equal footing with its adversary, the apartheid government. And then, in 1960, after Sharpeville, Mandela called on the government to hold a national convention to negotiate a consensus by the entire South African nation.

The ANC's policy of diplomacy also meant that it formed alliances with other black organisations such as Abdullah Abdurahman's African People's Organisation, the All-African Convention, the South African Indian Congress – when the so-called Doctors' Pact was signed in 1947, and then again in the mid-fifties, to form the Congress Alliance. Tambo himself was directly involved in many of these diplomatic initiatives. In fact, one of his first diplomatic experiences was the particularly sensitive circumstance of the Afro-Indian violence in 1949. The communiqué that emerged from the negotiations, in which the delicate issue of Afro-Indian relations on the ground was placed in its social context, squarely held the state responsible for the violence. The statement was considered to be 'a major act of diplomacy'.[3]

In 1960, Oliver Tambo was venturing beyond the borders of South Africa. New to overseas travel, the early members of the Mission in Exile were pioneers, voyagers of discovery in their journey from south to north. For them the international terrain was uncharted, often hostile territory, and the only way forward was a rocky, uphill path. Decades of quiet, steady toil would be needed to map out and cultivate an unlevelled, unmapped, unknown quantity of land that would yield fertile results.

In this way, the ANC's holistic approach to diplomacy aided rather than hindered self-determination and the achievement of an inclusive and accepted sovereignty. For Tambo and the ANC, the endeavour was more than simply getting international support against a repressive regime. It was a strategy to internationalise the struggle against apartheid without allowing international forces to take it over. Once again, South Africans themselves would have to find solutions, but with international opinion and sanctions helping to balance the superior firepower of the apartheid state.

Tambo had always believed that to achieve lasting change, a carefully planned process would produce longer-lasting results than a single, dramatic event – his response to the pass law campaigns in the 1950s, and his analysis of the Sharpeville massacre bear testimony to that approach. But, as a pragmatist, Tambo was always open to strategies. He, for instance, gave Kwame Nkrumah's request for a United Front with the PAC due consideration and had made himself open to the SACP because their members were people whose understanding and judgement he respected.[4]

Tambo's careful, patient, step-by-step advances, in accordance with the differing needs of each situation, meant that the ANC, under his guidance, was able to venture into the uncharted terrain of the international arena until worldwide support was able to make a major contribution to the success of the struggle in South Africa.

In 1963, Tambo had led an ANC delegation to the historic formation of the Organisation of African Unity in Addis Ababa, Ethiopia, the oldest state in Africa and once a member of the defunct League of Nations. The diplomatic party included Robert Resha, Johnny Makathini, Joe Matthews, all of whom were moved by the historic event. As its first act, the OAU had mandated its members 'to decolonise the rest of the African continent' and appointed a Liberation Committee.[5] But, despite warm moral support for the liberation movements, the collapse of the United Front in 1961 led to complications, and it was clear that long-term diplomatic footwork was needed.

With the announcement of armed struggle, the task of selling the new face of the ANC to the world required both political and financial support in the struggle against apartheid. The outlay for every cadre, his or her fighting equipment, the months of training, the subsistence expenses, was immense. It entailed, as far as Tambo was concerned, an even more carefully thought-out approach, in which each segment of the terrain needed to receive attention. Viewing the options holistically, Tambo was obliged to accept with gratitude generous support from the socialist countries in Eastern Europe. But this support came at a price, for it would need further diplomacy to nurture warm personal relations between Tambo and officials in the Scandinavian countries, whose governments rejected communism. The situation also required work – from scratch – to build up support from other Western nations.

In essence, the diplomacy of the ANC amounted to assessing what each country could do to help, according to its objective position. 'There were other ways (besides giving armed support) of assisting,' commented chief ANC representative in Sweden, Lindiwe Mabuza.[6] Similarly, 'to sell armed revolution to a party which already has a democracy, and especially in Britain where by and large there has been a history of parliamentary and democratic evolution... is more difficult,' commented Bob Hughes, Labour Party MP and a trustee of the Anti-Apartheid Movement. 'But Oliver never sought from people in this country arms, ammunition to fight the armed struggle'.[7]

Tambo worked systematically – *indima* style – and with deep commitment towards these diplomatic goals, well aware of their crucial value. Within the ANC itself, too, he had to maintain a finely honed balance between the revolutionary struggle and the need for material and moral support.

'As you will surely agree,' wrote Tambo to UN official and friend of the ANC, ES Reddy, 'it is absolutely imperative that we confront apartheid at its base in an effective manner if work done at the international level is, in the long run, to yield any fruit. This is why I have lately featured so little in international work.' Of course, the demands of armed struggle – its need for finance, arms, training, accommodation, subsistence and welfare – were always played out against a background of the impatience of young cadres for action. Yet the growing numbers of departments and increasing running costs of the ANC required accessible and friendly dialogue with organisations and/or governments across the globe for their wide-ranging variety of assistance. Indeed, Tambo had to take the process much further – he had to not only win over new allies but also persuade existing ones to maintain, and even *increase*, their support.

'As usual I am hoping to get out of here and go round the world begging for moral and material support for our struggle,' wrote Tambo to Reddy on another occasion. 'But, as usual also, I am likely to stay pinned down to the day-to-day problems imposed on us by apartheid, racial discrimination and colonialism in southern Africa.'[8]

Generally, however, there was little popular appreciation inside the ANC and MK for the necessity of diplomacy. Rather, at times, there was even resentment against what appeared to be the relatively comfortable lifestyle of those in the ANC's diplomatic corps. In 1965 senior theoretician Ben Turok, who arrived in Tanzania after serving three years in prison, impatiently made no bones to Tambo that the ANC had failed to get back home. The movement's energies seemed to him to be increasingly absorbed in surviving in exile rather than sending trained cadres back to continue the revolutionary struggle inside.[9] From the beginning, therefore, even in relation to the liberation movement's warmest supporters, a high level of skilled and delicate diplomacy was demanded.

For Tambo, it was a difficult time. His uncertain, peripatetic lifestyle was hardly glamorous. In fact, it proved extremely stressful, and as a result asthma attacks became more and more frequent – so much travelling, regular change of climate, flight delays, and hours at under-resourced airports. So often, he waited for days at a time for interviews with heads of state and patronising officials. 'He was not accepted anywhere, he had to battle,' commented Turok. 'People don't know this generally, but if you talk to people who knew him well, Canon Collins and people like that, they will tell you that [Tambo] was a very unhappy man... It affected his personality: a little bit introspective, quiet.'

Some of the observers to the OAU conferences recall being struck by the sight of Tambo sitting patiently outside the closed doors of the main sessions, waiting to be called in to make a presentation.[10] It was surprising to them that the leader of an African liberation movement could be so excluded. But this second-class status applied to all liberation movements – despite the fact that OAU members consisted largely of governing parties that had themselves until recently been liberation movements. At the founding of the OAU, however, a Liberation Committee had been formed and began to function immediately.

'So the leaders of the liberation movements,' explained Julius Nyerere, 'although they were not heads of state, had their own status, and they always came to the meetings. They were obviously not treated as heads of state, but for many of us they were leaders of the liberation movements. We were lucky, we were also leaders of liberation movements; the difference between themselves and ourselves was that we had made it earlier than they had. We gave them all the other facilities with the exception of formal facilities for heads of state. So Oliver was treated with that respect.'[11]

But during the era of the United Front, Tambo was frequently chosen as its spokesperson and in 1961, when Ghana's Attorney-General tried to persuade the two liberation movements to form a government in exile, it was Tambo who was chosen to head it. There was at the time, however, a thriving ANC underground base at home, and as the PAC was not willing to fall in with the scheme either, the proposal fell through. As early as 1960, Tambo had, in fact, addressed the United Nations Fourth (Trust and Non-Self-Governing Territories or Decolonisation) Committee, and then again during the Rivonia Trial in order to pre-empt the expected death sentence. In 1963, he went on to address the inaugural meeting of the OAU. There was no doubt that as an individual he made a favourable impression.[12]

Nyerere, who himself became an international icon and spokesman for the iniquities bestowed upon the Third World, was a humble and unassuming person despite his position and status. Indeed, Trevor Huddleston, who served in Tanzania for eight years as Bishop of Masasi, reflected that the two men he most loved and respected were Oliver Tambo and Julius Nyerere. Nyerere, too, readily appreciated Tambo's qualities: 'He was a very modest person. He never wanted to push himself around. Others pushed around. Oliver never did. He was a very considerate person… Oliver came to see me only when he felt it was necessary to come and see me. He was that type of person.'[13]

And when the UF was dissolved, despite the public acrimony surrounding the break-up, Tambo was generally acknowledged in the PAC as having been genuine in trying to make a go of the project while it lasted.[14]

'Tambo was one of the ANC leaders about whom the PAC dissidents spoke respectfully,' wrote George Houser, a founder of the American Committee on Africa and a seasoned traveller in the continent and friend of many liberation movements. 'They seemed to trust his word.'[15]

After the dissolution of the UF, the ANC's External Mission lost no time in setting up its own offices in the places that had once accommodated UF appointments. ANC diplomacy had already secured MK training bases in several countries – in Algeria, Morocco, Egypt, Tanzania and Zambia – and for South Africans meeting independent Africa for the first time, these were heady days indeed. The experience of black people moving around freely and expressively in their own country was deeply inspiring. MK was generously given accommodation by these friendly countries, and there was a keen appreciation of the succour that 'Mother Africa' was able to provide.

There was, though, a gradual realisation of political and cultural differences in some places. Ghanaian officials, for example, made it clear that the PAC ideology was preferable to the ANC's. They were also touchy about anyone who appeared less than enthusiastic about the personality cult that George Padmore was building up around Kwame Nkrumah and, at the end of 1961, they expelled the ANC's Tennyson Makiwane from their territory. But, as time passed, there came also an understanding of the limitations of the OAU. Its members were unable to keep up the subscriptions that would maintain growing numbers of revolutionary armed forces on the continent and, after listening to the relative proposals of the PAC and the ANC (the Unity Movement was rejected outright), the OAU announced that 10 per cent of its budget for liberation movements would be given to both the PAC and the ANC. The amount varied every year, and it was but a small percentage of what the ANC needed for even the barest survival of its exile population. ANC members, and Tambo himself, felt strongly that the decision was failing to recognise the unevenness of the achievements of the two movements. The ANC was working very hard to deliver on the revolutionary outcome, while the PAC, it felt, was frittering away its energies in self-destructive and irresponsible behaviour.

So it was that, in the first decade in exile, Tambo and his team worked very hard with little return. Many suffered under the strain and either dropped out (Makiwane and Hadebe were expelled) or asked to be transferred to other departments (Piliso went into the military and Matthews became Attorney-General in Botswana). Gertrude Shope, who headed the Women's Section, recalled Tambo's abiding worry over funds. Around 1972, three young men suffered food poisoning. One of the men died, and Tambo attended the funeral. It was a low point in the organisation. Nothing seemed to be happening, and there was even a feeling at times that the ANC was on its way out.

'There was no food, there was no money,' recalled Gertrude Shope. 'The OAU had promised to give us 10 per cent because they must give 10 per cent to the PAC, who did not even have a liberation movement.'

But what stuck in Gertrude's mind was OR's response in his funeral oration. He was uncharacteristically disheartened. '"Ten per cent or no 10 per cent, the struggle will carry on," he said, '[but] we could just see small tears running down his eyes and we knew exactly what that meant.'[16]

Impatient of the liberation movements' lack of progress in engaging South Africa militarily, Zambia and Tanzania – both friendly countries – had, much to the horror of the ANC, attempted détente with South Africa. It was clear that even the ANC's friends like Kaunda and Nyerere were not convinced that the ANC – or the PAC – would be able to pull off a revolution. Nevertheless, Tambo insisted that the ANC should make a consistent effort to attend every OAU conference, to imprint on the organisation that the ANC was an integral part of Africa. In time to come, he was adamant, the tide would turn...

But, apart from its work with the growing number of newly independent states in Africa and Asia, the ANC also enjoyed the support of Third World countries in general. As long ago as 1955, when Tambo was Secretary-General of the ANC, it had been part of the Asian-African Conference in Bandung. Officially, ANC members had been refused passports to attend the conference – in the wake of Walter Sisulu and Duma Nokwe's successful visit to China, the USSR, Israel and the UK[17] – but NEC member Moses Kotane and the SAIC's Maulvi Cachalia did manage to acquire travel documents from India and had indeed been able to attend. Tambo celebrated this history in his 1979 speech, 'The Spirit of Bandung', in support of the Front Line States in Lusaka,[18] and reminded his audience of the defining principles of Afro-Asian solidarity – non-alignment, anti-colonialism and anti-imperialism.

Eventually, two organisations sprang from the Bandung initiative: the Afro-Asian People's Solidarity Organisation (AAPSO), to which the ANC belonged, and the Non-Aligned Movement (NAM).

From the beginning, the ANC was permitted to attend as a guest or observer. At the launch of the NAM in Belgrade in 1961, Tambo, as the representative of the United Front, presented the southern African case. But, while they were 'welcome to present their views', when the NAM defined its policy towards national liberation movements the following year, it resolved that the OAU should decide which movements to recognise.[19] In 1970 the NAM again confirmed that as the liberation movements did not have the status of independent sovereign states, they could participate only as observers at summit conferences.

And yet, despite these setbacks, Tambo retained warm, personal relations with many leaders of independent states, both in Africa and Asia. Many African countries, often at the risk of being attacked by the apartheid regime, hosted the ANC. Tambo was careful to show his appreciation of their support. The ANC's strategy was to attend unfailingly all the non-aligned conferences – far more often, it was noted, than the PAC, for example.[20] And it was outside the conference sessions that the ANC had its most useful exchanges, networking and lobbying non-aligned heads of state. Informal and semiformal meetings proved extremely valuable – for example, at the Algiers Conference in 1973, the heads of the liberation movements had arranged separate meetings with Indira Gandhi, Castro and Nyerere.[21]

At times, though, the ANC had to be selective in its support for certain NAM members. For instance, the issue arose as to whether socialist countries could be considered non-aligned. Cuba, for example, supported the Soviet Union, yet maintained (in contradistinction to Yugoslavia) that the chief criteria for membership were whether members were anti-colonial and committed to

Afro-Asian solidarity. In 1970, the ANC stressed that it was 'non-aligned, but committed' – the South African government's policy of fighting communism was a pretext for aggression in Africa, similar to the US policy of aggression in Vietnam and the Dominican Republic. When Castro was nominated in 1978 as the next chairman of the NAM, the ANC defended the Cuban, Tanzanian and Afghanistan contention that the Soviet Union was the 'natural ally' of the Third World. Cuba itself had come to the aid of the MPLA government in Angola at its request. Yugoslavia, on the other hand, maintained that the USSR and Cuba's interventions in Africa could become 'new forms of colonial presence'.

The ANC was given a high profile at the Havana Conference when Tambo spoke on behalf of all the liberation movements.[22] The ANC had come a long way since the days when the NAM lumped together all African liberation movements, simply calling for the 'immediate termination of colonialism'.[23] More than a decade later, in Havana, Tambo was able to raise issues facing the PLO, SWAPO and Polisario, the liberation movement in Western Sahara.[24] His support earned an enduring appreciation from the latter movement. 'Oliver Tambo was the father also of our nation,' asserted Mohamed Beissat (who was later to become the Saharawi ambassador to a democratic South Africa). 'He never failed to being our cause to the international attention.'[25]

Tambo also flagged the need for the Canary Islands – as well as Swaziland and Lesotho, which had 'not as yet been bombed' by the apartheid government – for the protection and support of the NAM, and drew parallels between the anti-imperialist and anti-colonialist struggles: 'Thus, Mr Chairman, the liberation movements and the independent countries of the Non-Aligned Movement are joined not only by their common experience but also by the fact that they share the present with common objectives and a common enemy.'[26]

Tambo's approach was recorded in the Final Declaration of the Conference itself. Non-alignment was to be identified with the struggle against colonialism, imperialism, apartheid and racism, but the Declaration also included a general condemnation of 'any form of foreign aggression, occupation, domination, interference or hegemony as well as the struggle against great power or bloc policies'.[27] Notably, after the Havana Conference the new revolutionary governments of Nicaragua, Iran and Grenada all broke off relations with the apartheid regime, with Iran stopping all oil shipments to South Africa.[28]

Soon after, the ANC sent emissaries to Nicaragua, Iran and Grenada and, in 1983, Tambo accepted an award on behalf of Nelson Mandela in Venezuela. He also led the delegation to the seventh NAM summit in New Delhi, India, in that year. In its Final Declaration, the liberation struggles of southern Africa were identified with the worldwide struggle against oppression, inequality and racism, thus universalising apartheid evils as a crime against humanity. The ANC was thus increasingly sensitising Latin American, Caribbean and Asian countries to its diplomatic strategy of isolating South Africa as widely as possible.

In 1987, Tambo visited Nicaragua. Since the early 1970s, the ANC had observed and acted on the strategic interests it shared with the liberation movements of Argentina, Brazil, Paraguay, Uruguay and (after the 1973 coup) Chile, whose governments were cultivating relations with the apartheid state, together forming a South Atlantic Treaty Organisation (SATO). At the NAM preparatory meeting in 1970, the ANC denounced SATO as 'part of the sinister plot against the national liberation struggle and national independence in Africa, Asia and Latin America'.[29] The Caribbean countries supported the ANC's call for sports boycotts at the Colombo Summit in 1970 (Jamaica was the first country officially to introduce a boycott against South African goods), while in 1975 the ANC also expressed its concern about the South African government's trade activities in Mauritius and the subsequent participation of South African mercenaries in an abortive coup d'état in the Seychelles. This issue of the Indian Ocean as a zone of peace was taken up regularly at NAM conferences, preparing the way two decades later for 'South-South' initiatives as a strategy to deal with the sweeping power of globalisation.

The ANC had a somewhat easier path with the Afro-Asian People's Solidarity Organisation (AAPSO), which was aligned to the Soviet bloc and included other liberation movements such as Makarios's Patriotic Front of Cyprus, struggling for independence from what remained of the British colonial legacy in the Mediterranean. Tambo, in fact, formed warm relations with a number of its representatives. Vassos Lyssarides of Cyprus recalled how he had met Tambo many times at Social Democratic conferences in Sweden, at meetings in London, Cairo and other AAPSO gatherings. Tambo once stayed at his home. As he walked in the streets of Limassol, Lyssarides introduced Tambo to perfect strangers, and the people, including children, were taken by his sincerely unaffected interest in their lives and opinions.

'We become very close – it didn't take long – he was such a likeable personality. I had a high esteem for him,' Lyssarides commented. He observed Tambo's 'double approach' – he was 'soft-spoken, an excellent orator, and had a good heart; but you could feel that underneath, when it came to the necessity to do something, he was iron... He didn't stay out of controversy, because if you did not take a stand for others, how can you expect them to take a stand in your case? You understood that if it came to a fight, you were dealing with someone absolutely determined'.[30]

Since its launch in 1959, AAPSO had been a staunch supporter of the armed struggle and MK, and AAPSO solidarity committees in the member states provided crucial practical support. Even less well-resourced countries, such as Poland, Romania and Bulgaria, themselves experiencing difficulties with foreign exchange, were able to send MK goods and supplies such as cloth, equipment, fertiliser, food and medical supplies. In 1971, in his speech to AAPSO at Tripoli, Tambo emphasised the huge challenges that still remained – 'the bitterest battles have yet to be fought in the course of Africa and Asia for the complete defeat of imperialism' – and urged AAPSO to work with like-minded bodies (such as the NAM) to 'initiate a new and powerful campaign to sink all differences and forge a solid united front of all anti-imperialist forces'.[31]

ANC support was greatly enhanced by the formation of the Front Line States in 1975, following the collapse of the Portuguese regime and the independence of Guinea-Bissau, Mozambique and Angola. The new presidents of Angola and Mozambique, Aghostino Neto and Samora Machel, came together with Nyerere of Tanzania, Khama of Botswana, and Kaunda of Zambia. After the convincing objections of the ANC and the other liberation movements in southern Africa, they formed a regional security grouping in response to JB Vorster's détente initiative to woo African states with trade and political agreements. When the South African army invaded Angola in 1975, the Front Line States formed a crucial negotiating team at a time when the UK/USA's proposals on Rhodesia required South Africa's cooperation. Vorster was applying for membership of the OAU and visiting more conservative countries such as Liberia as part of his plan to revive diplomatic expansion.

The ANC was, of course, deeply suspicious of these moves and produced a major policy document in response, which the Secretary-General, Alfred Nzo, delivered at the OAU conference in February 1975. (Ironically, ministers from the Central African Republic were absent from that meeting because they were visiting South Africa!)[32] The apartheid regime, alleged Nzo, aimed to divide the African states and isolate the liberation movements. Its granting of 'independence' to the Bantustans (beginning with the Transkei, planned for 1976) was a ploy to placate international opinion. The ANC's intervention seemed to be effective and by the end of the conference two resolutions had been unanimously adopted. The first called for a special ministerial meeting in April 1975 to consider ways of countering Vorster's détente policy, while the second specifically cautioned member states against South Africa's attempts to 'confuse and divide' them. It also called on all members to condemn apartheid and the Bantustans.[33]

In April the following year (1976), Tambo called a *lekgotla*-style meeting of an enlarged NEC. It was time, Tambo said, for the ANC to identify their position. 'Much has happened in Africa,' he said, 'to require of us to restate the objectives of our struggle.'[34]

In his delegation to Dar es Salaam for the special session of the OAU's Council of Ministers, a committee of representatives of member countries, to discuss the South African situation, Tambo brought some of his most talented people – Josiah Jele (ANC head of International Affairs), Secretary-General Alfred Nzo, Johnny Makathini (ANC representative in Algeria), Florence Mophosho of the Women's Section, and NEC member Moses Mabhida. In his preparatory speech to the Council, Tambo set out to show how the racism of apartheid was inseparable from the economic exploitation of black people.

'[In] South Africa, coloniser and colonised live side by side within the same country. Colour and race are used as a dividing line between the resident white army of occupation and their subject population – the black people. The extreme exploitation of labour is the *raison d'être* of this system... As a fundamental condition of its survival, the apartheid regime maintains a complete monopoly of State power and seeks by terrorist methods to make the people acquiesce in their own servitude.'[35]

Reform of such a system, therefore, was not possible. Tambo and the ANC were also concerned about the tendency of the OAU to give priority to some liberation movements over others, for example the struggles of Namibia and Rhodesia over South Africa. 'The OAU in our opinion,' he commented, 'must adopt a strategy that recognises not only the indivisibility of the enemy, but also the dominant role of the South African regime in the area.'[36]

The difficulty for the ANC and for Tambo in particular lay in the perhaps understandable ambivalence of President Kenneth Kaunda of Zambia. He wanted to try the diplomatic approach, and defended this by arguing that 'non-alignment needs purity for us to keep [that] right, [and] demands that we speak our minds on any issue regardless of who is involved'.[37]

He had no illusions about the South African regime, which encouraged, he said, 'racism unstinted'. He made it quite clear, he said, that he was meeting Vorster as an equal. He had not come to discuss trade, even though it was quite clear that the Zambian economy, particularly in the early years, was heavily dependent on South African supplies. 'Even the soap we were using to bath with came from South Africa.' But this very economic dependence created a limited interdependence between the two countries. 'Oliver understood that very well,' he added.[38]

Kaunda, in fact, respected Tambo profoundly and held him in great affection. He was 'a great African leader', remarked Kaunda, who had both 'humility' and was a master of diplomacy. Kaunda's party, UNIP, the governing party of Zambia, had given warm support for all the liberation movements in the region, and as soon as Zambia became independent, they hosted the ANC, providing headquarters, accommodation for its members and even transit camps for MK cadres. But this proved to be both 'expensive and dangerous'. As a landlocked country, Zambia needed access to a port and its efforts to avoid South African trade routes for the export of their copper by developing the Tanzam railway line to Tanzania met with hostility.

'They began bombing the railways by supporting Savimbi in Lobito Bay, Angola, the Benguela railways, and bridges on the roads we were using towards Tanzania and Malawi. They began bombing those bridges so that they could stop us from using those other routes.' (In the 1980s, the domino theory became even stronger, suggesting that Namibia and Angola be 'de-linked' from South Africa. The ANC argument was that only the freeing of South Africa could produce independence for Angola and Namibia. The ANC did not, however, oppose the UN focus on Namibia.)

As a humanist, said Kaunda, he always looked for a negotiated way. He had, for example, as head of the OAU, suggested that Neto's MPLA and Savimbi's UNITA form a government of national unity for an independent Angola. But, to Kaunda's disappointment, 13 days of talks eventually broke down.

For Kaunda, the concept of non-alignment meant an open-minded approach. He first met JB Vorster over negotiations on Rhodesia, and managed to persuade him to agree to release the imprisoned leaders of that country's liberation movements. He knew, he said, that it was South Africa that called the shots in the region, and he was undertaking these talks as one head of state to another. Tambo was, of course, not happy about the direction Kaunda was taking, especially as he had not consulted the ANC, but nevertheless used his personal relationship with Kaunda to put across the perspective of the ANC.

The two men had significant experiences in common. Both had been schooled by missionaries, both became schoolteachers, both were practising Christians, and both loved music. Kaunda, more emotional and demonstrative of his feelings, often played his guitar and sang at meetings, including Christian hymns. In their conversations, both enjoyed discussing issues such as the nature of humanism and Christianity as well as political strategy.[39]

He recalled that Tambo had once told him the story of how Tambo and Mandela had both been opposed to the ANC making common cause with the SACP when they were Youth Leaguers. Later, Tambo told Kaunda, he had been impressed with Luthuli's reply to objectors: 'Look, we are not fighting communism here, we are fighting apartheid. And these are our allies.'[40]

Kaunda offered hospitality to the ANC, undeterred by the apartheid regime or the link with the communists. Like so many colonised leaders in Africa and indeed in the ANC itself, he had learnt to communicate in a way that left a window half open, ready to consider its view at a more opportune time.

Despite political differences, however, Tambo – spokesperson for the ANC – was always discreet and expressed appreciation to his hosts at every opportunity. With traditional courtesy, Tambo behaved 'like a guest in their house'.[41] There was no question of replicating colonial mores, or a culture of entitlement.

As a result, Tambo's personal influence in Africa grew and, by his own style and insight, he – in the words of Marcelino dos Santos, the vice-president of Mozambique when Frelimo came to power[42] – acquired 'stature as a leader'. Tambo's seniority and political experience were readily appreciated, and this image was to stand the ANC in good stead in the even harder times to come.

Besides the diplomatic initiatives with independent organisations the world over, the policy of Tambo's Mission in Exile also focused on the United Nations. Disputes over South Africa were not new to the UN. Indeed, South African issues had been raised at its very inception in 1945. The UN's predecessor, the League of Nations, had mandated South Africa to administer South West Africa as far back as 1919, and now South Africa's detractors argued that the mandate had run its course. As a society that officially promoted racial discrimination, South Africa did not adhere to the Universal Declaration of Human Rights. In 1946, South Africa was again challenged by India over its discriminatory treatment of South Africa's Indian population, yet the Security Council, consisting of Great Britain, the United States, the Soviet Union, France and China, was not unanimous in its condemnation. Great Britain, in particular, was not prepared to act against its interests – South Africa was a member of the British Commonwealth, Prime Minister Jan Smuts (one of the founders of the League of Nations) continued to be a highly respected international figure, and his country was a strong trading partner to both Britain and the USA. The UN was thus 'a white man's club',[43] and there were powerful friends lobbying for South Africa. In fact, in 1959, South Africa's Foreign Minister was elected to the vice-presidency of the UN's General Assembly.

The UN saw its brief as resolving disputes between states and, although there existed a Special Committee, which dealt with other issues as they arose, there was no formal place for liberation movements in the General Assembly. In

1960, after Sharpeville, the enlarged Africa Group pushed for a debate on apartheid as an issue that affected international relations. While he was waiting in Bechuanaland in April 1960, Tambo had written to Dag Hammarskjöld, UN Secretary-General, requesting an audience, but the request had been denied. He was invited to address the General Assembly's Fourth Committee (on Decolonisation) instead, on the subject of South West Africa. But when Tambo applied to the USA for a visa to address a South African emergency conference at the end of May, this was refused. The ACOA organised protests to the Secretary of State, and finally in June the government granted Tambo a visa, confining him to a 25-mile radius of New York City. The ACOA was able to reschedule Tambo's speaking engagements, and while he was there, he managed to speak to United Nations delegates in New York and members of the Special Political Committee and brief them about the Mission in Exile.

His statement to the Fourth Committee required Tambo to confine himself to the dispute on South West Africa but when he spoke, he represented, he said, his country's 'voteless millions'. In his statement, not only did Tambo remind the international body of the illegality of South Africa, 'perhaps the only international delinquent since Hitlerite Germany', but was able to give vivid personal testimony of the aftermath of the police massacre of 13 South Africans at a human rights demonstration on 10 December 1959. The blatant partiality of the resultant Commission into the deaths and injured could, he said, only be attributed to the 'ceaseless lies pronounced under oath by members of the Department of Justice, the police'. The resultant 'reign of terror and murder' was 'closely identifiable with... apartheid and white supremacy'. But, he urged, 'the United Nations is not powerless to act and act effectively'.[44]

Tambo's statement was not without impact even among his monitors. Immediately after his address, Washington inquired of the South African ambassador whether Tambo 'had at any time been behind the Iron Curtain', but the commissioner of the South African Police was unable to confirm or deny the truth of this possibility.[45]

Now a new composition of the UN membership was taking shape. Indeed, South Africa's Minister of External Affairs, Eric Louw, complained of the large increase in the single session of the General Assembly of October 1960, 'no less than 16 new Member States from the continent of Africa',[46] and their voices began to be heard. Nevertheless, it was no easy task to deliver action against apartheid, for despite the General Assembly's increasing weighting of developing countries, the Security Council's five permanent members – Britain, the USA, France, the Soviet Union and China – had veto powers.

But within the United Nations, a warm and enduring friend of the ANC was to be found in ES Reddy, secretary of the Special Committee on (later 'Against') Apartheid. Enuga Reddy came from a background of resistance in his native India. His father had been jailed during the struggle for independence. Reddy knew that Mahatma Gandhi had fashioned the philosophy of non-violent resistance in South Africa, and he took to heart the call of Pandit Nehru to South African Indians to join hands with Africans in their struggle. Like many bright middle-class students, he was sent to study abroad in New York in 1976. Realising that the United Nations had the potential to shape a better world, Reddy joined the UN. He was delighted to join the South Africa desk.

In 1960, Reddy met Oliver Tambo and responded readily to his warmth, deeply impressed by the man's unassuming manner and quiet intellect.[47] From then onwards, Reddy was to become a dedicated partner 'in trying to make the United Nations go beyond speeches and resolutions to ensure effective support to the liberation struggle in southern Africa, and especially of the friendship, thoughtfulness, integrity and statesmanship of OR'.[48]

Reddy next met Oliver Tambo on the eve of the Rivonia Trial in 1963. The previous November, the Afro-Asian group had pushed through a resolution that called for sanctions against the South African regime, calling also for a 'special committee against apartheid'. The Special Committee was formed and, ironically, was able to make headway largely because the major First World powers were not interested in it, and it was allowed to proceed without interference. Within the first year of its existence, the committee filed two reports. Its break came when President Kennedy's UN ambassador, the former presidential liberal candidate Adlai Stevenson, indicated sympathy for the committee's call for sanctions. Shortly afterwards, Washington announced an arms embargo. The item appeared on the agenda of the Security Council (which now had 10 non-permanent members, including five from Africa and Asia, two from Latin America and one from Eastern Europe). Although Britain and France abstained from voting, the Council resolved to support a voluntary ban on sales.

Two years later, on 8 October, the day before the commencement of the Rivonia Trial, Tambo was granted a hearing by the chairman of the Special Political Committee to 'appeal for action to stop repression and trials in South Africa'. (He was the first leader of a liberation movement to be honoured in this way.)[49] Since the Treason Trial, Tambo pointed out, the South African laws had been so engineered as 'to make it practically impossible for an accused person to escape conviction'. Already there were 5 000 political prisoners languishing in jail, and Tambo called for urgent action to protect the accused in the Rivonia Trial. It was already known that the state would demand the death sentence.

On 11 October, the General Assembly adopted Resolution 1881 (XVIII), condemning South Africa and requesting it to abandon the Rivonia Trial and release unconditionally all political prisoners. (Reddy and Tambo had worked on the wording of the resolution.) Only South Africa voted against the resolution (Portugal had quietly left) and the passing was greeted with cheers. Bram Fischer was able to pass on the news to Mandela. Three weeks later, Tambo again addressed the Special Committee. His purpose was to situate apartheid more fully in the political economy of the system, of which the Western world was a part. He pointed out that this was the first time black South Africans were being heard directly by the UN – unhappily, their major leaders were in prison, some 'at this very moment facing trial' in 'farcical' conditions, while ill-treatment and torture was escalating. Tambo quoted a recent informant from home. A number of African accused in another political trial alleged that they had been 'suffocated with wet bags, given electrical and other treatment'. (Some 35 years later, the perpetrators confirmed and demonstrated these inhuman methods to the Truth and Reconciliation Commission.) While European immigrants were being wooed to South Africa, 'foreign natives' were deported or removed under the country's pass laws. South Africa was being partitioned into Bantustans, 'like the locations we already have, patched outside cities where Africans are concentrated and kept in subjection, available as labour,' said Tambo. Apartheid was nothing more than crude white supremacy, which Verwoerd had defined in Parliament as 'White domination – not "leadership", not "guidance", but "control" – supremacy'. By contrast, the Freedom Charter opened with the all-inclusive and ringing statement, 'South Africa belongs to all who live in it' – 'a drastic concession,' said Tambo pointedly, 'on the part of the African people'.

But apart from the barbarism of apartheid, it was 'impossible to separate racial discrimination in South Africa from the economic structure of that country'. Even as Tambo spoke, the bodies of dozens of black migrant workers were being excavated in a mining disaster that had just befallen Coalbrook. These workers, who had sacrificed their lives for the mining companies' profits and foreign exchange, had been living and working under semi-slave conditions.

In describing the context and effects of apartheid, Tambo's statement was calculated to demonstrate that the international community had both a responsibility and the capacity to act against these iniquities. The logic of apartheid rested on its exploitative political economy. 'The United Kingdom is South Africa's greatest trading partner... it is therefore the greatest source of strength for apartheid.' It was thus possible to isolate South Africa through economic and cultural sanctions and so smash the apartheid system.

As soon as he had made his presentation, Tambo followed up with a further comment on the resolution, which was published by the ANC's *South Africa Freedom News* in Dar es Salaam the following January. It confirmed the ANC's determination to lead the boycott initiative. To this end, Tambo also sought to strengthen the arm of the United Nations. He noted that the South African regime had entirely ignored the UN resolution, and was continuing apace with the Rivonia Trial. The resolution's 'request' to South Africa was not strong enough, he felt. 'South Africa should not be allowed to continue reducing the UN, including the Security Council, to a debating society and nothing more.'

Tambo also had a firm response to a follow-up draft resolution by Norway. The resolution expressed its 'abhorrence for apartheid' and the country had warmly welcomed Chief Luthuli in Oslo the previous year as well as hosting ANC delegations in their visits to the World Assembly of Youth and in a meeting with the Norwegian Ministry of Foreign Affairs. The reason for Norway's intervention was an attempt to moderate what seemed to be extreme proposals from the Afro-Asian bloc, which had no hope of being passed by South Africa's trading partners, the UK and the USA. Instead, Norway proposed a small body of experts 'to examine methods of resolving the present situation... through full, peaceful and orderly application of human rights and freedoms... and to consider what part the UN might play in the achievement of that end.'[50]

Tambo, however, had problems with the resolution – it lacked 'the sense of urgency which underlies demands for sanctions', he wrote to Reddy. 'People who are sacrificing or are willing to make sacrifices to end apartheid immediately react to the idea of a group of experts by asking: "What exactly are they supposed to do?" This has turned out to be a difficult question... Of course, I respect every one of the names so far mentioned, but I do think the UN ought to exercise great care in its use of such terms as "experts" for they necessarily relate to the scale or standard of values which it observes and employs.'[51]

In his press report, Tambo elaborated. In the first place, he pointed out, South Africa would reject out of hand the opinions of such a group; secondly, the idea itself was problematic. It was 'born of the feeling that the white man's fears should be considered', rather than addressing 'what the white man is doing to the African'. The solution was to intensify economic sanctions, not relax the pressures by postponing sanctions while the 'experts' deliberated. Certainly the arms embargo was inadequate – it served merely to prevent Western assistance in the murder of the opponents of apartheid. 'It does not operate to prevent the murders, much less the policy which must inevitably lead to such murders.' He suggested that the UN should make 'more use of' the Special Committee and continue to locate decision-making within the General Assembly.[52]

But by the time this considered objection was published, the Security Council had already unanimously adopted Norway's resolution. Secretary-General U Thant established a Group of Experts, chaired by the Swede, Mrs A Myrdal, and they then consulted Tambo, who conveyed his arguments to them. The Group submitted its report in April 1964. Needless to say, South Africa ignored the report, and the international critics of apartheid experienced for themselves the stubborn intransigence of the regime.

For Tambo, his dismay over Norway's well-meaning exercise was to be repeated a few years later by the episode of the Lusaka Manifesto. The lesson for the ANC was that much as one valued one's good friends and was grateful to them, the ANC should never relinquish the lead in the liberation struggle. Only that organisation knew the enemy; only that movement could appreciate the extent to which strategic, diplomatic nuances could be employed, and assess their place at any given moment in the revolutionary struggle.

Tambo made another submission to the Special Committee on Apartheid in March 1964, in which he reminded the committee of the ANC delegations in the previous July, who proposed a blacklist of companies involved in arms manufacture 'such as De Beers Limited [and] African Explosives and Chemical Industries'.[53] Again, he urged the General Assembly to impose mandatory sanctions, citing the support of the Organisation of African Unity in its most recent congress. It was particularly provoking that the South African economy was enjoying an unprecedented boom. 'This is no doubt encouraged by a sense of security induced by the belief that with arms supplied by its friends, the South African government is able to ensure stability for South Africa'. Who, asked Tambo, was the greater 'racialist' – the formulators of racism, or 'those who furnish the capital, technical knowledge and manpower for the execution and maintenance of these policies?' In this missive, Tambo was again situating the half-dozen political trials – including trials in Pietermaritzburg, Ladysmith and Cape Town, as well as the Rivonia Trial, which was drawing to a close – in the context of ongoing resistance against increasing oppression. 'Let the United Nations and the world save what it can,' he said. And if diplomacy should fail, warned Tambo, 'What [the UN] cannot, will either be destroyed or destroy itself' by other means. 'This, to us, seems inevitable enough.'[54]

The ANC's barrage of interventions in the United Nations did not have the long-term effect of imposing mandatory sanctions – this vision was still a long way away – but it seemed to many that by the time the Rivonia Trial had drawn to a close, South Africa had been sufficiently intimidated (even if they would never admit to it) by the international pressure (including the Group of

Experts, whose final report came to Tambo as 'in many respects a happy surprise, considering my apprehensions last year')[55] and worldwide publicity. It was generally agreed that the diplomacy of the ANC both in the United Nations and at the 1964 International Sanctions Conference in London in sensitising international public opinion on the Rivonia Trial contributed to the sentence of life, rather than the death penalty, which so many had feared.[56]

Most Western states were unresponsive to the urging of the ANC to withdraw their lucrative trade with apartheid South Africa. So it was that Oliver Tambo began working with two other Western sources of support. The first fountainhead of solidarity came from below, from ordinary men and women throughout civil society – churches, trade unions, women's organisations, sports clubs, the youth (students in schools, colleges and universities) and organisations dedicated to the struggle against apartheid.[57]

Perhaps the most effective initiative throughout the years of struggle in exile was the drive against apartheid that originated in the United Kingdom and spread steadily across the Western world. The founders of what grew to become a social movement of international proportions were also Tambo's warm friends – Bishop Trevor Huddleston and Canon John Collins. Since those early days, when Tambo was staying in the Canon's Amen Court, the movement had grown considerably. The Treason Trial and the near certainty of the death sentence had galvanised the two clerics into raising funds for the best legal advice available. This British-based Treason Trial Defence Fund, to develop into the Defence and Aid Fund, was administered by Bishop Ambrose Reeves in Johannesburg until he, too, was to all intents and purposes driven out of the country. That fund was beholden to Canon Collins for at least two thirds of its support. The Defence and Aid Fund also had offices in Johannesburg, Cape Town and Durban, and later branches in East London and Port Elizabeth, all of which were overrun with the outbreak of trials that followed the banning of the ANC and PAC. These offices also attempted to assist the families of the accused and imprisoned. The Quaker communities undertook the welfare side of the project, and two or three times a week these offices would be packed with distraught and stranded families of detainees or accused.

But Collins was not without his critics, who came from a wide spectrum. Right-wing conservatives detested him – during his campaign against the death penalty, the walls of Amen Court were daubed with crude slogans such as 'Hang the Canon!' But there were others, even anti-apartheid activists, who intensely disliked Canon Collins for his outspoken, almost hyperactive and dominating personality. Shrewd, gifted, passionate and able to juggle many projects at the same time, he was once affectionately defined as 'God's stockbroker'. Lord Astor, owner of *The Observer,* though a warm admirer of Oliver Tambo, had no patience with Collins' clear intention to control the disbursement of funds (though, as everybody knew, with the noblest of intentions).[58] Along with other liberals, Astor was also suspicious of Collins' friendly working relations with communist countries such as the Soviet Union, which he and Diana Collins visited. Ironically, Canon Collins himself was wary of communism but remained open-minded, particularly as he deeply admired the intellect and altruism of individuals such as Bram Fischer. Collins was also influenced by Tambo, who once explained to him: 'If you are drowning and somebody throws you a rope, you don't stop to ask about his political beliefs.'[59]

In 1961, the PAC suffered huge losses as a result of detentions and arrests. It was also the year in which Robert Sobukwe lost his appeal against his three-year sentence for urging his followers to hand in their passes. In that year, the PAC received more funding than the ANC, but thereafter its internal activity seemed to decline – if the number of arrests and detentions are an indication. The Defence and Aid Fund also financed the trials of the African Resistance Movement, whose members – such as John Harris (executed in 1966 for his fatal bombing at Johannesburg's Park Station), Eddie Daniels (sentenced to 15 years on Robben Island) and others – were also members of the Liberal Party.

Tambo himself continued to emphasise a non-sectarian approach to all the organisations that raised funds for the welfare of the oppressed in South Africa. Indeed, he himself would recommend people from outside the ANC, including those from other organisations, for assistance.[60]

Then, in December 1963, the United Nations General Assembly invited governments and organisations to contribute to relief and assistance to families of persons persecuted by the South African government for opposing apartheid. Interestingly, Tambo asked the question whether humanitarian assistance might not divert attention from political action, especially sanctions.[61] Reddy spoke to Tambo several times on that topic.

'Finally,' Reddy remembered, 'late in November Diallo Telli spoke to him and he agreed to the proposal, and one of the two resolutions tabled by the Non-Aligned Group dealt with assistance.' A further concern of Tambo's firm response was to emphasise that assistance should be provided to all political prisoners and their families, irrespective of their affiliations. 'There are many organisations and people who are interested in handling the relief fund. Some are good organisations and I think all are manned by honest people,' he wrote to Reddy. '[But] I trust you will bear in mind the necessity of keeping the fund outside of any area of conflict or rivalry, which would tend to give it a party-political complexion.'[62] This approach yielded excellent results in the long term.

In time, Canon Collins was able to bring on board millions of pounds in donations from the world over, especially from the Scandinavian countries, the Netherlands and the UN Trust Fund for South Africa. The Trust Fund, in particular, garnered considerable funds following an appeal from the Special Committee to governments in November 1964 to contribute to the Defence and Aid Fund and other agencies assisting political prisoners and their families in South Africa and refugees from South Africa. In January 1965, the Swedish government announced a grant of $100,000 to the Defence and Aid Fund and $100,000 to the World Council of Churches. Substantial contributions from Scandinavian countries, the Netherlands, and other countries followed.[63] All these funds were to be channelled through the International Defence and Aid Fund (IDAF), renamed in order to be able to access the UN donations, as well as to widen its scope of building awareness and support.

But all the IDAF's activity aroused suspicion among South African authorities, particularly as Collins' high-profile fundraising campaign was exposing the iniquities of apartheid to the public through South Africa's own court cases. Large amounts of money arrived from the UN Trust Fund (via Reddy), from Sweden, Norway, New Zealand, Canada, Nigeria, Tunisia and Jamaica.

Then, in 1966, the IDAF was banned in South Africa. Shortly beforehand, local newspapers had splashed a claim that the US$20,000 donation from the Netherlands to the Defence and Aid Fund had actually been laundered behind the Iron Curtain. The regime was also clearly excited by an impassioned statement made by Collins at the United Nations Special Committee Against Apartheid. 'Because of the tyrannical legislation of the present South African government,' he had charged, 'no political organisation which seeks to change South Africa's racial policies can function properly in the open. Black political organisations are banned. Those who wish to continue the struggle have to go underground.'[64] For the South African government and its supporters, his speech was a golden opportunity to demonstrate to the international community that the Defence and Aid Fund was clearly supporting violent revolution.

The banning of IDAF under the Unlawful Organisations Act imposed a 10-year sentence for any recipient in South Africa if it could be proved that the financial assistance received was linked in any way to the IDAF. After his initial dismay, the ever-resourceful Collins talked to selected friends and eventually came up with two strategies. The one was to form three funds or foundations, with trustees not previously associated with Amen Court. The accounts for the funds were channelled to them from Amen Court through Swiss banks renowned for their discretion. The three new foundations were to act as fronts for the filtering of funds through several layers to defend political trials and aid the families of political prisoners and victims of opposition to apartheid.

An elaborate strategy was devised, using two sets of respectable legal firms. The identity of the two London solicitors (attorneys) was kept top secret. One of the two would brief a second set of solicitors that included lawyers from the UK, Canada, New York, France, West Germany and Zurich. They had not the faintest clue of the connection of the trial funds to IDAF. They would receive the money from the first solicitor through the Swiss bank account of one of the three specially created foundations. They would then brief an attorney in South Africa. The attorneys and advocates undertaking the defence of the political accused were under the impression that the funding came from individual wealthy benefactors, such as Lord Mitchison, a Conservative with a conscience. Other aristocrats, labour and liberal establishment figures as well as respected scholars (archaeologist Jacquetta Hawkes, for example) and literary luminaries (JB Priestley) willingly lent their names to serve as front donors.[65] The South African lawyers tended to be drawn from a small group of brave souls – attorneys Joel Carlson, Raymond Tucker, Priscilla Jana, Shun Chetty, Himie Bernadt and Michael Richman, and advocates George Bizos, Sidney Kentridge, Denis Kuny, Arthur Chaskalson, David Soggot, Ernie Wentzel and others. As part of the smoke screen, these lawyers received market fees for legal services, whereas in the early days they had worked *pro deo*. Tambo, who informed Collins that a number of cases had cropped up without defence, found that this oversight was quickly rectified. Subsequently Tambo admitted, 'We knew large sums of money were sent through, but we didn't know the means.'[66]

The second strategy for disbursing welfare was equally resourceful. Phyllis Altman, an intelligent and extremely dedicated South African exile, made a simple suggestion. She had worked for years in the South African Congress of Trade Unions, was now Collins' right-hand person in Amen Court and had herself been recruited by Rica Hodgson, the Treason Trial's most talented fundraiser and former secretary of the Defence and Aid Fund in Johannesburg. When Collins first set up the IDAF, he had employed Hodgson despite complaints from some quarters that she was a known communist. Hodgson herself could see that her presence would eventually become a stumbling block to the objectives of the organisation, so she stepped down in favour of Phyllis Altman.

Even before she arrived at Amen Court, Altman used her network to raise funds for banned trade unionists. The funds were donated by the Czech-based World Federation of Trade Unions, as well as unions in the UK and the USA.

The British unions included the seamen's and fire brigades' unions, as well as the musicians' union which imposed a cultural boycott of South Africa, while major American unions included the United Auto Workers and the Longshoremen. Prior to the ban, these donations had been sent on to the Johannesburg office of the Defence and Aid Fund for disbursement, but Altman now suggested that, as with the legal funding system, the process should be interrupted so that neither the sender nor the recipients could identify the links along the chain. Recruited pen pals would receive a registered package containing cash and a covering letter with instructions from a fictitious 'Reverend Williams'. They, in turn, would send a letter and a money order to a specified person in South Africa. They were not to discuss politics, send photographs of themselves or provide telephone numbers. The thank-you letter served as a receipt, which would then be mailed to another cleric, who passed it on to St Paul's church or priory. These would be collected and taken to Amen Court.

It was Rica Hodgson who recruited the letter writers. It was important that they were impeccably trustworthy and also untraceable by South African authorities – 'free of political microbes', as she put it. After a while, these first contacts then recommended other correspondents, all of them being asked, without being told too much, to maintain confidentiality and steer away from politics in their letters. In time, the project grew into a multimillion-pound welfare scheme, involving up to 700 letters at one time.[67]

'We finally had correspondents all over the world who were sending the money to the families of political prisoners and to released prisoners... it was such an intricate operation to get the funds into South Africa, I think it was really rather a miracle that we got so much in.'[68]

The letters made their way to the families of the detained or exiled; to the house arrested, the banned, those banished to the notorious 'dumping grounds' of Winterveld, Dimbaza and elsewhere; to ANC and PAC ex-prisoners, to the families of those still locked up. The £40 international money orders found their way into shacks, township 'matchbox' houses, hostel dormitories, or huts in remote rural homesteads. The money paid for funerals, schooling, food, and in at least one case to call a taxi to replace the long and arduous monthly trip in a wheelbarrow by an ailing ex-prisoner to collect his tiny pension. Wives and children were now able to save for the twice-yearly visit to Robben Island or to Barberton Women's Prison. In their replies, the recipients were astute enough not to discuss politics, but quite often would mention the solace of 'the church', which eased their lives.

Tambo, who continued to drop in at Amen Court whenever he was passing through London, would regularly contribute to the mailing list, gleaned from the debriefing sessions of released prisoners and new exile arrivals. 'He would give us details of people he felt needed money,' recalled Altman. 'But, other than coming to ask about trials or suggesting people who were in need of help, he knew how we did it, but he never let on.'[69]

In the meantime, Tambo and the pen pals knew – as did the South African regime – that support, whether legal or material, was also a message of approval and encouragement to continue the struggle. As General Johan Coetzee, head of the Security Police, put it, 'If you come and say if you are arrested we'll see that you've got the best defence, we'll see that your wife is looked after whilst you are in prison, you've got a prison education scheme running for you and once you are through all this we'll see that there is work for you – isn't this removing the ordinary inhibitions which are operative among ordinary societies?'[70]

But important as the support might be, Tambo felt that one should not lose sight of the end objective – to increase the pressure of sanctions. And this indeed was the prime focus of the Anti-Apartheid Movement (AAM) founded by Trevor Huddleston as long ago as 1959 in response to Luthuli's call for the international isolation of South Africa's apartheid government. Since the early days, the AAM had grown. After Sharpeville, it organised demonstrations, marches, campaigns and rallies. Supporters stood outside supermarkets, picketed in Trafalgar Square, argued in public places about the inequities of apartheid. They pointed out Britain's dominant role in the South African economy and Britain's influence in shaping policy. 'The more we could expose that to the public and generate pressures in Britain and internationally, the greater the prospects of bringing about our change of policy,' remarked Mike Terry about the AAM programme, whose audience was firmly geared to the British public, and 'directing its discourse to British values of democracy and non-racialism'.

Activities included the campaign to expel South Africa from the Commonwealth, the demonstrations and marches during the Rivonia Trial, the vigil at the execution of Vuyisile Mini in November 1964. At Tambo's urging, the Anti-Apartheid Committee (as the Anti-Apartheid Movement was previously known) conducted a major public-awareness campaign (suggested by Tambo)[71] about the growing use of torture, especially following the deaths in detention of Looksmart Ngudle in September 1963 and Babla Saloojee in September 1964. The vigils attracted tens of thousands to Trafalgar Square, which was overlooked by the imposing heritage building, South Africa House. Tambo himself joined many a march, and on a number of occasions addressed the protesting crowds. He had insisted from the beginning that the AAM, like the IDAF, should never become an extension of the ANC, that it should be the voice of the British people.[72] Nevertheless, like the IDAF and the British

Defence and Aid Fund (BDAF), the AAM's relationship with the PAC was, in comparison, 'very patchy', admitted trustee and Labour MP Bob Hughes.[73] The ANC's wide-ranging approach included talking to local councils and, after the popularisation of Mandela as the personification of the struggle on Robben Island, local authorities in cooperation with the AAM began to grant Mandela the freedom of the city or naming public places or buildings after Mandela, and joined in the campaigns for boycotting South African goods. 'So, I mean, they were conscious of South Africa, and they were conscious that apartheid was wrong; and a lot of people had been convinced of the overall leadership of the ANC and its kind of policies, the Freedom Charter, the ANC's non-racialism.[74]

'They developed an understanding that the ANC was in a leadership position more strongly,' continued Mike Terry, 'and that was being reflected across the board so that in that period, the British government came under a tremendous amount of pressure to have some sort of a relationship with the ANC.'[75]

It was with Tambo's enthusiastic approval that Ronald Segal convened an International Conference on Economic Sanctions Against South Africa in London in April 1964, with the sponsorship of the AAM and with a number of heads of state or government as patrons. The Conference Steering Committee commissioned papers from independent experts to argue the feasibility and urgency of mandatory economic sanctions, and the case was further popularised in a paperback, entitled *Sanctions Against Apartheid*,[76] published by Penguin. Tambo's speech at the conference left a deep impression that was to set the strategy for the entire sanctions campaign.

But Tambo also emphasised the need to widen public awareness to other parts of the world, and so the AAM began to organise internationally on a number of other terrains. Sport, white South Africa's soft underbelly, was an easy target to identify. Sport was part of its national identity; even Chevrolet advertised South Africa's attractions – 'sunny skies, *braaivleis* [barbecues] and rugby'. Yet black South Africans were excluded from all the mainstream games. Their local resources, both in their neighbourhoods and at school (if they were able to attend school at all), were pathetically few. Black children did, however, play games, and their communities tried to sponsor youngsters as best they could from their own pockets, but their training grounds were the street or an empty piece of veld. Cricket required more than a ball, and of course tennis, golf and swimming needed courts, courses, pools and trainers. Even the talented few who were able to overcome these impediments would not be accepted because of their colour. If the international sports community could be persuaded to boycott matches with South Africa, it would hit where it hurt most.

The AAM linked up with two South African activist athletes – Chris de Broglio and the poet Dennis Brutus. Brutus had been instrumental in forming the South African Sports Association (SASA) in Port Elizabeth in 1959, with himself as secretary. To popularise the association nationally, it had 20 vice-presidents, all well-known sportsmen in the black community. In 1962, the organisation changed its name in order to be able to lobby the Olympics Committee. Although South Africa already had an Olympics committee, this was all white – the committee maintained that it was against the law to include black athletes, so in October 1962, SASA became the South African Non-racial Olympics Committee (SANROC). From then on, they were able to negotiate with the World Olympics Committee.

Brutus arrived in London after he had been incarcerated on Robben Island for breaking his banning by trying to leave the country[77] – and he hit the city running. Within two weeks, in August 1966, he was able to attend a meeting in Jamaica, which was in the process of organising the Commonwealth Games. On his return, he held a press conference in Fleet Street and started an anti-South Africa campaign. Canon Collins, who had followed Brutus's fortunes with interest, and on Tambo's recommendation, offered him a post in the IDAF.[78]

'In those early days, people told us not to mix sports and politics, so it took some time before our campaign brought us support', recalled Abdul Minty, who would become a long-serving secretary of the AAM and had been asked by Brutus to represent SASA in the UK. In 1968 the South African government again played into the hands of the UK boycott movement when Prime Minister JB Vorster refused to allow the MCC to tour the country if South African coloured cricketer Basil d'Oliviera, who had left the country (and became a star in England), was included as part of the UK team.

SASA was able to lobby FIFA (Federation Internationale de Football Association) to drop South Africa from the World Cup, the first sports body to do so.[79] This was a major blow to South Africa, and the government raged at this unprecedented step. But soccer was still considered a second-class, 'black' activity. Brutus realised that sanctions against the sport that came closest to the hearts of white males – rugby, dubbed 'Afrikaners at play' – would hurt most. In 1969 the British rugby union invited the South African team to a test series and Brutus immediately hit the campaign trail, and thus the 'Stop the Seventy Tour', organised in the UK by exiled South African Peter Hain, was born.

When Brutus was in the USA, he was offered an academic post at North West University, but before he accepted it, he went to see Tambo. 'I had a high regard for him,' said Brutus (who was later to become a left-wing critic of the ANC's orthodox economic policies after it came into power). 'A man of consistent integrity... I said I was at his disposal. He should use me in any way he saw fit.' Tambo thought for a while and recommended that Brutus take up the offer, since he could be useful in the States. Brutus, however, was reluctant, believing that much more was happening in the UK. Nevertheless, he took Tambo's advice and proceeded to build an impressive US network. Through his visiting lectureships, he reached a student constituency. 'The base of the struggle was students, but we built on that a community layer, a black layer, a church layer, a trade union layer and ultimately a congressional level. That was the most difficult. But when we reached that point, then we could get legislation.'[80]

As with ANC diplomacy in general, Tambo's concern was to widen the sports lobby to draw in as many active boycotters as possible. He emphasised that, in the interests of building the broadest base, the sports sanctions drive should not side with either of the liberation movements, and that the ANC should not hold senior positions. This was the policy he also advocated for the AAM, although the most articulate speechmakers and writers did seem to come from the ANC. The UK was now the new home of many Congress of Democrats and non-African exiles, who were not necessarily welcome in African countries – not least of whom were Hilda and Rusty Bernstein and Ruth First. They tended to be drawn from the activist intelligentsia and had had experience in talking to people who often knew little about the black experience under apartheid. Highly educated individuals such as Mendi Msimang and Raymond Mazisi Kunene also staffed the London office. Often, therefore, the AAM took on campaigns that were conceived along ANC lines. The 'Release Political Prisoners' campaign, the sports boycott, the cultural projects, and the movement for economic sanctions closely linked the two organisations. ANC members did much AAM legwork, and ANC-supporting students helped establish AAM branches at universities and polytechnics.

In Europe, local anti-apartheid activists were already being identified. Collins' Trust Fund has been described as 'the world's most generous underwriter of Africa's non-violent struggle'.[81] But this would not have been possible without the moral and material support of the Scandinavian countries, primarily Sweden, Norway and Denmark. 'Perhaps more than any other Southern African politician,' writes archivist Tor Sellström, '[Tambo] contributed to the partnership between Sweden and the liberation movements of the region.'[82]

While Tambo worked on trying to acquire support from the governments of the Scandinavian countries, he also systematically developed relationships with civic organisations – since, in the democratic societies of Scandinavia, these audiences were the voters who would support and even drive government into anti-apartheid initiatives.

Tambo's speeches to rallies on May Day in Denmark in 1960 and Sweden in 1961 were well publicised. In 1962, he addressed the Afro-Scandinavian Conference at the University of Norway. He called on the youth to convince their governments and people 'that it is not the South African goods that are cheap, but the forced labour of the Africans'.[83] The conference resolution, in response, demanded an imposition of 'total economic, diplomatic and cultural sanctions' and 'unreserved material and moral support for the liberation movements in South Africa'. The Scandinavian governments, however, were not yet ready to take up such a radical policy.

After 1962, when he met Olof Palme, Tambo's relationship with Sweden reached a more personal level. From their first meeting, the two men took to each other, talking easily, sharing their experiences of personal growth into political activism. Both had warm personalities and were earnestly involved in the politics of social change. 'What did you and Palme talk about?' I once asked Tambo, on learning about their 'special relationship' and Palme's habit of frying up a plate of sausages for Tambo in his home.

'Politics,' he replied, smiling. The subject closest to their hearts, politics was an integral part of both personal identities. The two leaders were 'like brothers in the struggle', observed Lindiwe Mabuza. 'As ANC chief representative... I have been privileged to hear secrets being exchanged: "Which front should we try to deal with? Which country could then be approached? How, as a liberation movement, should you be going about this?"'[84]

The Swedish press gave Tambo's 1964 visit wide coverage. His ability to portray the devastation of apartheid for black society in his low-key manner enabled him to get through to the more sceptical. A conservative newspaper, *Svenska Gedagbladet*, portrayed Tambo – somewhat patronisingly – as a 'good representative of the leading layer of educated Africans. He speaks in a cultivated and modulated way. He is calm and logical and presents his points of view without showing a hint of fanaticism'.[85]

Per Wästberg, an influential writer, and trustee of IDAF, commented on Tambo's personal skills and warmth. He was able, said Wästberg, to reach 'the middle terrain, the political and diplomatic'. In so doing, he dispelled 'the frightening features [of the ANC], the terrorist's shadow'.[86]

Palme, highly intelligent and perceptive, rapidly grasped the multifaceted nature of ANC strategy. 'Without underestimating the difficulties,' reflected Tambo 15 years later in a posthumous tribute to Olof Palme, he 'understood our resolve to set ourselves free – free to think and act independently, free to differ from him without losing his support'.[87] Palme had an abhorrence of violence and actively campaigned against the military Cold War blocs developing at the time. 'And yet he was not a pacifist,' maintained Tambo. He would not 'allow hypocritical positions about the issue of violence to pass as immutable and inherited wisdom'.[88] Per Wästberg observed that in their mutual understanding of the economy, there were so many similarities that there was a trust and dialogue which 'had so much reference, the one to the other, that I think [Tambo] was influenced by us and we influenced by him'.[89]

Palme had, on May Day 1965, observed Tambo's differences with his Prime Minister Tag Erlanger, when Tambo, 'in a quite spectacular manner',[90] 'stood under the Prime Minister's very nose and stated that the time had come for Sweden to introduce sanctions against South Africa'.[91] Public debate elicited fierce criticism of the Social Democrats, particularly by the Liberal Party. Indeed, the Social Democrat newspaper *Tiden* itself argued it was essential that the Swedish government support the ANC if it was 'not to be taken over by Communists and Liberals'. It was then that Palme made a crucial speech. While his chief was on holiday, and acting as Foreign Minister, he argued (like Tambo) that apartheid posed a threat to international peace, and warned against 'a division of the world between rich and white, poor and black'.[92]

Palme was later to become Foreign Minister and then Prime Minister. Unlike the USA, France and the UK at the time, whose governments, recalled Tambo, were 'making it a condition for the support for the national liberation... that we must reproduce ourselves in their image', the Swedish government was able ultimately to override its tradition of hands-off neutrality. Nonetheless, ironically, the ANC was the last of the liberation movements in southern Africa to be given official sanction – largely because of their relationship with the South African Communist Party. The 1968 visit of Robert Resha and Joe Matthews to Sweden and their meeting with the senior Social Democrats in government, Olof Palme and Alva Myrdal,[93] evoked 'near hysteria' in the South African press. *Dagbreek en Landstem* blared in its headline news: 'Two South African Communists announce offensive: Sweden gives money for terror regime.'[94] The following year, the Swedish Parliament almost unanimously voted to give official support to the ANC and other liberation movements in southern Africa.[95] After Sweden's lead, other Scandinavian and Nordic countries followed suit, and began providing financial and material support (though not for arms) to the ANC and other liberation movements.

Government support included the provision of skills as well as the means for providing welfare, health care, clothing, food and education for the thousands of South African exiles in the Front Line States. These governments took a conscious decision to include moral values as a justification for foreign policy; but the argument was strongly supplemented by the assertion that the Soviet

Union and its allies should not be seen as the only bloc to support the anti-apartheid struggle, for this would create a dependency on the Eastern Bloc and exclude the influence of progressive sympathisers in the West.

But, as important was what Tambo called Scandinavia's 'people-to-people' relationship with the ANC – the support of civil society for the anti-apartheid project. As early as 1962 Tambo had written to Swedish activist Joachim Israel commending the solidarity of the Swedish South Africa Committee and urging it to use its respected status to embark on international solidarity action: 'It seems to us that you could raise the efforts in Britain and the United States to the level of practical action by coordinating your plans with those of the British Anti-Apartheid Movement and the American Committee on Africa.'[96]

For the 1962 launch by the World Assembly of Youth (WAY) of the public boycott campaign, 'on the recommendation by the South African Nobel peace laureate Albert Luthuli and his oppressed brothers', Tambo had telephoned a message of encouragement directly from London. As the campaign had taken off, WAY activists, as well as the Swedish South Africa Committee and the Isolate South Africa Committee, had targeted shops and individual customers, naming South African consumer products such as fruit (Outspan oranges), wine and cigarettes. By April 1963, the retail trade organisation ICA, representing about 9 000 shops in Sweden, and the wholesale society KF, announced the stoppage of South African imports.

In July, Swedish dockworkers refused to unload South African cargo from a Swedish ship. It was, therefore, rerouted, but Danish stevedores also refused to handle the South African goods – Tambo's address to Danish workers on May Day, 1960, and his call to the ports of Copenhagen and Aarhus, to isolate apartheid South Africa was still fresh in their minds.[97] In Sweden, activists continued to distribute leaflets to dockworkers in the Stockholm harbour area: 'We *demand* blockade against South Africa', declared the banners in October 1963. In that year the Scandinavia Transport Workers had issued a strong statement that went to the international trade-union federation of the West, the International Confederation of Free Trade Unions (ICFTU). Noting the continued and increased racial oppression in South Africa, the statement argued that 'experience shows us that the consumer boycott must be expanded to include actions that will hit harder... We therefore propose,' it continued, '... comprehensive boycott actions in the form of an end to oil deliveries, refusal to buy South African gold, an end to all shipping to and from South Africa and a termination of diplomatic relations'.[98] Within a year, imports from South Africa had fallen by nearly four-and-a-half million Swedish krona.

In 1964, the Davis Cup Tie took place in Oslo, between South Africa and Norway. Tennis was a popular pastime in Norway, but many people had come to realise that in South Africa the sport was a 'white sport'. Alert to popular feeling, albeit by a vocal minority in Oslo, the government forbade demonstrations. Two hundred activists, members of the Norwegian Action Against Apartheid, then bought seats in the stands for the opening match. Once the match was in progress, on a prearranged signal, the protestors stood up and began to throw black tennis balls onto the court. They then invaded the court and sat down, linking arms and holding onto the net. The match was thus abandoned, and thereafter, tickets were not available to the public.[99]

In 1985, a newspaper photograph showing Oliver Tambo shaking hands with a smiling US Republican Secretary of State, George Schultz, startled the ANC and its sympathisers. They were all the more surprised as Cold War warrior President Ronald Reagan was in power. The ANC had been kept at arm's length for over a quarter of a century by even Democratic presidents, and in recent years Reagan had been echoing Margaret Thatcher's allegation that the ANC was a 'terrorist organisation'.

By comparison with the Scandinavian countries and the UK, Tambo's 'acre by acre', *indima* approach had developed slowly in the US. Tambo himself had made public appearances there as early as 1960, when he addressed a meeting organised by the American Committee on Africa and had located South Africa on a conceptual map for his audience.[100] He also addressed church congregations, which were to prove staunch supporters of anti-apartheid initiatives. To many congregations, apartheid was morally repugnant, and preachers in particular were to play an influential role in the divestment campaigns to come.[101]

The American Committee on Africa was one of the earliest anti-apartheid organisations and had supported the ANC's position on sanctions from the beginning. Gradually it helped to build up a critical constituency, going from state to state, city to city.[102] But after Tambo's initial interaction, more than a decade was to pass before the ANC engaged seriously with the USA. The ANC was, for many years, kept out as a 'terrorist' organisation because it was involved in armed struggle. Its members could go to the UN and move within a radius of 25 miles. In fact, Oliver himself had to obtain a special visa. The ANC's diplomatic energy was, therefore, focusing on friendlier countries in Europe, the United Nations, the Eastern Bloc and the developing countries. But in 1976, the world was sharply reminded of the violence that sustained apartheid, and the African-American Institute took the step of raising funds to give direct support to Sowetan students who had fled to Lesotho. From then onwards, African-American bodies increasingly interested themselves in the issues of racial oppression in South Africa.

From an early stage, Tambo was determined to clarify the nature of the struggle against apartheid. The struggle in South Africa was qualitatively different from one of civil rights, he maintained. It was not about gaining rights in a constitutional system, but changing the system entirely. 'We have a system,' he explained, 'where you have the white population organised into a state, and the majority of the people are outside that state. Now, that's not a question of civil rights at all. It's a question of colonialism. It is just that the colonial power is separated not by geographic boundaries but by colour.'[103]

The wave of vocal support began with the students, largely radicalised by the mounting, militant Civil Rights Movement from the late fifties onwards, by growing resistance to the US war in Vietnam. The opposition to apartheid was given substantial impetus and focus with the murder of Steve Biko in detention in October 1977. Students challenged their universities and colleges to withdraw their investments in South Africa, picketed the offices of their trustees, and interacted with the media. But, as one anti-apartheid activist observed, it was almost impossible to build a united British-style anti-apartheid movement because 'US politics is much more complicated'.

The American Committee on Africa was able to build an extremely powerful movement based on linking independent groups together, for example the Yale Students. 'We never tried too hard to put them all under one national umbrella but told people what to do,' explained its director, Jennifer Davies. 'In fact, the anti-apartheid movement managed sometimes to bring together people who wouldn't talk to each other on any other issue.'[104]

What many people, black or white, had in common was that they saw anti-apartheid as part of a larger liberation support movement, which had started with Vietnam and then spread to Latin America, including Brazil, Argentina, Salvador and Chile (where the CIA had been instrumental in the 1973 military coup that confronted the democratically elected socialist Allende and secured his death). This then came to encompass Angola, Mozambique and, crucially, South Africa. Support for one movement strengthened the solidarity movement as a whole.[105] Gradually, groups that in the normal course of events did not have much to do with one another began to cooperate on anti-apartheid campaigns.

During the 1970s, influential figures in the African-American community began to develop a more substantial commitment to opposing apartheid. Until then, the Civil Rights Movement had tended to take precedence. But, given their own historical experiences, they were easily aroused to action as they became more aware of what was happening in South Africa. Some conceptual difficulties nevertheless remained.

'I can remember in a meeting,' recalled Dr Sylvia Hill, one of the founder members of the Southern African Support Group, 'where we were trying to debate – because the word ["apartheid"] was so unused in this country in the early seventies and late sixties – and trying to decide: should we call it racism, should we call it slavery, what can we call this to make sense to people?'[106] But within a few years, the notion of apartheid became commonplace, and indeed began to be applied to many situations in the USA itself.[107]

The best-organised black solidarity organisation, TransAfrica, was formed in 1971, and aimed to create awareness in black communities of Africa's liberation movements. They lobbied various sectors, including government and civil society, to support their cause. The solidarity initiatives began to concentrate on mobilising at a local level. Despite race and class differences, various groups drew inspiration from the accomplishment of putting an end to the Vietnam War. In the anti-apartheid campaign, black and white were urged to lobby their local councillors and Congress.[108] Local groups proved to be productively inventive, and on one occasion, a group of people even waylaid Republican Congressman Luger at a Saturday football game. His response, he later revealed, was 'that if people were going to start raising this issue with him at the football game, that's when he really had to take it seriously'. As a good politician, he had long ago grasped the importance of listening to his own constituency.[109]

The anti-apartheid groups also took to heart Tambo's strategy of replacing simple material aid for the liberation struggle with a more muscular form of solidarity to help isolate the apartheid regime. Civic society could best achieve this pressure through sanctions, divestment and lobbying the politicians, national and local, who represented them. Sanctions, they began to argue, could reduce the violence by helping to overthrow apartheid peacefully. Divestment had to be understood as a political act, and served also to educate students on the campuses. 'In turn, the students educated their parents.'[110]

TransAfrica had set out to create a black lobby within 'the helm of Congress' and the State Department in order to influence legislation and policy. Parallel with this thrust was a conviction that the grass roots, as consumers, had to be mobilised. Later, when the ANC and PAC were granted observer status at the UN, they opened offices there. It was then that the ANC representative in New York, Johnny Makathini, met labour leader William Lucey of the African-American Labor Centre. The coalition of black trade unions, TransAfrica and other community-based organisations was 'canalised into a major anti-apartheid movement'.[111] For trade unions, Lucey observed, apartheid was also a form of labour control. Lucey was in touch with David Sibeko of the PAC, which received considerable support from the black community, mainly because of its strong Africanist stance but also for its critique of the ANC's alliance with the SACP and the Soviet Union's bank-rolling of the armed struggle.

But some conservative politicians manipulated the differences between various black organisations that were not always clear to people. For instance, conservative organisations such as the Heritage Foundation invited public figures to 'a glitzy reception' to meet Mangosuthu Buthelezi.[112] Here was a black leader of South Africa's largest ethnic group, they conveyed, who opposed sanctions and armed struggle.

'I knew many Zulus who supported the ANC through my visit to Natal,' responded Dr Hill. 'But Americans don't know that... and the whole notion of Shaka, you know, that's a positive image to young Americans.'[113]

In 1986, Buthelezi received an honorary doctorate from Boston University amid indignant student protest. Along with Helen Suzman, lone opposition member of parliament, Buthelezi's argument was that sanctions would hurt the very people they were intended to defend – the black workers and the black poor. But this was no more effective in deflecting protest than the well-meaning attempt by the Reverend Sullivan, an African-American who was horrified at the ultra-low wages of black workers in South Africa and who devised a code of criteria to guide the US investor there. It became the purpose of the solidarity groups to oppose any investment in South Africa, even a 'human face' of capitalism.

Equally, despite the occasional cries that boycotts jeopardised American jobs,[114] the effectiveness of support for the ANC was reinforced by the progressive unions' growing links with the democratic labour movement within South Africa. The National Union of Metalworkers of South Africa, the National Union of Mineworkers, the Food and Canning Workers' Union – all unions that would help to form the federated Congress of South African Trade Unions (COSATU) in 1985 – developed a relationship with the ANC in Lusaka. The American unions thus launched a vigorous support campaign during the long detention of Moses Mayekiso in 1987.[115] Joined by students and community solidarity groups, they produced buttons, leaflets and posters, demanding his release. They organised street marches and pickets outside the South African Embassy, chanting 'No Aid, No Trade'. Campuses protested outside university offices, demanding to know whether their institutions' pension and investment funds were directly or indirectly benefiting the South African economy.

Events in South Africa helped to clarify the issues. In 1984, following the angry response in the townships to PW Botha's 'bogus constitution', which separated coloureds and Indians from black Africans by giving coloureds and Indians the vote in a 'Tri-cameral Parliament', the black mayor of Washington himself suggested civil disobedience.

'I think we should have a sit-in,' he declared at a support meeting.

He was inspired by the black comedian, Dick Gregory, who every year staged a sit-in at the South African Embassy. His arrest and fine were always covered in the papers. The year 1984 was the one in which Archbishop Desmond Tutu won the Nobel Peace Prize and was fêted in the streets of New York, but it was also the year of presidential elections. Jesse Jackson, in his campaign, frequently raised the issue of southern Africa. The re-election of Reagan further fired the African-American community to pressurise their political representatives for more militant action. In the process, observed Sylvia Hill, the popular perception of the liberation movements, especially the ANC, shifted from a discourse of communism to one of race. Quite clearly, apartheid was simply and crudely a form of blatant legalised racism. Black intellectuals were writing papers and delivering them at strategic events to communicate the nature of apartheid, and therefore mobilise support for the national liberation movements.

Harry Belafonte, Bruce Springsteen, Mr T of the television series *The A Team* and many more celebrities came out in public solidarity for the anti-apartheid movement. In the eighties, as the momentum accelerated, the ACOA drove a campaign in which artists performed and cut a record against the Sun City casino and entertainment centre in the homeland of Bophuthatswana. 'I don' wanna go to Sun City!' was the hit that topped the charts, and the artists were able to hand over a cheque for $100,000 to Oliver Tambo at a reception hosted by Harry Belafonte. Tambo, the guest of honour at the event, afterwards stood for hours, shaking hundreds of hands. Someone observed:

'Americans have a terrible habit of looking over people's shoulder to see who is important. And OR never did that once. He talked to everyone who wanted to talk to him, and lots of people wanted to tell him what a great contribution they had made to the anti-apartheid struggle in the United States.'[116]

It was this personal encounter with the man himself that imbued people with a strengthening commitment.

As the level of popular pressure increased, it began to make an impact within Congress itself. The Secretary of State and his assistant, Chester Crocker, persuaded President Reagan to intervene in what they considered to be the growing threat from the Soviet Bloc in southern Africa. Cuba was already stationed in Angola, at the invitation of its elected government, the Marxist-oriented MPLA. Crocker described the region as 'a rough neighbourhood', but what he did not mention were the historical circumstances that had made it 'rough' for the people of Africa. Nor did he acknowledge the more recent interventions on the part of his country's CIA, which had kept in close touch with South African intelligence in monitoring liberation activities in the region, making it even 'rougher'.[117] However, this noxious involvement had been surreptitious. Now the Reagan administration was persuaded to follow a policy of 'constructive engagement' with the apartheid regime. This meant working on a diplomatic level to persuade the South African government that it was better to institute reforms itself than ultimately submit to outside pressure. The policy was continued, however, in the context of a Cold War.

By 1984, the US administration had become aware of an 'air instantly charged with the electric currents of racial politics'. A culture of anti-communism seemed to be bumped in favour of racial politics. Crocker described this phenomenon as the 'sanctimonious' setting off on 'a race for the moral high ground'.[118]

But a shift was being discerned across the Atlantic Ocean. On Sharpeville Day in 1984, Tambo addressed the Anti-Racist Day meeting hosted by the Greater London Council and paid tribute to its grass-roots citizens. For Tambo, the participation of ordinary people in striking a blow against apartheid was a major weapon. While many Western countries were ignoring calls for sanctions, men and women on the ground were gradually building up an awareness of apartheid as 'a crime against humanity'.

'Our people,' he pointed out, 'have known London as the imperial capital that betrayed both its principles and the African people. To this day, the heir to Imperial London continues to see the creature it spawned in 1910 as its ally... Its institutions pour investments into the apartheid economy and harvest the profits of our dispossession and exploitation.'

But, he added, 'Tonight, we are meeting with another London... [the] *People's London* – to distinguish and dissociate it from that centred in Whitehall and the City... This is the London of Fenner Brockway, who met and welcomed Solomon Plaatje at the time. It is the London we have known as the birthplace of the British Anti-Apartheid Movement.'

Tambo went on to celebrate more than 100 other UK cities and towns that had broken apartheid ties, and linked them with towns and cities in the USA – 'three states and more than 22 cities' that were rupturing relations with apartheid. These citizens had created 'anti-apartheid zones' by boycotting South African sporting links as well as South African products such as wine and fruit. But there was still some way to go, he pointed out. The balance of power still lay in the hands of the oppressors, supported by heads of state such as Thatcher in the UK and Reagan in the USA.[119] The solution was to be inclusive, to encourage all prospective opponents of apartheid rather than drive them into a corner. OR's comment on a draft speech on imperialism – the identity of the writer is not known – is an example of his strategic thinking and diplomacy:

'It sounds as if,' responded Tambo, 'we are attacking the West as the West – that apartheid merely gives us an excuse that if they complied with our demands, we would want to look for something else to use against them.'

The purpose, he explained, was to win them over to oppose and, therefore, to isolate apartheid; to raise other issues that would hinder the primary objective. Other problems should be tackled once the task at hand was completed. Step by step, acre by acre.

'Tactical retreat only,' he continued. 'Strategic objective remains. What are we all about? Who is our immediate enemy and what are we doing about him? What are our priorities? How do we at this stage handle imperialism?'[120]

Oliver Tambo's *indima* style ensured that he did not take short cuts. He insisted that funds earmarked by donors for specific purposes not be diverted. What sometimes came to be known as 'struggle bookkeeping' inside South Africa was not for Tambo. For practical reasons, he did not want to risk losing the enormous goodwill that was steadily and painstakingly being achieved through the building of trust relationships, be they in the West or East. The Swedes, for example, knew that their contributions were going to welfare and education; Tambo had made the political adjustments to channel military aid and training from the socialist bloc and also from India – those countries willing to arm the national liberation movement. Personal relations became important here, and Tambo's identity as a nationalist and a democrat rather than a communist was a significant factor in the choice of the ANC for many countries.

Tambo and ANC Treasurer Thomas Nkobi kept impeccable books. Tambo would systematically suggest to sympathisers where they could best lend their support for the cause, according to their abilities and skills.

Peggy Delaney (née Rockefeller), who together with her husband had a useful network of industrialists, visited Oliver Tambo in 1985 when he happened to be at Muswell Hill. She asked him how she could help the movement.

'I said in a rather naive way, "Well, I really want to help", and in a self-mocking way, "but I am sure what you are not looking for is for me to join your guerrilla army, so how can I help?" He laughed and said that he definitely would not think of that, and he said that I mustn't think of going about getting arrested in front of the South African Embassy either. They had plenty of people who could do that; they didn't have a lot of people who could help them to make connections with the business community. And now that they would be moving into that phase, that is what they needed me to help them do.'[121]

Civil society for Oliver Tambo included the corporate world. He was already making contact with South African and UK businesspeople. In 1980, he had met with American multinationals, including both Citibank and General Motors at their request, and he was interested to talk to more corporations. 'The ANC must explain itself to everybody. It was a very welcome opportunity,' he explained.[122]

Influencing them, though not easy, was germane to the sanctions project, and as the 'owners of the means of production', they were influential with their governments. To members who were uneasy about talking to those who were not 'natural allies' in race struggles, ANC leaders reminded them of Tambo's approach – 'don't ever lose sight of the real enemy – the apartheid state'.

By the 1980s, the ANC was thus receiving enough support from increasingly vocal constituencies to have brought certain US Congressmen to Lusaka.

'Even conservatives,' remarked Frank Ferrari of the Ford Foundation, 'were impressed with this sensitive person.'They were quite unprepared for Tambo's warmth and his clarity of presentation. Indeed, Senator Warren commented on how the leadership of the ANC 'defied the stereotype'.[123]

Personal contacts with Johnny Makathini (who was clearly no communist) and Oliver Tambo's more frequent presence, which attracted great interest wherever he went, had turned the tide in black American support. Tambo's lecture at Georgetown University in January 1987 and his comments on constructive engagement captivated US supporters.[124] Using the discourse of his audience, Tambo brought them on board, carefully assembling for his rapt listeners the pain of racism and structural inequity that in many ways both societies shared. He spoke about the need for the oppressed to emancipate themselves in the context of some Western universities that had once promoted scientific racism. He went on to examine the structural violence of apartheid, citing continuing atrocities both at home and in the broader region. No part of apartheid, 'correctly categorised as a crime against humanity,' he emphasised, 'can be left intact… A crime cannot be reformed or amended.'

'We therefore', he added to applause, 'take issue with those who argue that to end violence in South Africa the ANC must end armed struggle.' The oppressed in South Africa had no option but to follow the path American forebears had taken for their own independence.

Tambo thanked the two major political parties and 'the American people as a whole', first for 'moving Congress not only to pass sanctions against apartheid South Africa but also to override President Reagan's veto'. American aid had helped to save millions of lives during the great drought in Africa – 'Now the American people can move to save hundreds of thousands more lives by acting to help bring about the dismantling of apartheid and the establishment of a non-racial and democratic society in South Africa.'

The time had come for the USA to review its policy to southern Africa as a whole. It had the potential to make an important contribution towards resolving some of the problems afflicting the region. But – and this was a message he had imparted to the Secretary of State the previous year as well as to Gorbachev in Moscow – 'These problems should not be viewed through the distorting prism of the East-West conflict.'

'Why,' he suggested, 'does not the US meet the Soviet Union and discuss together how they could cooperate to help bring about a new system?' Perhaps surprisingly, Schultz accepted the proposition. He told Tambo that a US meeting with the Soviet Union was imminent, and he would raise the issue there.[125]

'We, for our part, are ready to deal with the United States government honestly and openly for the sake of the cause of justice in our country and peace in southern Africa... We shall live up to that responsibility and expand the frontiers of democracy to our country as well. To carry out this task, which faces all humankind, we count on your support. We're certain you'll not fail us.'[126]

Soon afterwards, a San Francisco television documentary on the ANC was viewed by large numbers of Americans. ANC spokesmen and -women, including Tambo, did not shy away from explaining why the armed struggle was necessary, and also why it had to be intensified. Balancing that facet of the struggle was the call to the international community. It could minimise that violence by isolating the apartheid regime through economic and political sanctions, so as to hasten the day of liberation. Their vision of the future South African society, Tambo made clear (his mild expression belied by the excited movement of his eyes and finger often directed heavenwards as he made his points), was of a shared yet diverse and tolerant democratic society.[127]

The ANC had established links with the Nordic countries in the sixties; in 1977 Tambo and Thomas Nkobi met the Dutch prime minister and his Cabinet for the first time, and they subsequently provided assistance and medical supplies for the camps in Angola and for educational facilities in Mazimbu. But it was only in 1986 (around the same time as the US) that the liberation movement seemed to have developed links with West Germany.

What had been holding back the West Germans, including the Social Democrats on the left of the political spectrum in that country, was the ANC's warm relations with the GDR. East Germany supported the armed struggle, the training of MK cadres, journalists and mass-media workers, generously supplied food and clothing to the camps and ANC members in Tanzania, Zambia and Angola, and provided publications free of charge of both *The African Communist* as well as the ANC's *Sechaba*.[128]

Interestingly, the GDR also gave support 'from below', through the congregations of various churches. The Gosner Mission, which had sister churches in the West, also belonged to the World Council of Churches. When that body, encouraged by Tambo in 1967, began a programme for all its members to combat racism, the Gosner Mission began to raise funds directly. The funds it made available to certain liberation movements (Frelimo, MPLA, SWAPO, the PAC, the ANC) did not exclude support for armed struggle.

'The churches didn't want to control that money,' said Friedriche Schultz, a Gosner staff member. But there was 'a gentleman's agreement that the liberation armies didn't use that church money for purchasing weapons, and I am sure they got their weapons from governments' – including of course the GDR. The funds were not huge – perhaps $100, 000 for all of southern Africa – but they came from people who had been made aware of conditions inside South Africa. WCC pastors such as New Zealander John Osmos (later wounded by a parcel bomb in Lesotho), Beyers Naudé, as well as ANC representatives such as Anthony Mongalo, Indres Naidoo, Sthembiso Mhlangana, Jane Ngubane and others, contributed to an understanding of apartheid and its effects. Schultz also recalled Tambo speaking at a Solidarity Conference in the GDR, and being impressed with his message, 'referring to the situation in the GDR that Communists and Christians must go together, and here he gave the Solidarity Conference a quite impressive opening'.[129]

Social Democrats and the communist parties in the eastern bloc were deeply suspicious of each other, however. But while the communists had resigned themselves to Tambo's friendship with Social Democrats of the Nordic countries, France and the Netherlands, it took West Germans a little longer to overlook the ANC's alliance with the SACP as well as its benefactors in eastern Europe.

In the meantime, though, Tambo had met and got to know Social Democrats Willie Brandt and Francois Mitterand of France through the Socialist International (SI). When Brandt became its president in 1976, he began to steer the SI towards a focus on the Third World, with special recognition of the struggle in South Africa. Warmly supported by Olof Palme, the SI recognised the ANC and SWAPO in 1977 as the authentic liberation movements in South Africa.

Finally, in 1985, the development arm of the Social Democratic Party, the Friedrich Ebert Stiftung (FES), invited Tambo to be their guest in Bonn to present the ANC case. Tambo arrived in April of the following year.

Before Tambo and his delegation arrived, the FES prepared a report on the ANC, which drew from an interview given by Tambo to the FES a few months earlier.[130] First, the report assured its readers, 'the ANC is not the Communist Party'. Nor was it controlled by the SACP – the SACP had its own position and the ANC had its own identity. The vision for the ANC was the Freedom Charter, which was closer to a Social Democrat view of society and economy. Finally it pointed out, the ANC was not a terrorist organisation – it had turned to armed struggle only when all other options had been exhausted.[131]

In his speech at Bonn, Tambo reiterated: 'The ANC has grown and developed over the last 74 years into the powerful force it is today because the masses of our people see it as the embodiment of that perspective of a free and peaceful South Africa for all the people of our country, regardless of colour.'

Furthermore, he reassured his audience, once apartheid was defeated (and the ANC was 'the decisive factor' in any future political arrangement), the ANC was 'acutely aware... that our task would be that much simpler if we were to inherit a country with as little destruction as possible, and with as little antagonism among its peoples as possible'. The ANC was interested 'in as peaceful a resolution of the South African problem as is practicable'.[132]

Tambo made a most favourable impression during his visit. He convinced his hosts that the ANC was not only enlightened but competent to transform and run a democratic country. The FES were to host Tambo twice more in the next two years in western Germany, and provided resources for the ANC.

But even as the ANC network was growing steadily wider, the South African regime was hitting back. At the same time as it was embarking on a series of reprisal raids into neighbouring countries hosting ANC members, it was also promoting military and terrorist groups to oppose the Marxist-oriented, new governments of MPLA in Angola and Frelimo in Mozambique. In Mozambique, Renamo (the national resistance movement) had been founded by the Rhodesian security forces in the seventies to counter Frelimo's harbouring of Robert Mugabe's ZANLA cadres. With financial and technical support from South Africa, it now began an offensive in central Mozambique that involved the indiscriminate killing of anyone in government-connected areas. It destroyed railway lines, roads, hospitals, schools, shops and government buildings. It increased its numbers through methods of coercion and terror on the peasantry – there was no intention of winning over 'hearts and minds'.[133] The aim of the South African government was to increase the economic dependency of the region on South Africa, to make Frelimo's socialist project unworkable, and to obliterate the ANC presence in Mozambique. Gradually, through its violent methods of recruitment, the Renamo presence spread to most rural districts, able to take advantage of Frelimo's tendency to pay less attention to the peasantry, leaving the cities under Frelimo control.

Samora Machel, though aware of his country's economic dependence on South Africa – tens of thousands of Mozambicans laboured in its gold mines, returning home with precious foreign exchange – tried to create a balance between hospitality for the liberation movement and political pragmatism. He and Tambo agreed that Mozambique was not in a position to offer military camps. What is more, Tambo gave a strategic interview in which he asserted that there was 'a gap between what Frelimo will do for us and what we would like them to do'. Machel himself emphasised that Mozambique would be an example 'for peaceful change in South Africa'.[134]

Observers who looked for tensions between Frelimo and the ANC tended to miss the importance of the warm, personal relations between Tambo and Machel. The first time Tambo met Machel's family, Mr Machel Senior exclaimed when he saw the younger man, 'This is my son, whom I lost in the mines of South Africa! Now he is restored to me.'[135]

In Mozambique, Tambo spent more than one happy seaside holiday with the family. Later he became a godfather to Samora's children, Josina and Maluga Machel. Tambo was at Machel's house one evening in 1981. It was a difficult moment, for Tambo had come in the wake of the traumatic, first massacre in Maputo of ANC members by the apartheid regime. And it was perhaps not surprising that Tambo suffered one of his more severe asthma attacks. Machel immediately sent for a specialist doctor.

'My mother was plagued for years by asthma,' the doctor told Tambo, 'until I cured her with this method.' He prescribed a certain spray, to be squirted into the mouth last thing every night and first thing in the morning. From that day onwards, Tambo's asthma never again interfered with his hectic programme.[136]

The South African pressure was, in the meanwhile, putting an intolerable strain on the Frelimo government. On 30 January 1981, soldiers of the South African Defence Force (SADF) had attacked houses in the Maputo suburb of Matola, where ANC members were known to be staying. They killed 13 people, not all ANC. The dead included senior members. Obadi (his nom de guerre) had led the Special Operations team and had commanded the bombing of the SASOL oil refinery the previous June; SACTU official and ex-Robben Islander William Khanyile, and MK commander and lawyer Mduduzi Guma, as well as other valued cadres, were killed.

Tambo responded immediately. The crime perpetrated in Maputo was a lesson, he said to an audience of thousands two days later. The attack on residences had been unprovoked, for there were no MK camps in Mozambique.

'It was not covered by any of the normal excuses for aggression… We have not been told that every white household, every residence occupied by families in South Africa is such a base or camp,' he elucidated. 'If the qualification to make a house a camp is that people living in it can use a gun, we need to know.'

This was a crime perpetrated against the people of Mozambique as well as the people of South Africa. He again reminded his audience that the struggle in the region was indivisible: 'Mozambique will never grow, Zimbabwe will never – for as long as there is oppression and racist domination in South Africa, we shall not know independence. And the enemy is attacking: *Let us reply!*'[137]

Certainly, Tambo's earlier warnings to the OAU that apartheid was a danger to peace in the entire region, and that they could not separate the struggle in South Africa from the struggles in the region, had proved to be tragically correct – the South African regime was to go on to spread its destabilising tactics to Angola, Zambia, Zimbabwe, Tanzania, Botswana, Lesotho and Swaziland.

Mozambicans had also suffered fatalities. Dozens more bombings, assassinations, shootings and massacres were to follow in the next three years, and the USA's failure to condemn the attacks seemed to give the South African government the go-ahead. Indeed, East German intelligence conveyed to Mozambique that the CIA had supplied the SADF with useful intelligence on the ANC.

By 1983, Machel was desperate, and he approached Western countries for support, touring Europe in the hopes of winning some respite. It was quite clear to Frelimo, though, that South Africa held the trump card. Machel dreaded telling Tambo that his government had resolved to do a deal with South Africa. A meeting for May 1983 was postponed three times, and then an end-of-June appointment with Tambo was also cancelled. In the meantime, reports of the continuing talks between Mozambique and South Africa elicited a response from Tambo in a *Guardian* interview: 'The ANC has tried desperately to place as little weight as possible on the neighbouring countries,' he explained. 'But South Africa wants… a constellation of puppets. Then they would feel safe.'

'But,' he added, 'it is not possible for these governments not to support our struggle. The Machels, Dos Santos, Kaundas, Mugabes – they are all creations of liberation struggles… If they did what South Africa wanted them to do, to destroy the liberation struggle, they would be destroying their own independence.'[138]

In the meantime, Swaziland was also affected. King Sobhuza II, now in his nineties, considered himself a member of the ANC. Indeed, the Queen Regent Labotsueni had inducted him into the ANC when he succeeded to the throne. Like other kings and queens of her generation, she had been a founder member of the ANC. Sobhuza, therefore, had a connection to the ANC President. Not long before he died, he called for Tambo. 'It will not be long before I pass away,' he told Tambo. 'What do I tell the ancestors when I join them? Because they will ask me, "What has happened to our organisation, the ANC?"'[139]

And Tambo gave him a report on the state of the organisation. The king had protected the ANC and harboured its members as far as he could risk it. But after his death, which occurred in 1981, around the time of the Matola massacre, many ANC members in Swaziland were rounded up and deported.

On 16 March 1984, unable to hold out any longer, Samora Machel signed an agreement with PW Botha's regime, which presented itself as a government 'looking for change'. The Nkomati Accord compelled both parties to cease helping each other's enemies. For the ANC, this meant that all MK members, including Joe Slovo, head of Special Operations, had to leave Mozambique. Torn between guilt and necessity, Machel had not told Tambo of his intentions beforehand, and Tambo himself was taken aback that his friend had not shared with him his painful dilemma. He would have understood, and they might have worked out a compromise together.

It was on this occasion that Adelaide Tambo recalled the tension between the two friends. On the first morning of an international conference organised jointly by UNESCO and the OAU in Brussels a few months after the Accord, Machel's face lit up when he saw Tambo.

'Shall we breakfast together?' he suggested. Tambo's face clouded over.

'No, Samora,' he said sternly. 'What are we saying to the people? They have been chased out of Mozambique.'

Afterwards, Adelaide urged her husband, 'Don't let the Boers divide us.'[140]

On a diplomatic level, Thabo Mbeki recalled Tambo's handling of the situation and the gentle direction that he provided. Part of the Accord required that ANC members in Mozambique be given notice to leave the country. Even those who were in hospital – including pregnant women receiving treatment in antenatal clinics – were asked to leave. This was shoddy treatment, felt the ANC.

'There was a tremendous amount of anger among our people; among the majority of the leadership there was an insistence that we must denounce, publicly, this betrayal,' recalled Thabo Mbeki. What was particularly galling, he added, was that Mozambique sought to portray this as a victory. Machel, it seems, sincerely believed that the South African regime had been propelled into an agreement that the West would ensure would be honoured.[141] 'It wasn't a victory, but even if it was, it was achieved at a cost of great pain and a great reversal. Angry meetings wanted tough measures to be taken. It was a hard time.'[142]

But Tambo's answer, remembered Thabo Mbeki, was considered and strategic: 'Let us look at this as it affects us now, but let us also think of tomorrow', advised OR. 'How will this decision influence that tomorrow that we seek? How will our response to this matter, determine the situation in a year's time?' In public, Tambo responded in a statesmanlike way.

'I am not sure that in their position I would have gone quite as far as they have,' he told a press conference in London. 'But it must be accepted that the South African government, the South African regime, had decided to destroy Mozambique, to kill it as a state, and got pretty close to doing so. Mozambique, the leadership of Mozambique, were forced to choose, as it were, between life and death. They chose life, and life meant talking to the butchers of southern Africa; it meant hugging the hyena... For the rest of us, we must accept our position, but defend our own positions, defend our struggle.'[143]

'Tambo had the capacity to move from concrete to abstract', explained Mbeki. 'He could deal with the particulars of the current situation but at same time look into the abstract of the future'.

Soon after the Accord, a Front Line States meeting was held in Arusha, with Julius Nyerere in the chair. Everyone spoke. Clearly, there was general criticism of the Accord. Machel spoke, and explained that it was a victory for Mozambique to get South Africa to agree to cease interfering and destabilising its socialist neighbour. But when his turn came to speak, Kaunda corrected Machel.

'Let us agree that this is a defeat,' he recommended. 'Then we can strategise how to overcome the situation, rather than accept the status imposed on you.'

Nyerere called upon Tambo to speak last. Tambo spoke in his usual slow, deliberate way, to make sure that his audience was following his line of reasoning, his eyes moving from left to right, as if fixed on an imaginary text.

'The Mozambican people have made great sacrifices in the struggle for our liberation,' he began. 'It is a newly independent country, and it is in a weak position.' He then went on to outline the difficult economic relationship between Mozambique and South Africa. They had stood up to their powerful neighbour, he acknowledged, but the balance of forces had prevailed. 'If they did not retreat, Mozambique would be destroyed. We need to support them. They had to retreat – if they did not, they would not have survived. This has, of course, negative consequences for us, but we should think through the steps to overcome the situation.'[144]

Afterwards, Nyerere expressed his amazement: 'I do not understand the ANC. I would have thought you would be the angriest in our meeting – we are angry and you are not.'

'Yes, we all understand it...' agreed Tambo, '– its consequences and so on... Intrinsically there is nothing wrong with that response; but if you look at the abstract, the future, it is not necessary to respond that way. Respond differently to get different results in the future. Don't fight Mozambique.'

For Thabo Mbeki, this was an 'outstanding example' of how Tambo educated the ANC and provided leadership. 'The result was [that] we did not need Mozambique; they did not treat us as a hostile force. In fact, we did not leave Mozambique at all. In reality, the Nkomati Accord didn't do much to change our situation in Mozambique... That was the style of OR's leadership. And, of course, people would question it: "But why is OR being so soft? Why is he busy protecting Samora Machel?" But, of course, in a little while, when they saw what was happening, they then understood that it was much better not to have denounced Samora Machel, no matter how wrong the Nkomati Accord was. If you were looking at *the future*, it was much better not to.'[145]

Practically and strategically, Tambo's response was to reaffirm that 'in the totality of this situation' the ANC had 'to stand up and make revolution!'[146] And indeed, the South African regime was to learn that there were unintended consequences to its supposed success. As Tambo commented to sympathetic journalists at the time:

'The Matola Raid increased the readiness of neighbouring states to support us to the extent that they refused to be terrorised; they refused to be bullied... I detected a determination which I was not quite aware of, in reaction to the Matola raid. Mozambique, far from feeling that we were a source of danger and that we should keep out of their country, faced South Africa very squarely, and it started to mobilise to meet any other invasion that might come.'[147]

The Nkomati Accord proved to be a positive turning point for the ANC. It pushed the movement back to its most fundamental 'rear base', to the people of South Africa, back home, thus escalating the struggle and hastening the demise of the apartheid regime.

By the mid-1980s, Tambo's *indima* diplomacy had garnered support from far corners of the world, and had exposed the iniquities of apartheid to many layers of the international community. In the streets of the Western world, in Austria, the Netherlands, Ireland and Scotland, the USA and Canada, people marched in protest against apartheid South Africa. In Indian schools, children had learnt the story of the struggle, and sang 'Nkosi Sikelel' iAfrika', the anthem of the movement. In New Zealand and Australia, warm support for the anti-apartheid movement was amassing – indeed, some changed the name of their local organisations to the 'Anti-Apartheid Movement to Support the ANC'. Governments, both national and local, East and West, were bestowing honours on the ANC and its icons. In the region, special relations had been put together, and South Africa's neighbours had come to understand, from experience and from Tambo, that their fate was inseparable. With liberation movements further north, as Thabo Mbeki observed, 'countries like Algeria and Morocco, because of their own struggles, had taken particular positions, and we had very close relations with them'.[148]

In relation to the independent countries in Africa, the ANC had become 'more interactive, more part of the common army for the liberation of the continent rather than... coming to them as petitioners... there was something also that was particularly special'.[149]

Far, far away from the Engeli Mountains, Oliver Tambo's ANC was helping to chart a new, rich atlas of struggle. Its team had fashioned a landscape of several 'political geographies' – the international, the national, the regional and the 'people-to-people' terrain of the local.[150] This worldwide territory was mapped out with the generous support of the socialist bloc, the anti-apartheid movements, the churches, the trade unions and civil society in England, Scandinavia and the capitals of Western Europe and North America. Its landscape swept across the vicinities of the United Nations, the Organisation of African Unity, the Non-Aligned Movement, AAPSO and the Socialist Bloc. Tambo's ANC was steadily revealing the universality of apartheid, the crude and brutal injustices perpetrated on the 'other'. Its relevance was global. It was a concept that was to continue to blight the world and spread its stain into the next millennium. The anti-apartheid struggle, led by the ANC, sensitised the international community, laying the foundations of other struggles for democracy and respect for humanity in its diverse peoples and cultures.

Indeed, as one commentator remarked, 'No other post-World War Two struggle for decolonisation has been so fully globalized; no other has magnetised so many people across such national divides, or imbued them with such a resilient sense of common cause.'[151]

This outstanding phenomenon owed the major part of its success to Oliver Tambo's *indima* diplomacy, laid down step by step, acre by acre, in the long hard years of struggle.

CHAPTER SEVENTEEN

The Road to People's Power

EARLY IN 1988, OLIVER TAMBO TOOK AN UNUSUAL STEP that set alarm bells ringing in the upper echelons of Umkhonto we Sizwe. He called for a full emergency meeting of the Politico-Military Council (PMC) to determine exactly what was happening within South Africa. The previous year had seen a record 234 armed attacks inside the country by MK.[1] For the movement's army, this was grounds for satisfaction. But some of the 'soft' targets, such as the bombing of two popular fast-food outlets, were clearly causing Tambo some uneasiness. Apprehensively, Joe Modise, Chris Hani and Steve Tshwete, Commander, Chief-of-Staff and Commissar of the army respectively, held a quick caucus.

'We are not going to escape OR's censure,' Steve Tshwete predicted.[2]

Tambo's disapproval could, they knew, be devastatingly bruising. He would not become angry: even worse for those who prided themselves on their senior positions and their political acumen, he would be coldly analytical.

'These are the implications,' he would say, 'and this is how they are going to affect the image and the integrity of this organisation.'

The outcome was inescapable: the perceived culprits felt intellectually inadequate and politically immature. After all, there was no way that, as the top MK officials, any of the three could plead ignorance, or excuse themselves that they had not issued instructions to attack civilian targets. The best tactic, they agreed, was to say nothing rather than try to defend ill-chosen targets.[3]

All 18 members of the PMC turned out. Tambo spoke quietly.

'If there is anything systemic about apartheid,' he said, 'it is its criminal character, its structural violence, its systematic and ongoing injury to life and property; while the ANC's most meaningful, symbolic strength – despite its tactical shift since the SADF massacres on our members as well as civilians in Mozambique, Lesotho and elsewhere – lay in its moral high ground. It is therefore essential that the heavy sacrifices made in the 27 years since the movement was driven underground should not be undermined by short-sighted actions.'

In response, those in the political machinery came out one after the other to agree that the attacks had been morally and politically wrong. Soft targets contradicted the ANC's non-racial struggle and the inclusive message that the movement was aiming to send to the people of South Africa.

Chris Hani, the most outgoing of the three military men, could hold back no longer. Despite Tshwete's warning scowl, he spoke out. The problem was, Hani was anxious to explain, that MK was not always on the ground; it was sometimes impossible to pilot that kind of activity, given the distance from Lusaka to Johannesburg or Durban. The lines of communication were long – it was an achievement even to get the cadres to reach their destination.

There was no question of disputing the policy itself. Despite more than 20 years of avoiding the loss of life, as Tambo and others had so often explained, the ANC still maintained a policy of selective targets. A target such as Johannesburg's Ellis Park Stadium, which was bombed immediately after a rugby match in July 1988, causing the deaths of white rugby fans, 'does not fall within our practice', Tambo declared. Tambo was speaking to Radio Maputo, a station accessed by supporters in South Africa. 'It is not part of our policy. We are clear in our policy. We attack the military, we attack the police, and we warn that in those actions people not intending to be hit, will be hit. But the targets will be perfectly clear.'[4]

Since 1985, when the ANC conference in Kabwe had determined that while it would continue to avoid 'soft' targets, it could no longer allow the possibility that civilians might be accidentally injured in attacks to constrain the actions of MK as it had done in the past. Therein lay the blurring or nuancing of tactics and principles, providing grounds for misunderstanding. It would require highly dextrous leadership to convey even to the senior members of the movement the fine balance between encouraging mass insurrection on one hand, and regulating a revolution on the other. The way forward was through the agency and power of the people themselves to render, in a multiplicity of ways, the apartheid regime unworkable and therefore the country ungovernable.

The roots of 'people's power' lay in the visit of a Tambo-led delegation of the ANC to Vietnam in October 1978. The sojourn proved to be 'a watershed in our strategic approach'.[5] Disturbed by the ANC's failure to take advantage of the 1976 uprising in Soweto, Tambo had called together a meeting of the senior organs to assess and undertake a strategic review of the movement's performance. Seven years after Morogoro, it seemed that the restructuring of the movement to facilitate a closer synergy between the military and the political had failed to function as planned. The ANC had not been ready to seize the momentum of that explosive event. Soweto 1976 might have been the spark, the conflagration for which the liberation movement had been waiting 15 years, and which Oliver Tambo had warned of time and again in his speeches to the

ANC, to the regime and to the world at large. It had been an opportunity unforgivably missed.

The ANC underground, although operating fitfully and able to reach some of the youth in the urban areas, had not been able to take root. In part, this was because a 'mechanical attitude' had developed over the years. In practice, underground activity within the country tended to be confined to recruiting members for the armed struggle.[6] For young black men, the more dramatic and confrontational action of joining the armed struggle, to travel abroad, to train in a socialist country, to carry arms and to be prepared to pay the ultimate price for a noble cause seemed the natural and manly course to espouse. The less visible, slow and patient work inside, in the bleakly familiar dusty townships was far less glamorous. Even those who had started off in the political underground – such as Steve Tshwete, who had served 14 years on Robben Island, and after his release in 1978, built underground structures at home – were eventually spotted by the security. Tshwete himself had been instructed to leave the country immediately. The political structures had thus been 'denuded' of people operating at home.

The military, on the other hand, whose 'detonator' strategy had been to focus on the peasantry in rural terrain had not only suffered heavy losses in their attempted incursions back into the country via the homelands, but were nowhere near the townships when the countrywide urban uprisings spread. Where had the strategy gone wrong?

One thing that had become clearer to the ANC leadership was that the massive influx of young people to the ANC had occurred because of the reputation enjoyed by MK. So it was agreed to return to MK's first tactic, its concept of armed propaganda. This approach did not employ classic military combat, and eschewed confrontation with the other side in a direct encounter of military personnel. Rather, explained Joe Slovo, it entailed 'military activities... which inspired and gave people new courage inside, and hope'.[7] The agreement to adopt this tactic led to the establishment of a Special Operations Unit under Slovo's direction, which would select highly symbolic targets and mount 'spectacular armed propaganda attacks'.[8]

But the NEC and the Revolutionary Council could not but fail to observe that little of the upsurge of political and labour opposition at home seemed to have been directly initiated by the ANC underground. The question for the ANC now was, firstly, how to respond to these rapidly developing disparate activities and, secondly, how to direct these towards a coherent programme of national liberation. For too long, the ANC had acted as if the repressive conditions made mass legal and semi-legal work impossible.

'If the people had taught us anything through the initiatives they had taken in the preceding five years,' said Slovo, 'it was that the potential for political struggle [was] never exhausted... And if our own independent efforts had taught us anything, it was that our efforts would reach a dead end unless they had a broader political base.'[9]

Comparing their progress in this regard with other successful national resistance movements, the committee shifted its gaze from the armed insurrections of Algeria, Cuba and China to Vietnam, a small country that had succeeded in reuniting its people after decades of resistance against French colonialism and, more recently, US imperialism, and in pushing back foreign aggression by harnessing all the elements of opposition in that country.

In Vietnam, the Tambo delegation – senior leaders Moses Mabhida, Cassius Make, Joe Modise, Joe Slovo and Thabo Mbeki, now a member of the NEC – underwent an intensive programme of lectures and site visits. Tambo's notes on the sojourn convey the instructive and inspiring nature of the experience. The group were taken to the tunnels near Saigon – intricate networks leading from homes and spreading for kilometres underground. These had been dug clandestinely by young people ostensibly walking into the woods and emerging from the tunnels with bags of soil, which they discreetly sprinkled on the ground. The tunnels provided extensive shelter and sustenance for military cadres, activists, refugees and villagers hiding from the devastation of shootings and napalm bombs. Vast storage operations of munitions, food, water and clothing were set up there; even cattle were kept in pens, feeding on the grass brought to them in students' backpacks. Deeper underground was a small command centre that oversaw all operations.[10]

Talks were given by activists and theoreticians, including workers ('the most exploited in our society, also equipped with Marxist-Leninist ideology, therefore possesses the most revolutionary spirit', Tambo summarised in his notebook); an activist Christian minister and a nun, whose testimony particularly interested Tambo; community women, youth, students, artists and intellectuals.

The church minister described his activities in the community: 'We participated in the student struggle against the rise of fees, joined workers in demanding the rise of salaries... we put up slogans close to the aspirations of the people. Because I was a priest, people did not think I could work with communists.'[11]

He was able to shelter four Party members in his house, and when the authorities posted agents to spy on him, he even managed to convert the informers to the cause, protecting both his operation and the turned agents. What struck Tambo most was the connection between the spiritual and material influences on the dedication of the young revolutionaries. The priest had spoken eloquently of the dangers of the corruption of values and morality by an evil regime. The delegation heard how social, cultural and sports organisations of women, youth, and even children were given missions to undertake liaison work, the distribution of leaflets, take part in community, student and worker demonstrations and strikes, organise sports events as well as social relief work, including funerals.

Trade unions, perhaps the most powerful sector in the country, had been encouraged to form alliances with the peasantry, who comprised 90 per cent of the population but were dispersed and engaged in individual forms of production. The arts, too, were marshalled into revolutionary work. 'The enemy distorted Vietnamese culture,' they were told, 'to pervert the youth.' Concerts with patriotic music, songs, public poetry readings and theatre all sought 'to facilitate the broad alliance through knowledge and education'.[12] Tambo noted with interest a student presentation, 'using all forms of struggle – all idiosyncrasies, characteristics and features of different strata of society'.[13]

The group met with General Vo Nguyen Giap, and from him they heard how the Vietnamese Workers' Party (the VWP – or LaoDong – which would become the Communist Party of Vietnam) had constructed a National United Front (NUF) in Vietnam, building contacts with both legal and semilegal forms, taking care to keep these strictly separate.

'A military person in Saigon was never allowed to be in possession of a party pamphlet – for security, in case they were caught and linked,' explained Joe Slovo. 'And a political cadre underground was never allowed to possess a weapon in case there was a raid and he was linked then with the military.' The NUF had been careful not to be domineering but to be guided by the organisations on the ground. Tambo noted Ho Chi Minh's comment, also relevant to the ANC's aim of re-entering popular consciousness. 'Only through [the Party's] daily actions and struggles,' Ho had said, 'will its leadership be recognised by the masses.'[14]

The 'important, vital strategic principle: politics is the foundation for successful armed struggle', Tambo summarised. 'This accounts for the fact that a small country, a small population, a backward country, a small army, could defeat the most powerful imperialist country.' The guiding strategic slogan for the NUF was: 'Walk on Both Feet (military and political).'

Tambo was deeply moved and excited by what he saw. There were lessons to be learnt, though they need not be derivative, he noted. There were similarities in their colonial history and in the inclusiveness of their struggle, but the visit also highlighted the ANC's own weaknesses thus far. The trip to Vietnam had provided the Tambo delegation with an opportunity to witness first-hand the synergy, in the revolutionary pursuit, of mass struggle, the underground and the army. The experience was to confirm the ANC's vision of calling on all South Africans to unite under the Freedom Charter. The Vietnam strategy had supplied just such an inclusive programme; under the guidance, often discreetly, of the National Liberation Front, the population was mobilised into underground and semi-legal organisations with one aim in mind, noted Tambo – to bring about revolutionary social change to achieve 'one people, one country'.

Following the 1978 Vietnam visit, Tambo chaired a report-back meeting to the NEC and the RC in Luanda in December. They noted the 'golden thread of the strategic thinking of the VWP', and mandated a Politico-Military Strategy Commission to consider a strategy on mass mobilisation. The Commission consisted of Tambo, SACP General-Secretary Moses Mabhida, Joe Gqabi, Joe Modise, Joe Slovo and Thabo Mbeki. Mac Maharaj, who, after 10 years on Robben Island, had arrived in exile shortly before with news and political interpretations, participated in the Maputo meetings that followed.[15] Their brief was fourfold: to consider ways of creating the 'broadest possible national front for liberation'; the reinforcing of the underground by drawing in 'activists thrown up by mass struggle'; the proliferation of political operations; and the establishment of a central coordinating body inside the country.[16]

First, though, members had to spell out 'fundamental propositions',[17] which led to some intriguing debates. Tambo himself had been exhilarated by the visit, and had been struck by the adeptness of the Vietnamese Workers' Party in elevating the values of virtually the entire population and hence drawing them into the liberation struggle. In the context of the successes of the Marxist-Leninist liberation movements of Frelimo and Angola's MPLA and the burgeoning of the democratic labour movement at home, he seemed to look with favour upon Slovo's question as to whether the time had not come for the ANC to position itself more clearly as a socialist party – Was the feeling, perhaps inspired by Vietnam, to return to the African culture of communal sharing and humanism? This was a bold and surprising proposition, especially if Oliver Tambo supported it. Thabo Mbeki, though himself a leading member of the SACP at the time, reminded the group that the ANC was a broad, multi-class national liberation movement that had to appeal to all sections of the populace. 'It was wrong,' Mbeki recalled much later, 'the notion that the ANC was a party of socialism. I said, "Well, if that is the case, then what is the SACP doing? You might as well dissolve it."'[18]

He obtained the agreement of Moses Mabhida that the SACP existed to promote socialism.[19] There was to be, therefore, no immediate subtext in the ANC's quest for broad, mass support.

In the process of the discussion, Tambo wanted to ensure a thorough understanding of the consensus. 'Consensus, too,' pointed out the report, 'needs to be explicitly spelt out to avoid misperceptions.'[20] This was another intriguing turn – an awareness that consensus could be a double-edged sword. Its downside could be the coercion of people into agreeing in meetings to something against their convictions in order to please the powerful and articulate. It was thus to Tambo's credit that he was consistently aware of this danger, and patiently allowed discussion to be prolonged, scrupulously making certain that everyone had expressed their views before summarising what he perceived to be the import of the views, reconciling the opinions into a workable decision. Joe Slovo, himself tending to argue forcibly for his own passionate, Marxist-revolutionary convictions, was nevertheless able to observe and appreciate Tambo's style as head of a collective leadership as a skilful listener. Tambo, he remarked in admiration, was able to pull together the tendencies expressed in the meeting so that the group as a whole was able to own the decisions and indeed articulately and convincingly represent them to their constituencies.[21]

Tambo summarised the concern of the meeting for the minutes:

'We've been forced by events into a false, a bad strategic situation in which armed struggle is and remains the basis of political struggle – an impossible equation. [It is] necessary to correct this distortion... Necessary to recognise that our approach is an external approach: we see the struggle as being built up from outside, introduced from outside by people who are outside... This approach wholly excludes the people, the masses, as the decisive factor not only for victory, but for any progress at all in our struggle... [We] see a serious strategic problem to solve before we can hope to make advances. Hence the view that we slow down on [military] operations and work for a change in the order of priority as between political work and military operation.'[22]

The strategic review (also known as 'The Green Book'[23]) issued its findings in March 1979. A wide range of senior ANC members had been consulted – Yusuf Dadoo and Reggie September were invited to discuss the effects of the imposition of apartheid institutions on coloured people and Indians. The SACTU executive committee submitted a written briefing that was reproduced in the final report, and the SACP tabled a discussion document on the Bantustans. The women's and youth sections also submitted reports, and the regions, too, provided inputs. The strategic review was praised, in the words of Chris Hani – who was operating in Lesotho, for 'creating an organisational structure which, from top to bottom, is designed to plan and coordinate all aspects of internal work under the immediate direction of a single political collective, serviced by specialist departments'.[24]

The Commission proposed a bolder intervention – as Tambo himself had pointed out, apartheid's contradictions were emerging and mass resistance was growing. The review recommended that two policy decisions be implemented: military struggle was to be subordinated to the political imperatives through acts of sabotage on symbolically selected targets – that is, armed propaganda; and a programme of non-collaboration. Spelt out, this meant the employment of the boycott weapon as a way of actively involving every South African opponent of apartheid. The logical consequence would be that every opposition organisation would be active in rejecting apartheid.

The priority, then, was to 'attract the broadest possible spectrum of groups, organisations, and individuals engaged against the regime'.[25] Lacking a significant base at home, the ANC leadership realised they had missed opportunities to assess the potential of the Black Consciousness Movement and the re-emergence of the labour movement because the ANC had not kept their ear to the ground by means of a widespread internal base. They saw, too, the mistake they had made in rejecting the 'workerist' tendency of the FOSATU unions, with their emphasis on shop floor rather than political issues.[26] Rather than engaging with organisers of the trade-union federation (if only to prevent the formation of a 'third force' in the labour movement), the ANC tended to rely on the armed struggle. Yet it had been the militant agitation of FOSATU's affiliated unions that had forced the regime to grant the black unions official recognition. There was a growing respect among the ANC, despite the narrow outlook of some FOSATU unions, for their organisational and mobilising ability. 'The ruling class is no longer able to evade some form of recognition of black trade unions,' remarked the report. While black men and women had been stripped of almost all legitimate means to oppose the apartheid regime, workers were still in possession of their most potent weapon – the power of their labour. It was imperative, urged the report, that the ANC ensure that the regime did not succeed in cultivating 'trade unions concerned solely with petty reforms and isolated from the national liberation struggle... Time,' it continued, 'is indeed very short for our movement to ensure the emergence of a trade union movement which will have the capacity to act in the interests of our revolution'.[27]

The way forward, therefore, was 'to join hands with all opposition groups based around a broad, minimum programme'. Slovo, who had written a summary of the findings, commented on the essence of the report: '"Every organised act of opposition and defiance to tyranny and racism, every struggle for better conditions", was a "blow struck for the revolution". The ANC realised that it could not afford to slight any organisation simply because it did not embrace immediately the ANC.'[28]

The challenge, though, was to facilitate sectoral political struggles and direct them towards an over-arching national vision. 'Many of the struggles that our people had waged were around local issues,' recalled Tambo in 1985. 'The situation had therefore arisen in which it was necessary and possible to bring the mass movement together, to influence it to act as one and to focus the minds of our people beyond local national issues.'[29]

Once again, the ANC had demonstrated its strategic pragmatism – it drew on its long tradition, learning to play situations by ear, as it had done in the fifties. The Internal Reconstruction Department estimated that its underground membership was a mere 300–500 operatives, with whom the movement was able to maintain limited and uneven communication. The Commission conceded that its customary vanguard role might not be the best option in rebuilding a mass base; the movement could derive significant advantages by being flexible, recognising the autonomy of its potential constituencies in existing opposition organisations inside the country while attempting to influence them.

There came also the realisation that the terrain of struggle needed to be shifted from the rural areas, which had not succeeded in igniting the spark of resistance. 'Sending strangers to villages no good,' Tambo had scribbled in a memo. 'Sending strangers to terrain dangerous for the strangers. They can only be reported to the police because they are strangers.' And he added: 'Start with militia, self-defence etc., from among politically active masses.'[30]

Popular political consciousness was being rekindled in the urban terrain. It offered more resources, better communication lines and an accessible array of media. The concept of armed propaganda had already been reformulated earlier by a structure called the Senior Organ. In a sense, it helped to rationalise the losses of MK thus far. From 1976 and 1978, according to the South African Police, out of 37 incursions, 35 cadres were rendered inoperative – either killed or arrested.[31] Of course, these figures did not take into account the obvious – that the apartheid institutions were covering up both the number of MK attacks and their successes. Be that as it may, the Senior Organ was mindful of the impact of armed incursions on the public. While many were not reported at all, where MK cadres were captured, there were trials. Even when held in camera, these were reported by the papers, and though subject to restrictions, largely welcomed by the black population.

The notion of armed propaganda, then, which had been formulated in MK's infancy in the early sixties, was reactivated to become official policy. In addition, the decision at Morogoro in 1969 – which essentially had not been carried out – was also reaffirmed: military actions should be guided by political imperatives. Classical armed struggle was therefore to be 'temporarily' shelved until such time as it might be employed to mobilise the populace towards conducting a 'People's War'. But this could only happen once political structures, both underground and those operating legally in various community structures, were in place. The Commission's 'strategic' review was discussed and adopted by the NEC in August 1979. Thereafter, the ANC structures began to attempt to implement the resolutions.

High-profile military acts were now stepped up, demonstrations of armed propaganda. A team was set up. The skill of Special Operations Unit head Joe Slovo was such that, despite the conscious shift towards the political, funding for the project was acquired directly from the President's Office. Almost immediately, a crack team was selected from the many hundreds of eager cadres in the camps. Those chosen felt privileged to become part of the Unit. They were grouped into small teams and were carefully briefed on their particular operation. Adhering to the principle of 'hard targets' – that is, attacking state installations and only those personnel serving the most oppressive institutions of the apartheid regime, such as the army or police force – each operation sent a small advance team on reconnaissance missions. The scouts were selected because they were fluent in the language of the local community and were sufficiently familiar with the local landscape to stake out the proposed site.

Rashid, for instance, who had taught in the camps and had been seconded to 'Special Ops', was posted to Natal to assess the feasibility of blowing up a power station in Durban. Working on a shoestring budget, he had just enough money to stay in a cheap boarding house with meals provided, but not enough to hire a car. After a month of 'casing the joint', he concluded that the task itself would be easy to undertake, but the snag was that collateral damage might occur, as the tower adjoined the township of Merebank. 'If the tower went off and there was a cloud of gas, it could have carried over the residential area... a gas cloud explosion would have been detrimental to us politically. And, therefore, a decision was taken that we should not go for that target.'[32] So, on Rashid's return and report-back, Special Ops decided to scrap the project.

In all, MK managed to inflict 17 recorded armed incidents between November 1978 (after the Vietnam visit) and March 1980. These included economic installations such as railway tracks and fuel depots, the most spectacular and highly publicised being the oil refineries in Sasolburg and Secunda, 'when Umkhonto we Sizwe set racist South Africa ablaze', to quote Tambo.[33] Special Ops hit four police stations, a magistrate's court, a labour bureau that administered passes, and executed two hit-and-run attacks – one in Soweto and the other in the Northern Transvaal village of Soekmekaar – as well as two civilian targets.[34] One of the latter, highly publicised, was not planned by Special Ops, but was a spontaneous action undertaken by a unit that had been isolated from its command due to a breakdown in communications. It involved an unprecedented siege of a Volkskas Bank in Silverton, Pretoria, in which three armed combatants held customers hostage before they were shot dead by the police.

Tambo, while praising the courage and sacrifice of the combatants, was not comfortable about all the events. He was aware that the cadres had been caught out and had to make an instant, desperate stand that would publicise their act. The formal statement issued by the ANC leadership was ambiguous – it did not specifically endorse the action of those MK cadres. Yet, despite the losses, there could be no doubt that the overwhelming majority of the people inside the country responded positively to MK attacks.[35] People recognised its message as an example of military propaganda, and a warning to the apartheid regime. The funeral in Soweto of one MK combatant in the siege drew 10 000 mourners. Durban's *Daily News* reported an opinion survey, which revealed that three out of four residents of Soweto were sympathetic to these MK men.[36]

To the international audience, Tambo explained the context of not so much a change as a 'development of strategy'. He was speaking on the day three MK militants were hanged in Pretoria, and was reaffirming the determination by the ANC to pursue the armed struggle until South Africa was liberated. 'For 20 years,' he explained, 'we have resorted to prudent and selective violence.

'We have attacked material targets and not individuals. We wanted to be sure that nobody suffered the slightest scratch. In reply to that, our people were killed, imprisoned, and tortured, and it is becoming unreasonable to pay so dearly for our actions.

'When we attacked the SASOL installations, we did not kill anybody. They responded by killing 12 of our militants in Matola. During the raid on Maseru in Lesotho, they killed several dozens of our people, and their supporters congratulated them. Their own operations show an escalation in the conflict.'[37]

Meanwhile, international media constantly raised the issue of civilian deaths.

'Each time there is talk of civilian victims, it is whites that are referred to,' observed Tambo. 'How many black civilians have been killed in 30 years of apartheid? Thousands. The people who died in Sharpeville and Soweto were not soldiers. Steve Biko was a civilian.'

Oliver Tambo had the ability of always convincingly inserting an element of humanism into MK actions. He reminded his interrogators that the armed struggle had been imposed on the ANC. 'When a woman dies or child dies because they were at the scene of an explosion, we are heartbroken. Our target is the enemy forces, the apartheid regime.'[38]

Besides creating diplomatic flak for Tambo internationally, the attacks on civilians also emphasised for him and the Revolutionary Council the need to achieve greater synergy between the military and the political. The lack of an organised political base had more than once forced MK cadres to handle crises on the spot, resulting in abandoning the rules, executing unplanned, panic attacks and incurring greater losses. Sue Rabkin, who worked in the political structures in the forward area of Mozambique, recalled MK cadres reporting back to their bases in Mozambique or Swaziland after their assignments saying: 'We can't do it like this. We can't just go in and hit. What are we doing it for? We've got to get the people to help us. We've got to get them involved. Because only then can we be protected.'[39]

Steadily, the ANC underground was growing, both formally and informally, not least because of the impact of armed propaganda. In one of those repeated ironies of apartheid, the detention after the death of Steve Biko of 47 activists of various persuasions brought them together for the first time in a communal cell in a prison in Modder B. Among the 47 were members of the underground ANC: Popo Molefe, Diliza Mji, Jackie Selebi and Curtis Nkondo. For these activists, it had become clear, as Popo Molefe put it, that: 'the only instrument through which our freedom could be attained was the African National Congress and in particular through its armed wing, Umkhonto we Sizwe. It was clear to all of us at that stage that the movement [the ANC] was the only organisation which had the facilities to train us, to prepare us to fight for our freedom'.[40]

The 47 held intensive discussions about strategic ways forward. 'These leaders,' Tambo was to observe later, 'had the opportunity to discuss the perspectives of our struggle. Thanks to the position taken by many of these, including leaders of the now-banned SASO, a majority view had emerged clearly in favour of the ANC as the authentic representative of our people.'[41]

It was decided to begin by forming a new student body following the banning of the South African Students Movement (SASM). Astutely, the ANC caucus was able to acquire the leadership positions as well as a significant minority of the grass-roots membership. Curtis Nkondo was elected as chairman of the historically BC-oriented AZAPO. The scheme was assisted by the work of Joe Gqabi, who had developed networks in Soweto before he 'skipped' in 1978 and was now deployed in Botswana. He and Aurelia Gqabi, who had remained behind in Soweto, made contact anew with the students and briefed them to support the formation of AZASO for school students, and COSAS for those in tertiary education. Underground members were told to go easy on ideology at first, concentrating on building cordial relations, sharing platforms with BC speakers or indeed, as stated by COSAS at its launch in September 1979, with 'any progressive group whose policy and politics are similar to those of ours'.[42] Within months, dozens of AZASO branches were established around the country, and steadily, many endorsed the principles of the Freedom Charter. By 1980, the ANC had reached a critical mass in the student bodies and was entering broad popular consciousness.

Mac Maharaj, who had brought messages of concern for Tambo from the Island regarding the slow progress of building the political structures at home, was appointed to head the Internal Reconstruction Department. Sitting in on the strategic review commission in Luanda, he had argued vigorously for prioritising the political base. Even before the Vietnam visit, he had set in motion initiatives for making contact at home through the political structures set up in the forward areas in Lesotho, Mozambique, Botswana and Swaziland. Instructing the underground cadres from their bases in Mozambique and Swaziland, he counselled them: '[Go] down to the people. This is a people's struggle. You know we have to build from the grass roots... [If] people... are complaining about their window panes being broken, take it up, write a leaflet. Deal with it. Organise around it. There is no issue that is too small.'[43]

Maharaj also recruited pharmacist Pravin Gordhan in Durban, who set up an underground unit of young professionals there. Their tactic was to avoid confrontational activities. Rather, in order to survive, like the FOSATU tactics with the workers on the shop floor in the seventies, they addressed bread-and-butter issues in the communities – at first in the Indian townships, but hoping to expand into the African areas. Their patient hard work resulted in the formation of the Durban Housing Action Committee. In the Eastern Cape, Chris Hani operating from Lesotho, helped to set up a black civic organisation PEBCO – the Port Elizabeth Black Civic Organisation – which was to play a significant, militant role in the 1980s. In the Transvaal, underground operatives were also working in both the African and Indian communities – in the schools and in civic organisations, beginning with the Soweto Civic Association.[44] Other initiatives were also being quietly probed.

Molefe recalled: '[By] 1980, in Soweto, I had started encouraging discussion around the need to create a mini-front. We were looking at the situation in Soweto, how we could draw in organisations in common campaigns and a common programme. We were thinking of FOSATU at the time, thinking of AZAPO, civic associations, women's groups and so on, student organisations – discussion was taking place, including the Black Municipality Workers' Union, you know the Joe Mabis, Martin Seris and Philip Dlaminis of the PAC.'[45]

Tambo's 8 January speech in 1979, Pallo Jordan pointed out, 'was the first example of Vietnam mission outcomes being translated into action'. Declaring the centenary of the Zulu battle of Isandhlwana 'The Year of the Spear', his speech set out to revive memories of military traditions of resistance to colonialism. He linked these memories to contemporary battles – not excluding smaller grass-roots struggles such as the resistance to removals and the 'Third Force' at Crossroads.[46] The following 8 January speech, in 1980, was another tool designed to reach South Africans. Broadcast on Radio Freedom and then published in March in *Sechaba*,[47] Tambo declared 1980 to be 'The Year of the Charter'. The following 26 June would be the 25th anniversary of the Congress of the People. Just two months earlier, Tambo was observing meticulously in his notebook the relevance of an inclusive programme of action that would bring together all opposition. 'Significant cracks are appearing in the monolith of racist domination,' he wrote. 'Democratic and progressive white South Africans, including in particular the youth and students, have recognised that the apartheid system is leading them to a disastrous dead-end and are fighting it with mounting vigour… Many are deserting from the army.'

As in Vietnam, apartheid as a system had worked 'to undermine the humanity of white South Africans... Racism has been used by a few to distort the normal humane nature of white people into bigoted racialists'.[48]

In his speech, Tambo also called for a campaign to popularise the Freedom Charter. Evoking the struggles of the 1950s, he called for united, mass action. He again rejected cooperation with apartheid's divisive structures, including the Bantustans and Botha's cosmetic reforms. 'How much longer shall we allow ourselves to be bought to serve the perpetuation of our own oppression?' he asked pointedly. In his own mind, Tambo was going over the Inkatha episode.

'The question of united action… ANC's historic function, role of leadership,' he jotted down in his notebook in November 1979. And that depended on 'how this function [is] performed in practice... Recently in circumstances which were as stunning to ANC leadership as it was to the mass of our people, reports of meeting between Inkatha and ANC'.

But the real issue, he observed, was 'not meeting with Inkatha but meeting with any one at all: Have spoken to leaders of Inkatha. It is up to them to use such meetings to strengthen or destroy the basis of mutual confidence, trust and understanding. The ANC supports patriotic organisations (not necessarily revolutionary) and, far from stabbing them in the back, it will go out of its way to strengthen their operational capability... and the ANC will never abandon them, no matter in what part of the country they have been *kraaled* and caged by the brutal racist regime'.

Tambo was still hoping to win over Inkatha as 'a patriotic organisation (not necessarily revolutionary)', by persuading them about the value of a united front. In his 1980 speech, Tambo left the door ajar. He warned against 'encouraging false divisions and antagonisms, as for instance between one ethnic group or so-called tribe and another, between one nationality and another, between our rural people and our urban people, between the young and the old, between the liberation movement inside the country and those described as "in exile", and indeed, strange to say, between the ANC and the rest of the patriotic forces in our country. It is understandable that the enemy should try to promote these antagonisms. It makes no sense that we should want to do it for them'.[49]

For Tambo and the ANC, the conditions for mass action seemed to be in place at last. It was the 'historic duty that rests on us as a people to liberate our country'. And, in an early hint of a more developed concept to come, Tambo spoke of considering the question of how 'to destroy or render inoperative' apartheid 'in all its forms'.

'The need for the unity of the patriotic and democratic forces of our country has never been greater than it is today... [It] has become clear to us that more dialogue is called for amongst us, the oppressed, to seek and find common responses to our common oppression.'[50]

Almost immediately after the speech was published in *Sechaba,* South Africa's two largest black newspapers, the *Post* and the *Sunday Post*, edited by Percy Qoboza, published the full text of the Freedom Charter.

In the meantime, faced with popular insurgency, the apartheid government was similarly reviewing its strategy and tactics. Following the resignation in 1978 of JB Vorster in a corruption scandal, PW Botha now stood at the helm. A paid official of the National Party since his youth, Botha had served the government for many years as Minister of Defence. It had been he, Tambo reminded the world, who 'had masterminded the Angolan invasion'.[51] Now prime minister, Botha appointed his disciple Magnus Malan as the new Minister of Defence. Malan had received training in the USA and with the colonial French forces in Algeria. He brought back with him the argument that a state needed to develop not merely a military but also an ideological strategy for war. Malan was influenced by the proposition from anti-Soviet writers who argued that the Western world faced a 'total onslaught'. The concept had been used by Winston Churchill to mobilise the British people against the Nazi threat of invasion during the Second World War, but it was now seen to be applied by the Soviet Bloc and also by the People's Republic of China to conquer the entire capitalist system. Botha and his think-tank were also influenced by a thesis on counter-revolutionary war, which advocated the implementation of counter-terrorism and the elimination of revolutionaries.[52] The ANC and its military wing, which had been tutored in Soviet Bloc camps, were not only a threat to apartheid, but to 'Western civilisation' and to Christianity itself. Certainly the ANC's 'four pillars' of struggle, which Tambo often expounded in his speeches, seemed to embody an all-encompassing terrain of revolution – a 'total onslaught'.

In reply, the Botha regime proposed a 'total strategy'. This was conceived as a policy of both carrot and stick that would woo the black elite in the Bantustans, nurture and co-opt a black middle class in the cities, and carry over JB Vorster's earlier plan to co-opt Indians and coloureds into separate legislative chambers of Parliament – to which Tambo had responded in 1977: 'This is yet another attempt by Vorster to win time for apartheid, which of course we reject. It is also an attempt to destroy the growing unity among the victims of oppression. We demand a parliament for the entire population.'[53]

'Botha's Total Strategy (for what?),' figured Tambo in his notebook in 1982; 'to be assured of support among black bourgeoisie in urban areas and upper ruling class in bantustans', Botha had pulled a fast one on those who had tried to negotiate some space within the apartheid system. He had, for example, 'taken the ground from under the... feet of the Committee of Ten by giving them what they asked for – semi-autonomy in Soweto'.[54]

The move was ideological as much as tactical, Tambo saw, for in 'modernising' apartheid, the total strategy included changing the African culture of sharing and collective problem-solving.

'The people have been nurtured in capitalistic expectations,' reflected Tambo. '[The] racist strategy is to meet these expectations: (You want a big house and a big car – *voila!* You want to be a big business man – Done! Dinner at the Carlton – *Pajalsta!*' But for the ANC, this stratagem also revealed a defensive retreat by the enemy, and needed a tactical response. It was essential to examine the enemy's new tactics.

'How do we exploit it?' Tambo asked. 'How [to] defeat its intention and counter its objective effects? How [to] expose enemy strategy as dangerous and win new opposition to [the] enemy over and against that strategy?'

The new prime minister was overbearing and domineering – his nickname was '*Groot Krokodil*' (Great Crocodile). Botha had created an Office of the Prime Minister soon after his succession, and set up an interdepartmental State Security Council (SSC), in which the military was paramount.[55] To contain opposition, Botha's 'total strategy' embraced legal as well as illegal methods: 'dirty tricks' now became a regular occurrence. These included murder and assassinations, at home and abroad; disinformation provided by fake pamphlets; plants; smears on individuals, accusing them of being apartheid informers; harassment (death messages, poisoning clothes, and hanging dead animals at activists' front doors); and actively encouraging divisions in the black community (for example, by issuing false and provocative leaflets, fanning intolerance between AZAPO and the UDF, Inkatha and the UDF, and AZAPO and Inkatha), and the detention and torture of thousands of people. As Tambo pointed out, Botha's 'total strategy' dramatically elevated the conflict and violence inside South Africa to a new level.[56]

The SCC had powers to vote massive sums of money, operate secretly in the 'interests of the state' and bypass accountability to Parliament. Apartheid legislation already gave the authorities a wide range of powers to harass and oppress opponents – indeed, it encouraged the creation of a police state, with a 'cop-culture' that absolved them from public accountability, or even the need to give convincing explanations for torture, murder or abductions to the law courts.[57] The memorandum of the Detainees Support Committee, initiated by relatives of detainees, published in April 1982 claimed that 82 per cent of a sample of 175 detainees claimed to have been physically tortured. The Department of Psychology at the University of Cape Town came to the same conclusion.[58]

But this generous licence was not enough; it was but a small step from torture to assassination. In November 1981, human rights lawyer (and in the ANC underground) Griffiths Mxenge was stabbed to death in a staged robbery. Eight years later, three security policemen confessed to assassinating him. 'Make a plan with Griffiths Mxenge,' Brigadier Jan van der Hoven, the security chief in Natal, is alleged to have said. 'We tried to build a case against him, but failed. We just do not have enough evidence to charge him.'[59]

In the years that followed, at least 81 more men and women were killed inside South Africa by the death-squad operation. Abroad, ANC members also suffered grievous losses. In the same year as the killing of Mxenge, Joe Gqabi was shot at point-blank range in his car in Harare, Zimbabwe. Then, in August 1982, Ruth First was killed in her office at the Eduardo Mondlane University in Maputo by a parcel bomb doctored under the orders of Craig Williamson, the spy who had earlier infiltrated the ANC in Europe. Two years later, ANC member Jeanette Schoon and her six-year-old daughter Katryn died in Botswana by the same method. In 1986, prominent activists Dr Fabian and Florence Ribeiro were gunned down in their home in Mamelodi. The numbers escalated as the decade wore on. Mass killings through SADF attacks on ANC quarters in the southern African states occurred again and again – in Botswana, Lesotho, Mozambique, Zambia and Zimbabwe, not only of ANC members but also civilians. Individual ANC members, such as Ebrahim Ebrahim, were kidnapped in Swaziland and driven across the border with impunity into South Africa. MK cadres were seized or captured in neighbouring countries, and either 'turned' through torture, or were killed. Those who were forced to confess, betray and kill for apartheid's security system became known as Askaris.

Botha's total strategy included, too, the introduction of a 'Third Force', as Tambo himself observed in 1982: 'A third force. Deliberately created by those who could not, who failed to manoeuvre the ANC into an instrument for their own ends. Our history (the history of our struggle) is not without striking examples of attempts to defeat that struggle by sponsoring rival groups.'[60]

This comprehensive range of methods was to be applied, with devastating effect, throughout Botha's turbulent reign of office, and well beyond. But the one area the Botha regime, despite all its attempts to modernise white minority rule, was powerless to reform was the inbuilt, contradictory nature of apartheid. The wealth generated by the blatant exploitation of black workers created an ironic negation in the system. As the economy grew, so did the need for labour. The state was thus forced to allow more and more black workers into the towns and cities in order to service the growing industries – despite the policy of discouraging blacks from 'white' areas. Government's response was a more determined implementation of the migrant labour system, with the construction of more and bigger single-sex hostels for black workers in townships adjoining industrial areas, such as Alexandra township in Johannesburg and East Rand townships like Vosloorus, Thokoza or KwaThema. At the same time, the regime continued to execute the pass laws, harassing black men and women in their homes, in the streets, at work or at leisure, with harsh determination.

In the 1980s, South Africa was hit by a major economic recession. In 1982, the price of gold fell in the wake of OPEC's sudden increase in the price of oil. Gold continued to drop through 1983 and 1984. The government, desperately short of cash to pay its foreign debts, introduced a general sales tax, which contributed to a huge jump in the cost of living (16,9 per cent). This occurred at the same time that economic growth declined. Unemployment aimed another huge blow at the people. In the metal industry, for example, 84 000 workers lost their jobs between 1982 and 1984, and by 1985, a quarter of the population had no jobs. Most of these unemployed were young people under the age of 30. As if these hardships were not enough, the 1980s also saw a massive drought, pushing up the price of food and driving hundreds of thousands of people from the rural areas into the cities to look for jobs.

The regime was also coming under financial strain. In response to the armed struggle of the liberation movements, the government was allocating massive amounts to defence in order to finance its military operations in the region – in Angola to stop the advance of SWAPO, as well as indiscriminate attacks on ANC houses and local civilians in Lesotho, Zambia and Mozambique. As the ANC's drive for international sanctions began to be felt at home, the regime was hard-pressed to find extra income for the townships, and the result was a steady deterioration of conditions there. Despite vigorous prosecution of the pass laws, the black urban population was steadily growing – thanks, in part, to the creative ability of hundreds of thousands of men and women to beat the system – but with the regime's unwillingness to pay for maintenance costs, townships became rundown. Services such as sewerage systems and drainage had decayed, rubbish lay in piles in the streets, and shack settlements were beginning to spread across the landscape. Black South Africa was simmering.

Time was ripe for appropriate intervention by the ANC. Tambo's notes revealed that 'a structured nationwide liberation front [needs to be] created – more precise content and shape will emerge in the course of actual unfolding of struggle'.[61] In January 1983, Tambo called for 'The Year of United Action'.

'Fellow South Africans,' he exhorted. 'We must organise ourselves... The people of South Africa [must] form a strong mass democratic action.' Pointing out the growing crisis in the apartheid system and its increasingly desperate and violent attempts both in the broader region and inside the country to shore up its power, he restated the broad and inclusive vision of the ANC's Freedom Charter. He urged all 'patriots and revolutionaries [to] work tirelessly to strengthen and expand the mass democratic organisations among the youth and students, among the women, among the cultural and sports workers, the religious community and at the civic level'.

He went on to commend the trade unions and also point out the importance of organising 'landless, unemployed or agricultural workers' and 'deportees who have been dumped in the so-called resettlement areas'.

He called on coloured and Indian communities to resist Botha's proposed new constitutional attempts to co-opt them and divide them from the majority of the people. The time was ripe. He suggested that a start be made with a 'release political prisoners' campaign: 'For every Mandela, Sisulu, Mbeki, Kathrada, Goldberg; for every Motsoaledi, Gwala, Nyembo or Hogan that the enemy has captured, we must produce a thousand others to take their places.'[62]

Not two weeks later, the gifted orator and church minister Allan Boesak spoke at an event to oppose the government-appointed South African Indian Council (SAIC), which had been set up to promote Indian and coloured candidates for a new Parliament consisting of three chambers in the apartheid government. (Perhaps deliberately on the part of the government, the South African Indian Congress, which had been part of the Congress Alliance since the 1950s, had the same acronym.) The expanded legislature would exclude Africans, since they were supposed to have their own 'homeland' parliaments.

In his speech, Boesak made a compelling suggestion. 'The only dignified response that [all] blacks can give in this situation,' he declared, 'is the politics of refusal. There is no reason why churches, civic associations, trade unions, student organisations and sports bodies should not unite on this issue, pool our resources and inform the people of the fraud that is about to be perpetrated in its name, and on the day of the election expose these plans for what they are.'[63]

To what extent were Tambo's and Boesak's speeches connected? Allan Boesak declared that the meeting of minds was pure coincidence; that he, Boesak, was unaware of Tambo's January call. Prior to the speech, though, there had been some discussion among the anti-SAIC people who had invited Boesak. Some of them, like Pravin Gordhan, were members of the ANC underground. Although the annual Tambo speech usually took time to reach South Africa, the underground was probably aware of the ANC's general call for the Year of Unity in Action. During the planning session, Cassim Saloojee – a member of the anti-SAIC group – suggested the idea of forming a front. Gordhan readily agreed. When Boesak arrived and commented informally that 'this is not just a thing for the coloured people', Saloojee responded: 'We also met for the Anti-SAIC and thought it's a damned good idea, you know, if we try and call for a front of organisations and people against the tricameral system and all that... I am going to make a plea for that in my speech.'[64]

Whether the convergence of the two historic speeches was coincidental or not, the purport of both was 'an idea whose time had come'.[65] Boesak's public and aboveground suggestion, though initially meant by him to be an ad hoc tactic, received a ready response. A growing awareness of the ANC was in the air. It was enough that the liberation movement seemed to give its blessing to Boesak's proposition. There was no doubt that thousands were managing to tune in secretly to Radio Freedom to listen to the ANC President's annual message. In the townships, groups would be huddled around short-wave radios, curtains drawn and someone on the lookout for the police or eavesdroppers, to listen to ANC news and the speeches of Oliver Tambo. Dumisa Ntuli, for example, recalls his older brother Sam, a charismatic trade-union and civics organiser on the East Rand, arranging get-togethers on Sunday evenings in Thokoza and Vosloorus. These events were disguised as parties, where young people would gather for a drink. As a prelude to the main happening, Sam Ntuli would talk to the group about an aspect of the history of the ANC such as the Freedom Charter or the formation of the Youth League. At 7pm the guests would cluster around the radio to listen to Tambo's speech.[66]

What was the influence of the ANC on the increasing number of organisations that became affiliated to the UDF? In reply to a question on whether the UDF was a mere front of the ANC, Tambo expressed consternation. 'No, no!' he protested. 'It does not follow. To say the UDF is a front for the ANC is to say that all these constituent bodies – more than 700 of them – are each a front of the ANC... The UDF is its own Front. We have encouraged the formation of organisations, [but] these organisations were not created by the ANC.'[67]

Nevertheless, despite the lack of a visible ANC presence inside the country, the liberation movement proved to be skilful in winning over the loyalty of a critical mass of the UDF leadership as well as its grass-roots members. The ANC's political maturity impressed the new activists, who realised that they had much to learn from their seasoned comrades. Over more than two decades, the movement in exile had garnered a rich experience in the art of symbolism and promotion through propaganda and select targeting of apartheid emblems. MK's attack on Secunda's oil refineries, for example, followed by assaults on police stations and military quarters, created a deep and unambiguous popular impression. (Indeed, the very date of its launch – 16 December – in 1962 was the most emotive day in the year for both whites and blacks.) In the eighties, the annual 8 January speeches, workshopped by the NEC, and canvassed and discussed, became a national institution, and it was Tambo, as chairperson of the NEC, who read the speech every year, who became associated with the political education of the people on strategy and tactics.

The ANC was also able to challenge its rivals – above all, it was imperative, Oliver Tambo noted, that the ANC 'avoid being isolated; discourage attempts, surreptitious goings-on aimed at creating a supposed alternative to the ANC'. Wherever possible, the struggle should be inclusive, drawing in more adherents to a mass democratic movement, under the leadership of the ANC. The ANC had to stimulate joint action, cutting across racial boundaries. The struggle, which was being waged by different communities over different specific issues, had to find common ground in mass action and in the vision of a unified state with one Parliament, based on 'one person, one vote'.[68]

There had, in addition, been the years of prior preparation. By the 1980s, a significant number of black consciousness activists had embraced the ANC vision and the Freedom Charter. Recruitment had taken place on all ANC fronts – on Robben Island, in the External Mission and in the underground at home. Wally Serote, the prominent poet and activist in the Black Consciousness Movement, was one example of an ANC underground operative able to send information to the ANC outside.[69] These patient beginnings slowly built up a growing awareness of the ANC's message. The Charterist vision made firm inroads, inexorably undermining the BC organisations. AZAPO, although it had already formed a national forum, which it defined as 'a loose grouping of non-collaborationists' open to blacks only, and which also advocated the boycott tactic, proved itself to be less experienced in organisational and campaign follow-ups. The Inkatha movement was more complex – being ethnically based, it was not a national organisation. In both cases, violent clashes for hegemony between ANC/UDF activists and rival organisations took place, further escalating a spiral of confrontation.

In turn, the UDF was able to rest on the gravitas of the ANC's 70 years of struggle and so claim legitimacy. This experience gave its senior leaders a perceptive insight. Tambo, as one of the ANC's most experienced strategists, had pinpointed the concept of ungovernability in his personal notebook in 1977, commenting on the apartheid state's savage murder of Steve Biko. 'As in 1960, so in 1977,' he had written, 'the regime resorted to bannings because the level of the struggle of the people was making the country ungovernable.'[70]

Increasingly, the UDF saw itself as carrying out the ANC's broad strategic direction. Tambo's speeches, including his two key messages of 1983 and 1985, were providing this direction.

But the relationship was reciprocal. The dissemination of the ANC's messages was facilitated by its close relationship with the UDF. It was able to monitor more closely than before the activities and day-to-day sufferings of the ordinary people. It was able to ensure that the 8 January speech and other statements had a message for every sector. And, regardless of where they were, local communities could interpret the messages and find tasks in the civics, in education, in the unions, in church or any other area of activity. So it was that the messages, though comprehensive, provided the means of empowering local people. In this respect, the grass roots often surprised and delighted, but sometimes also dismayed the ANC, especially when their suggestions were applied in forms that were very different from what Lusaka may have intended. The connection between the two organisations, therefore, was marked by a relative autonomy as well as a connection between the two,[71] so that while many of the campaigns undertaken by the UDF emanated in general terms from the ANC, the form they took on the ground often differed from the original intention.

The months following Tambo's January speeches saw much organisational activity. Meetings, public rallies, 'interim committees' and 'Anti-PC' (President's Council) organisations were set up. On 20 August 1983, a huge launch was held in Rockville, Cape Town. The new United Democratic Front enlisted scores of organisations and, in a declaration reminiscent of Nelson Mandela's call in his 'No Easy Walk to Freedom' in 1953[72] and indeed Tambo's 1982 call, the UDF aimed to unite 'all our people... in the cities and the countryside, the factories and mines, schools, colleges and universities, houses and sports fields, churches, mosques and temples, to fight for our freedom'.[73]

One of PW Botha's 'bogus reforms' to which Tambo had referred included Botha's proposed tricameral constitution, by which coloured and Indian people would be represented in Parliament, but as separate caucuses. In a response to an early question by *Newsweek* in August 1980, Tambo had commented: 'The majority of the people of South Africa are left out of it. It is not a constitution that includes the people of South Africa as a whole. It has all the features of racism and apartheid. It is designed to maintain the status quo and keep power in the hands of the white minority – to the total exclusion of the blacks. We reject it completely.'[74]

Opposition to the constitution came decisively in the Transvaal from many coloured and Indian communities such as Riverlea, Noordgesig, Actonville, Eldorado Park, Lenasia and Laudium. Polls in that province for apartheid's 1984 tricameral elections in 'coloured areas' ranged from 6 per cent to 47 per cent. In Lenasia, only 2.8 per cent to 6.1 per cent of the voters voted. To what extent had the communities been aware of Tambo's urgent message to them?

'[We] address an appeal to our Indian and so-called Coloured compatriots to *stand firm* with the oppressed majority,' he urged, 'to *refuse* to join the doomed apartheid system on the eve of the triumph of our long and bitter struggle. The ANC's call to them, this valiant month of June, is: "*Don't Vote! – Don't!*"'[75]

The Transvaal Indian Council (TIC) hailed the laughably low poll results as a 'massive victory' and called on those elected to resign immediately because they were not working in the interests of the people they claimed to represent. Opposition to the Coloured Management Committees (CMCs) spread to the western and eastern Cape, and in Natal, many residents rejected the Indian Management Committee (IMC) as a 'dummy body'. In Lenasia, the federation of residents' associations demanded direct and equal representation in a single body with Johannesburg.[76] The Coloured and Indian Management Committees controlled sports facilities, such as the soccer, rugby, cricket and hockey fields, and they soon clashed with SACOS-affiliated bodies, which were not allowed by their constitution to negotiate with 'dummy bodies'.

But the most intense opposition came from African townships. Local councils faced severe cash-flow problems. With the Black Local Authorities Act, the government had dumped township expenses on to the councils. These included debts from the years before. Soweto, for example, had a debt of R33 million, but the country's biggest civic was determined to fight the system. To secure the widest support, it initiated the Anti-Community Council Committee – a coalition of student, youth, women's and labour organisations – to boycott the 1983 elections. This coalition mirrored the thinking behind the UDF.

Although a prior organisation initiated by AZAPO was also urging boycott and opposition, from its launch in 1983, the UDF, by picking up on day-to-day grass-roots grievances, was to lead the enterprise almost constantly. As the UDF grew, so too did the civic movement. The civics, mobilised and supported by the UDF, aimed to tackle everyday problems such as rent, transport, schooling and services. These were issues that concerned people deeply, and they participated in opposition campaigns through their various organisations. These groups included student and youth groups, women's organisations, churches and trade unions. Civics sprang up around the country, and included areas away from the political centres in the urban townships.

In the dry, sheep-farming Karoo, a small group of activists led by popular ex-political prisoner and school teacher Matthew Goniwe, founder of the Cradock Residents' Association (Cradora) in his home town, went from house to house canvassing support for the opposition to rent increases. He and his colleagues introduced a grid system, reminiscent in concept of Mandela's M-plan, of street committees, block by block, so that 'even the family is seen as the structure of the organisation', explained Goniwe.[77] Within just months, a chain of tightly coordinated civic and youth organisations had been set up in 10 or more small Eastern Cape towns. The initiative received an enthusiastic following.

In the year following the UDF launch, the organisations began to work more purposefully towards the UDF's vision of a popular front of resistance. Inspired by the initiative, ordinary people began banding together to form civic organisations to join the larger national umbrella of the United Democratic Front. The civics drew on a growing pool of supporters. While in Soweto it had started as an initiative of leaders – many of them veterans of the 1950s such as former Youth Leaguer Nthatho Motlana and, notably, Winnie Mandela – the initiatives from below set an example to civics throughout the country. On the East Rand, ERAPO grew to a number of township-based civics, which later formed a federation of the Civic Associations of the Southern Transvaal (CAST).

Then, in 1984, a shift occurred in the nature of the struggle of the civics. It began with the uprising in the townships in the Vaal Triangle, home of Sharpeville. The outcome was to trigger a wave of activism that swept the country and developed into a broad, popular wave of community-based resistance. The depth and breadth of the response was one that drew a response from the ANC leadership.

In August 1984, Lekoa Town Council announced a R5.50 increase in service charges in the townships of Boipatong, Bophelong, Sebokeng, Sharpeville and Zamdela (Sasolburg). At the same time, Everton announced a R6.00 increase in residents' permits. In line with the Black Local Authorities system, the townships received no subsidies – services had to be paid for by the poorest communities through rents and service charges. The new rent increase was yet another heavy blow for a community that was not only badly underpaid but also had to cope with growing unemployment against a rising cost of living.

Throughout August, angry Lekoa and Evaton residents held protest meetings. Sello Morake, later of the Vaal Civic Association, recalled: 'On Saturday, we had the final meeting in the Anglican Church – there were Casspirs all around. When we moved out, we were shouting, "Viva Oliver Tambo!" – excited.'[78]

At the meetings, residents called for the resignation of all councillors; not only were the councillors not accountable to the community they were supposed to serve, but there was also strong evidence that many were corrupt. There were hundreds of experiences of people having to pay anything from R100 to R1 000 into private councillors' accounts in order to obtain houses, business licences or amenities that should have been every resident's right.[79]

The Vaal Civic called for a stayaway on 3 September. On that day, nearly all the 93 000 school children boycotted classes and about 60 per cent of the workers stayed away. The civic resolved to march on the council. But the Sebokeng march did not reach the council offices. The police broke it up.

'We went to stop the buses and started making barricades, piling up rubbish and stones, very early in the morning. By 7am it was not easy for the police to move around. And when we saw police vehicles coming, we stoned them and they sort of ran away. Then we went, we marched towards the councillors. We went to Mahlatsi's place... When he saw the big mob approaching, he started shooting into the air. But when he saw that we were really meant business, he ran away, on foot. We started doing our job with the house. We took the car, drove it off to the township. It was burned there... From there, it was just going. You could see these houses burning. You'd actually see an office burning in Zone 13, another one in Zone 12, Zone 11.'[80]

On that day, 3 September 1984, 33 people were killed. Further repression followed. Evictions increased. The collection of rubbish stopped. Those who had electricity had their lights cut off. The government moved the army into another Vaal township, Sebokeng.

This was the first time that military troops were brought into a township, and their presence seemed effective. Thereafter, the state was to use the tactic of an army presence in the townships many times over in community clashes, sending a message of war and playing into the hands of the ANC's call for a 'People's War'. The authorities had thus responded to the resistance movement by further repression, and attempted to tie up the movement by apprehending the leaders. Civics leaders, especially those discerned as being 'Charterist' and therefore ANC supporters, such as Popo Molefe and Mosiua 'Terror' Lekota and others, were arrested and charged in the Delmas Treason Trial.

Resistance to higher rents and service charges spread, in many cases, violently. The Belabela campaign, for example, included the boycott of councillors' shops, and some of their shops and houses were burnt after a community member was shot. The councillors then resigned. In Soweto alone, 24 councillors' houses were petrol-bombed in 1984. Civics were rapidly gaining support across the spectrum of the township populations, and developed a multiclass composition – workers, unemployed, housewives, taxi owners, businesspeople, even former councillors now joined their local civics.[81]

But perhaps the most significant input into the practical organisation and resistance techniques of the civics and the UDF in general came from the democratic trade-union movement. The government had been forced to acknowledge the power of organised black labour as the state, with all its apparatuses – the army, the police force, the security and the law courts – had been unable to crush the labour movement. Police regularly broke up strikes and pickets. Trade-union leaders were harassed, banned and arrested. Union offices were bombed. But, through these many struggles, the government was eventually forced to accept black and non-racial unions in 1979.

The unions brought to the table a wealth of organisational experience. In 1979 events had taken place that seemed to consolidate the policy of political unionism. In Cape Town, the Food and Canning Workers Union, originally a SACTU union, had called on traders and consumers to boycott Fattis & Monis products and demand the reinstatement of dismissed workers. After months of boycott, with the help of the community, the union won its demands. In the same year in Port Elizabeth, workers at the Ford plant went on strike after organiser Thozamile Botha was dismissed for leading the Port Elizabeth Black

Civic Organisation (Pebco). With the support of Pebco, the strike spread to other factories, and Thozamile Botha was offered his job back. Unfortunately, he was detained during the strike and, immediately after his release, was banned from all factories. He then 'skipped' the country and joined the ANC in exile. The following year, the Garment Workers' Union went on strike for the right of workers to elect a non-racial factory committee. The community in Cape Town also supported a boycott of red meat until the union won its demands.

The consumer boycotts and the Ford strike were significant in that they proved that, given the right conditions, unions could count on the community for support in workers' struggles. The campaigns indicated that a new kind of union strategy was developing, and a new kind of community movement was being born. Many felt that alliances between labour and the community were opening up exciting possibilities for the success of future struggles. State and employer oppression had the opposite effect to what they had intended.

In the 1980s, the democratic trade unions in South Africa were the most rapidly growing worker organisations in the world. It was, of course, the urban black working class that was crammed into the hostels, the yards and the matchbox houses of the townships, and exploitation and racism at the workplace was also leading to growing worker militancy. Unions were fighting low wages with a series of ongoing, or 'rolling', strikes. In July 1981 the unions called for the communities to boycott Colgate Palmolive products. This boycott action was followed by a series of strikes on the East Rand. Workers at the firms of Salcast, Hendler & Hendler, Bison Board, Langeberg Co-op and Vaal Metals downed tools. There were over 50 strikes in five months, involving 24 000 workers.

This cooperation created the opportunity for the unions to develop links between the workers and the community. Major FOSATU-affiliated unions such as the Metal and Allied Workers Union (MAWU), later the National Union of Metalworkers of South Africa (NUMSA) and later still the massive National Union of Mineworkers (NUM) began to assist civics with their hard-won skills. The FOSATU unions themselves were beginning to develop a greater awareness of the connection between community issues and workplace issues.

This entry of the organised working class into the political domain was watched with bated breath by the ANC. Clearly, it assessed, the UDF was operating in a dramatically responsive and propitious environment. 'The people expect us to lead them to victory,' Tambo urged.[82] It was time for the ANC to intervene more openly and decisively with a specific plan of attack.

Infiltration of MK cadres back into South Africa occurred more rapidly. Many were stationed conveniently nearby (in Mozambique) and it was South Africa's Nkomati Accord with the Frelimo government that, ironically, put pressure on MK cadres to speed up the process of their return home. But, with few underground reception structures, there were scores of casualties. Only 45 armed incursions took place in 1984, police reported – a drop from the previous year. And 177 guerrillas were captured or killed.[83]

But the Vaal uprising in September 1984 and its impact on other parts of the country changed this dismal outlook. MK operatives were now able to reach more civilians through the street committees in the townships, and set up training units. Young militants, using the same rudimentary weapons as before – stones and petrol bombs – learnt how to hijack hippos by digging trenches in the road and captured their weapons.

By the end of 1984, a bigger picture was beginning to emerge: popular insurrection was taking shape as a conscious strategy – it was no longer a spontaneous, hit-and-miss happening. 'The reality is,' said Oliver Tambo, 'the apartheid system cannot be reformed.' In practice, 'reform' meant a string of further oppressive laws – the 'feverish attempts to strengthen the bantustan system' through legislation that sought to 'transform Africans into foreigners in the land of their birth and banish them to starvation and death... the continuing pass raids and the genocidal programme of forced removals'.[84]

A growing awareness began to combine, under the bright umbrella of the UDF, the organisational strength of the labour movement, the grass-roots millions in the civics, the churches, and the combat units (with or without MK guidance) of the township militants.

On 8 January 1985, Tambo summed up the ANC methodology of people's insurrection: 'Render South Africa Ungovernable!'[85] The 1985 speech, discussed as usual with the NEC, was to become perhaps the most dramatic in Tambo's career. On 22 July, 48 hours after the declaration of the State of Emergency, the ANC responded with Tambo's 'Address to the Nation'. The militant discourse of his reasoned argument was all the more effective for being broadcast in his calm, light, measured voice. By declaring a State of Emergency, he contended, Botha had admitted that his organs of government had collapsed: 'The regime can no longer conceal its true face. What has become plain for all to see is the reality of military dictatorship and not the comforting but spurious image of a reformer that Botha has sought to cultivate and protect.'

The reply to Botha, Tambo suggested, was to break down and destroy the old order. 'We have to make apartheid unworkable and our country ungovernable.'

Already, great progress had been made in this offensive, particularly in 'the weakest link', apartheid's local government authorities in the black urban areas, and the police. It was now necessary to intensify the struggle 'exactly in those areas that are under martial law'. In that struggle, 'we must make it impossible for our enemy to govern even in the new way'. Unity was of paramount importance. In town or countryside, 'there is not a single black person anywhere in our country who can say that he or she lives in conditions of freedom'.

There were, nevertheless, pockets of unevenness in the struggle, which strengthened the enemy in certain areas. The offensive of ungovernability therefore had to be spread to reach all parts of the country – 'In all our localities, wherever they may be, we must rise now and destroy apartheid organs of government that are used to hold us in bondage. We make this call to all black people – African, Indian and so-called Coloureds.'

The call was extended to white South Africans too. It was 'a special responsibility' to white democrats to make apartheid supporters realise that Botha could not guarantee their security: 'To guarantee its own security, white South Africa must come over to the side of the forces fighting for a democratic non-racial society... The alternative... of pitting themselves against the overwhelming majority of the people of our country – is nothing but a death trap.'

The struggle, therefore, was to be extended into the white areas of South Africa. The call to Umkhonto we Sizwe was to work with the people and 'act together to inflict the greatest possible number of casualties on armed enemy personnel... If need be, let us force the apartheid regime to deploy its armed forces in every village and township in our country.'

The people would not be alone. The international community, Tambo promised, was at that very moment adopting new measures to isolate the apartheid regime. 'The order of the day to all units of Umkhonto we Sizwe is that they must strengthen links with the people.'

'Make Apartheid Unworkable!' Tambo concluded. 'Make South Africa Ungovernable! Prepare the Conditions for the Seizure of Power by the People!'[86]

The broadcast had an electric effect in townships. Young people in particular thrilled to his words. 'When we heard OR's voice that evening,' recalled one young man, eyes shining at the memory, '*Ey!* – Our eyes were opened!'[87] The youth swelled with pride when Tambo hailed them as 'the Young Lions'.

In this January speech, Tambo had already demonstrated the ANC's detailed knowledge of the situation inside South Africa. He outlined the momentous events of that year and the build-up of organised resistance across the sectors, providing an analysis of their significance. He noted the rejection of the tricameral constitution by the very people whom Botha had tried to co-opt, the vast majority of coloured people and Indians; the strikes and the increasing political consciousness of workers in their stayaways; the Sebokeng resistance to local authorities, and the ongoing education struggles of the youth – 'the pride of our nation'. Indicative of the attempt to 'de-gender' MK, Tambo observed that more women had joined MK in the 1984 Year of the Women than ever before. He praised the women of Sebokeng and elsewhere, who were fighting 'in the front ranks' against 'forced removals, starvation wages, increased rents and taxes, inferior education and health services'. He called for more grass-roots mobilisation in towns and also in the dispossessed rural areas.

'The land question is inextricably tied to the struggle against the bantustans... Last year we said we must begin to use our accumulated strength to destroy the organs of the apartheid regime. We have now set upon this path. We have taken impressive strides towards rendering the country ungovernable. This has not only meant the destruction of community councils; our rejection of the illegitimate rule of the Botha regime. Other struggles, including those on the issue of education as well as the stay-at-home, themselves pitted our democratic power against the forces of oppression, racism and counter-revolution, for the defeat of the latter and its replacement with popular power.'[88]

The regime had been knocked off balance by the intensity of the popular uprising. It was now time for a combined strengthening of the ANC's underground structures with 'the armed offensive spearheaded by MK', paying particular attention to building up a well-organised revolutionary cadreship.

'Who are these revolutionary cadres about whom we speak? Where are they? They are not special people. It is we – men and women, young and old, black and white – who are involved in daily struggles, making sacrifices in pursuit of the people's cause. It is we, the workers in the factories, the mines, the farms, the commercial establishment and offices of various kinds; we, who work in health and educational services as well as those of us within residential areas.'[89]

These cadres would work 'to shift our posture to the offensive... to cultivate the spirit of rebellion... Through struggle and sacrifice, we have planted the seeds of people's war in our country.'

The substance of Tambo's electrifying broadcast was indeed a message of 'total onslaught', and a State of Emergency was declared. Thousands, mainly UDF activists, were detained. The spiralling and countrywide escalation of resistance redoubled PW Botha's determination to use any methods to fight off the forces of opposition. The state's declared enemies were the banned organisations – the ANC, the PAC and the SACP – but the UDF, too, was seen as an extension of the ANC and anyone who supported the UDF was considered to be a danger to the state. Even clerics like Bishop Desmond Tutu and Frank

Chikane were treated with hostility by the media and persecuted in their everyday lives. Assassination attempts included the poisoning of Chikane's clothes, which landed him, seriously ill, in a US hospital, where his malady was diagnosed, to the contemptuous disbelief of some of the white South African press.

Tambo's call received an immediate and heady response. He was a national hero. Young men and women, students on campuses and in the township streets sang praise songs to Tambo, dancing to the seductive new beat of the *toyi-toyi*, imported from the ranks of the MK who were beginning to infiltrate back into the country. 'Oliver Tambo, Oliver Tambo!' they sang boldly, ignoring the Security Police and the photographers, openly spreading the reputation of both the man and the movement he led.

Daily confrontations in the townships became commonplace. The army was brought in, in increasingly large numbers, to patrol the townships. South Africa was witnessing unrest, which the Law and Order Minister Louis le Grange described as more serious than the Soweto uprising of 1976.[90] Systematically, as more people enlisted in MK, small arms were being sneaked into South Africa via underground routes in the Front Line States. There were also more creative undertakings by, for example, Mannie Brown's African Hinterland tour company in London. European sympathisers posing as tourists on safari smuggled arms into South Africa in false-bottomed four-by-fours.[91] In the townships, ill-equipped young men were mockingly apt to throw hand grenades at the soldiers, who responded with a ferocity fuelled by fear. They shot, often at random, from the interior of Casspirs, but photographs showed SADF soldiers more than once standing openly in the street, taking a smoke break next to a dead body. In June 1985, black South Africa was anguished to learn that Matthew Goniwe and three of his comrades, Fort Calata (grandson of the Reverend James Calata, ANC Secretary-General of the ANC from 1939 to 1949), Sicelo Mhlauli and Thomas 'Sparrow' Mkhonto, had disappeared. The dismissal of Goniwe and Calata from their teaching posts in 1984 had sparked a protest boycott by the pupils, followed by widespread student unrest and riots throughout the area. Boycotts continued through 1985 – statistics show that 907 schools countrywide, involving 674 275 pupils, were hit by stayaways.[92] A week after the disappearance of the four men, their bodies were found, mutilated and burnt, on the side of the road.

Afterwards, Tambo asserted that the barbarous method of necklacing – forcibly placing a petrol-filled tyre around the hapless victim's neck and then setting it alight – employed by police assailants on the Cradock Four was deliberately introduced by the security machinery through instigation at crowded gatherings. The accusation seemed far-fetched, but it was years later that the Truth and Reconciliation Commission found the charge to have been true. To the ANC, Tambo urged that they keep their gaze fixed on the real enemy.

'Who is the enemy of the people? Let's get on with the business of fighting him – from wherever we are, with whatever we have. The process of our struggle will itself deal with our secondary enemies – the spies, agents, stooges, collaborators. There are self-confessed... traitors who have closed ranks with and are part of the enemy. *But we must not place in the category of traitors those who do not in fact belong there.*'[93]

At the funeral of the Cradock Four, attended by many thousands, ANC and SACP banners were unfurled in the open for the first time. Victoria Mxenge, widow of the murdered Griffiths Mxenge and human rights lawyer who had defended many young people, students and scholars, spoke passionately at the funeral, referring to the deaths of the four comrades as 'a dastardly act of cowardice'. The dead, she said, had gone to deliver messages to the ancestors. 'Go well, peacemakers. Tell your great-grandfathers we are coming because we are prepared to die for Africa!'

Twelve days later, Victoria Mxenge was stabbed and shot as she climbed out of her car at her front door in Umlazi.[94] At her funeral, messages were read out from Oliver Tambo and from Nelson Mandela.

Increasingly, throughout the country, weekends were taken up by the funerals of young victims, usually killed by the police or the army. In fact, the funerals themselves became 'sites of struggle'. Mourners were attacked and killed during militant rhetoric, the unfolding of ANC and SACP banners, the singing of resistance songs and performances to the rhythmic *toyi-toyi* beat.

Thousands of supporters were also aware of the major event of the year – the ANC's National Consultative Conference in June 1985, the first in 16 years. It was being held on the anniversary of Soweto, 16 June, at a conference centre in Kabwe, Zambia. Preparations required massive organisation, including research, input and requests for items on the agenda from branches around the world.

The conference had been preceded by an 18-month open-discussion period, during which all structures were encouraged to deliberate and prepare papers for submission to the Preparatory Committee. Every centre held regional conferences, and delegates were chosen to represent various structures and branches.

'It was probably the most participatory conference held outside South Africa,' remarked Pallo Jordan.[95] The 250 delegates, observed Oliver Tambo, represented the entire organisation. There were cadres from every country as well as from home – anywhere where branches, MK and the diplomatic corps existed, from 'political organisers, trade unionists, administration, production, health and cultural workers, propagandists, students and other members who are employed outside the ranks of our organisation'.[96] The conference also heard messages of support from the political prisoners on Robben Island and at Pollsmoor.

'It is most satisfying,' wrote Mandela (mindful of complexities beginning to manifest themselves in a subtext of changing tactics not yet in the public domain), 'to belong to a tested organisation, which exercises so formidable an impact on the situation in our country, which has established itself firmly as the standard bearer of such a rich tradition, and which has brought us such coveted laurels… We find it rewarding indeed to know that despite the immense distance and the years that separate us, as well as the lack of effective communication channels, we still remain a closely knit organisation, ever conscious of the crucial importance of unity, and resisting every attempt to divide and confuse.'[97]

The conference had been conceptualised as a 'Council of War'. At its opening, Tambo had spoken about an earlier decision 'to take our country through the terrible but cleansing fires of revolutionary war to a condition of peace, democracy and the fulfilment of our people'.[98]

'Even as we opened our meeting,' reported Tambo afterwards, 'the continuing massacre of our people loomed large in our minds, highlighted by the criminal invasion of Botswana and the murder of innocent people in Gaborone.'

The conference had generated earnest discussion and a demonstration of participatory democracy, an ideal that had been practised all too seldom in the constraints of exile, distance, enemy infiltration and a war mode. The branches had sent an array of thoughtful observations, raising concerns to do with leadership inside the country, representation, the need to draw the organised working class and the rural population into the political. Summarising the reports from the regions, the Preparatory Committee flagged the issues.

'Underground leadership should be set up within RSA, and this is the most vital phase ahead.' In its recommendations, it commented: 'ANC leadership has acquitted itself well in spite of difficulties; hence we are in a position to raise the struggle to a higher plane. There can be no justification for continued exclusion of capable comrades from the NEC. We should consider whether the ANC's original mission has been fulfilled. Care should be taken not to dilute the national character of the ANC. Perhaps one member of the NEC should come from minorities.' Ways of improving participatory democracy, despite the context of security threats and underground operations needed to be considered: 'though centralism is important', it commented, 'democracy in the governance of our activities is equally important'.[99]

The key decisions were a confirmation of armed struggle, with the demand that any negotiated settlement 'of the South African question' could not even be entertained while political prisoners languished in jail. The cardinal importance of unity was stressed, not only within the ANC, but among all who were 'true liberators'. 'Let us not allow the enemy's dirty tricks department to succeed in getting us to fight one another,' was Tambo's plea.[100]

Kabwe was critical for the decade that followed. Firstly, its strongly democratic character sent an important message about the ANC to its members. Debate was open, free and vigorous, and the NEC was elected for the first time since 1959 by a conference. Some incumbents, anticipating unpopularity, wanted a slate, for which delegates could vote as a whole, but Tambo insisted on open elections by secret ballot.

'The delegates cheered, and then got a fright,' recalled Albie Sachs. 'The organisation was so scattered that people did not know each other, so they asked Tambo for his list!' In the end, Tambo gave a list longer than the number of places to be filled. Two former NEC members, who had been disgraced by the events in Angola, were not re-elected. Meanwhile, the conference overwhelmingly supported the right of non-Africans to be on the NEC. After a passionate debate, Slovo, Maharaj and September (who had been on OR's list) were among those voted elected.

Secondly, the conference carefully balanced intensifying insurrectionary struggle with giving a mandate for the leadership to negotiate, if the conditions were ripe. This balance proved to be vital in the complicated period to come.

Thirdly, the conference adopted ANC statutes, updating constitutional structures, and adopted the Code of Conduct. The democratic processes, secret ballot, open debates and thought-through mandates gave the ANC buoyancy for the final thrust.

It was becoming increasingly clear to many inside South Africa, including the influential Broederbond members, that a constructive intervention, though risky, was necessary. In August, Botha made a speech that was widely expected, nationally and internationally, to announce sweeping reforms. Pressed by the influential Afrikaner nationalist insiders' club, the Broederbond, as well as international cohorts in the West, the ever-dextrous Foreign Minister Pik Botha was alleged to have written most of it. But on the appointed evening, to an audience of millions of television watchers around the world, Botha discarded the speech. He refused, he declared bombastically, to 'take the road to abdication and suicide'. He blamed the troubles on the 'barbaric communists and agitators' and wagged his finger at the cameras, threatening 'Do not push us too far!'

'Posturing like a pathetic dictator,' said Tambo the next day in Lusaka, comparing Botha with 'his predecessor and mentor', Mussolini.[101] Botha's speech had been accompanied by a video broadcast of a necklacing, which had taken place a few days earlier, of a tragically ill-fated young woman who attended the funeral of a man killed by the Security Police. She was the girlfriend of a known informer (this was confirmed years later by the man himself at the Truth and Reconciliation Commission in the 1990s). She had been spotted, recognised, stoned and necklaced by a screaming crowd.

The 'People's War' increasingly displayed this darker side. Tambo's call to 'make apartheid unworkable and our country ungovernable', in the context of troops in the townships, the death squads, arrests and torture, disappearances, informers and collaborators, was interpreted by some to mean the discipline and punishment of 'puppet local government authorities' – town councillors and informers – by death. The deep-seated anger of thousands of people sometimes boiled over into summary trials and mob executions by 'necklacing'. The fine houses and cars councillors had gained at the expense of poor and struggling township people were often the symbolic targets of their anger. On the part of MK, collaborators in the prosecution of apartheid were seen as legitimate 'hard targets'. The eagerness with which the general populace had grasped the import of Tambo's call for ungovernability was a sign – both to the enemies of the ANC and its sympathisers – that the ANC was prevailing.

The clauses of the Freedom Charter became popular slogans: 'The People Shall Govern!', 'All Shall be Equal Before the Law!', 'There Shall be Houses, Security and Comfort!'[102] It was 'on the basis of the Freedom Charter', pointed out Tambo, that people were able to propose an alternative democratic vision.[103] Tambo and Mandela were folk heroes – people were being arrested for the possession of banned books or material reproducing their speeches. In 1983, even a nun, Sister Bernard Ngcube, was arrested and sentenced to 12 months' imprisonment for being in possession of a photograph of Oliver Tambo and a copy of the ANC's *Sechaba* magazine, which featured Tambo's January speech. One young man was jailed for possession of a coffee mug sporting Mandela's image. It seemed clear that the UDF was indeed a 'front' for the national liberation movement – the Mass Democratic Movement, as it now came to be known. The UDF sponsored the Five Freedoms Forum, aimed especially at white liberals. At the event, a white man from the Eastern Cape stood up and declared, 'It's ten freedoms, not five!' referring to the Freedom Charter. Indeed, Charterism was rapidly being formally adopted by a range of organisations, including, significantly, the massive National Union of Mineworkers.

Tambo was quick to respond to Botha's Rubicon speech, which had coincided with the first full plenary of the NEC, which was presided over by an elections commission consisting of Jack Simons, Brian Bunting and Tambo. The very next day, Tambo called a press conference, based on discussions with the new NEC. Botha had suddenly suffered an attack of cold feet, he remarked. He called on 'the business community of our country, the professionals and intellectuals, the religious community and others' to reach out to the ANC. It was a significant call because it received a run of responses that was to give the struggle a new dimension.[104] Ten years later, looking back on the highlights of the struggle in the eighties, Mandela was to cite this call as an example of Tambo's strategic mind.[105] Within the following months, representatives of all these constituencies made their way to meetings with the ANC.

Sheena Duncan, spirited chairperson of the white middle-class anti-apartheid Black Sash movement, was a member of those early groups who openly met the ANC in 1985. The event was ostensibly a World Council of Churches symposium, and Duncan went with Beyers Naudé.

'The ANC had asked the World Council to please put up this umbrella [group] so that we could all be together,' she recollected. 'That was when I first met Oliver Tambo. He flung his arms around me, and asked "And how is your dear mother?" [herself a Black Sash chairperson].'[106]

The ANC had wasted no time in communicating with their underground members to urge them to arrange to both give and receive briefings in Lusaka or other less patent venues. One of the early aboveground groups to meet with the ANC was a UDF delegation to Sweden in February 1986. Arnold Mankekisi Stofile, Valli Moosa, Cheryl Carolus, Yunus Mahommed and Raymond Suttner represented the internal delegation.[107] The seniority of the ANC delegation conveyed to the fairly youthful group from South Africa how seriously the ANC was taking the meeting.

One of their first impressions was the warmth of the ANC's welcome. Raymond Suttner recalled particularly Tambo's friendly manner. 'Raymond! How are you?' He seemed to know all about him, and proceeded to ask him detailed questions about his personal progress. 'We were made to feel that the ANC knew exactly who we were; that they had gone to some trouble to find out about each and everyone of us.' They were overwhelmed – these were figures 'who we sang songs about'. Suttner, who regarded himself as very junior, was struck and moved by the observation that, as he gave his report, Tambo listened carefully, and sat quietly taking notes.[108]

To another delegation, Tambo's question, 'Do you have any suggestions about what we should do to ensure the success of your mission; to help build the "protective shield" around you?' taught them the value of prioritising collective, united struggle.[109]

As the ANC in exile prepared to return home, Tambo's persona had become increasingly inseparable from the growing status and image of the movement. Some ANC members noticed what they felt was the cultivation of a needlessly deferential manner to Tambo. He was in danger, they felt, of being smothered by obsequiousness. Possibly, his minders were anxious to protect him and his health from too many demands. In his personal interactions, however, Tambo cut through the pomp in the most natural, unaffected manner. While the ANC's relationship with the UDF was positive and stimulating – in both directions – in time, differences in approach emerged from different experiential circumstances. Visitors from home observed that while the UDF learnt a lot from the ANC, its strategies and tactics and how it operated, 'the ANC learnt too –about the culture of consultation'.[110]

In the meanwhile, the ANC continued to encourage the labour movement to utilise its organising skills in the service of national liberation. Tambo's speeches reflected this concern and in 1987 he issued a special May Day call to the people of South Africa. Like the other January speeches of that decade, it summarises the escalating situation in South Africa, and the ANC's responses.[111] Tambo pointed out that Botha's regime was on the defensive. It had been compelled to impose a State of Emergency for the third time in three years. It had undertaken another racially defined election, but only with the assistance of an unparalleled show of force and suppression. It had perpetrated acts of vicious external aggression – only five months earlier, Samora Machel's plane had been diverted into South African air space and was brought down by a false beacon, killing all on board.[112] Assassinations and bombings in the region and of ANC offices abroad were continuing. Inside the country there was evidence of growing attempts to recruit spies and informers and the assiduous cultivation of a Third Force, demonstrated by the murderous attacks on communities by black men wearing white bandannas – '*witdoeke*' – in the informal settlement of mostly Eastern Cape work-seekers at Crossroads in Cape Town. The resulting fear and anger of the cultivated divisions were calculated to generate tensions between coloured workers and the black underclass, which, many coloured people feared, would take away their jobs and undercut their wages. And it was becoming increasingly clear that the killings in hostels on the Rand of those inmates perceived to oppose Inkatha were sponsored by state appendages. Saracen tanks were seen to monitor areas prior to the routing of township houses adjacent to the hostels. Buthelezi, leader of Inkatha, was also caught up in a 'sprial of contradiction'. Given frequent access to the media, and free to travel abroad with his public relations consultants, he had 'allowed himself to be used by the regime in a remarkable way', commented Tambo to *The Times* in London. Playing his typically skilled game of double messages, Buthelezi had also attracted much publicity in his call to the regime to release Mandela. 'He says all the things they say,' explained Tambo; 'he takes all the positions they are taking', for Buthelezi was vehemently opposed to sanctions internationally and the boycott, 'people's education' and stayaway campaigns at home. Contrarily, while insisting that he was opposed to apartheid, 'he continues to make speeches against the ANC'.[113] For the ANC, said Tambo, the common enemy was apartheid, not other organisations opposing apartheid.

'Ungovernability', a concept originally authored by Thabo Mbeki, had a significant corollary. As the structures of apartheid were being made increasingly inoperable, something had to replace them. Tambo outlined the importance of converging all the acts of resistance towards a larger aim. 'We are not fighting and are not dying to have a better system of waste disposal. We are engaged in struggle for the inalienable right to govern our country in all its parts.[114]

'We have virtually lifted the ban on our vanguard movement, the ANC,' he claimed. 'In some areas of our country, having destroyed the puppet organs of government imposed on us by the apartheid regime, we have reached the situation where even the enemy has to deal with the democratic forces as the legitimate representatives of the people. The establishment of people's power in those areas, however rudimentary and precarious, is of great significance for the further advancement of our struggle... We are the alternative power... We must impose on our country our own popular legality.'[115]

Tambo had also explained the import of People's Power at a press briefing following the ANC conference at Kabwe. 'We are making the point here,' he said, 'that power in South Africa must be held by the majority of the people of South Africa as a whole, not by a white minority, not even by a black majority, but by a majority of the people of South Africa as a whole. Such a government will be legitimate; it will derive its mandate and authority from the people.'[116]

In May 1986, the ANC's NEC followed up the January speech with a 'Call to the Nation', in which it projected the swelling acts of resistance as the building up of People's Power.[117] 'The mass offensive,' it commented, 'is reaching new levels in ever-widening areas of our country. More and more of our people are being awakened to action in organised contingents against apartheid's evil forces. Inspired by the leadership of the ANC and its allies, the people are continuing to show unending revolutionary inventiveness and creativity.'

The call went on to summarise ways in which ungovernability was operating in tandem with power exercised by the people themselves: 'The seeds of people's power are beginning to germinate and spread their roots. People's committees, street committees and comrades' committees are emerging on a growing scale as popular organs in place of the collapsed racist stooge administrations. People's courts, people's defence militia and other popular organs of justice are, in many cases, challenging the legitimacy of the racist's machinery of justice and their uniformed forces of repression.

'Our working class has created a mighty trade-union federation – Cosatu – and has demonstrated its strength in the two-million-strong May Day strike.

'The schools and universities continue to be flashpoints for freedom. Youth stand poised to strike organised blows for liberation from their reoccupied bases. The forthcoming 10th anniversary of June 16 will fan the flames of resistance to slave education and reinforce the surge towards a free South Africa.'

Consumer and rent boycotts, and the 'shedding of the uniform of apartheid' supplemented these activities by growing numbers of soldiers (including white South Africans resisting call-up) and police. 'Those who continue to carry out its orders and who work with and for the enemy are shunned by the communities and can find little rest living among the people.'

The concept of People's Power introduced an important balance to the popular understanding of ungovernability, for it initiated a creative and enabling dimension. This was further promoted by the ANC's understanding that the communities on the ground were in the best position to interpret the principle and translate it into action – in the civics, in schools, in the labour movement.

'For me,' commented UDF activist Raymond Suttner, 'one of the main strengths of those messages is that one could look at the message and find tasks that you had to interpret wherever you were. The messages were comprehensive in that sense, while still leaving space for the individual activists and sectors to find their own way of implementing [the ideas].'[118]

The creative aspect of People's Power was, in his view, 'possibly the central, creative part of this period, in that people through that experience went beyond ungovernability towards building alternatives in a variety of creative ways, in a number of areas of the country'. The outcome was an exhilarating experience of agency for the common people. Phrases like 'mass creativity' were popularised, and tangible evidence of popular democracy was emerging.

The UDF put forward two senses of the latter, both of which had to be struggled for. There was the struggle for the right to the franchise, but there was also the taste of participatory democracy as an alternative to unworkable apartheid. These 'elementary' organs of People's Power manifested themselves in street committees, which won the support of the community and were able to set up crèches and 'People's Parks' and also control local crime. Sometimes these surfaced in particular sectors and sometimes in particular localities. The consumer boycotts in Port Alfred and Soweto; struggles in the schools in Cradock and other Eastern and Western Cape townships; the distinctive mobilisation of civic associations in tandem with the trade unions in the East Rand, Alexandra and Soweto, for example, developed broad community support for People's Power. At the same time, these were relevant to local concerns.

The next couple of years revealed an encouraging testimony of a growing unity of purpose in South Africa. In the first four months of 1987, Oliver Tambo noted in his May Day speech, more workers' strikes had taken place than in the entire preceding year. The growing numbers of workers in the 'giant democratic trade union federation, COSATU' had supported these general strikes. There were also other sectors of South Africans that were actively opposing apartheid. Under the guidance and training of MK, affirmed Tambo, people were joining self-defence units and combat groups. The underground was also making progress instructing 'growing contingents of the oppressed people' on the art of clandestine resistance. The youth, in particular, were 'the shock troops of the national democratic struggle'. The newly formed South African Youth Congress (SAYCO), headed by the fiery young militant Peter Mokaba, was the 'largest democratic youth organisation ever seen in our country', while 'most significant' was 'the growing unity of our women', whose Federation of South African Women had close ties with the ANC Women's Section. In this context, Tambo also commented on the potential for more white people to join the struggle. In the now regular funeral services of township youth killed by the police and army, middle-class white women of the Black Sash were often to be seen mingling among the mourners, their presence effectively protecting the crowd from further attacks and shootings.

In his address on May Day, Tambo made a range of powerful calls, demonstrating the ANC's knowledge of events on the ground and suggesting further campaigns to consolidate the 'unworkability' of apartheid. For the approaching anniversary of the Soweto uprisings, he exhorted South Africans to stage 'a most massive demonstration... through general strikes and heightened mass and armed actions'. In particular, the event should focus sharply on the struggle for people's education. To the 'noble' working class, he called on 'factories, mines, farms and other enterprises' to become the bases of the democratic trade-union movement, and exhorted growing civics in town and countryside to strengthen street and village committees. He called on people to refuse to pay rents and for the Defence Units to protect those persecuted for boycotting rents.

'Let us build and strengthen grass-roots organisations, engage in action to make the system unworkable and move ahead to establish organs of people's power. The ghetto councils and Parliament stooges should not be allowed to operate in our midst.'

Tambo also called on the people in the homelands to rise against the collaborationist administrations. He was, of course, referring particularly to the insistent attempts by the apartheid regime to foist 'independence' on the latest Bantustan, KwaNdebele. He also appealed to the coloured and Indian communities to 'act in unity with the rest of the democratic forces'.

The theme was the unity of democratic opposition in all sectors. Above all, the regime's divisive aggression had to be countered: 'Let the regime's death squads – the vigilante hordes – be made inoperative in all localities. It is the task of the democratic movement to deny the regime the social base from which it recruits these forces. The extent of our work among the unemployed and rural communities will determine the extent to which the regime can use our brothers against us.' And, more fatefully, he stated: 'Let us identify and isolate the incorrigible and professional hirelings and let them feel the wrath of the people.'

There was a widespread response to these calls, demonstrating to the world and to a harassed regime the upsurge of the ANC inside the country. In general, the direction suggested by the speeches was closely followed. A large part of the ANC's success lay in its style and, above all, the *language* of the ANC.

'It knew precisely how to strike a chord with people in a number of sectors, and whether we like it or not it was the military chord that was often the most effective,' commented Raymond Suttner.[119] 'You find all sorts of people using words like "combatant" and "detachment" to describe themselves and their structures.' It was a language, he pointed out, that had a way of often achieving what the UDF on its own could not do. In 1985, for example, the UDF, through its affiliate, the Soweto Education Crisis Committee, was struggling to persuade children to return to school. A delegation went to Lusaka to discuss the issue with the ANC, who then put out a call for the students to go back to the classrooms – these were their 'trenches'. Its militaristic metaphor and idiom, 'which may still be part of the problematic legacy that is with us today', was taking the education struggle seriously in its own right and placing it in the main body of the struggle.

Often, language was transferred literally. 'Now is the time to take action to realise the objectives of one democratic council for each municipality', prompted Tambo in his January 1986 speech. And soon afterwards, activist poet Mzwake Mbuli published his memorable 'Now is the Time!' and it became a hit, quoted throughout the country. From the same speech, in the year of the centenary of the discovery of gold in Johannesburg, was Tambo's remark, 'We... confined in black ghettoes on the periphery of the city, have nothing to celebrate', and the slogan 'nothing to celebrate' became so popular and vocal that the city was obliged quietly to drop its festival plans. Another widespread slogan turned the conservative argument for 'normal sports' on its head – 'no normal sport in an abnormal society', echoed Tambo, who in that same speech had called on all sports enthusiasts to 'help end the apartheid system so that in a normal society we can all have normal sport with all the benefits that will accrue to the people'.

On a broader, more practical level, within months of Tambo's prodding for 'an alternative system of education during this year, the tenth anniversary of the Soweto Uprising', a parents' Soweto Crisis Committee set up commissions to draw up curricula for democratic Mathematics, English and History school subjects. Activist educators and scholars were commissioned to provide alternative texts for democratic schooling for community discussion.

The following year, the committee (now called the National Education Crisis Committee) produced a History text and Maths and English curricula, which included indigenous methods of calculation and indigenous literature. Its text included the Freedom Charter for literary analysis.[120] Not surprisingly, these efforts were angrily rejected – with a perfectly straight face – by the Minister of Education as coming from an 'unrepresentative' source, and banned.

Tambo's January speeches emphasised the importance of organisations; very rapidly, effective new organisations would be formed. In 1987 alone SAYCO, the UDF Women's Congress, the Congress of Traditional Leaders and the National Association of Democratic Lawyers were set up. Tambo's 1989 call was for 'militant mass defiance... targeted against the many restrictions of the States of Emergency; the attempts to intensify racial segregation, group areas, anti-squatting measures and forced removals; rent, service charge collection and taxation'.[121] Many of these calls were already being heeded; Johannesburg's inner-city quarter, Hillbrow, was rapidly becoming a 'grey area' – blacks were simply moving into this whites-only-designated high-rise section of the city; rent boycotts were already a reality; laws against 'furthering the aims' of organisations were increasingly ignored – ANC and SACP banners were regularly unfurled at funerals and other community gatherings. The point made by Tambo, though, was a conceptual one, giving ordinary people status and ownership to their resistance on day-to-day issues. 'The spirit of defiance should permeate all the other campaigns we undertake.'[122]

Within weeks, unions and other MDM leaders called for a defiance campaign. 'We are unbanning the banned organisations,' they announced, referring to the UDF, the severe restrictions on COSATU, and the banning of the opposition newspapers named by Tambo himself: *New Nation, South* and *The Weekly Mail.* Areas of resistance were identified as 'sites of struggle'. A year later Tambo was able to celebrate the advances made in 'the theatre of struggle... on all fronts.

'The 1980s have seen us muster the most gigantic, organised and active political force for the liberation of our motherland. The township and the workplace, schools and universities, churches, mosques and temples, and villages and farms have become important sites of struggle for the eradication of racial tyranny.'[123]

An interesting outcome of one January call was the meeting in Lusaka with a delegation of black shopkeepers, victims of the 'people's wrath'. They wanted Lusaka to tell the people not to burn their shops. Said Albie Sachs: 'And the line the NEC took was, "If you join in the people's struggle, they will stop burning your shops. It is not for us to tell them. We are not in control of them; we certainly didn't order them to burn your shops. But if they see that you are part of the struggle, they will automatically stop burning your shops."'[124]

Sachs also recalled debates that arose from these developments during this time. Senior member and intellectual, Pallo Jordan, revisited the conventional wisdom of the role of the African 'petty bourgeoisie', a topic that was dealt with in the ANC's 'Strategy and Tactics' document of the late sixties.[125] 'The line had been that the enemy, the ruling class, would attempt to recruit a powerful collaborationist class, not just a few little bureaucrats, but a black middle class that will align itself with the existing racist power and become the oppressors of the people,' explained Sachs. 'In many respects, these were stigmatised as the main enemy because they were black, and because they would help to de-racialise oppression.'

It was Pallo Jordan who pointed out that the 'black petty bourgeoisie' were, in reality, treated with great hostility by the apartheid regime and were extremely marginalised. 'But if we give them the lead,' he argued, 'to become part of the mass movement while not dominating it, then they have a very positive role to play.'[126]

For Tambo's part, commensurate with his overall design to maximise unity, he welcomed the shopkeepers' visit to Lusaka. His message to them was, 'You are part of the nation. Think like a patriot, don't become a traitor. Don't betray the cause of the African people.'[127]

In the meantime, however, there was the danger of the degeneration of People's Power. Some of the more antisocial activities of the self-defence units and summary mob executions by necklacing continued. Although not widespread, the latter practice was growing, and many were accompanied by sensational coverage by the media. The atmosphere was reaching climactic proportions. By the mid- to late 1980s, it was Winnie Mandela who personified the spiral of unrestrained violence that was gripping the popular understanding of 'ungovernability'. Winnie, who had flouted her banishment to Brandfort and had returned to Soweto, had been rescuing vulnerable young people. Widely admired for her recalcitrance, she formed the Nelson Mandela United Football Club under the ANC call to campaign for the release of political prisoners.

It had long been the movement's policy to recruit and provide direction to the youth. Tambo noted with concern that 'a whole generation is growing up and has known nothing but daily violence meted out in the streets by the armed killers of the apartheid regime'.[128] In his 1986 speech, he called students, parents and teachers to campaign for an alternative system of education and to force the lifting of the ban on the Congress of South African Students. Tambo also praised the 'collectives of revolutionary cadres' that were being constituted – 'organised, rooted among the masses, ready to pay the supreme sacrifice if necessary'. In the Year of the Cadre (1986), the ANC was adopting new youth structures. 'We refer here to the mass combat units... to carry out various tasks, including those related to the destruction of the organs of the apartheid regime and to making the country ungovernable.' He called on these units 'to protect our leaders and to maintain revolutionary law and order'.

Direction was indeed sorely needed, for not all the youth were in formal structures. As UDF treasurer Azar Cachalia commented in post-apartheid years to the Truth and Reconciliation Commission, 'unaffiliated youths lacking direction or cohesion, many of them badly affected by detention, saw themselves as soldiers in the liberation struggle'.[129] Many constituted themselves into armed gangs and staked out their own turf, ostensibly to protect the communities from right-wing attackers and informers. But, in the context of states of emergency, mass arrests and the detention of many UDF leaders, the links of these gangs to MDM organisations or to MK were tenuous. They were lacking in political direction or indeed revolutionary discipline.

The fierce methods of Winnie Mandela's followers of harassing those who were seen to be lax in executing the stayaways and boycott campaigns led to uneasiness among some UDF affiliates. Public criticism of their bullying tactics in the community surfaced in a written attack by a black journalist,[130] but Winnie Mandela's speech in April 1986 also led to adverse publicity. She seemed to be encouraging the unarmed masses to intensify their struggles in whatever ways they could. 'We have no guns – we have only stones, boxes of matches and petrol,' she was quoted as saying and, to the embarrassment of the UDF, this was an endorsement of necklacing. 'Together, hand in hand, with our boxes of matches and our necklaces,' she proclaimed, 'we shall liberate this country.'[131]

By now, Tambo – who was travelling more widely and more frequently – had to deal with the international flak created by the feverish events inside South Africa. Frequently, he met with close interrogation on the meaning of 'hard and soft targets' and was asked to explain the nature of the insurrectionary armed struggle. Time and again, he had to remind his questioners that 'it is perfectly clear that the source of violence throughout our region is the apartheid regime'.[132] He also pointed out that the ANC had signed the Geneva protocols in 1980, which protected civilians in time of war, although in the South African context it was difficult to define 'civilians'. 'The ordinary white people are not those whom we are fighting,' he also told the AFP in Lusaka, following the car bomb outside the Air Force headquarters in Pretoria's central business district in 1983. 'However, most whites in South Africa are liable for military service and thus take part in the state's repression of black people.'

'We are not against civilians,' Tambo reiterated to the British newspaper *The Guardian* a few days later. 'We do not include them in our definition of the enemy... But implicit in the practices of the South African regime is that when you shoot an African you are not killing a civilian. We don't want to kill civilians. But some will be hit, quite accidentally and regrettably.'[133]

To his own constituency, Tambo explained the context and the reasons for the often frantic emphasis on popular violence rather than on apartheid's structural brutality. 'Our movement is currently subject to a determined onslaught which seeks to divide it, to weaken it, to destroy it,' he reported to the ANC UK region in 1987. They were now facing a duel to the death.

'The enemy's strategy is aimed at separating our movement from the people and attacking it... Not only externally but even from within. These [assaults] have grown out of our strength: the point has been reached when either the enemy succeeds or we succeed. And Botha's behaviour in the recent past demonstrates clearly that they have taken this decision. At all costs the movement must be destroyed; every effort must be put into eliminating and liquidating our movement. We have therefore a challenge to look at some of their methods.'[134]

Besides resorting to their routine bogey of communism, hostile factions were propagating hostile publicity on violence and terrorism in an attempt to wean support away from the ANC.

'They have taken advantage of the necklace to heighten the offensive against our armed struggle,' said Tambo. 'They have decided to sow confusion in every area of activity.'

Anxious over divisions within the country and misunderstandings between the ANC and the MDM, he warned: 'Our people are showing a manifestation to talk in different voices; to speak in different voices about crucial strategic questions of armament, disinvestments, sanctions... This offensive has been translated into neighbouring countries. It is an attempt – I'm not saying it has succeeded – to sow division and confusion... It is necessary that they recognise what they are trying to do and [for us to] fight back. We find they have extended this kind of offensive and joined forces with their own allies. Elements in the US, elements in the US Congress, conservative groups in the US have picked up this thing – the communism of the ANC, the terrorism of the ANC.'[135]

Then, in October 1985 Tambo was asked to give evidence to the Foreign Affairs Committee of the House of Commons in London. In reply to their questions on violence, he yet again explained how for half a century the ANC had tried to reason with the white minority rulers and communicate to them the oppression of black people. Even when it took up arms, it had avoided loss of life. But since 1976 there had been an intensification of bloodshed. Unarmed civilians had been killed by both the army and the police. Accordingly, the 1985 consultative conference at Kabwe had made a mindful policy decision that, in the course of attacking military establishments and other 'agencies of the regime', bloodshed would be unavoidable – even innocent blood.

'In the course of all this, there are excesses that we do not condone, but we understand the circumstances in which all this is happening. There has been such an onslaught on our people by the regime – the shooting of children.'[136]

A member of the Committee, Peter Thomas, asked, 'The children of black policemen and black officials have been killed and their houses burnt. You say you do not condone it. Are you willing to condemn it?'

'What I condemn, with all the vehemence I can muster,' replied Tambo, 'is the fact that for... three-quarters of a century we have been victims of white minority rule, which has progressively become more violent against us up to the point where it now assumes the forms we are witnessing.

'If the apartheid system stopped – and it is violent, it maintains itself by violence – if it is stopped, all this would not be happening... All this must be taken into account before one condemns an individual act. I regret all these things. I regret them, but I refuse to be asked to condemn individual acts when I know these acts would not have been there in the first instance had there not been this criminal system, this crime against humanity.'

Another member, Ivan Lawrence, then rephrased the question. Reminding Tambo of speeches he had made in 1981 and 1983 in which he had spoken of an 'onslaught' of armed struggle on apartheid, and of armed struggle as an 'overall strategy to seize power from the racist tyrants', he asked: 'Will you disown attacks in the ANC's name on African security policemen, councillors, former ANC members who have turned state witnesses, any bombing in city centres, shopping areas, public buildings and places of entertainment?'

In the sophisticated, uninformed white comfort of the West, phrases like 'racist tyrants' sounded bombastic and farcical. A timely reminder of the black experience of the fruits of apartheid was needed.

'In 1981,' began Tambo, 'one of our most outstanding leaders was assassinated by South African agents. In that year, South Africa had raided our people – raided Mozambique – and massacred very brutally some 13 of our people who were simply living in houses in Mozambique.

'That was in 1981. In 1982, the South African army invaded Lesotho and massacred not 19 but 42 people, shot at point-blank range [including] 12 nationals of Lesotho... I think your question fails to address this aspect: that we were victims of assassinations, of massacres. And in return for what? We were not killing anybody... It has been fortunate perhaps, in that time, that there have not been so many people dying on the other side of the conflict, but [there have been] many on our side. They have been hanged, they have been sentenced to long terms of imprisonment for exploding a bomb that destroyed a pylon; sentenced to life imprisonment. *That* is violence.

'This country,' he continued, referring to the United Kingdom, 'fought a war 45 years ago. How many children were not killed when the RAF was bombing away in Germany and other places? How many? Why is it so strange with us? After all, we have a fascist nazist [sic] regime that came to power in 1948, immediately after the defeat of Nazism in Germany.'

It was ironic, he pointed out, that the very paucity of armed struggle in the preceding two decades had only served to highlight the few targets that had caused loss of life. 'It has been an armed struggle with so much restraint that we have tended to draw attention to the few acts of violence that we have carried out, diverting attention from the massive violence that comes from the operation of the apartheid system.'

Tambo's explanation seemed to be effective, for the questions that followed then focused on how sanctions could assist the struggle and so minimise the violence of armed struggle. There were also questions, fielded by Thabo Mbeki, on the ANC's conditions for negotiations to take place. The meeting was to have a practical effect – the following year, the UK, as a member of the

Commonwealth, sent an Eminent Persons Group to South Africa to investigate the situation for themselves and to try to influence the Botha regime to offer conditions favourable to a détente.

It was often the ability of Tambo, the committed Christian, to communicate without affectation the earnestness of the ANC's 'moral high ground'. On the 20th anniversary of the founding of Umkhonto we Sizwe, Tambo invoked its opening justification for the turn to armed struggle. 'We have no choice,' he confirmed, 'but to hit back by all means within our power in defence of our people, our future and our freedom.'[137] In Sweden, where on a few occasions he addressed congregations from the pulpit, Tambo's integrity was unhesitatingly accepted. He was 'almost sad, when all these things happened', observed writer Per Wästberg, recalling just such an occasion at the height of the turmoil in the eighties. Tambo's credibility was enhanced by the fact that 'he didn't really try to excuse it – as many others did in the ANC'.[138]

After the bombing of several 'soft targets', and having spelt out clearly and firmly to his own Politico-Military Council the delicate nature of MK strategy, Tambo was determined to find a way to arrange to speak not only to leaders but also to guide grass-roots members of the MDM. His opportunity came in 1987, at the Children's Conference in Harare. Presided over by Bishop Huddleston, it had been organised mainly by the churches and supported by UNICEF and the International Commission of Jurists to protest the detention and torture of children in South Africa. For the first time, scores of delegates from home, many of them women and also children, were able to meet senior ANC leaders. Speaker after speaker from South Africa gave devastating witness to the torture and deaths of children, and the tragic rate of infant mortality particularly in the poverty-struck rural areas. Children themselves gave testimony. Then came a closed session where, for the first time, women and men from inside would meet the members of the ANC's NEC. Per Wästberg, who was invited by Oliver to attend the closed session – ('Squeeze in. I regard you as a South African and you can sit there') – described the atmosphere: 'To see the applause, the enthusiasm, the weeping of these people when Oliver introduced one by one all those unknown fighters in exile, and the roar when Joe Slovo stood up, was something more than anybody else. That was very touching.'[139]

Then Tambo spoke about the necklacing. He outlined his appreciation of the trauma that men and women were undergoing during this intensification of the struggle, and commended the courage of those who were fighting these last decisive battles. But neither the summary sentencing of suspects, nor the necklace method of execution was an acceptable method of discipline – they contributed to the propaganda interests of the apartheid state rather than serve the people as a whole. A sober audience listened carefully and took his message back home.

Uncoordinated acts of violence also resulted in the concern that the alliance was under strain. The episode involving Winnie Mandela was perhaps the most publicised symbol of the dangers of undirected and unaccountable 'ungovernability'. In late 1988, it was revealed that Mandela Football Club had kidnapped the 14-year-old Stompie Sepei at Winnie's behest. Stompie was accused of having slept with the white Methodist minister of the manse where he was staying with other children, and of selling out to the system. He was now nowhere to be found, and there were rumours he had been killed. The boy was not the first in the care of the Mandela Football Club to have been denounced and then gone missing.[140] Extremely perturbed, the Mandela Crisis Committee – there were many crisis committees at the time – met with Winnie and asked to see other children under her protection. They saw that some of the boys displayed fresh wounds. Reverend Frank Chikane then sent a report to Oliver Tambo, describing what the Committee had found, and imploring him to use his standing to intervene in 'this ghastly situation that is developing before our very eyes... [Mrs Mandela] shows utter contempt for both the Crisis Committee and the community'.[141] Shortly afterwards Tambo learnt that another boy, Katiza Cebekhulu, had also disappeared. He urgently contacted Chikane and asked him to call on Winnie immediately and not to leave the house without the boy. After hours of hard talking, Chikane finally discovered the boy's whereabouts and saw to it that he received medical attention.

The TRC later revealed that Winnie Mandela's entourage had been heavily infiltrated by *agents provocateurs*, and that some of those she counted among her friends were informers. The year before the scandal, a rival gang had burnt the Mandela house to the ground. The police had stood by and watched. Winnie's paranoia was thus not without foundation. The UDF had, however, tried unsuccessfully to draw her into an organisational haven – but she claimed to have her own underground contacts. In the meantime, indignant at the increasing number of stories circulating, 150 community leaders called a meeting to protest against the behaviour of the Mandela Football Club.

Then came the discovery of Stompie's body buried at the edge of a riverbed. He had evidently died of multiple stab wounds. A few weeks later, Soweto doctor Abu Baker Asvat, who had a month earlier examined Stompie and had found him badly bruised but not to have been raped, was himself murdered in his surgery. For the MDM, the tragedy brought with it a painful situation.

After much agonising, the organisation mandated Publicity Secretary Murphy Morobe to make a press statement denouncing the wife of their revered leader. 'We couldn't afford for our people to do something on their own,' Morobe later explained to Nelson Mandela's biographer, Anthony Sampson. Two days later, Tambo was obliged to issue a press statement in Lusaka on behalf of the NEC.

Tambo had been deeply disturbed at this turn of events and very worried about Winnie's psychological wellbeing. Winnie, the kinswoman from Bizana, whose beauty and talent had entranced the nation and indeed the world; who through her own suffering and defiance had (together with Tambo) kept alive the name of Nelson Mandela and raised his image into a universal symbol of principled and heroic resistance to a brutal racist regime. 'We must pray for her,' Oliver told Adelaide.

But he was also very anxious to maintain unity in the movement.[142] Winnie was widely admired as the 'mother of the nation' in her own right and had a broad and loyal following among ordinary people. Tambo was determined that the scandal should not lead to weakening and divisions in the movement. He had always emphasised the importance of political leaders, even more so in exile, being supportive.[143] He had been troubled to learn from Reverend Beyers Naudé, who had come to Lusaka to report to Tambo after having visited Nelson Mandela, that Winnie's 'irrational' and irresponsible behaviour had raised suspicions that she 'might be cooperating with the enemy'.[144] In response to the news that Winnie had broken away from the Federation of South African Women and started her own women's organisation, Tambo was dismayed. 'But that is exactly what we tried to prevent – division!' he exclaimed.

His press statement provided strategic guidelines for damage control, taking care to affirm the MDM and pointing to the dangers of individualistic initiatives. 'It is with a feeling of terrible sadness that we consider it necessary to express our reservations about Winnie Mandela's judgement in relation to the Mandela Football Club,' he said. 'Our organisation, complementing the initiatives of leading personalities of the Mass Democratic Movement, tried to use its influence to bring about the disbanding of the group... Unfortunately, our counsel was not heeded by Comrade Winnie Mandela. The situation has been further complicated by the fact that she did not belong to any structures and therefore did not benefit from the discipline, counselling and collectivity of the Mass Democratic Movement. Under these circumstances, she was left open and vulnerable to committing mistakes which the enemy exploited.'

Referring to the 'unbecoming activities' of the club, which had angered the people and their organisations, he added: 'We have every reason to believe that the club was infiltrated by the enemy, and that most of its activities were guided by the hand of the enemy for the purposes of causing disunity within the community and discrediting the name of Nelson Mandela and the organisation of which he is the leader.'

In this dangerous situation it was crucial that the problem be 'resolved within the ambit of the democratic movement as a whole, both at local and national levels'. For this to happen, it would be imperative that Winnie cooperate to effect a resolution. And in an appeal to the MDM, Tambo asked that it 'open its doors to her in the interest of our people and the struggle'. A climate needed to be created, he said, 'in which all problems facing the community be discussed to foster unity rather than let the enemy use them to achieve its ends'.[145]

As it happened, in the months that followed, Winnie Mandela was reinstated through the intervention of her husband, without consulting the MDM leadership. The challenge of disciplining and rehabilitating erring ANC leaders behind the scenes in the interests of the party, rather than publicly and in the media dazzle, was a tactical tradition that was to continue into the future.

It was in the context of this kind of turmoil, and with the risk that events might spin out of control, that Tambo called his PMC together. Skilful tactics, political maturity and attention to detail had to be navigated to maintain a finely honed balance in a changing situation. Tambo, with 45 years of struggle behind him, expressed his sense of the momentous epoch of the decade to his NEC and to visiting MDM leaders Murphy Morobe and Valli Moosa in 1989: 'Those of us who have lived through the fifties and witnessed the intensity of the struggle leading to Sharpeville and the armed struggle are seeing something new... As a result of that struggle, South Africa will never be the same again.'[146]

As resistance was increasingly manifested, with all sectors of the population joining in strikes, marches, boycotts and other forms of resistance, it seemed that at last the 'pillars' of the military, the underground and the masses were firm enough to support People's Power. As Tambo attested, 'The people had lifted the ban on the ANC and imposed on our situation their own legality.'[147]

The support of the international community, too, was coming together for a coherent thrust of sanctions against the regime – they had heeded Tambo's 'sanctions or bloodshed'. The 'balance of forces', said Tambo, had shifted. The state had lost... This was now in the hands of the ANC and the people.[148]

The four pillars seemed to be firmly in place. But would they be able to sustain the weight of the massive shift required for revolutionary transformation? Would they be able to stand firm in the midst of the gathering upheavals of violence, terror and the threat of civil war? Or (as some in the movement itself were suggesting) would a fifth pillar need to be put in place?

CHAPTER EIGHTEEN

Negotiating the Revolution

OLIVER TAMBO ONCE CONFESSED TO THABO MBEKI that for many years he was plagued by a recurring nightmare. He dreamt that a day would come when the regime would send a signal to the ANC. 'We want to talk,' they would indicate. 'We want to sit down with you and make an agreement to end the system of apartheid.' Tambo's nightmare was that the ANC would not understand the message. The ANC and the apartheid government were on opposite sides of the barricades; they had never managed to get through to one another before; they did not speak the same language, so they would not be able to respond to the signals. 'We would end up in a situation of greater disaster,' explained Tambo, 'whereas the situation could have been rescued.'[1]

What was one to make of this subconscious message? In his role as political leader, Tambo had always to think ahead and to plan strategically. The problem was that with such foresight inevitably came anxiety – often suppressed until it surfaced in his dreams. At times, Tambo confronted these feelings in his daily meditations and prayers. His reflections would serve to affirm his inborn, profound *ubuntu* – the sense that all human beings, no matter how far they might seem to stray, are human after all. As both a Christian and a humanist, he accepted that the Prodigal Son must always be welcomed back into the fold.

At the turn of the 21st century, most published literature on South Africa's negotiated revolution and the 'miracle' that followed has focused, correctly, on the crucial role played by Nelson Mandela in pushing the diplomatic option on the agenda at a strategic moment in the struggle. What the narrative has left virtually unrecorded, however, is the role of the ANC leadership in Lusaka. In particular, it is necessary to acknowledge the difficult, distinctive and comprehensive strategy employed by Oliver Tambo and his team of select cadres in an increasingly complex situation.

Under Oliver Tambo's leadership, the ANC's relationship of armed struggle versus negotiations was crafted into a bow with many strings. The goal was to end apartheid by isolating the regime. Armed struggle and negotiation were the means, rather than the end. The product of this extremely complex and delicate scenario was Tambo's achievement of the Harare Declaration, conceptualised by the ANC and endorsed by African states. This was *not* a 'Western plan'.

As Tambo often reminded the world, the ANC had for 50 years attempted to communicate and negotiate with the whites-only regime. It had continued to try to keep the lines open in the fifties, after the state extended racial discrimination and moved to suppress black and democratic opposition. Even after the movement was banned in 1960, an All-in African Conference called for a national convention. Indeed, as we know, Umkhonto we Sizwe declared at its launch that state-imposed repression had forced it into an armed struggle. Tambo confirmed this view in his 1979 diary. 'The half a century of brilliant oratory by our fathers and leaders up to and including Chief Albert Luthuli,' he wrote, '...33 years of speeches and resolutions by the United Nations, three decades of the Universal Declaration of Human Rights, and two decades of demands and denunciations by the collective voice of 350 million people of Africa speaking through their governments, and mass organisations and through the liberation movement' had failed to shift the powers that be.[2]

No, a more tangible response needed to be manifested; a call to arms, to goad the apartheid regime into a qualitatively different relationship, and a qualitatively different liberation movement.

And yet the ANC's door was always left slightly ajar. Despite his warnings and sober predictions of bloodshed, Tambo himself throughout the exile years left clues for those who could discern them. He would indicate, for example, that armed struggle, though necessary, was not and had never been a first option. He often urged the West to use economic embargoes against apartheid to minimise the carnage. 'Without sanctions a bitter war will be inevitable,' he stated in Amsterdam in 1981. In another note to himself in 1982, reflecting on the process of independence in Zimbabwe, he wrote: 'It is a question about the best solution: durable, viable, realistic. The facts of experience and the realities are these: we do not have to try a radical or a moderate solution. We decide on the *best* – not the best for the colonialists and racists; the best for the people of Z[imbabwe]. Armed struggle is not a solution, it is a *means* to a solution, and a solution is not a solution if it does not end the problem.'[3]

In January 1981, Ton Vosloo, in the Afrikaans newspaper *Beeld* (Mirror), raised the tricky subject of communicating with the ANC. Only a courageous figure within the establishment could get away with it. Vosloo argued that the ANC was 'the mother body of organised black politics'.[4] Perhaps he had been talking to BC newspaper colleagues – the concept was certainly part of its political culture.[5] Probably millions of blacks, he said, were supporters of the movement.

'The day will yet arrive when a South African government will sit down at the negotiating table with the ANC.' But the conditions, he speculated, rested on the ANC's ridding itself of its 'Marxist strivings' and accepting a federal structure – including the Bantustan system. The article raised eyebrows not only because of its startling content but also because *Beeld* was generally seen as a government-supporting newspaper. Was the publication of this bold speculation in any way significant? Unthinkable!

But a few years later, the regime itself dropped a hint that it might be interested in talking to the ANC. By 1984, the political circumstances of the region had altered. Having assisted in destabilising independent Mozambique, the regime's Nkomati Accord[6] seemed to have successfully defused the Frelimo government. Andima Toivo ya Toivo had been transferred after 17 years' imprisonment from Robben Island to a Namibian prison, then released – possibly, it was speculated, to foster division in SWAPO. The regime was clearly feeling more confident to experiment with new tactics.

'Anything is possible,' declared the South African ambassador to France just after the Nkomati Accord, 'even rapprochement with the ANC.'[7] Botha himself was preparing for his tour of Western Europe, a move that the ANC opposed.[8]

A few days after the ambassador's comment, Tambo was at the ANC's Solomon Mahlangu Freedom College in Mazimbu, Tanzania. He talked to the youth about this latest development.

'Some genuinely think that that is a natural thing to do. If Botha is travelling around talking to everybody in southern Africa, to leaders, why does he think there are no leaders in Africa? How genuine are his talks with Mozambique and everybody else? And therefore his *bona fides* – his *honesty* is being questioned. And so he is answering, "Well, we have no objections in talking to the ANC, but the ANC must throw away its weapons first, and surrender. Then we can talk to them." That is the effect of their language. But they are under pressure to talk to us – they are under pressure.'

Tambo acknowledged, though, that the pressure to talk was also building up for the ANC.[9] He promised, to a cheering audience, 'next time we are approached by somebody about talking to Botha', the ANC would consult the youth; because 'the future belongs to our youth'.

Two months later, the press asked Tambo, in Gaborone for a Southern African Development Coordination Conference (SADCC) summit meeting, to comment on these recent hints by South African officials. The ANC had not been approached directly, he told them, 'But we know the question is being discussed.' The ANC would be prepared to meet Mr Botha only after they were persuaded that there would be 'serious dialogue aimed at bringing about an end to apartheid'. A precondition for such a channel of communication would be the direct participation of imprisoned leaders such as Nelson Mandela. 'The participation of these leaders is crucial.'[10]

Scarcely a few weeks later an unofficial and oblique contact surfaced. In August 1984, Professor HV van der Merwe, an Afrikaner academic at the University of Cape Town, who had personal links with influential people in the establishment, and also – as a Quaker – international links with certain friends of the Anti-Apartheid Movement, made contact with the ANC. The ANC agreed to meet him – because, Mzwai Piliso explained later in an ANC news briefing, he was 'an individual of apparently good faith' – and also, no doubt, out of tactical curiosity.

Two meetings took place with Van der Merwe, but not at top level, the first in August, when Penuel Maduna accompanied him to Tanzania. Van der Merwe was 'the first Afrikaner to address a meeting in Arusha, which was basically an All-African meeting… He made a tremendous impression on me', confided Penuel Maduna.[11] After a follow-up meeting in December – when Piet Muller, a senior journalist from *Beeld*, accompanied Van der Merwe – ANC representatives Penuel Maduna, Thabo Mbeki and Johnny Makathini reported to Oliver Tambo and the NEC. Van der Merwe and Muller had suggested that the ANC meet certain members of the South African Parliament, either in Lusaka or in Grenoble, France. But for this to happen, Van der Merwe reported to them, Pretoria insisted on the precondition that the ANC drop all its contacts with the socialist bloc in Eastern Europe. Although nothing further developed from this particular initiative, it served to put the 'unthinkable', if only tentatively, on the agenda.

Muller's newspaper subsequently urged dialogue with the ANC. *The Argus* newspaper responded by quoting a survey revealing that 43 per cent of white South Africans favoured negotiations with the ANC. The National Party youth, who had begun steps to send a delegation to Lusaka and had been angrily stopped by PW Botha, were also said to favour negotiations. The government itself, said *The Argus*, was faced with evidence that the ANC had wide support among black South Africans. A growing number of people might also start seeing the irony, it continued, of the government talking to a Marxist-oriented Frelimo government and engaging in negotiations aimed at a settlement in Namibia, but not talking to the ANC.[12]

The ANC responded guardedly. Piliso pointed out that Van der Merwe had no official mandate to talk, although he had said that he knew 'at least one NP MP who was eager to meet the liberation movement'. The ANC had replied that if this person was able to get to Lusaka, an ANC official would be willing to receive him or her. At the same time, the ANC delegates had pointed out that Botha's condemnation of 'ANC terrorism' was hypocritical, since the apartheid regime itself was responsible for the ongoing brutality against civilians. The ANC reiterated its commitment to armed struggle, 'since the apartheid regime has blocked all avenues to talks'.[13] As Tambo had clarified in his 1984 tour of Western Europe, 'We cannot rely solely on the gun, but it would be disastrous if we abandoned it. Non-violence has brought more, not less apartheid.' On the other hand, said Piliso, 'The ANC is not saying there never will be talks.'

In fact, the ANC's National Working Committee (NWC) had – in anticipation of the Nkomati Accord the following year – called an extended meeting in 1983, to explore proactively scenarios for negotiations, lest they be caught flat-footed. They commissioned a group chaired by Pallo Jordan (deputy head of the Department of Information and Publicity at the time), including Joe Slovo, James Stuart and Simon Makana. Their brief was to examine this scenario in the event of negotiations. Such a situation could only come about, they argued, under three circumstances: '1. outright defeat of the apartheid regime; 2. stalemate; 3. or a 'Patriotic Front dilemma' (referring to the situation of the Zimbabwe Patriotic Front in 1979, when the [Front Line States] gave them an ultimatum – to go to Lancaster House or get out of our countries).'

If the ANC was subjected to 'irresistible pressure' by the Front Line States, the commission pointed out, it would need to be well prepared in order to avoid being dominated by the agenda of the other side; it would, therefore, be important to set their terms on the table. In another paper, drafted right after the 1985 Kabwe conference, Pallo Jordan discussed the constitutional debates among the National Party's strategists. The paper argued that the Freedom Charter needed more fleshing out to make itself understood by a wider audience. The ANC also needed to reassure the world on its own stance on political pluralism. Jordan suggested that the ANC needed a Bill of Rights and a set of constitutional guidelines that set out the political rights South Africans could expect under an ANC government.[14] Negotiations would at least create a situation in which the regime would be obliged to acknowledge the ANC, not as 'terrorists' but as interlocutors in the process of talks.

Soon afterwards, Tambo acted to appoint a constitutional committee, which presented its draft in 1987. According to Albie Sachs, 'OR came to us and he said that there was quite a lot of pressure on the ANC from various international bodies to produce an ANC constitution. People said, "We know what you are against, but we don't know what you are for. What kind of country do you want?"'[15]

It was a distinguished team, indicating the high level of the ANC's top legal skills. Led by Zola Skweyiya, it included Kadar Asmal, Zingisile Jobodwana, Penuel Maduna, Bridgitte Mabandla, Shadrack Pekane, Albie Sachs and Jack Simons. Tambo suspected that the task might not be easy, but the team thought it would be a fairly quick exercise. After all, they reasoned, they knew what the ANC policy was. But, as they began to work on it, they discovered it was far more problematic than they had anticipated:

'In the first place, to write a constitution in advance, not knowing the circumstances within which liberation would be achieved, and to tie everybody down was quite wrong. Secondly, a constitution shouldn't come from a committee of the ANC, or from the whole ANC; a constitution by its very nature should come from the people of South Africa, through a properly elected constitution-making body. Already in '87 we were saying that... On the other hand, people wanted to know where did we stand on all sorts of questions. So we came up with a formula [for] constitutional principles.'[16]

The idea had been implemented in Nicaragua, when, towards the end of the insurrection, the opposition groups agreed on four principles around which they would campaign. These were political pluralism, a mixed economy, participatory democracy, and non-alignment. These 'laconic statements' were not fully spelt out. They set out the ANC policy, yet left the door open for popular consultation. The advantage of this approach was that it would not be necessary 'to express the whole political philosophy... The style doesn't matter. What matters is that it just sounds and feels right'.

Tambo sat in on the meetings, taking a personal interest in this important update on the ANC constitution since he had led the construction of the 1958 document. '[He] would guide those meetings,' recalled Maduna, 'like an old rural headmaster who wanted everything done correctly. Words mattered so much with him and we enjoyed the debates we engaged him in – all of us.'[17]

In successive 8 January speeches, Tambo expressed support first for multi-party democracy (reflected in his 1986 speech), and then for an entrenched Bill of Rights. Looking back on the process in 1993, Albie Sachs saw 'the hand of Oliver Tambo' in both principles.

'In today's climate, these are very banal self-evident things; but one must remember that those positions were adopted at a time when we were in exile – we were underground, we were being bombed. We saw ourselves as a revolutionary movement, the slogans were "seizure of power" and there was very strong People's Power... The NEC adopted these positions. Partly, the Freedom Charter calls for multiparty democracy. That has always been our policy. Partly, we had seen, we had lived under one-party states, in various

African countries and seen that the general population gets alienated. We just could see that it wasn't actually serving the purpose of nation-building and national unity, which was its main justification.'

Tambo realised that the Bill of Rights was the answer to group rights – the critical question at that stage. The government was insisting on group rights for racial groups, and even the *Indaba* proposals from KwaZulu-Natal for a national convention were arguing for group rights. The ANC's Bill of Rights gave protection against abuse of minorities and individuals. Ironically, radical opinion inside South Africa was wary of a Bill of Rights because it was seen as a mechanism for protecting property over people. The direction given by Tambo and the NEC, commented Sachs, legitimised human rights 'from being something someone called a Bill of Whites – simply to protect the interests of the minority – into an instrument that could enlarge freedom for everybody and protect South Africans in future from abuse, even by an ANC government.[18]

'And again... it was on these questions, that Tambo was particularly strong... forward-looking; he always had that broad view. Anticipating many steps ahead. Because he wasn't tied down to a particular vocabulary, a tight, narrow vocabulary of power, he was able to utilise a language that is universally acceptable.'

In the meantime, the ANC was continuing with its multilateral struggle – the added dimension was the preparation for the eventuality of negotiations. It was planning to launch its 'ungovernability' strategy, which included the escalation of popular armed struggle. But while the ANC continued to arrange for military training in the Soviet Union, in international diplomatic circles as well as within the ANC, the message was advanced – a political solution was no longer beyond the pale. At the end of 1984, Gorbachev's Soviet Union, which, surprisingly, had not thus far had formal state relations with the ANC, received the movement's delegation in the Foreign Ministry.[19] This, in fact, was the first time that the ANC had been accorded an official state reception in the USSR. Then, in November 1986, for the first time a discussion took place between the President of the ANC and the Soviet head of state, Mikhail Gorbachev. The meeting was significant precisely because it was the first time. A few weeks earlier there had been a summit between Gorbachev and Reagan; two months later, Tambo was to meet with the USA's Secretary of State. The most positive outcome of the Washington meeting was the US acceptance that the ANC did not need to suspend hostilities in order for negotiations to start.[20]

The ANC was growing in significance. To Gorbachev, Oliver Tambo presented a proposal that the Soviet Union investigate the possibility of a joint

USA–USSR programme against apartheid. The ANC was reluctant to leave the field of Africa to the USA's policy of 'constructive engagement'. The USA seemed, to them, to want to be the only mediator in future talks. The Cold War was being acted out in Africa. Gorbachev's reforms aimed to end the costly Cold War. He was due to meet Reagan again, and the issue would be on the table. In a follow-up press statement, the two leaders said that they had agreed that a political settlement could be achieved in South Africa provided that Pretoria granted independence to Namibia, ended its acts of aggression and dismantled the apartheid regime. It left the issue of the USSR's continuing support for the armed struggle unspoken for the present.

The pace was accelerating. In 1985, Kenneth Kaunda who proposed an informal meeting between corporate businessmen and the ANC. Since independence, Kaunda had become friendly with investors in the Zambian copper mines. One of these businessmen was a director of Anglo American, Gavin Relly. Stationed in Zambia in the early years of independence, Relly had witnessed first-hand the peaceful transition from colonial to independent rule in that country. It was Relly whom Kaunda contacted. He and a number of other South African entrepreneurs were observing with concern PW Botha's political gaffes – as well as the highly organised strikes and stayaways – but they were also hesitant to intervene.

'You could see that PW Botha was trying to move forward and get rid of some of the formalities of apartheid; and I think moved towards letting Mandela out,' commented Relly afterwards. 'So some businessmen were afraid that this process might be upset if we appeared to interfere.'[21]

But pushing the corporations also had a broader context. By 1985, financial sanctions were beginning to bite. In the short term, they led to a mini boom as local capital was invested in a market vacated by the departing multinational companies. But now the leakage of capital was amounting to a haemorrhage, and organised black labour was turning political. Its strikes were becoming larger and its demands encompassed the calls of the community. The South African Foundation (headed by Relly) and other businessmen began to call for reforms. Botha had assured them that these were on the way. But his strategy of co-opting coloured and Indian communities in a 'tricameral' parliamentary system served only to anger the excluded majority even further. The black public, the democratic labour movement and the UDF itself were turning to the ANC for tactical guidance. The bombing of the Anglo American and Anglo Vaal buildings after the dismissal of 14 000 and 3 000 workers respectively in May 1985, for instance, clearly demonstrated the armed struggle's active support for opposition organisations and for the labour movement.

Unlike some of the bankers and relatively recent investors in the apartheid economy who were threatening to disinvest, the huge mining companies had an immense, century-old immovable venture in South Africa. With a 54 per cent stake in the Johannesburg Stock Exchange (according to a 1985 survey),[22] South Africa's massive mining corporations were not in a position to pull out in a hurry. They needed to explore an intelligent alternative to Botha's crude tactics. Quiet diplomacy seemed to be the best option.

Relly solicited support for talking to the ANC. A number of businessmen, including Afrikaner entrepreneurs such as Anton Rupert of Rembrandt and Fred du Plessis of Sanlam, as well as directors Tony Bloom of Premier Milling, Chris Ball of Barclays Bank and Mike Rosholt of Barlow Rand, were interested.

And all the while, Tambo was pushing for the strengthening of international economic pressure on the apartheid regime to hasten transformation, and so ward off further bloodshed. In the event, the date fixed for the meeting had to be changed more than once – as did the composition of the delegates from South Africa. When the plan was leaked, Botha made it clear that he was opposed to the initiative, and Rupert and Du Plessis withdrew. But two intrepid editors, Harold Pakendorf of *Die Vaderland* (the newspaper Verwoerd had edited) and Tertius Myburgh of the *The Sunday Times*, plus the enthusiastic publisher of the up-market *Leadership* magazine, Hugh Murray, braved it out. Former Progressive Federal Party leader – and Anglo board member – Zach de Beer joined the team from South Africa. The meeting finally took place on 13 September, after Botha's 'Rubicon' speech put paid to any expectations the progressive businessmen might have had in the prime minister. On the appointed day, the small group landed discreetly at an airstrip in the Luangwa Valley, where they were joined by Peter Sorour, a South African businessman in Zambia. They were all dressed as if on safari, in cool, open-neck shirts. A smiling ANC team, on the other hand, welcomed them warmly, formally attired in suits.

Forever afterwards, Relly retained fond memories of his meeting with Tambo. 'You know, Gavin,' he remembered Tambo laughing, more than seven years later, 'before the meeting we had in Zambia, I was scared stiff. I would never have come to meet you if Kenneth Kaunda hadn't forced me to.'

Relly replied, 'Well, Oliver, as far as I am concerned I was scared too!'[23]

But the ice was broken amid jokes about who most resembled revolutionaries and who capitalists. The two parties sat down around a table at Kaunda's game lodge, to a formal reception by their host. Kaunda was delighted to be talking to South Africans from both sides of the border. The purpose of the meeting, he said, was to ascertain just how much the two groups had in common, as opposed to focusing on the issues that divided them.[24]

Tambo soon suggested that the seating should not reflect a division between the two groups, and so they rearranged themselves around the table to form a 'mixed' group. Relly then put his cards on the table.

'We have come to this meeting,' he began, 'as businessmen, firm in our conviction that one cannot create a stable society or introduce reform measures without economic growth. Reform is simply not possible without economic growth, and our belief in reform is as avid on these grounds as indeed on moral grounds.' The ANC were coming face to face with capitalism at this particular meeting, he went on, 'whereas we are coming face to face with your policies in South Africa'.

Tambo replied with traditional African courtesy. First, he thanked their host and praised his 'unquestionable sincerity'. President Kaunda had always considered South Africa an integral part of the region and therefore considered its problems those of Zambia as well. Nothing would bring KK greater joy than to see the apartheid problem resolved. He also thanked the business delegation for its foresight in breaking through the barriers of resistance and coming to the meeting.

Tambo then turned to the ANC's fundamentals: 'The ANC believes that South Africa belongs to all South Africans, and all South Africans belong to South Africa,' he said. 'History has ordained it so (and some say God has ordained it so).'

It was an aside that reflected the conclusion that he himself had reached more than 30 years earlier when he received his 'calling' from the ANC to head the Mission in Exile. The aim now, continued Tambo, was to find the quickest way out of the present situation.

'This meeting is a rare opportunity to exchange views. The expressions of disfavour which surfaced in relation to your coming to the meeting oblige all of us present here to prove the worth of the meeting. All of us present owe

the world a task – South Africa is at the centre of world opinion, not for its achievements, but for what it is failing to do.

'We are not happy to see South Africa as an international pariah,' he added, 'and we look forward to making a contribution to the development of the entire region'.

Zach de Beer spoke of the delegation's impression of sterility, indeed retrogression, in South Africa's human relations in the previous 30 years. Recently, though, it seemed to have dawned on the South African government that there was only one South Africa – the dropping of the pass laws was extremely significant, he said, in this respect. All the same, the government had skirted the hardcore issue of political power sharing – this had remained untouched.

'Two questions arise,' said De Beer, raising their core concerns. 'How much bloodshed will there be before this takes place? And, secondly, how good a country will we have left at the end?'

This set off an animated discussion. The familiar questions about the influence of the SACP and the use of violence were raised. Everyone had a lot to say, debating energetically on the respective merits of private initiative versus economic justice, group protection versus one-person-one-vote, armed struggle and the ANC's understanding of 'soft targets', the relationship between big business and the trade unions in industrial disputes, and the duty of big business to press for the release of political prisoners. Relly flagged the possibility of official negotiations. He believed, he said, that there was a sincere and real undertaking by PW Botha for genuine negotiation.[25]

Tambo pointed out the under-utilised power of business to intervene. 'The government will not defy the views of business if business is insistent,' he said. It was unfortunate that 'the ANC will have to escalate the struggle and hundreds will probably have to die before the international community takes notice'.

During the outdoor lunch break – Tambo was asked by the businessmen to say grace – they spontaneously arranged themselves at tables in small mixed groups, talking animatedly. By then they had taken to calling each other by their first names. Asked afterwards about his impression of the ANC delegation, Relly commented: 'Mac Maharaj seemed to be very fierce, Mbeki gave a very good impression, Pallo Jordan seemed to be fierce; but nobody was very fierce at all. Nothing was very fierce. I mean, people said to us afterwards in [South Africa], when we said that they all seemed very, very reasonable people, like any other cross-section you find in South Africa, they all said: "That's where they are clever, these people."' (Significantly, Relly omitted to mention Chris Hani, who was to remain an insurrectionist until almost the end of his life.)

The businessmen were impressed by what they felt was the openness of the ANC. They had not been evasive in answering difficult questions, yet in their frankness, even Maharaj, Hani and Jordan were not abrasive. They respected the intelligence of these men and assumed their sophistication in accepting and understanding the imperatives driving a liberation movement. Tambo, Relly acknowledged, had a rare grace. He was, for example, able to convey that he was not a member of the SACP in such a way that he did not undermine allies.

'Members of the ANC are just that – members of the ANC,' Tambo said. As a youth, he explained, he had campaigned for the expulsion of Communist Party members. 'We were defeated. With the benefit of hindsight, we were wrong.'

Against that background, Tambo was on the lookout for the possibility of being overtaken by a Marxist agenda. 'In all frankness, I have great respect for those members of the SACP who are members of the ANC. I feel that they have absolute loyalty to the ANC, despite the fact that they are members of the SACP as well.' The ANC, he pointed out, was a national movement that could embrace communists, Muslims, Christians and anyone else who wished to join.

'I am often asked whether the new South Africa will be communist or capitalist,' he observed. 'It is not possible to say that the fight is for a capitalistic state or a communistic state – the fight is simply to be free.'

Of course, freedom had an economic dimension, and Tambo touched on class: 'The "haves" cannot continue to exist at the expense of the "have-nots" – freedom has to reflect a difference in the conditions of life.' But the details of nationalising monopoly capitalism would have to be worked out in a democracy. Beyond that, Tambo added, he was certain that private capital would exist.

Hugh Murray posed a question on the possibility of consensus. 'Would you vote for a government of national unity?' he asked.

'If I were a member of a party with South Africans, I would even vote for Tertius Myburgh if he were the best man,' replied Tambo. ('Much laughter', wrote Tony Bloom in his notes. 'Harold Pakendorf said that obviously reflected a basic lack of judgement!')[26]

Everyone thoroughly enjoyed the exchange. 'It was one of the nicest days I've ever spent,' confided Relly to Anthony Sampson – 'a picnic among South Africans talking about their future together.'[27] Bloom came away with the impression that the ANC's brand of Marxism was no more radical than a Swedish form of social democracy. For the business delegation, the meeting had the effect of 'demystifying and de-demonising the ANC', Relly concluded.

'I think the effect was that [if] the South African businessmen could go and meet these people and apparently came away unscathed, the odds were that some other people, including the governmental agencies, should look for themselves. And I think it opened that sort of doors.'[28] And at a press meeting back in South Africa, Relly said, with feeling, 'they want to come home. We must find a way for them to do so'.[29]

The immediate outcome of that encounter was discerned a week later. While South Africa was still labouring under a State of Emergency and mass detentions, a prominent advertisement appeared in several national newspapers. It was signed by 91 business leaders and was headed, 'There is a Better Way'. Expressing deep concern, the signatories advocated the abolition of all racially discriminating laws, the negotiation of power-sharing with acknowledged black leaders, granting citizenship rights to all the people of South Africa, and the restoration of the rule of law. Extracts of the advertisement were also published in the UK and the USA, where 10 chief executive officers of multinational companies endorsed the contents of its message.[30]

The white businessmen's meeting, while disturbing many in the ANC, proved to be a breakthrough. It was followed closely by the visit to Lusaka of magnate Sam Motsuenyana, head of the National African Confederation of Commerce (NAFCOC), with a delegation of African and coloured businessmen. He, too, was well pleased with the ANC's assurances that they were not against private enterprise but visualised a mixed economy.

But, to the disappointment of the businessmen, ANC attacks on hard and arguably even soft targets continued. They had perhaps overestimated the extent to which their advice could change ANC policy. 'Ungovernability' at home was whipping up more brutal reprisals, including mass detentions without trial, death squads, SADF raids and assassinations. Tambo and Radio Freedom continued an unequivocally militant rhetoric. The businessmen were puzzled at the fierce image that some of Tambo's official speeches conveyed, which was at variance with the warm, benevolent and conciliatory manner Tambo had demonstrated in Zambia.

'Some of us don't like violence at all,' he had said to the group. 'I have an abhorrence of violence – I even take insects out of the bath! But we are forced into violence. I, for example, won't hunt to kill because I do not like to kill.'[31]

In person, Tambo had displayed an intelligent awareness and sophistication. But what the businessmen had not understood was the ANC's holistic approach to struggle. There was no way that the movement could even entertain the undermining of any one of the 'four pillars of struggle', for it was on these foundations that success relied.

'The challenges we face are ones that arise out of success,' Oliver Tambo had observed in his opening statement at the Consultative Conference at Kabwe in 1985. Indeed, failing effective sanctions, he insisted, the regime would not be galvanised into talking without violence. It was, he said on Radio Freedom, 'the armed component of our struggle which causes the greatest threat for the apartheid system and its economy, and under conditions of struggle there is instability.

'Without the urgency of the counter-violence to apartheid's violence, there would be no rapid change transformation… We would be talking and arguing about things while they are making profits, for 10 years, 20 years or 30 years… It is the armed component which has made them come to the ANC.'[32]

This was a concept echoed by Commonwealth representatives to the South African Cabinet a year later, when they pointed out that violence 'was the only power available' to the ANC.[33]

A month or two later, Tony Heard, editor of the Argus Group's *The Cape Times*, published a long interview with Tambo.[34] The Minister of Justice had transgressed his own legislation by allowing the prime minister to quote Tambo selectively – naturally, only seemingly bloodthirsty extracts from one of his speeches, out of context. Heard managed, through colleague John Battersby, to arrange to get together with Tambo while he was in England. Heard met him one fine autumn morning in the Tambo household in Muswell Hill. Looking 'more like a British banker than the leader of a guerrilla movement', Tambo seemed to Heard to convey 'an old-world charm'. He noted, too, Tambo's style of speaking in 'slow, measured tones', without ever 'a word or thought misplaced. He knew exactly what his attitude was on the many subjects I raised'.[35] The questions were, of course, very familiar to Tambo, but knowing that the interview would for the first time reach a white audience in South Africa, he welcomed the talks that the ANC had enjoyed with their fellow South Africans and spoke reassuringly about their undoubted place in the country and their identity as Africans. He clarified the ANC's stand on soft targets – 'We will not go into cinemas and bars and places like that. We will not do that... We are not fighting against people, we are fighting against a system.' Tambo also spoke of the prospect of negotiations with the government.

'Is there a possibility of a truce?' asked Heard.

'There is always the possibility of a truce. We see the possibility of a truce. It would be very, very easy if, for example, we started negotiations... with the government, when they are ready because at the moment they are not ready.'

And he went on to give a description of the right climate for such talks. They were the conditions identified by the NWC subcommittee a year or two earlier: 'Lift the State of Emergency; pull the troops from the townships, and the police. And release the political prisoners. We have even said unban the ANC. Do all these things to create a climate.'

The interview, published as soon as Heard returned to Cape Town, cost him his job. But it also caused a major stir, and exposed thousands of white South Africans to the thinking of the ANC.

Meanwhile, the international meetings with the ANC intensified – in Lusaka, in London and in New York. In the United States, a quiet symposium had taken place in the spring of that year, arranged by sympathiser and doer-and-shaker Franklin Thomas, the first black president of the Ford Foundation. It was not Tambo's first meeting with corporate business.

In London, despite Margaret Thatcher's firm opposition to the ANC as a group of 'communist terrorists',[36] British businessmen, bankers and industrialists representing a range of multinationals, met with Tambo a few months later, first discreetly in the home of Anthony Sampson and then in a more public venue.[37] It was a major breakthrough. Lord Barberton of Standard Bank, Sir Timothy Bevan of Barclays, the oil giant Shell (boycotted by the ANC) and BP (which along with Shell supplied the South African defence system with fuel), Consolidated Goldfields and Courtauld textiles (which had invested in a joint venture with the apartheid government) were joined by Tony Bloom of Premier Milling as well as Chris Ball of Barclays South Africa.

Over lunch in the imposing Connaught Rooms in London, Tambo once again quietly portrayed the life of black men and women under apartheid. He again outlined the history of the ANC – its attempts to communicate with successive white governments until, banned, it was driven to armed resistance. He reminded the group how he had pleaded with the international community to impose sanctions on this 'crime against humanity' to minimise the foreseeable bloodshed. South Africa and her people had now reached a crisis point. An intransigent PW Botha – now carrying the title of President – claimed that he had not yet used a tenth of his military capability – nor, added Tambo, had the ANC. But 'governments often negotiate while there is war being fought'.

In the same month, Thatcher attended the Nassau meeting of Commonwealth heads. Shridath (Sonny) Ramphal, Commonwealth Secretary-General, who six years earlier had prepared the way for the UK to reach negotiations with Zimbabwe, was looking to do the same for South Africa. But Mrs Thatcher's determined opposition to sanctions and the ANC ensured only a minimal ban. ('Whoever entertained the idea', she asserted, that the ANC might ever become the government of South Africa was living in 'cloud-cuckoo-land'.) The resulting Commonwealth Accord confined itself to a call for the dismantling of apartheid, the ending of the State of Emergency, the release of Mandela and the unbanning of the ANC. Sanctions were limited to a prohibition on the purchase of Kruger Rands and new government loans. The most far-reaching decision, however, was the appointment of seven 'eminent persons' whose objective would be to encourage dialogue with South Africa.[38] One member of the Eminent Persons Group (EPG) was the former Nigerian head of state, General Olusegun Obasanjo. A shrewd and worldly-wise negotiator, he had the respect of Western diplomats and politicians, including Mrs Thatcher. But the idea also had to be sold to the South Africans, both black and white.

'White South Africa, Botha didn't like it – Pik or PW – but black South Africa didn't like it either,' recalled Ramphal. And, for Tambo's part, he too was sceptical. The ANC was 'not excited' about the plan, Penuel Maduna recalled.[39]

A similarly high-profile group had failed to reach agreement with the regime over a settlement for Namibia. Tambo feared that an EPG presence in South Africa might serve to reduce pressure on the regime. It might also cause the international community to let up on sanctions.

'The ANC was very cautious, very uneasy,' admitted Ramphal. 'I had to sell it to Tambo... My credibility, the Secretariat's credibility, the Commonwealth's credibility was a very critical element in selling it to the ANC which of course was absolutely crucial.'[40]

It was Thatcher who overcame PW Botha's doubts about the EPG, and persuaded him to allow them to visit South Africa. Tambo was pleased to learn that Botha had agreed to allow the EPG to visit Mandela.

What, in the meantime, of communications between Mandela and Tambo? When, in April 1982, Mandela was unexpectedly transferred from Robben Island to Pollsmoor in the Cape Town suburb of Tokai, he was isolated from all of his comrades bar three – Walter Sisulu, Raymond Mhlaba and Andrew Mlangeni. Rivonia Trialist Ahmed Kathrada joined them a few months later. Significantly, the prison's most senior leader, Govan Mbeki – 'the leading Marxist' as Anthony Sampson noted[41] – was not included. Prison authorities were no doubt aware of earlier disputes around various issues, including Mbeki's unequivocal insistence on the formal recognition of Oliver Tambo as President of the ANC while the movement dragged its feet.[42]

While more facilities were made available to the group, including the use of television and increased access to correspondence, the prisoners had no contact with nature as they had had on the Island and the accommodation was dark and damp. But Mandela was now able to write to Adelaide Tambo, whom he addressed as 'Matlala' – her African name – through a circuitous route, using fairly easily decipherable code names to pass on his views and responses to ANC policy.

One reason for the move to the mainland was probably Mandela's growing international fame and the regime's desire to isolate him for closer observation. The South African government was also taken by surprise at the extent of popular black support for Mandela. A year or two earlier, the ANC had shifted from its policy of a collective image to the tactical utilisation (with Tambo's keen participation) of Mandela as an icon of the struggle against apartheid. Successive visitors to Mandela bore out Tambo's observation of the striking impression Mandela made. His physical appearance, his bearing and assured but easy manners of an aristocrat impressed even reluctant cabinet ministers and senior officials, Kobus Coetzee, Minister of Justice, aggressive 'hawk' Louis le Grange, Minister of Law and Order, and the intelligence head Niël Barnard. Unlike Tambo, Mandela had not been tested in the outside world. As an enforced observer yet receiver of special treatment, he was in a better position to reassure his select, conservative visitors and address their concerns without having to worry unduly about his own constituency. Mandela had not been given detailed mandates, as Tambo always had, and so was freer to put a more flexible emphasis on interpreting ANC policy and events.

In January 1985, Thatcher sent Conservative Party House of Lords member, Lord Bethell, to visit the increasingly famous prisoner. 'The ANC is doing its best to restrain the armed struggle,' Mandela assured him. Bethell reported that Mandela 'deeply regretted the Pretoria bomb which killed innocent civilians' in 1983. This was, of course, indeed the case – the response echoed Tambo's personal feelings over the incident. But Tambo had many more constraints and considerations placed on him before he could speak publicly on the nature of MK targets. Tambo's dual role as both president of the movement and Supreme Commander of MK at times put an intolerable strain on him.[43]

As the campaign to release Mandela gained momentum, the ball fell into Botha's court. During Botha's European visit in 1985, he was faced with noisy campaigns, public demands and private questions about Mandela. In Germany, he was given tactical advice by a group of right-wing politicians: 'Offer Mandela his freedom,' they suggested, 'provided he unconditionally renounces violence.'

Botha liked the idea. In that way, he reasoned, if Mandela turned down the proposal, the world would realise that here indeed was a man who espoused violence as a political weapon.[44] 'Botha wanted the onus of violence to rest on my shoulders,' commented Mandela in his autobiography.

'I wanted to reaffirm to the world that we were only responding to the violence done to us. I intended to make it clear that if I emerged from prison into the same circumstances under which I was arrested, I would be forced to resume the same activities for which I was arrested.'[45]

It was clear to Mandela that Botha was attempting to drive a wedge between him and the ANC. He would address the nation directly, he determined. He prepared a speech in which he not only replied to Botha but also affirmed his commitment to the ANC and Tambo. On 10 February 1985, Zindzi Mandela read out her father's words to an ecstatic crowd at Orlando's Jabulani Stadium.

'My father says,' she began, and then went on to utter, for the first time in 20 years, Mandela's words directly – 'I am a Member of the African National Congress' – and flagging the banned organisation from the start:

'I have always been a member of the African National Congress and I will remain a member of the African National Congress until the day I die. Oliver Tambo is more than a brother to me. He is my greatest friend and comrade for nearly 50 years. If there is anyone among you who cherishes my freedom, Oliver Tambo cherishes it more, and I know that he would give his life to set me free.'[46]

The statement, with its Shakespearian cadences, was to be learnt by heart and repeated in the townships, the schools and in the streets. As for violence, Mandela's speech went on: 'It was only then, when all other forms of resistance were no longer open to us, that we turned to armed struggle. Let Botha show that he is different to Malan, Strijdom and Verwoerd. Let him renounce violence. Let him say that he will dismantle apartheid. Let him unban the people's organisation, the African National Congress. Let him free all who have been imprisoned, banished or exiled for their opposition to apartheid. Let him guarantee free political activity so that people may decide who will govern them… Only free men can negotiate. Prisoners cannot enter into contracts… I cannot give any undertaking when I and you, the people, are not free. Your freedom and mine cannot be separated. I will return.'

The message was an audacious move – it had effectively unbanned Mandela, bringing the ANC openly back inside South Africa, directly linking the Mission in Exile with political prisoners and people on the ground. Tambo was delighted with the outcome. Adelaide wrote to Mandela, congratulating him on her husband's behalf. Tambo's draft notes outlined the points in the letter:

'A short while ago, Bishop Madibane [Mandela] delivered a brilliant and stirring message on behalf of the Bishops' Synod… International support due in no small measure to role of Reverend Pokelmanb [Mbeki], Bishop Xamaza [Sisulu], Bishop Cartwright [Kathrada]; the family as a whole, particularly the elders, preaching to a packed congregation – a stirring sermon, which to this day continues in even more demanding terms of time, to draw favour – from the world religious community, raising the level of goodwill and fraternity. I do not know how much you keep yourself informed about the Church. We believers listen to the voice of the Church very intently. Highly commended worldwide.'[47]

It was not long before the regime made a tactical move. Mandela had a prostate problem and required minor surgery. On his discharge from hospital, he was removed from even his four comrades and ensconced in a three-room suite in Pollsmoor. It seemed clear to Mandela and his colleagues that the move was an attempt to wean him away from his comrades' influence. But, on reflection, Mandela decided that the move was an opportunity for him to initiate talks with the government and take individual responsibility for the consequences if they should rebound against the movement.

Removed from society and direct experience of the struggle out there in the dusty township streets, Mandela had observed with concern the negative aspects of ungovernability – the escalation of violence and the ensuing chaos. In hospital, he had received a visit from Kobus Coetzee, to whom he had written months earlier asking for an audience. He had also been taken for scenic drives by the prison warder. Mandela's 'quarantine' and the special treatment accorded him were causing ripples of uneasiness in the wider liberation community, even before his startling plans became more widely known.

Tambo continued to keep the political prisoners in the forefront of the ANC consciousness. In nearly every speech, he reminded the ANC members of their presence, acknowledging the sacrifices they continued to endure. In 1987, Tambo again read to members and students in the UK the Pollsmoor and Robben Island message originally sent to the Kabwe Conference two years earlier: 'We find it rewarding indeed to know that despite the immense distance and years which separate us, as well as the lack of effective communication channels, we still remain a closely-knit organisation, ever conscious of the crucial importance of unity and of resisting every attempt to divide and confuse.'

Tambo was worrying about more than one divisive issue in the movement, and he repeatedly emphasised the importance of unity. Although he did not mention directly the disturbing emergence of dissidents in camps, he used the legitimacy of the political prisoners to emphasise 'the over-riding principle of maximum unity... To lose sight of this basic principle is to sell our birthright'.[48]

On Mandela's part, as he formulated his bold resolution, he realised he had to find a quick way of reaching Oliver, who had sent a message asking him what he was up to. '[OR] said he knew I had been alone for some time and separated from my colleagues... Oliver's note was brief and to the point: What, he wanted to know, was I discussing with the government?' The tenor of his note suggested that he thought Mandela might be making an error of judgement.[49]

The best way to respond was to send a personal emissary, trusted advocate George Bizos. 'He was afraid that the story may go out that he was negotiating without the knowledge of Oliver Tambo,' explained Bizos, 'whom he acknowledged as the leader of the African National Congress. And he sent me off to Lusaka in order to brief Oliver, and also to assure him, assure Oliver, and through him the movement as well, that Nelson was in control.'[50]

In the words of Mandela, 'I was convinced that the time was right for us to act.' He sent a memorandum with Bizos, assuring the ANC in Lusaka that he would not act without Tambo's approval. He motivated his action and asked them to support him. 'They did so without hesitation... But of course our people were outside and conducting the armed struggle; and it was not easy for them, and especially because I was isolated, not only from the leadership outside, but [also] from the leadership inside prison. And this is human, when a man starts a move, without consultation, to say what is happening. So there was this reluctance at first. Has the government corrupted this man, won him over?'[51]

Mandela had confidence in Tambo's grasp of strategic thinking to deal with this new stratagem. Tambo consistently shielded Mandela from any uneasiness by ANC members, emphasising the importance of unity and assuring the leadership that he was in contact with Mandela.

The Commonwealth's Eminent Persons Group was finally able to pay a visit to Mandela in March 1986, stopping over in Lusaka to give an account of their overall plan and anticipated meeting with Mandela. The previous month, their emissary, General Obasanjo, had been permitted to see Mandela alone, and reported back to his colleagues that the man 'was no communist, simply an African leader'.[52] When the EPG as a whole met with Mandela, they too were impressed. The March visit was a preliminary one and they returned in May, but after an absence of only two months, they found deteriorating conditions in the country.[53] In Cape Town's informal settlement of Crossroads, they observed an increase in the activities of black vigilantes, who 'with active backing from the security forces, were attacking supporters of the UDF, including women and children, and setting fire to their shanties'.

In this second May meeting with Mandela, the EPG ascertained that he was willing to go some way towards creating a calmer atmosphere in preparation for negotiations, provided the government demonstrated a similar programme. But again Mandela emphasised the necessity for him to be able to consult with representatives of the Mass Democratic Movement and other internal groups, and for the EPG to talk to the ANC in Lusaka. On the same day, the EPG met with Foreign Minister Pik Botha, who wanted the EPG to emphasise to the ANC that it was not possible to topple the government through violence – the government could generate enormous military power. In any case, he said, there was no point in pursuing this route, because in the final analysis negotiations were inevitable. The EPG arranged to meet with the Cabinet a few days hence.

The group left immediately afterwards for Lusaka – their third visit there. They had already determined, having undertaken at an early stage formal consultations with Tambo and the NEC, that the role of the ANC's external leadership, because of the nature of its struggle, its popular credibility and support inside the country, was 'central to the South African political problem'.

Now, on 17 May, they met again with Oliver Tambo and NEC members. They were able to give them news of Mandela, whom they had seen the day before, and to reiterate his insistence that despite their extensive discussions, he was but an individual member of the ANC. The EPG reported on their consultations with the UDF, COSATU and AZAPO. Without exception, they found, 'government was regarded as deceitful and untrustworthy' – a huge credibility gap would have to be bridged before there could be negotiations. The churches, too (in particular, the members of the South African Council of Churches – to which the Call of Islam was also affiliated – and the South African Catholic Bishops Conference), were revealed to be 'a force for change'. They had day-to-day knowledge of the problems of ordinary people, having regularly to provide shelter to men, women and children fleeing detention and violent harassment. They all 'shared a deep-seated fear that South Africa stood on the brink of catastrophe'. The government's reform programme, they felt, was inadequate as it left apartheid's 'fundamentals' intact. The EPG had also had discussions with businessmen (overwhelmingly in favour of talks with 'moderate blacks'); the PAC (like the ANC, insisting that violence was self-defence); 'homeland' leaders and the parliamentary opposition, the Progressive Federal Party.

The EPG then shared their suggested negotiation concept with the Tambo group. Only now, after putting it to the Botha government nine weeks earlier and talking extensively to the opposition inside, did they feel ready to present it to the ANC. Basically, their key suggestions for negotiations were:

'For the South African government to terminate the State of Emergency; unconditionally release Mandela and other political prisoners; lift the ban on the banned organisations and initiate (in the context of all sides suspending violence) a process of dialogue across lines of colour, politics and religion, with a view to establishing a non-racial and representative government.'[54]

Tambo listened keenly. Expressing appreciation, he said that they would not be able to give a considered response before they had consulted more widely. The ANC, based in Lusaka, was in a difficult position: 'The organisation is spread out – it has responsibilities to many people, including our leaders in jail and all of those at home who support our endeavours and influence our thinking.'

'Insofar as the concept corresponds to the Nassau Accord,' he added, 'it will command the support of the ANC.' In principle, Tambo had no objection to negotiations, as long as they did not become a 'device to quell internal demands and weaken external pressures'. The government had demonstrated its bad faith again and again – its double-dealing with SWAPO, its violation of signed agreements in Angola over the Lusaka Accord, and in Mozambique with the Nkomati Accord, were ample testimony to their diplomatic unreliability.

'The regime,' pointed out Tambo, 'after all these weeks has still not given you a substantive answer.'

Other NEC members then raised questions for clarification. What did the government have in mind by the concept of 'power-sharing'? Was this a code word for black participation in the tricameral constitution? If so, there would be no basis for negotiation. On the question of the suspension of violence, the EPG made clear that a simultaneous action had to be undertaken. On the issue of the removal of troops from the townships, the NEC pointed out, free speech and assembly did not necessarily follow. The EPG agreed that the latter was an additional demand that had to be made separately, in its own right.

At the end of the discussion, Tambo summed up. He affirmed that both groups had an interest in reaching a point where apartheid would cease to exist, and the EPG concept could help them achieve that. 'We would want about 10 days for consultations before we can give you a firm answer,' he concluded.

Encouraged, the EPG returned to South Africa, looking forward to making progress in their meeting with Cabinet on Monday. On Sunday, they briefed Cosatu, UDF and Azapo representatives. But the next morning, the EPG were stunned to hear on the radio that the SADF had raided 'ANC bases'. The air strike in Lusaka had targeted the Department of Information and Propaganda headquarters, but had in fact hit the refugee centre run by the UN Commission on Human Rights; in Zimbabwe, they bombed a house; in Gaborone, they attacked the homes of ANC personnel. None were military targets. The attacks were all in 'capitals we had visited in the course of our work'.[55]

Why this blatant violation of international law? It certainly forcibly reminded the EPG and its opponents of 'the other dimension of the government's strategy', which was to 'force its immediate neighbours to submit to South Africa's economic and political domination of the region'. The Botha government was not happy with the headway that the EPG was making amid the accompanying unfavourable publicity – Botha had four days earlier broadcast a speech spelling out a 'new constitutional dispensation', and warning against 'interference by outside bodies'. It galled Botha that the EPG had been freely moving around, commenting, listening to grievances and making glib recommendations. They were a potential hazard to the regime, threatening to eclipse Botha's initiatives and weaken his upper hand – all this in the face of the ANC's continuing campaigning for 'ungovernability' and the escalation of violent resistance in the townships. With high expectations for the release of Mandela now reaching fever pitch worldwide, Botha did not relish appearing to have lost control of events. Defiantly, he asserted his position as president by approving his minister's proposal for a military strike, without consulting the Cabinet. The move would strengthen his hand prior to negotiations. Botha did not see any problem with cross-border attacks – Israel had indulged in them several times and, more to the point, the USA had bombed Libya only a week earlier.

For the EPG, the attacks cast serious doubts on all possibility of a negotiated settlement. Nevertheless, the Group kept their appointment with the Cabinet, wanting to keep doors open. It transpired at the meeting, though, that the government had retreated to its former position – there would have to be a visible reduction in violence before it would be prepared to even consider talking. Botha had demonstrated his goodwill, he said, by announcing sweeping reforms – the ball was now in the court of the opposite side.

Later, the ANC issued a statement asserting that the regime's response to the Commonwealth initiative 'was crystal clear'. Mandela, who had invested much in the preparations for talks, was deeply disappointed. The raids had 'utterly poisoned the talks'.[56] To the EPG, the raids appeared to confirm all warnings not to trust the regime. In their concluding report, the EPG pointed out that there could be no negotiated settlement in South Africa without the ANC.

'Among the many striking figures whom we met in the course of our work, Nelson Mandela and Oliver Tambo stand out. Their reasonableness, absence of rancour and readiness to find negotiated solutions which, while creating genuine democratic structures, would still give the whites a feeling of security and participation, impressed us deeply.'

'If the government finds itself unable to talk with men like Mandela and Tambo,' they concluded, 'then the future of South Africa is bleak indeed.'

The attempt at talks had collapsed after all the hard work, the sensitive and sincere efforts to understand and reach out to the widest possible range of interest groups. The EPG had had to contend with suspicions from both the government and the opposition; nearly all groups had been cautious of outside interference. Nevertheless, the EPG had been able, through their legitimacy – conferred, ironically by Thatcher herself – to shuttle back and forth, conveying messages from prison, the internal movement and the external mission. To the extent that they opened doors for talks by civil society to take place, the EPG had managed to take the process forward. But it was to take more time, and cost many more lives, before negotiations could even begin.

While PW Botha was bent on his course of full onslaught, a broad spectrum of groups continued to make journeys, crossing borders and oceans to meet with the ANC. Franklin Thomas of the Ford Foundation had already arranged a discreet meeting between Thabo Mbeki, Mac Maharaj and former Robben Island prisoner and Oxford graduate Seretse Choabe with influential Afrikaners, including Pieter de Lange, head of the Broederbond. That the encounter made a favourable impression was borne out by the resulting pressure that the Broederbond was to exert on the government to agree to negotiations – but this was to come later. In August, Frederik van Zyl Slabbert, having resigned from Parliament earlier in the year as leader of the Progressive Federal Party, led a delegation of 50 intellectuals and journalists to meet the ANC in Dakar – there were, after all, Afrikaners who opposed apartheid. (To a delegation of students from the famous Afrikaner university, Stellenbosch, which had bred generations of prime ministers and members of the Broederbond, Tambo said, *'Julle het die moeilikste taak'*.)[57] The outcome was a joint call for the unbanning of the ANC and a negotiated settlement.

But it was the meeting in November 1987 with a group of elite Afrikaner academics that was to prove in the long term to be the most significant. Professor Willie Esterhuyse, political philosopher of Stellenbosch University, brought a few Afrikaner colleagues to a meeting with the ANC arranged by Consolidated Gold, the holding company for Goldfields. Esterhuyse was well qualified to undertake this risky political venture: he had both the legitimacy in establishment circles and the leeway as a respected academic and public intellectual; he was active in debates and regularly wrote articles for *The Sunday Times*; he was *'verlig'* (enlightened), close to influential people including cabinet ministers and the Broederbond; he had also recently written *Afskeid van Apartheid*, which had caused a stir, and had indeed been translated into English under the title *Apartheid Must Die*.

It all began early in 1987 when Esterhuyse talked on the telephone with a journalist friend, Fleur de Villiers (niece of ANC activist and ex-Treason Trialist, Jan Hoogendyk), who was living in London. Discussing Esterhuyse's book, Fleur suggested to him that the ANC needed to meet and understand Afrikaners who were critical thinkers yet still in the fold. He should have a confidential meeting with the ANC, and she could arrange for him to participate in such an event through a friend in Consolidated Gold. A week or two later, National Intelligence contacted Esterhuyse and asked to see him in Stellenbosch – it did not need great powers of deduction to realise that they had been tapping his telephone. They were keen, they said, to find out what the ANC was thinking.[58] Later, Esterhuyse made direct contact with Niël Barnard, who was pressing for making discreet contacts with the ANC. Esterhuyse was so serious about the project that he resigned from the Broederbond and even gave up attending the church committee. 'I did not want to be institutionally involved,' he explained.

And so began a two-track exercise. In his first meeting, Esterhuyse was part of the Consolidated Gold delegation that met openly with the ANC. Here Esterhuyse spoke privately to someone from the ANC and requested a confidential, separate conversation with an ANC delegation. As insurance, Mbeki first sent 'explorers' to assess whether a follow-up would be worthwhile. These were Aziz Pahad, Tony Trew, Harold Wolpe and an uneasy and suspicious Wally Serote, fresh from military training in the Soviet Union. By the end of the meeting, the 'explorers' formed a favourable impression, and reported back to Mbeki and the NIS. Several meetings followed over the next few months between Mbeki and Jacob Zuma and Esterhuyse and other colleagues. These included constitutional scholar Marinus Wiechers, economist Sampie Terreblanche and Willie Breytenbach, also from Stellenbosch, but there were some 15 others during the course of the get-togethers. The meetings were held in a secluded manor house, Mells Park, owned by Consolidated Gold, whose chairman had been persuaded to finance the secret project. In the discussions, Esterhuyse made clear that he was approaching them as an emissary and would be reporting to the National Intelligence Service (NIS) as well as the ANC.

'The first talk was an exploratory talk; it was only academics,' explained Esterhuyse, although everyone understood the subtext: that it might lead to more significant exchanges in the future.

Esterhuyse had no idea what to expect from ANC revolutionaries. He had approached the meeting with some trepidation but as soon as he met Mbeki, he said, his misgivings melted away. Mbeki had read *Apartheid Must Die* and, as they shook hands, he mentioned with insight an argument in a passage even the author had forgotten. Esterhuyse was impressed. The man was an intellectual, Esterhuyse observed; he seemed to have judgement and an appealing low-key, sophisticated style.[59] The small gathering concurred that the purpose of the get-together was merely to convey informal messages and exchange ideas. The meetings took on a mode of small social conversations over dinner and drinks, in which they shared each other's political, cultural and even sporting perspectives, exchanging anecdotes. The talks often went on until late into the night.

'Niël Barnard accepted that it was necessary to develop avenues to interact informally,' said Esterhuyse. And indeed the whole exercise served to break down barriers, prejudices and stereotypes. The ANC emissaries proved to be as judicious as the Afrikaners, and convincing.

'Thabo ran rings around them,' remarked Michael Young, Consolidated Gold's public relations manager and convenor of the publicly known meetings. 'The Afrikaners had never seen anybody like him: he moved in the international circles to which they aspired.'[60]

Gradually, the successful personal interactions evolved into a trust relationship, paving the way for more formal, direct interaction.

On 31 May 1989 (the anniversary of the South African Republic, Esterhuyse noted), he supplied Mbeki with a code name and a telephone number. When Tambo gave him the go-ahead, Thabo called Esterhuyse. 'That meant I could set up the meeting (between the NIS and ANC),' recalled Esterhuyse.

It was after that telephone call that Mbeki reported to Tambo, asking permission to go ahead with the talks. Tambo agreed that the event should be unofficial, and that it should be kept under wraps for the time being. Clearly, the project was hazardous. It might well be a trap calculated to expose the ANC and consequently lead to division. And indeed, the ANC now realised, the NIS was trying to persuade Mandela to renounce armed struggle, which could then be used as a lever to discomfit and weaken the ANC in exile. But, as Tambo explained to Mbeki, his nightmare had been that a singular opportunity would be lost. These people were part of the political elite, deeply embedded, by birth and status, in the Afrikaner ruling oligarchy, yet able to reach out in a communicable way to their corresponding equals in the ANC.

According to Esterhuyse's understanding, 'Tambo was the one who was very, very emphatic about the fact that they should get to know Afrikaners within the establishment to find out what was going on in their head, because at that stage a small group in the ANC also realised that negotiations were inevitable; but they couldn't say it; so they had to build a plank.'[61]

Mbeki corroborated this impression: 'OR's position had been, you can't *not* want to talk to people – it's incorrect. We are after all organising everybody to get involved in the struggle against apartheid. And you can't say I want to talk only to those people who are already converted.'[62]

While that these clandestine talks were proceeding (there were two before 1990), Niël Barnard had arranged for himself and senior prison personnel to meet Mandela on a regular basis at Pollsmoor. Only 36 years old, Barnard's smooth style and coldly cerebral logic bestowed on him the self-assured confidence to challenge accepted procedures in a highly authoritarian context.

'He also had to fight with Military Intelligence, because MI was running the show. This was an important point because if there was a leak, he would be able to say it's the job of NIS to spy on people,' explained Esterhuyse. It would be easier to protect not just the NIS at this sensitive stage, but also the ANC. Over this period of preparations for talks, Barnard had skilfully moved closer to PW Botha. It seems highly likely that Botha knew what was going on, but looked the other way – he could not afford to acknowledge these moves.[63]

In the meantime, Tambo also had to handle tensions over contested terrain. The leadership were acutely aware of the changing circumstances in the region, and the pressures that were being exerted by the USA on Angola. The Soviet Union, along the *perestroika* course of 'new thinking' on foreign policy, made it clear that it was opting for a political solution. In December 1988, a 'non-aggression' agreement between Angola and South Africa was signed in New York (along with Cuba). The quid pro quo was that South Africa would cease to support Unita in return for the departure of ANC and Cuban troops from Angola.[64]

'It was clear,' recalled Thabo Mbeki, 'that there was a process leading to the independence of Namibia, the withdrawal of Cuban troops in Angola, an implication similar to Nkomati, so troops had to be moved to Uganda as part of the deal – the price that was extracted in the process of those negotiations. It became clear that we were moving towards negotiations.'[65]

With typical foresight, Tambo was able to assess the inevitable implication when it came, and was instrumental in the decision to pull out of Angola without further ado and relocate the camps to Uganda.

But there were also concerns inside the movement. Many younger cadres, especially, had been disturbed by the Lusaka meeting with the businessmen – discussions with the multinational corporate world seemed to be marginally more acceptable because of the need to push for sanctions. But with the managers of South Africa's racial capitalism? Tambo's antennae picked up this unease, and he gave an analysis in his report, published shortly afterwards in *Sechaba*.

Much of this burning debate was playing itself out in the pages of the ANC monthly, *Sechaba*, as well as the *African Communist*.[66] Tambo's strategy of employing a multifaceted approach was to continue to foreground the primacy of mass mobilisation and armed struggle. In his talk to the ANC intelligentsia in the UK in October 1987, the apartheid regime was still 'the enemy' as opposed to 'the other side' (as the conceptual phrase became a couple of years later). In 1987, Tambo was still publicly spelling out the terms before negotiations could even begin. He illustrated the ANC's approach in discussions he had undertaken six months earlier with US Secretary of State, George Shultz:

'We explained to him that in our experience, negotiations have started when the parties were ready to go into negotiations, notwithstanding that hostilities were continuing. We cited a number of instances like Vietnam, Zimbabwe, Nkomati, Lusaka Agreement or Lusaka Accord, Namibia; we cited all those instances as to how, in each of those cases, negotiations were in progress while hostilities were also in progress. And an agreement about a cease-fire was reached at some point in the negotiations.'

The ANC was conducting the struggle on two fronts – one openly and the other behind the scenes. It was perhaps the latter that Tambo bore in mind when he subtly hinted at possible alternatives to come: 'Whatever variations in the tactical area, in strategic terms we have the initiative. When Botha makes our movement the issue for the elections, he is acknowledging the fact that we even dictate what should be the issue of elections in SA. Our power dictates that.'[67]

In the meantime, the 'four pillars' had to be maintained, and the official policy focused on these, rather than the 'fifth pillar' of preparing for negotiations. 'The reality in our country,' stated Tambo on 26 June 1987, 'is that the regime confronts the perspective elaborated in the Freedom Charter with states of emergency, massacres, mass detentions, torture, repression and aggression.

'To our demands for one person one vote in a unitary state and the sharing of the wealth in our country, the oppressor replies with military rule, vigilantes and state terrorism. To all this... we have no alternative but to unite in action and to mount an all-sided concerted offensive against the apartheid system.'[68]

The truth was, Tambo told a number of people, that 'we will have to develop our own perspective on negotiation'.[69] To the NEC and the other committees, the issue was thoroughly canvassed. Penuel Maduna, who attended one such meeting, remembered Tambo's guidance on this difficult issue. He confirmed what by now had become the popular wisdom about Tambo.

'Tambo was the kind of leader who would never suppress a viewpoint. Even if he didn't agree with you, he would grant you the right and the opportunity to be heard completely. Completely, completely, completely. And he would tell you he benefited from the views and the wisdom of all. And at the end of it all, beautifully summarise the debate – and we would have a policy on that issue.'[70]

Arising from discussions, in 1988 Tambo appointed a President's Team on Negotiations under his stewardship to develop the ANC's perspective on negotiations, taking his cue from broad discussions that had taken place in the NEC, talking to the Mass Democratic Movement and from Mandela. The ANC also had discussions with the OAU, sketching out the concept of negotiations from a 'Pan-African' viewpoint. Tambo-style, warmly and with a sense of comradeship, there was a gentle insistence that the ANC drive the process.

But pressures were escalating on all fronts, not least the pressure of time. Tambo was driving hard to push through the sanctions that would shift the 'balance of forces' towards the ANC. And the escalation of events brought other unexpected setbacks. Despite the tumultuously rapid developments at home and the enthusiasm for the movement everywhere, the organisation was coming under increasing strain. One young man even wrote to resign from the movement just five years after his arrival in Dar: 'Nothing is forcing [me] to resign. I just want to forget the struggle for a bit, relax my mind and try to live [an]other life away from the South Africans.'[71]

The movement in exile had become such a large and, in many ways, unwieldy operation that the leadership could easily overlook nooks and crannies in the structures and, in the process, neglect the wellbeing of individuals. Certainly, many unhappy and unacceptable experiences of the exile movement's cadres 'from below' were not foregrounded. The ANC discourse was one of sacrifice for the enhancement of the movement as a whole; many cadres embraced this vision and tolerated the hardships experienced on the ground in exchange for the anticipated happy outcome.[72] Indeed, the processes of leadership formation itself – the manner by which people were delegated to undertake tasks and why they often remained in those positions – needed periodic review, but were not always able to be undertaken; accountability tended to slip by the wayside.

For Tambo, freedom was the end vision of the struggle – the apex, the 'mountain top' – and he tried to ensure that democracy would as far as possible also be the means. Consultation, participation and human rights were his preferred means of reaching a goal. 'OR is a natural democrat,' observed Pallo Jordan.[73] His unhesitating acceptance of the Bill of Rights drawn up by his Commission included freedoms probably beyond his immediate experience.[74]

But there were certain structural constraints on the best of intentions. Firstly, there was the restriction of exile, which removed the movement from its base, and put additional pressures on security and on unity. Tambo was, above all, dedicated to keeping the movement together, and sometimes this involved withholding information that might destabilise sections of the movement. He was careful about the particulars he had garnered about Mandela beginning to talk to officials of the government. He had counselled Mbeki to go ahead clandestinely with his project with the Afrikaner academics and the Broederbond.

At the same time, Tambo headed the top secret Operation Vula (for *Vulindlela*, meaning 'Open the Way'), a covert project of which not even the ANC's Security Department was aware. The simultaneous sponsorship of the Mells Park and Vula initiatives was an example of Tambo plucking the 'bow of many strings' – the strings of quiet diplomacy, armed struggle, the underground and the mass base. It was Tambo who selected the operatives and sent them inside to work underground politically, among the various opposition organisations burgeoning at home. Joe Slovo was instrumental in reorienting the Politico-Military Council (PMC) for insurrection. Some restructuring of personnel took place. Steve Tshwete was moved from Military Headquarters to head the Internal PC of the PMC, responsible for mass organisations. Chris

Hani resumed his post as Commissar, and Tim Ngwenya (Bra 'T') was promoted to Chief of Staff. The first mention of the operation (code-named the President's Project), Jordan pointed out, was at an NEC meeting in 1987.

'No minutes were taken of OR's remarks. He set it out... to establish a beachhead inside the country. The next report was in 1988 – again, no minutes were taken, but OR announced he had drawn Joe Slovo into running the project.'[75]

Security and Tambo's solemn duty to protect the people in his care prioritised concern and secrecy over open debate. The ANC Security Department – like any other, Chris Hani observed – did not operate openly.[76]

The ANC was experiencing the most tumultuous period of its history. While resistance was building up inside South Africa, the movement at home and abroad was also hit hard by assassinations, counter-attacks – the total onslaught. It was still experiencing difficulty in getting the cadres back into the country and the patience of many soldiers was reaching breaking point; the escalation of tension as the People's War intensified was being manipulated by the regime.

Further pressures to negotiate came from unexpected quarters. In 1986, Tambo made a visit to Cuba. Mbeki, who was part of the entourage, recalled Fidel Castro's intensive engagement with them on the Freedom Charter. What precisely did it imply? he wanted to know. Was it capable of implementation? It seemed to him, said Castro, that there were many clauses that would be incapable of implementation; for instance, the clauses that asserted that the wealth – banks and monopolies – 'shall become the property of the people'.

'You would have to ask the same people you expropriated to run the companies,' he pointed out, 'so this is strategically wrong.'[77] Castro was drawing on the experience of Cuba when it tried to appropriate the profitable export products of rum and cigars, only to find that the owners of these industries had registered the brand names in Florida during the process of the revolution.

'He gave that as an illustration of how unready they were to deal with economic questions,' explained Mbeki. '"You have to coexist with enemies... You have to enter into an arranged conclusion. You've got to share power... except you must control the central bank [and] educational systems. You've got to compromise. You will enter in reality into a negotiated settlement."'[78]

Coming from Castro, this emphatic observation was sobering to the ANC delegation, for the ANC was still attempting to withstand the Soviet line from Gorbachev that emphasised dialogue, which for the moment was premature. OR led an ANC delegation at a subsequent meeting of liberation movements, with Soviets, Cubans, the GDR in East Berlin, in which the issue of negotiations in relation to the armed struggle was raised. The ANC's purpose was to explain why armed struggle was an integral part of the negotiations process.

The international landscape was changing – just how rapidly was beyond even the wildest imagination of the West, much less the ANC. But as Gorbachev began to withdraw from the Cold War and meet with President Reagan of the USA, peace initiatives were implemented, one after the other. Resolution 435 began to free Namibia. In the Middle East, in Afghanistan, in Vietnam, in Latin America, adversaries were coming together to explore peaceful resolutions. The OAU responded to these developments with euphoria, and began to plan a procedure for a negotiated resolution, which – prompted by Tambo and the ANC – they had long since maintained was a regional conflict.

There was 'No need for armed struggle; no need for that', some said.[79] Some West African countries took their own initiatives, even attempting to draft a post-apartheid constitution. Many universities, too – in the USA, Sweden, Germany and Switzerland – were beginning to study the form of democracy that a post-apartheid South Africa might take. In a secret document, the ANC expressed its concern on outside initiatives aimed at imposing negotiations.

'We presume that these powers are preparing this initiative with the Pretoria regime', it stated. It went on to list steps taken by the governments of the USA, the UK and the Federal Republic of Germany to set out the parameters for a negotiated resolution of the South African question.[80]

Within the country, too, the uprising in the Vaal Triangle in September 1984 – followed by the hammer blows of the political stayaways – indicated that the UDF and Cosatu had seized the initiative and were able to stay with it. But this effective resistance was not in the realm of armed struggle so much as in organised resistance. Their discourse of resistance (particularly the labour movement), while confrontational, was one of making demands rather than a call to arms. Cosatu publicly supported sanctions, yet had to deal with its members feeling the loss of jobs as more and more multinationals pulled out. The success of the stayaways demonstrated the relative strength of the UDF/Cosatu alliance and, ironically, encouraged the feasibility of a move towards negotiations. It meant, wrote the exiled scholar Sylvia Neame from the GDR, 'that they would be in a position to come together with white representatives in order to find a solution on a more-or-less equal footing'.[81] Tambo himself, while insisting on the importance of armed struggle, continued to stress that armed struggle and negotiations were complementary, not contradictory, processes – two of the strings to the same bow aimed at dismantling apartheid.

These were all signs for Tambo that it was imperative that the ANC be prepared, if and when the time came, to enter into negotiations. For him, the significant element of his nightmare had been that even if the ANC were able to 'hear' and translate the message from the regime, the movement would not be *politically* prepared for such a meeting. The result would be that the ANC would lose its initiative and so the balance of power would once again become skewed. As president, Tambo could not afford to spell out openly the complexities and contradictions of the situation and so risk division within the ANC at this sensitive time. He certainly could not allow himself to talk directly to the preliminary emissaries. He therefore quietly encouraged his informal representatives, Thabo Mbeki and Jacob Zuma, to pursue steadily the diplomatic route (though, of course, to remain highly alert during the process of exploring these 'negotiations about negotiations'). The information gathered from the talks with the UDF, Cosatu and other South African groups, including the 1985 meeting with businessmen and other representatives from civil society, also gave valuable pointers towards the issues that would need to be addressed.

To the Western world, Tambo made clear the ANC's bottom line. 'Many in the West,' he told his audience in Bonn during a visit there in April 1986, 'are arguing that democracy is not good for South Africa… [It] is suggested that we replace it with some complicated arrangements which, it is said, are dictated by the objective situation in South Africa.'[82]

'It is argued,' he went on to explain, 'that we should not demand one person one vote in a unitary state. Rather, we should accept and strive for a system whereby the white population, as a group, has a right of veto or a federal structure based on the separation of our people according to racial and ethnic norms or a combination of these two.

'But we cannot buy a false peace by tolerating racism because it has assumed a new guise,' he summarised succinctly. 'We must state it here categorically and unequivocally that the ANC does not and will not accept any arrangements which impose racial formulae on our country. Nowhere in the world is there a country as racist in its policy as our country. Our struggle is anti-racist. It aims at uprooting racism and creating a non-racial society.'

And Tambo spelt out again the ANC's basic conditions: a united, democratic and non-racial South Africa. 'Any outcome short of that would not be permanent. Neither would it bring peace and stability to our country.'

The necessary conditions included the dismantling of the Bantustan system, agrarian reform, a 'publicly controlled' economy in a context where all business people could compete on an equal basis. 'The perspectives we are putting forward are no more than an assertion on our part that the people of South Africa must enjoy the same democratic rights for which the French and the American revolutions were carried out,' he added pointedly.

Tambo was making it clear to the world and to the movement itself that it was crucial to put the initiative firmly into the hands of the ANC.

In the meantime, the NEC was discussing the way forward. Johnny Makathini, head of the International Department, had earlier voiced the fear that international pressures for a negotiated settlement might catch the ANC flat-footed, just as NIBMAR had done in Zimbabwe.[83] Tambo suggested that the ANC prepare 'a bottom-line position,' recalled Pallo Jordan, 'to be sold first to Africa, then to the UN in 1987'.[85]

'In 1988, following the Battle of Cuito Cuanavale, OR put together a team, headed by Neo Mnunzana, former ANC Rep at the UNO, to prepare such a document. The team included Joel Netshitenzhe, Propaganda Head of the Internal Political Committee, [and] Ngoako Ramathlodi, OR's Deputy PA.'

Tambo asked the working group to prepare a preliminary draft on its terms for negotiations. In response to the OAU, he clarified the importance of the input of the South African people. It needed to carry their stamp of approval and ownership and, as the OAU's recommended custodian of the liberation movement, the ANC had the right to draw up the terms. He persuaded the OAU to wait for the ANC to reveal its plan and then present it as a joint declaration, 'built up from the ground, but resting on our thinking'.[86]

In 1989, FW de Klerk replaced PW Botha. Margaret Thatcher decided to intervene. She invited, one by one, the South African Minister of Foreign Affairs, the Minister of Finance and De Klerk, to strategise the shape of negotiations. If their plan should be adopted, the ANC would be 'locked into somebody else's plan, somebody else's thinking', explained Mbeki a few months later.[84]

In the meantime, it was necessary to convey the real possibility of negotiations to the members of the ANC. This would not be easy, nor would it take just one meeting to find acceptance. In military quarters especially, there was vehement opposition to the first draft of the plan (ultimately, to become the Harare Declaration).

'I don't think we succeeded in pushing it across, partly because we were half-hearted ourselves,' recalled Steve Tshwete.[87] Given the climate in the camps, the losses incurred at the hands of Unita, the assassinations and infiltrations and facing death on many fronts, it seemed a tall order to ask the cadres to accept negotiations with the enemy. However, as a national commissar, Tshwete accepted that this was 'part of my job, to say to the army that we are not fatally committed to war... We went to war because there was an objective situation that forced us to go to war; but if this situation changes we have to change our tactics as well, to accord with [the] objective reality we wanted to influence.'

Acceptance was greatly facilitated, said Tshwete, by Tambo's persuasive argument that the movement needed to conduct, in his words, its 'own Implementation 435'. Tambo pointed to the experience of Zimbabwe, when, after a Commonwealth meeting, Mozambique gave the liberation movements an ultimatum. In Tshwete's words:

'Those guys had to be taken to Lancaster kicking and crying. It was said to them, if then you don't want to go to negotiate, then you are pulling out of Mozambique... *A Luta Continua* – from home. End of story. So we must avoid this situation. When the moment for negotiations comes, it must find us ready; and we should not start to fumble.'[88]

How did ANC branches deal with the question of negotiations? To an extent, argued Lindelwe Mabandla, the rationale for meeting the business people had been 'soundly laid out' in 1985. 'OR was very strong in that kind of thing – in other words, to say, "These are South Africans; it is time to talk to them."'[89]

The Lusaka branches were particularly well informed, because senior leaders attended branch meetings; Tambo gave habitual report-backs at rallies, reminding members of the holistic approach to the struggle symbolised by the four pillars. Lindelwe and Bridgitte Mabandla recalled lively, unconstrained debates at their Lilande branch meetings in Lusaka. An example of the membership's insistence on dialogue survives in a memorandum following a meeting with Oliver Tambo in 1987. They raised such issues as 'the Movement's general strategy and the conduct of the liberation struggle at the home front'; 'the general breakdown of discipline and internal political life in the movement'; and urged the movement to provide access to the leadership of the hard-working and dedicated commanders on the front. They also raised forthrightly the questions: 'Is the leadership preparing to go into negotiations?' 'Has the movement changed as regards the seizure of power?'[90]

Tambo had also promised the youth at the Solomon Mahlangu Freedom College that they would be consulted. He wanted to ensure that this rather tricky process would be understood and 'owned' by the younger members.

'We will tell [our friends], "You know, if we are talking to Botha we are talking about the future... And the future belongs to our youth. Before we start talking we will have to go and get permission." Is that all right? [Cries of 'Yes!'] So we will come back. Is that all right? ['Yes!'] We will come back and find out what you say.'[91] Where possible, students were represented in decision-making structures, and their representatives informed of ANC developments.[92]

'Students used to monitor news, they used to receive information about what is the process, what is happening and they would discuss it, they would make their input,' said Bridgitte Mabandla. In so far as consultation was imperfectly imparted, this was the fault of human weakness, not the structures, she added.

But the deadline also meant working under great pressure. The draft essentially called for 'a fundamental change in South Africa'. Before negotiations could take place, the document repeated the conditions put by the ANC to the EPG. It was then sent home – at first 'to selected people on a confidential basis to seek their input', reported Tambo to his National Working Committee. It went to Mandela, to Govan Mbeki and Harry Gwala (both released from prison in 1988) and to leaders of the MDM as well – asking them in particular how the people would receive the position outlined. Tambo also spoke to the PAC, hoping to work towards an anti-apartheid coalition. It was also sent to Nyerere, Kaunda, Mugabe and Masire of Botswana as well as the Soviet Union and Cuba.[93] All except Nyerere, who was worried the document might restrict the ANC's flexibility to meet unexpected situations, were enthusiastic about the idea. Later, Nyerere accepted Tambo's argument, but emphasised the importance of spelling out a Statement of Principles. Interestingly, the Soviet Union approved of the draft but, reported Tambo to his NEC, 'thought our language was a little tough, and drew attention to words such as "racist regime"'.[94]

The modified draft had to be taken back to the Front Line States, 'so that it becomes the proper expression of the South African people, and then secondly the region'.[95]

In the interim, Tambo was concerned to emphasise two points: that the movement should continue with a multiple approach – 'from our point of view, negotiations will succeed if the struggle is intensified' – and, taking Nyerere's point, focus on the ANC's principles based on the Freedom Charter so that 'our people know and have confidence that we are not moving away'.[96]

Tambo asked Jack Simons to assist with the preamble, its key import to assert African agency. A week before the OAU meeting, set for 10 August, Tambo toured the Front Line States. Steve Tshwete, Thabo Mbeki, Penuel Maduna, Pallo Jordan and Ngoako Ramathlodi accompanied him. Kaunda offered Tambo his small jet – had they relied on commercial flights, they would not have made the deadline[97] – but the trip, over three days, was gruelling, and flying at such altitude impacted on Tambo, more than 20 years older than the others. In Dar es Salaam, the younger team encountered argument on the detail from Salim Salim, the Foreign Minister, who had experienced the pitfalls of the unilateral settlement in Namibia. Discouraged, they reported to Tambo.

'Chief, we failed,' they said disconsolately.

That night, Tambo sat with the team and refined the document, clause by clause, taking in Salim's arguments and clarifying the stance of the ANC – 'into the evening and into the night with OR sitting and making a contribution'.[98] The next morning Tambo led the delegation to Nyerere.

'OR had a clean grasp of the situation [that] he wanted to influence in South Africa,' explained Tshwete, 'that's why he was always able to carry the day.'[99]

Early the following morning the team left for Zimbabwe, where Tambo had done so much to mend the ANC's relations with ZANU. There they met Robert Mugabe, who suggested some fine-tuning of one of the clauses. From there to Botswana, which had originally not been in the itinerary. Tambo was anxious that they might not meet their deadline with this extra stop, but the eagerness of the younger men prevailed.

'Somewhere in mid-air, the pilot beamed: "Comrade President and entourage, we are now crossing the Limpopo"' and Tambo, clearly tense, muttered, 'We are a nice little parcel for them.' No doubt the death of Samora Machel was on his mind. The entourage joked and laughed and, to make him smile, sang in chorus an impromptu song, 'Crossing the Limpopo with Father Tambo'.

The Batswana were delighted to see them and they were 'given lots of meat'. After seeing Ketumile Masire, they moved on to Angola, where again Tambo was very persuasive and President Eduardo dos Santos endorsed the document.[100]

Penuel Maduna recalled vividly how Dos Santos warned the ANC not to repeat the mistake of the MPLA, which had failed to take into account the needs of Unita, and were now enduring the bitter consequences.

'We made that mistake and we've had a war for a decade, as a result,' Dos Santos told them. 'You don't agree with them on many things, but involve them in these processes. You'll never regret it.'[101]

Maduna was confident that the ANC leadership was equipped to follow that approach. In the 30 years of exile, said Maduna, Tambo consistently upheld the values of consensus, collective leadership and attention to the opponent.

The team returned to Lusaka at about 6am the following morning, tired, dishevelled and with swollen feet. Tony 'Gabs' Msimang, the President's driver, met him at the airport. He noticed that Tambo's left eye was watering, and he was dabbing it with a handkerchief.

'Chief, you look very tired,' he said.

'Yes, I am tired,' admitted Tambo. Gabs drove him to his office.

After a quick shower, the team congregated at Mbeki's apartment and settled in front of his computer to consider the additional inputs and finalise the document so that it could be presented to the National Working Committee the following day. At 10am, Tambo walked in.

'Chief, but you are supposed to be resting!'

'No, no, no, I've come to raise a few things about the document.'

He had brought with him his copy of the document, marked with his habitual red pen. It was so important that the declaration be perfectly presented.

'He literally baby-sat that document,' said Tshwete. 'Looked after every comma, every word, every spacing and what it looked like on paper.'

The group eventually prevailed on Tambo to go home and rest and Tshwete walked him out. As he left, Tambo whispered to him, 'Steve, all is not well with me.' But Tshwete did not grasp the import of what he had said.

The following morning, on 7 August, Tambo joined the National Working Committee. Surprisingly, he was late. He explained that the delegation was still drafting the report, and he was also suffering the effects of air travel. Tom Nkobi then proposed a motion to postpone the session until the afternoon to allow the president to rest.

'This is dictatorship of the masses!' protested Tambo, to much laughter.[102]

Finally, at 3pm Tambo gave a preliminary report, explaining the responses of the Front Line States. The ANC had drafted a separate document that differed slightly in some clauses from the Front Line suggestions – for example, on an interim multiparty government, which the ANC wanted – in case the OAU did not accept the ANC version.

From the NWC meeting, Tambo went to the house of John Nkadimeng, where he had been asked to meet a comrade from home – Comrade Tsholo, who had been sent by his organisation to see the leadership outside. Gabs waited in the car and, as the hours went by, he became jittery. Suddenly, the electricity failed. The entire house was in darkness, and and he flew into the house.

'That's it!' he exclaimed. 'We are no longer staying. We don't know whether this is deliberate.'

So they returned to the cars. Tambo was upset. 'But this person is from home,' he protested.

'I am concerned about your security,' Gabs retorted. 'And another thing – you are tired; you haven't been resting.'

'Yes, but I will be going for a holiday soon.'[103]

In silence, they drove back to the office, where Tambo put in some more work before retiring.

The NWC met again the following morning to discuss the draft declaration, comment on the wording, and then move to adopt it. The document, which ultimately was to become the Harare Declaration, linked quite clearly the fate of South Africa to the welfare of the region. It acknowledged that, as a result of many years' struggle, there might now be an opportunity for negotiations.

'We believe,' it declared as a statement of its principles, 'that a conjuncture of circumstances exists which, if there is a demonstrable readiness on the part of the Pretoria regime to engage in negotiations, genuinely and seriously, could create the possibility to end apartheid.'[104]

It then enumerated its principles, many of which were an elaboration of the Freedom Charter: 'We reaffirm our recognition of the rights of all peoples, including those of South Africa, to determine their own destiny, and to work out for themselves the institutions and the system of government under which they will, by general consent, live and work together to build a harmonious society.'

It went on to spell out the climate necessary before negotiations could begin. 'At the very least,' it declared, drawing on previous ANC documents and existing popular demands, that political prisoners be released, restrictions and bans be lifted, troops be removed from the townships, the State of Emergency end and political executions cease. Then, celebrating its own heritage 40 years earlier, the ANC team ended the document with a flourish – a 'Programme of Action', which included monitoring and advocacy by the OAU and Front Line States to hasten the liberation of Namibia and South Africa.

The declaration, Tambo pointed out at the meeting, set out the climate and the principles, 'but still doesn't cover the *process* negotiations should take'. This aspect would need to be looked at afresh, he said (and indeed, in due course, it was added to the final document). '[But] let's report back after the meeting [of the Front Line States], because that will also determine the shape of our own [ANC] document; let's be ready for another meeting.'[105] The delegates for the meeting with the OAU were chosen.

'No liberation movement on the continent of Africa had ever produced a document of that integrity,' commented Steve Tshwete in later years. 'The ANC was being hailed all over the world, and that was because of OR; his foresight to see that the conjuncture of circumstances wanted us to come up with a document of this kind – the Harare Declaration.'[106]

Tambo's process of consultation of those who had a stake in a free South Africa had been taken in earnest, and at great cost to himself – just how great, the ANC was shortly to find out.

There were a few other matters on the agenda, including Chris Hani's report on his inspection of all the military camps and his concern about the continuing serious lack of health facilities in some camps in Tanzania. The Treasurer-General promised to pursue this matter and then Tambo thanked the members for their attention, adjourning the meeting at 12.30pm. It was to be the last meeting in which he was to participate fully.

That afternoon, Tambo had appointments in the ANC office. First there was Thenjiwe Mthintso, who had been appointed six months previously as the new ANC representative in Uganda, and who had the disagreeable task of setting up accommodation for the detained suspects waiting to be charged or cleared. They had been moved according to the December 1988 accord signed in New York, in which it was agreed that the ANC (and Cuba) would withdraw its troops from Angola, while Namibia would be decolonised and would hold free and fair elections under the supervision of the UN. The MK cadres had been relocated to Uganda after leaving Angola. Mthintso had also come to ask OR to help her with logistical problems. She was struggling to control her dismay with the enormity of the challenge.

'Six months down the line,' she explained to him, 'the ANC has not sent us uniforms… no food, no uniforms, no tents, no training equipment – nothing... We are just living on handouts.'[107]

As the chief representative, she still did not have a house but was staying in the camps, and when she went to town for supplies, she would have to sleep in the Land Rover. As Thenjiwe conveyed her acute anxiety to Tambo – how, for example, she had to scout the streets of Kampala looking for the best price for beans, because the Ugandan army had offered to lend her money until the ANC could repay them – to her mortification, she burst into tears.

'So, I gave these details to Comrade OR in between my tears and my emotions and my sobs. And he was listening. And, unfortunately, Comrade Nkobi was not there, because I felt at least something could be done from the Treasury.'

Thenjiwe stayed for a long time. 'He had taken the matter so seriously. I had cooled down a bit; he had cooled me down.'

As Thenjiwe left, Zola Skweyiya, the Officer of Justice, came in. By now, it was already dark.

A short while later, Gabs heard Tambo's bell ringing repeatedly and urgently, and he rushed into the office.

'I could see him stretching his left arm and asking Zola to pull him up.'

Gabs immediately called Thabo Mbeki. Mshengu, OR's personal attendant, rushed into the room. Everybody panicked; they loosened Oliver's clothes and lay him on a sofa. Oliver could not move. He was silent. Bodyguard regulations demanded that the room be cleared, and Gabs had the office locked. They then carried Tambo into the car and drove him to Kaunda's doctor. The exposure of a public hospital was not appropriate, and Tambo was instead rushed to the military hospital.

The following day, a Front Line States meeting convened in Lusaka.

'People were wondering why OR was not there. Where was OR? The Harare Declaration was adopted there at the summit. Nzo came to tell OR. But his speech was gone.'[108]

CHAPTER NINETEEN

'Freedom is the Apex'

WOMEN'S DAY FALLS ON 9 AUGUST. In 1989, the ANC Women's Section hosted an event in London, attended by Adelaide Tambo. That afternoon, Adelaide received a call from Lusaka. It was Thomas Nkobi.

'We need to consult you about something,' said Nkobi. 'We have organised a ticket for you to get here today.' He said he could not explain anything further.

Mystified, Adelaide went to the airport with Dali. Was it an underground errand, an important task to be communicated only in person? But while she was waiting , she was called to a telephone. This time it was Kenneth Kaunda.

'Stay where you are, my dear. I am afraid Oliver has had a stroke, and I have arranged a plane to bring him to you in London... Have an ambulance waiting, so that he can be taken straight from the airport to the London Clinic.'

A few hours later, the private jet landed.

'By coincidence,' recalled Tony Mongalo, 'Tiny Rowland's executive jet was in Lusaka and due to return to London the next morning. KK asked Rowland to assist by giving OR a lift to London. Together with KK's physician, Gabs, Distance and two other bodyguards and myself as OR's PA for the trip, we flew to London. OR was admitted to a private hospital on Harley Street.'[1]

Rowland had been asked to carry the cost for medical attention. Adelaide nursed OR every day, while the children took turns to be with him at night. Oliver could not speak, she found, but was able to walk with some assistance. On the fifth morning, Adelaide walked into his ward to be greeted by a 'Good morning!'

Those who worked closely with Tambo had long been anxious about his health. Beneath the surface, and unknown by most of those he served, Tambo had suffered from bouts of ill health. An appropriate response, as his doctors had so often advised him, was to ease up on his hectic travel schedule. For a quarter of a century, Tambo had been passing through dozens of cities, taking only the occasional break in quiet retreats or clinics in friendly host countries.

The constant movement itself was stressful – 'I am in space,' he wrote to Adelaide, 'landing here and there now and again, which means you cannot even write to me about anything'[2] – and travel was cumbersome and unreliable.

On one occasion in the early years, Tambo described an exhausting trip from Addis Ababa to Nairobi, then on to Dar es Salaam. After an overnight flight from London, a two-hour delay from Addis to Nairobi resulted in a missed connection on the Friday, so he was booked on a flight the following morning.

'I resisted this intensely, insisting that I had to be in Dar before Saturday. Somehow it worked, for although the air hostess and immigration officers told me there was no other flight before Saturday, they later turned up… to tell me there was a 6pm flight and I was booked on it.'

But that plane was also delayed and the passengers waited 40 minutes to take off. As it finally began to motor along the runway, it suddenly slowed down and then turned back. After a further wait, the plane did finally take off and landed a little before midnight.

'In my usual superstitious bent, I began to wonder what there was about the Dar trip – why I had to face the restraining forces before getting there.'[3] And, as it happened, a number of problems awaited him in Dar, not the least of which was an immediate meeting in Tennyson Makiwane's apartment with Joe Matthews. This meeting lasted until 4am. But, as Tambo commented another time, 'the redeeming feature in all this is the nobility of the cause'.[4]

Confronted with tough decisions daily, long hours and exhausting schedules, each trip also demanded preparation on many levels – the speeches, formalities, strange beds, irregular and unsuitable meals, social interaction and change in climate. However much Tambo might have enjoyed the human contact, the gruelling lifestyle affected his health. Doctors were worried.

Oliver once took ill in Cairo, and was advised by the doctor that 'having descended from the lofty and icy Alps to the suffocating humidity and unrelenting heat of Cairo in the month of August, my asthma reacted violently'.[5] He knew that he was working himself too hard. Just after his return from New York in 1973 he wrote to scholar Tom Karis: 'I need a break very badly. Now that I'm back from the US, a thousand decisions are waiting to be taken urgently. This means two things: (1) an urgent holiday, (2) no holiday just yet.'[6]

But as the tempo of struggle diplomacy escalated, trips became more frequent and more demanding. In 1980, he had to cancel his plans to attend Moses Kotane's funeral in Moscow when a doctor in Maputo strongly advised against the trip. The journey would simply be too stressful and too risky.

Then, one day in 1982, Tambo suffered a mild stroke. He was attending a rally in Dar es Salaam, and had retired to bed late the previous night. At the stadium, he suddenly felt strange and passed out. He was immediately taken to hospital, but was released after just a couple of days. The diagnosis was a mild stroke, and he was advised to rest and take a holiday.[7]

Then, the following year, he suffered another, more serious attack. He was at home in London, delighting in holding his first grandchild, Sacha, on his lap. Seconds after he handed the baby to Adelaide, he collapsed. He had been struck by an arterial spasm. As Tambo struggled with this violent assault on his body, he heard his wife calling on him to 'fight back!'[8]

'I heard your voice as it reached me somewhere beyond my conscious being – somewhere below the surface of my normal existence. Your message must have registered. The rest of the time witnessed a battle to return. I recall Nini [Thembi] joining in to reinforce me. For the rest of the time, the excellent nurse in you came to the fore and took charge, armed with deep love.'[9]

It was fortunate that the attack had taken place in London. His children 'smoothed the road towards normal', backed by the doctors and the support of friends. But back at his desk in Lusaka, he realised 'the fight was not over'. He found 'the most tricky problem is how to isolate and insulate yourself from a situation which by its very nature defines the parameters of your basic concerns and constitutes the very essence and purpose of your being' – his heart.

The attack had occurred in a time of 'gruelling conflict',[10] and it was difficult to take time off. He was faced with a conscious decision to balance the need to facilitate developments as much as possible – including more delegating, which in itself required careful management – with the need to conserve his strength in order to serve the movement in the crucial months and years ahead. There was also the reality that, despite the collective nature of leadership, it was Tambo who had come to symbolise the ANC. His image was distinct, and his personal opinion, albeit on behalf of the ANC, was respected and sought after.

In the context of increasing dangers, it was important to play down any idea of Tambo's ill health. From time to time, he was able to slip away for a rest, usually in the Eastern European socialist countries. On several occasions he spent a week or two undergoing thorough medical check-ups, and also had brief holidays at the Black Sea in the GDR and twice in Bulgaria.[11]

Scholar and long-standing friend of the ANC, Vladimir Shubin, recalled several occasions when Tambo received treatment in Moscow: '[In October 1984], when we fetched him from the airport, he was exhausted. After a month in hospital and then in a sanatorium, his health improved.' Tambo was then able to join a delegation in Moscow for discussions in the wake of the Nkomati Accord, but had to miss Nyerere's invitation to a meeting in Arusha.[12]

By 1985, Tambo publicly admitted that he was ailing. As if to warn his movement, at the end of his summation of the Kabwe Conference, he put aside his notes and spoke directly to his audience: 'Comrades, my health is not good; but,' he pledged 'what remains will be consumed in the cause of the struggle.'[13]

His hectic schedule continued nonetheless. In October 1985, in the wake of gruelling preparation for the Kabwe Conference and its aftermath of evaluations, press conferences and meetings,[14] Tambo received the following missive:

'Dear Mr Tambo, I have just written to Dr Hindley to say that the various tests show that there has been no worsening of any measurements in the last year and that this was a reflection of the fact that you had been taking things a little more easily and taking some rest every day.

'From the papers, it is clear that you have had a very strenuous time recently, both physically and emotionally. I understand from your wife that you may be going to the Cameroon on Saturday. I would advise you strongly against this on medical grounds because the stress of flying, change in climate and almost certain overwork when you get there, may well push a fragile balance out of equilibrium: it can result in another stroke or put excessive strain on your heart whose rhythm, as you know, is already irregular. I hope you will forgive me for being rather didactic, but concern for your health demands it.'[15]

But Tambo found that he was unable to take Dr Robert Mahler's advice, and proceeded to the Cameroon and other countries. The schedule took its toll.

'In the past few days since returning I feel the strain. Every day I am dragging my right leg except for a short while after I have been resting.' The NEC thus cancelled all engagements and arranged rest and treatment in the Soviet Union.

But, just two months later, he was travelling again. In February, he addressed the Swedish parliament: 'The Stockholm trip – and preparation to be away from Lusaka – was crowded with work and flying. But I have recovered from the strain, although I felt it for four days since returning,' he confessed.[15]

The following month he attended the funeral of Moses Mabhida in Maputo, at which time an important rapprochement was effected with the Mozambique government.[17] He then crossed the hemisphere to visit Cuba. In May, Tambo accepted the Third World Prize on behalf of Winnie and Nelson Mandela in Malaysia, before going on to receive an honorary doctorate in New Delhi. He was in Paris later that month to prepare for a consultation with the USSR, Angola, Cuba and SWAPO. Although a date had formerly been fixed for the end of June, Tambo stood up and announced that he would not be available. It emerged that he was booked into a GDR sanatorium for heart treatment.[18]

The warm hospitality of the Eastern European governments was an added reason to be grateful to the Socialist Bloc. They had provided resources, education and financial support throughout the exile. They looked after ANC representatives and stood by the ANC in lean times. But, in addition, they had provided attentive and expert medical care where technical resources were not always available in the young African countries.

But the most advanced medical care could do little more than contain the strain as long as Tambo continued his hectic schedule.

'It gives me sleepless nights,' he confessed in an interview when Nairobi's *Sunday Nation* asked him what troubled him most, 'to think we are not moving fast enough.' A relentless sense of urgency drove him.[19]

In the same year, for example, that Tambo was making high-profile American appearances – at Washington DC, in Chicago, at the Riverside Church in New York and other East and West Coast venues where he was received by film-makers, actors, artists and African-American businesspeople – he was also moving across hemispheres. After the whirlwind US tour in January 1987, he hastened back to Lusaka to meet George Schultz, US Secretary of State. Then, in April, he and his entourage set off to Australia. In May, it was Sweden, then Lusaka, then London. In July, Tambo visited Jamaica, Nicaragua, Venezuela and Ethiopia, giving speeches and interviews at every stop. In August, he was back in North America, this time in Canada, then on to Harare in September, Moscow and Leipzig in November, finishing the year with the ANC conference in Lusaka.[20] After that event, Tambo was left with three weeks in which to organise and prepare for the next 8 January speech, which was now being delivered to larger numbers of avid listeners, both in South Africa and abroad.

The stress of the massacres and murders, of identifying and containing infiltrators, curbing both the zealous Mbokodo and mutiny in the camps, as well as handling the happier but demanding tasks of meeting the many diverse people from home, giving guidance during the 'people's war' while simultaneously conducting highly sensitive and perilous negotiations took up all his waking hours. In an ironic tragedy, it was at the climax of the struggle of the movement that Oliver Tambo's own hidden and private struggle over his health was brought into the open. That he survived as long as he did could only be attributed to his own willpower and anxiety to complete his mission, of seeing through the ANC's 'historic task of leading the political and military assault on the apartheid regime', as he had been mandated to do nearly 30 years earlier.[21]

Now, in September 1989, having been struck down by this heaviest blow, OR began to make steady progress in London. Adelaide arranged for a neurosurgeon to attend to him, particularly as his right hand was not responding. Working with a physiotherapist, OR was given a set of exercises and it was not long before he was able to move. Adelaide had him admitted to a rehabilitation centre in Surrey, engaging also the services of 'a fantastic West Indian' nurse, so that they could alternate nursing him in shifts.

But no sooner had OR arrived than he began running a high temperature, so Adelaide decided to take him back to the London Clinic. She diagnosed him as having malaria, and treated him with an indigenous medication – a remedy given to her by KK's nurse, Camellia. In a few days he was discharged.

It was at this point that the Swedish government sent a neurosurgeon, Beth von Schreeb, to examine Tambo. The ANC decided to accept Sweden's offer of treatment for OR. They felt that a private clinic would provide more rest, particularly away from the hurly burly of London, where visitors constantly jostled to see him. The NEC was also not comfortable that a controversial tycoon was footing the bill. It seemed inappropriate that their president should be beholden to an individual.[22] But Adelaide opposed the idea. First, there was excellent care in London, boasting fine neurologists. Furthermore, her husband had spent nearly 30 years away from home. Now, when he was ill, and she a respected senior in her profession, she was again to be deprived of her husband – and this at a time when she could nurse him, and when he could be with his family.

Was this an old replay of the tense dialogue between 'the family and the nation' and 'the family *or* the nation'?

Tambo – registered as 'Mr Reginald', for security reasons – was nevertheless admitted to a hospital in Stockholm. He fretted that there might not be an Anglican minister to give him communion, but this was soon remedied.[23] The suite at the clinic was supplied with protection glass and there was also police protection – Stockholm had its share of Neo-Nazis roaming the city.[24] He also had his ANC bodyguards, who watched his door day and night. They slept in the library not far away. In the clinic itself, once he was able, he walked freely.

His medical condition, diagnosed Dr Von Schreeb, was an infarction, damage in the left area of his brain, so that it affected his right side. He also had high blood pressure, which was always aggravated by stress.

Neurologists are inclined to put more weight on heredity when it comes to explaining the causes of brain aneurysm, but Dr Von Schreeb conceded that, together with aggravated high blood pressure, 'in a stressful situation these conditions are not getting better – they're getting worse – so [stress and overwork] probably contributed to the development of the stroke'.

When OR was admitted, he was walking without a stick but had a little paralysis of the arm and leg. His speech was slow, with a noticeable stammer.

'I found him intellectually intact; he could keep a conversation and tell me a lot of things and he could answer … he could use the language but didn't find the correct words. He had a little stutter when he talked and he was slow and tried to be very articulate; but we could understand and he understood.'

In Lusaka, a historic three-day ANC meeting was taking place with the seven released prisoners led by Walter Sisulu, the NEC, representatives of the Mass Democratic Movement and 700 ANC delegates. An open meeting followed for all ANC members. A member of the ANC in the audience recalled the uncertainty and heated discussions regarding the status of the armed struggle during these secret talks and what some termed 'negotiations with capitulation'. It was Sisulu who replied. He reassured them that the ANC was working on a two-track strategy. The ANC would not abandon armed struggle – indeed it would intensify the struggle on all fronts in order to exert pressure on Pretoria.

The level of anger from the rank and file disturbed Sisulu. He 'felt the absence of Oliver Tambo's leadership had been an unsettling factor, and the issue of communication within the organisation had to be addressed urgently'.

And indeed, while the ANC had developed the practical ability to replace leaders through collective leadership and Tambo had groomed a generation of leaders, he himself was sorely needed at this time. On his part, Tambo too was worried that this period of rapid transformation should be managed as sensitively as possible. He was distressed at 'letting down' the movement.

But a joyous prospect awaited him. Govan Mbeki, Walter Sisulu, Raymond Mhlaba, Wilton Mkwayi, Andrew Mlangeni and Elias Motsoaledi and others were making their way to Sweden. Tambo was still frail, hardly able to speak, and his doctors were unsure whether he was ready for such extreme emotion. But Tambo, determined to get well, intensified his rehabilitation and made sufficient progress for Dr Von Schreeb to consent to this exceptional event.

The meeting was deeply moving. To be reunited with his comrades and long-standing friends, for whom Tambo had fought ceaselessly to remind the world of their sacrifice, brought them all to tears. To OR's astonishment, Walter's ample hair had turned snow white! Displaying his familiar tooth-gapped grin, Sisulu again attested to his role of the astute, genial senior mentor of the ANC. The genuine delight of the two men was obvious, with not a hint of strain in OR as he broke out in a delighted exclamation on seeing his beloved mentor.

Sweden owed this eminent ANC delegation to Tambo's presence, and the government requested Dr Von Schreeb to act as the doctor for the entire contingent. Besides the internal consultations held in Tambo's room, the team held discussions with the Swedish government, with aid authorities and solidarity organisations. All were aware of the import of their visit at this time. Remarkably, on the day of the reunion (2 February), President FW de Klerk announced the unbanning of the ANC and other liberation organisations. Later that day the team held a press conference, announcing that the move would 'go a long way towards creating a climate of negotiations'.[26]

A week later Nelson Mandela was released. Like millions around the world, OR watched the events on television, and heard his opening tribute to Tambo.

'I salute our President, Comrade Oliver Tambo, for leading the ANC even under the most difficult circumstances.'[27] Bittersweet emotions washed over him – Oliver longed to go home.

Then, at last, Mandela arrived. Hada Castle, reserved by the government for distinguished guests, was filled. 'Mr Mandela was coming', recalled Von Schreeb, 'there was the foreign minister, and everybody was excited. Mr Tambo and Mr Mandela – famous people. Adelaide was there and Winnie Mandela was there.

'And then Mr Mandela came in, I remember it… He had such a presence… He came in and walked into the room and, of course, he saw Oliver Tambo and they just grabbed each other and they sort of laughed... I cried almost and the wife cried – it was just joy and a sort of sentimental crying. But these emotions were very, very warm and I'll never forget it! That was the first time they met. And I was happy that I was his doctor, and able to see this.'[28]

After that remarkable reunion, Tambo went back to the clinic. Mandela saw him frequently, and had telephone conversations with him several times a day.

Then it was time for Mandela to go. Tambo felt the parting keenly.

'[OR] wanted to get back; he wanted to come back. He hoped that he would be good for the ANC even in the future, and I think he was really disappointed when he noticed that that might not be the case…'

Tambo was determined to get well. His rehabilitation included an English-speaking speech therapist whom he met every day, and of his own accord he wrote letters to well-wishers, and had regular sessions with Von Schreeb.

Days later, Mandela addressed an audience at Wembley Stadium in England.

'There is no man in [South Africa] and anywhere else in the world,' he announced, 'who could have performed as magnificently as [OR] has done over the last 30 years. He kept our organisation united and strong under the most difficult conditions and we say that our prayers are that he should be able to recover sufficiently to take his position of leadership of this organisation.'[29]

On the night of 1 April, Dr Von Schreeb received a call from a nurse: 'Mr Tambo is talking; he seems not to understand what we are telling him and I don't understand what he is saying and he is getting paralysis...'

It was another stroke, a seizure of blood vessels. The paralysis on his right side was more noticeable. His medication was changed and the therapy and rehabilitation exercises were intensified, though his speech was a little further impaired. Then a week later OR contracted pneumonia, which was treated with antibiotics. By 24 April, Tambo had recovered and slowly began to walk again.

Adelaide, who had stayed with him when she could, was distressed by these setbacks, particularly as she was so far away. She began to insist on his return home and, after some hesitation, the doctors finally discharged her husband.

'He was like a prisoner,' said Dr Von Schreeb. 'He was looked after, of course, but it wasn't his room... he was in a different country. He was taking care of all the others, [but] he could not really say what he really wanted.'[30]

Adelaide once again asked Tiny Rowland if he could assist. Tambo and members of the family, accompanied by Rowland's doctor, flew back to London. Oliver was now able to stay at home, though he was admitted to the College Hospital as a day patient. At home, he was received by a children's choir in their London garden. The stream of well-wishers increased – they came from all over the world. OR improved slowly. He itched to return home.

In December 1990, the entire family flew home, stopping on the way to greet the ANC in Lusaka and to thank Kaunda for his loving care. More than 30 years had passed. The three Tambo children, their son-in-law and three grandchildren accompanied Oliver and Adelaide. The children all spoke with English accents, were well educated, and had in varying combinations inherited their father's creativity and their mother's vitality. Thembi and Dali had been too young to remember South Africa when they left all those years previously. Tselane, born in England, had only oral history to supply her imagination. But, she had told a British journalist in 1986, 'I will not go to South Africa until I can return with my father on my arm – he as a free man and our country liberated from the shackles of apartheid.'[31] This had at last come to pass.

At the airport there was a tumultuous reception. The students' organisation, SASO, had organised a phalanx of Radio Freedom admirers. Tambo stood above the multitude and smiled and lifted his right arm with his left hand to wave. '*Khuluma!*' (Speak!) shouted the crowds, amid ululation and chanting.

Tambo attempted to speak but could not. The 11-hour journey and the anticipation and profound emotion had left him exhausted. One member of the welcoming crowd expressed shock at seeing the 'Comrade President'.

'Why did they not tell us he was so sick?' he asked.[32]

But a city council worker, plastered with ANC stickers, was dancing for joy. 'This is the man who kept the ANC fires burning throughout the world,' he said excitedly, 'when they were being extinguished in South Africa. This is the man we have been waiting for!'[33]

Tambo's welcome-home rally at Orlando Stadium was huge – and Mzwake Mbuli's poem on 'ORT: Organise, Resist, Takeover!' urged a crowd of 70 000 to its feet. A few days later the ANC held the first Consultative Conference in

South Africa since 1959. Tambo was acclaimed. Still frail, his speech offered members a glimpse of his political wisdom. Knitting together the audience by recalling a shared struggle, he evoked 'the heroic traditions of your forebears, Shaka, Hintsa, Sekhukhuni, Moeshoeshoe and others'.[34]

'At no time,' he observed, 'have a people heading warring camps in this country come together to find a common way out.'

The halting words came out slowly; it was nevertheless a personal message to every man and woman in the audience. 'I am back', his very presence implied. 'I have devotedly watched over the organisation all these years. I now hand it back to you, bigger, stronger – intact. Guard our precious movement.'

Tambo's unsullied reputation was so strong that the leadership had chosen him, as president and for his unquestioned integrity, to flag two unpopular issues. He first sketched out the background:

'The massacres in the townships and elsewhere are a painful reminder that apartheid is still in place. Accordingly, the struggle should be intensified at all fronts.' Tambo acknowledged 'the crucial role of the international factor in our struggle'. Their support of 'political, military, cultural and economic sanctions' was a significant contribution. But, he cautioned, in the rapidly transforming landscape of South Africa, 'it is no longer enough for us to repeat tired slogans. We should, therefore, carefully re-evaluate the advisability of insisting on the retention of sanctions, given the new developments in the country and abroad.'

'If peaceful negotiations will result in the formation of a united, democratic, non-racial and non-sexist South Africa, we are not only willing but ready to enter into such negotiations. Consequently, the ANC has suspended the armed struggle in order to give peace a chance as well as indicate our serious concern for the future of the country and all its citizens'.[35]

At the conference Mandela paid tribute to Tambo, 'who deserves a special place in the annals of our struggle for liberation both because of the longevity of his service in the ranks of the ANC and for his outstanding stewardship during the most difficult and trying phase'. He pointed out that Tambo had, in effect, been the leader of the ANC for 23 years. He referred to key events, such as Rivonia, the death of Luthuli and Wankie:

'The road ahead looked dark and daunting. What communication there was between the movement abroad and the home base was slender and irregular... You [Tambo] took up the challenge boldly and creatively. From that winter of 1967, under your guidance and unwavering leadership, the ANC rebuilt its strength. From the crippling reverses our movement had sustained in the early 1960s you laboured to rekindle the fighting spirit of our people. Today our people are ready as never before to use their organised strength to destroy apartheid, thanks to you and the team of men and women you led.'[36]

And then, notwithstanding the collective tradition, Mandela acknowledged the singular importance of Tambo in ANC history – an answer, perhaps to the question of the important role of every individual in a collective culture.

'In paying tribute to our Comrade President, I am addressing not only the unrivalled qualities and achievements of the individual, I am addressing the man as the crystallisation and personification of what the ANC is and became under his leadership. When we assess the processes that brought about the events of February 1990, we should never underrate the importance of the individual personality in determining the pace at which matters moved to that point.'[37]

At the following ANC Congress in July, Tambo effortlessly and gracefully relinquished the presidency for his comrade in arms, Nelson Mandela.

'It would... be easy to measure the consensus of the masses in the country as to who should be the President-General, and the whole movement would be guided, appropriately, by such a consensus. None of us outside here have any doubt as to what that consensus is', OR had written to his friend years ago.[38]

At the Congress, Tambo declined to stand, and Mandela was elected president. A new position was created in OR's honour – National Chairman. The conference was attended not only by ANC members, but also by friends, including Cuban ambassador, Angelo Dalmao, who knew OR well from his days in Angola.

'For President Tambo to have been the main figure in exile, and for Comrade Oliver Tambo to have had that modesty as a revolutionary – to have always defended the idea, the principle, the right that Mandela should be freed, released – day after day, after all those 29 years,' he commented afterwards.

'And then waiting for the moment when Comrade Mandela would come out of jail to deliver him the banner of the leadership of the ANC. That in itself is an outstanding personal behaviour of a man who is not a common, simple man. For that you have to be a superior kind of man, to have been able to do that... He came at the end so clean... He puts the flags of the ANC in the hands of Mandela without hesitation... For him it was reinforcing the ANC as the vanguard of this country, of South Africa.'[39]

As soon as he could, Tambo visited Wattville – the old house in Maseko Street. The family were considering building a house in Benoni when Tiny Rowland offered them the use of a home in fashionable Sandown, north of Johannesburg. It was also large enough to take in the three generations of the family.

They were home, and new terrains lay before them. For Tambo there was the enjoyment of the hitherto rare company of his own family. He delighted in showing them Bizana, Kantolo and the Engeli Mountains. He introduced his children and grandchildren to the Amapondo people, and to the king in his palace in Lusikisiki. Wherever he went, he was fêted. As in ancient lore, the victorious hero had come home at last. He had performed great deeds, and was honoured. It was deeply moving to observe Tambo's undisguised delight in savouring Pondoland, gazing once more on its green and gentle fields, and on the cherished landmark imprinted on him since infancy – the Engeli Mountains.

Sitting in the back seat of the car, the window rolled right down as it moved slowly through the welcoming throngs, he watched and listened with tangible delight to the children's greetings.

'Hello, hello,' he smiled and waved his left hand. He loved the performances of the unexpected blending of voices in the village choirs – in Bizana, in Flagstaff, in Lusikisiki, in schools and churches – beating time with his stick. He savoured the celebratory feasts, watching over the preparations as men deftly slaughtered and skinned sheep and cattle in his honour. Tambo felt regenerated. His health improved. His speech became more distinct.

In the ANC's new multistoreyed Shell House, Tambo had a large office, and he was driven to work every day, although Adelaide insisted that he come home for an afternoon rest. In Shell House, 'the great three' – Sisulu, Mandela and Tambo – came together every day. Mandela (now more commonly and affectionately known by his clan name, 'Madiba') would consult Tambo daily about issues as they arose. Tambo attended NEC meetings, but seldom spoke.

Mandela would first consult with his friends on issues of national concern and the growing evidence of 'Third Force' activity. There were also the personal disappointments and heartache in his domestic life. Both Oliver and Walter were by his side when he made a painful public statement announcing his divorce.

During this period, the different personalities of the three became evident to the committees and workers in Shell House. Their vision was indivisible, for they had forged it together and apart through nearly half a century of struggle and political experience. Each had a specific, individual contribution to make. Mandela was able to win over old enemies with his message of reconciliation, his common touch, his charisma. Sisulu, the perceptive kingmaker and modest exemplar, resumed his schedule as he had 40 years earlier, visiting towns and villages around the country, meeting and talking to people on the ground.

And Tambo? 'OR has qualities of his own,' observed Walter Sisulu in a discussion about the ANC's tradition of consensus decision-making. '[OR] is one of the best men in assessing a position. He speaks less. He observes and comes to a conclusion when everybody has spoken, everybody has expressed an opinion. This, I think, is the characteristic which made him so successful in mobilising the exile; in bringing about stability to a community... He has got that characteristic. Even today it is a remarkable thing... Even in a situation which you have had abroad, you hardly come across anybody who was hostile. I think he was the most loved leader. I know Luthuli was, but OR has got that exceptional gift of moulding people.'[40]

And while 'comparisons are odious' because they leave out context, circumstances and individuality, a number of ANC members observed many years later that, despite their close personal friendship and shared political culture, Tambo and Mandela differed in their style and approach to consensus.

In meetings, 'Comrade OR would always be the last to speak', was one NEC member's comment, 'whereas Madiba makes clear his view up front.'

Tambo gave direction to policy and strategy in the form of 'traditional leader as wise listener' in order to keep the large, diverse movement together over three decades, whereas Mandela, needing to assert the strategy of negotiations in a highly contested, increasingly violent, highly charged political and historic environment, clearly felt it necessary to 'lead from the front'.

Even so, there were many members who expressed a sadness that after his return home, OR did not receive the recognition he deserved for his achievements – his creativity in interpreting the ANC's role for its members and for the world as circumstances altered over the years, his strategic intelligence and foresight, and his ability to effect collective shifts of emphasis in such a way as to carry the membership along with him and ensure collective ownership, not only by the leadership and members on the ground, but by the newly recruited in the seventies and eighties – the advocates of black consciousness, organised workers, white radicals and many others. They missed OR's ability to employ his calming, reassuring approach, his insights and participatory methods that had the potential to bring opponents on board, reducing stress and perhaps also the number of lives lost during the pre-election period. But OR – the custodian, the intellectual whose central role had been to work collectively with others to make meaning of situations as they altered while never losing focus on the core vision, the 'complete diplomat', a humanist of quiet wisdom – had preferred to be in a supportive role; he had been tossed into the limelight by necessity. In the exile period, he had gained generations of experience, with the Cold War, MK, the prolonged struggle forcing generations out of South Africa, the necessity of running a virtual government whose people were scattered worldwide. The special sadness was that people at home could not see him functioning as 'OR'; he was there physically, but not able to give active leadership as before.

'The contrasting personalities,' wrote Rusty Bernstein (himself a dedicated and long-serving member of the Alliance) of the 'golden three', 'complemented each other so fully that their combined influence was far greater than the sum of their individual parts.'[41] Their very political identity had been forged by a unique constellation of circumstances that formed an enduring bond. It was a phenomenon that was grasped and appreciated by the younger comrades in exile. Jacob Zuma, one of that cohort, spoke with reverence of the Govan Mbeki, Sisulu, Tambo, Mandela generation. There was a realisation that they, the kingmakers, had consolidated the best of the traditions of the oldest national movement in South Africa. They had 'a quality of leadership that South Africa has produced which I am not certain, after that generation, we will ever have again'. The trio had been shaped by the struggles of an earlier generation – articulate, strategic, shrewd and substantial, there was no question of their being manipulated.

Among the returned exiles, there was a growing appreciation of the principled tradition OR had borne, almost single-handed, the responsibilities of leadership as older comrades passed away. Many were experiencing difficult adjustments:

'The inescapable fact is that no return is solely a return; it is a new migration,' a scholar of the exiled condition observed. 'Those who return are not the same people they were when they left, and the place they return to is not the same.'[42]

'It was such a shock when the exiles returned home to look after themselves. It was painful to experience the almost palpable hostility from our own people, and encounter suspicion and gossip,' confessed one seasoned comrade.[43]

That Tambo had been struck down on the eve of their homecoming was a double blow, a symbol of the passing of a political landscape.

'When I first met OR here inside the country,' remembered Thenjiwe Mthintso, 'I looked at him and just felt so sad, I just cried, because that was the last serious time that I had seen and talked to him – that time of the beans!' Thenjiwe was, of course, referring to her tears when her cadres had little more than beans to eat.[44]

A great wave of love and appreciation for Tambo's integrity and honesty, and his cultivation of a culture and acceptance, swept those struggling to find a place for themselves back home. Reconciliation, so crucial a retort to the counter-revolution and the bigots and to survival itself, was simply an extension of *ubuntu* translated into the inclusiveness and the human rights of the Freedom Charter. These values had been inscribed in the ANC's Constitutional Guidelines in the new Constitution of South Africa at Oliver Tambo's instigation.

Tambo, however, played a more vigorous role in ANC activities in the early nineties than is popularly perceived. He attended NEC meetings but also participated in international areas – behind the scenes, he hosted a steady stream of international guests who loved him and grieved for the fell blow on his health. In his living room, there were constant visitors, old friends of the movement – governors, heads of state, ministers of state, mayors, famous artists and other dignitaries – come to share and savour with him the return of the ANC.

There were also many old veterans who had never left the country during the long years of struggle. With him they had joyous reunions, recalling past campaigns and debates and struggles and prayers. They recalled Chief Luthuli's words, widely distributed, more than 30 years earlier.

'The history of mankind is the history of man struggling and striving for freedom,' Luthuli had asserted in the 1950s. 'Indeed, the very apex of human achievement is *Freedom,* and *not* slavery. Every human being struggles to reach that apex.' In their old age, they were thankful to be alive, so close to the top.

Tambo very much wanted to see as many communities as possible, and visited informal settlements, including Tamboville, which had sprung up in the late-1980s near Benoni, and had developed into a functional community, able to plan and design its space in a collective and creative manner. But excessive travel was not advised.

A lifetime of self-discipline was embedded in his very being. 'He had a strong will,' Dr Von Schreeb observed. 'Even [with] the damage he had, he had the possibility to function because he had compensatory mechanisms – which might have been helped by the fact that he was so intellectually alert before.'[45] Tambo gradually improved, although his progress was uneven.

In October 1991 Tambo was installed as Chancellor of Fort Hare, and gave a fascinating account of the university 60 years earlier.[46]

There were times when he felt frustrated by some people's misguided compassion. In August 1992, he was invited to attend an event at the University of the Western Cape to commemorate the 10th anniversary of the assassination of Ruth First. After the introductions and his presentation of the Ruth First Memorial Prize for Courageous Journalism, Tambo prepared to deliver his speech. But, perhaps to save him from discomfiture, the chairperson moved on to the next item on the agenda. Tambo's innate wisdom and vast experience were sorely missed.

'His mind was on the struggle all the time. Is this going right, is that other one going right, is that thing corrected?' remarked Tony Mongalo at Shell House. 'I thought to myself, who is there like him? If we were all, even half – say half of him – oh, I think we would have done very, very well.'[47]

Years later, whenever there were disputes between questions of interpretation and representation – of the poor, of democracy, participation and consultation – it was Oliver Tambo's name that was invoked. He remained an exemplar, called upon particularly in times of contested interpretations of the ANC – for it had been Tambo who had steered the African National Congress through its darkest days, through massacres, betrayals and tactical confusion.

In February 1993 Tambo opened a large international conference held in Johannesburg and chaired by Thabo Mbeki. Dozens of foreign dignitaries and eager representatives of anti-apartheid organisations filled the hall to capacity. Tambo had invited them in order to thank their countries and organisations for their valuable contribution to the freeing of the South African people from the bondage of apartheid. Perhaps the conference should have been held in Pretoria, said Tambo, 'to make the point that soon the country will be under new management'.

One of the ANC's most significant tasks was 'to liberate the oppressors... from fear of democracy and the future, to free them from a guilt-ridden fear of retribution and to dissuade them from any foolhardy temptation to seek an ephemeral security by imprisoning themselves within an armed laager'.[48]

'What we certainly can never be,' he added, 'is black racists who turn their back on the philosophy which has inspired the ANC since its birth – the sacred undertaking that the cause we serve is the emancipation of all humanity.'

The resolutions adopted by the conference agreed to mobilise the international community to help ensure that the first democratic elections would be 'free and fair', to promote maximum material support to the ANC to assist in this process, and to develop new forms of solidarity for the reconstruction and development of a new South Africa.[49]

As the pace of events spiralled, Tambo's schedule became fuller. 'He comes to the office every day,' reported Mongalo, his former PA, in March 1993. 'He contributes, he goes out addressing meetings – like Saturday, he addressed the Gandhi march; this weekend he will be going to the Transkei to address another rally and the chiefs in Lusikisiki.'[50]

On 9 March 1993 Tambo and other ANC senior leaders had a meeting with Lars-Åke Nilsson, Sweden's Foreign Under-Secretary, who broke the news that Sweden's support was 'approaching a point where "the present forms of support must come to an end"'.[51] The announcement was a blow to the ANC; huge expenses were still essential for managing transformation and survival in a hostile environment. Cadres needed to come home, pensions granted, staff at head office maintained, the township youth politically educated, branches to be set up countrywide. The struggle was not over. Clearly, the ANC was moving on to a new level abroad as well as at home, and it decided to renegotiate its relationship with Sweden and other donors. It was time for the wealthy of South Africa to make a contribution to the dismantling of apartheid.

In the meantime, Tambo was optimistic that his health was improving, and he wanted to be able to contribute to the challenges facing the movement. His speech was improving steadily, but his assistants were concerned that he might be straining his health for he could not bear to be away from the negotiations process.

'He went on holiday in January to the Transkei. He said, "I'll go only two weeks. Things will be happening here and I won't be able to give my input."'[52]

Then, on the fateful Easter Saturday of 1993, Chris Hani was shot in the head in the driveway of his house in a suburb of Boksburg. By then General Secretary of the SACP, Hani had enthralled the public with his engaging and articulate arguments on television. He had continued to argue for militancy and preparation for insurrection, if necessary, until a few weeks before his death, when he spoke out clearly in favour of reconciliation. He was beginning to express the possibility that negotiations might indeed be the best way to peace and democracy. His assassination traumatised the country. Most blacks were overwhelmed by a hitherto suppressed rage, whites by fear. Mandela's statesmanlike appearance on television to appeal to the entire nation to remain calm seemed to have prevented a conflagration of national proportions.

Thenjiwe Mthintso, who was on the funeral committee, saw that OR was at the Hani house every day. 'I just see OR – that way that he cared… OR used to go there, *e-v-e-r-y d-a-y!* I couldn't get him out of that house. And I could not understand what he was doing. But he would get there, day in and day out, and sit hours on end and we would have to persuade him to leave in the evening. And he would not even sit in the room where Limpo [Hani] was. He was just sitting in the lounge. Just caring, in that piercing [way], but very far away. Sad, but I think more far away than anything. And I used to just feel that I would just hug him and he would say things like, "I thought Chris was going to bury me, not me bury Chris."'[53]

It was a sign that OR was withdrawing in his grief. He was mourning, not only for Chris, but for the scores of cadres who had been lost in the struggle – in battle, through raids and assassinations, the toll of liquor and betrayal. People like Obadi, Dulcie September, Joe Gqabi, Duma Nokwe, Solomon Mahlangu, the innocent children, and many, many more – all heroes who fell during the long, uphill battle to reach that apex of freedom.

'We had one beautiful afternoon with OR,' Thenjiwe remembered. 'Beautiful in that we just sat. I think half of that time we just sat and looked at each other and just smiled; but just sat... In that condition, I couldn't relate to him in that same way – that flippant way. And he also sounded removed and it was because of the speech, I think, in the main. So, in between, we would throw in some of the things that we were remembering about each other – he and I. And he was reminding me of the *nyopa nyopa,* which is the syrup, Illovo syrup [which he loved so much].'[54]

Is it fanciful to imagine that, as he sat in the wake of the death of one of his political sons, OR's mind would have gone back – back to the beginning, back to his earliest memories – of the brown and green fields of Pondoland, and of his homestead at the foot of the mountain range? He could no longer speak with ease, but he might have listened again clearly to the rural sounds of his childhood – of children at play, the parting songs of his uncles and older brothers as they set off for the coal mines of Natal; of his grandmother, his aunts and other mothers' voices in sociable conversation across the open spaces as they ground mealies, carried the fire wood, hoed the fields or suckled their babies; of the quiet conversations of the adults around the fire; the call of the birds, the chickens and the goats and the donkeys and the cattle. He would have thought, gratefully, of his large, extended family, which had functioned economically and socially as a coherent, shared whole; recalling fondly his parents – his mother's laugh, at prayer, at work, and her wood-smoke smell, and his father's serious and dignified bearing – the farsighted, even-handed father who retained an interest in the welfare of each member of the family; and how he had grasped the import of the future, identifying for his son the gift of education. OR had long since realised that long before his discovery of Christianity, his traditional home and family had laid the foundations for his own integrated self, and his capacity for love and respect.[55] His rich oral culture had endowed him with the art of listening with care, in order to remember what was being said, and with patience and courtesy. In that tradition, human relations were of greater significance than material interests – indeed one's interests were inextricably tied to other human beings. He might have again recalled the thrill of his first encounter with Holy Cross Mission School, and his pleasure in learning, with its exhilarating rewards of good marks, problem-solving, the savouring of exotic words – words that would open other, magical doors of learning in time to come. And his father's inference that education and technical expertise, the prime skills of the white rulers of the country, could become powerful tools for independence; and the first time that he began to realise that to be black and think independently was an act of defiance; the lessons he had learnt from his comrades, too, from Nelson and Walter and Trevor Huddleston and all the others in shaping a new identity – the Africanists, the communists, the militants, the wise and the witty, the profoundly spiritual; and the support provided by the collective – greater than the sum of its parts. For where would the ANC have been without the maturity of so many comrades – Mda, Lembede, Marks, Kotane, Dadoo, Nokwe, Nkobi, Makatini and many, many others?

Above all, his mentor, Chief Luthuli, had shown him the way of combining the best of their African heritage with the accomplishments of modernity. He was the 'good chief', whose mantle he himself was honoured to wear before passing it on to Nelson. But in exile, once deprived of their guidance and partnership, he had utilised his exceptional mind and finely honed sense of strategy to draw on the best of the ANC's political culture of inclusiveness, collective ownership, adaptability and a moral vision, to achieve unity in the movement through the three decades of exile. This formidable, indeed unparalleled, effort had come at great personal cost. A few weeks earlier, Tambo recalled what he had missed in life, and how he had gently tried to nudge the present generation to push towards reconciliation so that they could more quickly come to lead a normal life. For a speech he made in Benoni, he had written some simple points: '(1) Disunity – unity in general; (2) Call all the people of Benoni to support the call. All the people to respond. When you have spent 75 years in struggle, you wish you had spent half the amount in enjoying life.'[56]

The dedicated, single-minded struggle denied him a normal family life, the pleasures of loving and sharing with his children his artistry: of music, sports, books, and heritage. So many missed opportunities. But then, all his life he was convinced that Divine Providence was guiding him. His frustrations and disappointments had turned into valuable lessons or unanticipated opportunities. Once, when Adelaide reprimanded her husband for driving himself too hard, he gave her one of his piercing looks.

'I had other plans for my life,' he said. 'I wanted to be a minister of the Anglican Church with Bishop Clayton. After we married, I was going to train for the ministry in Cape Town. But God had other plans for me. God's plan was for me to fight in the political liberation for my people.'[57] In his daily prayers, he continued to place his life in the care of God.

Chris Hani's funeral was a national expression of grief and controlled anger. The vigil at the FNB Stadium lasted all day. It was cool and damp, and Max Sisulu noticed that Oliver was without a coat.[58] At the cemetery, Tambo was alongside the grave. He sat through the long speeches, the hymns and liberation songs, MK's haunting farewell melody. The coffin was lowered into the grave, and OR scooped some reddish earth onto the casket.

At home that evening, he began to cough, spitting up the dust. His cough persisted until, after a few days, the family took him to Milpark Hospital. Mshengu, his faithful comrade and nurse-aide for many years, went with him. But even in hospital, OR seemed to get worse.

On the evening of 22 April, OR watched proudly as Tselane appeared on television. Then he went to sleep.

Late that night, Adelaide was woken by the ringing of the telephone. Oliver had had a heart attack. It had been caused by congestion of the heart. The family rushed to the hospital, where he was put on life support.

Oliver Reginald Tambo died in the early hours of Friday, 23 April 1993.

An extraordinary life had ended.

Oliver Tambo had worked hard and intelligently and selflessly. He had been fortunate to have survived the struggle to see apartheid come to an end. He had been with his wife and children when they returned home to South Africa. He had shepherded the family of the nation towards the apex, freedom. It was now time for him to cross once again, to his ancestral and spiritual home, to be received and embraced by the mountains.

Adelaide, in her grief, recalled an exchange concerning his health: 'At the rate you are working and the pace you are putting the nation through, when we reach freedom you might not be there!'

Oliver had replied in his slow and deliberate way: 'Perhaps I shall not live to see the Promised Land, but my people shall have reached it.'[59]

Thousands attended the funeral, many coming from faraway places to take leave of Oliver Tambo. They included heads of state, politicians, artists, public figures, and also thousands who had fought in the struggle and received his inspiration. The atmosphere was muted. It had scarcely been a fortnight since the people had buried Chris Hani.

Speakers expressed themselves with passion. Biblical images prevailed. In a lyrical homage to Tambo, Nelson Mandela's funeral oration was in essence a traditional praise poem.

'A great giant, who strode the globe like a colossus, has fallen. A mind whose thoughts have opened the doors to our liberty has ceased to function. A heart whose dreams gave hope to the despised has forever lost its beat. The gentle voice whose measured words of reason shook the thrones of tyrants has been silenced. Peoples of the world, here lies before you the body of a man who is tied to me by an umbilical cord which cannot be broken. We say he has departed, but can we allow him to depart while we live? Can we say Oliver Tambo is no more, while we walk this solid earth? Oliver lived not because he could breathe. He lived not because blood flowed through his veins. Oliver lived not because he did all the things that all of us as ordinary men and women do. Oliver lived because he had surrendered his very being to the people. He lived because his very being embodied love, an idea, a hope, an aspiration, a vision…'

Oliver Tambo was forever associated with the noble aspirations of humanity. 'We know that black and white, across the globe – the Pole, the Greek, the Ethiopian, the Cuban, the Brazilian and the Eritrean, people of all nationalities, are all united in their opposition to apartheid and injustice. While these exist, Oliver Tambo cannot perish. Let he or she who dares, stand up and tell us that it will happen that, while humanity survives, it will come to pass that OR Tambo will cease to be.

'Let all of us who live, say that while we live, Oliver Tambo will not die! May he, for his part, rest in peace. Go well, my brother, and farewell, dear friend. As you instructed, we will bring peace to our tormented land. As you directed, we will bring freedom to the oppressed and liberation to the oppressor. As you strived, we will restore the dignity of the dehumanised. As you commanded, we will defend the option of a peaceful resolution of our problems. As you prayed, we will respond to the cries of the wretched... As you loved them, we will, always, stretch out a hand of endearment to those who are your flesh and blood.'[60]

Then the Reverend Frank Chikane spoke: 'He led us to be free, so we can be free from the bondage of struggle... Like Moses, Oliver Tambo chose to go into exile. Like Moses, he pointed at the suffering of the people to those who hardened their hearts. Our father Tambo. He died near the top of the mountain... He has taken us along to the mountaintop. We thank you, Tata.'[61]

Like Moses, Oliver Reginald Tambo had led his people to the Promised Land, but did not live to reach the top. The demise of the apartheid regime still lay ahead.

Ten years into democracy, this architect of the struggle still had relevant lessons to impart on the quality of leadership – lessons on how to marry commitment to non-racialism with redress and nation-building; to attach black empowerment to integrity and public service. It was now for the next generation to pick up Oliver Tambo's gleaming spear as they continued their climb up to the apex, lest his strength of purpose, of character and endurance, lie rusting on the ground. The struggle for freedom, dignity and quality of life continued.

'Beyond the mountains – more mountains.'[62]

R NOTES

CE

1. This description is based on a video of Tambo's visit to Perth in April 1987, ANC Video Archives and OR Tambo Collection, Fort Hare Archives.
2. They were referring to the use of 'necklacing' – the placing of a petrol-filled tyre over the intended victim's head, and then lighting it. This practice was performed in public in parts of South Africa against perceived collaborators of the apartheid regime.
3. The charred remains of activist Matthew Goniwe and his four comrades had been found close to the coast in the Eastern Cape weeks after they had gone missing. Tambo's claim that they were 'necklaced' by their captors was to be confirmed 10 years later in the Truth and Reconciliation Commission's enquiry.
4. My thanks to Dr Morley Nkosi for his assistance in the translation of this traditional proverb.
5. From a proposal by Luli Callinicos (hereafter referred to as LC) submitted to the Tambo family and accepted, November 1992.
6. Per Wästberg, interview by LC, Stockholm, 21 October 2002.
7. Letter to Adelaide Tambo from Oliver Tambo, Lusaka, 11 October 1987.
8. Ibid.
9. The traditional name, as used by natives of the region, is Mpondoland; the colonial corruption, seen almost universally on maps, is 'Pondoland'.
10. Oliver Tambo recorded his memoirs on 12 audiotapes, mostly undated. Tape 1, however, from which this quote is taken, begins on 24 January 1988. *See also* Note 1, Part One, Chapter 1.
11. This is the original spelling of the family name *See also* Note 1, Part One, Chapter 2.
12. The Kantolo community recently decided to revert to the traditional spelling of 'Nkantolo'. For reasons of authenticity – as with 'Pondoland' versus 'Mpondoland' (*see* Note 9 *above*) – I have retained the spelling used by Tambo in his personal notes.
13. Richard Sennet, *The Corrosion of Character*, WW Norton & Co., 1998.

PART ONE *Chapter One*
'This Was My World'

1. Unless indictated, all quotations by Oliver Tambo are drawn from his taped memoirs to his daughter, Thembi Tambo, who transcribed them in October 1988. OR Tambo Collection, Fort Hare Archives.
2. William Beinart, *The Political Economy of Pondoland: 1860–1930,* Ravan, 1982, p42.
3. Ibid.
4. Matshilo Motsei, 'Sacred Rocks, Ancient Voices, Spiritual Significance of Rock and Water in African Healing', Paper prepared for Freedom Park, 2003.
5. Oliver Tambo, Cassette 1.
6. Oliver Tambo, interview by LC, Johannesburg, 2 February 1993.
7. Samson Mabhude, interview by LC, Kantolo, 24 January 1993.
8. Monica Hunter, *Reaction to Conquest*, Oxford University Press, 1936, pp264–5.
9. Tshongwana Mchitwa, interview by LC, Kantolo, 24 January 1993.
10. Oliver Tambo, Cassette 2.
11. WD Hammond-Tooke, *Command or Consensus: The Development of Transkeian Local Government*, David Philip Publishers, 1975, p155.
12. Ibid.
13. Ibid., pp65–8.
14. See Chapter 16.
15. Luli Callinicos, *Gold and Workers*, Ravan Press, 1981.
16. Oliver Tambo, interview by LC, op. cit.
17. Erik Erikson, *Gandhi's Truth: On the Origins of Militant Violence*, Faber & Faber, London, 1970, p43. Erikson describes the mother in Gandhi's extended family, 'in which she must respond to each and, at the same time, to all, and thus belong to the individual child only in fleeting moments and to nobody for good or for long'.
18. Ibid.

PART ONE *Chapter Two*
The Reluctant Schoolboy

1. Later in Oliver's school years, the spelling of 'Thambo' was changed to 'Tambo'.
2. William Beinart, *The Political Economy of Pondoland: 1860–1930*, Ravan, 1982, p102.
3. Ibid.
4. Tshongwana Mchitwa, interview by LC, Kantolo, 24 January 1993.
5. Rumford Qwalela, interview by LC, Holy Cross Mission, Flagstaff, 20 January 1993.
6. Madlhamba died in 1992.
7. Sindiso Mfenyana, interview by LC, Johannesburg, 23 March 1993.
8. That boy became an activist in the Unity Movement and a Robben Island prisoner in the 1970s and '80s. His sister, Brigalia, was known for her work in the Council of Churches, and was to become Chief Electoral Officer for the 2004 national elections.
9. Johnson Makaula, interview by LC, Holy Cross Mission, Flagstaff, 20 January 1993.
10. MJ Ashley, 'Features of Modernity: Missionaries and Education in South Africa, 1850–1900', *Journal of Theology for Southern Africa.*

PART ONE *Chapter Three*
The Mountain of Knowledge

1. Victor Sifora, interview by LC, Rustenburg, 4 October 1994.
2. Alan Wilkinson, *The Community of the Resurrection: A Centenary History*, SCM Press, 1992, p213.
3. Ibid., p215.
4. David Mankanzana, interview by LC, Johannesburg, 1 July 1993.
5. Trevor Huddleston, *Naught For Your Comfort*, Fontana Books, 1977, p190.
6. Wilkinson, op. cit., pp6–7.
7. Huddleston, op. cit., p304.
8. In 1889, Gore edited *Lux Mundi*, which scandalised the 'Old Church' for his suggestion that the Bible should not necessarily be taken literally. Similar views expressed 30 years earlier by Bishop Colenso caused him to be deposed for heresy. See Jeff Guy's *The Heretic*, Ravan, 1983.
9. Wilkinson, op. cit., p224.
10. Ibid.
11. Ibid., p216.
12. Ibid.
13. Ibid., pp210–11.
14. Ibid., p207.
15. Ibid., p215.
16. Alban Winter, 'Till Darkness Fell', cited in Wilkinson, p362.
17. *CR Quarterly*, 1971, cited in Wilkinson.
18. *The Autobiography of William Plomer*, Jonathan Ball, 1975, cited in Wilkinson, p20.
19. *CR Chronicle*, 1934.
20. Wilkinson, op. cit.
21. *CR Chronicle*, 138, 1937.
22. Edmund Maponya, 'Thoko, The Joyful One: Responses Within and Without', *The Bulletin*, 1938, pp7–8.
23. Sifora interview, op. cit.
24. Wilkinson, op. cit., p218.
25. See also Martin Jarrett-Kerr, 'African culture', *CR Quarterly*, 1960.
26. Sifora interview, op. cit.
27. Ibid.
28. St Peter's Collection, CPSA Archives, Wits University Historical Papers.
29. Wilkinson, op. cit., p214.
30. Letter to Miss Hill from Oliver Tambo, *c.*1935.
31. Basil Davidson, *Black Man's Burden*, Times Books, 1992, p297.
32. Tony 'Gabs' Msimang, Jacob Zuma and Joe Slovo, interviews by LC, Johannesburg, 22 June 1993, 27 July 1993 and 7 January 1994 respectively.
33. Letter to Miss Hill from Oliver Tambo, extracts typed by Trevor Huddleston, courtesy Thembi Tambo.
34. Oliver Tambo, interview by LC, Flagstaff, 23 January 1993.
35. Letter to Miss Hill from Oliver Tambo (undated).
36. David Mankazana, interview by LC, Johannesburg, 1 July 1993.
37. Nimrod Tubane, interview by LC, Johannesburg, 1 July 1993.
38. Ibid.
39. Mankazana interview, op. cit.
40. Tubane interview, op. cit.
41. Lancelot Gama, interview by LC, KwaThema, 2 March 1994.
42. KT Motsete, MA BD (Lond.), 'The Aim of African Education', *The Bulletin*, 1945.
43. Letter to the Misses J and R Goddard from Miss Whittington, 5 March 1936 (reproduced for Tambo by Huddleston).
44. *CR Chronicle* 138, 1937, p16.
45. Ibid.
46. Gerty Tambo, interview by LC, Kantolo, 21 January 1993.
47. St Peter's Logbook, 5 February 1937, Wits University Historical Papers.
48. Osmund Victor, CR, *The Salient of South Africa, Society for the Propagation of the Gospel in Foreign Parts*, 1931, pp44–5.
49. The Reverend Joel Jolingana, 'A Christian Circumcision School', *The Bulletin*, 1938, pp11–12.
50. South African Native College, Calendar for 1939, Fort Hare, Alice, p46.
51. Bruce K Murray, *Wits: The Early Years*, Wits University Press, 1982, p303.
52. Bruce K Murray, *Wits: The Open Years*, Wits University Press, 1997, Chapter 2.
53. Alexander Kerr, *Fort Hare 1915–48: The Evolution of an African College*, C Hurst & Co., 1968, p150.

PART TWO *Chapter Four*
'The Starting Point'

1. South African Native College, Calendar for 1940, Fort Hare, Alice, pp82–6.
2. Annual Report, Beda Hall, Fort Hare, 1941.
3. Alexander Kerr, *Fort Hare 1915–48: The Evolution of an African College*, C Hurst & Co., 1968, p22.
4. Ibid., p25.
5. The speech is reproduced in Richard Rive and Tim Couzens, *Seme*, Skotaville, 1991, p75ff. (Thabo Mbeki, as Deputy President of South Africa, drew on the legacy of Seme's speech when he delivered his own 'I am an African' address to Parliament in 1996.)
6. DT Mweli Skota, *African Yearly Register: Being an Illustrated National Biographical Dictionary (Who's Who) of Black Folks in Africa*, 1930. Skota was ANC Secretary-General at the time. Plaatje was Congress's first Secretary-General.
7. These names are invoked in HIE Dhlomo's ode to the poet BW Vilikazi, 1949, cited in Tim Couzens, *The New African: A Study of the Life and Work of HIE Dhlomo*, Ravan, 1985.
8. Quoted in Luli Callinicos, *Gold and Workers*, Ravan, 1981, p92.
9. Victor Sifora, interview by LC, Rustenburg, 4 October 1994.

10. ZK Matthews, *Freedom For My People: The Autobiography of ZK Matthews, Southern Africa, 1901–1968*, David Philip Publishers, 1986, p51.
11. Kerr, op. cit., p31.
12. Ibid.
13. Matthews, op. cit., p55–6.
14. Ibid., pp51 and 54.
15. Kerr, op. cit., p14.
16. Ibid., p10. The book in question here was Maurice Evans' *Black and White in South-East Africa* (date unknown).
17. In 1924 the white electorate put Hertzog's Afrikaner Party, in alliance with the English-speaking Labour Party, into power. In that same year, at Fort Hare's graduation ceremony, speaker Professor GF Dingemans gave a pointed message that Kerr summarised in his history of Fort Hare: 'Dingemans hoped that the College... would ever strive to be a Native College, giving to its students a training not in any way inferior to that given in the European centres of Higher Education, but more specifically adapted to the needs of Native students and the circumstances in which they were to exercise their particular calling. He recalled that there had been a time when European education in South Africa was but a copy of a system developed under entirely different conditions overseas. And Native education, in its turn, was a copy of a copy.' Most English-speaking South Africans agreed with the segregationist approach. In 1928, JR Sullivan published his book on the policies of Sir Theophilus Shepstone, the 19th-century governor of Natal, and compared these with the 'Native Policies' of the contemporary government. Hertzog's, he said, was 'the fullest and sincerest attempt to deal with the relationship between black and white'. 'To denationalise the Bantu race would be dangerous to both white and black as it would result in racial amalgamation and consequently in deterioration and bitter struggle. Tribal communities... should be preserved... and under white guidance... they should be assisted along their own path of evolution'.
This was the general feeling on black education, and was to find many variations, from African traditionalists, to African nationalists, to white segregationists, until it found its crudest form in the Bantu Education policy.
18. Kerr, op. cit., p130.
19. Ibid., p14.
20. Ibid., p129.
21. It was in this context that the Fort Hare students were offered the challenge of preparing productively for the wider South African society. Chief Inspector of Native Schools in the Cape and son of a prominent missionary, WK Bennie, counselled the alumni to adopt a more accommodating approach that was to excite the fierce criticism of Africanists. Ironically the stance of moral excellence in the face of racism and bigotry, fortified by the African tradition of courtesy and *ubuntu*, did not fail, ultimately, to influence a number of future leaders of the ANC, many of whom had passed through the portals of Fort Hare. Nelson Mandela acknowledged the sway of the missionaries: 'Our generation was produced by Christian schools, by missionary schools... when the government took no interest whatsoever in our education. It was the missionary that piloted black education... So Christianity is really in our blood...' (Nelson Mandela, interview by LC, Johannesburg, 20 August 1993.)
In years to come, Oliver Tambo himself, as Supreme Commander of the ANC's military wing Umkhonto we Sizwe, became the very personification in the eyes of its members of 'the moral high-ground' with which it justified armed struggle.
22. Matthews, op. cit., p76.
23. Ibid., p78–9.
24. Calendar for 1939, op. cit., p94.
25. The Beda Hall Chapel had started as a rondavel commandeered by Bishop Smythe on his arrival. When, after 14 years in a bungalow, the Anglican Church erected the Beda Hall residence, an adjoining chapel was added as a matter of course. It was Bishop Smythe who had influenced the naming of the hostel: St Bede had been a great classical scholar who had translated the Bible from Latin into English, the language of the common people. After his retirement, Smythe commissioned a stained-glass window for the chapel, in which he himself sat for the portrait of St Bede dictating the Gospel and, 'over my embarrassed objections', recruited ZK Matthews to pose for the figure of the disciple and scribe. (Matthews, op. cit., p79.)
26. Matthews, op. cit., p65.
27. Nelson Mandela, interview by LC, Johannesburg, 31 August 1993.
28. Kerr, op. cit., p19.
29. Lancelot Gama, interview by LC, KwaThema Springs, 2 March 1994.
30. David Bopape, interview by LC, Johannesburg, 2 November 1994.
31. Gama interview, op. cit.
32. Matthews, op. cit.
33. VJ (Joe) Matthews, interview by LC, Cape Town, 28 February 1995. At the time of this interview, Matthews was Deputy Minister of Safety and Security and a member of the Inkatha Freedom Party.
34. Gama interview, op. cit.
35. Ibid.
36. Couzens, op. cit., cites *Ilanga Lase Natal*, 9 August 1929, which claimed that 77 had matriculated at Fort Hare and 10 had graduated from the University of South Africa.
37. Letter to the Misses J and R Goddard from Oliver Tambo, Beda Hall, Fort Hare, Alice, 20 October 1940.
38. Reference by Principal, Alexander Kerr, (11 September 1942), Rhodes University, Grahamstown, courtesy Dr Robert Edgar.
39. Mandela interview, op. cit.
40. Kerr, op. cit., p97.
41. Phyllis Ntantala, *A Life's Mosaic: The Autobiography of Phyllis Ntantala*, David Philip Publishers, 1992.

42. Letter to the Misses J and R Goddard from Miss Tanqueray, Holy Cross Mission, 25 August 1940, extracts typed by Trevor Huddleston, courtesy Thembi Tambo.
43. Letter to Misses J and R Goddard from Oliver Tambo, Fort Hare, Alice, 20 October 1940, extracts typed by Trevor Huddleston, courtesy Thembi Tambo.
44. See Skota's account in *The African Yearly Register* (1892) of Mr and Mrs Paul Xiniswe's choral tour of Europe in 1892, p109.
45. Medical explanation provided by Professor John Kalk, epidemiologist, Wits University.
46. Letter to Bishop Ferguson-Davie from Dr Rogers, Holy Cross Hospital, 12 May 1939, Rhodes University, Grahamstown, courtesy Dr Robert Edgar.
47. Subsequently, Kerr (op. cit., p31) was convinced through experience of the social significance of women. Female graduates succeeded in the fields of social work, nursing and medicine, as well as education at nursery, school and adult levels. Kerr observed: 'We shall never know the whole story of quiet work done by the majority... there is no record of the unspectacular but nonetheless valuable leadership given in... communities.'
48. Ntantala, op. cit., p71.
49. Matthews, op. cit.
50. Memoir by Monica Wilson, cited in Matthews, op. cit., p120.
51. Skota, op. cit.
52. Couzens, op. cit., pp5–6.
53. Ibid., p6.
54. Wilson in Matthews, op. cit., p120.
55. Gama interview, op. cit.
56. Letter to Misses J and R Goddard from Oliver Tambo, Fort Hare, Alice, 20 October 1940, extracts typed by Trevor Huddleston, courtesy Thembi Tambo.
57. Govan Mbeki, interview by LC, Port Elizabeth, 2 November 1993.
58. Gama interview, op. cit.
59. Ibid.
60. South African Native College, Calendar for 1944, Fort Hare, Alice, p68.
61. Gama interview, op. cit.
62. Mandela interview, op. cit.
63. Kerr, op. cit., p167.
64. Annual Report of Beda Hall, Fort Hare, 1942, sent to the Archbishop of Cape Town, Cory Library PR3362, Rhodes University, Grahamstown.
65. Gama interview, op. cit.
66. Kerr, op. cit., p167.
67. Ibid., p243.
68. Ibid.
69. VJ (Joe) Matthews, interview by LC, Cape Town, 31 August 1994.
70. Calendar for 1944, op. cit.
71. Matthews interview, 1994, op. cit.
72. Ibid.
73. Kerr, op. cit., p245.
74. Huddleston, op. cit., p106.
75. Calendar for 1944, op. cit.
76. Thomas Tlou, Neil Parsons and Willie Henderson, *Seretse Khama: 1921–80*, Rhino Press, 1994, p52.
77. Gama interview, op. cit.
78. Calendar for 1944, op. cit.
79. Huddleston, op. cit., p106.
80. Ibid., p107.
81. Reference for Oliver Tambo, 11 September 1942, by Dr Alexander Kerr, Fort Hare, Alice, courtesy Dr Robert Edgar, Rhodes University, Grahamstown.
82. Oliver Tambo, interview by LC, Johannesburg, 2 February 1993.
83. Ibid.

PART TWO *Chapter Five*
The Trumpet Call

1. Letter to the Misses J and R Goddard from Miss Tanqueray, Holy Cross Mission, 20 January 1943, extracts typed by Trevor Huddleston, courtesy Thembi Tambo.
2. Fertz Ngakane, interview by LC, London, 23 September 1993.
3. Henry Makgothi, interview by LC, Johannesburg, 24 February 1993.
4. Ibid.
5. Ibid.
6. VJ (Joe) Matthews, interview by LC, Cape Town, 20 October 1994.
7. Rumford Qwalela, interview by LC, Holy Cross Mission, Flagstaff, 19 January 1993.
8. Ibid.
9. Vella Pillay, interview by LC, Johannesburg, 21 September 1993. At the time of this interview, Pillay was Director of the Economic Policy Unit to advise the ANC.
10. Obed Musi, 'Musin', *City Press*, 2 May 1993, copy courtesy Phyllis Naidoo.
11. Qwalela interview, op. cit.
12. Vuyiswa Tambo, interview by LC, Umtata, 17 January 1993.
13. Qwalela interview, op. cit.
14. Ibid.
15. Any non-manual work in a society that was generally poor was accorded an aura of authority. White-collar work meant exposure to formal education beyond primary school, with a lifestyle to match – the literate read newspapers and joined libraries; they wore suits to work, had Western furniture and often cooked European food. Skilled workers were more likely to be economically stable. They formed part of the occupational cream of African society. Added to the tiny handful of doctors and lawyers, a modest number of teachers ranked alongside court interpreters, journalists, clergy, nurses and social workers, government-appointed chiefs and businessmen, such as shopkeepers and estate agents in status.
16. By the 1940s Johannesburg was a metropolis. For the black elite the hub of activity was the Witwatersrand. Just 50 years earlier, the locus

of the black intelligentsia had been in the Eastern Cape, with its educational institutions, two Xhosa newspapers, black liberals, writers and politically active, enfranchised elite. Later, Kimberley also attracted the educated, including Sol Plaatje. As the century progressed, the axis steadily shifted northwards. The Witwatersrand gold industry increasingly dominated the local economy. The region benefited further from the 1913 Land Act, with its commercialisation of white-owned farms. By blocking off South Africa's supply of goods from Britain, the two world wars also stimulated the Witwatersrand's manufacturing industry.

17. Now the province of Gauteng.

18. Alan Gregor Cobley, *Class and Consciousness*, Greenwood Press, 1997, p38–9.

19. See Mitchell Duneier, *Slim's Table*, University of Chicago Press, 1992.

20. Elinor Sisulu, *Walter & Albertina Sisulu: In Our Lifetime*, David Philip Publishers, 2003 (Second Edition).

21. Walter Sisulu, interview by LC, Johannesburg, 31 October 1994.

22. Walter Sisulu, interview by LC, Johannesburg, 24 November 1994.

23. Walter Sisulu, interview by LC, Johannesburg, 5 February 1993.

24. Ibid.

25. Lancelot Gama, interview by LC, 1 December 1994.

26. These included the Council of Non-European Trade Unions. In addition, the ministers of Education and of Native Affairs also received queries from the Natal Indian Physical Culture League, the African Historical Association, the Transvaal African Congress, the Johannesburg Communist Party, the National Liberation League of South Africa, the Non-European United Front, the Communist Party of South Africa, the Natal Indian Association, the Liberal Study Group and the Natal University College Students' Union.

27. Letters, telegrams and minutes of the Native Representative Council, South African National Archives, Pretoria, courtesy Dr Robert Edgar.

28. Minutes of the Meeting of the Governing Council, NTS 9294 22/373, South African National Archives, Pretoria.

29. Ibid.

30. Dan Khoza was a labour and community activist from Alexander. Self Mampuru was a member of the African Democratic Party, an organisation of socialists critical of both the inertia of the ANC and the 'Stalinism' of the Communist Party of South Africa.

31. Walter Sisulu, interview by LC, Johannesburg, 10 June 1990.

32. David Bopape, interview by LC, Johannesburg, 6 July 1990.

33. Lancelot Gama, interview by LC, KwaThema Springs, 2 March 1994.

34. Xuma was the son of a peasant in the Eastern Cape and had earned bursaries to study in mission schools. In 1912, he – having saved for the fare from his earnings as a teacher – went on to receive medical training in North America, Hungary and Scotland. After 14 years, he returned to Sophiatown. In 1938 he received a Public Health degree from London University. He was committed to a vision of non-racial cooperation. He believed that it was necessary to use the African elite as a vanguard for the reconstruction of his people.

35. Introduction to Nelson Mandela's *No Easy Walk to Freedom*, Heinemann, 1965, pxiv.

36. Peter Molotsi, interview by LC, Johannesburg, 1 August 1995.

37. Nelson Mandela, *Long Walk to Freedom*, Abacus, 1994, p15.

38. David Bopape, interview by LC, Johannesburg, 2 November 1944.

39. Sisulu interview, October 1994, op. cit.

40. Oliver Tambo, interview by Thomas Karis and Gail Gerhart, London, 3–4 and 6 March 1991, courtesy Karis and Gerhart.

41. Ibid. *Thomas Karis:* 'So, it was merit only, as Luthuli said – that he wanted a South Africa where advancement would be based on merit?' *Oliver Tambo:* 'Yes!'

42. Peter Walshe, *Rise of African Nationalism in South Africa*, Paper Books, 1987, p1.

43. Thomas Karis and Gwendoline Carter, *From Protest to Challenge*, Volume 2 (*Hope and Challenge*), edited by Thomas Karis, Hoover Institution Press, 1973, p82.

44. Ibid. JB Marks, secretary to Councillor Baloyi, recalled: 'We toured the Transvaal and Free State, visiting almost every village and *dorp*, and took the message that the ANC is back.'

45. Centenary address to Lovedale, 1941, and report on proceedings of the Native Representative Council, Pretoria, December 1942, cited in Walshe, op. cit., p269.

46. *Bantu World*, 21 January 1942.

47. *Umteteli*, 31 January 1942.

48. Prison biography of Walter Sisulu, Mayibuye Archives, University of the Western Cape, courtesy Elinor Sisulu.

49. Karis and Carter, op. cit., p89.

50. Luli Callinicos, *A Place in the City: The Rand on the Eve of Apartheid*, Ravan/Maskew Miller Longman, 1993.

51. Sisulu interview, October 1994, op. cit. Sisulu rated Nkomo highly. A member of the CPSA, Nkomo had a vision of marrying African nationalism with Marxism-Leninism. His ideas influenced Sisulu to look more kindly upon communists. Ironically, he turned away from the CPSA and joined the Moral Re-Armament Movement, becoming a leading influence in the formation of the Black People's Convention before he died of a stroke in 1972.

52. Robert Edgar and Luyanda ka Msumzi (Eds), *Freedom in Our Lifetime*, Ohio/Skotaville, 1996, p38.

53. Letter to the Director of the Hoover Institute from Congress Mbata, 12 May 1961, ANC AD1189, Box 9 La1, Mayibuye Archives, University of the Western Cape.

54. Edgar and ka Msumzi, op. cit., Introduction.
55. Victor Sifora, interview by LC, Rustenburg, 4 October 1994.
56. The son of a poor farm labourer in Natal, Lembede was passionate about learning and was awarded a bursary to train as a teacher at Durban's Adams College. When Lembede arrived in Johannesburg in 1943, he was working on his Master of Arts thesis on concepts of God by European philosophers since Descartes. He was a devout Catholic, and was taken up with theories of nationalism. Having experienced poverty and hardship, he went beyond notions of armed resistance or liberal assimilationist ideas; the root of the African predicament, he argued, was the low self-esteem imposed by whites to create dependence. Yet Africans had rich spiritual and cultural resources they could use to overcome injustices. Pride in African culture and wisdom had to be overcome before political and economic equity could be achieved. He coined an enduring name for this empowering form of nationalism: 'Africanism.'
57. Bopape interview, 1990, op. cit.
58. Sisulu interview, October 1994, op. cit.
59. Dr Robert Edgar, interview by LC, Johannesburg, 3 July 2000.
60. Michael Worsnip, *Between the Two Fires*, University of Natal Press, 1991, p16.
61. Letter to Trevor Huddleston from Oliver Tambo, 25 September 1990, courtesy Robin Denniston.
62. Robin Denniston, *Trevor Huddleston: A life*, Macmillan, 1999, p3. As a schoolboy, Huddleston's visits to London at the height of the Depression exposed him to hardship and social deprivation, and made him receptive to the Christian Socialist movement. He read history at Oxford and in 1941 took his monastic vows with the Community of the Resurrection (CR). Two years later, he was posted to Johannesburg to head the CR mission there, which centred on the Church of Christ the King, Sophiatown. Unlike most white clerics, he chose to live among his flock, and became a much-loved figure. To residents, Huddleston was a living example of what they had been taught were the characteristics of a Christian – protective, understanding of frailties and ready to do battle against injustice and injury towards others. He even impressed other whites and Alan Paton, stirred by Huddleston's lifestyle, modelled *Cry, the Beloved Country*'s Father Vincent on him.
63. Adelaide Tambo, interview by LC, Johannesburg, 9 August 1993.
64. Letter to Huddleston, 1990, op. cit.
65. Adelaide Tambo interview, op. cit.
66. Huddleston linked the divine law of the church by placing it in the paradigm of humanism. Drawing on the words of Jesus, 'If ye do this unto the least of these, my little ones, ye do it unto me', he argued that one could only love an unseen god 'by serving those you are sent to serve'. Apartheid was blasphemy because it humiliated creatures of God. It was this drawing together of spiritual fulfilment through service to humankind that drew Tambo to him.
67. Anthony Sampson, *Drum: A venture into the new Africa*, Collins, 1956, p169.
68. Letter to Trevor Huddleston, undated.
69. Huddleston, op. cit., p107.
70. Karis and Carter, op. cit., p308–9.
71. Mzala, 'How the ANC Was Revived by the Youth League: A 70th Birthday Tribute to President Tambo from one of the Soweto Generation', *Sechaba*, 1987.
72. Karis and Carter, op. cit., p316.
73. Letter to Nelson Mandela from IB Tabata, 16 June 1948, cited in Karis and Carter, op. cit., pp366–7.
74. Karis and Carter, op. cit., p316.
75. Ismail Meer, interview by LC, Durban, 20 January 2000.
76. Sisulu interview, February 1993, op. cit.
77. Sisulu interview, October 1994, op. cit.
78. 'A Message to African Youth by OR Tambo, National Secretary and Acting National President of the Congress Youth League', undated (before October 1949), courtesy Dr Robert Edgar.
79. Sisulu interview, June 1990, op. cit.
80. 'The African Mine Workers' Strike – A National Struggle', flyer issued by the ANC Youth League, 1946, cited in Karis and Carter, op. cit., p318.
81. Sisulu interview, June 1990, op. cit.
82. Mandela, op. cit., p119.
83. Meer interview, op. cit.
84. Sisulu interview, June 1990, op. cit. See also Elinor Sisulu, op. cit., p77.
85. Oliver Tambo, interview by Chutter, unpublished, 15 November 1963, courtesy Thomas Karis and Gail Gerhart.
86. Sisulu interview, June 1990, op. cit.
87. The concept of the 'organic intellectual' who develops an intellectual understanding of the organisation or community from which he or she springs is from Antonio Gramsci, in his writings in prison. See his *Prison Notebooks and Letters from Prison*, Quartet Books, 1979.
88. Thabo Mbeki, written correspondence, 4 September 2003.

PART TWO *Chapter Six*
'Holding a Snake by its Tail'

1. Hermann Giliomee, *Sunday Times*, 22 May 1998.
2. 'Statement by Dr Xuma, President of the ANC', 5 April 1948, cited in Thomas Karis and Gwendoline Carter, *From Protest to Challenge*, Volume 2 (*Hope and Challenge*), edited by Thomas Karis, Hoover Institution Press, 1987 (paperback edition), p274.
3. Albert Luthuli, *Let My People Go*, Fontana Books, 1963, p97.
4. Nelson Mandela, *Long Walk to Freedom*, Abacus, 1994, p128.
5. Walter Sisulu, interview by LC, Johannesburg, 11 February 1993.
6. Nelson Mandela, interview by LC, Johannesburg, 20 August 1993.
7. Rusty Bernstein, *Memory Against Forgetting*, Viking, 1999, p110.

8. Walter Sisulu, interview by LC, 27 June 1990.
9. Ibid.
10. Mandela interview, op. cit.
11. Ibid.
12. Sisulu interview, June 1990, op. cit.
13. Ibid.
14. 'A Message to African Youth by OR Tambo', *Bantu World*, 1 April 1950. The white 'Native' representatives in Parliament were two CPSA members – Sam Kahn and Ray Simons – who were forcibly ejected from the Legislature because they were communists.
15. Oliver Tambo, interview by Gail Gerhart, New York, 6 November 1973, notes courtesy Gail Gerhart.
16. Sisulu interview, June 1990, op. cit.
17. Ibid.
18. Letter to *Bantu World* from AB Xuma, 15 March 1951.
19. Ibid.
20. Ibid.
21. Letter to *Bantu World* from WM Sisulu, NR Mandela and OR Tambo, 1 April 1950.
22. Memoirs of MB Yengwa, unpublished interviews by Beverley Naidoo, London, 1982, courtesy Dr Beverley Naidoo.
23. Sisulu interview, June 1990, op. cit.
24. Meer interview, op. cit.
25. Sisulu interview, June 1990, op. cit.
26. 'The Programme of Action – Statement of Policy Adopted at the ANC Annual Conference', 17 December 1949, cited in Karis and Carter, op. cit., pp377–8.
27. *The Guardian*, 21 January 1949.
28. Meer interview, op. cit.
29. Yengwa interview, op. cit.
30. 'Statement issued by Joint Meeting of African and Indian Leaders', 6 February 1949, cited in Karis and Carter, op. cit., p287–8.
31. Meer interview, op. cit.
32. David Bopape, interview by LC, Johannesburg, 6 July 1990.
33. Elias Motsoaledi, interview by LC, Johannesburg, 9 July 1990.
34. Sisulu interview, October 1994, op. cit.
35. Meer interview, op. cit.
36. Godfrey Pitje, interview by LC, Daveyton, 3 August 1996.
37. Ibid.
38. Document TAB/TPD 964/1951, Supreme Court, Transvaal Provincial Division, Certificate: 'Admission of Oliver Tambo as an Attorney', South African National Archives, courtesy Dr Robert Edgar.
39. Sisulu interview, October 1994, op. cit.
40. George Bizos, interview by LC, Johannesburg, 12 December 1998.
41. Ralph Tuch, interview by LC, Sydney, 8 December 1999.
42. Ibid.
43. Ibid.
44. Thomas Nkobi, interview by LC, Johannesburg, 12 August 1993.
45. Tuch interview, op. cit.
46. Ibid. *Ralph Tuch:* 'Mandela says something in his book which is not correct; he used to call regularly. He often came to spend lunch hour at our offices. Oliver had an office of his own. We didn't have separate offices. Mandela says that we had in our general office chairs marked "Whites Only" at our reception. That is not correct. Whoever called at our offices, never saw that... Oliver had full access to his clients from the reception room, with personal, private offices for himself.'
47. Ibid.
48. Ibid.
49. Ibid.
50. Bernstein, op. cit., p114ff.
51. 'Programme of Action', cited in Karis and Carter, op. cit., p338.
52. Elinor Sisulu, *Walter & Albertina Sisulu: In Our Lifetime*, David Philip Publishers, 2003 (Second Edition), p126.
53. Sisulu interview, October 1994, op. cit.
54. Ibid.
55. Mandela interview, op. cit.
56. Sisulu interview, op. cit. It was later revealed that Moroka had racially separate waiting rooms for his white patients, but this, while embarrassing for the ANC, hardly amounted to his being an informer.
57. Draft Report of the National Executive of the ANC, submitted to the Annual Conference, 15–17 December 1950, cited in Karis and Carter, op. cit., pp452–8.
58. Sisulu interview, op. cit.
59. James Phillips, interview by LC, London, 27 July 1987.
60. Certificate: 'Admission of Oliver Tambo as an Attorney', op. cit.
61. Tuch interview, op. cit.
62. Sisulu interview, op. cit.
63. Oliver Tambo, Introduction to *No Easy Walk to Freedom*, Heinemann, 1965, pxii.
64. Mandela interview, op. cit.
65. Introduction, *No Easy Walk*, op. cit.
66. Oliver Tambo, interview by LC, Umtata, 17 January 1993.
67. Ibid.
68. Ibid.
69. Mandela interview, op. cit.
70. Ahmed Kathrada, interview by LC, 14 February 2002.
71. Introduction, *No Easy Walk*, op. cit.
72. Mandela interview, op. cit.
73. Ibid.
74. Mendi Msimang, interview by LC, Johannesburg, 10 March 1993.
75. George Bizos, interview by LC, Mafikeng, 18 December 1998.
76. Msimang interview, op. cit.
77. Lancelot Gama, interview by LC, KwaThema Springs, 2 March 1994.
78. Ibid.
79. Albie Sachs, interview by LC, Johannesburg, 4 February 1993. Sachs commented, 3 June 2004:

'Pitje was convicted for not occupying the black section. Chief Justice, Lucas Steyn, upheld the conviction, saying Pitje could save his client as well from one section of the Bar as from another. See State v Pitje.'
80. Bizos interview. op. cit.
81. Mandela interview, op. cit.
82. Msimang interview, op. cit.
83. Mandela interview, op. cit.
84. Sisulu interview, op. cit.
85. Tom Lodge, *Black Politics in South Africa Since 1945*, Ravan, 1983, p59.
86. 'Letter Calling for Repeal of Oppressive Legislation and Threatening a Defiance Campaign, from Dr JS Moroka and WM Sisulu to Prime Minister DF Malan', 21 January 1952, cited in Karis and Carter, op. cit., pp476–7.
87. Ibid. See also Endnote 34, p434.
88. Sisulu interview, op. cit.
89. Ibid.
90. Jacob Zuma, interview by LC, Johannesburg, 27 July 1993.
91. Karis and Carter, op. cit., p424.
92. Meer interview, op. cit.
93. Yengwa interview, op. cit.
94. Ibid.
95. Meer interview, op. cit.
96. Yengwa interview, op. cit.
97. Ibid.
98. Karis and Carter, op. cit., p419.
99. Nkobi interview, op. cit.
100. Mandela, op. cit., p159.
101. Oliver Tambo, interview published by *New Age*, 13 November 1958.
102. Ibid.
103. Executive Committee of the All-African Convention, 15–16 December 1952, cited in Karis and Carter, op. cit., p430.
104. 'A Declaration to the People of South Africa from the Non-European Unity Movement', April 1951, cited in Karis and Carter, op. cit., pp494–505.
105. WM Sisulu, 'Statement before sentencing for pass offence', 21 July 1952, cited in Karis and Carter, op. cit., p484 (author's emphasis).
106. Yengwa interview, op. cit.
107. See biographical sketch of AJ Luthuli in Thomas Karis and Gwendoline Carter, *From Protest to Challenge*, Volume 4 (*Political Profiles*), edited by Thomas Karis, Hoover Institution Press, 1973, p61.
108. Albert Luthuli, *Let My People Go*, Fontana Books, 1962, p110.
109. Nkobi interview, op. cit.
110. Presidential address by Chief AJ Luthuli, ANC Annual Conference, 16–19 December 1954, cited in Thomas Karis and Gail Gerhart, *From Protest to Challenge*, Volume 3 (*Challenge and Violence 1953–1964*), Hoover Institution Press, 1977, p135.
111. 'The Road to Freedom is via the Cross', Statement by Chief AJ Luthuli, issued after the announcement on 12 November 1952 of his dismissal as chief, cited in Karis and Carter, Volume 2, op. cit., pp486–8.
112. Tambo interview, Chutter, op. cit. Kotane was an innovative intellectual, developing a communist perspective from an African point of view. Even more than other black intellectuals of the CPSA such as JB Marks and Edwin Mofutsenyana, Kotane made an enduring impact on political debates, and went on to deepen the Party's theories on the 'national question'. Kotane went so far as to declare publicly, 'I am an African first and a Communist afterwards.'
113. Brian Bunting, *Moses Kotane*, Nkululeko Publications, 1975, p230.
114. Ibid.
115. Bernstein, op. cit., p137.
116. Tambo interview, *New Age*, op. cit.
117. Ben Turok, interview by LC, Johannesburg, 10 August 1993; Ben Turok, *Nothing But the Truth*, Jonathan Ball, 2003.
118. Ibid.
119. Jack Unterhalter, interview by LC, Mafikeng, 20 April 1995.
120. Tambo interview, *New Age*, op. cit.
121. Ibid.
122. Msimang interview, op. cit.
123. Ibid.
124. Andrew Mlangeni, interview by LC, Johannesburg, 13 October 1994.
125. Karis and Carter, op. cit., p453.
126. 'Letter to all Congress Branches of the Province', December 1952, Karis and Carter, op. cit., p488.
127. Tuch interview, op. cit.
128. See chapters 2 and 4.

PART TWO *Chapter Seven*
Negotiating Partnerships

1. Walter Sisulu, interview by LC, Johannesburg, 22 July 1993.
2. Albertina Sisulu, interview by LC, Johannesburg, 10 September 2001.
3. Victor Sifora, interview by LC, Rustenburg, 4 October 1994.
4. Ibid.
5. Adelaide Tambo, interview by LC, Johannesburg, 18 October 1994.
6. Ibid.
7. Introduction, Nelson Mandela's *No Easy Walk to Freedom: Letters from Underground*, Heinemann, 1965, pxiv.
8. Robert Edgar and Luyanda ka Msumzi (Eds), *Freedom in Our Lifetime*, Ohio/Skotaville, 1996, p10. Edgar and ka Msumzi relate the story of how once, reading in the press about scholar Caroline Ntseliseng Ramolahloane, a graduate of Fort Hare, Lembede vowed to meet her. On his next holiday, he travelled to Lesotho and cycled to the Thabana Morena School, where she was teaching. But she was away at the time. A few years later, however, he met and became engaged to Cherry Mndaweni. Cherry had been reared in a rural homestead, but her father was working as a mine clerk in Germiston, and she had trained as a nurse. Lembede was in the process of negotiating *lobola* with the family when he died.

9. The township was demolished in the 1960s and all its residents were removed to Soweto.
10. Laura Longmore, 'A Study of Changes in African Marriage and Family Systems Under the Impact of Urbanisation with Specific Reference to Eastern Native Township – and to Conditions in and around Johannesburg', PhD in Social Anthropology, Wits University, 1957.
11. Ibid., p514.
12. Adelaide Tambo, interview by LC, Johannesburg, 12 May 1995.
13. Ibid.
14. Ibid.
15. Prisoners included Mahatma Gandhi in 1913 and Taffy Long, who was sentenced to death after the 1922 strike, to ordinary folk who fell foul of the apartheid laws. The women's prison, too, was densely populated, not only by those who broke the usual laws of crime and social taboos but also beer brewers, black rural women who had come to the city and used their traditional brewing skills to supplement the meagre wages of the men.
16. Adelaide Tambo interview, 1995, op. cit.
17. Ibid.
18. This hostel was demolished in the 1960s.
19. Adelaide Tambo interview, October 1994, op. cit.
20. Ibid.
21. Ibid.
22. Longmore, op. cit., p200.
23. Adelaide Tambo, interview by LC, Johannesburg, 12 February 1995.
24. Reverend Tuge, interview by LC, Johannesburg, 1 July 1993.
25. Mrs Gladys Tuge, interview by LC, Johannesburg, 1 July 1993.
26. Adelaide Tambo interview, 12 February 1995, op. cit.
27. Ibid.
28. *Lobola* is the price paid, traditionally in cattle, by the bridegroom to the bride's family in compensation for 'losing' a valued daughter.
29. In 1954, Father Zulu (later Bishop) – with a wife and seven children – was earning £20 a year, while a newly ordained, unmarried white priest would start on £35 a year. See also Diana Collins, *Partners in Protest*, Victor Gollancz, 1992, p203.
30. Adelaide Tambo, interview by LC, Johannesburg, 23 August 1993.
31. Victor Sifora, interview by LC, Rustenburg, 4 October 1994.
32. I am grateful to clinical psychologists Tony Hamburger and Hillary Hamburger for their insights on this topic.
33. See Chapter 3.
34. Ralph Tuch, interview by LC, Sydney, 8 December 1999.
35. Thomas Karis and Gail Gerhart, *From Protest to Challenge*, Volume 3 (*Challenge and Violence 1953–1964*), Hoover Institution Press, 1977, p35.
36. Sidney Kentridge, interview by LC, Johannesburg, 2 March 1999.
37. B Rose and R Tunmer, *Documents in South African Education*, Ad Donker, 1975, p266.
38. Minutes, ANC NEC Meeting, 21 May 1955, cited in Karis and Gerhart, op. cit., p88.
39. Report of the NEC, 17–18 December 1955, cited in Karis and Gerhart, op. cit.
40. Trevor Huddleston, *Naught For Your Comfort*, Fontana Books, 1977, p132.
41. Prison biography of Walter Sisulu, Mayibuye Archives, University of the Western Cape, courtesy Elinor Sisulu.
42. Leaflet of the Society of Young Africa, *New Age*, 12 May 1955, cited by Karis and Gerhart, op. cit., p89.
43. Karis and Gerhart, op. cit., p87.
44. Ibid., p234.
45. Ibid.
46. Huddleston, op. cit.
47. Karis and Gerhart, op. cit., p27.
48. Nzana (Robert Sobukwe), *The Africanist*, May 1955, cited in Karis and Gerhart, op. cit.
49. Karis and Gerhart, op. cit., p27.
50. ANC NEC Report, op. cit.
51. Oliver Tambo, interview by *Drum*, 1955.
52. Report of the NEC, 16–19 December 1954, cited in Karis and Gerhart, op. cit., p159.
53. An earlier version of this cell-based strategy had been forwarded to Mandela by AP Mda in 1951. Gail Gerhart reports in her *Black Power in South Africa* (University of California Press, 1979, p132): Mda argued that the proposed Defiance Campaign was to most likely result in harsh repression and it was advisable to develop structures [for] an underground movement capable of developing guerrilla tactics. When Mandela raised this at the NEC meeting, it was considered too sensitive, and the issue was shelved for the time being.
54. Raymond Suttner and Jeremy Cronin, *Thirty Years of the Freedom Charter*, Ravan, 1986, p17.
55. Thomas Nkobi, interview by LC, Johannesburg, 12 August 1993.
56. Ibid.
57. Nkobi Senior was a Zambian who arrived in South Africa in 1913. Employing his 'natural talents', he saved up to buy property, open a store and then a pharmacy in Alexandra. He was able to provide his son with a good education, sending him to Natal's Adams College, where Thomas Titus (TT) did well scholastically, and went on to study for a BCom at Lesotho's Roma University. But TT was expelled, like so many others, for 'militancy'. 'I remember we used to say to Father: "You want us to behave like you; we are not fathers, neither nuns. We are going to face the world and therefore our tuition must be geared to us becoming leaders of our people not leaders of the church."'
58. Rusty Bernstein, *Memory Against Forgetting*, Viking, 1999, p151.
59. Rusty Bernstein, interview by LC, Woodstock (UK), 19 February 1995; see also Bernstein, 1999, op. cit., p155.
60. Bernstein, op. cit., p145.

61. Nelson Mandela, *Liberation*, June 1956, cited in Karis and Gerhart, op. cit., p246.
62. Karis and Gerhart, p228.
63. Ibid.
64. Ibid.
65. Gerhart, op. cit., p138.
66. PK Leballo, 'The Nature of the Struggle Today', *The Africanist*, December 1957, cited in Gerhart, op. cit., p149.
67. PK Leballo and Z Mothopeng, 'The Kliptown Charter', *The Africanist*, June/July 1958, cited in Gerhart, op. cit., p158.
68. Joe Slovo, interview by LC, Johannesburg, 7 January 1994.
69. Nkobi interview, op. cit.
70. Sisulu interview, July 1993, op. cit.
71. Ibid.
72. Report of the NEC, December 1958, cited in Karis and Gerhart, op. cit., pp435–56.
73. Nkobi interview, op. cit.
74. Karis and Gerhart, op. cit., p237.
75. Ibid.
76. Letter to Wilson Z Conco, 15 May 1955, cited in Karis and Gerhart, op. cit., pp39–40.
77. *New Age*, 20 November 1958.
78. Oliver Pelesane, interview by LC, Pretoria, 8 October 1996.
79. Huddleston, op. cit., Chapter 8.
80. Ben Turok, interview by LC, Johannesburg, 10 August 1993.
81. Mrs Gladys Tuge interview, op. cit.
82. Prison biography, op. cit.; Elinor Sisulu, *Walter & Albertina Sisulu: In Our Lifetime*, David Philip Publishers, 2003 (Second Edition).
83. Ibid.
84. Robin Denniston, *Trevor Huddleston: A life*, Macmillan, 1999, p277.
85. Oliver Tambo, unpublished interview by Thomas Karis and Gail Gerhart, London, 3 March 1991.
86. Anthony Sampson, *The Treason Cage*, Heinemann, 1958, p165; Sisulu interview, July 1993, op. cit.
87. Karis and Gerhart, op. cit. (p81), list Joe Molefe and Vus Make, who led the Everton bus boycott, AB Ngcobo, Elliot Mfaxa and TE Tshunungwa.
88. Joe Slovo, *The Unfinished Autobiography*, Ravan, 1995, p97.
89. Ben Turok, interview by LC, Johannesburg, 10 August 1993.
90. Oliver Tambo, interview by LC, Flagstaff, 22 January 1993.
91. Adelaide Tambo, interview by LC, Johannesburg, 12 May 1995.
92. Memoirs of MB Yengwa, unpublished interviews by Beverley Naidoo, London, 1982, courtesy Dr Beverley Naidoo.
93. Adelaide Tambo interview, 1995, op. cit.
94. Gama interview, op. cit.
95. Ibid.
96. Report of the NEC, 17–18 December 1955, cited in Karis and Gerhart, op. cit.
97. Adelaide Tambo interview, 1994, op. cit.
98. Karis and Gerhart, op. cit., p472.
99. Ibid., p76.
100. Huddleston, op. cit., pp171 and 183.
101. Izzie Maisels, unpublished memoirs on the Treason Trial.
102. Ibid.
103. Oswald Pirow, interview by Thomas Karis, 20 January 1959, cited in Karis and Gerhart, op. cit., p275.
104. Oliver Tambo, *New Age*, 13 November 1958.
105. Prison biography, op. cit. 'Duncan left a disappointed man; this explains why he later joined the PAC. He would have loved to join the ANC'; Walter Felgate, interview by LC, Durban, 14 March 1998. In 1997, Felgate resigned from the IFP and was received as a member of the ANC, 'where I always belonged in the first place'.
106. Letter to Adelaide Tambo, Lusaka, October 1969.
107. Letter to Adelaide Tambo, Morogoro, 1 March 1966.
108. Benjamin Pogrund, *How Can Man Die Better? The Life of Robert Sobukwe*, Jonathan Ball, 1990, p87.
109. Adelaide Tambo interview, 1995, op. cit.
110. Oliver Tambo, interview by LC, Johannesburg, 11 January 1993.
111. Report of the NEC, December 1958, cited in Karis and Gerhart, op. cit., p444.
112. Pogrund, op. cit.
113. Oliver Tambo, *c*1972, Document A.11.3, Wits University Historical Papers, now part of the OR Tambo Collection, Fort Hare Archives.
114. Ibid.
115. Benjamin Pogrund, interview by LC, Johannesburg, July 2000.
116. Pogrund, op. cit., pp87–88.
117. Albert Luthuli, *Let My People Go*, Fontana Books, 1963.
118. Adelaide Tambo interview, 1995, op. cit.
119. Mrs Gladys Tuge interview, op. cit.
120. Karis and Gerhart, op. cit., p280.
121. Walter Sisulu interview, op. cit. Sisulu remembered the correspondence, but this disappeared in the wake of raids and confiscations in Luthuli's home, the homes and workplaces of NEC members and the ANC offices.
122. Jacob Zuma, interview by LC, Johannesburg, 27 July 1993.
123. Karis and Gerhart, op. cit., p443.
124. Report of the NEC, December 1959, cited in Karis and Gerhart, op. cit., p472.
125. Peter Delius, *A Lion Amongst the Cattle: Reconstruction and Resistance in the Northern Transvaal*, Ravan, 1996.
126. Ibid. Whenever Bapedi migrants returned home, they brought with them a new political awareness they had developed through their experiences of community organisations and trade unions in the cities. They were at the forefront of developing a rural resistance movement (*Fetakgomo*) in Sekhukhuneland.

127. Stephen Franklin, *An Ordinary Atrocity*, Wits University Press, 2001.
128. Oliver Tambo, 'Statement made at the 1053rd Meeting of the Fourth Committee', United Nations, October 1960, Document 1/18/11/13, South African National Archives, Pretoria.
129. Collins, op. cit., p205.
130. Ibid., p207.
131. Martin Bauml Duberman, *Paul Robeson: A Biography*, Ballantine, 1989, p340.
132. Ibid., p341.
133. Denis Herbstein, 'White Lies: Canon Collins' Secret War Against Apartheid', unpublished manuscript.
134. Per Wästberg, interview by LC, Stockholm, 18 May 1993.
135. Ronald Segal, interview by LC, Walton-on-Thames, 12 May 1993.
136. This label originated in *New Age*, 13 November 1958.
137. 'Sobukwe Outlines Africanist Case', cited in Gerhart, op. cit., p195.
138. Report of the NEC, December 1958, cited in Karis and Gerhart, op. cit., p447.
139. Report of the NEC, December 1959, cited in Karis and Gerhart, op. cit., p473.
140. Ibid.
141. Ibid.
142. May Brutus, interview by LC, Boulder, Colorado, USA, 12 October 1993.
143. Karis and Gerhart, op. cit., p329.
144. Tambo, Document A.11.3, op. cit.

PART THREE *Chapter Eight*
Into the Wilderness

1. Adelaide Tambo, interview by LC, Johannesburg, 23 August 1993.
2. Ronald Segal, *Into Exile*, Jonathan Cape, 1963, p276.
3. Frene Ginwala, interview by LC, Johannesburg, 9 April 1993. Frene, daughter of a progressive Indian merchant from Mozambique, was well travelled and gaining experience in radio and newspaper journalism and was the representative of *Africa South* in Tanganyika (Tanzania). Resourceful and self-confident, she had excellent contacts with influential people in East Africa. In South Africa, Frene was a member of the Transvaal Indian Youth Congress.
4. Oliver Tambo, interview by LC, Johannesburg, 1 November 1993.
5. Adelaide Tambo, interview by LC, Johannesburg, 14 April 1995.
6. Adelaide Tambo interview, ibid.; Oliver Tambo interview, op. cit.; Ronald Segal's account (interview, op. cit.) differs slightly – he writes that Adelaide accompanied her husband to the house where Segal was staying.
7. Ronald Segal, interview by LC, Walton-on-Thames, 12 May 1993; Segal (1963), op. cit.
8. Document LCO 2/6966, Public Records Office, London.
9. Joe Podbrey, interview by LC, Johannesburg, 24 February 1995.
10. Adelaide Tambo interview (1993), op. cit.
11. Segal (1963), op. cit., p284.
12. Document LCO 2/6966/541/13362, Public Records Office, London.
13. Ibid.
14. Mac Maharaj, interview by LC, Johannesburg, 1 August 1995. Maharaj claims that the SACP cell in London organised the airfare.
15. Julius Nyerere, interview by LC, Johannesburg, 29 October 1994.
16. Ibid.
17. David Wirmark, interview by LC, Stockholm, 18 May 1993.
18. Tor Sellström, *Sweden and National Liberation: Southern Africa*, Nordiska Afrikainstitet, 1999, pp102–3.
19. Ginwala interview, op. cit.
20. Oliver Tambo interview, op. cit.
21. Aziz Pahad, interview by LC, Johannesburg, 11 August 1993.
22. Kwame Nkrumah, *Ghana: The Autobiography of Kwame Nkrumah*, publisher unspecified, 1957, p164.
23. The term 'Pan Africanism' was coined by Trinidadian barrister Henry Sylvester Williams and first found formal expression in the Pan-African Congress organised by WEB Du Bois in London, 1900. See David Levering Lewis, *WEB Du Bois: Biography of a Race*, Henry Holt & Company, 1993, p248.
24. Peter Molotsi, interview by LC, Johannesburg, 8 January 1995.
25. Oliver Tambo, interview by LC, Johannesburg, 6 February 1993.
26. Sellström, op. cit.
27. Ibid., pp107–8.
28. Maharaj interview, op. cit.
29. Oliver Tambo interview, op. cit.
30. Diana Collins, *Partners in Protest: Life with Canon Collins*, Victor Gallancz, 1992, p370.
31. Diana Collins, interview by LC, Surrey, 6 May 1993.
32. Ibid.
33. Mzwai Piliso, interview by LC, Umtata, 17 January 1993.
34. Document C1.1.1/1.1.2, OR Tambo Collection, Fort Hare Archives.
35. Maharaj interview, op. cit.
36. Abdul Minty, interview by LC, Johannesburg, 9 September 1993.
37. Mike Terry, interview by LC, London, 28 April 1993; Rosalynde Ainslee de Lanerol, interview by LC, Johannesburg, 11 June 1993.
38. Per Wästberg, interview by LC, Stockholm, 17 May 1993.
39. Ibid.
40. Minty interview, op. cit.
41. ES Reddy Collection, 'Speeches of Oliver Tambo', unpublished. Grateful thanks to Mr Reddy and Judge Albie Sachs for making this collection available.

42. Adelaide Tambo interview, op. cit.
43. Molotsi interview, op. cit.
44. Adelaide Tambo interview, op. cit.
45. Ibid.
46. Correspondence (1960), OR Tambo Collection, Fort Hare Archives.
47. Document LCO 2/6966/541/3362, Public Records Office, London.
48. George Houser, *No One Can Stop the Rain: Glimpses of Africa's Liberation Struggle*, Pilgrim Press, 1989, p269.

PART THREE *Chapter Nine*
Reinventing the ANC

1. Jane L Guy, quoting Nuruddin Farah in the foreword to Kofi Anyidoho (Ed.), *The Word Behind Bars and the Paradox of Exile*, Northwestern University Press, 1997.
2. Wilton Mkwayi, interview by LC, King William's Town, 29 June 2000.
3. See, for example Brian Bunting, *The Rise of the South African Reich*, IDAF, 1986.
4. In the words of the African-American Christian, Steven Carter, in a forum discussing 'The Future of the Public Intellectual', *The Nation*, 12 February 2001, p30.
5. Alex Moseley, 'Just War Theory', *Internet Encyclopaedia of Philosophy*, 24 June 2003.
6. VJ (Joe) Matthews, interview by Sifiso Ndlovu and Professor B Magubane, SADET Archives, unpublished, undated. Joe Matthews represented the ANC at two meetings of the World Council of Churches to follow up Tambo's initiatives in the early 1960s.
7. The ANC's initial misreading of the politics of Chief Gatsha Buthelezi and Bishop Desmond Tutu, for example, or the agenda of the emerging democratic labour movement in the 1970s were examples of dangers to come.
8. See also Chapter 16. Tambo and the ANC had to undertake damage control when Kenneth Kaunda and Julius Nyerere issued the Lusaka Manifesto, which advocated negotiating with the apartheid state without consulting the ANC, and this ultimately affected Tambo's approach to directing the negotiations process in exile in 1989.
9. Kofi Anyidoho (Ed.), *The Word Behind Bars and the Paradox of Exile*, Northwestern University Press, 1997, p3.
10. William Mervyn Gumede, 'Consensus isn't harmony, but dialogue', *Sunday Independent*, 24 May 1998.
11. It was, of course, to take more than 30 years before Nelson Mandela, President of the ANC in the Transvaal, would be able to fulfil Chief Luthuli's mandate.
12. David Wirmark (Stockholm, 18 May 1993), Per Wästberg (Stockholm, 17 May 1993), Erik Mechanik (16 May 1993), Carl Tham (Stockholm, 17 May 1993), Lisbet Palm (Stockholm, 17 May 1993) and Abdul Minty (Johannesburg, 9 September 1993), interviews by LC.
13. Lumford Gunyile, interview by LC, Bizana, 23 January 1993.
14. See also Chapter 7.
15. Howard Barrell, *MK: The ANC's Armed Struggle*, Penguin Forum Series, 1990, p5.
16. Nelson Mandela, *Long Walk to Freedom*, Abacus, 1994, p322.
17. Brian Bunting, *Moses Kotane*, Nkululeko Publications, 1975, p269; also cited in Vladimir Shubin, *ANC: A View from Moscow*, Mayibuye Books, 1999, p18.
18. Joe Slovo, *Dawn*, cited in Barrell, op. cit., p24.
19. Mandela, op. cit., p324.
20. Joe Slovo, interview by LC, Johannesburg, 5 January 1994.
21. Oliver Tambo, interview by Chutter, unpublished, 15 November 1963, courtesy Thomas Karis and Gail Gerhart.
22. VJ (Joe) Matthews, interview by LC, Pretoria, 28 February 1995.
23. Oliver Tambo interview, Karis and Gerhart, op. cit.
24. Ibid.
25. Mac Maharaj, interview by LC, Johannesburg, 1 August 1995; Tom Karis, interview by LC, New York, 12 November 1995.
26. Joe Slovo, 'No Middle Road', in Basil Davidson, Joe Slovo and Anthony R Wilkinson (Eds), *Southern Africa: The New Politics of Revolution*, Penguin Books, 1976, p179.
27. Document C2.69, OR Tambo Collection, Fort Hare Archives.
28. Frene Ginwala, interview by LC, Johannesburg, 9 April 1993.
29. Ibid.
30. Colin Legum, interview by LC, London, 20 May 1993.
31. South African Congress of Trade Unions, an alliance partner of the ANC.
32. Both Rob Lambert in his PhD and Eddie Webster in 'Stayaways and the Black Working Class' in *Labour, Capital and Society*, Volume 14, 1981, have argued that the 1961 stayaway was surprisingly successful – they draw on an assessment by SACTU and suggest that there were further opportunities for trade union struggle which were not developed because SACTU leaders were drawn into the political imperatives of armed struggle.
33. See Chapter 10.
34. Barrell, op. cit., pp11–12.
35. Matthews interview, op. cit.
36. 'He was a dear friend, and I think by being himself he personified gentleness and democratic attitudes... It was a horrible injustice that was committed to the black and coloured people': Wirmark interview, op. cit.
37. At least some of the UF offices, such as London and Dar es Salaam, had supported the stayaway (Chutter interview, op. cit.).
38. Thomas Karis and Gail Gerhart, *From Protest to Challenge*, Volume 3 (*Challenge and Violence 1953–1964*), Hoover Institution Press, 1977, p639.

39. Vella Pillay, interview by LC, London, 21 September 1993.
40. Legum interview, op. cit.
41. Ibid.
42. Maharaj interview, op. cit.
43. Ibid.
44. Letter to Adelaide Tambo from Oliver Tambo, Dar es Salaam, 30 June 1962. The five were Adelaide, her three children and her sister, Lydia.
45. Letter to Oliver Tambo from Adelaide Tambo, London, 4 July 1962.
46. See Njabulo Ndebele, *The Cry of Winnie Mandela: A Novel*, David Philip Publishers, 2003.
47. Letter, Oliver Tambo to Adelaide Tambo, op. cit. The 'hot problem' was probably to do with Chief Albert Luthuli's unhappiness with armed struggle, which would have affected Tambo too.
48. Shortly after Mandela's release in February 1990, he was to visit his friend – by then President of the ANC, but struck down by a massive stroke – in Stockholm.
49. *Atlanta Journal and Constitution*, 4 July 1990; also cited in Barrell, op. cit.
50. Document C2.69, op. cit.
51. Slovo interview, op. cit.
52. Albert Luthuli, *Let My People Go*, Fontana Books, 1963, p208.
53. Slovo in Davidson, Slovo and Wilkinson, op. cit.
54. Thanks to Pallo Jordan for this suggestion.
55. Karis and Gerhart, op. cit., p760.
56. Pallo Jordan, correspondence with Luli Callinicos, May 2003.
57. Slovo interview, op. cit.
58. Karis and Gerhart, op. cit., p763.
59. 'Operation Mayibuye', document found by the South African Police, Rivonia, 11 July 1963, cited in Karis and Gerhart, op. cit., pp760–8.
60. Ibid.
61. Ahmed Kathrada, interview by LC, Cape Town, 20 June 2003; Rusty Bernstein, *Memory Against Forgetting*, Viking, 1999, pp251–2.
62. Slovo interview, op. cit.
63. Bram Fischer died in 1975, still a prisoner, but released to his deathbed in his brother's care and under restricted access. His ashes were appropriated by the police.
64. Slovo interview, op. cit.
65. Ibid.
66. Adelaide Tambo, interview by LC, Johannesburg, 12 May 1995.
67. Trevor Huddleston, interview by LC, London, 10 May 1993.
68. Legum interview, op. cit.
69. See Chapter 3 for Tambo's response to being nominated as Head Prefect.
70. 'United Nations must take action to destroy Apartheid', Statement at the meeting of the Special Political Committee of the United Nations General Assembly, New York, 29 October 1963 (ES Reddy Collection).
71. Matthews interview, op. cit.
72. James Kantor and Bob Hepple were acquitted; Mosie Moola, Abdul Jasset, Harold Wolpe and Arthur Goldreich escaped from prison while awaiting trial.
73. Statement at press conference, Dar es Salaam, concerning sentences in the Rivonia Trial, 12 June 1964.
74. *Dawn* (Souvenir Issue), 25th Anniversary of MK.
75. Among the documents seized by the Security Police in Rivonia was a report on funding written by Nelson Mandela, in which he concluded: 'Visit to socialist countries has become imperative'; cited in Shubin, op. cit.
76. Oliver Tambo in *Meeting the Challenge: The Story of the American Committee on Africa*, New York, 1981, p9, cited in Shubin, op. cit., p47.
77. Shubin, op. cit.
78. Aziz Pahad, interview by LC, Johannesburg, 11 August 1993.
79. Shubin, op. cit., p39.
80. Ibid., p51.
81. Nyerere interview, op. cit.
82. Ibid.
83. Oliver Tambo, verbal communication with LC, Johannesburg, January 1993.
84. Luli Callinicos, 'Oliver Tambo and the Politics of Race, Class and Ethnicity in the African National Congress', *African Sociological Review*, 3 January 1999.
85. UN Statement, 1963, op. cit.
86. Oliver Tambo, 'Statement to the United Nations Special Committee Against Apartheid', New York, March 1964 (ES Reddy Collection).
87. Matthews interview, op. cit.
88. See Elinor Sisulu, *Walter & Albertina Sisulu: In Our Lifetime*, David Philip Publishers, 2003 (Second Edition).
89. Matthews interview, op. cit.
90. Introduction to Nelson Mandela's *No Easy Walk to Freedom*, Heinemann, 1965, pxiv. The description was not an invention by Tambo. Anthony Sampson's *Mandela: The Authorised Biography* (Harper Collins, 1999) traces the long and patient road taken by Mandela, the angry though astute younger man, to his ultimate destination of reconciliation.
91. Anthony Sampson, *Mandela: The Authorised Biography*, Harper Collins, 1999 (author's emphasis).
92. Devised in the late 1950s in preparation for underground activity, the M-plan was designed as a series of cells by Mandela.
93. Stirring words that might well have raised a cynic's eyebrow, yet – remarkably – Tambo's perceptive observations were to be brilliantly confirmed more than 26 years later.
94. Matthews interview, op. cit.
95. See Chapter 14.

PART THREE *Chapter Ten*
The Freedom Train

1. Langston Hughes, 'Freedom Train'.
2. See Sifiso Mxolisis Ndlovu, 'Heritage routes for liberated South Africans: Using oral history

to reconstruct unsung heroes and heroines' routes into exile in the 1960s', *Historia* 47(2), November 2002, pp479–510; Sifiso Ndlovu, interviews for SADET Oral History Project, SADET Archives; Michael Dingake, *My Fight Against Apartheid*, Kliptown Books, 1987; Archie Sibeko, *Freedom in Our Lifetime*, Mayibuye Books, 1997.
3. See Chapter 9.
4. Thomas Nkobi, interview by LC, Johannesburg, 18 March 1993.
5. George Bizos, *No One to Blame? In Pursuit of Justice in South Africa*, David Philip Publishers/ Mayibuye Books, 1998, p13.
6. Howard Barrell, *MK: The ANC's Armed Struggle*, Penguin Forum Series, 1990, p13.
7. Ibid., pp11–13.
8. Ibid., p15.
9. Jacob Zuma, interview by LC, Johannesburg, 27 July 1993.
10. Ibid.
11. *Natal Mercury*, 15 September 1965; *Eastern Province Herald*, 20 September, 1965.
12. Sibeko, op. cit.
13. Julius Nyerere, interview by LC, Johannesburg, 29 October 1994.
14. Vladimir Shubin, untitled, unpublished, Part 1. The information here is drawn mainly from this source. Grateful thanks to the author and to Barry Feinberg for granting access to this manuscript prior to publication.
15. Joe Slovo, 'No Middle Road', in Basil Davidson, Joe Slovo and Anthony R Wilkinson (Eds), *Southern Africa: The New Politics of Revolution*, Penguin Books, 1976, p107.
16. Mannie Brown, interview by LC, Johannesburg, 17 May 2001.
17. Ben Turok, interview by Howard Barrell, London, 21 February 1990, unpublished, Document IVS.4.
18. Ibid.
19. Letter to Tom Karis from Oliver Tambo, 24 November 1973.
20. Eleanor Kasrils, interview by LC, Cape Town, 16 May 1995.
21. Eleanor Kasrils, interview by LC, Cape Town, 12 May 1995.
22. JB Marks, who had arrived in Dar at the same time as Joe Slovo to discuss issues with the Mission in Exile, had many years of the struggle behind him. As an early black CPSA member, he had infused a black perspective in the Communist Party and had sensitised many Marxists to the interplay between race and class. He was an important influence in directing the Party towards wanting to work with the ANC.
23. Ibid.
24. Mosie Moola, interview by LC, Johannesburg, 2 April 1994.
25. Sibeko, op. cit., p77.
26. Ibid.
27. Chris Hani, interview by LC, Johannesburg, 30 March 1993.
28. Ibid.
29. Eleanor Kasrils interview, op. cit.
30. Ronnie Kasrils, interview by LC, Johannesburg, 5 November 1993.
31. Roughly translated as 'We are tightening our trouser belts [to stave off hunger pangs]'.
32. Document A1.1.1, undated, OR Tambo Collection, Fort Hare Archives.
33. Matthews interview, op. cit.
34. Letter to Adelaide Tambo from Oliver Tambo, 21 July 1965, OR Tambo Collection, Fort Hare Archives.
35. Adelaide Tambo, interview by Heidi Kingstone, *The Independent*, 29 December 1986.
36. Adelaide Tambo interview, Callinicos, op. cit.
37. Ibid.
38. Zeph Mokgetla, interview by LC, Johannesburg, 27 July 2003.
39. Ibid.
40. Hani interview, op. cit.
41. Mac Maharaj, interview by Howard Barrell, November 1990, London, Document IVS.2.
42. Joe Slovo interview, op. cit.
43. Raymond Suttner, 'Masculinities and Felinities within the ANC-led Liberation Movement, Paper for Wits Institute of Social and Economic Research Symposium on 'Manhood and Masculinity: Struggles with Change', August 2004.
44. Isaac Makopo, interview by Sifiso Ndlovu, undated, SADET Oral History Project, SADET Archives
45. Ronnie Kasrils, *Armed and Dangerous: My Underground Struggle Against Apartheid*, Part II, Heinemann, 1993.
46. Ibid.
47. Document 'Operation Mayibuye', cited in Thomas Karis and Gail Gerhart, *From Protest to Challenge*, Volume 3 (*Challenge and Violence 1953–1964*, Hoover Institution Press, 1977, p35.
48. 'Statement of the NEC of the ANC on Heroes' Day, 16 December 1986 on the occasion of the 25th Anniversary of MK', cited in *Dawn* (Souvenir Issue).
49. Document A11.2, OR Tambo Collection, Fort Hare Archives.
50. Letter to ES Reddy from Oliver Tambo, 31 August 1967 (ES Reddy Collection).
51. Sibeko, op. cit.
52. Hani interview, op. cit.
53. Document A11.3, OR Tambo Collection, Fort Hare Archives.
54. Letter to Thomas Karis from Oliver Tambo, 28 November 1973.
55. Lumford Ganyile, interview by LC, Bizana, 23 January 1993.
56. See Howard Barrell, *MK: The ANC's Armed Struggle*, Penguin Forum Series, 1990.
57. Thomas Karis and Gail Gerhart, *From Protest to Challenge*, Volume 5 (*Nadir and Resurgence, 1964–1979*), Indiana University Press, 1997, p29.
58. Sibeko, op. cit., p91.
59. Mzala (Jabulani Nxumalo), cited in Karis and Gerhart, Volume 5, op. cit., p29.
60. Ronnie Kasrils, interview by Howard Barrell, unpublished, Document IV, p332.

61. Cited in George Houser, *No One Can Stop the Rain: Glimpses of Africa's Liberation Struggle*, Pilgrim Press, 1989, p232.
62. Publicity and Information Bureau, ANC/AANCZAPU Military Alliance, South African Studies 1: Guerrilla Warfare, London, 1971, cited in Karis and Gerhart, Volume 5, op. cit.
63. Oliver Tambo, interview by Howard Barrell and Jenny Cargill, Salisbury (Harare), 10 August 1981.
64. Karis and Gerhart, Volume 5, op. cit.
65. Hani interview, op. cit.
66. Cited in Karis and Gerhart, Volume 5, op. cit., p30. 'Askaris' were captured members of the liberation movements who were tortured until information was extracted from them, after which they were under the control of the SADF and SAP. They were employed thereafter to reinfiltrate their organisations and report back to their new masters.
67. 'Presidential Address, Morogoro Conference', April 1969, OR Tambo Collection, Fort Hare Archives.

PART THREE ***Chapter Eleven***
Mapping the Way Forward

1. Extensive research has been unable to uncover the names of the remaining four individuals who initiated the document of complaint.
2. Joe Slovo, 'The Sabotage Campaign' and 'No Middle Road', in Basil Davidson, Joe Slovo and Anthony R Wilkinson (Eds), *Southern Africa: The New Politics of Revolution*, Penguin Books, 1976, pp24 & 187; Chris Hani, interview by LC, Johannesburg, 10 March 1993.
3. Hani interview, op. cit.
4. Albie Sachs, interview by LC, Johannesburg, 2 March 1993.
5. Amin Cajee, 'Account of experiences in ANC camp', unpublished, *c.*1969, courtesy Gail Gerhart.
6. Sachs interview, op. cit.; Pallo Jordan, correspondence with C, May 2003.
7. Document A11.3.1a, OR Tambo Collection, Fort Hare Archives.
8. Cajee, op. cit.
9. Document courtesy Gail Gerhart. (It has been pointed out that these accusations were made by a dissatisfied MK deserter, whose complaints were subsequently disseminated by the SAP.); Jordan correspondence, op. cit.
10. Document A11.3.1a, op. cit.
11. Ibid.
12. Ibid.
13. See the 'Statement on the Expulsion from the ANC (SA) of T Bongo, AM Makiwane, JD Matlou, GM Mbele, AK Mqota, P Ngakane, TX Makiwane, OK Setlhapelo', issued by the eight expelled members, London, 27 December 1975, p22, courtesy Fertz Ngakane.
14. VJ (Joe) Matthews, unsigned reply to Ben Turok's 'What is Wrong?' Memorandum before the Morogoro Conference, April 1969, cited in Thomas Karis and Gail Gerhart, *From Protest to Challenge*, Volume 5 (*Nadir and Resurgence, 1964–1979*), Indiana University Press, 1997, p386.
15. Document A11.3.1a, op. cit.
16. Letter to Adelaide Tambo from Oliver Tambo, *c.*1968.
17. Ibid.
18. VJ (Joe) Matthews, cited in Karis and Gerhart, op. cit.
19. Letter to Adelaide Tambo from Oliver Tambo, Dar es Salaam, 20 August 1968.
20. Ibid.
21. Grant Farred, 'Victorian with Rebel Seed: Post-colonial Intellectual', *Social Text*, 38, 1994.
22. Slovo, op. cit.
23. Ibid.
24. Ben Turok, 'What is Wrong?' Memorandum, Morogoro Conference, April 1969; see also Karis and Gerhart, op. cit., pp383–7.
25. Ibid.
26. Jordan correspondence, op. cit.
27. Document A11.3.1a, op. cit.
28. Ben Turok, interview by LC, Johannesburg, 10 August 1993.
29. Brian Bunting, *Moses Kotane*, Nkululeko Publications, 1975, p280ff.
30. Karis and Gerhart, op. cit.
31. Chris Hani, interview by LC, Johannesburg, 29 March 1993.
32. Turok interview, op. cit.
33. Ibid.
34. Ibid.
35. Oliver Tambo, interview by Thomas Karis, New York, undated, courtesy Thomas Karis.
36. Letter to Adelaide Tambo from Oliver Tambo, 23 November 1969.
37. Fertz Ngakane, interview by LC, London, 23 September 1993.
38. Oliver Tambo, speech on behalf of the NEC to the National Consultative Conference of the ANC, Kabwe, June 1985.
39. Ibid.
40. Slovo interview, op. cit.
41. Stephen Ellis and Tsepo Sechaba, *Comrades Against Apartheid*, James Currey/ Indiana University Press, 1992, p42.
42. Observation in Tambo's notebook, Document A11.3.1, *c.*1970, OR Tambo Collection, Fort Hare Archives.
43. Ibid.
44. Julius Nyerere, one of the initiators of the Manifesto, agreed that, in hindsight, this had indeed been a lapse: 'I don't know how much we consulted the Liberation movement... I think that, perhaps, we did not consult [them] movements very much, that is probably true...'; Julius Nyerere, interview by LC, Johannesburg, 29 October 1994.
45. Ibid.
46. Observation in Tambo's notebook (Tambo's emphasis), Document A11.3.1, *c.*1970, OR Tambo Collection, Fort Hare Archives.
47. Ibid.
48. Kenneth Kaunda, interview by LC, Johannesburg, 19 August 1993.
49. Ibid.

50. Hani interview, op. cit.
51. Wilton Mkwayi, interview by LC, King William's Town, 29 June 2000. For many years, senior leaders on Robben Island declined to divulge the methods of smuggling information in and out of prison for fear of punishment bearing down on prison officials who were still working for the Department of Corrections in the 1990s. However, in 2000, Wilton Mkwayi admitted that warders gave valuable assistance in that regard.
52. 'Presidential Address, Morogoro Conference', April 1969, OR Tambo Collection, Fort Hare Archives.
53. Letter to Adelaide Tambo from Oliver Tambo, *c*.1969.
54. 'Moulding the Revolution: The Morogoro Conference of the African National Congress', *The African Communist* (38), 3rd Quarter, 1969; Tom Lodge, *Black Politics in South Africa Since 1945*, Ravan, 1983, p300.
55. 'Presidential Address', Morogoro, 1969, op. cit.
56. Ibid.
57. The tactical response of the ANC to the Transkei elections had been a hotly debated issue on Robben Island, with Mandela wanting to find a way of working with the opposition to Matanzima to build up a mass base in the Transkei. The Lobatse meeting had, however, voted to boycott the elections, and the High Organ on the Island outvoted Mandela. See Nelson Mandela, *Long Walk to Freedom*, Abacus, 1994, p605, and Anthony Sampson, *Mandela: The Authorised Biography*, Harper Collins, 1999, p241.
58. 'Moulding the Revolution', *African Communist*, op. cit.
59. Ibid.
60. Karis and Gerhart, op. cit., pp35, 387–93.
61. Ibid.
62. Ibid.
63. Hani interview, op. cit.
64. Slovo interview, op. cit.; Turok interview, op. cit.
65. Thami Mhlambiso, interview by LC, New York, 20 October 1993.
66. Slovo interview, op. cit.; Hani interview, op. cit.; Pallo Jordan, interview by LC, Johannesburg, 2 December 1993; Albie Sachs, interview by LC, Johannesburg, 2 March 1993.
67. Slovo interview, op. cit.
68. Mhlambiso interview, op. cit.
69. Ibid.
70. Ibid.; Slovo interview, op. cit.
71. 'Political Report of the NEC delivered by Acting President OR Tambo to the Consultative Conference of the ANC', Morogoro Conference, 25 April 1969 (ES Reddy Collection).
72. Sachs interview, op. cit.
73. 'No Middle Road' is the title of a major section of *Southern Africa: The New Politics of Revolution* (Penguin Books, 1976), by Basil Davidson, Joe Slovo and Anthony R Wilkinson (Eds). Part II of this section was written by Slovo to contextualise and justify ANC strategy following the Morogoro Conference.
74. Isaac Makopo, interview by Sifiso Ndlovu, undated, SADET Oral History Project, SADET Archives.
75. 'Political Report by OR Tambo', Reddy Collection, op. cit.
76. Ibid.
77. Oliver Tambo, interview by Howard Barrell and Jenny Cargill, Salisbury (Harare), 10 August 1981.
78. Sachs interview, op. cit.
79. Karis and Gerhart, Volume 5, op. cit., p57.
80. Oliver Tambo interview, Barrell, op. cit.
81. Ibid.
82. 'Presidential Address', Morogoro, 1969, op. cit.
83. 'Moulding the Revolution', *African Communist*, op. cit.
84. Matthews interview, op. cit.
85. Oliver Tambo, 'Message to the People of South Africa on the 68th Anniversary of the African National Congress', 8 January 1980.
86. Karis and Gerhart, op. cit.
87. Cited in 'Moulding the Revolution', *African Communist*, op. cit.
88. Kasrils interview, op. cit., Matthews interview, op. cit.
89. Matthews interview, op. cit.
90. Oliver Tambo, NEC speech, Kabwe, op. cit.

PART THREE *Chapter Twelve*
The Winding Path

1. 'In Defence of the African Image and Heritage: Reply to the Central Committee of the South African Communist Party statement entitled "The Enemy Hidden Under the Same Colour"', African National Congress of South Africa (African Nationalists), Dar es Salaam, February 1976.
2. In his comment on the initial draft of this chapter, Pallo Jordan wrote: 'There was a document, authored by Joe Slovo, circulated among the senior ANC leadership, that raised the issue of the marginalisation of the other Congress Alliance leaders in exile after Rivonia – *circa* 1967.'
3. Document A11.1.3, OR Tambo Collection, Fort Hare Archives.
4. Thami Mhlambiso, interview by LC, New York, 20 October 1993.
5. 'Against Manipulation of the South African Revolution', Tennyson Xola Makiwane, African National Congress of South Africa (African Nationalists), Dar es Salaam, October 1975.
6. Mhlambiso interview, op. cit.
7. Jean Middleton, interview by LC, Johannesburg, 17 November 1995.
8. Mhlambiso interview, op. cit.
9. Ibid.
10. Letter to Adelaide Tambo from Oliver Tambo, *circa* September 1962.
11. The operation culminating in 1971 to land cadres on the shores of the Transkei, for example, had deployed two non-South African communists – Alex Moumbaris and Sean Hosey – to assist in infiltration. See also Chapter 13.
12. Ibid.

13. Neo Moikangoa, interview by LC, Johannesburg, 14 June 1993.
14. Breyten Breytenbach, telephonic interview by LC, 14 August 1993.
15. Pallo Jordan, interview by LC, Johannesburg, 2 December 1993.
16. Bill Anderson, interview by LC, Johannesburg, 23 June 1993.
17. Glenn Moss, correspondence with LC, Johannesburg, 12 April 1996.
18. Jordan interview, op. cit.
19. Anderson interview, op. cit.
20. Jordan interview, op. cit.
21. Breyten Breytenbach, *The True Confessions of an Albino Terrorist*, Farrar Straus Giroux, 1983, cited in Thomas Karis and Gail Gerhart, *From Protest to Challenge*, Volume 5 (*Nadir and Resurgence, 1964–1979*), Indiana University Press, 1997.
22. South African Institute of Race Relations, *Survey of Race Relations in South Africa 1977*, 1977, p136.
23. Jordan interview, op. cit.
24. Okhela members, disenchanted, turned to the Black Consciousness Movement. They shook off some of Okhela's more controversial members, including Schuytema, and later reinvented themselves as a new organisation, trying to raise funds by approaching potential donors who would be sympathetic to any anti-communist approach.
25. Jordan interview, op. cit.
26. Observation in Tambo's notebook, Document A11.3.1, undated, OR Tambo Collection, Fort Hare Archives.
27. Ibid.
28. Evidence by Duma Nokwe, OR Tambo Collection, Fort Hare Archives.
29. Fertz Ngakane, interview by LC, London, 23 September 1993.
30. Ibid.; see also Chapter 14.
31. Document A11.3.1, Fort Hare, op. cit.
32. Oliver Tambo, interview by Thomas Karis and Gail Gerhart, London, 3–4 and 6 March 1991, courtesy Karis and Gerhart.
33. Ibid.; see also Thomas Karis and Gail Gerhart, *From Protest to Challenge*, Volume 4 (*Political Profiles 1882–1964*), Hoover Institution Press, 1977.
34. Oliver Tambo interview, Karis and Gerhart, op. cit.
35. Document A11.3.1, Fort Hare, op. cit.
36. Oliver Tambo interview, Karis and Gerhart, op. cit.
37. Sachs interview, op. cit.
38. 'Reply to SACP Central Committee', 1976, op. cit.
39. Mhlambiso interview, op. cit.
40. 'Speech delivered by Mzimkulu Ambrose Makiwane on the occasion of the unveiling of the tombstone of the late Robert Resha', London, 19 July 1975, cited in Karis and Gerhart, op. cit.
41. Oliver Tambo interview, Karis and Gerhart, op. cit.
42. Karis and Gerhart, op. cit.
43. Document A11.3.1, Fort Hare, op. cit.
44. Karis and Gerhart, op. cit.
45. Sachs interview, op. cit.
46. Thabo Mbeki, recorded response to questions from LC, 20 January 2001.
47. Sachs interview, op. cit.
48. Draft of code letter to High Command on Robben Island, OR Tambo Collection, Fort Hare Archives.
49. Oliver Tambo, speech on behalf of the NEC to the National Consultative Conference of the ANC, Kabwe, June 1985.
50. Mbeki, recorded response, 2001, op. cit.
51. 'Statement on the Expulsion from the ANC (SA) of T Bongo, AM Makiwane, JD Matlou, GM Mbele, AK Mqota, P Ngakane, TX Makiwane, OK Setlhapelo', issued by the eight expelled members, London, 27 December 1975, p22, courtesy Fertz Ngakane.
52. Karis and Gerhart, op. cit.; Frene Ginwala, interview by LC, Johannesburg, 18 February 1993.
53. 'Against Manipulation', TX Makiwane, 1975, op. cit.
54. Oliver Tambo interview, Karis and Gerhart, op. cit.
55. Karis and Gerhart, Volume 5, op. cit.; Mac Maharaj, interview by LC, Johannesburg, 1 August 1995.
56. Thabo Mbeki, recorded response, 2001, op. cit.
57. Almost all of the dozens of interviewees who discussed this issue – including Matthews, Slovo, Zuma, Maharaj, Kasrils – agreed (perhaps with the benefit of hindsight) that the Group of Eight had been led as much by personal grievances as ideology.
58. Draft code letter to Robben Island, op. cit.
59. Oliver Tambo, interview by LC, 4 February 1993.
60. Moikangoa interview, op. cit.
61. Albie Sachs, interview by LC, Johannesburg, 13 July 2004. Sachs pointed out that, now years later, he was happy to resume friendships with at least two of the Eight – Ambrose Makiwane and Pascal Ngakane.
62. Ibid.
63. The phrase is Mhlambiso's.
64. Mhlambiso interview, op. cit.
65. Ibid.
66. Chris Nteta, interview by LC, Boston, 10 April 1993.
67. Ibid.
68. Matthews interview, op. cit.
69. Ibid.
70. Wilton Mkwayi, interview by LC, King William's Town, 29 June 2000. Mkwayi related that the correspondence had been lost in prison – not surprisingly, since South African newspapers had a field day broadcasting the news of the split in the ANC and the disenchantment with Oliver Tambo.
71. The High Organ consisted of Govan Mbeki, Walter Sisulu, Raymond Mhlaba, with Nelson Mandela as the elected leader.
72. Andrew Masondo, interview by Sifiso Ndlovu, undated, SADET Oral History Project, SADET Archives.
73. Ibid.

74. Walter Sisulu, interview by Anthony Sampson, 25 January 1996, cited in Sampson's *Mandela: The Authorised Biography*, Harper Collins, 1999, p213.
75. Ahmed Kathrada, interview by LC, Cape Town, 20 June 2003.
76. Verbal communication with several ANC members in the UK during the 1970s.
77. Wandile Kuse, interview by LC, Stellenbosch, 20 January 1995.
78. See Chapter 13.
79. Sachs interview, op. cit.
80. See, for example, the summary of press reports discussed in *The Post* (21 March 1971), *Beeld* (31 December 1975), *Sunday Times* (4 January 1976), *Rand Daily Mail* (5 January 1976) and *The Natal Mercury* (12 January 1976).
81. Draft letter, *c.*1976, OR Tambo Collection, Fort Hare Archives.
82. Ibid.
83. Ibid.
84. Maharaj interview, op. cit.
85. VJ (Joe) Matthews, interview by Sifiso Ndlovu and Professor B Magubane, SADET Archives, unpublished, undated.
86. Maharaj interview, op. cit.
87. Oliver Tambo, interview by LC, Johannesburg, 11 January 1993.
88. Thomas Karis and Gail Gerhart, *From Protest to Challenge*, Volume 5 (*Nadir and Resurgence, 1964–1979*), Indiana University Press, 1997, p789.
89. Karis and Gerhart, op. cit.
90. Vladimir Shubin, untitled, unpublished.
91. Vladimir Shubin, *ANC: A View from Moscow*, Mayibuye Books, 1999.
92. Ibid., p139.
93. Joe Slovo, interview by LC, Johannesburg, 7 January 1994.
94. Ben Turok, interview by LC, Johannesburg, 10 August 1993.
95. Hani interview, op. cit.
96. Oliver Tambo, 'Speech at meeting to observe the 60th Anniversary of the South African Communist Party', London, 30 July 1981 (ES Reddy Collection).
97. For example, Frene Ginwala was in the first category and Vella Pillay in the second.
98. Sachs interview, op. cit.
99. Slovo interview, op. cit.
100. Mark Gevisser, 'The Big Carrier', *Sunday Times*, 6 June 1999.
101. Sachs interview, op. cit.
102. Maharaj interview, op. cit.
103. Letter to the author from Jack Simons, 9 February 1993.
104. Karis and Gerhart, Volume 5, op. cit. My thanks to the authors for granting access to this material prior to publication.
105. Hani interview, op. cit.
106. 'Statement on Expulsion', 1975, op. cit.
107. Document A11.3.1, undated, OR Tambo Collection, Fort Hare Archives.
108. Ibid.

PART THREE *Chapter Thirteen*
The Search for the Road Home

1. Document A11.3.1, 1971, OR Tambo Collection, Fort Hare Archives.
2. Ibid.
3. Deborah Potts, 'The Geography of Apartheid: The Relationship between space and ideology in South Africa', *Geography and Education*, Volume 2 Number 1, Spring 1985, p2.
4. Ben Turok, *Strategic Problems in South Africa's Liberation Struggle*, LSM Information Center, 1974, p39.
5. Document A11.3.3, 1977 Report, OR Tambo Collection, Fort Hare Archives.
6. Ibid.
7. Ibid.
8. Ibid.
9. Flag Boshielo was among the first to arrive in Dar es Salaam.
10. Peter Delius, *A Lion Amongst the Cattle: Reconstruction and Resistance in the Northern Transvaal*, Ravan/Heinemann/James Currey, 1996, p177.
11. Vladimir Shubin, untitled, unpublished.
12. Joe Slovo, interview by LC, Johannesburg, 5 January 1994.
13. Document A11.3.3, 1977 Report, op. cit.
14. Ronnie Kasrils, 'The Adventurer Episode', *Dawn* (Souvenir Issue), 25th Anniversary of MK.
15. Oliver Tambo, press conference introducing Moumbaris, Lee and Jenkin, Lusaka, 2 January 1980 (ES Reddy Collection).
16. George Bizos, *No One to Blame? In Pursuit of Justice in South Africa*, David Philip Publishers/ Mayibuye Books, 1998.
17. Rita Ndzanga, interviews by Sifiso Ndlovu, Johannesburg, 24 January 2001 and 3 August 2001, SADET Oral History Project, SADET Archives; *Trial by Torture – The Case of the 22* (pamphlet), International Defence and Aid Fund, May 1970.
18. Ronnie Kasrils, *Armed and Dangerous: My Underground Struggle Against Apartheid*, Heinemann, 1993.
19. Slovo interview, op. cit.
20. Document A11.3.1, 1971, op. cit.
21. Oliver Tambo, New Year address to the ANC External Mission, 1971, cited in Adelaide Tambo (Ed.), *Preparing for Power: Oliver Tambo Speaks*, Heinemann, 1987.
22. Turok, op. cit.
23. Gerhard Maré, *The Durban Strikes*, Institute of Industrial Education, 1974.
24. Luli Callinicos, 'Labour History and Worker Education in South Africa', *Labour History Journal*, 65, November 1994.
25. Howard Barrell, unpublished Document IVS.2.
26. Chris Hani, interview by LC, Johannesburg, 29 March 1993.
27. 'Report of SACTU Activities to the Enlarged NEC of the African National Congress of South Africa', May 1974, OR Tambo Collection, Fort Hare Archives.

28. Ibid.
29. Document A11.3.1, 1971, op. cit.
30. Lindelwe Mabandla and Bridgitte Mabandla, interview by LC, Johannesburg, 18 June 1994.
31. Document A11.3.3, op. cit.
32. Raymond Suttner (18 January 2003), Farouk Timol (22 July 1993) and Jacob Zuma (27 July 1993), interviews by Luli Callinicos, Johannesburg.
33. Albie Sachs, interview by LC, Johannesburg, 3 February 1993.
34. Zuma interview, ibid.
35. Document A11.3.5, 1979 Report, OR Tambo Collection, Fort Hare Archives.
36. Barrell, op. cit.
37. Ibid. (citing Jacob Zuma).
38. South African Institute of Race Relations, *Survey of Race Relations in South Africa 1977*, 1977, p305.
39. Kasrils, op. cit., p123.
40. Raymond Suttner, *Inside Apartheid's Prison*, University of Natal Press/Ocean Press, 2001.
41. The accused were University of Natal Durban lecturer Eddie Webster and NUSAS students Cedric de Beer, Glenn Moss, Charles Nupen and Karel Tip.
42. 'Presidential Address to the Extended Meeting of the NEC of the African National Congress', April 1975, OR Tambo Collection, Fort Hare Archives.
43. Bizos, op. cit., p38.
44. Race Relations Survey, 1977, op. cit., p150ff.
45. The accused were H Gwala, W Khanyile, Z Mdlalose, J Nduli, C Ndlovu, A Xaba, V Magubane, M Meyiwa, A Ndebele and J Nene. Race Relations Survey, 1977, op. cit. p133.
46. The five were D Ntsebeza, L Ntsebeza, M Silinga, M Goniwe and M Mgobizi.
47. Shubin, op. cit.
48. Pam Christie, *The Right to Learn: The Struggle for Education in South Africa*, Sached/Ravan, 1985, p100.
49. Nozipho Diseko, 'The South African Students' Movement (SASM): 1968–1976', *Journal of South African Studies*, Volume 18 Number 1, March 1991, p46.
50. Ibid., p48.
51. Ibid., p49.
52. Christie, op. cit.
53. Diseko, op. cit.
54. Ngoako Ramathlodi, interview by LC, Johannesburg, 24 April 1993.
55. Samples of protest literature and art were to be found in the pages of *Staffrider*, a popular literary magazine. Ravan Press and Skotaville Press also published works by black artists.
56. Ramathlodi interview, op. cit.
57. Harry Mashabela, *Black South Africa: A People on the Boil, 1976–1986*, cited in the NECC's *What is History? A New Approach to History for Students, Workers and Communities*, Skotaville, 1987. The quote is cited in Paul Hausse, *Brewers, Beerhalls and Boycotts: A History of Liquor in South Africa*, Ravan, 1988, p67.
58. See Sifiso Ndlovu, *The Soweto Uprisings: Counter Memories of June 16*, Ravan, 1997.
59. Ndzanga interview, op. cit.
60. Pallo Jordan, interview by Howard Barrell, Lusaka, 4 July 1989.
61. Ibid.
62. Ramathlodi interview, op. cit.
63. Slovo interview, op. cit.
64. Barrell, op. cit.
65. *The Star*, 14 June 1996.
66. Tony 'Gabs' Msimang, interview by LC, Johannesburg, 22 June 1993.
67. Ibid.
68. 'Statement by the ANC on the Current Situation in South Africa', 23 June 1976.
69. Oliver Tambo, 'Message to the People of South Africa', 26 August 1976.
70. Oliver Tambo, 'Political Report of the NEC to the National Consultative Conference of the ANC', Kabwe, 16 June 1985.
71. Pallo Jordan, interview by LC, Johannesburg, 12 April 1993.
72. Ibid.
73. Political Report, 1985, op. cit.
74. Steve Biko, *I Write What I Like: A selection of his writings edited with a personal memoir by Aelred Stubbs CR*, The Bowerdean Press, 1978.
75. Statement to the Truth and Reconciliation Commission, African National Congress, August 1996. The ANC named Carl Edwards and Craig Williamson as the probable informers. Williamson had bought Biko the ticket that was to take him to the meeting with Tambo in Botswana.
76. Prakash Naidoo, *The Sunday Independent*, 2 February 1997.
77. Oliver Tambo, speech on behalf of the NEC to the National Consultative Conference of the ANC, Kabwe, June 1985.
78. Ibid.
79. Ibid.
80. Document A11.3.3, 1977 Report, op. cit.
81. Statement to the TRC, 1996, op. cit.
82. Jordan interview, Callinicos, op. cit.
83. Delius, op. cit.
84. Document A11.3.3, 1977 Report, op. cit.
85. Ibid.
86. Maharaj interview, op. cit.
87. Document A11.3.5, 1979 Report, OR Tambo Collection, Fort Hare Archives.
88. Ibid.
89. Ibid.
90. Document A11.3.3, 1977 Report, op. cit.
91. DT (Desmond Tutu), NM (Nthato Motlana) and PQ (Percy Qoboza).
92. Document A11.3.3, 1977 Report, op. cit.
93. Walter Felgate, interview by LC, Durban, 14 March 1998.
94. Document A11.1.1, OR Tambo Collection, Fort Hare Archives.
95. Rumford Qwalela, interview by LC, Holy Cross Mission, Flagstaff, 21 January 1993.
96. Thomas Karis and Gail Gerhart, *From Protest to Challenge*, Volume 5 (*Nadir and Resurgence, 1964–1979*), Indiana University Press, 1997.

97. Document A11.3.5, 1979 Report, op. cit.
98. Document A11.3.4, OR Tambo Collection, Fort Hare Archives.
99. Gatsha Mangosuthu Buthelezi, interview by LC, Cape Town, 2 August 1994.
100. Ibid.
101. Adelaide Tambo, interview by LC, Johannesburg, 18 July 1996; Buthelezi interview, op. cit.
102. Karis and Gerhart, Volume 5, op. cit.
103. Pallo Jordan, verbal communication with LC, Johannesburg, 25 July 1996.
104. Minutes of the NEC, Lusaka, 1973.
105. Kari and Gerhart, Volume 5, op. cit.
106. Rick Turner was assassinated in his home in January 1978, dying in the arms of his daughter.
107. Buthelezi interview, op. cit.
108. Oliver Tambo, interview by Thomas Karis and Gail Gerhart, New York, November 1973, courtesy Karis and Gerhart.
109. Buthelezi interview, op. cit.
110. Oliver Tambo, interview by Thomas Karis and Gail Gerhart, New York, December 1991, courtesy Karis and Gerhart.
111. Document A11.3.5, 1979 Report, op. cit.
112. Ibid.
113. Document A11.3.4, 1978, OR Tambo Collection, Fort Hare Archives.
114. Political Report, 1985, op. cit.
115. Ibid.
116. See Shula Marks, *The Ambiguities of Dependence in South Africa: Class, Nationalism and the State in Twentieth-Century Natal*, Ravan, 1986.
117. Buthelelzi interview, op. cit.
118. Ibid.
119. Ibid.
120. Ironically, Tennyson Makiwane, one of the Group of Eight who criticised Tambo's attempts to get through to Buthelezi, took up a senior post in the Matanzima government in 1979. Believed by some in the ANC to be revealing classified information, he was shot dead in Umtata by an unknown gunman in July 1980. In a press conference, Tambo denied that the ANC was responsible, although it is generally assumed that the assassin was indeed a member of the ANC.
121. Document A11.3.3, 1977 Report, p cit.
122. Document A11.3.5, op. cit.
123. Buthelezi interview, op. cit.
124. Ibid.
125. Parliamentary Question, Democratic Party, source unspecified, 1992/3.
126. Document A11.3.5, op. cit.
127. Buthelezi interview, op. cit.
128. Document A11.3.5, op. cit.
129. Ibid.
130. Buthelezi interview, op. cit.
131. Document A11.3.5, op. cit.
132. Ibid.
133. Oliver Tambo, interview by LC, Johannesburg, 11 January 1993.
134. Buthelezi interview, op. cit.
135. Document A11.3.5, op. cit.
136. Press statement by the ANC, 5 November 1979.
137. Ibid.
138. Oliver Tambo, interview by *De Volkskrant*, Amsterdam, October 1991.
139. Political Report, 1985, op. cit.
140. Maharaj interview, op. cit.
141. Ibid.
142. Oliver Tambo, interview by Anthony Sampson, London, 12 May 1993.
143. Zuma interview, op. cit.
144. Maharaj interview, op. cit.
145. Ibid.
146. Ibid.
147. Document A11.3.5, op. cit.
148. Lindelwe Mabandla and Bridgitte Mabandla interviews, op. cit.
149. Victor Mayekiso, interview by LC, 26 August 1996.
150. Ramathlodi interview, op. cit.

PART FOUR *Chapter Fourteen*
Family in Exile

1. Memorandum (34), 1982–4, OR Tambo Collection, Fort Hare Archives.
2. Micere Githae Mugo, 'Exile and Creativity: A Prolonged Writer's Block', in Kofi Anyidoho (Ed.), *The Word Behind Bars and the Paradox of Exile*, NWU Press, p86.
3. Hilda Bernstein, *The Rift: The Exile Experience for South Africans*, Jonathan Cape, 1994.
4. Katleho Moloi in Bernstein, *The Rift*, op. cit., p185.
5. Moeletsi Mbeki, interview by LC, Johannesburg, 12 September 1998.
6. See Chapter 12.
7. A phrase eloquently coined by Grant Farred, the biographer of CLR James, the black radical who lived and died in exile. See Grant Farred, 'Victorian with Rebel Seed: Post-colonial Intellectual', *Social Text*, 38, 1994.
8. Edward Said, *Reflections on Exile*, Harvard University Press, 2000, p183.
9. 'Bella Copia', Tambo's notebook, *c.*1972, OR Tambo Collection, Fort Hare Archives.
10. Jacob Zuma, interview by LC, Johannesburg, 27 July 1993.
11. Zeph Mokgetle, interview by LC, Johannesburg, 21 May 1999.
12. Said, op. cit., p176.
13. Pallo Jordan, correspondence with LC, June 2003.
14. Ibid.
15. Oliver Tambo, 'Statement on the Tenth Anniversary of Umkhonto We Sizwe', 16 December 1971.
16. Hermanus Loots, interview by LC, Johannesburg, 3 September 2001.
17. Ibid.
18. Zuma interview, op. cit.
19. Loots interview, op. cit.
20. Mugo, op. cit., p9.

21. Mzwai Piliso, interview by LC, Umtata, 17 January 1993.
22. Ibid.
23. See, for example, Hilda Bernstein's interview with Thuso Mashaba and other refugees from apartheid in *The Rift*, op. cit.
24. Jane Dumasi in Bernstein, *The Rift*, op. cit., p107.
25. Piliso interview, op. cit.
26. Letter to Adelaide Tambo from Oliver Tambo, *c.*1969.
27. Adelaide Tambo, interview by LC, Johannesburg, 2 May 1995.
28. Adelaide Tambo, interview by Heidi Kingston, *The Independent*, 29 December, 1986.
29. Letter to Adelaide Tambo from Oliver Tambo, Lusaka, 8 July 1982.
30. Letter to Adelaide Tambo from Oliver Tambo, 18 November 1969.
31. Fertz Ngakane, interview by LC, London, 23 September 1993.
32. Ibid. My emphasis.
33. Adelaide Tambo, interview by LC, Johannesburg, 11 July 1995.
34. Ibid.
35. Ibid.
36. Eleanor Kasrils, interview by LC, Cape Town, 16 May 1995.
37. Adelaide Tambo interview, 11 July 1995, op. cit.
38. Dali Tambo, interview by Victoria Brittan, *The Guardian,* 29 July 1987.
39. Dali Tambo, quoting Adelaide Tambo, in Bernstein, *The Rift*, op. cit., pp476–81.
40. Ibid.; Olusola Oyelele, interview by LC, Johannesburg, 14 August 1993.
41. Bernstein, op. cit.
42. Adelaide Tambo, interview by LC, Johannesburg, 18 July 96.
43. Thembi Tambo, interviews by LC, Johannesburg, 11 July 1994 and 19 August 2003.
44. Thembi Tambo, Obituary: Oliver Tambo, London, 8 May 1993.
45. Adelaide Tambo interview, 12 May 1995, op. cit.
46. Ibid.
47. Ibid.
48. Gertrude Shope, interview by LC, Johannesburg, 3 September 1993.
49. Ngakane interview, op. cit.
50. Bernstein, op. cit., p18.
51. Gloria Nkadimeng in Bernstein, *The Rift*, op. cit., pp132–3.
52. Penuel Maduna, interview by LC, Pretoria, 6 June 1994.
53. Neo Moikangoa, interview by LC, Johannesburg, 14 June 1993.
54. Phyllis Altman, interview by LC, Johannesburg, 3 February 1993.
55. Letter to Adelaide Tambo from Oliver Tambo, Lusaka, 7 January 1978.
56. Letter to Adelaide Tambo from Oliver Tambo, Lusaka, 11 October 1987.
57. Document courtesy Lindiwe Sisulu-Guma.
58. See, for example, letter from Baleka Kgositsile to the Women's League, requesting permission for her 14-year-old daughter to live with her, undated, Mayibuye Archives, University of the Western Cape.
59. Mac Maharaj, interview by Howard Barrell, London, November 1990, unpublished Document IVS.2, p86. 'Bernie' is not his real name.
60. Moikangoa interview, op. cit.
61. Ibid.
62. Maduna interview, op. cit.
63. Moikangoa interview, op. cit.
64. Thabo Mbeki, interview by LC, 20 January 2002.
65. Ibid.
66. Ibid.
67. Ibid.
68. 'Briefing to ANC membership UK Region', 30 May 1987, recording courtesy Sipho Pityana.
69. Thabo Mbeki interview, op. cit.
70. Ibid.
71. Moikangoa interview, op. cit.
72. Bridgitte Mabandla, interview by LC, Johannesburg, 3 June 1995.
73. John Pampallis, interview by LC, Durban, 4 April 1995.
74. Thabo Mbeki interview, op. cit.
75. Mabandla interview, op. cit.
76. Pampallis interview, op. cit.
77. Shope interview, op. cit.
78. Shireen Hassim, 'Identities, Interests and Constituencies: The South African Women's Movement 1980–1999', PhD Dissertation, York University, Toronto, 2002; Shireen Hassim, 'Nationalism, Feminism and Autonomy: The ANC in Exile and the Question of Women', *Journal of Southern African Studies*, Volume 30(3), 2004; see also Helen Joseph, *Side by Side*, AD Donker, 1986.
79. Hassim, 2002, op. cit., p501.
80. Shope interview, op. cit.
81. Ibid.
82. Shope interview, op. cit.
83. Hassim, op. cit.
84. See Dumasi in Bernstein, *The Rift*, op. cit., p107, and also p224, for example.
85. Albie Sachs, interview by LC, Johannesburg, 3 February 1993.
86. Thenjiwe Mthintso, interview by LC, Johannesburg, 10 March 1998.
87. Oliver Tambo, 'Speech to the Women's Section of the African National Congress', Luanda, 10 September 1981.
88. Sachs interview, op. cit.
89. *Natal Mercury*, 17 April 2000.
90. Shope interview, op. cit.
91. Zuma interview, op. cit.
92. Mthintso interview, op. cit.
93. Mabandla interview, op. cit.
94. Bridgitte Mabandla and Lindelwe Mabandla, interviews by LC, Johannesburg, 18 July 1994.
95. Bridgitte Mabandla interview, 1995, op. cit.
96. Lindelwe Mabandla interview, 1994, op. cit.
97. Ibid.

98. Lindiwe Mabuza, interview by LC, Johannesburg, 7 May 1993. At the time of writing, Mabuza was South Africa's High Commissioner for the UK.
99. Lindiwe Sisulu, interview by LC, Johannesburg, 9 August 1993.
100. Stuart Commission Report, 1984; Appendices to the African National Congress Policy Statement to the Truth and Reconciliation Commission, August 1996.
101. Sean Morrow, 'Dakawa Development Centre: An African National Congress Settlement in Tanzania, 1982–1992', *African Affairs*, 1998, pp497–521.
102. Television documentary, 'SOMAFCO', *Special Assignment*, SABC 3.
103. 'Statement by the African National Congress on the Current Situation in South Africa', ANC Press Release, 23 June 1976.
104. Ronald Segal (Walton-on-Thames, 12 May 1993), Joe Slovo (Johannesburg, 7 January 1994) and Jacob Zuma (op. cit.), interviews by LC. In an informal conversation between the author and Nelson Mandela, he recalled with fondness what he felt was Tambo's excessive patience in their law practice. More clients chose to go to Mandela, because Tambo – too courteous to interrupt – spent too much time on the endless details of every client's story.
105. Zuma interview, op. cit.
106. Violet Weinberg, interview by LC, Johannesburg, 28 October 1993.
107. Letter to Ronald Segal from Oliver Tambo, Lusaka, 8 July 1983, courtesy Ronald Segal.
108. Chester Crocker, interview by LC, Washington, 29 September 1993.
109. Thoma Nkobi, interview by LC, Johannesburg, 24 August 1993.
110. Rusty Bernstein, interview by LC, Kidlington, 19 May 1993.
111. Tambo's notebook, *c.*1982, OR Tambo Collection, Fort Hare Archives.
112. Adelaide Tambo interview, 12 May 1995, op. cit.
113. Moikangoa interview, op. cit.
114. Oliver Tambo, interview by Rixaka, January 1985.
115. Ibid.
116. Piliso interview, op. cit.
117. Maharaj interview, Barrell, op. cit.
118. Piliso interview, op. cit.
119. Sachs interview, op. cit.
120. Zuma interview, op. cit.
121. Maduna interview, op. cit.
122. Ibid.
123. Moikangoa interview, op. cit.
124. Piliso interview, op. cit.
125. Letter to Adelaide Tambo from Oliver Tambo, Nairobi, 12 January 1972.
126. Lisbet Palme, interview by LC, Stockholm, 6 May 1993.
127. Dr Beth von Schreeb, interview by LC, Stockholm, 1 October 2002.
128. See Chapter 17.
129. Maharaj interview, Barrell, op. cit.; the names supplied by Maharaj have been omitted.
130. Sean Jacobs and Richard Calland, *Thabo Mbeki: Politics and Ideology*, University of Natal Press, 2001.

PART FOUR *Chapter Fifteen*
'Shishita' – Sweeping the Path

1. Oliver Tambo, interview by *Sechaba*, April 1968.
2. Helmoed-Romer Heitman, *Some Possibilities in Counter-Insurgency Operations*, SADF, 1977.
3. Wolfie Kodesh, interview by LC, Cape Town, 8 August 1994.
4. Ronnie Kasrils, *Armed and Dangerous: My Underground Struggle Against Apartheid*, Heinemann, 1993.
5. See, for example, HJ Simon, *African Women: Their legal status in South Africa*, Hurst, 1968; HJ & RE Simons, *Class and Colour in South Africa 1850–1950*, Penguin 1969, republished by IDAF, 1983.
6. Marion Sparg, Jenny Schreiner and Gwen Ansell (Eds), *Comrade Jack: The political lectures and diary of Jack Simons, Novo Catengue*, STE Publishers, 2001.
7. Sparg, Schreiner and Ansell, op. cit., p48.
8. Ibid.; Chris Hani, interview by LC, Johannesburg, 16 August 1991.
9. See Chapter 10.
10. Mzwai Piliso, interview by LC, Umtata, 17 January 93.
11. Episode 2, *The History of Political Parties*, African Renaissance Media and Entertainment, SABC 2.
12. ANC Statement to the Truth and Reconciliation Commission (TRC), August 1996, p69.
13. Pallo Jordan, interview by LC, Johannesburg, 2 December 1993.
14. ANC community leader (not identified), Truth and Reconciliation Commission (TRC), SABC 3, 26 July 1996.
15. ANC Statement to TRC, op. cit.
16. Motsuenyane Commission Report, 20 August 1993, p33.
17. Stuart Commission Report: Commission of Inquiry into Recent Developments in the People's Republic of Angola, 14 March 1984, Appendices to ANC Statement to TRC, op. cit.
18. 'Struggle Against Bandits'.
19. Motsuenyane Report, op. cit.
20. Ibid., p24.
21. Stuart Commission, op. cit.
22. Sean Morrow, 'Dakawa Development Centre: An African National Congress Settlement in Tanzania, 1982–1992', *African Affairs*, 1998, pp497–521.
23. ANC Statement to TRC, op. cit., p71; Piliso interview, op. cit.
24. Gertrude Shope, interview by LC, Johannesburg, 24 March 2003.
25. Ibid.
26. Skweyiya Commission Report, Appendices to ANC Statement to TRC, op. cit., p21.

27. Piliso interview, op. cit.
28. Motsuenyane Report, op. cit., p45.
29. Mwezi Twala and Ed Benard, *Mbokodo*, Jonathan Ball, 1994.
30. Farouk Timol, interview by LC, Johannesburg, 22 July 1993.
31. Hani interview, op. cit.
32. Penuel Maduna, interview by LC, Pretoria, 6 June 1994.
33. ANC Statement to TRC, op. cit.
34. *Dawn* (Souvenir Issue), 25th Anniversary of MK.
35. Siphiwe Lubambo, interview by LC, Johannesburg, 7 August 1995.
36. Jonas Gwangwa, interview by LC, Johannesburg, 6 April 1995.
37. Motsuenyane Report, op. cit., p35.
38. Ibid.
39. Nat Masemola, interview by LC, Johannesburg, 29 July 1995. Thelma Masemola was tortured in South Africa when it was discovered that she was Nat's wife, in order to extract information from her about her husband.
40. Jordan interview, op. cit.
41. ANC Statement to TRC, op. cit.
42. Ibid.
43. Piliso interview, op. cit.
44. Ibid.
45. Bridgitte Mabandla, interview by LC, Johannesburg, 3 June 1995. Ironically, some people felt that if executions had been permitted, there may have been fewer tortures, remarked Bridgitte Mabandla, a member of the Skweyiya Commission.
46. Joe Slovo, interview by Howard Barrell, Lusaka, 12–16 August 1989.
47. Ibid.
48. ANC Statement to TRC, op. cit.
49. Slovo interview, Barrell, op. cit.
50. See chapters 17 and 18.
51. Thabo Mbeki, interview by LC, 20 January 2002.
52. 'Rashid' (Aboobaker Ismail), interview by LC, 26 March 1993.
53. Motsuenyane Report, op. cit., p28.
54. Ronald Segal, interview by LC, Walton-on-Thames, 12 May 1993.
55. Rashid interview, op. cit.
56. Stuart Commission Report, 1984: Report on Death of Thami Zulu, 1989, Appendices to ANC Statement to TRC, op. cit., p4.
57. Chris Hani, interview by LC, Johannesburg, 30 March 1993.
58. Rashid interview, op. cit.
59. Maduna interview, op. cit.
60. Albie Sachs, interview by LC, Johannesburg, 3 February 1993.
61. Maduna interview, op. cit.
62. Motsuenyana report, op. cit., p50.
63. Ibid., p46.
64. Alex Boraine, *A Country Unmasked: Inside South Africa's Truth and Reconciliation Commission*, Oxford University Press, 2000, p142.
65. Mbeki interview, op. cit.
66. Mazisi Kunene, interview by LC, Durban, 20 October 1998.
67. Thenjiwe Mthintso, interview by LC, Johannesburg, 10 March 1998.
68. Hani interview, op. cit.
69. Motsuenyane report, op. cit., p36.
70. 'Statement made by President OR Tambo on behalf of the African National Congress and Umkhonto we Sizwe, on signing the Geneva Convention', 28 November 1980.
71. Albie Sachs, interview by LC, Johannesburg, 13 July 2004.
72. Mbeki interview, op. cit.

PART FOUR *Chapter Sixteen*
***Indima* Diplomacy – Acre by Acre**

1. Thomas Nkobi, interview by LC, Johannesburg, 18 August 1993.
2. Wilton Mkwayi, interview by LC, King William's Town, 20 June 2000.
3. Ismail Meer, interview by LC, Durban, 20 January 2000; Raymond Suttner, interview by LC, 20 August 2002.
4. Oliver Tambo, interview by LC, Johannesburg, 12 February 1993.
5. Joe Matthews, cited in 'Inspired by the Leaders', *Sunday Times*, 25 May 2003.
6. Lindiwe Mabuza, in Tor Sellström (Ed.), *Liberation in South Africa: Regional and Swedish Voices*, Nordiska Afrika Instutet, 1999.
7. Bob Hughes, interview by LC, London, 26 May 1993.
8. Letter to ES Reddy from Oliver Tambo, Lusaka, 25 January 1970 (ES Reddy Collection).
9. Ben Turok, interview by LC, Johannesburg, 9 August 1993.
10. Carl Tham and Lisbet Palme, interviews by LC, Stockholm, 8 May 1993.
11. Julius Nyerere, interview by LC, Johannesburg, 29 October 1994.
12. David Wirmark, interview by LC, Stockholm, 19 May 1993.
13. Nyerere interview, op. cit.
14. Costa Gazi, interview by LC, Johannesburg, 12 September 93; Peter Motlatsi, interview by LC, Johannesburg, 19 February 1995.
15. George Houser, *No One Can Stop the Rain: Glimpses of Africa's Liberation Struggle*, Pilgrim Press, 1989, p129.
16. Gertrude Shope, interview by LC, Johannesburg, 3 September 1993.
17. Elinor Sisulu, *Walter & Albertina Sisulu: In Our Lifetime*, Chapter Four, David Philip Publishers, 2003 (Second Edition).
18. Cited in *Sechaba*, July 1979 (ES Reddy Collection).
19. Scott Thomas, *The Diplomacy of Liberation: The Foreign Relations of the African National Congress since 1960*, Taurus, 1991.
20. Ibid.
21. Ibid.

22. 'Speech on Behalf of the National Liberation Movements at the Opening Session of the Sixth Conference of Heads of State or Government of Non-Aligned Countries', Havana, 3–9 September 1979 (ES Reddy Collection). (An edited version was published in *Sechaba*, December 1979.)
23. Cited in Thomas, op. cit.
24. The Polisario was 'fighting a surprising war,' said Tambo, 'not deserved by the people of Morocco', since it was 'having to fight for the liberation of Western Sahara not from Spain but from a brother African country'.
25. Mohamed Beissat, interview by LC, Pretoria, 1 August 2003.
26. 'Statement by Tambo at Sixth Conference of Heads of State', Havana, op. cit.
27. Thomas, op. cit., p100.
28. Ibid.
29. Ibid.
30. Vassos Lyssarides, interview by LC, Johannesburg, 3 March 1993.
31. 'Bitter Battles to Come', Message to the Council of the Afro-Asian People's Solidarity Organisation, Tripoli, January 1971, cited in Adelaide Tambo (Ed.), *Preparing for Power: Oliver Tambo Speaks*, Heinemann, 1987.
32. Ibid., p135.
33. *Africa Research Bulletin*, February 1975, Political. Social and Cultural Series; also cited in Thomas, op. cit., p278.
34. 'Presidential Address to the Extended Meeting of the NEC of the ANC', April 1975 (ES Reddy Collection).
35. Statement at the 9th Extraordinary Session of the Council of Ministers of the Organisation of African Unity, Dar es Salaam, 7–10 April 1975 (ES Reddy Collection).
36. 'The OAU Dar Meeting', *Mayibuye*, 30 May 1975.
37. Kenneth Kaunda, interview by LC, Johannesburg, 23 February 1993.
38. Ibid.
39. Kenneth D Kaunda, *A Humanist in Africa: Letters to Colin M Morris*, Longman, 1966. While President Kenneth Kaunda objected to the arrival of Cubans in Angola, he did so on practical rather than ideological grounds: 'I disagree with many things that Marxist Leninists have done in their time, but their concept is similar to Christianity... Precisely, brotherhood of man... Love thy neighbour and do unto others as you would have them do unto you. They were real Christians. And socialists indeed!'
40. Kaunda interview, op. cit.
41. Cited in Carol Paton, 'Prince of Paradox' *Financial Mail*, 25 July 2003.
42. Marcelino dos Santos, interview by LC, Johannesburg, 6 May 1993.
43. Thomas, op. cit.; Denis Herbstein, 'White Lies: Canon Collins' Secret War Against Apartheid', unpublished.
44. Oliver Tambo, 'Statement made at the 1053rd Meeting of the Fourth Committee', United Nations, October 1960, Document 1/18/11/13, South African National Archives, Pretoria.
45. Ibid.
46. Quoted by Oliver Tambo, Document 1/18/11/13, ibid.
47. ES Reddy, 'Extracts From Letters, 1964–1973' (ES Reddy Collection).
48. Ibid.
49. Ibid.
50. Ibid.
51. Letter to ES Reddy from Oliver Tambo, London, January 1964 (ES Reddy Collection).
52. Ibid., citing *South Africa Freedom News*, No. 24, Dar es Salaam, January 1964.
53. Ibid. The ANC delegation of July 1963 consisted of Duma Nokwe, Tennyson Makiwane and Robbie Resha.
54. 'Make Accomplices of Apartheid Account for their Conduct: Statement at the Meeting of the United Nations Special Committee Against Apartheid', New York, 12 March 1964.
55. Letter to ES Reddy from Oliver Tambo, Dar es Salaam, 6 May 1964.
56. Thomas, op. cit.
57. Various interviews by LC. See Appendix.
58. Lord David Astor, interview by LC, London, 8 May 1993.
59. There were also those who denounced Collins' favouritism. But while his personal politics favoured the non-racialism of the Freedom Charter, and the vision of the ANC helped persuade him to accept the armed struggle, the Canon was also highly principled, and would not consciously allow personal preferences to interfere with the aims of the Defence and Aid Fund; Ethel de Kayser, interview by LC, Johannesburg, 20 February 1993.
60. On 10 July, 1970, Oliver Tambo wrote to ES Reddy from Lusaka: 'Mr X is not a member of the ANC, or indeed of any South African political organisation, and yet I have been moved to support him fully in his desire and aim. Several cases of non-ANC persons seeking assistance... have been brought to my attention from time to time, and wherever I could I have readily helped my fellow countrymen, notwithstanding their being members of what we call rival Parties in some instances. But in none of these cases have I discovered such a deep-seated but silent and noiseless commitment to the cause of one's people as I did in the case of Mr X.'
61. ES Reddy, *Defence and Aid Fund and the United Nations: Some Reminiscences*, unpublished, courtesy ES Reddy
62. Letter to ES Reddy from Oliver Tambo, 30 January 1964 (ES Reddy Collection).
63. Note by ES Reddy on correspondence with Oliver Tambo, ES Reddy Collection.

64. Cited in Diana Collins, *Partners in Protest*, Victor Gollancz, 1992, p312.
65. Herbstein, op. cit.
66. Ibid.
67. Ibid.
68. Phyllis Altman, interview by LC, Johannesburg, 3 February 1993.
69. Ibid.
70. cited in Herbstein, op. cit.
71. Mike Terry, interview by LC, London, 2 May 1993.
72. Abdul Minty, interview by LC, Johannesburg, 12 November 1993.
73. Hughes interview, op. cit.
74. Terry interview, op. cit.
75. Mike Terry, interview by LC, London, 10 May 1993.
76. Ronald Segal (Ed.), *Sanctions Against Apartheid*, Penguin Special, 1964.
77. Dennis Brutus, interview by LC, Boulder, 12 October 1993.
78. Ibid.
79. Minty interview, op. cit.
80. Ibid.
81. Herbstein, op. cit., Chapter 10.
82. Tor Sellström, *Sweden and National Liberation in Southern Africa – Volume 1: Formation of a popular opinion 1950–1970*, Nordiska Afrika Institutet, 1999, p19.
83. Ibid., pp107–8.
84. Lindiwe Mabuza, in Sellström (Ed.), 1999, op. cit., p141.
85. Ibid., p111.
86. Per Wästberg, interview by LC, Stockholm, 17 May 1993.
87. Cora Weiss (Ed.), 'Olof Palme Memorial Lecture on Disarmament and Development', Riverside Church Disarmament Program, 1987, pp55–6.
88. Ibid., p56.
89. Wästberg interview, op. cit.
90. Sellström, op. cit., p227.
91. *Orebro-Kuirren*, 3 May 1965, cited in Sellström, ibid.
92. Sellström, op. cit., p510.
93. Myrdal was Minister without Portfolio and later became the United Nations representative for Sweden. In 1982 she was awarded the Nobel Peace Prize for her work on international disarmament.
94. 27 February 1968, cited in Sellström, op. cit., p246.
95. The story of how the Swedish government came to officially provide this support is related by Pierre Schori, *The Impossible Neutrality – Southern Africa: Sweden's Role under Olof Palme*, David Philip Publishers, 1994.
96. Letter to Joachim Israel from Oliver Tambo, 18 September 1962, cited in Sellström, op. cit., p185.
97. Sellström, op. cit., pp176–209.
98. Ibid., p198.
99. Erik Erikson, *Gandhi's Truth: On the Origins of Militant Violence*, Faber & Faber, London, 1970, p211.
100. George Houser, interview by LC, New York, 23 October 1993.
101. Wayne Fredericks, interview by LC, New York, 20 October 1993; Peter Weiss, interview by LC, New York, 22 October 1993.
102. Cora Weiss, interview by LC, New York, 22 October 1993.
103. Oliver Tambo, interview by Howard Barrell and Jenny Cargill, Salisbury (Harare), 10 August 1981.
104. Jennifer Davis, interview by LC, New York, 20 October 1993.
105. Ibid.
106. Dr Sylvia Hill, interview by LC, Washington, 29 September 1993.
107. See Douglas S Massey and Nancy A Denton, *American Apartheid: Segregation and the Making of the Underclass*, Harvard, 1993.
108. 'Congress' is the equivalent of Parliament in South Africa and Europe.
109. Davis interview, op. cit.
110. Dr Gillian Hart, interview by LC, Johannesburg, 28 August 2002.
111. William Lucey, interview by LC, Johannesburg 30 April 1994.
112. Davis interview, op. cit.
113. Hill interview, op. cit.
114. Lucey interview, op. cit.
115. Joshua Brown, interview by LC, New York, 18 October 1993.
116. Peter Weiss interview, op. cit.
117. See Chapter Nine.
118. Chester A Crocker, *High Noon for Southern Africa: Making Peace in a Rough Neighbourhood*, Jonathan Ball, 1992, p256.
119. Oliver Tambo, 'Address to the Anti-Racist Day Meeting of the Greater London Council', London, 21 March 1984 (ES Reddy Collection).
120. Tambo's notebook, 1977, OR Tambo Collection, Fort Hare Archives.
121. Peggy Delaney, interview by LC, New York, 18 October 1993.
122. Oliver Tambo interview, Barrell and Cargill, op. cit.
123. Frank Ferrari, interview by LC, Johannesburg, 19 May 2003.
124. Oliver Tambo, Speech at Georgetown University, 22 January 1987.
125. Oliver Tambo, audiotaped briefing to UK ANC members, 31 May 1987.
126. Ibid.
127. 'South Africa Under Seige', source unspecified, San Francisco.
128. Indres Naidoo, interview by LC, Johannesburg, 15 March 1993.
129. Friederiche Schultz, interview by LC, Johannesburg, 17 April 1994.
130. Background information on the visit of ANC President Oliver Tambo, courtesy

Dr Hubert Schillinger of the Africa Desk, Friedrich Ebert Archives, Bonn.
131. Ibid.
132. Oliver Tambo, 'Economic and Political Perspectives of the ANC for a Liberated South Africa', Bonn, 8 April 1986, courtesy Dr Hubert Schillinger of the Africa Desk, Friedrich Ebert Archives, Bonn.
133. Alex Vines, *Renamo: Terrorism in Mozambique*, CSAS/James Currey/Indiana, 1991; Ellis and Sechaba, *Comrades Against Apartheid: The ANC and the South African Communist Party in Exile*, Indiana/James Currey, 1992.
134. Thomas, op. cit., p145.
135. Tambo became a 'family member' and Samora's brother there and then. In the fifties, the other young Machel had lived in Wattville, Benoni, worked on the East Rand Propriety Mines and had been crushed to death by an underground rockfall. Oliver Tambo had got to know him in Wattville, and he and Adelaide would meet him at the occasional community event. Adelaide Tambo, interview by LC, 31 July 2003.
136. Ibid.
137. 'Statement on South African Raid on Matola', February 1981, *Mayibuye*, No. 1. 1981 (ES Reddy Collection).
138. Stanley Uys, *The Guardian*, 6 August 1983.
139. Thabo Mbeki, interview by LC, 24 January 2002.
140. Adelaide Tambo interview, op. cit.
141. Pam Christie, *The Right to Learn: The Struggle for Education in South Africa*, Sached/Ravan, 1985, p117.
142. Mbeki interview, op. cit.
143. Oliver Tambo, Press Conference, London, 21 March 1984 (ES Reddy Collection).
144. Ibid.
145. Mbeki interview, op. cit.
146. ANC press release, 21 March 1984 (ES Reddy Collection).
147. Oliver Tambo interview, Barrell and Cargill, op. cit.
148. Mbeki interview, op. cit.
149. Ibid.
150. Barbara Harlow, *Afterlives: Legacies of Revolutionary Writing*, Verso, 1996, p131.
151. Rob Nixon, *Homelands, Harlem and Hollywood: South African Culture and the World Beyond*, Routledge, 1994, cited in Harlow, ibid.

PART FOUR *Chapter Seventeen*
The Road to People's Power

1. Patrick Lawrence, 'Slide into Terror', *The Star*, 11 June 1988, cited in Anthony Marx, *Lessons of Struggle: South African Internal Opposition 1960–1990*, Oxford University Press, 1992, p186.
2. Steve Tshwete, interview by LC, Johannesburg, 20 March 1993.
3. Ibid.
4. Oliver Tambo, interview by Radio Maputo, 16 July 1988 (ES Reddy Collection).
5. Joe Slovo, interview by LC, Johannesburg, 5 January 1994.
6. Mac Maharaj, interview by LC, Johannesburg, 7 August 1995.
7. Slovo interview, op. cit.
8. Howard Barrell, 'Conscripts to their Age: African National Congress Operational Strategy, 1976–1986', PhD thesis, Oxford University Press, 1993, Chapter 4, p213.
9. Joe Slovo, interview by Howard Barrell, Lusaka, 16 December 1989.
10. Ibid.
11. Tambo's notebook, 1978, OR Tambo Collection, Fort Hare Archives.
12. Ibid.
13. Tambo's wire-bound writing pad on visit to Vietnam, undated, OR Tambo Collection, Fort Hare Archives.
14. Tambo's notebook, 1978, op. cit.
15. 'The Green Book', Report of the Politico-Military Strategy Commission to the ANC National Executive Committee, August 1979, OR Tambo Collection, Fort Hare Archives. The 'Green Book' is a typed ANC report, extracts from which are published by Thomas Karis and Gail Gerhart, *From Protest to Challenge*, Volume 5 (*Nadir and Resurgence, 1964–1979*), Indiana University Press, 1997.
16. 'Green Book', Karis and Gerhart, ibid., pp302–3.
17. Preamble, 'Green Book', Karis and Gerhart, op. cit.
18. Mark Gevisser, 'The Bag Carrier', *Sunday Times*, 6 June 1999.
19. Ibid.
20. Ibid.
21. See Slovo's comment on Tambo's sophisticated consensus style in Chapter 12.
22. Writing pad, Vietnam notes, op. cit.
23. 'Green Book', Karis and Gerhart, op. cit.
24. cited in Karis and Gerhart, op. cit., p304.
25. 'Green Book', Karis and Gerhart, op. cit.
26. Ronald Press, interview by LC, Johannesburg, 5 August 1991.
27. 'Part V – The Trade Unions', 'Green Book', Karis and Gerhart, op. cit.
28. Joe Slovo, Barrell thesis, op. cit.
29. Oliver Tambo, Political Report of the NEC to the National Consultative Conference of the ANC, Kabwe, 16 June 1985.
30. Writing pad, Vietnam notes, op. cit.
31. Evidence of General Hermann Stadler, SAP to Harms Commission, cited in Howard Barrell, *MK: The ANC's Armed Struggle*, Penguin Forum Series, 1990.
32. Ibid.
33. Oliver Tambo, Statement on 16 June 1984, *Mayibuye*, No. 5, 1984 (ES Reddy Collection).
34. Barrell, 1990, op. cit., Chapter 5.

35. Joe Slovo, cited in Barrell, ibid.
36. Ibid.
37. Oliver Tambo, interview by *Le Monde*, Addis Ababa, 8 June 1983 (ES Reddy Collection).
38. Ibid.
39. Cited in Barrell, op. cit.
40. Ibid.
41. 'Political Report', Kabwe 1985, op. cit.
42. Karis and Gerhart, op. cit., p766.
43. Sue Rabkin, interview by Howard Barrell, cited in Barrell, op. cit., Chapter 5.
44. According to Barrell, ibid., who claims his source to be confidential.
45. Popo Molefe, unpublished interview by Howard Barrell.
46. Pallo Jordan, correspondence with LC, June 2003.
47. 'Message to the People of South Africa on the 68th Anniversary of the ANC', 8 January 1980 (ES Reddy Collection).
48. Tambo's notebook, 1979, OR Tambo Collection, Fort Hare Archives.
49. Ibid.
50. 'Message to the People', op. cit.
51. Oliver Tambo, 'Address to the Anti-Racist Day Meeting of the Greater London Council', London, 21 March 1984 (ES Reddy Collection).
52. Peter Stiff, *Warfare by Other Means: South Africa in the 1980s and 1990s*, Galago Press, 2001, pp75–77.
53. '[The] cosmetic reform of apartheid from local through to national level, while acting mercilessly to crush extra-parliamentary opposition. Its security arm learnt lessons from the USA's Central Intelligence Agency and Israel's Mossad on state-of-the-art methods of intelligence, infiltration, elimination through assassination, terror, detention, torture and destabilisation of the enemy', *Svenska Dagbladet*, Stockholm, 30 August 1977.
54. Tambo's notebook, 1982, OR Tambo Collection, Fort Hare Archives.
55. Stiff, op. cit., Chapter 5.
56. Tambo interview, *Le Monde*, op. cit.
57. Jacques Pauw, *In the Heart of the Whore: The Story of Apartheid's Death Squads*, Southern Book Publishers, 1991, p98.
58. Ibid., p100.
59. Ibid., p13.
60. Tambo's notebook, 1982, op. cit.
61. 'Green Book', op. cit.
62. 'We must organise ourselves into a conquering force', Message of the NEC of the ANC on the 71st Anniversary of the ANC, January 1983 (ES Reddy Collection).
63. Cited in Ineke van Kessel, *Beyond our Wildest Dreams: The United Democratic Front and the Transformation of South Africa*, University of Virginia Press, 1999, p16.
64. Barrell thesis, op. cit., p295.
65. Elinor Sisulu, *Walter & Albertina Sisulu: In Our Lifetime*, David Philip Publishers, 2003 (Second Edition).
66. Dumisa Ntuli, interview by LC, Johannesburg, 20 November 2002.
67. Oliver Tambo, *Mayibuye*, No. 10, 1984 (ES Reddy Collection).
68. Slovo interview, Barrell, op. cit.
69. Wally Serote, interview by LC, Kempton Park, 16 August 2003.
70. Tambo's notebook, 1977, op. cit.
71. Raymond Suttner, interview by LC, Johannesburg, 21 January 2003.
72. Thomas Karis and Gail Gerhart, *From Protest to Challenge*, Volume 3 (*Challenge and Violence 1953–1964*), Hoover Institution Press, 1977, p35; Luli Callinicos, *The World That Made Mandela*, STE Publishers, 2000.
73. 'Declaration of the United Democratic Front', August 1983.
74. Oliver Tambo, interview by *Newsweek*, August 1980.
75. Oliver Tambo, 'Statement on June 16, 1984', *Mayibuye*, No. 5, 1984 (ES Reddy Collection).
76. Interestingly, this echoed the demands put forward for 'one town council' exactly 50 years earlier when David Bopape, member of the CPSA and the ANC Youth League, led a protest stayaway in Brakpan location in 1944. See Luli Callinicos, *A Place in the City: The Rand on the Eve of Apartheid*, Ravan, 1993, pp44–7.
77. Cited in Tom Lodge and Bill Nasson, *All, Here, and Now: Black Politics in South Africa in the 1980s*, Ford Foundation/David Philip Publishers, 1991, p75.
78. Sello Morake, interview by LC, Johannesburg, 22 August 1991.
79. James Rantata, *On the Third Day of September*, Ravan, 1985.
80. Morake interview, op. cit.
81. Moses Mayekiso, interview by LC, Johannesburg, 30 July 1991.
82. Oliver Tambo, Speech on 8 January 1984 (ES Reddy Collection).
83. Barrell, 1990, op. cit., p53.
84. Tambo, *Mayibuye*, 1984, op. cit.
85. 'Message of the NEC of the ANC on the 73rd Anniversary of the ANC', 8 January 1985 (ES Reddy Collection).
86. Oliver Tambo, 'Address to the Nation on Radio Freedom', 22 July 1986 (ES Reddy Collection).
87. Lucky Leseane, interview by LC, 3 December 1991. On learning that I was writing OR's biography, many young people singled out this speech as a profound influence on their political development.
88. 'Message of the NEC', 1985, op. cit.
89. Ibid.
90. *The Guardian*, 15 January 1985.
91. *Secret Safari*, produced and directed by David Max Brown and Sally Browning, eTV, 2001.
92. Stiff, op. cit.
93. Document A11.3, OR Tambo Collection, Fort Hare Archives.

94. Pauw, op. cit., p8.
95. Jordan correspondence, op. cit.
96. 'Communiqué of the Second National Consultative Conference of the African National Congress, Presented by Mr OR Tambo at a Press Conference in Lusaka', 25 June 1985 (ES Reddy Collection).
97. Document A11.3, op. cit. See also Chapter 18.
98. Political Report, op. cit.
99. National Preparatory Committee Composite and Organisational Report, Kabwe Conference, 1985 (ES Reddy Collection).
100. 'Communiqué', 25 June 1985, op. cit.
101. 'Press Statement presented by Mr OR Tambo', Lusaka, 16 August 1985 (ES Reddy Collection).
102. Van Kessel, op. cit.
103. Political Report, op. cit.
104. Tambo, 'Press Statement', op. cit.
105. Nelson Mandela, interview by LC, 8 August 1993.
106. Sheena Duncan, interview by Rupert Taylor, location and date unspecified.
107. Raymond Suttner, interview by LC, 21 January 2003. Confidence Mhlopho, a medical student studying in Sweden, also attended the meeting.
108. Ibid.
109. 'Minutes of Meeting of ANC NEC', 11 January 1989, Mayibuye Archives, University of the Western Cape.
110. Eric Molobi, interview by LC, Johannesburg, 4 September 1996.
111. Oliver Tambo, 'A Call to the People of South Africa', May 1987 (ES Reddy Collection).
112. 'Samora Machel's death no accident', *Soweto Sunday*, 13 January 2003.
113. Oliver Tambo, interview by *The Times*, London, 13 June 1988.
114. 'Message of the NEC of the ANC on the 74th Anniversary of the ANC', 8 January 1986 (ES Reddy Collection).
115. Ibid.
116. Press conference, Lusaka, 25 June 1985.
117. 'From Ungovernability to People's Power, ANC Call to the People', May 1986.
118. Raymond Suttner, correspondence with LC, 18 January 2003.
119. Ibid.
120. See, for example, the NECC's *What is History? A New Approach to History for Students, Workers and Communities*, Skotaville, 1987.
121. 'Message of the NEC of the ANC on the 77th Anniversary of the ANC', 8 January 1989 (ES Reddy Collection).
122. Ibid.
123. 'Forward to Mass Action for People's Power!', 'Message of the NEC', 8 January 1989, op. cit.
124. Albie Sachs, interview by LC, 3 February 1993.
125. The theme was particularly interesting for post-apartheid South Africa as the issue continued to be hotly explored into the early 21st century.
126. Sachs interview, op. cit.
127. Ibid.
128. 'Attack, Advance, Give the Enemy No Quarter', 'Message of the NEC', 8 January 1986, op. cit.
129. Anthony Sampson, *Mandela: The Authorised Biography*, Harper Collins, 1999, p373.
130. N Mathathiane, *Front Line*, July 1987.
131. cited in Sampson, op. cit.
132. 'Statement at the World Council of Churches', Liberation Movement Dialogue, Lusaka, 5 May 1987 (ES Reddy Collection).
133. Oliver Tambo, interview by *The Guardian*, 6 August 1983.
134. Transcription of a tape recording of Tambo's report to the ANC's UK region, London, 1987, courtesy Sipho Pityana.
135. Ibid.
136. Evidence before the Foreign Affairs Committee of the House of Commons, London, 29 October 1985 (ES Reddy Collection).
137. 'Statement on the 20th Anniversary of Umkhonto we Sizwe', Radio Freedom, Addis Ababa, 17 November 1981.
138. Per Wästberg, interview by LC, Stockholm, 18 May 1993.
139. Ibid.
140. Others included Lolo Sono and Sibuniso Tshabalala, who were never traced; Sampson, op. cit., p376.
141. Mandela Crisis Committee to Oliver Tambo, January 1989, cited in *Mail & Guardian*, 12 September 1997; also cited in Sampson, op. cit., p377.
142. Billy Jardine, interview by LC, Johannesbug, 8 October 1998.
143. Tony 'Gabs' Msimang, interview by LC, 24 June 1993.
144. Cited in Sampson, op. cit., p380.
145. 'Statement on Mandela Football Club', Press Statement, NEC of the ANC, Lusaka, 18 February 1989.
146. 'Minutes of the NEC of the ANC', Lusaka, 11 January 1989, Mayibuye Archives, University of the Western Cape.
147. Political Report, op. cit.
148. 'Attack, Advance...', op. cit.

PART FOUR *Chapter Eighteen*
Negotiating the Revolution

1. Thabo Mbeki, interview by LC, Johannesburg, 20 January 2002.
2. Tambo's notebook, 1979, OR Tambo Collection, Fort Hare Archives.
3. Ibid.
4. *The Cape Times*, 15 January 1981, cited in Vladimir Shubin, *ANC: A View from Moscow*, Mayibuye Books, 1999, p266.
5. Eric Molobi, interview by LC, Johannesburg, 4 September 1996.
6. See Chapter 15.
7. Shubin, op. cit.

8. Open letter to Archbishop Trevor Huddleston, President of the Anti-Apartheid Movement, 'Appeal to the British People to Oppose the Visit of PW Botha', *Morning Star*, 21 May 1984.
9. 'We are a Force', Speech at Solomon Mahlangu Freedom College, Tanzania, May 1984.
10. *Zimbabwe Herald*, 7 July 1984, reproduced by *ANC Weekly News Briefing*, London, 7 July 1984.
11. Penuel Maduna, interview by LC, Pretoria, 6 June 1994.
12. *ANC Weekly News Briefing*, extract from *The Argus* editorial, 7 January 1985, ANC Archives, Luthuli House, Johannesburg.
13. Ibid; *West African* magazine, 14 January 1985.
14. Pallo Jordan, correspondence with LC, August 2003.
15. Albie Sachs, interview by LC, Johannesburg, 3 February 1993.
16. Ibid.
17. Maduna interview, op. cit.
18. Sachs interview, op. cit.
19. Shubin, op. cit., p271.
20. Ibid., p208; *ANC Weekly News Briefing*, London, 31 May 1987.
21. Gavin Relly, interview by LC, Johannesburg, 31 August 1993.
22. Robin McGregor, *The Investor's Handbook*, Purdey Publishing, 1985, cited in Anthony Sampson, *Black and Gold: Tycoons, Revolutionaries and Apartheid*, Pantheon Books, 1987, p190.
23. Relly interview, op. cit.
24. Tony Bloom, 'Notes of Meeting at Mufuwe Game Lodge', 13 September 1985, courtesy Gavin Relly.
25. Ibid.
26. Bloom, op. cit.
27. Sampson, op. cit., p195.
28. Relly interview, op. cit.
29. Gavin Relly, interview by Howard Barrell, Johannesburg, 29 June 2000.
30. Sampson, op. cit., p210.
31. Bloom, op. cit.
32. Oliver Tambo, interview by Radio Freedom, reproduced by *Sechaba*, February 1986.
33. 'The Findings of the Commonwealth Eminent Persons Group on Southern Africa', *Mission to South Africa: The Commonwealth Report*, Penguin, 1986, p119.
34. Tony Heard, *The Cape of Storms*, Ravan, 1990, p203.
35. Ibid.
36. Sampson, op. cit., pp25–27.
37. 'Notes on Meeting of Oliver Tambo with British Businessmen', 24 October 1985, courtesy Anthony Sampson.
38. Sampson, op. cit.
39. Maduna interview, op. cit.
40. Sonny Ramphal, interview by Patti Waldmeier, location and date unspecified.
41. Anthony Sampson, *Mandela: The Authorised Biography*, Harper Collins, 1999.
42. See chapters 12 and 13.
43. Molobi interview, op. cit.
44. Sampson, *Mandela*, op. cit.
45. Nelson Mandela, *Long Walk to Freedom*, Abacus, 1994, p621.
46. Ibid.
47. Tambo's notebook, 1985, OR Tambo Collection, Fort Hare Archives.
48. *ANC Briefing*, London, op. cit.
49. Mandela, op. cit., p638.
50. George Bizos, interview by Rupert Taylor, location and date unspecified.
51. Nelson Mandela, interview by Patti Waldmeier, location and date unspecified.
52. Sampson, *Mandela*, op. cit.
53. 'Findings', *Mission to Southern Africa*, op. cit.
54. Ibid., p138.
55. Ibid., p126.
56. Mandela, op. cit.
57. Jo Beale, interview by LC, London, 14 January 1996.
58. Professor Willie Esterhuyse, interview by LC, Cape Town, 13 March 2003.
59. Professor Willie Esterhuyse, interview by Patti Waldmeier, location and date unspecified.
60. Sampson, *Mandela*, op. cit.
61. Esterhuyse interview, Waldmeier, op. cit.
62. Mbeki interview, op. cit.
63. Esterhuyse interview, Waldmeier, op. cit.
64. Scott Thomas, *The Diplomacy of Liberation: The Foreign Relations of the African National Congress since 1960*, Taurus, 1991.
65. Mbeki interview, op. cit. It would be another two years before negotiations about Namibian independence would begin.
66. Sylvia Neame, telephonic interview by LC, 17 March 2003. See also the debate between Brenda Stalker (aka Sylvia Neame) and Thando Zuma in *Sechaba*, November 1987 and February 1988 (ES Reddy Collection).
67. 'Findings', *Mission to Southern Africa*, op. cit.
68. 'The Way Forward: South African Freedom Day – 26 June 1987', ANC Statement, 26 June 1987.
69. Maduna interview, op. cit.
70. Ibid.
71. Correspondence, January 1989, Mayibuye Archives, University of the Western Cape.
72. A careful study of the exile movement, particularly from a grass-roots experience, still needs to be undertaken. See also Hilda Bernstein, *The Rift: The Exile Experience for South Africans*, Jonathan Cape, 1994; Wolfie Kodesh, taped interviews, Mayibuye Archives, University of the Western Cape; Bernard Magubane (Ed.), *The Road to Democracy*, SADET, 1994.
73. Sachs interview, op. cit.
74. In commenting on the ANC's constitutional guidelines, which accepted sexual preference, Albie Sachs added that Tambo's approach was that if he did not understand the question of sexual preference, 'he would understand that there are people who are gay – that is their life, that is the way they are'.

75. Pallo Jordan, correspondence with LC, June 2003.
76. Chris Hani, interview by LC, Johannesburg, 30 March 1993.
77. Mbeki interview, op. cit.
78. Ibid.
79. Steve Tshwete, interview by LC, Johannesburg, 20 October 1993.
80. 'Pointers Towards an Initiative Aimed at Imposing Negotiations on the ANC', 23 July 1987, Document E22, Mayibuye Archives, University of the Western Cape.
81. Letter to Professor Dr Franz Ansprenger from Sylvia Neame, 30 August 1991, Document A2729/B9, Wits University Historical Papers.
82. Oliver Tambo, 'Economic and Political Perspectives of the ANC for a Liberated South Africa', Bonn, 8 April 1986, courtesy Dr Hubert Schillinger of the Africa Desk, Friedrich Ebert Archives, Bonn.
83. Jordan correspondence, op. cit.
84. Ibid.
85. 'Minutes of an Emergency Meeting of the NWC', 29 July 1989, Mayibuye Archives, University of the Western Cape.
86. Thabo Mbeki, speech to anti-apartheid activists, Switzerland, September 1989, cited in *Sechaba*, December 1989.
87. Tshwete interview, op. cit.
88. Ibid.
89. Lindelwe Mabandla, interview by LC, Johannesburg, 18 June 1994.
90. 'Memorandum to the NWC on Membership Questions That Need Our Attention', Lusaka, *c.*1987, Mayibuye Archives, University of the Western Cape.
91. Tambo, 'We are a Force' speech, op. cit.
92. Bridgitte Mabandla, interview by LC, Johannesburg, 18 June 1994.
93. 'Minutes of Emergency Meeting', 1989, op. cit.
94. Ibid.
95. Tshwete interview, op. cit.
96. 'Minutes of Emergency Meeting', 1989, op. cit.
97. Tshwete interview, op. cit.
98. Maduna interview, op. cit.
99. Ibid.
100. Tshwete interview, op. cit.
101. Maduna interview, op. cit.
102. 'Resumed Special Meeting of NWC at 09:00 Hours', 29 July 1989, Mayibuye Archives, University of the Western Cape.
103. Tony 'Gabs' Msimang, interview by LC, 24 June 1993.
104. 'Harare Declaration: Declaration of the OAU Ad-Hoc Committee on Southern Africa on the Question of South Africa', Harare, 21 August 1989.
105. 'Special Meeting of NWC at 08:00 Hours', 8 August 1989, Mayibuye Archives, University of the Western Cape.
106. Tshwete interview, op. cit.
107. Thenjiwe Mthintso, interview by LC, Johannesburg, 10 March 1998.
108. Msimang interview, op. cit.

PART FOUR *Chapter Nineteen*
'Freedom is the Apex'

1. Anthony Mongale, interview by LC, Johannesburg, 30 March 1993.
2. Letter to Adelaide Tambo from Oliver Tambo, Nairobi, 12 January 1972.
3. Letter to Adelaide Tambo from Oliver Tambo, Dar es Salaam, 30 June 1962.
4. Letter to Adelaide, January 1972, op. cit.
5. Letter to Adelaide Tambo from Oliver Tambo, Morogoro, 27 August 1966.
6. Letter to Thomas Karis from Oliver Tambo, 1973, courtesy Thomas Karis.
7. Mongale interview, op. cit.
8. Adelaide Tambo, interview by LC, Johannesburg, 31 July 2003.
9. Letter to Adelaide Tambo from Oliver Tambo, Lusaka, 1 January 1984.
10. Oliver Tambo, interview by *Mayibuye*, 1 September 1981.
11. Thembi Tambo, interview by LC, Johannesburg, 18 August 2003.
12. Vladimir Shubin, *ANC: A View from Moscow*, Mayibuye Books, 1999, p269.
13. Nat Masemola, interview by LC, Johannesburg, 29 July 1995.
14. See chapters 15 and 17.
15. Letter to Oliver Tambo from Dr Robert Mahler, London, 31 October 1985.
16. Letter to Adelaide Tambo from Oliver Tambo, Lusaka, 27 February 1986.
17. Shubin, op. cit., p259.
18. Ibid., p302.
19. Oliver Tambo, interview by *Sunday Nation*, Nairobi, 27 June 1982 (ES Reddy Collection).
20. Thanks to Clarity Films for this chronology.
21. 'Speech on Occasion of 20th Anniversary of Umkhonto we Sizwe', New York, 16 December 1981 (ES Reddy Collection).
22. NEC Minutes, Lusaka, 9 October 1989.
23. Masemola interview, op. cit.
24. Dr Beth von Schreeb, interview by LC, Stockholm, 1 October 2002.
25. Elinor Sisulu, *Walter & Albertina Sisulu: In Our Lifetime*, David Philip Publishers, 2003 (Second Edition).
26. Tor Sellström, *Sweden and National Liberation: Southern Africa*, Nordiska Afrika Instutet, 1999, pp818–9.
27. Nelson Mandela, Cape Town, 11 February 1990, cited on www.anc.org.za
28. Von Schreeb interview, op. cit.
29. Nelson Mandela, Wembley, April 1990, cited on www.anc.org.za
30. Von Schreeb interview, op. cit.
31. *The Independent*, 29 December 1986.

32. A few years later, the same individual was working in the Johannesburg Metro and we had the opportunity to meet. I reminded him of this remark. He was shamefaced: 'I did not know as much about the late Comrade OR as I do now.'
33. Gavin Bell, 'Crowds Greet "Hero" Tambo as 30-year Exile Ends', *The Times*, 14 December 1990.
34. Oliver Tambo, 'Opening Address to the ANC National Consultative Conference', Johannesburg, 14 December 1990.
35. Ibid.
36. Nelson Mandela, 'Address to the ANC National Consultative Conference', Johannesburg, 14 December 1990.
37. Ibid.
38. Document A11.3, OR Tambo Collection, Fort Hare Archives.
39. Angelo Dalmao, interview by LC, Johannesburg, 13 February 1993.
40. Walter Sisulu, interview by LC, Johannesburg, 11 February 1993.
41. Rusty Bernstein, *Memory Against Forgetting*, Viking, 1999, pp145–6.
42. L and R Grinberg, *Migration and Exile*, Yale University Press, undated.
43. Hermanus Loots, interview by LC, Johannesburg, 14 August 2001.
44. Thenjiwe Mthintso, interview by LC, Johannesburg, 10 March 1998. See also Chapter 17.
45. Von Schreeb interview, op. cit.
46. Oliver Tambo, 'Speech at the Installation as Chancellor of the University of Fort Hare', 19 October 1991.
47. Mongalo interview, op. cit.
48. Oliver Tambo, 'Opening Address at the International Solidarity Conference', Johannesburg 19 February 1993.
49. Footnote by ES Reddy in his collection of Oliver Tambo's speeches, Wits University Historical Papers.
50. Mongalo interview, op. cit.
51. Tor Sellström, *Sweden and National Liberation: Southern Africa, Volume II: 1974–1994*, Nordiska Afrika Instutet, 2002, p849.
52. Mongalo interview, op. cit.
53. Mthintso interview, op. cit.
54. Ibid.
55.These memories are based on his taped interviews with Thembi Tambo, OR Tambo Collection, Fort Hare Archives.
56. Personal note on a scrap of paper, OR Tambo Collection, Fort Hare Archives.
57. Adelaide Tambo interview, op. cit.
58. Max Sisulu, interview by LC, Johannesburg, 2 May 1993.
59. Adelaide Tambo interview, op. cit.
60. Nelson Mandela, 'Oliver Tambo: Funeral Oration', 2 May 1993.
61. Reverend Frank Chikane, 'Oliver Tambo: Funeral Oration', 2 May 1993.
62. Haitian proverb, cited in Ronald Segal, *The Black Diaspora*, Faber & Faber, 1995. (This book bears the following dedication: 'In memory of Oliver Reginald Tambo 1917–1993 – A great leader in the cause of freedom and a beloved friend.') Thanks to Ronald Segal for pointing this proverb out to me.

APPENDIX

The following individuals graciously granted interviews with the author, Luli Callinicos, between January 1993 and August 2004.

Abubaker (Rashid); Rosalynde Ainslee de Lanerrol; Phyllis Altman; Bill Anderson; Emeka Anyaoku; Kadar Asmal; David Astor; Ismael Ayob.

Ben Baartman; Jerry Bender; Mary Francis Berry; Jo Beale; Elias Bantshi; Howard Barrell; Mary Benson; Jane Bergerol; Rusty and Hilda Bernstein; George Bizos; Paul Boateng; David Bopape; Breyten Breytenbach; Julius and Selma Browde; Caroline Brown; Mannie Brown; Joshua Brown; Dennis and May Brutus; Brian and Sonja Bunting; Sakhela Buhlungu; Mangosuthu Buthelezi.

Carlos Cardoso; William Carmichael; Diana Collins; Chester Crocker; Jeremy Cronin.

Angel Dalmao; Jennifer Davis; Natalya Dinat; Marcelino dos Santos; Pam dos Santos.

Willie Esterhuyse.

Frank Ferrari; Walter Felgate; Michael Fleshman; Wayne Fredericks.

Lancelot Gama; Costa Gazi; Gail Gerhart; Frene Ginwala; Lumford Ganyile; Denis Goldberg; Jonas Gwangwa.

Chris Hani; Gillian Hart; Nadine Hack; Hillary and Tony Hamburger; Sylvia Hill; Rica Hodgson; Barbara Hogan; George Houser; Trevor Huddleston; Bob Hughes.

Albert Isengwa.

Bill Jardine; Pallo Jordan.

Temma Kaplan; Ronnie Kasrils; Eleanor Kasrils; Ahmed Kathrada; Kenneth Kaunda; Sidney Kentridge; Ethel de Keyser; Neil Kinnock; Wolfie Kodesh; Masizi Kunene.

Colin Legum; Aubrey Lekwane; Esther Levitan; Hermanus Loots (aka James Stuart); Siphiwe Lubambo; Bill Lucey; Vassos Lyssarides.

Lindelwe Mabandla; Bridgitte Mabandla; Eddie Mabitse; Samson Mabhude; Lindiwe Mabuza; Penuel Maduna; Mac Maharaj; Sipho Makana; Henry Makgothi; Nelson Mandela; David Mankazana; Nat Masemola; VJ (Joe) Matthews; Victor Mayekiso; Govan Mbeki; Moeletsi Mbeki; Thabo Mbeki; Gay McDougal; IC Meer; Erich Mechanik; Sindiso Mfenyana; Wilton Mkwayi; Andrew Mlangeni; Thami Mhlambiso; Jean Middleton; Abdul Minty; Neo Moikangoa; Zeph Mokgetla; Noel Mokoti; Eric Molobi; Peter Molotsi; Ruth Mompati; Anthony Mongalo; Mosie Moola; Sello Morake; Graham Morodi; Agnes Msimang; Tony 'Gabs' Msimang; Mendi Msimang; Thenjiwe Mthintso; Ntshongwana Myshitwa.

Beverley Naidoo; Indres Naidoo; Beyers Naudé; Fertz Ngakane; John Nkadimeng; Thomas Nkobi; Marshall Nomqhiza; Cleopas Nsibande; Phyllis Ntantala; Chris Nteta; Dumisa Ntuli; Julius Nyerere.

Olusola Oyeleye.

Aziz Pahad; Essop Pahad; Lisbet Palme; John Pampallis; Mzwai Piliso; Vella Pillay; Godfrey Pitje; Sipho Pityana; Joe Podbrey; Ronald Press.

Rumford Qwalela.

Ngoako Ramathlodi; Brenda Randolph; Gavin Relly.

Albie Sachs; Anthony Sampson; Vladimir Schubin; Friederiche Schultz; Ronald Segal; Ann Seidman; Gertrude Shope; Victor Sifora; Jack and Ray Simons; Albertina Sisulu; Elinor Sisulu; Max Sisulu; Walter Sisulu; Joe Slovo; Colin Smuts; Duma Sokapa; Raymond Suttner.

Adelaide Tambo; Dali Tambo; Gertrude Tambo; Oliver Tambo; Thembi Tambo; Rupert Taylor; Mike Terry; Carl Tham; Farouk Timol; Steve Tshwete; Nimrod Tubane; Ralph Tuch; Nimrod & Gladys Tuge; Ben Turok.

Jack Unterhalter.

Themba Villakazi; Mpoyindo Vimba; Beth von Schreeb.

Patti Waldmeier; Per Wästberg; Sheila Weinberg; Violet Weinberg; Cora and Peter Weiss; David Wiley; David Wirmark.

Walter Zauer; Jacob Zuma.

INDEX

T